IQ and Human Intelligence

IQ and Human Intelligence

SECOND EDITION

N. J. Mackintosh

Emeritus Professor in the Department of Experimental Psychology,
University of Cambridge

OXFORD
UNIVERSITY PRESS

OXFORD

UNIVERSITY PRESS

Great Clarendon Street, Oxford OX2 6DP

Oxford University Press is a department of the University of Oxford.
It furthers the University's objective of excellence in research, scholarship,
and education by publishing worldwide in

Oxford New York

Auckland Cape Town Dar es Salaam Hong Kong Karachi
Kuala Lumpur Madrid Melbourne Mexico City Nairobi
New Delhi Shanghai Taipei Toronto

With offices in

Argentina Austria Brazil Chile Czech Republic France Greece
Guatemala Hungary Italy Japan Poland Portugal Singapore
South Korea Switzerland Thailand Turkey Ukraine Vietnam

Oxford is a registered trade mark of Oxford University Press
in the UK and in certain other countries

Published in the United States
by Oxford University Press Inc., New York

British Library Cataloguing in Publication Data
Data available

Library of Congress Cataloging in Publication Data
Library of Congress Control Number: 2010941708

Typeset by Newgen Imaging System Pvt Ltd
Printed in Great Britain
on acid-free paper by
CPI Antony Rowe
Chippenham, Wiltshire

ISBN 978-0-19-958559-5

1 3 5 7 9 10 8 6 4 2

For Alasdair, Lucy, Duncan, Douglas, and Angus

Preface to second edition

The last ten years or so have seen substantial advances in research on human intelligence, and I have attempted in this new edition to incorporate much of this new information. But there are other substantial changes from the first edition. One is the inclusion of new chapters on intelligence and the brain, developmental changes in intelligence, and aspects of intelligence not measured by conventional IQ tests, topics that were treated only very cursorily in the first edition. Some material in the first edition has been dropped to make room for these new chapters.

A second change is a fairly radical reorganization. The opening historical chapter is now followed by six chapters on the psychometric tradition, factor analysis (treated rather more briefly than before), and the experimental and theoretical analysis of the components of intelligence revealed by factor analysis; this part of the book ends with a discussion of g, the general factor apparently common to all tests of intelligence. Three chapters then discuss the reliability and validity of the tests, developmental changes in intelligence, and whether IQ tests fail to capture all aspects of intelligent behaviour. They are followed by four chapters on heritability, environmental effects, and group differences and, as in the first edition, a final epilogue.

In response to some helpful comments from several anonymous reviewers, I have also tried to make this edition slightly more student friendly. Each chapter now ends with a discursive conclusion which seeks to bring together some of the more important points and issues discussed in that chapter. This is then followed by a brief 'bullet point' summary, and a few suggestions for further reading. The non-mathematically inclined reader, with whom I sympathize, may find an appendix containing a brief discussion of some statistical issues helpful and, I hope, take comfort from my attempt to keep the mathematics to a really bare minimum (no doubt some readers will disapprove).

One feature of the book has not changed. As I wrote in the preface to the first edition, I have not hesitated to express my own views. Some are bound to be wrong, and I do not expect all readers, especially those I criticize, to agree with them all. For what it is worth, however, my criticisms are, I think, directed equally often at the staunchest defenders of the psychometric tradition and at that tradition's fiercest critics.

I have taken the opportunity to correct some embarrassing errors that made their way (how did that happen?) into the first edition. I am grateful to those who drew my attention to them.

As before, I am deeply grateful to Robert Sternberg, who read an early draft of many of the new chapters. His criticisms were occasionally harsh, but always deserved, and mixed with enough encouragement that the task of further rewriting became almost a pleasure. I was also able to persuade a former student, Scott Kaufman, to read a complete later draft. He provided many, many helpful comments. Kate Plaisted-Grant and Kristof Kovács also read some chapters for me. Since I have not always heeded the advice they gave, none of them can be blamed for the errors and misjudgements that remain. I must add that I have shamelessly borrowed some ideas on working memory from Kristof Kovács's Ph.D. thesis.

Finally, I am seriously indebted to my daughter, Lucy, who compiled the new reference list, a labour of filial duty made unduly laborious by my frequent failure to have kept proper notes of the new papers and book chapters I referred to.

N. J. Mackintosh
Cambridge, July 2010

Acknowledgements

With one exception, all the figures and tables have been especially drawn and compiled for this book. I am grateful to the following for permission to copy material directly.

Table 5.2 reprinted with permission from *Intelligence*, 2006, 34, Williams, B. A. and Pearlberg, S. L. Learning of three-term contingencies correlates with Raven scores, but not with measures of cognitive processing, pp. 177–91. With permission from Elsevier.

Table 5.3 reprinted with permission from *Intelligence*, 1988, 12, Roberts, R. D., Beh, H. C., and Stankov, L. Hick's law, competing-task performance, and intelligence, pp. 111–30. With permission from Elsevier.

Figure 7.2 reprinted with permission from *Intelligence*, 1989, 13, Detterman, D. K. and Daniel, M. H. Correlations of mental tests with each other and with cognitive variables are highest for low-IQ groups, pp. 349–59. With permission from Elsevier.

Table 7.2 reprinted with permission from *Journal of Verbal Learning and Verbal Behavior*, 1978, 17, MacLeod, C. M., Hunt, E. B., and Mathews, N. N. Individual differences in the verification of sentence-picture relationships, pp. 493–507. With permission from Elsevier.

Figure 8.2 reprinted with permission from *Journal of Personality and Social Psychology*, 2004, 86, Deary, I. J., Whiteman, M. C., Starr, J. M., Whalley, L. J., and Fox, H. C. The impact of childhood intelligence on later life: Following up the Scottish Mental Surveys of 1932 and 1947, pp.130–47.

Contents

The early development and uses of IQ tests

Introduction

In one sense 'human intelligence' is something all humans share in common: it is what traditionally marks us out from other animals and has made *Homo sapiens* one of the more successful (if not necessarily more admirable) species on the planet. It involves language and the capacity to develop and transmit a culture, to think, reason, test hypotheses, and understand rules, and so on. For the greater part of the twentieth century, however, the psychological study of human intelligence attempted to understand how and why people *differ* in intelligence. Until the development of cognitive psychology in the 1960s, indeed, this focus on individual differences quite overshadowed any attempt to study the general nature of human intelligence, what people share in common rather than what sets them apart.

This focus on differences is, of course, one part of the meaning of the word 'intelligence'. The *Oxford English dictionary* gives as the second meaning: 'Understanding as a quality admitting of degree; *spec.* superior understanding; quickness of mental apprehension, sagacity', and similarly of 'intelligent': 'Having a high degree or full measure of understanding; quick to understand; knowing, sensible, sagacious'.

Everyday use of these and related terms is firmly comparative and evaluative. When someone exclaims: 'What a clever idea', or 'That was a stupid thing to do', they are contrasting this idea or that action with others. And when everyone agrees that Mary is clever and poor Johnny is not, they are comparing them with one another, even if they would be hard pressed to specify precisely what they meant by saying this. What *is* this intelligence they are talking about?

If people use these terms, and are understood when they do so, they must have at least some implicit or intuitive theory of what intelligence is. Indeed, from the earliest Greek philosophers to the present day, many writers have explicitly enunciated their ideas about the nature of intelligence (see Sternberg, 1990). For Plato, it was the love of learning and the love of truth; for Aristotle, it was the ability to infer causal relationships between events. In *Leviathan*, the seventeenth century British philosopher Thomas Hobbes went into more detail, arguing that superior intelligence involved a quick wit, and the ability to see similarities between different things, and differences between similar things (ideas that have certainly found their way into some modern intelligence tests). Others have been more sceptical of the value of intelligence: St Augustine, for example, believed that superior intelligence might lead people away from God. All these writers clearly implied that people differed in intelligence, but that belief was not universal. Adam Smith, in *The wealth of nations*, argued that the division of labour was responsible not only for that wealth, but also for the apparent differences in the talents of a philosopher and a street porter.

Few, if any, of these ideas constitute anything one could call a proper *definition* of intelligence. Perhaps such a definition had to wait for proper scientific inquiry. If so, we are still waiting. But is this what is really needed at the outset? It might seem that the proper place for scientific enquiry into intelligence to start is by providing a proper, scientific definition. Is it not a common practice for books on the psychology of learning, memory, attention, or whatever, to begin with a definition of these terms? Should not a book on intelligence begin in the same way? The trouble is that the question 'What is intelligence?' may seem simple, admitting of a straightforward answer. It is not, and does not.

For a start, to pose the question in this form may imply that there is a single process or faculty, which can be labelled 'intelligence' and distinguished from other human faculties, such as learning, memory, etc. But is there? Terms such as intelligent, unintelligent, clever, or stupid, are used to describe some of the things that people, or sometimes other animals, or even machines, can do. For example:

> The pianist played that piece with great insight and intelligence.
> The footballer committed a really stupid foul.
> Computers are not really intelligent; they are just programmed to follow instructions.
> What a clever baby she was to find the hidden toy.
> It was stupid of me to say that to John in front of Mary.
> Chimpanzees are more intelligent than monkeys, because they can use tactical deception to manipulate other members of their group.

Everyone can understand these sentences. But is it really plausible to suppose that they are all referring to a single process or faculty (or lack thereof)? Is the intelligence displayed by a performance of a piece of music the same as the intelligence so obviously lacking in a tactless remark made in casual conversation? Is the baby who finds the hidden toy exercising the same faculty as the chimpanzee who pretends not to notice the hidden food so that she can get it for herself when the dominant male's back is turned? Are computers and some football players unintelligent in the same way? The answer to all these questions might be yes; indeed some psychologists seem to have thought so, for they have insisted that 'intelligence' is a single, very general process entering into all that we do or say. But even if this turns out to be true, it is surely not true by definition. Whether this is a plausible idea will be determined only by further enquiry.

People have, no doubt, a rough and ready idea of what they mean by 'intelligence' and other cognate terms. The objective of scientific enquiry, however, is to advance beyond this primitive, common-sense understanding (often termed 'folk psychology') to a more securely grounded set of ideas, based on empirical evidence and capable of ordering the world in possibly new and illuminating ways. That goal will not be achieved by insisting on a precise definition of terms at the outset. New definitions are the end product of scientific enquiry, not its starting point.

All that is needed at the outset is a rough and ready understanding of the area of proposed study—sufficient to draw some tentative boundaries round it, so that the enquiry is confined, at least in the first instance, to some topics to the exclusion of others. There is, in fact, some measure of consensus here. Sternberg *et al.* (1981) asked two groups of people, one consisting of psychologists whose main research was in the area of human intelligence, the other non-psychologists, to say how characteristic of an intelligent person certain courses of action or patterns of behaviour were. The replies of the two groups were not identical, but they were quite similar, and agreed on three important aspects of intelligence: problem-solving ability, verbal intelligence, and practical intelligence or social competence.

There are, it goes without saying, strict limits to this consensus. While some psychologists, such as Sternberg himself, have accepted that there are at least these three aspects to human intelligence (e.g. Sternberg, 1985), others have disagreed sharply. At one end of the continuum there are psychologists, such as Spearman (1927) and Jensen (1998), who have argued for the overriding importance of a single process of general intelligence, labelled *g*. Many others, such as Thurstone (1938), Guilford (1967), or Gardner (1993, 2006), however, have insisted that there is a multiplicity of different intelligences. Among these pluralists, most psychometricians (that is to say, psychologists interested in measurement and in the construction and interpretation of tests) would agree that verbal ability, abstract reasoning ability, and visuo-spatial ability constitute important and partially distinct aspects of the intelligence measured by IQ tests. But is there something that can be called 'practical intelligence' distinct from general intelligence, as Sternberg and Wagner (1986) have argued? Is social intelligence anything more than 'general intelligence applied to social situations', as Wechsler (1958) suggested? Is there such an entity as 'emotional intelligence', as proposed by Mayer *et al.* (2008)? What is one to make of Gardner's claim that there are at least eight different intelligences, which include musical intelligence, intrapersonal and interpersonal intelligence, and bodily, kinaesthetic intelligence (Gardner, 2006)?

I raise these questions here, not to answer them (it will take much of this book to suggest some answers), but to give the reader advance warning of some of the issues that will need to be discussed. But not at this point. Without prejudging the issue, I shall start, conservatively, by following historical tradition, and restrict my discussion to those aspects of human intelligence that first became the object of scientific enquiry.

From the outset, the main goal of the scientific study of human intelligence was measurement rather than abstract theory construction. Operationalism implied that only if it could be measured, would it be possible to understand the nature of intelligence, and measurement meant measuring a person's level of intelligence—which in effect meant comparing one person's level of intelligence with another's. The result was the development of intelligence or IQ tests—heralded by some as one of psychology's proudest achievements, denounced by others as instruments of oppression against the poor. Their controversial status continues to this day. For the past 40 years or more, each decade has seen a new round in the battle between proponents and opponents of IQ tests. In 1969, Arthur Jensen published an article in the *Harvard Educational Review*, in which he concluded that attempts to modify IQ by compensatory education had unsurprisingly failed, that the reason why they had failed was that differences in IQ scores were largely due to genetic differences between people, and finally that the difference in average IQ between Americans of European and African origin was probably partly genetic in origin. In 1974, Leon Kamin published *The science and politics of IQ*, in which he argued that 'there exist no data which should lead a prudent man to accept the hypothesis that IQ test scores are in any degree heritable' (p. 1), and concluded that the 'evidence' provided by Cyril Burt, on which Jensen had largely relied, was worthless. In 1981, Stephen Jay Gould published *The mismeasure of man*, a history of attempts to measure differences in cranial capacity and, later, intelligence, in which he argued that IQ tests were hopelessly biased—and that there was no such thing as general intelligence anyway. The 1990s saw a robust defence of the scientific credentials and social importance of IQ tests in Richard Herrnstein and Charles Murray's *The bell curve* (1994), whose publication was followed by a deluge of books denouncing their procedures and conclusions. The most recent contribution has been Stephen Murdoch's *IQ: The brilliant idea that failed* (2007): a title (of the English edition) suggesting a possibly more balanced approach, but Murdoch tends to emphasize the failure rather than the brilliance. All are more or less entertaining, and worth reading—but they all need to be approached with a measure of scepticism; they cannot, after all, all be right.

What cannot be disputed is that, for much of the twentieth century at least, IQ tests represented psychology's main contribution to the study of human intelligence, and in particular to the study of individual differences in intelligence. As a result of the way in which they developed, which I shall shortly describe, psychologists found themselves with a variety of test batteries, described as measures of intelligence or IQ tests, without knowing precisely what it was that these tests were measuring. Critics of the tests have often used this as a stick to beat them with (e.g. Murdoch, 2007). But for reasons implied by what I have already said, the criticism is largely misplaced. Eventually, of course, the scientific measurement of intelligence must be based on an adequate scientific theory of human intelligence, and such a theory will bring in its train a number of new definitions. But although IQ tests are undoubtedly far from perfect and were originally constructed on the basis of a mixture of common sense and relatively crude psychological theory, critically aided by trial and error, these much reviled instruments do seem to satisfy at least some of the criteria one would expect to see satisfied by any adequate measure of anything one might want to call intelligence (I hope that is sufficiently cautious). For example:

- A person's score on an IQ test does not vary capriciously from one moment to the next with changes in mood, etc. Indeed, after the age of 10 or so, people's IQ scores remain *relatively* stable for much of the rest of their life. This is at least consistent with the notion of intelligence as a relatively enduring trait—rather than something that fluctuates from day to day or even year to year.

- At least some IQ tests, such as Raven's Matrices or Cattell's 'Culture Fair' tests, require one to solve precisely the sort of abstract reasoning problems that seem central to many conceptions of the nature of intelligence. (In another survey of expert opinion, Snyderman and Rothman (1988) found that 'abstract thinking or reasoning' was named by 99% of their respondents as an important element of intelligence.)

- According to one distinguished, but not wholly well informed critic:

  IQ psychologists like to think that intelligence can be measured as if it were a simple scalar quantity. I recall in particular the barefaced impudence with which a notorious IQ psychologist has proposed that a person's IQ *is* his intelligence as much as his height might be five feet five inches. Unfortunately for IQ psychologists this is not so. Intelligence is a complicated and

many-sided business. Among its elements are s
cations and conversely to discern a *non sequitt*
formal parallels between outwardly dissimilar
else besides. One number will not do for all the

- It is certainly true that a single number, an
  want to know about a person's intelligenc
  scores on a standard IQ test may do so in v
  right. But it is also true that IQ tests come in
  ing for definitions of the meanings of words
  solve analogical reasoning, series completi
  others to detect hidden patterns, while yet
  tasks, but as rapidly as possible. In other wor
  of the abilities or skills that Medawar menti

- In spite of this diversity of content, however
  the sense that people who do well at one wil
  do poorly on one will tend to do poorly on
  the argument that a measure of *g* or general intelligence is the most important thing to
  know about someone's intelligence may well be debatable, but it does suggest that the
  various aspects of intelligence that Medawar was pointing to may not be wholly independent of one another.

- Finally, IQ tests succeed in predicting other aspects of human behaviour in a way that
  one would expect of a measure of intelligence. The intelligence measured by the tests
  seems to be something of significant value (but see Box 1.1). Children with high test
  scores, for example, tend to do better at school than those with lower test scores. An
  IQ score at age 10 predicts (far from perfectly, but substantially better than chance)
  whether children will drop out of school at age 16 or go on to university, as well as the
  kind of job they will end up in, and how well they will perform that job. Indeed, it is
  often claimed that they predict many of these later achievements better than any other
  single measure.

BOX 1.1   Is intelligence a good thing? The case of Odysseus

Homer's *Iliad* and *Odyssey*, the earliest examples of European literature, prove that the concept of
intelligence has been around for a long time. Odysseus, the hero of the *Odyssey*, although playing only a
small role in the *Iliad*, is quite different from the other heroes: he is portrayed as intelligent. The contest
between Odysseus and Ajax at the funeral games at the close of the *Iliad* is a classic contest between
brains and brawn. And the more conventional heroes, such as Ajax and Achilles, do not really approve
of someone who is so willing to resort to stratagem to gain his ends. But it was Odysseus's stratagem
of the Trojan horse that finally won the war for the Greeks. In the *Odyssey*, he fools the Cyclops,
Polyphemos, by a trick that only an intellectually challenged giant would fall for. He tells Polyphemos
that his name is Nobody. When, later, the blinded Polyphemos calls out for help to his fellow Cyclopes,
and they ask him who is troubling him, he shouts back 'Nobody'. The other Cyclopes retort that if
nobody is troubling him, his trouble must come from the gods and there is nothing he can do but pray.

(continued…)

epithets applied to all the heroes, handsome, lordly, god-like and so on,
us as resourceful, clever, wily-minded, full of wiles, of great intelligence, quick-
ough there are hints that Odysseus is occasionally a bit too devious and, in the
ps not as manly as some of the other heroes, it is hard to believe that Homer does
, and prefer his resourcefulness and subtlety to some of the more conventional heroic
ater Greek writers, followed by Virgil in the *Aeneid* and many other writers since, have
bed Odysseus with notably less sympathy. Rather than subtle, resourceful, and intelligent, he is
ibed as shifty, unscrupulous, smooth speaking, unprincipled, cowardly, and a typical, despicable
olitician (see Stanford and Luce, 1974; and Shakespeare's *Troilus and Cressida* as one notable example).
Of several morals that might be drawn from this tale, one is worth bearing in mind throughout this
book: *intelligence is not synonymous with virtue*. Ranking people by their IQ score is not the same as
awarding them badges for varying degrees of merit. Some people are too clever by half, or too clever
for their own, or anyone else's, good. Honesty and integrity are more valuable, and may be more
effective, than unprincipled sophistry. These banal platitudes really ought not to need saying, but much
writing about IQ tests, especially that from IQ testers themselves, has often appeared to imply that IQ
and general worth are one and the same thing. They are not.

It should go without saying that this very brief and glib account of some of the apparent virtues of IQ tests will need to be expanded, and seriously qualified, in later chapters.
It was intended simply to illustrate the argument that a start can be made to the task of
trying to measure intelligence without getting bogged down in interminable wrangling
about definitions. It was not intended as a definitive summary, still less to imply that IQ
tests are perfect measures of human intelligence. They are not. Some of the most widely
used test batteries have consisted of a pretty motley assortment of tests chosen for no good
theoretical reason. IQ tests surely fail to capture some important aspects of human intelligence. Neither of these assertions should come as a surprise, nor should they be a cause
for denunciation or despair. Trial and error combined with advances in theoretical understanding should serve to improve imperfect test batteries. Understanding what IQ tests fail
to measure, as well as what they do measure, will help to produce a better map of human
intelligence and its variation.

The remainder of this chapter, then, will describe the way in which IQ tests were first
developed, for an understanding of that development is necessary for a proper appreciation of their nature. But the history of IQ testing has been thought by several critics to show
something much more sinister: that the tests were used to advocate reactionary and often
evil social policies. Since these criticisms are still current (e.g. Murdoch, 2007), it is worth
considering how far they are justified, and the final part of the chapter reviews some of the
uses to which IQ tests were put.

The origins of IQ testing

Galton

The two most important figures in the early history of IQ testing are the Englishman,
Francis Galton, and the Frenchman, Alfred Binet. Galton was a cousin of Charles Darwin,

and the origins of some of his ideas on intelligence can be found in Darwin's theory of evolution by natural selection. Two of the basic premises of that theory are that there is variation among members of any species, and that this variation is inherited, differences between parents in one generation being transmitted to their offspring in the next. If these ideas are taken seriously, they suggest the possibility that there may be inherited differences among people in such an important characteristic as mental ability or intelligence. In *Hereditary genius* (1869), Galton set out to prove this conclusion. Although the book received decidedly mixed reviews (see Gillham, 2001), it greatly impressed Darwin himself, who wrote: 'I do not think I have ever in my life read anything more interesting and original... You have made a convert of an opponent... for I have always maintained that, excepting fools, men do not differ in intellect, only in zeal and hard work' (Galton, 1908, p. 290).

Galton's first task was to establish that people do differ in intellect. He did this partly by assertion:

> I have no patience with the hypothesis occasionally expressed, and often implied, especially in tales written to teach children to be good, that babies are born pretty much alike, and that the sole agencies in creating differences between boy and boy, and man and man, are steady application and moral effort. It is in the most unqualified manner that I object to pretensions of natural equality. The experiences of the nursery, the school, the university, and of professional careers, are a chain of proofs to the contrary.
>
> (Galton, 1869, p. 12)

He argued that the results of public examinations confirmed this conclusion. Even among undergraduates at Cambridge University, for example, there was an enormous range in the number of marks awarded in the honour examinations in mathematics, from less than 250 to over 7,500 in one particular two-year period. As a first (not entirely convincing) step in the development of his argument that this wide range of marks arose from variations in natural ability, he established that these scores (like other physical measurements) were normally distributed, the majority of candidates obtaining scores close to the average, with a regular and predictable decline in the proportion obtaining scores further away from the average.

The main part of *Hereditary genius*, however, was devoted to establishing the hereditary basis of these differences in ability. His argument was simple: eminence runs in families. For example, of the 286 judges appointed to the English bench between 1660 and 1865, 109 had one or more relatives who were also eminent. This proportion was even higher (24 out of 30) among those who were appointed Lord Chancellor. Moreover, close relatives were much more likely to be eminent than more distant relatives: 36% of the sons of these judges were eminent, but only 9.5% of their grandsons and 1.5% of their great-grandsons. Similar analyses of distinguished statesmen, military commanders, and scientists, as well as of poets, painters, and musicians, gave similar results. There were, of course, important differences, and Galton did not suppose that success in all walks of life depended solely on a single faculty of general intelligence. For example, successful military commanders, he noted, were often very small men. Rather than the more modish, twentieth century suggestion that explained this by reference to the inferiority complex that small stature supposedly confers, Galton proposed a rather simpler notion, that a necessary precondition for promotion to supreme command is that one should survive numerous battles: 'There is a principle of natural selection in an enemy's bullets which bears more heavily against large than against small men. Large men are more likely to be hit. I calculate that the chance of a man being accidentally shot is as the square root of the product of his height multiplied into his weight' (Galton, 1869, p. 136).

Galton was fully aware of the obvious objection to his conclusion that genius or outstanding ability is inherited. If the son of a successful judge is himself successful, this might be only because 'he was promoted by jobbery, and jobbed when he was promoted; he inherited family influence, not natural intellectual gifts' (p. 64). The test of this proposition was to find 'two large classes of men, with equal social advantages, in one of which they have high hereditary gifts, while in the other they have not' (p. 37). His ingenious idea was to compare the sons of eminent men with the adopted sons (often nephews) of popes and other dignitaries of the Catholic Church. Without providing much hard evidence, and acknowledging that he had 'not worked up the kinships of the Italians with any especial care', he concluded that these adopted sons were much less likely to achieve eminence than were the natural sons of other eminent men. 'The social helps are the same, but hereditary gifts are wanting' (p. 38).

The relative importance of nature and nurture (he borrowed the phrase from Shakespeare's *The tempest*) continued to preoccupy Galton in his later writings. In *Inquiries into human faculty and its development* (1883), he discussed the similarities and differences between twins. He knew that it was important to distinguish between identical (monozygotic or MZ) and fraternal (dizygotic or DZ) twins, although he did not use modern terminology and lacked modern techniques for determining zygosity.

> The word 'twins' is a vague expression, which covers two very dissimilar events—the one corresponding to the progeny of animals that usually bear more than one at a birth, each of the progeny devolved from a separate ovum, while the other event is due to the development of two germinal spots in the same ovum … The consequence of this is that I find a curious discontinuity in my results.
>
> (Galton, 1883, p. 156)

He collected from correspondents numerous examples of close similarities between twins in the latter group, who had looked and behaved alike from birth and, equally important, of differences between twins in the former group. Identical twins seemed to be astonishingly alike not only in physical appearance but also in character, temperament, tastes, and dispositions—and even in their associations of ideas. Where differences were found, they were usually said to have arisen when one of the twins suffered a serious illness or accident, which permanently altered their life. Galton acknowledged that identical twins had experienced similar nurture, and this might well explain their similarities. Here was the importance of the differences between fraternal twins (such as Esau and Jacob). He cited one correspondent: 'They have had *exactly the same nurture* from their birth up to the present time; they are both perfectly healthy and strong, yet they are otherwise as dissimilar as two boys could be, physically, mentally, and in their emotional nature' (Galton, 1883, p. 170). In effect, Galton was the first to see the importance of the twin method of behaviour genetics (see Box 1.2).

BOX 1.2 The twin method of behaviour genetics

The classic twin method of behaviour genetics compares MZ and DZ twins. Since MZ twins share all their genes, while DZ twins, like any other pair of siblings, are assumed to share only 50% of their genes, any difference in the extent to which MZ and DZ twins resemble one another is said to be due to this difference in genetic resemblance.

The heritability of any character in any population refers to the extent to which variation in that character in that population is caused by genetic differences between members of that population. The twin method gives one simple formula for calculating the heritability of any character as:

$$H = 2(rMZ - rDZ)$$

where H is the heritability, rMZ is the average correlation in that character between MZ twins, and rDZ is the average correlation for DZ twins. Since the difference in their resemblance is due to the difference between sharing 100% and 50% of their genes, you double the difference to get an estimate of the total genetic contribution. Chapter 11 discusses the heritability of IQ at some length, including some reasons to be a bit wary of this simple formula, but several earlier chapters will presuppose some understanding of heritability, which is why it is important to explain these ideas at this point.

One point that needs to be stressed is that to say that IQ is partly heritable is *not* to say that IQ is innate, and the statement that the heritability of IQ in Europe or North America today is, say, 0.50 is *not* to say that half of your IQ is genetically determined (see Chapter 11).

He was not content to rely on correspondents for anecdotal evidence of this nature. He wanted to *measure* differences in mental ability. The culmination of his endeavours was the Anthropometric Laboratory set up at the International Health Exhibition in London in 1884, where for a fee of threepence visitors could undertake tests of their: 'Keenness of Sight and of Hearing; Colour Sense; Judgement of Eye; Breathing Power; Reaction Time; Strength of Pull and of Squeeze; Force of Blow; Span of Arms; Height, both standing and sitting; and Weight' (Galton, 1908, p. 245). The basis of most of these tests had been laid in the *Inquiries into human faculty*, where Galton argued why they (or at least some of them) should be regarded as measures of intelligence:

> The only information that reaches us concerning outward events appears to pass through the avenue of our senses; and the more perceptive the senses are of difference, the larger is the field upon which our judgement and intelligence can act...The discriminative faculty of idiots is curiously low; they hardly distinguish between heat and cold, and their sense of pain is so obtuse that some of the more idiotic seem hardly to know what it is...During a visit to Earlswood Asylum I saw...a boy with the scar of a severe wound on his wrist; the story being that he had first burned himself slightly by accident, and, liking the keenness of the new sensation, he took the next opportunity of repeating the experience, but, idiot-like, he overdid it.

> (Galton, 1883, p. 19)

It is easy to disparage some of Galton's ideas, and his subsequent reputation has been severely, if not entirely fairly, tarnished by his advocacy of eugenics (see below). His arguments for the relative importance of nature over nurture were based on rather little hard evidence. It is even easier to object to the evidence of insensitivity and prejudice in his writings. He had no doubts about the intellectual inferiority of 'savages', and most readers will already have detected a certain element of male chauvinism even from the few extracts I have quoted. They would not be mistaken. Galton had no doubt of the general intellectual inferiority of women, and one reason he advanced for his belief that fineness of sensory discrimination was a mark of intelligence will convince few modern readers.

> At first, owing to my confusing the quality of which I am speaking with that of nervous irritability, I fancied that women of delicate nerves...would have acute powers of discrimination. But this I found not to be the case...I found as a rule that men have more delicate powers of discrimination than women, and the business experience of life seems to confirm this view. The tuners of pianofortes are men, and so I understand are the tasters of tea and wine, the sorters of wool, and the like. These latter occupations are well salaried, because it is of the first moment to the merchant that he should be rightly advised on the real value of what he is about to purchase or to sell. If the sensitivity of women were superior to that of men, the self-interest of merchants would lead to their being always employed.
>
> (Galton, 1883, p. 20)

Finally, as will soon be seen, the measures of intellectual ability which Galton proposed were rapidly discredited. But the list of his achievements remains remarkable, and it is a mark of his stature that, for better or worse, they have continued to influence IQ testing to this day.

Cattell

Galton's idea that intellectual ability could be assessed by measures of sensory acuity, reaction time, and the like was taken up by James McKeen Cattell (not to be confused with a more modern psychometrician, Raymond Cattell, who will appear in due course). Although American, Cattell had studied in Wundt's laboratory in Leipzig, and spent some time in Cambridge, before returning to the USA. In 1890, he published a provisional list of ten 'mental tests' (the phrase was his), designed to measure individual differences in fundamental mental processes. The tests included measures of two-point tactile threshold, just noticeable difference for weights, judgement of temporal intervals, reaction time, and letter span. It was later expanded to measures of pitch perception, more reaction time tasks, and a letter cancellation test (in a 10×10 array of letters of the alphabet the task was to cross out all the Xs as rapidly as possible)

It is not entirely obvious why this heterogeneous collection of tests would provide a good measure of anything anyone would want to call intelligence. It seems more likely that they were chosen simply because the techniques required were already available. These were the standard paradigms of nineteenth century experimental psychology, and whatever it was that they were measuring, at least they were measuring it accurately. But as Galton astutely noted in a comment on Cattell's article:

> One of the most important objects of measurement...is to obtain a general knowledge of the capacities of a man by sinking shafts, as it were, at a few critical points. In order to ascertain the best points for the purpose, the sets of measures should be compared with an independent estimate of the man's powers. We may thus learn which of the measures are the most instructive.
>
> (Cattell, 1890, p. 380)

The need for some independent validation seems obvious enough now, but it took another ten years or so before anyone acted upon it. When they did, it signalled the end of this approach. Wissler (1901), employing the new technique of correlation perfected by Karl Pearson from Galton's original ideas, compared the scores obtained by undergraduates at Columbia University on Cattell's tests with their college grades. His first finding was that there was essentially no correlation between any of Cattell's mental tests: in other words, a student good at one was not necessarily good at any of the others. The implication was that if one of the tests was actually measuring intelligence, none of the others could be. Wissler's second finding, however, was even worse, for it implied that *none* of the tests was measuring intelligence: although a student's grades on one course tended to correlate quite well with his grades on others, none of them correlated with his scores on Cattell's tests. The implication was that college grades and Cattell's tests could not *both* be measuring intellectual ability. The prejudices of the university teacher outweighed those of the research psychologist. The generally accepted conclusion was that Cattell's mental tests, whatever else they might be measuring, did not succeed in measuring intelligence. Cattell was, in fact, rather unlucky: a letter cancelling test appears in many modern IQ test batteries—which is to say that it correlates with other tests. And it is now clear that there is a modest, but significant correlation between reaction time and IQ (see Chapter 3). Wissler's experiment was in fact seriously flawed: most of his experimental measures were far too unreliable to reveal any correlation with anything (reaction time, for example, was measured with a total of only five trials); even more important, he ignored the problem of restriction of range: all his participants were students at a highly selective university and would therefore have been of well above average intelligence.

Both Galton and Cattell based their choice of test on psychological theory, Galton on the associationism of classical British empiricist philosophy, Cattell on the new experimental psychology pioneered in Wundt's laboratory. Whatever one may think of the particular theories they espoused, their reliance on theory was far from absurd. If you are trying to devise a test that will measure a particular trait or characteristic, it will surely help to have a psychological theory specifying the defining features of that trait, to ensure that the test maps onto them. The problem, of course, is that the theory may be quite wrong. What is also needed, as Galton pointed out in his comment on Cattell, is some way of verifying the success or otherwise of the whole enterprise; if you are trying to devise a test of intelligence, you need some independent criterion of intelligence to see whether your test agrees with it. Wissler's results seemed to show that Cattell's mental tests failed on this score. No doubt there are many attributes of the successful university student, but most people would suppose that intelligence is one of them. If Cattell's tests failed to predict university students' grades, it seemed unlikely that they were succeeding in measuring intelligence.

Binet

It is one thing to say that any test of intelligence must agree with some independent criterion of intelligence. It is another thing to find a suitable criterion. If we already knew who was intelligent and who was not, why should we need a new test to prove it? One of Alfred Binet's major achievements was that he showed a way out of this apparent dilemma. Binet had been charged, by the French Ministry of Public Instruction, with the task of finding a quick and reliable method of identifying any child who, 'because of the state of his intelligence, was unable to profit, in a normal manner, from the instruction given in ordinary schools' (Binet and Simon, 1905a, p. 163; here and elsewhere, my translation). The advent of compulsory primary education in France, as in Britain and the USA, had resulted in the appearance in school of a whole new class of children who were creating considerable problems for over-stretched teachers. If they were not coping with the curriculum, they were to be assigned to special classes. The intention was certainly benign, but as Binet and Simon noted: 'It will never be a good sign to have been a member of a special school. At the very least, we must ensure that those who do not merit it, are spared the record' (Binet and Simon, 1905a, p. 164).

Rather than base his tests on philosophical theory or esoteric laboratory experiments, Binet took a more pragmatic approach. It would be quite misleading to say that he had no theory of intelligence, but that theory owed more to common sense supplemented by careful observation of his two young daughters than to the experimental psychology of his day. He noted, for example, that the elder of the two provided much better definitions of the meanings of words than the younger (and so included vocabulary items in his tests); but they did not differ in their ability to say which of two lines was the longer—indeed they both responded as accurately, and rather more rapidly, than adults given the same test (Pollack and Brenner, 1969). So much for the idea that sensory discrimination might be a good measure of intelligence.

He spent some time discussing what he meant by the term 'intelligence', but his discussions are more inclined to stress what intelligence is not, rather than what it is. This is not necessarily a bad idea: an important part of specifying the nature of a somewhat indeterminate concept, as I have already argued, is to draw boundaries around it by making distinctions. Binet drew a firm distinction between intelligence and scholastic knowledge: 'Our purpose is to evaluate a child's level of intelligence. It should be understood that this means separating natural intelligence from instruction. It is his intelligence alone that we seek to measure, by disregarding as far as possible the degree of instruction which the child has enjoyed' (Binet and Simon, 1905b, p. 196). Although he thought of intelligence as pervading much of mental life, he was clear that it should also be distinguished from sensation, perception, attention, and memory. This was a radical departure from the philosophy underlying Cattell's tests, but one that seems rather reasonable today. But what of a positive definition? One of the few passages where Binet comes close to providing such an account is this:

> It seems to us that there is a fundamental faculty in intelligence, any alteration or lack of which is of the utmost importance for practical life. This is judgement, otherwise known as common sense, practical good sense, initiative, the ability to adapt oneself to circumstance. To judge well, to comprehend well, to reason well, these are the essential ingredients of intelligence.
>
> (Binet and Simon, 1905b, pp. 196–7)

Reasoning is mentioned, but hardly given special status. The stress is rather on practicality, common sense, the ability to cope with the world. Thus, it is not surprising that Binet's tests measured everyday practical knowledge and skills; they required children to point to various parts of their body; to name objects seen in a picture; to give definitions; to repeat a series of digits or a complete sentence; to copy a diamond; to say what is the difference between paper and cardboard, or a fly and a butterfly; to find as many rhymes as possible in a minute for a word such as 'obeissance' (remember, this was in French); to tell the time from a clock and to say what the time would be if the positions of the minute and hour hands were reversed; to fold a sheet of paper over, cut a shape out of the folded edge and say what shape would appear when the sheet was unfolded (a task which can be made harder by increasing the number of initial folds).

Regardless of one's precise definition of intelligence, at least some of these tasks seem more plausible candidates as measures of a young child's intelligence, than did most of the tests in Cattell's battery. But Binet's most important contribution to the development of intelligence tests was the simple insight that, since he was dealing with young children, he could use their *age* as an independent criterion of intellectual competence. As he had noted from his experiments with his two little daughters, as children grow older, they can produce better answers to more difficult questions. His measure of intelligence, therefore, amounted to discovering whether a child was advanced or backward for her age, and what that required was a measure of what was normal for any given age. He thus developed a series of test items ranged according to the age at which most children in his sample were capable of solving them. This constituted his 'measuring scale of intelligence': 'A scale composed of a series of tests of increasing difficulty, starting from the lowest intellectual level that can be observed, and ending at the level of average, normal intelligence' (Binet and Simon, 1905b, p. 194).

By giving their tests to samples of normal children of various ages, Binet and Simon found out which set of tests could be solved by the majority of 4-year-olds, 6-year-olds, 8-year-olds, etc. The further requirement was that relatively few 4-year-olds, but essentially all 8-year-olds, should be able to solve the 6-year-old tests, and similarly for the tests for other age groups. The process of test construction was one of continuing experimentation and refinement. To take one example: the task of copying a square drawn on a sheet of paper by the examiner appears as an item in the 4-year-old test, because the majority of 4-year-olds, and essentially all older children could do it. But it turned out that the task of copying a diamond was significantly harder, and it appears as part of the 6-year-old test. The final set of tests (Binet and Simon, 1911), published in the year in which Binet died, consisted of five tests for each year from age 3 to age 10 (except the 4-year-test which still had only four items), together with some further tests for 12 and 15-year-olds, and adults.

The tests were used to assign a child a 'mental age': a child who passed the 6-year-old, but failed the 7-year-old test, had a mental age of 6. The concept of mental age is still sometimes used, most usually in the context of disability, but it has been replaced by the concept of mental quotient, intelligence quotient, or IQ. Nevertheless, Binet's procedure still marks an important change from the ideas of Galton and Cattell. Their tests gave an absolute measure of mental performance (thresholds measured in intensity units, reaction times measured in milliseconds or whatever). Binet replaced this with a *relative* or *normative* measure of intelligence: a mental age of 6 was simply the average score obtained by normal 6-year-old children. A 6-year-old child with a mental age of 6 was average; a 5-year-old with a mental age of 6 was advanced; but a 10-year-old with a mental age of 6 was backward.

The Binet scales, as they were known, formed the basis of modern IQ tests, just as mental age formed the basis for IQ scores. Translated and expanded by Lewis Terman in America and by Cyril Burt in England, they became the norm against which later tests were judged. Although Galton was the first to try to measure individual differences in intelligence, it was Binet who appeared to have succeeded. He owed his success in part to his empirical, pragmatic approach, but also to his robust, common-sense attitude to psychological theory, which allowed him to ignore the limitations both of associationist philosophy and of the techniques of the new experimental psychology then available. He differed from his predecessors (and from many of his successors) in other ways also. He did not, for example, believe that his tests were necessarily measuring innate ability:

> Our purpose is, when a child is brought to us, to measure his intellectual capacities in order to ascertain whether he is normal or retarded. We need, therefore, to study his condition at the time and that only. We have no need to concern ourselves either with his past history or with his future; we shall consequently neglect his aetiology, and we shall make no attempt to distinguish between acquired and congenital idiocy;... we do not seek to establish or prepare a prognosis, and we leave unanswered the question whether his retardation is curable, or even improvable. We limit ourselves to ascertaining the truth about his present mental state.
>
> (Binet and Simon, 1905b, p. 191)

Goddard, Terman's Stanford-Binet test, and the Army tests

Most of the next steps in the development of modern IQ tests were taken in America, largely by three men: Henry Goddard, Lewis Terman, and Robert Yerkes. Henry Goddard was director of the research laboratory at the Vineland Training School in New Jersey, an institution for the 'feeble-minded' (see Box 1.3 for a note on terminology), a position that involved him in the assessment of their intellectual status (for an excellent study of Goddard and his work, see Zenderland, 1998). He came across Binet and Simon's papers of 1905 on a visit to Brussels in the spring of 1908, but thought little of them. When, the following year, he read their 1908 paper, the first to produce a systematic series of tests graded by year, his initial impressions were still unfavourable. As he wrote some years later, 'Probably no critic of the scale has reacted against it more positively than I did at that first reading. It seemed impossible to grade intelligence in that way. It was too easy, too simple' (Goddard, 1916, p. 5). When he eventually decided to give it a try, however, 'our use of the scale was a surprise and a gratification. It met our needs. A classification of our children based on the Scale agreed with the Institution experience' (Goddard, 1916, p. 5).

BOX 1.3 Terminology

'Feeble-minded' was the generic term to encompass those later called mentally deficient, mentally handicapped, or mentally retarded. But the changes in terminology have not, of course, stopped there. No doubt in an attempt to avoid the negative connotations of the term 'retarded', the American Association on Mental Retardation changed its name to the American Association on Intellectual and Developmental Disabilities. In Britain the preferred term today is 'learning disabled'. Although the term 'retarded' is still commonly used by psychologists and others outside these professional bodies, I shall usually use the term 'disabled'.

The problem with these continued changes has been well enunciated by James Flynn: 'history has shown that negative connotations are simply passed on from one label to another' (Flynn, 2007, p. 10). Nowhere is this better illustrated than by the fate of the term invented by Goddard to denote the third and highest grade of the feeble-minded: the two lower grades were 'idiots' and 'imbeciles', defined as those with a mental age of less than 3 or an IQ below 35, and a mental age between 3 and 7 or an IQ between 35 and 50 respectively; for those with a mental age of between 8 and 12, IQ 50 to 70, Goddard invented a new term 'moron'.

A further historical confusion is that the term 'feeble-minded', although usually used generically to include all three categories, was sometimes used to refer only to the highest grade.

Goddard became an enthusiastic user and advocate of Binet's scale. He translated the 1908 tests into English, and at the 1909 meeting of the American Association for the Study of the Feeble-Minded, argued that they provided the most reliable means of classifying the various degrees of 'feeble-mindedness'. At the Association's next meeting in 1910, he presented the results of a study of 400 residents of the Vineland Training School, showing the close agreement between their Binet scores and the staff's judgements of their degree of feeble-mindedness. He then persuaded the superintendent of a local school district in New Jersey to allow him to test ordinary schoolchildren, and in 1911 published the results in a paper entitled 'Two thousand normal children measured by the Binet measuring scale of intelligence' (Goddard, 1911). Other teachers and special educators were enthusiastic; by 1914, several dozen school districts were giving Binet tests, and by 1916 Goddard had distributed 22,000 copies of a condensed version of Binet and Simon's 1908 paper, together with 88,000 record blanks (Goddard, 1916; Zenderland, 1998, p. 141).

BOX 1.4 The Stanford-Binet test

The original Stanford-Binet consisted of a series of ten tests, each appropriate for children of one age between the ages of 3 and 14. Each test consisted of six different items. The 4-year-old and 9-year-old tests were as follows:

Four-year old test:

1. Say which of two horizontal lines is longer.
2. Find the shape which matches a target shape.
3. Count four pennies.
4. Copy a square.
5. Answer questions such as: What must you do when you are sleepy?
6. Digit span of four.

Nine-year-old test:

1. Dates: What day of the week is it today? What year?
2. Arrange five weights from heaviest to lightest.
3. Mental arithmetic.
4. Backward digit span of four.
5. Generate a sentence containing three particular words.
6. Find rhymes.

In terms of test construction, however, the real breakthrough was the work of Lewis Terman, who produced the Stanford revision of the 1911 Binet-Simon scale, generally known as the Stanford-Binet test (Terman, 1916; Burt's translation and adaptation of the Binet scales was not published for another five years (Burt, 1921)). Although based on Binet's 1908 and 1911 scales, the Stanford-Binet was a virtually new IQ test (see Box 1.4). Forty completely new items were added, which allowed Terman to drop some of Binet's less satisfactory items and to bring up to six the number of items comprising the test at each age. The standardization procedures, although still defective by modern standards, marked an enormous advance on Binet's. Whereas Binet had tried out his tests on no more than 50 children specified by their teachers as of normal intelligence, Terman tested approximately 1,000 children aged 4–14. They were sampled by taking all children of the appropriate ages from schools situated in communities of average social status. Terman thus obtained much more accurate information than had Binet on the true level of difficulty of the items making up the various tests, and found that it was necessary to relocate to a different age the majority of the items actually retained from the Binet-Simon scales.

Finally, although still employing Binet's method of scoring in terms of mental age, Terman also borrowed the idea of the intelligence quotient or IQ that had earlier been proposed by Stern (1912). The definition of IQ was:

$$(\text{Mental age} \div \text{Chronological age}) \times 100$$

On a properly standardized test, therefore, a child of average intelligence would necessarily have an IQ of 100, while a 6-year-old child with a mental age of 7 would have an IQ of 133, and so on.

As Terman wrote some years later: 'I knew that my revision of Binet's tests was superior to others then available, but I did not foresee the vogue it was to have and imagined that it would probably be displaced by something much better within a few years' (Terman, 1932, p. 324). In fact, Terman's tests became the standard against which later IQ tests were judged: the proof that a new test was indeed a good measure of intelligence was, in part, that its results agreed with those obtained with the Stanford-Binet. It was not superseded for more than 20 years, and then, at first, only by a revised version (Terman and Merrill, 1937). Subsequently, various versions of the Wechsler tests (Wechsler, 1944) became more popular. But in its fifth edition, the Stanford-Binet remains one the standard tests of intelligence to this day (Roid, 2003).

The Stanford-Binet and Wechsler tests are individual IQ tests, administered by an examiner to a single person at a time. The examiner needs to be trained in the correct procedures for administering and scoring the tests, and scoring often calls for potentially arbitrary decisions about the adequacy of particular answers. What, for example, counts as a satisfactory definition of the word 'revenge'? According to Terman's manual, 'You kill a person if he does something to you' is all right, but 'To hate someone who has done you wrong' is not. The tests abound with items calling for similar fine judgements. This may be sufficient for many purposes, but it would clearly be impractical if one wished to obtain IQ scores from a large number of people in a short space of time. To do this, what is needed is a group test, that is, one administered by a single examiner simultaneously to many participants; the format needs to be that of a multiple-choice questionnaire, since the answers will then consist in the selection of one of several alternatives and can be scored automatically.

The first such group tests were introduced in the USA shortly after the publication of Terman's Stanford-Binet test. They were devised by a group of psychologists, which included both Goddard and Terman and was led by Robert Yerkes, and were designed for use by the US Army. Yerkes believed that the Army's need to select, and train for various occupations, the large number of new recruits produced by America's entry into World War I, provided an opportunity for the new science of psychology to prove its worth. He and his colleagues produced two tests, the Alpha and Beta tests, which became the prototype for many subsequent group tests—and several of whose items were also incorporated in a different form into the Wechsler tests. The Alpha test included such items as verbal analogies, series completions, and synonyms and antonyms, which have since become familiar. The Beta test was specifically designed for people who were illiterate. Men were required, for example, to fill in the missing part from an incomplete picture of a supposedly familiar object, a pig without a tail, or a revolver without a trigger; they had to perform simple series completion problems, a visual search task where they had to decide whether two sets of digits were identical or different, and a recoding task where they had to match the digits 0–9 to ten different patterns. All the problems were strictly timed, and in several cases, such as these last two, the test was largely one of performing a simple task as quickly as possible (in other words, rather like Cattell's letter cancellation test).

The Army tests, although of questionable value in helping America's war effort, wrought a transformation in the public's attitude to mental tests. After the war, Yerkes received hundreds of requests for copies of his tests (which had remained a classified secret in wartime) and, supported by a grant from the Rockefeller Foundation, published a new National Intelligence Test in 1919, which sold over half a million copies in a year. The tests were used in primary and secondary schools, and soon by some universities as an entrance requirement, as well as by business firms. But in Yerkes's eyes at least, the major value of the Army tests lay in the huge body of information about the nation's intelligence provided by a programme that had tested approximately 1,750,000 young American men in a little more than a year. Yerkes was not the only person to draw a number of startling social implications from these supposedly authoritative data.

Uses, misuses, and abuses of IQ tests

Galton had no doubt that nature had a far greater effect on intellectual ability than nurture, and, typical of the society and class into which he was born, was similarly confident that the races of mankind were far from equally endowed with such ability. Binet, on the other hand, although insisting that there was all the difference in the world between natural intelligence and level of instruction, explicitly denied that his tests were intended to measure innate endowment. Goddard, Terman, and Yerkes, however, had few such qualms. In his book *Feeble-mindedness: Its causes and consequences* (1914), Goddard adopted the technique of Galton's *Hereditary genius* to prove that feeble-mindedness was hereditary: it ran in families. But his evidence was not very much better than Galton's: however useful the Binet tests were for assessing the intellectual level of the residents of the Vineland Training School, the tests could not be given to their ancestors. Although he was no doubt committed to proving the hereditary nature of feeble-mindedness, his methods were not quite as fallacious as some critics have suggested. He correctly concluded that Down's Syndrome was not hereditary, and that more severe forms of feeble-mindedness (as displayed by 'idiots' and 'imbeciles') were less likely to be hereditary than milder forms, 'morons'. Here, too, he was quite right: his argument foreshadowed the distinction, drawn by Lewis (1933) and many others since, between pathological, severe disability and sub-cultural or familial, mild disability. Both genetic and environmental factors contribute to both, but the causes of pathological disability, if genetic, are often harmful single genes or chromosomal abnormalities and, if environmental, often particular physical hazards before, during, or after birth. Mild disability is simply the lower end of a normal distribution of intelligence, and due to polygenic inheritance or general family environment. In other words, it is more likely to run in families: the siblings of mildly disabled children are themselves likely to have low test scores, while siblings of severely disabled children are likely to be of normal IQ (see Plomin *et al.*, 2008).

Terman was equally convinced that the feeble-mindedness identified by intelligence tests was permanent and therefore hereditary (e.g. Terman, 1916, p. 6); while Yerkes roundly asserted that the Army Alpha and Beta tests 'were originally intended, and are now definitely known, to measure native intellectual ability' (Yoakum and Yerkes, 1920, p. 27). They had essentially no evidence for these beliefs, which must be taken to reflect, in part, preconceived opinion. Binet himself did not doubt that there were biological causes of individual differences in intelligence, and had indeed spent some years studying differences in skull size and their relationship to intelligence (Binet, 1900). Where he was exceptional was in his declared agnosticism: he regarded his tests as measures of current intellectual performance without commitment as to the origins of the differences they measured. The prevailing opinion, however, was that expressed by Goddard, Terman, and Yerkes in the USA, and by Spearman (1927) and Burt (1912) in Britain: Burt's definition of 'intelligence' was 'innate general cognitive ability' (Burt, 1955). Intelligence, like most other human characteristics, was affected more by nature than by nurture, and differences in intelligence could now be measured by means of IQ tests.

Several later critics have argued that the hereditarian beliefs shared by these early pioneers of IQ testing, reinforced by the prestige accorded their new, scientific tests, had sinister and malign influences on public policy (see, for example, Evans and Waites, 1981; Gould, 1997; Kamin, 1974; Rose *et al.*, 1984). More recently, Murdoch has written: 'The history of the use of IQ tests is appalling. IQ tests have often been used for the vilest purposes, no matter that many of their originators had lofty social goals in mind' (Murdoch, 2007, p. 231). It is worth pausing briefly to examine some of these arguments, for they have formed a small, but significant part of the popular case against IQ tests. Early IQ testers were not wholly blameless, and as I shall show, made some very foolish claims, but the picture is not, I think, as black as it has sometimes been painted by the critics. Here, for example, is one of the critics' arguments:

The testing movement was clearly linked, in the United States, to the passage, beginning in 1907, of compulsory sterilization laws aimed at genetically inferior 'degenerates'... [And] the army IQ data figured prominently in the public and congressional debates over the Immigration Act of 1924. That overtly racist act established as a feature of American immigration policy a system of 'national origin quotas'. The purpose of the quotas was explicitly to debar, as much as possible, the genetically inferior peoples of Southern and Eastern Europe, while encouraging 'Nordic' immigration from Northern and Western Europe.

(Rose *et al.*, 1984, pp. 87–8)

A substantial body of legislation was indeed passed in the USA to control immigration and provide for compulsory sterilization. Most people would now deplore much of that legislation (although few modern states permit immigration on the scale of the American experience between 1880 and 1914). The question at issue, however, is the extent to which the IQ testing movement was implicated in the passage of this legislation. There is good reason to believe that the critics' charge both overestimates the influence of psychologists on social policy, and underestimates the pervasive influence of eugenic thought in the USA (and elsewhere) at the beginning of the twentieth century (see Box 1.5). The term 'eugenics' was coined by Galton to refer to: 'The science of improving stock…which…takes cognisance of all influences that tend…to give the more suitable races or strains of blood a better chance of prevailing speedily over the less suitable than they otherwise would have had' (Galton, 1883, p. 17).

BOX 1.5   The rise and fall of eugenics

The term 'eugenics' was introduced to the English language by Francis Galton, and defined by him as: 'The science of improving stock…which…takes cognisance of all influences that tend…to give the more suitable races or strains of blood a better chance of prevailing speedily over the less suitable than they otherwise would have had' (Galton, 1883, p. 17). Galton went on to establish a Eugenics Laboratory and endow a Chair of Eugenics at University College, London, and presided over the founding of the journal *Eugenics Review* in 1909 (all have since changed their name).

It is important to distinguish between 'positive' and 'negative' eugenics. The former sought to encourage reproduction of desirable stock, the latter to prevent the reproduction of the undesirable. Galton himself was far more interested in the former, and devised various means for advancing such a policy. And in Britain at least, the only eugenic legislation ever passed was to give tax breaks to well-educated parents for each additional child. Other countries, however, did not hesitate to pass legislation enforcing negative eugenic policies.

In 1927, the US Supreme Court, in the case of *Buck* v. *Bell*, ruled in favour of a new statute from the state of Virginia. The particular case concerned a 17-year-old woman, Carrie Buck, who, shortly before being committed to the Virginia Colony for Epileptics and Feebleminded, had given birth to an illegitimate daughter. Carrie's mother was also an inmate of the colony, and had a mental age of less than 8 on the Stanford-Binet test. Carrie's own mental age was 9. Although her daughter was still less than 1 year old, she was given an infant test and said to be below normal. In the words of Justice Oliver Wendell Holmes, who wrote the Supreme Court's opinion: 'The principle that sustains compulsory vaccination is broad enough to cover cutting the Fallopian tubes…Three generations of imbeciles are enough' (Lombardo, 1985).

The USA was not the only country where negative eugenics, in the form of compulsory sterilization, was widely advocated and sometimes practised. During the early part of the twentieth century, eugenic ideas were common and widely promoted throughout Europe. Although Britain never enacted sterilization laws, other countries did: some 60,000 people were compulsorily sterilized in Sweden—a far higher proportion of the population than was ever sterilized in America. Sweden had a Social Democratic government in power for virtually the entire period. Eugenic ideas were *not* the preserve of the right—on the contrary, they were widely seen as the enlightened application of science to human

(continued…)

affairs, and in England were advocated by such left-wing luminaries as George Bernard Shaw and Sydney Webb.

As is well known, of course, they found their most notorious champions in Nazi Germany, but long before Hitler came to power, German psychiatrists and others were seriously debating the question of what was to be done about the incurable, long-term inmates of asylums for epileptics, the insane, and feeble-minded. There were many advocates of compulsory sterilization, and some who talked of even more extreme measures (Burleigh, 1994). It was left, however, to Hitler's Government to put these ideas into serious practice. One of the first laws to be passed by the new Government in 1933 was a Eugenic Sterilization Law, under whose auspices, by 1939, some 350,000 people had been compulsorily sterilized (Kevles, 1985). The outbreak of war, and the perceived need to concentrate the state's resources on those who would benefit the state most, led to a new, more drastic policy of compulsory 'euthanasia'. Between 1939 and 1945, some 200,000 men, women, and young children were killed—by starvation, lethal injection, gas, or shooting (Burleigh, 1994). While these numbers pale into insignificance by comparison with the number of Jews murdered in the Holocaust, they are surely horrifying enough. Most, but by no means all, of the victims had been inmates of asylums for the physically or mentally disabled, or mentally ill. Although the largest single category seems to have been the feeble-minded (Burleigh, 2000), that term was used elastically to include the morally feeble-minded, that is, prostitutes, petty criminals, and anyone deemed antisocial. The Nazi Government also practised positive eugenic policies: the 'Lebensborn' project provided SS troops on leave with young women of impeccable Aryan stock, usually from occupied countries such as the Netherlands and Norway, with the intention that the resulting offspring would in due course replace the men being killed on the battlefield.

Murdoch's book has a chapter entitled 'Nazis and intelligence testing', in which he writes:

Intelligence tests were of prime importance in most sterilization decisions...[They] allowed the Nazis to argue that they were scientifically discerning who was worthy and who was unworthy to live.

(Murdoch, 2007, pp. 121 and 138)

This is a gross exaggeration. German doctors did indeed cobble together a few questions, 'Who was Bismarck?', 'Who discovered America?', which they could put to those suspected of mental disability, but they regarded the results of such tests with scepticism—especially when it was found that they failed to discriminate between normal and backward children in East Prussia, and that far too many members of the Nazi party were unable to give the correct answers (Burleigh, 2000). Proper IQ tests, after all, would have revealed the embarrassing fact that, on average, Jews obtain rather higher test scores than 'Aryans' (Lynn and Longley, 2006; Storfer, 1990). Doctors were more likely to rely on their impressions of the victim's behaviour at interview, and their interest in moral feeble-mindedness resulted in many of these questions being superseded by ones asking why people pray, or why you should tell the truth.

If the case of Carrie Buck marked a high point in the public esteem accorded to eugenic ideas, the evidence from Germany of what could happen when people took the ideas of negative eugenics to what they saw as their logical conclusion, marked the end, at least for the time being, of the eugenic ideal. But eugenic sterilization was, until very recently, still practised in China.

In a common misinterpretation of Darwinian theory it was widely believed that it was no longer the fittest, but the least fit, who were surviving and multiplying (a misinterpretation because the definition of 'fittest' in Darwinian theory is precisely those who survive and multiply). Organized charity and improved public health, it was said, were allowing the poor and perhaps even the feeble-minded to survive in ever greater numbers (left to herself, Nature would have eliminated most of them), while the more prudent and prosperous classes, on whom the future of civilization depended, were limiting their families and hence failing to reproduce themselves. The rise of eugenics at the turn of the century did indeed coincide with a 'demographic transition': the affluent middle classes had started practising birth control, but the poor had not. In the USA fears of this sort were fuelled by the rapidity of social change. In the ten years preceding World War I, some 10 million immigrants entered the country, crowding into the large industrial cities of the east coast and mid-west, and forming, according to many, a new and perhaps dangerously radical urban proletariat, undercutting the wages of established workers. Many concluded that it was time for society to act.

Curbing feeble-mindedness

In his most famous (now infamous) book, *The Kallikak family: A study in the heredity of feeble-mindedness* (1912), Goddard described 23-year-old Deborah Kallikak (the name was invented), an inmate of Vineland with a mental age of 9, and her family background. He traced her ancestry back to a soldier at the time of the American War of Independence, whom he named Martin Kallikak. Martin had children by two different women, one a nameless girl of 'ill repute' who bore him an illegitimate son, the other a respectable Quaker woman whom he married. From these two unions, two distinct families were born, one full of 'paupers, criminals, prostitutes, drunkards', the other producing 'nothing but good representative citizenship...doctors, lawyers, judges, educators, traders, landholders' (Goddard, 1912, pp. 29, 97). Although it was naturally impossible to ascertain the mental level of most of the 480 members of the 'bad' Kallikak family, in the 189 cases where sufficient information was supposedly available to pass judgement, 143 were judged to be feeble-minded and only 46 normal. Goddard saw this as a perfectly controlled study: the two families differed only in their maternal ancestor—one of superior or at least average intelligence, the other said to be feeble-minded (although of course Goddard had no evidence of this). Astonishingly enough, this was sufficient for him to conclude that feeble-mindedness was a 'unit character'—that is to say a character controlled by a single (recessive) gene. That conclusion was reiterated and buttressed in a larger study of the Vineland inmates: 'It is clear from the data already presented that feeble-mindedness is hereditary in a large percentage of the cases, and that it is transmitted in accordance with the Mendelian formula...If both parents are feeble-minded all the children will be feeble-minded. It is obvious that such matings should not be allowed' (Goddard, 1914, pp. 560–1). Where only one parent was feeble-minded, the position was more complex, since the immediate offspring might appear normal, but feeble-mindedness would appear in subsequent generations. The conclusion was inescapable: 'No feeble-minded person should ever be allowed to marry or to become a parent. It is obvious that if this rule is to be carried out the intelligent part of society must enforce it' (Goddard, 1914, p. 565). Terman believed that one of the main uses of IQ tests was to identify the feeble-minded so that they could be brought 'under the surveillance and protection of society. This will ultimately result in curtailing the reproduction of feeble-mindedness and in the elimination of an enormous amount of crime, pauperism, and industrial inefficiency' (Terman, 1916, pp. 6–7). Goddard himself advocated institutionalization as the best means of preventing the feeble-minded from reproducing. But others had different ideas: for many, the simplest way to curtail this reproduction was by sterilization.

It is one thing to show, however, that some early proponents of IQ tests advocated the sterilization of the feeble-minded. It is another to establish that they or their tests had any great effect on public attitudes, policy, or legislation. For in fact there had been enormous public pressure for eugenic measures long before Goddard and Terman brought Binet's tests to America. These measures were to be directed not only against the mentally retarded, and the pressure for them had often been successful. Remember that Binet's tests were unknown in America until Goddard brought them to the attention of teachers and those working with the feeble-minded between 1909 and 1911, by which date there were already six states with sterilization laws on their books and many others with laws restricting marriage between certain categories of undesirables (Kevles, 1985). Dr Isaac Kerlin, the superintendent of a training school for the feeble-minded in Elwyn, Pennsylvania had, with parental permission, started castrating some of the inmates in 1889, having earlier argued for 'the correlation of idiocy, insanity, pauperism and crime' and the need to segregate such people in 'villages of the simple' (quoted by Zenderland, 1998, p. 147). Dr Harry Sharp, the medical superintendent at the Indiana State Reformatory at Jeffersonville, pioneered the sterilization of criminals by vasectomy, and by 1907, when Indiana passed the first compulsory sterilization law, had already performed vasectomies on more than 465 inmates.

Early advocates of measures to curb the reproduction of certain members of society were not particularly concerned with the unintelligent. They cast their net a great deal wider to include the insane, epileptics, habitual drunkards, criminals, prostitutes, tramps, and paupers—a general class of undesirables corresponding to a later generation's 'underclass'? All these characteristics were said to be hereditary, but that term meant something quite different before the rediscovery of Mendel's papers at the beginning of the twentieth century: they were interchangeable symptoms of a more diffuse degeneracy, that would be passed down from one generation to the next, so that 'an insane parent may bear an epileptic child, or an epileptic parent a child who is a profound idiot' (Barr, 1896, quoted by Zenderland, 1998, p. 151).

It is obviously absurd to pretend that the IQ testing movement was responsible for the passage of any legislation in the USA before 1910 or 1911. But there can be little doubt that Goddard succeeded in bringing the 'problem' of the feeble-minded to wider public attention. In 1913, an excerpted version of The Kallikak family appeared as a Book of the Month in a popular magazine, and by 1930 the book had been reprinted 11 times. There can, moreover, be no doubt at all that IQ tests were later used in the USA to justify sterilization in cases of mental disability. Many of the earlier state laws were declared unconstitutional by the courts, but many survived and the total number of states with such laws on their statute books eventually rose to 30. By 1928 nearly 9,000 people had been subject to compulsory sterilization, and by 1964 over 60,000 (Kevles, 1985). Although all these laws provided a variety of different grounds for sterilization ('pauperism', which had always been popular with earlier eugenicists, became even more popular in the depression of the 1930s), mental disability accounted for nearly half the total number of victims, and IQ tests were used as one important measure of this.

Control of immigration

Some of the early American IQ testers also argued vigorously for the control of immigration. Goddard (1917) administered Binet tests to newly arrived immigrants at New York and discovered that an astonishingly high proportion tested at the feeble-minded level or below. But by far the most important information was provided by Yerkes's Army data. They showed enormous differences between men of different national origins. When results were collapsed across both Alpha and Beta tests and scores translated to a letter grade, some 20% of those of English origin, 15% of Scottish, and 10% of Dutch or German origin scored A or B, the two highest grades; but less than 1% of Italians, Poles, or Russians were in these grades. Conversely, less than 15% of the British, Dutch, or German, but over 60% of the Italian, Poles, and Russians scored D. The new immigration from southern and eastern Europe, so it was claimed, was leading to an inexorable decline in the national intelligence. As Carl Brigham wrote in *A study of American intelligence* (1923), based on the Army data:

> The decline in intelligence is due to two factors, the change in the races migrating to this country, and to the additional factor of the sending of lower and lower representatives of each race.
>
> (Brigham, 1923, p. 178)

What was to be done? 'The steps that should be taken to preserve or increase our present intellectual capacity must of course be dictated by science and not by political expediency. Immigration should not only be restrictive but highly selective' (Brigham, 1923, p. 210).

Brigham got his wish. The following year saw the passage of the Immigration Act of 1924 that established national quotas and, more to the point, based those quotas on the incidence of each national group in the 1890 census. No one was in any doubt why 1890 was chosen as the base year: it marked the beginning of the new immigration from southern and eastern Europe, and thus kept the number of new immigrants from these countries to a minimum. Gould (1997) and Kamin (1974) appear to see a simple case of cause and effect: IQ tests, and their interpretation at the hands of racist psychologists, were responsible for the passage of this act. Once again, however, the story is not quite as simple as those who enjoy conspiracy theories of history would like (Samelson, 1975, 1979; Snyderman and Herrnstein, 1983).

In spite of the claim by Rose *et al.* (1984) quoted above, that the Congressional debates leading to the passage of the 1924 Act made frequent reference to the Army data, the facts are rather different. The Act itself makes no mention of IQ tests of any sort at all; the six hundred-page record of Congressional debates leading to the passage of the Act contains *one* exchange on the subject of the Army data; the committee hearings contain the record of three occasions (all carefully cited by Kamin, 1974) on which the Army data were mentioned; the committee's report to Congress contains no mention of these occasions. No psychologist was called to give testimony before the committee (Snyderman and Herrnstein, 1983).

This may dispose of one specific claim, but still leaves open the question of whether the testing movement in general, and the Army data in particular, exerted a more subtle influence. In fact, IQ tests entered the debate on immigration very late in the day. Legal restrictions on immigration dated back at least to 1882, when an act barred the immigration of lunatics and idiots; an act of 1903 barred epileptics and the insane; and one of 1907 barred imbeciles and feeble-minded. This was not enough to satisfy those who professed to believe that native American stock (a term which in those days meant white, Anglo-Saxon, North-Europeans) was being diluted by the new wave of immigrants from southern and eastern Europe. But their objections were economic, political, and social, rather than intellectual: they believed that American values were being destroyed by radicals and Bolsheviks, who were disrupting society and would never be assimilated. It was the inability of the 'melting pot' to cope with such a mass of people of such different backgrounds, and the consequent threat to national unity and homogeneity, that worried most of the proponents of restriction. The Army data were certainly mentioned, and provided additional ammunition for those whose minds were already made up, but Yerkes himself believed that IQ tests should be used on an *individual* basis to screen out intellectually inferior immigrants. This impractical suggestion commended itself neither to politicians anxious for a simple solution nor to racists anxious to preserve America's Nordic heritage (Samelson, 1975, 1979). Samelson's conclusion seems more reasonable than Gould's or Kamin's: 'The eventual passage of the "racist" immigration law of 1924 was not crucially affected by the contributions of Yerkes or other psychologists' (Samelson, 1979, p. 135).

The decline of national intelligence

As I noted above, one of the social changes responsible for the rise of the eugenics movement at the beginning of the twentieth century was the adoption, initially by the educated middle classes, of some form of birth control. In mid-Victorian England, middle-class families contained, on average, about seven or eight children; by the early years of the twentieth century, the number had shrunk to less than three (Lynn, 1996a). But not all families were following this practice, and the implications of this fact were quickly seized upon. Here is Sidney Webb, one of the founders of the British Labour Party, writing in a Fabian tract, published in 1907:

> In Great Britain, at this moment, when half, or perhaps two thirds of all the married people are regulating their families, children are being freely born to the Irish Roman Catholics and the Polish, Russian, and German Jews, on the one hand, and the thriftless and irresponsible—largely the casual labourers and the other denizens of the one-roomed tenements of our great cities—on the other... This can hardly result in anything but national deterioration.

It may be surprising to find such remarks being expressed by a socialist, but fashions and sentiments change, and such attitudes were commonplace among progressive thinkers both in Britain and America (Kevles, 1985). For many eugenicists, the problem seemed to be compounded by the phenomenon of social mobility. As the more able and energetic members of the labouring classes moved up the social scale, it was supposed, they adopted the manners and habits of the middle classes, including the practice of birth control, thus ensuring that it was only their less successful, more feckless brethren who were producing large families. The discovery of the negative correlation between social class and IQ (Burt, 1912; Terman, 1916) added to the gloomy picture, and the final step in the argument was provided by the discovery that there was indeed a negative correlation, $r = -0.32$, between children's IQ scores and the number of children in the family (Cattell, 1937). Cattell was not slow to draw the conclusion: since IQ is inherited, it follows that IQ must be declining in each generation, and the end of civilization as we know it could not long be averted (see Box 1.6).

BOX 1.6 The fight for our national intelligence

In a book with this title, published in 1937, Raymond Cattell calculated that the available data indicated:

> A decline of average IQ for town and country of about three points per generation...or one point per decade. If this were to continue for three hundred years half the population would be mentally defective. Since the changes which mark the rises and declines of history are certainly not as drastic as to require wholesale mental deficiency, the present rate of change must be one of the most galloping plunges to bankruptcy that has ever occurred.

(Cattell, 1937, pp. 42–3)

But what were the data used to establish such doom-laden conclusions? Lacking a direct comparison of the IQ scores of one generation with the next, Cattell, like others before and after him, resorted to arguments based on differences in fertility. But even this was not measured directly. Instead of demonstrating, in a representative sample of the population, a negative correlation between adults' IQ scores and the number of children they produced, Cattell was content to follow earlier IQ testers in demonstrating a negative correlation between children's IQ scores and the number of children in the family. But this correlation, by itself, is quite insufficient to prove the point. Let us suppose that the experience of living in a large family somehow depresses a child's IQ score. What follows? Nothing. Cattell's argument depended on the assumption that the reason why such children had low IQ scores was because they had inherited them from their parents. He assumed that it was low IQ parents who chose to have large families, with the consequence that, in each generation, more children were born to parents of low IQ than to those of high IQ. Cattell did, indeed, seek to establish this point; he carried out a study of one hundred families, in which he measured both parents' and children's IQ scores, finding a correlation of 0.73 between mid-parent and mid-child IQ. But in his haste to accept the desired conclusion, Cattell brushed aside two other aspects of his data. First, there was essentially no correlation between parents' IQ and the number of their children. Second, the children's IQ scores were *higher* than those of their parents. The first observation implies that the negative correlation between family size and children's IQ has rather little to do with differential fertility on the part of parents with high and low IQ. The second would seem to demolish his entire argument: if children have higher IQs than their parents, IQ must be rising from one generation to the next, rather than falling. Cattell tried to explain this finding away by noting that IQ tests then available were not well standardized for adults, and, as a consequence, test scores declined sharply with age. But even when he applied a correction for age, the average IQ of the parents was only 112, compared to 120 for the children. It says much for the power of a preconceived idea that Cattell could continue to believe that IQ must be declining by three points per generation, when his own data suggested an increase of some eight points.

A few moments' reflection should be sufficient to reveal some of the flaws in this argument. Children's IQ scores may well be affected by the number of other children in their family, but that effect might be entirely environmental in origin: with more children parents have less time to interact with each one, less money to spend on them, etc. Cattell's argument really required him to show that *parents* of low IQ had more children than those of higher IQ. His own rather limited data actually suggested no such trend. What is the truth? It took a surprisingly long time for adequate data to become available, but by the end of the century, a series of American studies, with large and representative samples,

confirmed that there was, and had been throughout the twentieth century, a small negative correlation between IQ and fertility (Herrnstein and Murray, 1994; Retherford and
Sewell, 1988; Van Court and Bean, 1985; Vining, 1995; for a summary, see Lynn, 1996a).
In whites at least, this negative correlation, never greater than r = −0.20 and usually nearer
−0.10, was lower than that between children's IQ and the number of other children in the
family. The data for other countries are much sparser and rather less reliable, but at least
some European studies have also suggested that IQ is negatively related to fertility (see
Lynn, 1996a).

It is worth pointing out, however, that these negative correlations probably still overestimate the extent to which there could be any decline in average IQ from one generation
to another. What matters here is not just the number of children born to parents with different levels of IQ, but the number of those children who survive to have children of their own.
Since there is good evidence that IQ is negatively correlated with longevity (see Chapter 8),
the correlation between adults' IQ scores and the number of their *grandchildren* is likely
to be smaller than that between their test scores and the number of their children.

The Flynn effect

The question at issue, however, is whether IQ test scores are or are not decreasing from one
generation to the next. Although one might be able to answer this question by looking at
the relationship between IQ and fertility, there are surely more direct ways. Cattell's own
data (see Box 1.6) actually suggested that children had higher IQs than their parents, but
a very much more reliable procedure would be to obtain IQ scores from two generations
when they were both the same age, for example from a sample of 10-year-old children
in 1950 and from another sample of 10-year-olds in 2000. In 1933 and 1947, the Scottish
Council for Research in Education (1949) did more or less this, reporting the results of
group IQ tests on virtually the entire population of 11-year-olds in the country in these
two years. They found a significant increase, of some 2–3 IQ points, from the earlier to
the later year, and their findings were soon confirmed by Cattell himself, who reported an
increase of 1.3 IQ points in schoolchildren in Leicester between 1936 and 1949 (Cattell,
1950). In the USA, Tuddenham (1948) reported substantial increases in the test scores of
men called up for military service in World War II by comparison with World War I.

Subsequent research, documented and summarized by Flynn (1984, 1987, 2007; see
also Neisser, 1998) has shown that these studies actually underestimated the true rate of
increase in test scores. It is now clear that average test scores increased at a remarkable rate
in most industrialized societies throughout the twentieth century—a finding now known
as the Flynn effect. In France and the Netherlands, for example, where data are available for
virtually the entire population of 18-year-old males (given IQ tests on call-up for military
service), scores increased by some 20–25 points between 1950 and 1980. One way to reconcile these data with the earlier British studies, which reported much smaller increases, is to
note that World War II might have temporarily suppressed the rate of increase in European
test scores: a comparison of pre-war and post-war scores would show only a small increase,
while a comparison of immediately post-war scores and those obtained 20 years later would
show an unduly large increase. Be this as it may, there is now ample evidence that substantial increases have occurred in several other European countries, Australia, New Zealand,

Canada, USA, and Japan (Flynn, 1984; Lynn and Hampson, 1986; Lynn *et al.*, 1988). Are they still occurring? There is evidence that, at least in Scandinavia, they have come to a halt (Sundet *et al.*, 2004; Teasdale and Owen, 2000, 2008). However, there were significant gains on tests of non-verbal reasoning in Britain between 1980 and 2007/2008 (Lynn, 2009), and the latest standardization of the Wechsler tests has shown a steady increase in test scores in the USA that has continued into the twenty-first century (Flynn, 2007).

A difference in the performance of groups of Dutch 18-year-olds in 1980 and 1950 will not say anything about changes in Dutch IQ unless the two groups of 18-year-olds are equally representative. If the two samples were drawn from different sections of the population, the difference in their scores would be uninterpretable. Since many of the European studies tested virtually all male 18-year-olds, the problem does not arise—just as it did not in Cattell's and the Scottish studies, where the entire relevant population was studied. But few studies can hope to sample on such a generous scale, and where they cannot there must always be some question whether there has been some change in the constitution of the samples from one date to the other.

Fortunately, there is another technique which allows one to assess changes in IQ from smaller samples without too much concern for their representative nature. By definition, if a representative sample of the population in 2000 takes a test standardized in 2000, they will obtain an average score of 100. Suppose that they also took a test standardized in 1950, and they obtained an average score of 120. Since, in 1950, a representative sample would have obtained a score of only 100 on this test, it follows that there must have been a 20-point increase in average test score between the 1950 and 2000 samples. But much the same conclusion would follow from less representative samples. If a group of 15-year-old children in 2000 obtains a score of 110 on a 1950 test, and of only 90 on a 2000 test, this is good evidence that the 2000 test is 20 points harder than the 1950 test. Flynn has used this technique with earlier and later versions of the Stanford-Binet and Wechsler tests, to establish that there has been a relatively steady increase in American test scores of some 15 to 20 points between 1930 and 2000.

The Flynn effect is important, and clearly demolishes the fears of an earlier generation of psychometricians such as Cattell. It is also surely surprising. What has happened to cause these large increases in test scores? I defer an attempt to answer this question until Chapter 12. But one important question must be addressed right away: does the Flynn effect represent a real increase in *intelligence*, or just an increase in IQ scores? The problem can be put succinctly. If the increase is just in IQ scores, not really in intelligence, then IQ tests are not good measures of intelligence. But if the increase has been in intelligence, then the Flynn effect seems to imply that most people born in the early years of the twentieth century, with a score of no more than 70 to 80 when measured against today's norms, were bordering on the mildly learning disabled.

The paradox is surely real, although one way to draw at least some of its sting is to note that the Flynn effect has not seen a uniform increase in scores on all kinds of IQ test. Those with serious disabilities are those who obtain low scores on essentially *any* IQ test. The generation born in 1900 did not obtain drastically low scores (by today's standards) on all IQ tests, only on some. Chapter 2 will discuss the variety of different IQ tests that were developed after World War I, but it is important to understand at this point that this proliferation of new test batteries resulted in the discovery of a variety of rather different aspects or components of IQ, with the most obvious distinction being that between verbal and non-verbal tests: earlier versions of the Wechsler scales were divided into a verbal and a performance half. The largest gains have occurred on tests of non-verbal reasoning or figural analogies, such as Raven's Matrices, and on tests of visuo-spatial ability such as the block design from the performance half of the Wechsler scales. Tests of verbal ability and general knowledge, such as the vocabulary, information, and arithmetic tests from verbal half of the Wechsler scales, have seen very much more modest gains (see Figure 1.1). Indeed in both Britain and the USA, while tests of abstract reasoning have continued to show substantial gains, there has been essentially no increase in scores on tests of vocabulary for the past 25 years or more (Flynn, 2007; Lynn, 2009). Your great grandmother probably had a vocabulary about as extensive as (although no doubt different from) yours. In at least some respects, therefore, people born in 1900 may have been less intelligent on average than the generation born in 1980, but they were not disabled: their intelligence was *different* from that of today's generation of students. They were undoubtedly less proficient at solving the sorts of figural analogies and series completion tests that IQ testers have invented as measures of non-verbal or abstract reasoning, but they were perfectly intelligent in many other ways. I shall discuss some possible reasons for this in a later chapter.

As can be seen in Figure 1.1, two other examples of tests that have shown substantial gains over the past 50 years are the comprehension and similarities tests of the Wechsler scales. Although these are classified as tests of verbal ability, along with the vocabulary test, if they have shown gains while vocabulary has not, they cannot be measuring the

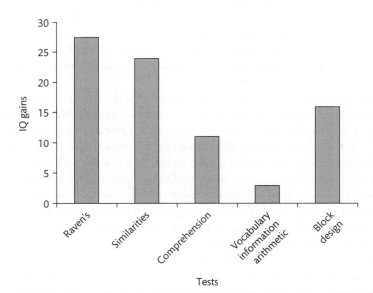

Figure 1.1 American gains in scores on various tests from the Wechsler Intelligence Scale for Children (WISC) from 1947 to 2002. 'Vocabulary information arithmetic' is the average gain on the vocabulary, information and arithmetic tests. The Raven's data are not American, but an estimate derived from the gains recorded on Raven's Matrices in several countries of western Europe, Israel, and Argentina (the data are from Flynn (2007), Figure 1, and Appendix 1, Table 1).

same thing. Why have they shown such gains? The comprehension test asks, among other things, for the meaning of various proverbs: what does 'One swallow does not make a summer' mean? What you have to do here is see the *abstract* meaning of this specific, concrete sentence, which would then allow it to be used in quite different contexts. This is rather similar to what is required to perceive analogies. The similarities test asks you to say in what way two different things are alike, thus 'In what way are a sword and a gun alike?' The correct answer would be to say they are both weapons. To say that they are both dangerous or that you can use both to kill people is not correct, and to point to any difference between them gets you no points at all. In effect, you are required to place items in the same taxonomic category. As Flynn (2007) has argued, this may seem obvious enough to a generation brought up in today's science-based industrialized societies, but it is clearly not the only way to categorize objects in the world—and actually seems quite unnatural to people brought up in many other cultures (see Chapter 13). Perhaps it also seemed less natural to people born in 1900.

Conclusion

It is commonly assumed that any psychological enquiry should begin with a clear and precise definition of the object of that enquiry. And since IQ testers have failed to provide such a definition of the 'intelligence' that their tests purport to measure, they have failed at the first hurdle. But good definitions are the end product of scientific investigation, not its starting point. Given a rough and ready idea of the subject of the enquiry, it is possible to proceed by trial and error. So it has been with the development of IQ tests: initial attempts by Galton and Cattell to measure intelligence by tests of sensory discrimination or reaction time were abandoned when it seemed that they failed to agree with an obvious external criterion of intelligence—students' college grades. On the assumption that children become intellectually more competent as they grow older, Binet used young children's age as an external criterion of intelligence and developed a series of tests based on this simple premise: an intelligence test for 6-year-olds should contain a series of items which the majority of 6-year-olds, but fewer 4-year-olds and virtually all 8-year-olds, could answer correctly. Further refinement and empirical trial and error, based on a standardization sample of some 1,000 children between the ages of 4 and 14, resulted in Terman's Stanford-Binet test, which for a long time served as the benchmark against which other IQ tests were measured.

Is the Stanford-Binet test a good measure of intelligence? Possibly. At least, it is possible to show that scores on this and other IQ tests do roughly what would be expected of a measure of intelligence (a point documented much more thoroughly in Chapters 8 and 9). A less strictly scientific question is whether IQ tests have served good or evil purposes—a common charge being that, from their inception, they were used as instruments of oppression against the poor and disadvantaged. IQ tests have not always been benign in their influence, and can certainly be criticized on other grounds. Many early IQ testers expressed some rather foolish, and as it turned out quite unjustified, fears about the decline in national intelligence. Many held social and political views that, although relatively commonplace at the time, are widely regarded as repugnant today; and some of them sought support for those views in the results of their tests. But whether or not it is the job of historians to pass moral judgement on the past, it is surely their job to try to *understand* the past, and that must involve, among other things, setting past actions, attitudes, and beliefs into the context of their time. A further danger arises when scientists start writing about social and intellectual history: they are likely to exaggerate the influence that their science had on that history. Neither IQ testers nor their tests were anything like as powerful as has sometimes been made out.

Summary

- It is important to distinguish between the 'intelligence' that is common to all people, and which serves to distinguish us from other animals, and the *differences* in 'intelligence' that distinguish the more from the less intelligent among us.
- For much of the twentieth century, psychologists studying human intelligence were concerned only with the second of these, that is, with differences in intelligence between different people. IQ tests were devised to measure these differences.
- The first successful intelligence test was developed by Alfred Binet in France at the beginning of the twentieth century. His success depended on two factors:
  - Unlike previous attempts to measure intelligence, Binet's tests measured everyday practical skills, rather than relying on the procedures of the experimental psychology of his day.
  - He used *age* as an independent criterion of intelligence. Since young children grow in intellectual competence as they grow older, Binet saw that a good test of intelligence must be one more likely to be passed by older than by younger children.
- Binet's tests were expanded and further developed by Terman, and became known as the Stanford-Binet test—now in its fifth edition.
- Contrary to early eugenic fears about declining national IQ, scores on IQ tests increased by 20–30 points over the course of the twentieth century—the so-called Flynn effect.

Further reading

Fancher (1985) gives an excellent and more detailed account of the development of intelligence tests from Galton to Goddard, and Cianciolo and Sternberg (2004) a rather more wide ranging history. Much of what has been written about the abuses of IQ tests is polemical and less than perfectly reliable, but Kevles (1985), a historian, and Samelson (1979), a historian of psychology, provide reasonably impartial accounts. The most illuminating account of the Flynn effect is, appropriately, by Flynn himself (2007). But an earlier book, edited by Neisser (1998), provides a spectrum of different opinions and explanations.

2 Psychometric theories of intelligence

Introduction

Although the initial development of IQ tests probably owed more to empirical trial and error than to profound psychological theorizing, early IQ testers, like those who followed them, did have theoretical views about the nature of the intelligence that their tests were supposedly measuring. Binet himself had tried his hand at defining intelligence—even if largely by exclusion. Charles Spearman, on the other hand, one of the other most influential figures in the early history of IQ testing, was solely concerned with theory. He did not himself devise new tests: his influence derives first from his theoretical argument that all measures of intelligence, however diverse they might appear, are in fact measuring a single underlying construct of general intelligence, which he labelled g, and second, from his development of a precursor of modern factor analysis, which he believed provided evidence for this theory.

Spearman's views did not go unchallenged, and as more and more different tests were developed, so it became clear that there was more to these tests than just g. The present chapter begins with a discussion of these newer tests and the psychometric theories of intelligence that informed their development. I then introduce the statistical techniques of factor analysis that underlie these developments, and show how an eventual (near) consensus has emerged in the form of a so-called 'hierarchical' model of the structure of the intelligence measured by IQ tests.

The variety of IQ tests: one intelligence or many?

Whether or not IQ tests served a malign purpose from the outset, what cannot be disputed is that the 1920s and 1930s saw, especially in the USA, a great expansion in their use. One consequence of this popularity was a proliferation of rival tests, as psychologists and publishers hastened to exploit a seemingly ever-expanding market. By 1935, Buros started publishing a yearbook, listing all mental tests (a term covering much more than IQ tests). Later editions included more detail and evaluation of the tests. The seventeenth edition, (Geisinger *et al.*, 2007), included details of some 3,500 tests—not all, of course, tests of intelligence.

There is no need to describe all, or even many, of these tests in any detail. But I shall start with a discussion of two of the more important, the Wechsler scales and Raven's Matrices, partly because they have been among the most widely used, but also because they differ very sharply from one another and thus give some idea of the diversity of tests and test batteries described as measures of IQ.

The Wechsler tests: WAIS and WISC

Although the Stanford-Binet test has been revised several times, most recently for the fifth time as SB5 (Roid, 2003), it has probably been overtaken in popularity. The most widely used individual IQ tests today are the Wechsler tests, first published in 1939 as the Wechsler-Bellevue Scale. Binet's original tests were designed for use with young children, and although Terman's original standardization sample included children up to the age of 14, and also some four hundred older teenagers and adults, he readily acknowledged that this older sample was far from representative of the population as a whole, and the next revision of the Stanford-Binet did not include adults at all (that is no longer true of recent revisions). The Stanford-Binet thus provided imperfect adult norms, and did not even pretend to provide norms for adults of different ages. The Wechsler-Bellevue test, designed for, and standardized on, a sample of some 1,500 adults (as well as some children), thus filled an important gap in the market. In 1955, it was revised as the Wechsler Adult Intelligence Scale (WAIS), with a standardization sample of over 2,000 people, aged 16–75, for by now Wechsler had also developed a version of the test suitable for children aged 5–16, the Wechsler Intelligence Scale for Children (WISC). Both have since been revised, first as WAIS-R and WISC-R and, more recently, as WAIS-III, and then WAIS-IV, and WISC-III and WISC-IV (Wechsler, 2003, 2008).

Both the Stanford-Binet and Wechsler tests are individual tests, administered by a single examiner to a single examinee. David Wechsler, however, introduced two major methodological changes, that have now been adopted by most other test constructors. Following Binet's original model, the early versions of the Stanford-Binet test consisted of a number of different tests, which were grouped by age. Thus a typical 6-year-old child would take a set of half-a-dozen tests designed for 6-year-olds, while a 10-year-old child would take quite a different set of tests (although, of course, a child could be given more than one set of tests). This was a reflection of Binet's original concept of mental age, which was still used in the original Stanford-Binet.

Wechsler's first innovation was to devise a single set of tests, suitable for all ages, with each test ranging from easy to difficult items. Those used in the WISC had almost exactly the same format as those from the earlier Weschler-Bellevue test and later WAIS, and, although incorporating many easier items than those used in the adult tests, still spanned a wide range of difficulty so that a single test was deemed suitable for children ranging in age from 5 to 16.

Wechsler's second innovation was the concept of the 'deviation IQ'. In the original Stanford-Binet test IQ was defined as:

$$\frac{\text{Mental age} \times 100}{\text{Chronological age}}$$

But this formula only makes any sort of sense when applied to children whose mental age, that is, ability to answer items in an IQ test, continues to increase as they grow older. As Terman discovered when testing his adult sample, mental age does not continue to grow indefinitely—that is to say, his adult sample did not obtain appreciably higher test scores than his sample of high school students. Strict application of the IQ formula above, therefore, would have meant that the average 32-year-old had an IQ half that of the average 16-year-old. To avoid this absurdity, Terman had to resort to another: he assigned all adults a chronological age of 16.

Although the World War I Army tests had, of course, been designed to assess adult intelligence, it was sufficient, for the purpose to which the tests were put, to rely on absolute test scores, or even a crude division of such scores into one of four categories, A–D. But when Wechsler introduced the first individual adult IQ test, he needed a new method for assigning IQ scores. His solution was to define IQ not in terms of mental and chronological age, but in terms of an individual's actual score on a test (the number of items correctly answered) relative to the score to be expected of people of the same age. The formula was:

$$\frac{\text{Actual test score} \times 100}{\text{Expected score}}$$

But what was this expected score? The answer was simply the average score obtained by a large representative sample of the population. Thus, to measure the IQ of a particular 30-year-old, what Wechsler needed was a representative (standardization) sample of 30-year-olds: he could then ascertain their average test score (number of items correctly answered), and compare any individual's score to this average, and so on, for every other age group. Thus Wechsler's standardization sample was carefully stratified by age as well as by other demographic characteristics (sex, social class, region of the country), and divided into age groups spanning 5–10 year ranges.

A test score equal to the average of one's age group defined an IQ of 100. But how does one convert test scores above or below this mean into IQ scores? Deviations from the mean of a set of scores are measured by calculating the standard deviation of that set of scores. If the scores are distributed approximately normally, as is shown in Figure 2.1, roughly 68% will fall within ± 1 standard deviation of the mean, 95% within ± 2 standard deviations, and so on. You can calculate the standard deviation of the actual test scores of the sample of 30-year-olds (20 in the illustrative example of Figure 2.1) and then convert these scores into IQs by adopting the wholly arbitrary convention that the standard deviation of IQ is 15 points. Thus, a test score of 100, one standard deviation above the mean of 80, translates into an IQ of 115; a score of 40, two standard deviations below the mean, translates into an IQ of 70, and so on.

Thus, an IQ score on the WAIS (a deviation IQ) is simply a reflection of an individual's relative standing with respect to others of the same age. It is not an absolute score. In the jargon of psychological measurement theory, IQ is not a ratio scale: there is no absolute zero for IQ, as there is for height or weight, and someone with an IQ of 150 is not twice as intelligent as another with an IQ of 75, in the sense that someone six feet tall is twice as tall as someone of three feet. Although many psychometricians have argued otherwise (e.g. Jensen, 1980), it is not immediately obvious that IQ is even an interval scale, that is, one where, say, the ten-point difference between IQ scores of 110 and 100 is the same as

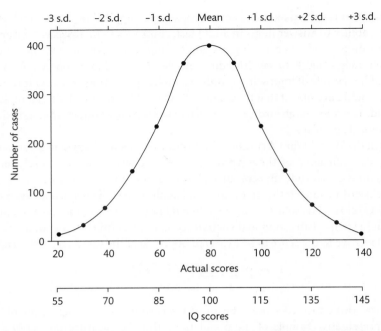

Figure 2.1 Hypothetical distribution of scores on an IQ test. The mean of the distribution of actual scores is 80, which thus defines an IQ score of 100 for this sample of individuals. The standard deviation (s.d.) of the actual scores is 20—that is to say a score of 60 is 1 s.d. below the mean of 80; by adopting the convention that the standard deviation of IQ is 15, a score of 60 translates into an IQ of 85 (100–15), and so on.

the ten-point difference between IQs of 160 and 150. The most conservative view would be that IQ is simply an ordinal scale: to say that someone has an IQ of 130 is simply to say that their test score lies within the top 2.5% of a representative sample of people of the same age. If this is accepted, then IQ scores are following the path set by Galton in the nineteenth century. Galton did not seek to measure ability or eminence on any absolute scale, but simply in terms of individuals' rank order in the population—whether they were in the top 1%, 5%, or 25%.

Content of the Wechsler tests

Earlier versions of the Wechsler tests divided them into verbal and performance halves, but this has since changed: the WAIS-III consisted of 13 tests and the WAIS-IV of 15, divided into four different groups, as shown in Box 2.1. The distinction between verbal and non-verbal or performance IQ is indeed one of the oldest in the history of IQ testing. As will become apparent, indeed as is apparent in the newer four-fold classification of the WAIS-III and WAIS-IV, this simple distinction is a serious oversimplification.

The origin of the verbal and performance tests can be traced back to the Army Alpha and Beta tests (verbal and non-verbal or performance respectively), which in fact provided the original source of many of Wechsler's original tests (with the exception of those marked with asterisks in Box 2.1, which are new to the WAIS-III and WAIS-IV). Given that the

BOX 2.1 The Wechsler tests

The WAIS-IV comprises 15 tests, divided into four groups, verbal comprehension, perceptual reasoning, working memory, and processing speed. One test from the old WAIS, object assembly, was omitted; three new ones, marked by an asterisk, were added for the WAIS-III and WAIS-IV, and a further two, marked by a double asterisk for the WAIS-IV only. The tests are briefly characterized as follows (the examples given are illustrative only; they are not the same as actual questions in the test):

Verbal comprehension

Information is a general knowledge quiz, with a careful mixture of questions covering science, religion, politics, geography, literature, etc.

Vocabulary asks for definitions of the meanings of words, such as interrupt, ambivalent, or sonorous.

Comprehension asks the meaning of various sayings or proverbs, or what is the appropriate thing to do in certain situations, or such 'good-citizen' questions as: why is it important to vote in a general election?

Similarities ask in what ways two things are alike, for example a hammer and a screwdriver, or avarice and gluttony.

Perceptual reasoning

Picture completion shows line drawings of more or less familiar objects or scenes, from which one important part is missing—exactly as in the Army Beta test.

Block design gives you nine coloured cubes, each with two red, two white, and two diagonally red and white faces. Your task is to arrange them so as to form certain patterns, and bonus points are earned for rapid answers.

Picture arrangement: each item consists of a number of pictures on separate cards which, when arranged in the correct order, tell a simple story (for WAIS-III only).

* *Matrix reasoning*: each item shows a 3 x 3 matrix of patterns, with the last pattern missing; your task is to select, from a number of alternatives on offer, the pattern that best completes the matrix. It is similar to Raven's Matrices illustrated in Figure 2.2.

** *Visual puzzles*: a completed puzzle is shown, and you must choose the response options that can be combined to form the puzzle.

** *Figure weights*: you must select the missing weights required to balance a scale.

Working memory

Arithmetic sets problems in mental arithmetic: if two men dig a hole in 1½ hours, how long would it take six men to dig the same hole?

Digit span requires you to repeat a series of digits, e.g. 7, 1, 6, 9, 3, read out by the examiner. In a second, harder part of the test, the task is to repeat the series in reverse order; thus 2, 8, 5, 4 would become 4, 5, 8, 2.

* *Letter-number sequencing*: the examiner reads out an alternating sequence of numbers and letters, e.g. 7, X, 4, M; your task is to repeat them, but putting the numbers first in ascending order, and the letters next, in alphabetical order, thus: 4, 7, M, X.

Processing speed

Digit symbol: a test sheet displays, at the top, the digits 1–9, in order, beneath each of which is a particular symbol; below this is a series of boxes, each with a digit on top and a blank space below; your task is to fill in the appropriate symbol in these blank spaces (with instructions *not* to go through the list filling in all the symbols for 1, then all those for 2, but rather to fill in each item in the random order in which they are printed).

* *Symbol search* shows a list of symbols, followed by a series of test items consisting of pairs of symbols; your task is to identify which symbol in each pair appears in the list.

** *Cancellation*: you must identify target shapes within a structured arrangement of shapes.

Only a short time is allowed for all three of these tests, and your score on each is simply the number of items correctly completed within this time limit.

Army tests are now nearly one hundred years old, the criticism that IQ tests have changed rather little since they were first introduced (Murdoch, 2007) seems fair enough when applied to the Wechsler scales before their latest revisions.

The nature of the items in each of the tests is illustrated in Box 2.1. Readers more familiar with IQ tests that require the solution of analogies, odd-one-out, or series completion problems may find the content of the Wechsler tests mildly surprising. Certainly, the tests carried over from earlier versions contain relatively little of this sort of problem solving or reasoning: the information, vocabulary, and comprehension tests seem tests of knowledge rather than problem-solving ability; other tests place a premium on rapid execution of a straightforward task which everyone could get right given the time (digit symbol); while yet others seem simply to require an eye for detail (picture completion). The only explanation given by Wechsler for the absence of reasoning problems in his own early versions of the WAIS is the cryptic and wholly false assertion that items demanding abstract reasoning are sometimes very poor measures of intelligence (Wechsler, 1958). One of the new tests marked with asterisks, matrix reasoning, is intended to fill this gap. A second, letter number sequencing, is designed to measure working memory—a construct that will figure largely in later discussions of the cognitive operations underlying test performance (Chapters 4 and 5). A third and fourth, symbol search and cancellation, provide additional tests designed to measure the speed at which people can carry out relatively simple operations. One salient characteristic of the scale as a whole, the remarkable diversity of the various tests that it contains, was quite deliberate policy.

This policy was initially based on the belief that particular types of test might favour or penalize particular people or even groups of people. Diversity of content was thus one way of ensuring that the test as a whole was fair. More generally, Wechsler argued, rather as Binet had earlier, that a person's intelligence could be manifest in a variety of different ways, and the wider the range of tests, and items within tests, the greater the chance that the test as a whole would provide a well-rounded view of that person's intelligence. But he stopped well short of the view espoused by Thurstone (1938), Guilford (1967), or Gardner (1993), which holds that intelligence should be conceptualized as a set of half-a-dozen or more relatively independent faculties. In the dispute between Thurstone and Spearman (1927), who argued that there was a single general factor of intelligence, g, common to all tests, Wechsler wanted it both ways. On the one hand: 'While intelligence may manifest itself in a variety of ways, one must assume that there is some communality or basic similarity between those forms of behavior which one identifies as intelligent' (Wechsler, 1958, p. 5). On the other hand, he insisted that: 'Other salient factors besides g enter into measures of intelligence... [and] the entity or quantity which we are able to measure by intelligence tests is not a simple quantity. Certainly, it is not something which can be expressed by one single factor alone' (Wechsler, 1958, pp. 12, 14).

Be this as it may, Wechsler tacitly accepted a central implication of Spearman's position: although the items and tests included were deliberately chosen to be as diverse as possible, they simultaneously had to satisfy a further essential criterion: they should all correlate with one another. This may seem an unnecessary restriction, but it is not an unreasonable one to impose. To see why, it is only necessary to recall the results of Wissler's experiment described in Chapter 1. Wissler (1901) found that the various mental tests devised by Cattell did not correlate with one another, and drew the conclusion that they could not all be adequate measures of intelligence: if one was, then the others, which did not agree with it, could not be. Once you are confident that you have found one test that measures intelligence, it seems only reasonable to insist that further tests should at least *tend* to agree with it. But however reasonable, such a strategy comes close to endorsing Spearman's key assumption that intelligence is a unitary process. It certainly guarantees that factor analysis will yield the strong general factor, *g*, which Spearman regarded as evidence for his view (see below).

Whether or not one insists that all parts of an IQ test should correlate positively with all other parts, a second sensible principle of test construction is that no two parts should correlate absolutely perfectly with one another. If they do, one of them must be redundant. Thus, the correlation matrix for most test batteries looks something like that for the WAIS-III, shown in Table 2.1: the correlations between each pair of tests are all positive, ranging from a low of 0.30 to a high of 0.77. A second feature of Table 2.1 is that the tests differ in the strength of their correlations with others: information and vocabulary correlate quite strongly with all other tests, while digit span and digit symbol show much more modest correlations. Finally, although there are many exceptions, there is some suggestion that the tests within a particular group, verbal comprehension or working memory, correlate more highly with one another (the average correlations are 0.73 and 0.55) than tests in one group correlate with tests in another (the average correlation between the four verbal comprehension tests and the three working memory tests is 0.49). It is this fact that justifies the division of the test as a whole into four groups. It also carries a further, important implication. If a strong positive correlation between two or more tests is consistent with the assumption that they both, in part, measure the same underlying trait or process, there is an even clearer implication that if two tests do *not* correlate with one another, they cannot be measuring the same thing. Thus, the *relatively* low correlations between tests in different groups suggest that the WAIS cannot be measuring *only* a single process of general intelligence, but that a distinction can and should be drawn between different aspects of intelligence. Much more on this later.

The fact that all parts of the WAIS correlate positively with one another (even if sometimes only quite modestly) is, of course, a consequence of the decision to include in the test battery only those tests that satisfy this criterion. In that sense, it is unsurprising and might even be thought to be without empirical implication. But it is, surely, somewhat surprising that tests of such diverse content should be able to satisfy such a criterion. Why should it be the case that people with a large vocabulary and fund of general knowledge should also be good at arranging coloured blocks to make particular patterns, or quick at filling in the appropriate symbol below each of a series of digits? There is no *a priori* reason why this should have been so, and in this sense it is an empirical discovery that such a wide variety of tests should satisfy this criterion. And it is an empirical discovery of considerable importance, for it serves to reinforce the test constructors' claim that their tests are probably not doing too bad a job at measuring something that we could call intelligence. But why that should be so will be answered more convincingly after consideration of some quite different tests.

Table 2.1 The correlation matrix, from the test's standardization sample, for the 13 tests of the WAIS-III (data from Wechsler, 1997, Table 4.12).

	Inf	Voc	Com	Sim	PC	BD	PA	MR	Ar	DSp	LN	DSy	SS
Information	–												
Vocabulary	0.77	–											
Comprehension	0.70	0.75	–										
Similarities	0.70	0.76	0.70	–									
Picture completion	0.46	0.47	0.46	0.48	–								
Block design	0.48	0.50	0.49	0.52	0.52	–							
Picture arrangement	0.54	0.53	0.50	0.52	0.49	0.49	–						
Matrix reasoning	0.53	0.54	0.52	0.54	0.48	0.60	0.50	–					
Arithmetic	0.63	0.60	0.57	0.57	0.40	0.54	0.44	0.58	–				
Digit span	0.40	0.45	0.39	0.40	0.30	0.36	0.33	0.42	0.52	–			
Letter number	0.50	0.50	0.44	0.46	0.41	0.43	0.39	0.47	0.55	0.57	–		
Digit symbol	0.38	0.44	0.37	0.44	0.39	0.41	0.37	0.40	0.43	0.36	0.44	–	
Symbol search	0.46	0.48	0.44	0.48	0.49	0.53	0.45	0.48	0.52	0.41	0.49	0.44	–

Raven's Matrices

According to Spearman (1927), the most important ingredient of general intelligence was the ability to see relationships between objects, events or ideas, and to draw inferences from those relationships. He called these the eduction of relations and the eduction of correlates, and termed them his 'noegenetic laws'. But these barbarous neologisms need not concern us further. To them, Spearman and Jones (1950) later added the further criterion that intelligence involved the ability to think in abstract rather than in particular, concrete terms. Spearman's arguments implied, it seemed to Penrose and Raven (1936), that a good measure of general intelligence would be a series of analogical reasoning or series completion tests. A simple analogy is:

Cat is to purr, as dog is to bark.

More generally, analogies can be represented as:

A is to A' as B is to B'.

Their solution requires you to see the relationship between A and A', and whether it is the same as the relationship between B and B'—this latter part of the problem often requiring you also to see the relationship between A and B.

A simple series completion task is:

B, C, B, C, D, C, D, E, … which letter comes next?

This particular example can also be conceptualized as requiring the solver to see the relationships between letters within groups (here groups of three), the relationships between each group of three, and thus the appropriate third letter in the third group.

Penfield and Raven also took seriously Spearman's notion that intelligence involved the ability to handle abstract terms. Thus, the result of their cogitations was a series of test items of the form shown in Figure 2.2. The main box contains a 3×3 matrix of diagrams with the third diagram in the third row missing. The examinee's task is to select, from the alternatives on offer below, that alternative which will complete the third row. The test was later published as the Standard Progressive Matrices (Raven, 1938), and has recently been substantially revised. There are two other versions of the test, the Coloured Progressive Matrices for young children, and the Advanced Progressive Matrices for students and adults of above average IQ. I shall usually refer to them all, indifferently, as Raven's Matrices. All three versions of the test consist of a number of items (up to 60) like that illustrated in Figure 2.2, covering a fairly wide range of difficulty. In the Advanced test, the items increase in difficulty as you progress through the test; the Standard test is divided into five blocks of 12 items, each block embodying slightly different rules which get harder to infer in later blocks, and beginning with easier and ending with harder items within each block.

The contrast between the Raven and Wechsler tests could hardly be greater. Raven's Matrices are a paper and pencil, multiple-choice test, which can be administered at the same time to an indefinitely large group of people. They are carefully constructed to start with extremely simple and straightforward items, which everyone can understand, and get right, with the absolute minimum of instructions (the Advanced Matrices begins with a set of practice items). One of their perceived virtues, therefore, has been that they can be

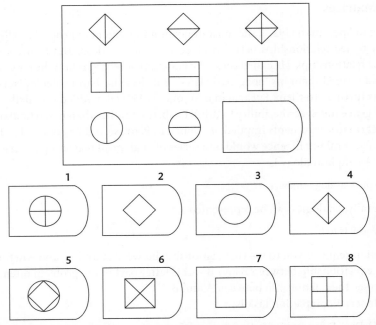

Figure 2.2 Illustration of the type of item appearing in Raven's Matrices. The task is to select, from the alternatives below, the diagram which best completes the 3 ×3 matrix above.

used with populations, such as the deaf or those whose first language is not the same as that of the examiner, who might find it difficult to follow all the examiner's instructions and questions during the administration of the WAIS or WISC. Deaf children, indeed, obtain scores on Raven's Matrices well within the normal range, in spite of a Wechsler verbal IQ significantly below normal (Conrad, 1979).

In addition to these differences in the way the tests are administered, the contents of Raven's Matrices seem to have virtually nothing in common with the original Wechsler tests—although, as noted above, a matrices test, clearly modelled on Raven's, was included in the WAIS-III. Yet the correlations observed between Raven's and earlier Wechsler tests in the general population were typically of the order of 0.40 to 0.75 (Court and Raven, 1995). A final difference between the two tests, which I have already noted, is that Raven's Matrices were explicitly designed to provide a direct measure of those cognitive processes theoretically supposed to underlie general intelligence. By contrast with Wechsler's approach, which deliberately sought diversity of content as a way of ensuring that he did not miss any of the ways in which intelligence might be manifest, Penrose and Raven equally deliberately concentrated on one particular class of test, which they believed would measure abstract reasoning ability and nothing else.

Why should two quite different IQ tests, constructed on different principles, administered in different ways, and containing entirely different kinds of items, still correlate so highly with one another? The intercorrelation between the various parts of the WAIS or

WISC could perhaps be attributed to the criteria adopted for the inclusion of items in the test. But that argument cannot seriously apply here. There is no evidence that Penrose and Raven tinkered around with the items that eventually contributed to their Matrices until they had found ones that correlated with existing IQ tests such as the Stanford-Binet (the Wechsler tests did not yet exist). Nor is there any reason to believe that Wechsler selected items for his tests on the basis of their agreement with Raven's Matrices (on the contrary, he believed that tests of reasoning were poor measures of intelligence). The correlation between such diverse tests, therefore, is of some theoretical significance, and surely poses a challenge to anyone who argues that IQ tests completely fail to measure anything they would want to call intelligence. The challenge can be spelled out thus: if no existing IQ test measures intelligence, then it ought to be possible to devise some other tests that do. And these new tests would, necessarily, show zero correlations with any existing IQ test, since the claim is that existing tests, unlike the new ones, fail to measure intelligence. But given the diversity of tests that do correlate quite substantially with one another (numerous other tests and test batteries have been developed, all of which satisfy the criterion of agreeing with existing test batteries—see Box 2.2), this challenge begins to look a serious one: it seems difficult to find a test, with any sort of face validity as a measure of intelligence, which will not correlate with existing IQ tests.

BOX 2.2 The variety of test batteries

I shall not bore the reader by listing all tests and test batteries that have been developed over the years, but since some of them will appear in later chapters, it is worth mentioning a few.

DAT or Differential Aptitude Test
This comprises eight different tests: language; spelling; verbal, abstract, and numerical reasoning; space relations; mechanical reasoning; and perceptual and clerical speed.

Woodcock-Johnson Test (W-J III)
The test, now in its third revision, was explicitly designed to measure the factors identified by the Cattell-Horn-Carroll model of intelligence (see later in this chapter), with separate tests of: comprehension-knowledge; long-term retrieval; visual-spatial thinking; auditory processing; fluid reasoning; processing speed; short-term memory; quantitative knowledge; and reading-writing ability. It also provides a summary measure of the general factor, general intellectual ability (GIA).

AFQT or Armed Forces Qualifying Test
As the name implies, a test introduced by the American military in 1950 as an entrance requirement. It comprises eight different tests: general science; arithmetic reasoning; word knowledge; paragraph comprehension; mathematics knowledge; electronics information; auto shop; mechanical comprehension; assembling objects.

   Although some of these tests are clearly vocational, many are similar to those appearing in traditional batteries, measuring verbal and visuo-spatial abilities.

SAT
This is the test most widely used for college entrance in the USA. Originally called the Scholastic Aptitude Test, it changed its name to Scholastic Achievement Test, but is now just plain SAT. There were originally two forms—SAT-Verbal and SAT-Mathematical. It is a multiple-choice test, similar in form to many group IQ tests, although a recent addition has been a written essay.

The variety of tests expands to include measures of specific abilities

The publication of Raven's Matrices prompted a number of similar group tests of non-verbal reasoning, among them Raymond Cattell's tests, which he explicitly and confidently described as a 'culture-fair' intelligence test (Cattell, 1940). Cattell's argument, which was accepted by many others, was that tests such as the Stanford-Binet or Wechsler scales could not give a fair picture of the intelligence of children from different backgrounds, because they asked questions about the meanings of English words or for evidence of specifically cultural knowledge that would simply not be equally available to all. By contrast, his tests used abstract and diagrammatic material that would be equally familiar or unfamiliar to all, and the tasks required, such as the solution of series completion tests, odd-one-out problems, as well as analogies and matrices, were testing skills that were not explicitly taught in school.

The idea that non-verbal tests were culturally fairer than verbal tests had its origin in the World War I Army tests (Alpha and Beta). Like many other long-cherished beliefs about IQ tests, it contains *at best* only a very small grain of truth (see Chapters 12 and 13). That is another matter. What is evident, however, and of more immediate concern, is that, in spite of the correlation between them, there does seem to be some sort of distinction between verbal and non-verbal IQ tests. In representative samples of the population, performance on a paradigmatic test of non-verbal reasoning, such as Raven's Matrices, correlates more highly with performance on other non-verbal tests than with scores on verbal tests. In a study of some 3,000 adults, Burke (1985) reported a correlation of 0.68 between Raven's scores and performance on the Shipley abstract reasoning test, but one of only 0.48 between Raven's and the Shipley vocabulary test. Several other studies have confirmed that the correlation between Raven's Matrices and various vocabulary tests is of the order 0.40 to 0.50 (Court and Raven, 1995: many of these studies have employed the Mill-Hill vocabulary test, specifically designed by Raven to complement the measure of abstract, non-verbal reasoning provided by his Matrices). But correlations between Raven's scores and other non-verbal reasoning tests, including Cattell's tests, have usually been of the order 0.60 to 0.85 (Court and Raven, 1995).

Although Spearman's main contribution to the theory of IQ was his concept of *g* or general intelligence, his influence can still be detected in these later developments. His argument, that there is a single, fundamental process of general intelligence which permeates all intellectual activities, and determines performance on any test properly described as a measure of intelligence, provided a simple and satisfying explanation of what came to be called the positive manifold—the finding of positive correlations between a wide variety of different tests. His further argument, which he called the principle of the indifference of the indicator, that the more diverse the set of tests included in a test battery, the better that battery would measure general intelligence, because idiosyncrasies in particular tests would cancel each other out, provided the justification for the construction of test batteries such as the WAIS and WISC. But at the same time, the very simplicity of Spearman's hypothesis, and its apparent eminent testability, encouraged some IQ testers to look for evidence that would contradict it. What they were searching for was evidence of the existence of more specialized sets of abilities. Thurstone and his followers were the most prominent champions of the view that human intelligence is better conceived as a set of independent faculties or relatively specialized abilities. But the first challenges to Spearman's hypothesis came from British psychologists. Burt (1917) argued that some tests revealed evidence of a more specialized set of verbal abilities, in addition to Spearman's general intelligence, while others were identifying a set of specifically visuo-spatial abilities (El Koussy, 1935). As in other cases, the basis of such claims was that certain tests tended to correlate more highly with each other than with other tests. Examples of the type of test used to identify a set of visuo-spatial abilities are shown in Figure 2.3.

Although there are some similarities between these spatial tests and tests of abstract or non-verbal reasoning, such as Raven's Matrices, it turns out that they are not necessarily measuring the same set of abilities. The correlation between scores on Raven's Matrices and scores on tests such as those shown in Figure 2.3 are hardly higher than those with specifically verbal tests, such as measures of vocabulary (Court and Raven, 1995). Non-verbal tests themselves, therefore, need further sub-division, into what we could call tests of general abstract reasoning, and other tests of more specifically visuo-spatial skills. The distinction between verbal, non-verbal reasoning, and spatial IQ is by now accepted by virtually all writers on the subject (see Carroll, 1993; Johnson and Bouchard, 2005). Even Gardner (1993, 2006) follows common practice by labelling three of his eight intelligences, linguistic, logical-mathematical, and spatial.

Thurstone (1938) went further, arguing that human intelligence consisted of some half dozen specific abilities, and attempting to devise tests which measured each of these abilities, as far as possible independently of the others. The result was a series of tests of seven 'primary mental abilities', which included verbal comprehension, verbal fluency, number, spatial visualization, inductive reasoning, memory, and possibly perceptual speed.

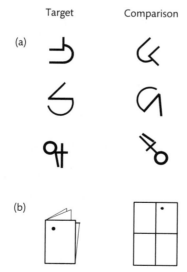

Figure 2.3 Examples of spatial IQ tests. In (a), the participant's task is to decide whether the figure on the right, if rotated, is the same as, or a mirror-image of, the figure on the left. In (b), the task is to mark where the holes would appear in the sheet of paper when it is unfolded. More examples of spatial IQ tests are shown in Chapter 4, Figure 4.4.

A proper understanding of these developments, however, requires some mathematical detail. It is no longer possible to postpone a discussion of the technique that psychometricians have used to elucidate what they refer to as the 'structure of human abilities'—namely factor analysis. And that means going back to the early work of Charles Spearman.

The factor analytic approach

Spearman's initial study, in which he outlined his 'two-factor' theory of intelligence, and identified the general factor of intelligence with general discriminative ability, was published the year before Binet's first tests appeared (Spearman, 1904). In other words, Spearman's theory was not based on any analysis of IQ scores as such: the initial empirical base for Spearman's theory of general intelligence consisted simply of the school marks, and teachers' and fellow pupils' assessments, of a small handful of schoolchildren in a few English village schools.

Nevertheless, Spearman's ideas, however weak their empirical basis, were (and remain) astonishingly influential. Even those British psychologists who disagreed with him worked on his agenda. Godfrey Thomson, although acknowledging the existence of Spearman's general factor, argued against his attempt to identify it with a single psychological process of general intelligence (see Chapter 7). Others, such as Burt and Garnett, developed techniques of multiple factor analysis which yielded evidence of 'group factors', that is, more specific components of IQ, as well as Spearman's general factor (Blinkhorn, 1995). In the 1920s and 1930s, the centre of gravity of factorial research moved across the Atlantic. Louis Thurstone (1931, 1938) developed other techniques of multiple factor analysis which, in his hands, initially seemed able to eliminate Spearman's general factor altogether, while other American factorists, such as Guilford (1967), surpassed Thurstone in their zeal both to dispense with the general factor, and to multiply the number of independent group factors or special abilities.

In what follows, I shall attempt only to describe the logic of factor analysis, and only in sufficient detail to enable the reader to judge the validity of certain conclusions supposedly implied by the results of such analysis. Those who want a much more detailed account, with a full explanation of the meaning of eigenvalues and communalities, or the distinction between principal components and principal factor analysis, are referred elsewhere (e.g. Bartholomew, 2004; Cudeck, 2000; Schulze, 2005). Carroll (1993) provides a magisterial summary of the empirical results of 50 years or more factor analytic research.

The fundamental assumption of factor analysis is that the correlation between any two tests may be explained as a consequence of each test's correlation with, or 'loading on' a third, hypothetical measure or factor:

$$r_{1.2} = r_{1.g} \times r_{2.g} \qquad (2.1)$$

The correlation between tests 1 and 2 ($r_{1.2}$) is equal to the product of each test's correlation with a hypothetical factor, here, in honour of Spearman, labelled g. The correlation between tests 3 and 4 is equally to be explained by their correlation with a hypothetical underlying factor, which may or may not be the same as that responsible for the correlation between tests 1 and 2. The aim of factor analysis, therefore, is to find a 'solution' to an observed correlation matrix which explains the large number of observed intercorrelations between the various tests or measures in terms of a smaller number of underlying hypothetical factors. The technique of factor analysis, properly understood, is a procedure for trying to simplify a large correlation matrix. Where there is a large number of different measures, whether they be scores on different IQ tests (see Table 2.1 above), performance on a variety of athletic events (100 metres, 1,500 metres, high jump, javelin, marathon, etc.) or the lengths of various bones in the body (femur, tibia, metacarpal, etc.), each of which can be correlated with every other, the resulting correlation matrices will usually be too large and unwieldy to be readily comprehended (look again at Table 2.1). Factor analysis allows you to see whether patterns can be detected in the raw matrix which would suggest a simpler story. You might imagine, for example, that taller people had generally longer bones than shorter people and therefore that a factor analysis of bone length scores would reveal a single, general factor corresponding to height. On the other hand, although some people may be generally more athletic than others and thus better at all athletic events, you might equally expect to find someone who was an outstanding sprinter, but not particularly good at long distance running, and hopeless at such field events as putting the shot. Factor analysis will enable you to find out whether there is any evidence for such clusters of different abilities in addition to, or rather than, any general athletic ability. This has been the goal of the factor analysis of IQ scores. Is there evidence of a single all-pervading factor (corresponding to Spearman's *g* or general intelligence) running through performance on all possible IQ tests? Is there only a set of more specialized abilities—verbal, spatial, etc.? Is there evidence of both?

General intelligence (*g*): Spearman's two-factor theory

Where all correlations between a large battery of tests are positive, as they are in the case of IQ, factor analysis will necessarily yield a general factor that accounts for this so-called positive manifold. This point should really not be controversial. All tests in the battery will 'load onto' this general factor, whose importance will depend on the size of the positive correlations between the various tests. Where they are all reasonably substantial, ranging, say, from 0.30 to 0.80, as is commonly observed with IQ test batteries, the general factor will account for something like 40–50% of the variance in the correlation matrix. Not content with this conclusion, however, Spearman went on to argue that this general factor, or *g*, provided a *complete* and *sufficient* explanation of the positive manifold. In other words, there is no need to appeal to any further underlying factors to explain the observed correlations between the tests. What was the basis of his argument? The important observation was one he made in data collected in another school, where he obtained somewhat more objective measures of academic performance, namely, each child's rank order in class for each of four different subjects, as well as measures of pitch discrimination and musical ability as rated by their music teacher. Interestingly, he anticipated Binet's appreciation of the importance of age by making an allowance for a pupil's age in adjusting their class ranking. The correlation matrix he reported between all these six measures is shown in Table 2.2. The correlations form what Spearman called a 'hierarchy'; that is to say, with one small exception, the correlations decrease as one goes down each column or across each row of the matrix. What was the meaning of this? Spearman's two-factor theory provided

Table 2.2 Spearman's correlation matrix for six measures of school performance (from Spearman, 1904, p. 275).

	Classics	French	English	Maths	Pitch	Music
Classics	—					
French	0.83	—				
English	0.78	0.67	—			
Maths	0.70	0.67	0.64	—		
Pitch	0.66	0.65	0.54	0.45	—	
Music	0.63	0.57	0.51	0.51	0.40	—
g-loading	0.95	0.88	0.80	0.75	0.69	0.65

the proposed answer: each test measures its own specific factor, but also, to a greater or lesser extent, a general factor that is common to *all* the tests in the battery. It is this general factor, *g*, that was said to explain why all tests correlated with one another. That this was a sufficient explanation of the observed correlation matrix, Spearman argued, was proved by the application of his 'tetrad equation'. If $r_{1.2}$ stands for the observed correlation between tests 1 and 2, and so on, then the tetrad equation was as follows:

$$r_{1.2} \times r_{3.4} = r_{1.3} \times r_{2.4} \qquad (2.2)$$

Substitute the appropriate numbers from Table 2.2 into this equation, and you have $0.83 \times 0.64 = 0.53$, and $0.78 \times 0.67 = 0.52$, as close as one could reasonably ask—and the same will hold for any other two pairs of correlations in this table. Why should this be? Spearman's explanation was straightforward. The reason why tests 1 and 2 correlate is because both measure *g*. But equally, the reason why tests 3 and 4 correlate is because they, too, measure the same *g*. The observed correlation between any two tests is simply a product of each test's separate correlation with *g* (as shown in equation 2.1 above)

And because this is true of all other pairs of tests, equation 2.2 can be rewritten as follows:

$$r_{1.g} \times r_{2.g} \times r_{3.g} \times r_{4.g} = r_{1.g} \times r_{3.g} \times r_{2.g} \times r_{4.g} \qquad (2.3)$$

which is clearly true. When the correlation matrix of a battery of tests forms a hierarchy such as that seen in Table 2.2, to which the tetrad equation applies, the explanation, said Spearman, is because the correlations between all tests are entirely due to each test's correlation with the single general factor, *g*.

Why then, you might ask, does the general factor explain only about half the variance in the correlation matrix of any large IQ test battery? Spearman's answer was that each test in the battery measured not only one and the same general factor, but also its own unique factor. A vocabulary test, for example, measured both *g* and also knowledge of the meaning of words. Some tests in the battery would be better measures of *g* than others: tests of vocabulary and of analogical reasoning were better measures of *g*, that is, loaded more strongly

THE FACTOR ANALYTIC APPROACH

onto the general factor than, say, letter cancelling or digit span. The variance in the matrix not attributable to g was explained by the specific factors unique to each individual test.

The bottom row of Table 2.2 shows the correlation or loading of each test on g. As can be seen, these loadings range from a high of 0.95 to a low of 0.65: classics is the best measure of g in this test battery. That the entire matrix can be explained by supposing that all tests correlate with a single general factor, g, is proved by showing that, within the limits of measurement error, the observed matrix can be reconstructed by multiplying, for each pair of tests, their correlation with g. For example, the correlation between classics and French is 0.95×0.88, or 0.84; that between French and maths is 0.88×0.75, or 0.66, and that between English and pitch is 0.80×0.69, or 0.55. When you go through the entire matrix in this way to obtain a 'predicted' matrix, and subtract the predicted matrix from the observed matrix, the residuals you get will be sufficiently small to make it safe to accept that the correlations between all tests in the battery are due entirely to each test's loading on g. A single general factor is sufficient to explain the entire correlation matrix.

What would count as evidence against Spearman's theory? One obvious answer is the absence of any positive manifold. But that evidence is not, on the whole, forthcoming. It is true that different techniques of factor analysis can appear to make g more or less important (see below), but in the case of traditional IQ test batteries none can eliminate it. However, Spearman's further claim, that g provides a *complete* explanation of the observed correlation matrix of any IQ test battery, that is, that there is no need to appeal to any further factors, is rather easily disproved. The correlation matrix of a large test battery does not always look like that shown in Table 2.2.

The disproof has already been foreshadowed by the earlier discussion of the correlation matrix of the WAIS-III shown in Table 2.1. Spearman's theory can allow that the correlations between various tests will vary quite substantially, as indeed they do, because he will say that some tests are better measures of g than others. But if a test is a good measure of g, its correlation with all other tests in the battery will be relatively strong, while conversely a poor measure of g will correlate only weakly with all other tests in the battery. What his theory cannot allow is that one test, a, correlates strongly with tests l, m, and n, but only weakly with tests x, y, and z, while a second test, b, correlates weakly with l, m, and n, but strongly with x, y, and z. Clusters of relatively high correlations between some groups of tests, separated by relatively low correlations between tests in one cluster and those in another imply that the two (or more) clusters are measuring, at least in part, two or more partially independent sets of skills or abilities. The picture is much the same as you might expect from factor analysis of performance on a variety of different tests of athletic ability: while some (younger and fitter) people may be better at everything than others, athletes who are outstanding at 100 and 200 metres will not necessarily be outstanding at longer distance races of 5,000 or 10,000 metres, let alone at throwing the discus or shot put. The correlation matrix of any large IQ test battery will show not only pervasive positive correlations between all tests, it will also reveal clusters of high correlations between different tests of abstract reasoning, vocabulary, or spatial visualization, separated by lower correlations between tests in one group (verbal) and those in another (spatial). Table 2.3 provides an example, from some of Thurstone's data, of a correlation matrix that clearly contradicts Spearman's tetrad equation. The six tests clearly form two clusters, the first three being 'spatial' tests, the second three tests of 'inductive reasoning'. The correlations between the

Table 2.3 Correlation matrix for six of Thurstone's PMA tests. Flags, figures, and cards are tests of visuo-spatial ability; letter series, pedigrees, and grouping are tests of inductive reasoning (from Thurstone and Thurstone, 1941, Appendix Table 4).

	Flags	Figures	Cards	Letter series	Pedigrees	Grouping
Flags	—					
Figures	0.64	—				
Cards	0.63	0.71	—			
Letter series	0.27	0.18	0.27	—		
Pedigrees	0.18	0.15	0.18	0.61	—	
Grouping	0.28	0.19	0.24	0.61	0.50	—

three tests in each cluster are high, but the correlations between the tests in one cluster and those in the other are much weaker.

Because all correlations are positive, it will still be possible to extract a general factor, *g*. But extracting this general factor will leave a residual matrix that will still contain six high numbers resulting from the high correlations between the three tests within each group.

Thurstone's primary mental abilities

Spearman's espousal of a general factor of intelligence arose in large part from his dislike of the prevailing 'faculty' psychology of his day, which sought to decompose the mind into a number of distinct components or faculties. Thurstone, on the contrary, precisely believed that human intelligence could and should be decomposed into a number of more or less independent components. Good IQ tests would be those that revealed these independent faculties. For Thurstone, the purpose of factor analysis was both to reveal these independent faculties and, if necessary, to guide the construction of better tests designed to be 'factorially pure', that is, measures of one factor at a time. Given a matrix of intercorrelations between a dozen or more tests, the goal of factor analysis for Thurstone was not to find the general factor that accounted for as much as possible of the variation in scores on *all* tests, but rather to find a series of separate factors, one of which accounted for the intercorrelation between one set of tests, a second for the intercorrelation between a second set, and so on. His principle of 'rotation to simple structure' implied that the factorial solution to aim for was one where each test loaded strongly onto some factors (preferably as few as possible), while simultaneously showing only negligible loadings onto other factors (preferably as many as possible).

In order to understand what is meant by 'rotation' of factors, it may help to outline an alternative, geometrical representation of the factorial structure of a battery of tests. Instead of expressing the results of factor analysis as a set of correlations between, or 'loadings' of test scores on hypothetical factors, that is, in numerical form, they can also, for those with more visual than numerical facility, be expressed geometrically. You can imagine (as Thurstone did) test scores as vectors, with the correlation between any two tests being represented by the angle between their two vectors. If they are highly correlated they will lie close together, and if uncorrelated far apart. More exactly, the correlation is represented by the cosine of the angle between two vectors, since the cosine of $0° = 1.0$ (i.e. perfect correlation) and of $90° = 0$ (i.e. zero correlation). Figure 2.4a, for example, shows six different test scores all correlated with one another, that is, with relatively small angles between them. If you draw the vertical axis, labelled g, through this cluster it will represent in effect the principal factor of a factor analysis, that is, the factor best correlated with all six tests.

One way to understand this is to realize that if you wished to summarize the overall performance of someone who had taken all six tests, the single number that would best do so, that is, capture most of the information from the original tests, would be a point on the axis labelled g. Such a hypothetical score would allow you to predict the actual scores obtained on all six tests with considerable, although by no means perfect, accuracy. Further accuracy would be achieved by placing a second axis, at right angles to the first. This would now allow you to distinguish, for example, between two people who obtained a similar total score on all six tests, but distributed differently between them. The one with higher scores on the right-hand group of tests would have a positive score on this second axis, the one with higher scores on the left-hand group would have a negative score on this axis.

In Figures 2.4b and 2.4c, I have introduced a small but critical change; all six tests still subtend relatively small angles with one another, but they also form two rather distinct clusters. It would obviously still be possible to draw a general axis through the middle of all six, and a second at right angles to it, as in Figure 2.4a. Given these two clusters of test vectors, however, an equally obvious alternative solution would be rotate the axes, that is,

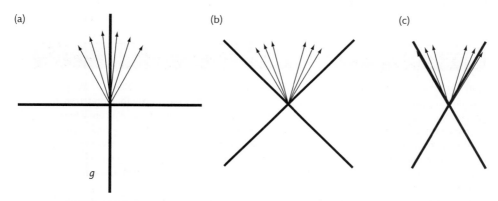

(a)   (b)   (c)

g

Figure 2.4 Geometric representation of correlations between scores on six tests. Each test score is represented as a vector departing from the origin (the six arrows radiating out from the origin in each of (a), (b), and (c). The correlation between each test is represented by the angles between the vectors, with small angles corresponding to high correlations. In (a), the vectors are equally spaced apart, but in (b) and (c), the six vectors form two distinct clusters. The natural factorial solution for (a) is thus to draw a first factor (labelled g) through the middle of the six vectors, and a second at right angles to the first. Although it would be perfectly possible to place two factors in the same place for the six vectors shown in (b) and (c), an alternative solution would be to place each of two factors as close as possible to one set of vectors. In (b), the constraint that the two factors be at right angles to one another means that they cannot be placed through the centre of each cluster. In (c), this constraint is relaxed and two oblique (i.e. correlated) factors are placed in the centre of each cluster. (This way of representing tests as vectors and their correlation as the angles between the vectors, although originally owing to Thurstone, is here taken from Gould, 1997.)

to draw two new axes, one through each cluster, as shown in Figures 2.4b and 2.4c. The only distinction between these last two figures is that in Figure 2.4b I have imposed the requirement that the two axes must be at right angles to one another, that is, uncorrelated with one another; while in Figure 2.4c I have allowed the two axes to be oblique, that is, correlated with one another. Both figures, however, are saying that the pattern of correlations between the six tests is best described by saying that three of the tests are measures of one factor and three of another. This is in effect 'rotation to simple structure'. In Figures 2.4b and 2.4c, the left-hand group of tests now correlate quite strongly with the left-hand factor, and quite weakly with the right-hand factor.

Thurstone (1938) administered a battery of 56 different tests to a sample of 240 students at the University of Chicago, and argued that his procedure of rotation to simple structure revealed seven different factors (his seven primary mental abilities), and at the same time eliminated the need for any general factor at all. This last claim was immediately challenged (Eysenck, 1939), and Thurstone conceded that his earlier conclusion was partly a consequence of the fact that his participants, students at a selective university, were all of well above average intelligence. When Thurstone and Thurstone (1941) administered their tests to a large sample of schoolchildren, clear evidence of a general factor emerged. The argument hinges on the question whether Figure 2.4b or 2.4c provides a better fit to the data. If the factors are all at right angles to one another, as in Figure 2.4b, they are all uncorrelated with one another, and that is the end of the story. But if Figure 2.4c provides a better fit to the data (as it clearly does here, since the two new axes lie within each cluster rather than outside them as in Figure 2.4b), the factors themselves are correlated with one another, and a further factor analysis will yield a higher-order factor to account for these intercorrelations. The answer was that the factors were indeed correlated with one another.

BOX 2.3 General factor or group factors first?

Although they ended up in rather closer agreement than their initial diametrically opposed theories would have suggested was possible, Spearman and Thurstone differed both in their preferred method of factor analysis, and in their interpretation of the results of the analysis. There is a connection between these two sources of disagreement. The general factor extracted by a principal factor analysis of the correlation matrix of any IQ test battery is the first to be extracted. It inevitably, therefore, accounts for a greater proportion of the variance in that matrix than any further group factor. This fact alone endows it with greater prominence and therefore apparently greater importance than subsequent factors. Thurstone's procedure of rotation to simple structure extracts the group factors first, and g is a second-order factor that accounts for the intercorrelation between these group factors. Now it is the group factors that have greater prominence.

The two procedures do not yield identical solutions, but they are not wholly dissimilar, and one solution can be mathematically transformed into the other (Gustafsson and Undheim, 1996). Given a large and diverse test battery, both will extract several group factors as well as a general factor, g. The difference is that if g has been extracted first, the group factors will be, so to say, residual factors shorn of anything in common with one another. If the group factors are extracted first, they will contain their share of g. The main difference is that when g is extracted first, it may be difficult to identify a group factor corresponding to Horn and Cattell's Gf. This is simply because, when group factors are extracted first, Gf is more closely related to the second-order g than is any other second-stratum factor, so if g is extracted first, there is little variance unique to Gf left.

Box 2.3 discusses an important difference between Spearman's and Thurstone's preferred procedures for performing factor analysis. Whichever procedure is employed, however, factor analysis appears to have shown that both Spearman and Thurstone were partly right, but also partly wrong. Spearman was right because the positive manifold implies that you cannot get rid of the need for a general factor, but wrong in supposing that this general factor is the *only* reason why IQ tests correlate with one another. Thurstone was right in supposing that there really are a number of different components of intelligence measured by IQ tests, but wrong in supposing that there is not also a general factor common to all tests. The obvious resolution is to incorporate both theories into a single 'hierarchical' model that has both a number of subsidiary 'group' factors at one level, as well as a single general factor at a 'higher' level. Such a model was first proposed by Vernon (1950), with *g* at the highest level, and two group factors, labelled *v:ed* and *k:m* at the next level: *v:ed* referred to verbal and educational abilities, and *k:m* to perceptual, spatial, and mechanical abilities (very roughly the distinction between verbal and non-verbal measures of intelligence).

Vernon's *v:ed* and *k:m* factors seem at first sight similar to the more widely known and influential distinction proposed by Cattell (1971) and Horn and Cattell (1966), between fluid (Gf) and crystallized (Gc) intelligence. In this model, fluid intelligence is engaged by tests such as Raven's Matrices or Cattell's own culture fair tests, while crystallized intelligence is measured by tests of knowledge, such as the information and vocabulary tests of the WAIS. Horn and Cattell also identified several other broad factors, including Gv or spatial visualization, Gr or retrieval, and Gs or a speed factor (Horn, 1985). Box 2.4 explains the reason for this difference in the models. As will become apparent below, however, there are other important differences between the Vernon and Cattell-Horn models—not least that Horn and Cattell saw no reason to postulate a general factor, *g*, superordinate to Gf and Gc.

BOX 2.4 What you get out depends on what you put in

The factorial structure revealed by factor analysis of a battery of IQ tests will always depend on the nature of the tests in that battery. Given the pervasive positive manifold, factor analysis of a set of IQ tests will inevitably reveal a general factor. But subsidiary group factors can only be revealed if more than one test loads onto them. Factor analysis of the earlier Wechsler tests, for example, revealed at best only three subsidiary factors in addition to *g*: verbal, performance, and a small third factor which the arithmetic and digit-span tests loaded onto. The verbal factor was more or less the same as Vernon's *v:ed*; but the performance factor, being based on a rather motley assortment of tests was not particularly closely related to Cattell's Gf or Gv, nor to Vernon's *k:m* (as can be seen in Figure 2.5, only two tests, block design and object assembly, had much spatial content) . And, as can also be seen in Figure 2.5, digit symbol was the only test loading onto a factor of perceptual speed, so no such factor appeared in factor analysis of the earlier Wechsler tests (hence the addition of speed tests in the WAIS-III and WAIS-IV).

One reason why the Horn-Cattell model has more broad group factors than Vernon's is simply that they analysed a very much larger and more carefully chosen battery of tests. This probably explains why the Vernon model does not contain any group factors corresponding to Cattell's Gr (and why it had to be added by Johnson and Bouchard, 2005, when they tried to fit the Vernon model to a much larger data set (see below)).

In his survey of twentieth century factorial studies, Carroll (1993) concluded that the structure of intellectual abilities revealed by factor analysis does include a general factor, *g*, at a third 'stratum', some half-dozen or more broad group factors, including Gf and Gc at a second stratum, as well as factors of visuo-spatial abilities (Gv), retrieval (Gr), and processing speed (Gs), and a large, perhaps indefinite number of specific factors at a first stratum. One important feature of the model is that there are substantial differences in the loadings of the second-stratum abilities on the third-stratum *g*, with Gf showing by some way the highest loading (to the point where authors such as Gustafsson (1988) have argued that the two are identical), and Gs one of the weaker loadings. This is now sometimes referred to as the Cattell-Horn-Carroll (or CHC) model (McGrew, 2009), and has been widely seen as the most plausible account of the structure of abilities measured by standard IQ tests (a view recently challenged by Johnson and Bouchard, 2005; see below). It is, in effect, a reconciliation between, or amalgamation of, Spearman's and Thurstone's accounts, the first and third strata corresponding to Spearman's general and specific factors, the second stratum to Thurstone's primary mental abilities. It should not be thought that *everyone* accepts this position (see Box 2.5).

BOX 2.5 Guilford's 'Structure of Intellect' model

Some factorists, most famously Guilford (1967, 1982, 1988), in his structure of intellect model, postulated a far larger number of abilities than Thurstone had ever dreamed of: Guilford started with 120, moved to 150 and ended up with 180 supposedly distinct and independent factors (although he did eventually acknowledge that there was probably also a general factor). The novel feature of his model was that the factors were derived from theoretical first principles, being defined by the execution of a particular kind of operation on a particular kind of product with a particular kind of content. There were five different kinds of operation, applied to five different types of content, expressed in terms of one of six different products (this produced the 150 number). Although Guilford claimed to be able to devise independent tests of most of these independent factors, his account has not commanded wide assent. The most devastating critique was provided by Horn and Knapp (1973), who showed that Guilford's factorial procedures, when applied to his test data, provided just as strong support for *randomly* generated factorial theories as they did for Guilford's own theory.

Many of Guilford's abilities should perhaps be seen as corresponding to the numerous specific first-stratum abilities in the CHC model. One of the important virtues of his approach is that he included measures of creativity and social intelligence that have not commonly appeared in traditional IQ test batteries. Suss and Beauducel (2005) have provided a sympathetic account, and Brody a notably less sympathetic one which concluded that 'Guilford's theory is without empirical support' (Brody, 1992, p. 34).

Guttman's radex model

A quite different way of representing the relationship between different IQ tests, or the 'structure of human abilities' was proposed by Guttman (1957) in what he called a radex model. Tests are represented in a circular space, with the complexity of the test inversely related to its distance from the centre of the circle (this is referred to as a 'simplex'). Tests loading strongly onto *g* would therefore be close to the centre, while those loading less strongly would be nearer the circumference. The second feature of the model is the 'circumplex', which describes the direction from the centre in which a particular test lies: tests more closely related to one another will lie in neighbouring directions from the centre, while those less closely related might lie in opposite directions.

All this is more readily comprehended diagrammatically. Figure 2.5 shows a drastically simplified version of the results of an analysis presented by Snow *et al.* (1984), which used multi-dimensional scaling to represent the relationships between various tests. The distance between any two tests in the figure is inversely related to the similarity (i.e. correlation) between them, and the heavy lines or boxes drawn round clusters of tests represent the broad second-stratum factors identified by the CHC model. As can be seen, tests of

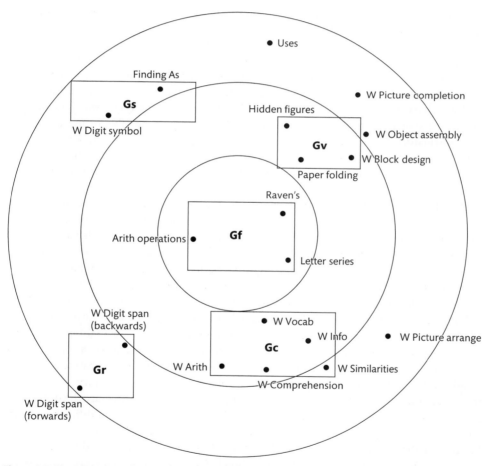

Figure 2.5 The interrelationships between various types of IQ test represented as distances between the tests in two-dimensional space. Tests at the centre of the space are more closely related to all other tests than are those nearer the periphery. Solid lines are drawn round groups of tests defining some of the major factors of the CHC model, Gf, Gc, Gv, Gs. Tests labelled W are tests of the WAIS (adapted and greatly simplified from Snow *et al.*, 1984, Figure 2.2).

reasoning, such as Raven's Matrices or letter series are at the centre, defining Gf, while verbal, spatial, memory, and perceptual speed tests form clusters round this central core. This is because tests of Gf correlate more strongly with tests of Gs, Gr, Gc, and Gv, than any of these do with one another. And this is also why, as noted above, Gf loads more strongly onto g than any of the other factors do. Although employing rather different techniques, this analysis implies a similar picture to that arising from the CHC hierarchical models.

Confirmatory factor analysis

The procedure I have been describing up to this point is usually termed 'exploratory factor analysis', designed, as its name implies, to explore a correlation matrix to see how many factors can and should be identified; it is not necessarily well designed to decide between alternative theories about the factorial structure of the test battery. Since more than one structure can always be found, there being in principle an indefinite number of factorial solutions to any given correlation matrix, how is the factorist to choose between them? One answer is by appeal to psychological or neuroscientific research and theory. In the last analysis, that solution is to be preferred that sits most comfortably with what is known about the functioning of the human brain. But that last analysis is probably still some way off (although Chapter 6 will discuss studies that have gone some way towards identifying the neural structures underlying Gf). In the meantime, it is possible to use techniques of 'confirmatory factor analysis' to choose between alternative factorial solutions. This involves specifying alternative theories of the factorial structure of a given test battery, and comparing how well the predictions made by these theories match the structure actually observed.

The procedure is illustrated by Benson *et al.* (2010), who compared the fourfold factor structure of the WAIS-IV preferred by the test's constructors with a fivefold structure suggested by the CHC model. They concluded that the CHC model provided a better fit to the data. The major difference between the two models was that in the former picture completion, block design, matrix reasoning, figure weights, and visual puzzles all loaded onto the perceptual reasoning factor, while in the CHC model this factor is divided into two, Gf and Gv. I earlier argued that this distinction between Gf and Gv could not be ignored.

Johnson and Bouchard (2005) investigated how well the Vernon, Horn-Cattell, and CHC models fit the data generated by a sample of over 400 people who took 42 different tests of mental ability. Standard measures of goodness of fit revealed that the Vernon model provided the best fit to the data, and its fit was further improved by incorporating an additional spatial factor alongside *v:ed* and *k:m*, and including a memory factor among the factors under *k:m*. At first sight, this might seem rather surprising: are the differences between these models so very great after all? Well, there are important differences that I have so far mostly glossed over. As already noted, the Horn-Cattell model, unlike Vernon, has no g, but that difference does not apply to the CHC model. A further difference, however, is that Vernon has no factor corresponding to Gf: in his model non-verbal or abstract reasoning is the function of g. There are also reasons why the mapping between Vernon's *v:ed* and *k:m* on the one hand and Gc and Gf is not in fact very close. For Vernon the distinction between the two factors is largely one of *content*: verbal and numerical on the one hand, and perceptual and spatial (but not abstract reasoning) on the other. So, one particular reason for the superior fit of the Vernon model was that it correctly predicted, for example, that tests that measured verbal reasoning should load only onto *v:ed* and not on to *k:m*, while the Horn-Cattell model predicts that they should load onto both Gf and Gc, which they did not. That may, however, be a consequence of the nature of the verbal reasoning test. In a study cited by Lohman (2000), Horn (1972) found that different verbal analogies might load either onto Gc alone or onto both Gc and Gf: in the former case the difficulty of the analogy was that the words used were relatively esoteric; in the latter case common words were used and the difficulty of the analogy lay in perceiving the relevant relationship between them.

In Cattell's original theorizing, the distinction between Gf and Gc was that the former was seen as the biological basis of intelligence, which could then become 'invested' in the acquisition of the knowledge appropriate to one's culture (measured by tests of Gc). There are good reasons, accepted later by Horn (1985), to reject this account. There is, for example, no reason to believe that the heritability of Gf is substantially higher than that of Gc. Cattell himself estimated the heritability of Gc as 0.73 and that of Gf as 0.77—not a very impressive difference (Cattell, 1971). Horn summarized a number of other studies that yielded entirely comparable estimates for the heritability of Gc and Gf, and in some cases higher heritability for Gc. Other evidence unambiguously demonstrates that performance on tests of Gf, such as Raven's Matrices, depends on schooling and other opportunities for past learning (see Chapters 12 and 13). Johnson and Bouchard, however, take the original version of the Horn-Cattell model literally, and this would seem to be why it failed to fit their data as well as the Vernon model. A plausible reconciliation would be to say that Gc should be conceptualized as verbal ability rather than *any* learned skill.

A second important feature of the original Horn-Cattell model was its prediction about the development of Gc and Gf over the lifespan: Gc was assumed to increase and then remain relatively stable well into old age, while Gf having reached a peak at the age of 20 or so, then started an inexorable decline. Although earlier studies may have exaggerated the extent of this decline, there is no doubt that this feature of the model has been strongly confirmed (see Chapter 8). Whether this important difference can be captured by the Vernon model is far from clear.

Another reason for continuing to use the CHC model is that although Gf may be highly correlated with *g*, there are reasons for distinguishing between the two (see Chapter 7) and the Vernon model would appear to conflate them by attributing all differences in reasoning ability to differences in *g*.

I shall therefore continue to use the terminology of the Horn-Cattell model (as I have in Figure 2.5), partly because it has become a standard way of talking about the structure of psychometric intelligence, and is likely to be more familiar to many readers.

Other examples of the use of confirmatory factor analysis will appear in later chapters.

Latent variables

A person's performance on any IQ test battery is usually summarized in a single number—an IQ score. This is derived from the sum of scores obtained from the individual tests in that battery. But if some tests in the battery have higher *g* loadings than others, this simple sum of test scores may not be the best way of estimating their general intelligence.

A better way would be to weight the scores on the individual tests by their g loadings. But this will still mean that the overall score will be a mixture of g and the specific factors unique to each test in the battery. A true estimate of g will be obtained only by discarding these specifics, and calculating the person's score on this g factor. By the same token, the best measure of a person's verbal or spatial intelligence may not be the simple sum of their scores on a variety of different verbal or spatial tests; the best procedure is to extract the verbal or spatial factor common to each of the two groups of tests, and calculate the score on these factors.

The same argument applies when the investigator is interested in whether performance on other cognitive tasks, for example tests of immediate memory, is associated with IQ. Rather than measuring the correlation between a single test of immediate memory and IQ, a far more powerful procedure will be to administer a number of different tests of immediate memory and extract the factor common to all these tests. You can then measure the strength of the association between IQ and the 'latent variable' of immediate memory, uncontaminated by the specifics of each individual test. Examples of this procedure will appear in later chapters.

Conclusion

After Binet's and Terman's pioneering work, the subsequent development of modern IQ tests was marked by a proliferation of different tests as psychometricians sought an answer to the question whether intelligence was best conceptualized as a single general process or a multiplicity of different abilities and skills. Some tests, such as the Wechsler scales, followed the Stanford-Binet tests in including a wide variety of different types of item, partly on the pragmatic intuition that different types of item might favour or penalize different people. The only fair test, therefore, would be one which ensured a careful balance between items favouring one person and those favouring another. On theoretical grounds, Spearman also believed that the more diverse the items in a test battery, the better it would measure the general factor, g, common to all IQ tests.

It soon became apparent, however, that different types of test were measuring rather different aspects of intelligence: a general consensus agreed that a distinction could be drawn at least between verbal IQ, non-verbal reasoning, and spatial IQ. According to Thurstone, a finer set of distinctions could be drawn between at least half a dozen 'primary mental abilities' (that included verbal, reasoning, and spatial IQ), but the fact remains that in the population as a whole, people who obtain high scores on one kind of test *tend*, on average, to obtain high scores on most others. At the very least, this perhaps allows one to talk sensibly of some people being generally more intelligent than others, and to use an overall IQ score as a useful, if imperfect, summary.

To go beyond this, psychometricians have used factor analysis as their chosen method for answering questions about the structure of human intelligence. Factor analysis, properly understood, is no more than a technique for trying to simplify, or see patterns in, large correlation matrices. It rests on the assumption that the reason why performance on two tests correlates is because these two tests are, partly, measuring the same thing. The correlation matrix of ten different tests contains 45 correlation coefficients: it can be rendered more intelligible if you show that the entire pattern of correlations could be accounted for by postulating a much smaller number of hypothetical factors with which the ten tests correlated to varying degrees.

In the limiting case, factor analysis may be able to show that the postulation of a single factor is sufficient to account for the entire pattern of correlations. Spearman believed that this was true for the correlation matrix of a battery of IQ tests, and labelled this single factor g. He thus claimed that IQ measured a single underlying process of general intelligence. Believing that human intelligence is better conceptualized as a set of largely independent faculties or cognitive abilities, Thurstone sought to dismiss Spearman's conclusion by showing that a different technique for factor analysis revealed evidence of clusters of tests which correlated quite strongly with one another, but not at all with tests in other clusters.

Both were partly right and partly wrong. Spearman's solution is wrong because in the correlation matrix of any large battery of IQ tests there will be clusters of tests that correlate more highly with one another than they do with tests in other clusters. Thurstone's solution is wrong because of the overall positive manifold: correlations between different clusters of tests are all positive. But both Spearman and Thurstone could take comfort from that aspect of the data which contradicted the other's theoretical preconception. Thus, there is a general factor common to all IQ tests, but there are also a number of more specific factors tapped by different groups of test. This has led to the consensus that the structure of human abilities is best described by 'hierarchical' models, such as the Cattell-Horn-Carroll (CHC) model, in which there is a single general factor at one level, with a number of (somewhere between five and ten) 'group' factors at the next level, and an almost indefinite number of specific factors describing the particular tests in the test battery. An alternative hierarchical model is Johnson and Bouchard's revision of a model first proposed by Vernon.

Factor analysis alone will never dictate any particular *psychological* interpretation of the nature of human intelligence. For that, what is needed is psychological research and theory. It is essential to keep clear the distinction between two quite separate questions. The first, empirical, question is whether the pattern of intercorrelations actually observed between different IQ tests does or does not imply that a single general factor, g, accounts for a sizeable proportion of the variance in the matrix. The second question is quite different: it is how to *interpret* the factorial solution or solutions most plausibly suggested by any observed pattern of intercorrelations.

Some of the criticisms advanced against Spearman's position have confused these two questions. Many of those who argue that there is no such thing as general intelligence, or that intelligence is too multi-faceted and complex an idea to be captured by a single number, often do not make it clear, perhaps even to themselves, which question they are addressing. Are they asserting that factor analysis of a battery of IQ tests will not, as a matter of fact, yield a significant general factor? If so, they are mistaken. Or are they insisting, as did Thomson (1916), for example, that the observation of such a general factor does not necessarily imply the existence of a single underlying *process* of general intelligence? The question of how to interpret or explain this general factor is taken up in Chapter 7.

Summary

- The Wechsler scales, WAIS and WISC, popularized a distinction between verbal and non-verbal or performance IQ tests.
- Non-verbal tests need to be further divided into tests of abstract reasoning, such as Raven's Matrices and tests of visuo-spatial ability.
- Factor analysis has provided the favoured procedure for analysing the structure of human abilities.
- Because all IQ tests tend to correlate with one another, Spearman was able to show that there was a general factor, labelled *g*, apparently common to all tests.
- But because of the distinction between verbal, spatial, and abstract reasoning tests, factor analysis also reveals a number of 'group' factors in addition to *g*.

Further reading

Fancher (1985) describes the further development of IQ tests between the two world wars, and Roberts *et al.* (2005) provide a critical discussion of several modern test batteries, including the WAIS-III (of which they are particularly critical). For factor analysis, an excellent introduction that provides much more detail than I offer is Kline (1994). Carroll's (1993) magisterial summary is not for the faint-hearted, but his introductory and concluding chapters are entirely accessible. Gould (1997) gives an admirably clear account of factor analysis, but his arguments for the unimportance of the general factor cannot be trusted. McGrew (2009) outlines the consensus Cattell-Horn-Carroll or CHC model, while Johnson and Bouchard (2005) should be consulted for their alternative model.

3

The search for cognitive processes underlying components of IQ: Gs or speed and efficiency of information processing

Introduction

Spearman and Thurstone eventually agreed that factor analysis of any large battery of IQ tests would yield both a general factor that explained the overall positive manifold or correlation between all tests in the battery, and several group factors needed to explain the observation of clusters of high correlations between some tests separated by lower correlations between tests in one cluster and those in another. By and large this consensus still holds today—as is evident in the general acceptance that either the CHC (Cattell-Horn-Carroll) model, or Johnson and Bouchard's modification of Vernon's model, provides the best summary of the conclusions yielded by factor analysis.

In spite of their agreements, however, as noted in Chapter 2 (Box 2.3) Spearman and Thurstone differed in their preferred method of factor analysis, and as a consequence also in their interpretation of the results of factor analysis. Spearman's procedure endows *g* with greater importance than any further group factor, while Thurstone's makes the group factors primary. Thus, when they advanced to the next step—that of *interpreting* the results of factor analysis, Spearman concentrated on offering an explanation of the general factor, while Thurstone, believing that his seven group factors were indeed 'primary mental abilities', wanted to understand the operations of these constituent faculties of the mind.

The psychological or biological interpretation of the general factor is something that has engaged psychometricians for the best part of a century, without any consensus having been reached—as will perhaps become apparent in Chapter 7. This suggests that the question is a difficult one. In the following chapters, therefore, I shall first review evidence on the cognitive and neurobiological underpinnings of some of the second-stratum factors of the CHC model, which correspond roughly to Thurstone's primary mental abilities. I start with speed of processing. Thurstone (1938) identified a factor labelled 'processing speed' as one of his primary mental abilities. Factor analysis of later versions of the Wechsler scales, as well as of other test batteries, has also revealed one or more speed factors (three in the case of Carroll, 1993). Horn's revision of Cattell's Gf-Gc theory had one such factor, labelled Gs. In most of these analyses, processing speed, or Gs, has never been one of the more prominent factors, and both Carroll, and Johnson and Bouchard (2005) relegate it to a lower stratum. But speed of processing has assumed much greater prominence in the writings of some theorists. Jensen (1998) and Anderson (1992, 2005), for example, have argued that it may be the psychological or biological basis of g itself. The evidence for this strong position is not compelling, but there is no doubt that speed of processing is a significant ingredient of the intelligence measured by IQ tests—and rather good evidence that Carroll was right to distinguish between more than one speed factor.

General intelligence as mental energy, speed, or efficiency

Spearman's factorial theory assumed that performance on any given individual test of intelligence is determined by two factors, one general, accounting for the correlation between this test and all others, the second unique, being specific to that particular test (Spearman, 1927). He suggested that the specific factors could be regarded as the nuts and bolts of cognition, the particular processes needed for solution of a particular type of problem, while the general factor was the 'mental energy' that powered these specific engines. It is not immediately obvious what 'mental energy' might be, but the underlying idea has resurfaced in several different guises, one of which forms the basis of the position taken by Anderson and Jensen. Anderson (1992, 2005) proposed a cognitive architecture of human intelligence consisting of a basic processing mechanism supplemented by a number of specific processors and modules. Variations in the speed and efficiency of the basic processing mechanism were said to be responsible for variations in g or general intelligence, because they set limits to the performance of the specific processors which operate on particular types of information, such as verbal and propositional or visuo-spatial. Thus, the single process underlying g is the speed and efficiency of the operation of this central processing mechanism. Jensen's argument was that the very diversity of IQ tests, which all correlate with one another, means that the basis of g could not be any specific cognitive process:

> Unlike group factors, g cannot be described in terms of the superficial characteristics or information content of the tests in which it is loaded. All mental tests have some degree of g loading and even extremely dissimilar tests (e.g. sentence completion and block designs) can have nearly equal g loadings ... It is wrong to regard g as a cognitive process ... At the level of causality, g is perhaps best regarded as a source of variance in performance associated with individual differences in the speed or efficiency of the neural processes that affect the kinds of behaviour called mental abilities.
>
> (Jensen, 1998, pp. 74, 91)

Intuitively, it seems reasonable to suppose that the speed and efficiency of information processing by the brain might be related to IQ. A more efficient nervous system must be a more intelligent one. Well, perhaps—but what does 'efficient' mean here? One possible answer was suggested by Eysenck (1982), who argued that the operation of the nervous system involves the transmission of signals, encoded as a series of pulse trains. Decisions about the nature of a signal, and therefore of the appropriate response in a later part of the system, are taken by sampling over a series of such pulses. Errors of transmission will add noise and hence make it harder to reach a decision, and further sampling may be required before a sufficiently unambiguous message is received. Intelligence, then, is a function of the fidelity and speed of transmission of these signals. The 'intelligent' nervous system will respond accurately to incoming signals, and will therefore also be able to respond rapidly; the less intelligent will make errors and respond slowly. This is the biological substrate of the general factor common to all IQ tests.

Anderson (1992) also discussed how such a theory could be tested:

> General intelligence cannot, by definition, be specific to any domain of knowledge. Thus it must be either a function of a cognitive control process that is involved in all domains or a non-cognitive physiological property of the brain. In either case it should be possible to find correlates of general intelligence in tasks that are relatively *knowledge-free*.
>
> (Anderson, 1992, p. 27, italics in original)

Behavioural measures of speed of processing

In the initial phase of this research programme, two particular behavioural tasks were widely used to test the theory, inspection time and reaction time. In a typical inspection time experiment, two vertical lines are briefly flashed on the screen and the participant's task is to report which is the longer (see Figure 3.3 below). The difference in length is well above threshold, but the task is made difficult by reducing the duration of exposure to the point where errors occur. In a simple reaction time experiment, you are instructed to press a key whenever a signal comes on: in choice reaction time experiments, there are several alternative signals, only one of which is presented on a given trial, and you must press the appropriate key for that signal. Significant correlations have been reported between IQ scores and the duration of exposure necessary for accurate discrimination in inspection time tasks, and the speed with which people respond in reaction time tasks.

Reaction time

The very earliest attempts to measure differences in intelligence relied on the recently developed techniques of the new science of experimental psychology (see Chapter 1). Prominent among these was the reaction time task, and Cattell's battery of mental tests included more than one measure of reaction time (Cattell, 1890). But when Wissler (1901) failed to find any relationship between reaction time or sensory thresholds and such apparent indices of intelligence as college grades, this approach was abandoned. The long-term consequence was that the development of modern IQ tests owed little to laboratory techniques, and everything to the work of Alfred Binet. However you judge the consequences of this, it is now clear that Wissler's results were misleading; his measures of reaction time, based on only a very small number of trials, were too unreliable, and his subject sample, undergraduates at Columbia University, too highly selected, to enable him to discover that there really is a small, but reliable relationship between IQ and reaction time (RT).

The first, systematic series of studies to establish this beyond serious doubt (Roth, 1964) came from Erlangen in Germany, and had relatively little impact on American or British psychologists. Much of the later work was conducted either by Jensen (1987), or by others employing apparatus and procedures similar to his (for reviews, see Deary, 2000, 2003; Jensen, 2006). The participants' task is to perform as rapidly as possible the appropriate response whenever a light comes on. Jensen's apparatus, illustrated in Figure 3.1, consists of a console containing a central 'home' button, above which is a semicircular array of eight response buttons, each with a small light immediately above it. Participants start each trial with their index finger on the home button; when one of the lights is illuminated they must press the button below that light as rapidly as possible. Anticipatory movements off the home button (i.e. before a light comes on) are not recorded, but prevent the occurrence of the next trial until the finger is replaced. This means that releasing the home button serves as a measure of RT or decision time, while the time taken to press the appropriate target button, after releasing the home button, is usually described as movement time (MT). Although I shall talk only of RT below, in many, but by no means all, cases movement time shows similar relationships with IQ.

One of the most reliable results of RT research, first documented by Merkel (1885) but more usually described as Hick's law (Hick, 1952), is that RT increases as a function of the number of alternatives between which the participant has to choose. Hick's law states that RT is a linear function of the logarithm of the number of alternatives. Since the eight-choice RT task is more complex and produces slower RTs, it seemed plausible to suggest, as Jensen initially did, that the correlation between RT and IQ would increase with an increase in the number of alternatives, that is, that IQ was associated with the slope of the function relating RT to number of alternatives. Perhaps surprisingly, this turns out to be a very small effect indeed. Jensen (1987) summarized the results of 26 studies with a total of some 2,000 participants: the correlation between overall mean RT and IQ was −0.20 (negative because higher IQ was associated with shorter RT). Approximately half of these studies had varied the number of alternatives between one and eight: the correlation between IQ and RT to a single alternative was −0.18; that between IQ and RT to eight alternatives was −0.23—hardly a dramatic increase. Jensen concluded that 'g is more highly correlated with a general factor common to all the Hick RT and MT variables than with any particular measure' (Jensen, 1987, p. 168).

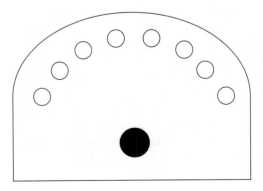

Figure 3.1 A schematic top view of the apparatus used by Jensen to measure reaction time. The black circle at the bottom is the 'home' button on which participants rest their finger at the start of each trial. The empty circles arranged in a semicircle at the top are eight different lights; reaction time is measured by the time between a light being turned on and the participant releasing the home button. Movement time is the time between releasing the home button and touching the correct light.

A correlation of −0.20 between RT and IQ may be significant, if based on a sufficiently large number of participants, but it is hardly going to revolutionize the understanding of IQ. It is, after all, marginally smaller than the correlation between IQ and height, which Jensen and Sinha (1993) have estimated as 0.23. There are, however, other sources of data to confirm that there is a real relationship between the IQ and RT, and it may be that these results underestimate its true magnitude. Most of the studies summarized by Jensen employed university students as participants, whose range of IQ scores is notably smaller than that of the population as a whole. Applying a correction for this restriction of range increases the correlation to −0.30. Such adjustments should, I believe, be viewed with considerable caution, but they may be justified here: in one of the largest single studies of the relationship between IQ and RT, employing participants of approximately average IQ and with a normal range of IQs (they were 141 17-year-old high school students with a mean IQ of 108 and a standard deviation of 15), Detterman (1987) found a correlation of −0.32 between IQ and RT. In a later study of 900 55-year-old Scottish people, whose social and educational characteristics were representative of the population as a whole, Deary *et al.* (2001) reported a correlation of −0.29 between IQ and simple RT, and one of −0.49 with four-choice RT.

The unusually strong correlation between IQ and four-choice RT in the Deary *et al.* study may have arisen from the effect of age on RT, which slows down after the age of 50. There is a similar decline at about this age in performance on a variety of IQ tests (see Chapter 8). If these correlated changes begin at different ages in different people, a random sample of 55-year-olds will include some where the changes are well under way, others where they have just started, and yet others where they have not even begun.

There is, then, a reliable correlation between IQ and RT. It may not be very large, but it still needs to be explained. One key to the explanation is that, in Jensen's summary, the correlation between IQ and a measure of the variability of RT was −0.21, almost exactly the same as that between IQ and mean RT. In one sense, this is not entirely surprising, since the average correlation between mean and standard deviation of RT in Jensen's analysis was 0.71. But what is the explanation? One possibility would be to appeal to differences in concentration or sustained attention between people of high and low IQ: there is good evidence that measures of sustained attention correlate with performance on RT tasks (Carlson *et al.*, 1983), and lapses of attention will presumably result in occasional long RTs, which would increase variability. More detailed analysis of the RT task suggests further possibilities. The participant's instructions are to respond as rapidly as possible without making errors, of which there are two kinds, pressing the incorrect button and releasing the home key before the start of a trial. There is an inevitable trade-off between speed and accuracy, and subjects need to titrate their own performance to find the fastest speed at which they can respond without making errors. Perhaps it is the precision of this titration process that distinguishes between people of high and low IQ. Brewer and Smith (1984), in an experiment with both normal and disabled participants, found that both groups showed a steady increase in speed of responding over a series of errorless trials; eventually such a sequence was followed by an error, which in turn was followed by an immediate slowing down of responding. This increase in RTs following errors was much greater for the disabled group.

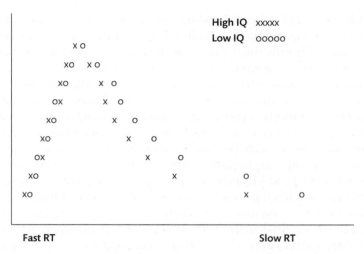

Figure 3.2 A schematic representation of typical RT distributions produced by participants of high and low IQ.

Consistent with this general line of reasoning, Juhel (1993), while observing a non-significant correlation of only –0.21 between IQ and mean RT, reported a significant correlation of –0.40 between IQ and the degree of skewness of participants' distribution of RTs. As is illustrated in Figure 3.2, RT distributions are invariably skewed, since there is a limit to how fast anyone can respond; the point is that low IQ participants are more likely to produce occasional long RTs than are high IQ participants. Larson and Alderton (1990) and Kranzler (1992) showed that the correlation between IQ and choice RT was significantly greater for each participant's slow responses than for their fast responses. Indeed, these findings are sufficiently reliable that they have been sanctified as the 'worst performance rule' (Coyle, 2003): it is their worst performance, not their best, that correlates with participants' IQ scores (see also Unsworth *et al.*, 2010). It is clear that the correlation between IQ and RT does not arise because the higher your IQ the faster you are capable of responding. It is because you make fewer slow responses. This hardly supports the idea that RT is a direct measure of the speed with which information is transmitted through the nervous system, let alone that differences in this speed are the cause of differences in *g*.

Finally, it is well established that practice affects RT. Not only do RTs continue to decrease with practice over many thousands of trials, prolonged practice will also decrease the slope relating RT to the number of alternatives (Teichner and Krebs, 1974). But if high IQ is associated with more rapid improvement in RTs over time (as implied by the results of an experiment by Widaman and Carlson, 1989), then this effect alone would presumably be responsible for some of the association between RT and IQ. It could certainly explain the very modest relation between IQ and the slope of the function relating RT to the number of alternatives.

Inspection time

In a typical visual inspection time (IT) experiment, two vertical lines are briefly shown side by side on a screen, one substantially longer than the other (see Figure 3.3). They are immediately followed by a mask designed to obscure the original lines. The participant's rather simple task is then to report whether the longer line was on the left or the right. Following a correct response, the exposure duration (more precisely, the interval between the initial onset of the lines and the occurrence of the mask) is shortened for the next trial, and so on, until the participant starts making errors, usually at exposures roughly between 50 and 150 msec. The briefest duration at which a participant is correct on a certain percentage of trials is the most commonly used measure of inspection time; an alternative procedure gives a fixed number of trials at various durations, and scores the percentage of correct responses. One or two early studies employing this procedure reported astonishingly high correlations between IT and IQ, in the range −0.70 to −0.92 (Brand and Deary, 1982; Nettelbeck and Lalley, 1976; as was the case for RT, the correlations are negative because high IQ was associated with short IT scores). It soon became apparent, however, that these early correlations had been inflated by the inclusion of a disproportionate number of people with *very* low IQ scores in the relatively small samples. Subsequent studies, reviewed by Nettelbeck (2003), Grudnik and Kranzler (2001), and Deary (2000) have reported much more modest correlations, never greater than −0.50, and in at least some studies not significantly different from zero. Grudnik and Kranzler reported the results of a meta-analysis of 92 studies with data from over 4,000 participants. The average correlation with IQ was −0.30. Once again, since the participants in many of these studies were university students, this may well be an underestimate of the true value of the correlation in the population as a whole, and by adjusting for restriction of range (and unreliability of the tests), Grudnik and Kranzler increased the correlation to −0.50. Although several reasonably large studies have reported correlations with at least some IQ measures ranging from −0.35 to −0.50 (Bates and Eysenck, 1993b; Chaiken, 1993; Deary, 1993), the largest single study, with a sample of 343 naval recruits, reported

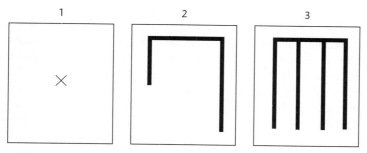

Figure 3.3 The sequence of stimulus displays, shown from left to right, in a typical inspection time experiment. In the interval between trials, the screen is blank except for a central fixation point (1); each trial consists in the brief presentation of the two vertical lines joined at the top shown in (2), followed after a predetermined interval by the masking stimulus shown in (3).

a correlation of only –0.25 between IT and a composite IQ score derived from the AFQT and Raven's Matrices (Larson and Saccuzzo, 1989).

There can be no doubt that there is a non-trivial correlation between IT and IQ. The precise value of that correlation may be a matter of some dispute. It is certainly a great deal smaller than the figure of –0.80 or so suggested by some early studies. An upper-bound estimate of the unadjusted correlation would be no more than –0.50, and that with only some kinds of IQ test (see below). But since a lower-bound estimate (at least for some kinds of IQ test) would have to be not much less than –0.25, it is clear that there is a moderate, significant correlation, which is probably rather higher than the correlation between RT and IQ. What is its explanation?

The IT task has some face validity as a measure of the speed and accuracy of transmission of information through the nervous system. According to the accumulator model of Vickers (1979), who developed the procedure, perceptual discriminations of this sort involve taking in information in a series of discrete samples: a decision is reached once sufficient information has been sampled or accumulated, and the time taken to reach such a decision will reflect both the accuracy with which one stage of the system produces different outputs for different inputs, and the reliability with which a later stage detects these differences in output. Vickers's model is thus very similar to that proposed by Eysenck (1982, see above) and implies that IT is a direct measure of a fixed property of the nervous system—the speed and fidelity with which it responds to different sensory inputs.

Is this all? Does performance on an IT task, like that on RT tasks, reflect a variety of other processes, which might be responsible for its association with IQ? There has been no shortage of alternative accounts. One possibility is that differences in IT (like differences in average RT) largely reflect differences in attention or vigilance. It seems reasonable to suppose that discriminating between two very briefly presented stimuli over a long series of trials must require sustained concentration on what is a relatively boring task, and one potential cause of longer ITs, as of occasional long RTs, must be occasional lapses of concentration. Several observations suggest that this may be important. In two experiments, Chaiken (1993) gave two separate IT tests in a single test session, separated by a series of other tests. In both experiments, performance on the second IT test, at the end of the session, was substantially worse than performance on the first. But the correlation between IT and IQ was higher on the second test (–0.50 and –0.38 in the two experiments) than it had been on the first (–0.35 and –0.27). A plausible explanation of the decline in IT performance from first to second test is that it represents a decline in vigilance during the course of a long, tiring session. If that is so, the increase in the correlation with IQ suggests that part of the IT-IQ correlation reflects a factor of vigilance or sustained attention. Bors and MacLeod (1996) gave participants a single, long IT session, consisting of 600 trials with a fixed set of trial durations ranging from 40 to 140 msec. Although their participants' IT scores averaged well under 100 msec, the accuracy of their performance correlated almost as strongly with IQ even at the longest duration of 140 msec. Low IQ participants must have been making errors at all durations. This is not quite the same as the 'worst performance rule' that described the relationship between IQ and RT, but it equally implies that the IQ-IT relationship is not simply a matter of how rapidly people can discriminate between the shorter and longer line.

Where there is a close parallel between IT and RT is that IQ correlates as much with the trial-to-trial variability of performance as with overall mean level of performance. Fox *et al.* (2009) reported that in a sample of 73 students, the correlation between IQ (Raven's Matrices) and mean IT was −0.25, but that between Raven's scores and the standard deviation of IT scores was −0.34.

Finally, performance on IT tasks, like that on RT tasks, improves with practice. Large practice effects are not usually observed during the course of a single session, presumably because they are masked by a decline in vigilance. But if trials are spread over several days, significant improvement has typically been found (e.g. Mackenzie and Bingham, 1985). Bors and MacLeod (1996) found that mean IT scores declined from over 80 to less than 70 msec over three days of practice. But even more important, the correlation between IQ and IT declined from −0.43 to −0.07 over the three days. That IT should improve with practice is not readily accommodated by the Vickers model. Bors and MacLeod's results suggest that the IT-IQ correlation may depend on differences in the rate at which high and low IQ participants show such improvement.

Odd-man-out RT and Zahlen Verbindungs test

Two other timed tests have shown significant correlations with IQ scores. The apparatus for the odd-man-out reaction time task (OMO RT) is the same, eight-light box, as that used for the Jensen's standard RT task, but as is shown in Figure 3.4, in OMO three lights are illuminated on every trial, two relatively close together, one further apart. The participant's task is to respond to this third, odd-man-out, light. Several studies have reported correlations between OMO RT and various IQ measures substantially higher than those between standard RT tasks and IQ (Bates and Eysenck, 1993b; Frearson and Eysenck, 1986; Frearson *et al.*, 1988). In the Frearson and Eysenck study, for example (although this is admittedly the most dramatic case), the correlation between OMO RT and scores on Raven's Matrices was −0.62, while those between various standard RT measures and Raven's ranged from −0.25 to −0.36. One parallel with the standard RT case, however, is that the 'worst performance rule' applies to OMO RT also; Kranzler (1992) reported that the correlation with IQ was −0.21 for participants' fastest RTs, but −0.36 for their slowest.

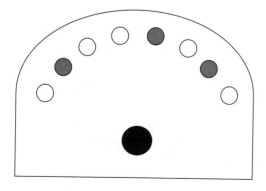

Figure 3.4 The RT apparatus used to study OMO RT.

1	7	6	14	12	18	19	21	22	23
2	5	8	13	15	11	17	20	24	26
77	3	4	9	10	16	29	30	27	25
76	78	83	84	85	86	31	28	34	35
75	74	79	82	87	88	32	33	38	36
73	72	81	80	90	89	49	39	40	37
71	65	64	63	58	50	48	47	46	41
70	66	62	59	56	57	51	53	45	42
69	68	67	61	60	55	54	52	43	44

Figure 3.5 The Zahlen Verbindungs Test (or ZVT): in a typical experiment, the participant starts at 1 in the top left corner, and has to trace a line connecting each number in ascending order until reaching 90 in the centre.

The Zahlen Verbindungs Test (ZVT) is illustrated in Figure 3.5. It is a trail finding task: the participant is shown a 10 × 9 grid containing a semi-random arrangement of the numbers 1 to 90. In the standard version, the requirement is to trace the line connecting the numbers in ascending order, that is, starting at 1, go to 2, then to 3, etc. The participant's score can be either the time taken to complete the test or the number of items correctly completed in a fixed time. As the name suggests, the task was developed and first used in Germany (again at Erlangen, by Oswald and Roth, 1978), but was taken up by Vernon (1993), who also developed variants of the simple task: tracing the numbers in descending rather than ascending order, connecting every alternate number in either ascending or descending order, interspersing numbers and letters, going from 1 to A to 2 to B, etc. Vernon reported correlations with scores on the Multidimensional Aptitude Battery (a multiple-choice version of the WAIS) ranging from 0.31 to 0.71, with an average of 0.53 (the correlations are positive when the score is the number of items completed in a fixed time). Williams and Pearlberg (2006) confirmed Vernon's findings, reporting a correlation of 0.42 between ZVT and Raven's Matrices.

Both OMO RT and ZVT are relatively straightforward, speeded tests, in the case of ZVT taking no more than a minute or two to complete. But performance on both appears to correlate with IQ in the range 0.30 to 0.60—a reliable and substantial effect, not far short of the correlation observed between, say, verbal and spatial IQ tests. It would be absurd to maintain that 'speed of processing' has nothing to do with IQ. At the same time, the OMO RT and ZVT correlations also pose a different challenge: why are they rather higher than those typically observed between RT or IT and IQ? In the case of OMO RT, I suggest one possible answer below. In the case of ZVT, the answer will have to wait until Chapter 5.

Interpretation of the correlations between IQ and speeded tests

There is no doubt that differences in performance on some superficially rather simple laboratory tasks are moderately correlated with differences in people's IQ scores. What do these relationships mean? It is worth starting off with the 'big' question. Do they provide good support for the position taken by Anderson (1992, 2005) or Jensen (1998) that the basis for g is the speed, accuracy, or efficiency of the brain as an information processing device? The answer must, I think, be: not really.

g or Gs

The first problem is that the correlations between IQ and the two simpler measures, IT and RT, are very much less impressive than initial enthusiasm led some proponents of this enterprise to claim. The correlation between IQ and IT is probably somewhere between −0.25 and −0.50. That between IQ and RT is probably only −0.20 to −0.30. Such correlations, especially those with IT, are far from trivial, and they may even be rather surprising, but they are hardly sufficient to justify the claim that either of these tasks provides a direct measure of the single, general process underlying g. As Detterman has noted, the claim to have found the single process underlying g is not easily satisfied: 'As a preliminary, it would be necessary to show that the candidate cognitive process had a high correlation with general intelligence, preferably above 0.80 before correction for unreliability. Such a correlation would indicate that the process in question accounted for most of the reliable variance in g' (Detterman, 2002, p. 230). This may be a rather stern requirement, but research on RT and IT has not even come close to meeting it. It is one thing to say that one *component* of general intelligence is related to speed of processing, and that it correlates with performance on laboratory tasks that also stress speed and accuracy. That is interesting and important, but it will not shed a blinding new light on the nature of general intelligence. It is quite another thing to claim that the most important central ingredient common to all forms of intelligent behaviour is speed of information processing. That sounds as if it might be a revolutionary idea. But it is not justified by the size of the correlations between IQ and IT or RT.

Indeed, the size of the correlation between choice RT and IQ is sufficiently small that no one could seriously argue that RT alone provides an explanation of g. But proponents of the IT paradigm, such as Anderson (1992), have sometimes insisted that the size of the correlation between IT and IQ, optimistically said to be at least 0.50, means that if the IT task really did provide a direct measure of the speed and efficiency of a basic information processing system, that system would have a fair claim to being the basis, or at least an important part of the basis, of g. There is, however, a serious problem with this claim: the correlation between IT and IQ is actually not a correlation with g.

It has been clear for a long time that the correlation between IT and IQ as measured by the WAIS was largely due to the performance half of the scale, rather than the verbal half. This was true in Nettelbeck and Lalley's (1976) early study, and has been amply confirmed since (see Nettelbeck, 1987, for a review of other early studies; and Crawford *et al.*, 1998, and McGeorge *et al.*, 1996, for two later studies). Factor analysis of earlier versions of the WAIS makes it clear that the verbal scale loads more strongly onto the general factor than does the performance scale (Silverstein, 1982). So IT scores do not correlate particularly well with the general factor of the WAIS.

Within the WAIS, there is in fact a *negative* correlation ($r = -0.65$) between tests' g-loadings and their correlation with IT (Crawford *et al.*, 1998): the test with the strongest correlation with IT is digit symbol, which has one of the lowest loadings on the general factor of the WAIS. This finding has been confirmed by two other studies (Nettelbeck *et al.*, 1986, and McGeorge *et al.*, 1996). McGeorge *et al.* employed a somewhat different visual IT task, tachistopic word recognition, which measured the shortest exposure duration at which subjects could correctly identify a certain proportion of a list of words presented one by one on the tachistoscope screen. Although the use of such verbal material might have been expected to increase correlations with verbal IQ, performance on this task correlated only -0.21 with scores on the WAIS-R verbal tests, but -0.47 with scores of the performance tests.

Digit symbol is a timed test that simply requires you to fill in, as rapidly as possible, the appropriate symbol under a series of 90 digits, and in the WAIS-IV loads onto a speed factor. The most obvious interpretation of these findings, therefore, is that IT correlates most strongly with Gs, not g. That implication is strongly supported by the results of other studies. In two large-scale experiments, for example, Chaiken (1994) found significant correlations, of about -0.40, between IT scores and performance on visual search tests, where you must find, as rapidly as possible, all instances of a particular target item embedded in a series of distractor items.

Several studies have explicitly tested the proposition that the overall correlation between IT and IQ arises largely from IT's association with Gs, not with g. Burns and Nettelbeck (2003), Burns *et al.*, (1999), and Mackintosh and Bennett (2002) all gave a series of marker tests of Gc, Gf, Gv, and Gs. The results of the last of these studies are shown in Table 3.1. Not only did IT correlate more strongly with Gs than with any other factor: once Gs was partialled out, IT did not correlate significantly with any of the other tests.

Table 3.1 Correlations between inspection time (percentage of correct scores) and measures of four components of IQ, Gc, Gf, Gv, and Gs. Partial correlations between inspection time and Gc, Gf, and Gv, are after controlling for Gs; the partial correlation between inspection time and Gs is after controlling for Gf (data from Mackintosh and Bennett, 2002, Tables 2 and 3).

	Gc	Gf	Gv	Gs
Raw correlations	−0.04	0.29	0.23	0.43
Partial correlations	−0.11	0.15	0.02	0.36

The conclusion seem inescapable: if performance on IT tasks shows a surprisingly strong correlation with IQ scores, this is not because IT provides a particularly good measure of the general factor common to all IQ tests, but because it measures one particular component of IQ, namely Gs or perceptual speed (see Box 3.1). Is this equally true for RT? Not entirely. Most earlier studies reported that, unlike IT, RT correlated as strongly with the old Wechsler verbal scale as with the performance scale (Jensen, 1987), although the latter includes several timed tests and the former none at all. Moreover, Vernon *et al.* (1985) reported that the size of the RT-IQ correlation remained much the same whether or not a time limit was imposed for the IQ test. However, Wilhelm and Schultz (2002) found that the correlation between various RT tests and Gf was greater when the tests of Gf were given with strict time limits than when they were not, and the picture is not as clear as Jensen (1998, p. 224), for one, has claimed. In the only study to have reported the correlation between RT and individual tests of the WAIS, Frearson *et al.* (1988) found that the correlation between four-choice RT and the digit symbol test was –0.32, while the next highest correlation, with block design (like most of the performance tests, this too carries bonus marks for fast solutions), was only –0.18.

BOX 3.1 Some questions about the correlates of inspection time

One of the more reliable sex differences in performance on IQ tests is that women outscore men on measures of Gs or perceptual speed (see Chapter 14). If individual differences in IT correlate not with any general factor common to all IQ tests, but largely with the factor of perceptual speed, it should presumably follow that women will also outscore men on IT tasks. In fact they do not (Burns and Nettelbeck, 2005). This would seem to imply that either IT or standard measures of Gs must be measuring some further process(es) that the two do not share in common. One possibility is that many measures of Gs also make demands on memory: the Wechsler digit symbol test, for example, requires you to write the correct symbol below each digit in a series of 90 randomly ordered digits. The correct symbol for each digit is given in a list at the top of the answer sheet. If you can remember which symbol goes with each digit, you will not have to refer back to this list each time you enter a new symbol—thus speeding up your performance.

What IT and measures of Gs presumably do share in common is the speed and accuracy of sensory registration. This suggests the possibility that the IT task may be the adult's or older child's version of the infant habituation test. The rapidity with which 6-month-old infants habituate to a novel stimulus predicts their IQ scores five or ten years later (see Chapter 8, where I discuss this evidence in more detail). Differences in speed of habituation may well depend on the speed and accuracy of sensory registration (although I half seriously suggest another explanation in Chapter 11). There is scope here for an interesting longitudinal study. Do infant habituation scores predict IT scores ten or twenty years later? Do they predict scores on tests of Gs better than other components of IQ?

The complexity of Gs

If the nervous system's speed of information processing really were the unitary basis of *g*, it would seem to follow that different ways of measuring that speed should all correlate with one another. They do not. Indeed, performance on one IT task does not necessarily correlate particularly well with performance on others. In addition to the standard visual IT task, there have also been studies of auditory and even tactile IT. In a typical auditory task, two brief tones are presented in rapid succession, followed by an auditory mask, and the participant's task is to decide whether the first or second tone has the higher frequency. Although auditory IT correlates with IQ, correlations between auditory and visual IT have ranged from only 0.15 to 0.39 (Irwin, 1984; Langsford *et al.*, 1994; Nettelbeck *et al.*, 1986; Saccuzzo *et al.*, 1986). The implication must be that much of the variance in IT scores is modality specific and can hardly be related to any general process of intelligence. Deary (1994) was able to show that there was a speed component to auditory IT performance that correlated significantly with IQ. It would be interesting to know whether this component represented the variance shared with visual IT.

In view of this, it is not surprising that numerous studies have reported only a trivially small correlation between IT and RT (Bates and Eysenck, 1993b; Kranzler and Jensen, 1991; Larson *et al.*, 1988; Larson and Saccuzzo, 1989; Nettelbeck and Kirby, 1983; O'Connor and Burns, 2003; Saccuzzo *et al.*, 1986). These correlations have ranged from zero to a maximum of 0.35, but the large majority, including those from the largest single study, with over 300 participants (Larson and Saccuzzo) have been 0.20 or lower. It seems reasonable to conclude that, whatever may be the cause of the observed correlations between IQ and IT or RT, it is not because these two tasks provide equivalent, interchangeable measures of a single underlying process of speed of information processing that is the biological basis of *g* or general intelligence. To a large extent, they must be measuring different processes.

In two of these studies (Bates and Eysenck, and O'Connor and Burns) participants were also tested on the OMO RT task. The correlations between OMO RT, IT, and two-choice RT from the latter study are shown in Table 3.2. As can be seen, the correlation between IT and RT was negligible, but both RT and IT correlated with OMO RT. The implication, consistent with Carroll (1993), is surely that there must be *at least* two distinct aspects of 'speed of processing', rapid or efficient sensory analysis, measured by IT, and rapid or efficient decision making, measured by RT. OMO RT measures both, which explains why it correlates more strongly with IQ than does either of the other two tasks. That OMO RT measures other more 'perceptual' aspects of timed performance than does ordinary RT is also suggested by results reported by Frearson *et al.* (1988). As noted above, they found that ordinary RT correlated modestly with the digit symbol test of the WAIS, but only negligibly with the other performance tests. While OMO RT also correlated most strongly with digit symbol ($r = -0.46$), it also correlated significantly with all other performance tests (between -0.30 and -0.40).

Factor analysis has confirmed and extended this conclusion. O'Connor and Burns (2003) took 18 different measures from a variety of speeded tests, and reported that a four-factor solution provided the best fit to their data. IT loaded onto a factor they labelled visualization speed, and RT onto a different factor they labelled decision time. OMO RT loaded onto both factors. Three of the four factors were correlated with one another (the exception was Movement time from the RT and OMO RT tests), and a higher order factor was therefore extracted, which O'Connor and Burns labelled Gs. Roberts and Stankov (1999) reported a relatively similar factorial solution from a slightly different battery of speeded tests.

There is a final problem. The discovery of correlations between IQ and performance on other psychological tasks will advance theoretical understanding of the nature of IQ

Table 3.2 Correlations between inspection time, two-choice reaction time, and OMO reaction time (data from O'Connor and Burns, 2003, Table 1).

	IT	RT	OMO RT
IT	—		
RT	0.13	—	
OMO RT	0.35	0.44	—

only if these other tasks are themselves better understood than is IQ, and there is some theoretical account of the reason for the correlations. It is most doubtful if these conditions have been satisfied here. Much of the research on RT and IT has been premised on the assumption that these tasks are so simple (even so non-cognitive in nature) that they will yield up their secrets without any need for the sort of theoretical and experimental analysis that might be provided by cognitive psychology. This seems wholly unwarranted. Performance on both RT and IT tasks improves with practice and probably reflects, among other things, the ability to maintain vigilance or attention on a repetitive task. In the case of RT, analysis of changes in speed over trials and after errors suggests that people are attempting to titrate their performance so as to combine maximum speed with the fewest possible number of errors. At the very least, the fact that differences in IQ are associated with differences in *slow* RTs rather than differences in fast RTs suggests that the critical processes being measured in the RT paradigm are not simply speed of transmission. Since IQ appears to correlate with errors at long as well as short stimulus durations in the IT task, a similar conclusion may also hold here.

Conclusion

One possible explanation of the general factor that can be extracted from any IQ test battery is that performance on all manner of IQ tests depends upon a single underlying process of 'general intelligence'. But what might such a process be? Several authors have argued that it must be some aspect of the efficiency of the brain as an information processing system, such as the speed and accuracy with which information is transmitted from one part of the system to another.

There are unquestionably modest/moderate/moderately strong (take your pick) correlations between scores on standard measures of intelligence and performance on several laboratory tasks: RT, IT, OMO RT, and ZVT, all of which measure the speed at which people perform relatively simple tasks—simple at least in the sense that, in the absence of time constraints, they could be performed without error by essentially anyone. The strength of some (but by no means all) of these correlations may be surprising, but they are hardly sufficient to substantiate the strong position taken by Anderson (2005) or Jensen (1998), that speed of processing is the psychological/biological substrate of *g* (but see Box 3.2). In the first place, the worst performance rule makes it clear that the correlation between IQ and both RT and IT is not a matter of the highest speed of which people are capable when required to decide which button to press or which of two lines is the longer. The correlation arises largely because the lower someone's test score the more likely they are to make occasional slow decisions. The implication is that neither RT nor IT is a direct measure of the speed of information processing by the nervous system. Both tasks are more complex than that. Second, the association with IQ is not so much an association with *g*, but rather an association with Gs or perceptual speed.

BOX 3.2 The rise and fall of speed of processing

Factor analysis may suggest that Gs or speed of processing is only a relatively minor component of IQ, but there is one further reason for supposing it may be more important. It is a commonplace observation that people slow down as they grow older, and numerous studies have shown that one of the first components of IQ to decline in middle to old age is Gs. Some writers, indeed (e.g. Salthouse, 1996), have argued that this decline in speed of processing is responsible for all changes in test performance in old age. There is also evidence that as young children grow up, one important change in their performance on any cognitive test is an increase in speed of processing. I discuss this evidence in Chapter 8, but it is worth drawing attention to it here as a possible counterweight to any tendency to relegate speed to a minor place in the IQ hierarchy.

At this point, the correlations become notably less surprising: most accounts of the factorial structure of IQ have identified at least one component, or group factor, labelled perceptual speed or some similar name—and one at least (Carroll, 1993) identified three such factors. The research reviewed above confirms Carroll's conclusion that 'speed' is certainly not a simple unitary factor, and this helps to explain why different speeded laboratory tasks do not necessarily correlate very strongly with one another. It makes little sense to insist that 'speed of processing' is the unitary basis of general intelligence. It is certainly one (perhaps more than one) component of the intelligence measured by IQ tests. But it is surely not the unitary basis of *g*.

Summary

- Performance on a variety of simple laboratory tasks, such as reaction time (RT) or inspection time (IT) shows modest correlations with IQ. Faster performance is associated with higher IQ.
- Although it has been argued that 'speed of processing' is thus the psychological or biological basis of general intelligence, this strong claim is not well supported.
- The correlation between IQ and both RT and IT is not a matter of the highest speed of which people are capable when required to decide which button to press or which of two lines is the longer. The correlation arises largely because the lower your test score the more likely you are to make occasional slow decisions.
- The correlations are less with *g*, than with Gs, a second-stratum factor in the CHC model.
- Moreover, Gs itself is probably divisible into more than one subsidiary factor.

Further reading

Anderson (2005) provides a rather more sympathetic account of his theorizing than I have, and Deary (2003) and Nettelbeck (2003) good reviews of the evidence relating reaction time and inspection time to IQ scores. Roberts and Stankov (1999) and O'Connor and Burns (2003) should be consulted for the complexity of the factor structure of 'speed of processing'.

4 Verbal, spatial, and fluid abilities: Gc, Gv, and Gf

Introduction

In the present chapter I look at three of the major components of IQ, first reviewing studies that have attempted to identify some of the processes or operations measured by tests of verbal or crystallized (Gc), and spatial (Gv) intelligence, finally examining attempts to understand fluid intelligence or reasoning (Gf). A question of some importance will be this: just as there is no *a priori* reason to suppose that there is a single cognitive or biological process underlying the general factor, *g*, so there is no necessary reason to believe that each of these second-stratum factors corresponds to a unitary psychological faculty, or (in more modern terminology) cognitive module. The answer to that question will require experimental and theoretical analysis. The previous chapter suggested that speed of processing is not a unitary construct, and the evidence reviewed below will equally suggest that verbal, spatial, and fluid abilities are not unitary, but that each depends on many partially distinct cognitive operations or processes. Particularly in the case of Gf, the nature of some of these processes is still shrouded in some mystery: the notion of a 'central executive' that formulates and implements plans for dealing with new problems is a case in point, and appeals to such a process to explain problem solving and other facets of intelligence sometimes seems to amount to little more than substituting one unknown for another. A second question that should be kept in mind is whether some of the processes that emerge from these analyses are common to more than one component of IQ; if they are, they may provide part of the explanation of the general factor.

Crystallized ability (Gc)

Although I shall here and elsewhere use the terminology and factor structure derived from the CHC model, in preference to Johnson and Bouchard's version of the Vernon model, this does not mean that the psychological interpretation Cattell gave his model should be accepted. As noted in Chapter 2, his interpretation of the distinction between Gc and Gf was that Gf was the biological potential for intelligence, which became manifest in Gc as people acquired knowledge and experience, absorbing the culture in which they lived, and profiting, or not, as the case may be, from the educational system provided by their society (Cattell, 1971). It is true that many of the typical measures of Gc, such as the vocabulary, information, and comprehension tests of the WAIS and WISC, seem to be little more than measures of acquired knowledge, rather than of innate ability (this also seems obviously true of the arithmetic test), but whether that is a sufficient account must be open to question.

Vocabulary

Vocabulary size is the quintessential measure of Gc. In group IQ tests, it is measured by multiple-choice questions—selecting from a list of alternatives the word closest in meaning to a target word, or in individual tests such as the Stanford-Binet or Wechsler scales, by the rather harder task of providing your own definition of the meaning of each target word. One striking feature is that scores on vocabulary tests, unlike most IQ tests, carry on improving up to the age of at least 50 or 60 before slowly beginning to decline (Chapter 8; Verhaeghen, 2003). An obvious explanation is that older people have simply had a longer time to learn the meaning of a larger number of words: once again Gc is just a measure of one's opportunity to acquire a certain kind of information. The assumption is that differences in acquired knowledge can be ascribed solely to differences in the opportunity to learn rather than to differences in the efficiency with which people take advantage of their opportunities. While this may help to explain the difference in vocabulary scores between middle-class and lower-class children (see Chapter 12), there is reason to question it as a complete explanation of all differences in vocabulary. There is good experimental evidence that differences in Gc predict children's ability to learn a new, arbitrary vocabulary rather than simply reflecting past familiarity with the material. Gathercole and Baddeley (1990) asked two groups of 5-year-olds to learn new names for each of four toy animals. The names were either ordinary proper names, Simon, Michael, etc., or nonsense names such as Tikal and Pemon. Children with higher scores on vocabulary and reading tests learned these new associations substantially faster than those with lower scores, even though the two groups were closely matched for scores on a measure of Gf—Raven's Matrices.

Moreover, young children do not acquire their vocabulary simply by a process of paired-associate learning of each new word with a definition kindly provided by parent or teacher. By the age of 6, the average child has a vocabulary of some 14,000 words; a rough calculation suggests that they must be learning a new word every waking hour. Ten years later, typical American high-school seniors have a vocabulary of some 40,000 words, and have learned about 3,000 new words a year throughout their time at school (Ellis, 1994). No one can seriously suppose that they are explicitly taught, or actually look up in a dictionary, each of these words.

Children acquire a vocabulary mostly by listening to what they hear people saying, and later by reading (Ellis, 1994; Krashen, 1989; Sternberg, 1985). They have to work out the meaning of new words in a variety of different ways. One is to analyse the structure of the word, and then infer its meaning from the known meaning of some of its parts. For example, what is the meaning of: Ingrate? The prefix 'in-' implies 'not', while 'grate' is perhaps the noun that forms 'grateful'—full of 'grate' (what is that?) or perhaps 'gratitude'. So an ingrate may be one who shows or feels no gratitude.

Whole sentences can usually provide much stronger clues to the meaning of unfamiliar words. What is the meaning of *thane* in the following sentence?

> Many thanes and their followers joined Harold at Hastings, but they did not save him from defeat.

It requires only a passing acquaintance with English history to infer that thanes are some sort of Anglo-Saxon soldier. And the mention of their followers implies that they were men of some authority and power, albeit below that of a king, in Anglo-Saxon England.

Acquiring a vocabulary depends on processes of inference and reasoning in the face of uncertainty; it is often possible to work out the meaning of an unfamiliar word, and it seems plausible to suppose that this is how people acquire much of their vocabulary. No doubt, the ability to do so often depends on prior knowledge; someone who has never heard of King Harold or the Battle of Hastings will find it difficult to work out what thanes are. But it also reflects one's ability to bring evidence to bear on the solution of a problem, to reject some hypotheses in favour of others, and so on. Given all this, it becomes less surprising to learn that vocabulary is a good measure of intelligence. Moreover, such reasoning skills must also contribute to one's ability to understand, and answer questions about, a passage of prose you have just read. Reading comprehension is another standard measure of verbal ability or Gc.

Experimental evidence is consistent with these observations. Sternberg and Powell (1983) gave American high school students passages of prose to read which contained some extremely rare and unfamiliar words, whose meanings they were asked to guess. For example:

> A middle-aged woman and a young man sat round a fire where the common meal was almost ready. The mother, Tanith, peered at her son through the *oam* of the bubbling stew. It had been a long time since his last *ceilidh* and Tobar had changed greatly. As they ate Tobar told of his travels and adventures of the past year. And all too soon their brief *ceilidh* over, Tobar got up, touched his mother's arm and left.

The students' task was to provide definitions of the italicized words. Measures of the accuracy and adequacy of their definitions correlated about 0.60 with verbal IQ scores. In a similar experiment, Van Daalen-Kapteijns and Elshout-Mohr (1981) gave Dutch university students a number of sentences to read, each containing a particular invented word, whose meaning they were asked to guess after reading the sentence. Students selected for high verbal IQ performed substantially more accurately on this task than those low in verbal IQ.

There is also evidence of the converse of this—that in young children, aged 5–7, verbal IQ correlates significantly with the ability to provide the appropriate word to fill a gap in a sentence (Hunt, 1985). An example:

> Aunt Jane was unhappy because the cat ----- her canary.

Information

The information test of the WISC and WAIS also forms part of the verbal comprehension group of tests—because it correlates strongly with vocabulary. It is a simple test of general knowledge—of facts about the world, for example, history, geography, literature, politics, science, and religion, rather than the meanings of words. The argument advanced above, to the effect that people work out the meaning of new words by a process of inferential reasoning, does not obviously apply to such general knowledge. So why is it a good measure of intelligence? Perhaps because more intelligent people have a wider range of interests, which translates into learning more about a wider variety of things? Be this as it may, in spite of its strong correlation with vocabulary, there is an important difference between the two: males and females obtain very similar scores on the vocabulary test of the WAIS, but males are substantially better than females on the information test (Ilai and Willerman, 1989). Lynn *et al.* (2002) reported a similar male superiority on a different test of general knowledge.

Speed of lexical access

Hunt (1987) reviewed a large number of studies (many from his own laboratory) documenting that measures of verbal ability or Gc show modest correlations with performance on several laboratory reaction time (RT) tasks, where the stimuli to which participants are required to respond are letters, words, or even sentences. Figure 4.1 shows a variety of possible tasks; in each case the decision required is to say whether two simultaneously presented stimuli are the same or different. The tasks differ in the basis of this decision. In the two simplest versions, usually referred to as Posner's letter-matching tasks, the stimuli are letters of the alphabet. In the physical identity (PI) condition, 'same' means two physically identical letters, A-A, or a-a, while 'different' means an upper and a lower-case letter, A-a. In letter name identity (NI) two As still count as the same, even if shown in different

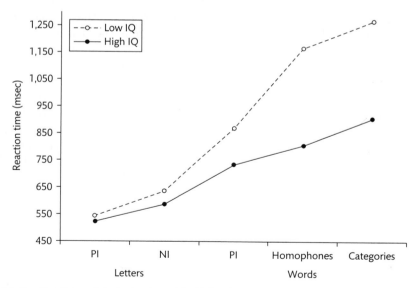

Figure 4.1 Reaction times of students selected for high or low verbal test scores on a variety of RT tasks. See text for further explanation. (The data for PI and NI to letters are from Hunt *et al.*, 1975, Table 1; and the data for the three tests with words are from Goldberg *et al.*, 1977, Table 1.)

type face, A-a. The stimuli for the remaining tasks of Figure 4.1 are words. Again, physical identity is a matter of whether two words are exactly the same, for example DEER—DEER. In the homonym identity condition, two words that merely sound alike are still to be judged the same, for example DEER—DEAR; while in categorical identity, two words from the same taxonomic category, e.g. DEER—ELK, count as the same, even if different in all other respects. People with higher Gc scores respond more rapidly than those with lower scores on all these tasks, but as can be seen in Figure 4.1, these differences become greater as one progresses through the list. In other words, there is an increase in the correlation between RT and Gc. The subjects in these studies were all university students and thus all of above average IQ. According to Hunt (1978), other populations take substantially longer to respond, and the *difference* in RT between letter NI and letter PI tasks (no data seem available for the other cases) is greater than that shown in Figure 4.1, ranging from 110 msec for young adults not at university, to 170 msec for adults over the age of 60, to over 300 msec for mildly disabled schoolchildren.

Vernon and Jensen (1984) reported actual correlations between scores on a test of Gc and RTs to various different stimuli: they ranged from no more than −0.05 when the stimuli were simple lights, to −0.25 when they were letters, to −0.33 when the task was to decide whether two words were synonyms or antonyms.

Performance on two other RT tasks also shows modest correlations with measures of Gc. One is Clark and Chase's (1972) sentence verification task, which requires you to say, as rapidly as possible, whether a given sentence provides a true or false description of a simple diagram (see Figure 4.2 for a further description). Lansman *et al.* (1982) reported a correlation of 0.28 with Gc in a group of 90 undergraduates. The other is a measure of the rapidity of retrieval from short-term memory devised by Sternberg (1975): participants are given a list of digits or letters to remember, and then asked to decide whether a given probe item was or was not in the list presented on that trial. Reaction time is a monotonically increasing function of the number of items in the list—a finding taken to imply that people normally engage in a serial search of the list held in memory. Bowling and Mackenzie (1996) found that performance on this task correlated with measures of Gc but not with measures of Gf.

What is the explanation of these correlations? Why should differences in Gc be associated with differences in RT in the letter or word-matching paradigm, in retrieval from short-term memory, or in the sentence verification problem? One possibility is that these differences in lexical access simply reflect differences in the amount of practice people have had with related tasks, such as reading, and are thus due to differences in the familiarity

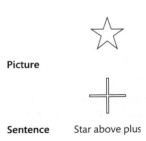

Picture

Sentence   Star above plus

Figure 4.2 The sentence verification task used by Carpenter and Just (1975). Participants are shown a picture, here of a star and a plus sign, and a sentence that may, or may not, accurately describe the spatial relationship between the elements of the picture. Their RT to respond true or false is measured.

of the material used in such experiments. If that were so, you would expect to see differences in test performance disappearing if people were tested with material that was equally unfamiliar to all of them, such as a novel set of symbols or hieroglyphics with which they had all had equivalent experience.

Jackson (1980) taught college students an artificial 'alphabet', in which arbitrary visual symbols were associated with nonsense syllables. By pairing two symbols with each nonsense syllable, he created two symbols with the same 'meaning', in a manner analogous to upper and lower-case versions of the same letter of the alphabet. He still found a significant correlation between measures of reading skill and RT on this stimulus-matching task. By equating his participants' experience with the symbols, he had presumably made them equally familiar to everyone.

Differences in Gc, then, are associated with differences in speed of access to, and efficiency of processing and retrieval of, lexical material, and this association is probably not simply a product of differences in the familiarity of the material used in lexical decision tasks. But the correlation between vocabulary size and speed of performance on letter matching, memory scanning, and sentence verification tasks is modest—of the order of 0.25–0.35. This alone should be sufficient to suggest that the two are measuring at least partially distinct processes. That conclusion is reinforced by an examination of age differences in the two types of test. As noted above, vocabulary scores tend to increase as people get older—at least up to the age of 50–60. But Lansman *et al.* (1982) reported that all these RT tasks correlated with measures of Gs as well as with Gc, and as one might expect therefore from other studies of age and RT (see Chapter 8), performance on the sentence verification task declines drastically with advancing years. Figure 4.3 gives the results of a direct comparison of the two.

Verbal fluency

In his list of primary mental abilities, Thurstone (1938) had two verbal factors: verbal comprehension and word fluency. Carroll (1993) also recognized this second factor. Tests of fluency typically require you to generate as many words as possible beginning with the letter F, or as many boys' names or animal names as you can in a minute. Although this may seem a rather trivial skill, it turns out to be a test remarkably sensitive to damage to frontal

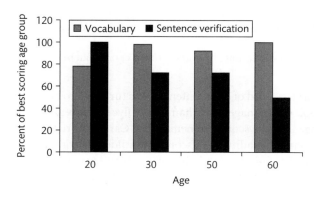

Figure 4.3 Vocabulary scores and performance on the sentence verification task as a function of age. Scores are all set relative to the best performing group on each task, whose score is set to 100 (data from Hunt, 1987).

cortex, the brain region generally regarded as the locus of 'executive function' (McCarthy and Warrington, 1990; see Chapters 5 and 6). Why should this be? The problem is not that such patients cannot remember any animal names: they perform quite adequately on cued recall or picture-naming tasks. The task is in fact a rather unusual one (you are not normally confronted with the need to generate animal names or words beginning with a given letter), and its solution therefore requires that you devise and execute an appropriate retrieval strategy, and monitor the items produced by such a strategy to ensure both that they are appropriate and that they are not merely repetitions of words you have already given. Frontal patients, indeed, make both types of error (Baddeley, 1997). In this sense, it is similar to another 'executive' task, random number generation, where you have to say the digits 0 to 9, but in a random order, that is, with not too many repetitions or ascending or descending sequences. There is, therefore, an unsuspected role to be played by cognitive psychologists' central executive systems in such a task.

Although it is undoubtedly a verbal task, and does correlate with other measures of verbal ability (Janssen *et al.*, 1996), it also correlates with other executive tasks such as the Wisconsin Card Sorting Test and Tower of Hanoi problem (Salthouse *et al.*, 2003; see Chapters 5 and 6). It can hardly be measuring the same thing as other measures of Gc, or Thurstone and Carroll would not have identified it as a separate factor. Moreover, unlike some other measures of Gc, such as vocabulary or lexical decision time, where there is at best only a small sex difference in average scores (see Chapter 14), females are substantially better than males at tests of verbal fluency (Weiss *et al.*, 2006). This is largely because they plan their search for new words more efficiently, by grouping their responses into better defined clusters, for example first giving boys' names beginning with A, then with B, C, etc. This both narrows down the search and reduces the load on memory (needed to ensure that you are not repeating a name already given).

Working memory

Daneman and Carpenter (1980) devised a 'reading span' task, specifically as an index of verbal comprehension and ability. Their participants, college students, were required to read aloud a series of sentences, visually presented one at a time, for example:

> I went to the theatre last night for the first time in over a year, and met a friend I had not seen for ages.
> I wish summer were here so that we could sit out in the garden after supper.
> Darwin's theory of evolution by natural selection relied on an analogy with artificial breeding.
> In most societies, the majority of aggressive crimes have always been carried out by young males, but females are catching up fast.

They were then required to recall the last word of each sentence. This turns out to be a surprisingly difficult task, and few people can manage more than four or five sentences. In spite of the inevitable restriction of range in these scores, Daneman and Carpenter reported a correlation of around 0.50 between various reading span scores and students' scores on the SAT-V, while Daneman and Green (1986) found a correlation of 0.57 between reading span and students' scores on a standard vocabulary test, and one of 0.69 between reading span and their ability to provide good definitions of very unusual words, such as *qualtagh*, from the context in which they appeared. Perhaps even more important, Daneman and Green found that the correlation of 0.61 between students' vocabulary scores and their ability to define words from their context was largely mediated by their reading span scores. The correlation was reduced to an insignificant value when reading span scores were taken into account. This is consistent with the suggestion that people acquire a large vocabulary by being able to infer the meanings of new words from the context in which they occur. Finally, Daneman and Carpenter (1980) reported remarkably high correlations, between 0.70 and 0.85, between students' reading span scores and their ability to answer factual questions about the contents of a passage of prose they had read.

There can be little doubt, then, that measures of reading or word span predict a variety of measures of verbal intelligence, including vocabulary, comprehension, and SAT-V scores. They are examples of what Baddeley (Baddeley and Hitch, 1974; Baddeley, 2007) has called 'working memory' tasks, which require you to remember some information (the last word of the last sentence) at the same time as processing some new information (reading the next sentence). I will give further examples of working memory tasks that correlate with different IQ measures later in this chapter, and Chapter 5 will provide a more general discussion of working memory.

Numerical ability

Daneman and Tardif (1987) devised a number span task, where each item consisted of three numbers, for example:

$$3, 7, 14,$$

and the requirement was to join (not add) two together to create a new number divisible by 3 (here, 714). Scores on the memory span part of this task, which required participants to recall the correct answer to each item at the end of the series, correlated 0.57 with the word span test and 0.51 with composite vocabulary and comprehension scores.

That working memory tasks with quite different materials and information processing requirements should continue to correlate with verbal intelligence scores implies, as did earlier results on speed of lexical access, that common content is not the underlying cause of correlations between IQ scores and various laboratory tasks. It is true that, in Daneman and Tardif's data and in other studies (e.g. Jurden, 1995), the correlations between measures of vocabulary or verbal comprehension and word span were rather higher than those with number span scores, but that is hardly surprising. This pattern of results is, in fact, entirely consistent with factorial studies of human abilities: as discussed earlier (Chapter 2), the higher-order factor, Gc, includes within it not only factors of verbal ability, reading comprehension, and general information, but also a factor of numerical facility (Carroll, 1993), and Vernon (1950) thought that his broad *v:ed* factor comprised distinguishable verbal and numerical factors. We should expect, therefore, that scores on verbal and numerical tasks should tap some overlapping processes. Of course, to the extent that both verbal and numerical factors can be extracted from large test batteries, they are partially distinct, but to the extent that they fall under the same broad Gc or *v:ed* factor, they must also be related.

It seems intuitively plausible that working memory will indeed be one of those overlapping processes, for solving problems in mental arithmetic surely places some demands on working memory. If asked to add 377 and 84, most people will solve this problem, as they were taught in school, by breaking it down into a series of sub-problems:

$$4 + 7 = 1 \text{ (carry 1)}$$
$$8 + 7 + 1 = 6 \text{ (carry 1)}$$
$$3 + 1 = 4$$

By holding the solution to each sub-problem in memory, it is possible to come up with the answer, 461. Hitch (1978) has provided good evidence that this intuition is correct—at least for most people; while Logie *et al.* (1994) have shown that performance on simple mental arithmetic tasks can be seriously disrupted by requiring people to perform concurrently another task that occupies the central executive memory store. The implication, then, is that a measure of working memory span would predict performance on mental arithmetic problems. But would all span tasks be equally strongly associated with mental arithmetic?

An experiment by Leather and Henry (1994) suggests that the answer is yes. They gave 7-year-old schoolchildren two working memory tasks: one involved listening to sentences and recalling their last words (listen span), the other required them to count the number of dots on each of a series of cards and recall the total number for each card (count span). They also gave them a standard vocabulary and reading comprehension test and the arithmetic test from the WISC. The correlations between the children's scores on all these tests are shown in Table 4.1. Listen span predicted vocabulary and reading comprehension rather better than count span did; count span predicted arithmetic better than it did the verbal tests. But the two span tasks correlated well, and also predicted arithmetic scores equally well.

What is verbal intelligence?

Traditional measures of Gc, such as vocabulary and comprehension tests, a general knowledge quiz, or mental arithmetic problems, have seemed to many critics to prove that IQ tests do not measure differences in anything they would normally want to call intelligence.

Table 4.1 Correlations between memory span, reading, vocabulary, and arithmetic tests in 7-year-old children (data from Leather and Henry, 1994, Table 2).

	Listen span	Count span	Vocabulary	Reading comp	Arithmetic
Listen span	—				
Count span	0.47	—			
Vocabulary	0.40	0.17	—		
Reading comp	0.61	0.36	0.48	—	
WISC Arithmetic	0.55	0.51	0.34	0.51	—

They appear to be measures of knowledge, not ability, and differences in performance on such tests, so the argument runs, can only be a consequence of differences in past opportunity to acquire the relevant information. Schools teach children to read and do arithmetic, so differences in schooling are bound to be reflected in these scores. The evidence reviewed above makes it clear that, at the very least, this is a serious oversimplification. Differences in Gc are reasonably described as differences in verbal *ability*, because they partly reflect differences in the way people take advantage of their opportunities. But what is verbal ability? According to Hunt:

> Verbal ability is the result of a somewhat correlated set of skills. These skills depend upon a variety of more primitive psychological processes, including access to lexical memory, rapid consolidation of information into long-term memory, the possession of knowledge about how to process discourse in general, and the possession of knowledge about the topic of the discourse being comprehended. Some of these primitive processes can be thought of as properties of the brain…[but] other processes…are learned, and are highly culture dependent.
>
> If the various verbal skills are distinct, why do psychometric analyses so consistently uncover a single dimension of verbal ability? It could be that all the primitive processes of language comprehension are derived from a single underlying brain process…[But] correlations between measures of different aspects of language comprehension could also be explained by interactions between them as they are developed. Being able to consolidate information into permanent memory rapidly would aid in the acquisition of lexical knowledge, and increasing one's vocabulary would increase one's ability to develop text and situation models, which could be used to increase lexical knowledge by defining new words in context.

(Hunt, 1987, p. 388)

Hunt's account, although persuasive, fails to mention one unifying process—working memory for verbal or numerical information. Not only are the correlations between measures of working memory and Gc quite high, ranging from 0.30 to as high as 0.60, but there is evidence that differences in working memory are responsible for the association between people's vocabulary scores and their ability to infer the meaning of unknown words from their context (Daneman and Green, 1986). Thus, size of vocabulary is a good measure of verbal ability, because we do not acquire our vocabulary by rote memorization of dictionary definitions, but rather by a process of inferential reasoning that appears to be dependent on working memory. As I have argued above, tests of verbal fluency tap into several different skills, one of which must be the ability to keep track of the items you have already produced in order to avoid repetition, that is, to hold items in working memory while generating new ones.

Spatial ability (Gv)

Factor analysis made it clear that there is an identifiable sub-set of IQ tests which can be distinguished from those that measure either verbal or crystallized ability (Gc) on the one hand, or non-verbal reasoning or fluid ability (Gf) on the other. A distinctive group of spatial tests was, in fact, the first to be reasonably securely identified by factor analytic techniques. Since then factor analysts have continued their study of spatial ability by arguing that it is not unitary, but can be decomposed into a number of subsidiary

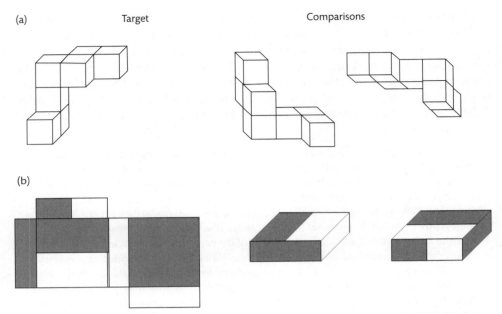

Figure 4.4 Examples of spatial IQ tests. (a) The Shepard-Metzler mental rotation task: which of the figures on the right is the same as the target on the left? (b) The DAT space relations test: if you folded up the target stimulus to form a box, which of the alternatives would it match?

abilities or skills, although with some disagreement both about the number of such subsidiary factors and their nature (Halpern, 2000; Hegarty and Waller, 2005). The general consensus is that the major factor, usually termed spatial visualization (not a particularly informative name), is defined by tasks such as three-dimensional mental rotation (3-D MRT), paper folding, form board, or the DAT space relations test (Figure 4.4; the paper folding test is illustrated in Figure 2.3). A second group of tests, which supposedly require you to orientate yourself in a wider, spatial frame of reference, or visualize a scene from a different perspective, has sometimes identified a second factor, called spatial orientation, although Carroll (1993) could find no really convincing evidence for such a factor. A typical test shows the view of the bow of a speedboat from the cockpit, and of the shoreline it is approaching. In a second picture, the boat has changed course slightly and the view of the shoreline has changed. The task is to state whether the boat has turned right or left, has rolled to the right or left, or has pitched up or down. A third factor has sometimes been defined by speeded tests of simple rotation—as in Thurstone's PMA test of mental rotation (see Figure 2.3). Although some commentators have argued otherwise, it does seem quite plausible that the solution of the seriously difficult Shepard-Metzler 3-D MRT task shown in Figure 4.4 here, should call into play psychological processes rather different from those required to solve simpler rotation problems. In order to improve the fit of the Vernon model to their data, Johnson and Bouchard (2005) added an image rotation factor to Vernon's *k:m*. Carroll also identified at least two further factors, one labelled flexibility of closure and measured by hidden or embedded figures tests

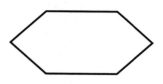 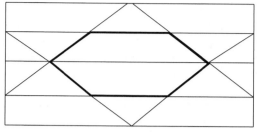

Figure 4.5 The embedded figures test: find the figure on the left in the more complex figure on the right. To make it easier, the embedded figure has been marked in bold.

such as that illustrated in Figure 4.5, and another labelled visual memory, interesting because it is one of the few spatial tests on which females generally do better than males (Chapter 14).

One reason for the confusion surrounding these different factors (apart from their confusing labels) is that not all analyses have identified the same factors. And one reason for that, as noted by Hegarty and Waller (2005), is that different people may adopt different strategies for solving the same problem, and sometimes the same strategy for solving what the test constructor had assumed were quite different tests. The distinction between visualization and orientation is a case in point. You might suppose that the set of skills being tapped by the speedboat test is more closely related than are tests of mental rotation to what we mean when we talk of someone as having a good sense of direction, and may be more relevant to the task of finding your way round a novel environment. But the problem is that laboratory versions of such tests are necessarily done with paper and pencil, and the small scale of the drawings means that they can be, and by many people are, just as readily solved by mentally rotating the scenes as by changing their own imagined orientation. And at that point, as some commentators have noted (Carpenter and Just, 1986; Lohman, 1988), factor analysis will not reveal distinct factors.

Spatial visualization

My discussion will largely focus on the first broad group of tests, those loading on the spatial visualization factor, since they have received most attention. The most common description of these tests (e.g. Carpenter and Just, 1986; Lohman, 1988) is that they measure the ability to form or construct representations of relatively complex visual patterns, shapes, or figures, representations that are sufficiently accurate, detailed, and durable that various operations can be performed on them, for example mental rotation of the entire shape, decomposing it into its constituent parts, recombining those parts into a new pattern, or adding or deleting various components. This seems, on the face of it, a reasonable starting point. To solve an item from the DAT space relations test shown in Figure 4.4, for example, it appears necessary to start by constructing a representation of what the two-dimensional target pattern will look like when each of the folding operations has been performed. All of these operations must be combined to construct a complete three-dimensional representation, which must then be operated upon, for example by mentally rotating it, to bring it into the same orientation as the various alternatives on offer. A similar account seems equally plausibly applied to the Shepard-Metzler 3-D MRT task: the task of aligning the target shape with the alternatives on offer presumably involves the operation of rotation in more than one plane and, given the three-dimensional nature of the shapes, is perhaps sufficiently complex that many people will find it necessary to decompose the shape into some of its constituent parts or blocks before carrying out these rotations. If so, these components must then be recombined to reconstruct the complete figure in order to compare it with the alternatives.

Lohman (1988) devised a simple set of laboratory tasks designed to separate out some of these component operations and assess their contribution to spatial IQ. Trials started with the brief presentation of a target stimulus on a computer monitor (see Figure 4.6); this was followed by instructions to perform certain operations on the target, and finally by the presentation of a comparison stimulus. The task was to decide whether the comparison stimulus matched the target stimulus presented at the outset of the trial, once account had been taken of the operations performed on it. Figure 4.6 illustrates a variety of types of trial. The first row depicts a simple matching task, no operations being required on the target. Two kinds of operation could be called for: addition of one (or more) further parts to the shape (row 2); or rotation through 90 or 180° (row 3). As illustrated in the final row, these could be combined.

The performance of students on these tasks was correlated with their scores on a variety of IQ tests, designed to give measures of Gc, Gv, and Gs. These correlations are shown in the right-hand three columns of Figure 4.6. Both verbal and perceptual speed scores showed only modest correlations with performance on any version of the task, but spatial scores predicted performance rather well. Even the simple matching task correlated 0.21 with spatial IQ; when the students were required to perform either the addition or the rotation operation on the target, their performance correlated over 0.50 with spatial IQ scores, and the combination of both operations led to even higher correlations.

Since the target stimuli were shown only briefly, the task required not only the establishment of a representation of the target, but also its retention. When additional operations had to be performed on the target, the task required simultaneous retention and processing of spatial information, that is, it became a working memory task in the sense defined earlier. Thus, Lohman's study is consistent with the idea that spatial ability depends on the

Task	Target stimulus	Operations	Comparison stimulus	Correlations		
				Gc	Gv	Gs
Simple matching		—		0.03	0.21	−0.02
Add 2				0.29	0.55	0.09
Rotate 180°				0.15	0.52	0.27
Add 1+ rotate 90°				0.26	0.67	0.20

Figure 4.6 Simple spatial addition and rotation tasks, and their correlations with measures of Gc, Gv, and Gs (from Lohman, 1988, Table 6.2).

Say whether letter is
normal or mirror image

Point to top
of each letter

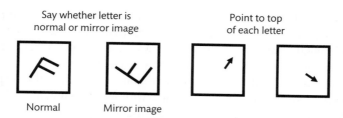

Normal   Mirror image

Figure 4.7 The spatial working memory task studied by Shah and Miyake (1996). The sequence of events on each trial goes from left to right. The first two panels show a normal or mirror-image letter rotated from the upright. You must report whether it is normal or mirror-image, at the same time as remembering its orientation. The last two panels illustrate the correct answers to this last test.

establishment and holding in working memory of representations that both preserve spatial information about an object and are sufficiently accurate and durable to allow various mental operations to be performed on them. Several studies have indeed reported substantial correlations between measures of Gv and of spatial working memory.

Shah and Miyake (1996) devised the spatial working memory task illustrated in Figure 4.7. Each trial consisted of a sequence of displays of a letter of the alphabet, here the letter F, on a computer screen. Each letter was presented at a different orientation, and the participants' task was to decide whether it was a normal F or a mirror-image ꟻ. At the end of each trial, after up to five letters had been presented, a grid appeared on the screen and, by pressing the appropriate button, participants had to indicate the direction in which the top of each letter in the series had been pointing. They were thus required to remember the orientation of a sequence of letters while simultaneously deciding whether each letter was normal or mirror-image. The correlation between performance on this task and a composite measure of Gv was 0.66. Another measure of spatial working memory is a noughts and crosses test. You are shown a series of screens that display successive moves by two people in a game of noughts and crosses, but each screen shows *only* the latest pair of moves and you have to remember what the earlier moves were. At the end of each trial, you are asked whether there was an actual winner, and if so what was the winning line. Performance on this test correlated 0.45 with scores on the Shepard-Metzler 3-D MRT task (Mackintosh and Bennett, 2003).

It is worth noting that several of the correlations with Gc and Gs in Lohman's study shown in Figure 4.6 were not negligible. When required to rotate the target, participants' performance correlated with Gs. There is indeed good evidence that speed of processing is involved in the mental rotation of simple figures. Shepard (1978) and Cooper (1975) recorded people's reaction times when they were required to decide whether two stimuli, one a briefly presented standard, for example the letter F in upright orientation, followed by a target rotated in one or other direction from the upright, were the same, or whether the target was the mirror-image of the standard (ꟻ). There was a linear increase in reaction time as the target was rotated away from the standard, suggesting that people do 'mentally rotate' the target to bring it into line with the standard. Consistent with this, if they were cued to expect that the target would be rotated clockwise from the standard stimulus on a given trial, but in fact it was presented 90° anti-clockwise from the standard, their reaction time corresponded to a 270° rotation (i.e. the clockwise discrepancy) rather than to one of

90°. In other words, it was the *mental* trajectory traversed that determined reaction time rather than the actual angular difference between standard and target. Individuals differ in their speed of mental rotation, and these differences are strongly correlated with overall levels of performance on tests such as the PMA space test (e.g., Mumaw *et al.*, 1984). Performance on more difficult tests of spatial visualization, such as the Shepard-Metzler 3-D MRT, however, is only very weakly correlated with speed (Lohman, 1986; Mumaw and Pellegrino, 1984). This is the justification for distinguishing a factor of speeded rotation from that of spatial visualization.

Carpenter and Just (1986) asked students to solve versions of the cube rotation task shown in Figure 4.8, and both monitored their eye movements and fixations during the course of their solution, and asked them for immediate retrospective reports on how they had succeeded in solving each problem. Both sources of information suggested that students typically rotated one face of the cube at a time in order to bring pairs of matching letters into alignment. In Problem 1 of Figure 4.8, for example, a 90° clockwise rotation of the target cube in the frontal plane (i.e. the plane of the A surface), which produces the comparison cube, not only changes the orientation of the A, it also moves the position and changes the orientation of the C, and finally produces a hitherto unseen letter, D in the position formerly occupied by the C. Although a single rotation simultaneously produces all three changes, most people typically operated on one change at a time. The greater the number of rotations required to solve a particular problem the greater the difference in solution times between people of high and low spatial ability. One reason for this was that those of low ability were able to rotate each face of the cube only around the three axes parallel to the faces of the cube. Problem 2 in Figure 4.8 requires two such rotations. But in principle it could be solved by a single rotation around an axis corresponding to a long diagonal of the cube. People of high spatial ability reported doing just this. A second reason for the difference in the time taken to solve the more complex tasks was that low ability participants often had to go back and rotate a particular face of the cube a second or third time within a single trial. An obvious interpretation of this would be that they were unable to remember the outcome of the rotation of the first face while rotating other faces, in other words that their problem was one of poor spatial working memory.

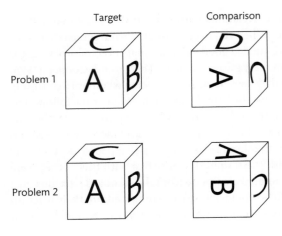

Figure 4.8 Two examples of the cube rotation test studied by Carpenter and Just (1986). As usual, your task is to decide whether the target and comparison stimuli could be the same.

A study by Heil and Jansen-Osmann (2008) suggests that males are more likely than females to solve complex mental rotation problems holistically (by a single rotation), while females break the problem down into separate components. In both men and women, reaction times to solve complex problems were longer than for simple problems, and increased with the size of the angular disparity between target and test figures (i.e. the amount of rotation required). Both of these effects were significantly greater in females than in males, and in females, but not in males, there was an interaction between the two: the effect of angular disparity was greater for complex problems than for simple problems. The implication is that females, unlike males, had to break the complex problems down into separate stages.

Spatial ability and visual imagery

Spatial tests often require you to operate on or otherwise transform mental representations of visually presented objects. Are these mental representations the same as visual images, and are differences in spatial ability caused by differences in visual imagery? The answer to both questions is no. People who have been blind from birth can still solve 'spatial' problems: they can, after all, navigate round their environment, and respond in much the same way as sighted people when tested on mental rotation tasks (e.g. Vecchi, 1998). It is true that among sighted people there are reliable differences in the reported vividness of visual imagery and that they predict other differences; but the one thing that is *not* predicted by differences in vividness of imagery is spatial ability: the correlations between such measures of imagery and scores on spatial IQ tests hover round zero, and in spite of the fact that males routinely outscore females on many spatial IQ tests, they obtain lower scores on self-ratings of vividness of imagery (Poltrock and Agnoli, 1986). Performance on many spatial tests may indeed require the ability to construct, retain, and manipulate internal representations of external stimuli, but nothing in that definition of spatial ability says that these representations have to be visual images accessible to conscious introspection. The brain constructs representations (in some sense of that term) of a whole variety of events of which we are not consciously aware: of the current position of our limbs and eyes, of the remembered size and weight of a familiar object which we pick up without being able to see it.

Moreover, although many people have talked of 'visuo-spatial' ability, or a 'visuo-spatial' sketchpad (Baddeley, 2007), as though 'visual' and 'spatial' were interchangeable terms, there are independent grounds for drawing a distinction between spatial and visual. For example, evidence from neuropsychological patients and PET scans (see Chapter 6) of normal human volunteers confirm a neuroanatomical distinction between spatial and non-spatial visual identification. Parietal and inferotemporal cortex are differentially activated when people are engaged in spatial and non-spatial visual tasks (Smith *et al.*, 1995), and patients have been observed who are seriously impaired on one kind of task, but not on the other (see Farah *et al.*, 1988; Hanley *et al.*, 1991).

Laboratory studies of concurrent interference have confirmed the independence of visual and spatial information processing. There are visual and spatial analogues of the digit span test of the WAIS as measures of immediate memory. In a visual immediate memory task, you are required to remember the shape of geometrical patterns, or the precise shade of patches of colour briefly displayed on a computer screen. In a spatial span task, a 3×3 matrix of blank squares is displayed on a computer screen; some of the squares are then filled, one at a time, with dots, and your task is to remember the positions of these dots and the order in which they appeared. Performance on these tasks is not necessarily dependent on verbal recoding of the material, since articulatory suppression, which seriously disrupts performance on word or digit-span tasks, has no more than a very small effect on retention (e.g. Smyth and Scholey, 1992). However, other distracters do prevent successful retention. Tresch *et al.* (1993) interpolated a ten-second interval between presentation of a visual task (remembering a geometrical shape) or a spatial task (remembering the position of a dot) and the test of retention. They then filled this ten-second interval with one or other of two distracter tasks, one requiring the discrimination of movement, the other discrimination of colour. Visual memory was disrupted by the interpolated colour discrimination, but not by the movement discrimination; spatial memory was disrupted by the movement discrimination but not by the colour discrimination. A similar dissociation between distracter tasks that disrupt retention of visual and spatial information has been reported by Logie and Marchetti (1991).

The implication of all these studies is that spatial visualization involves the ability to construct representations of the external world that preserve specifically *spatial* information about objects or scenes—what parts are to the left or right, or above or below others; how a complex object can be decomposed into its constituent parts, or reconstructed from those parts; how an object can be transformed or rotated, and how it would look from another perspective. This set of abilities is both broader and narrower than that involved in conscious visual imagery. A visual image of a patch of colour, or an object, or even of a visual scene, may not incorporate specifically spatial information at all. But conversely, there is no reason to suppose that spatial representations are necessarily visual at all, let alone that they are conscious visual images. The possession of a rich mental life, full of vivid imagery is neither necessary nor sufficient to guarantee high spatial ability.

Navigation and other spatial abilities

In the real world, spatial ability is about having a sense of direction, knowing where you are and how to get back to the place you started out from in a strange town, being able to read a map. It is surely not a matter of mentally rotating 3-D diagrams of strange objects, or imagining what a flat piece of paper would look like when folded up. Do the psychometrician's laboratory tests actually have anything to do with these real world abilities? The answer is that paper and pencil tests of Gv do indeed correlate with measures of navigational skill, although not *very* strongly: Hegarty and Waller (2005) reviewed 15 studies where the median correlation between paper and pencil tests of Gv and real world measures of spatial ability ranged from 0.09 to 0.52. A sophisticated study by Hegarty *et al.* (2006), in which they gave a number of different tests of both sets of abilities, reported an association between the two latent variables of 0.50.

Measures of Gv were first developed for the practical purpose of personnel selection in various settings. Ghiselli (1973) summarized older studies where Gv predicted performance on training programmes for jobs such as engineering drawing, drafting, design, or car mechanics, with correlations ranging from 0.35 to 0.46. Humphreys and Lubinski (1996) reported that tests of Gv were good predictors of aviation and piloting. Hegarty and Waller (2005) summarized a number of studies showing the relevance of Gv to medicine, and in particular to surgical skill. Finally, Friedman (1995) reported a meta-analysis of studies of the relation between Gv and mathematical ability, showing correlations between the two ranging from 0.30 to 0.45, although, consistent with the data reviewed earlier in this chapter, the relationship between mathematical and verbal abilities was marginally stronger ($r = 0.40$ to 0.50).

Fluid ability (Gf)

How many reasoning factors?

Logicians traditionally distinguish between inductive and deductive reasoning. Within psychology, typical examples of inductive reasoning problems would be analogies and series completion tasks (as exemplified by Raven's Matrices), while deductive reasoning problems would include syllogisms and transitive inference. Carroll (1993) tentatively suggested that factor analysis would distinguish three partially distinct reasoning factors—inductive, deductive, and quantitative. As Wilhelm (2005) has noted, however, most of the deductive reasoning problems in Carroll's data set were verbal, while most of the inductive problems were figural, so the distinction between the three factors is equally well described as one of content, verbal, quantitative, and figural. Indeed when Wilhelm gave a specially constructed set of reasoning problems (half deductive, half inductive, with either verbal, figural, or numerical material) to a large group of high school students, confirmatory factor analysis revealed that a model with distinct inductive and deductive factors fitted the data significantly less well than one with three content factors. It was also possible to reject a model with only a single general factor. It is worth noting that the DAT has three reasoning tests, called verbal, numerical, and abstract (whose content is indeed figural). The importance of content is consistent with one aspect of the Vernon (1950) model, but that model assigned reasoning to g, which perhaps makes it surprising that Wilhelm was able to reject a single general factor. For present purposes, however, it seems reasonable to argue that there is little need to draw a distinction between inductive and deductive reasoning, even if most psychometric tests of reasoning, such as Raven's Matrices or Cattell's Culture Fair tests, which include a somewhat wider variety of problems, such as odd man out, in addition to the series completion items of Raven's, are examples of inductive reasoning. Unfortunately, they are also examples of figural or abstract reasoning, and much less attention has been paid to understanding verbal and quantitative reasoning.

A componential model of analogical reasoning

Before turning to tests such as these, however, I start with a discussion of some rather simpler series completion and analogical reasoning problems that have been more widely studied by cognitive psychologists. Their simplicity has encouraged the development of some simple models, whose simplicity in turn may help to illustrate what needs to be

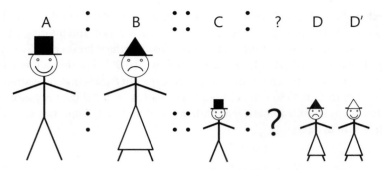

Figure 4.9 A figural, 'schematic picture' analogy, of the type used by Sternberg and Rifkin (1979).

added to explain the reasoning processes underlying solution of more complex problems. Analogies have been described earlier (Chapter 2). Although series completion problems seem superficially rather different, as noted there, they, too, require that the solver see the relationship between the terms of the series.

Consider the simple, figural analogy illustrated in Figure 4.9. The task is to choose, from the two alternatives on offer, D or D′, the one that correctly completes the analogy. A whole series of problems can be presented using the same basic figures, varying in the following attributes:

Male or female; square or triangular hat; black or white hat; happy or sad; large or small.

Sternberg (1977, 1985) and Pellegrino (1986) and their colleagues have argued that the solution of such analogies involves the following main components or sub-processes: encoding, inference, mapping, and application (later simplified by Sternberg, 1986, to include just selective encoding, comparison, and combination):

- *Encoding* is a matter of listing the attributes of each of the five terms. Thus, the encoding of A in Figure 4.9 would list the following attributes: large, happy, male, with square, black hat.
- *Inference* involves seeing the relation between A and B, which is a matter of listing the transformations that must be performed on A's attributes to turn A into B. In Figure 4.9, this means transforming three attributes: male to female; square to triangular hat; happy to sad.
- *Mapping* is the same process as inference, but now as applied to the relationship between A and C; so here, the one transformation called for is large to small.
- *Application* involves applying the A:B transformation to C. The inference process listed three transformations from A to B; applying those transformations to C yields a sad, small, female with a black triangular hat.

With very simple problems such as these, errors were rare; the measure of performance was reaction time, and the aim of the exercise was to measure individual differences in the time taken to perform the various component operations. Measuring inference or mapping time, for example, was achieved by varying the number of transformations needed to turn A into B or C. For example, if the transformation of A into B required two changes rather than one, and resulted in an increase in overall solution time of x msec, then x msec is the time that it took to perform one extra transformation.

Sternberg's and Pellgrino's experimental techniques seem both simple and elegant, and allowed them not only to obtain reliable measures of the time taken to execute various component processes, but also to choose between alternative versions of this general model as providing the most accurate account of the data. The general model seems to make sense: that is to say, it does seem to summarize, and put together in a plausible package, the various operations that, one might suppose, must be performed by anyone solving analogical reasoning problems of this sort. The terms of the analogy must be encoded; the relationship between the A and B, and between A and C must be worked out; and the A:B relationship must be applied to C.

But there surely remain some doubts (many of which have been raised by Sternberg himself). Is it likely that analysis of the way people solve a series of simple analogies, like that shown in Figure 4.9, will reveal all the cognitive operations involved in the solution of difficult analogies? Consider the problem of encoding the various terms of the analogy. What does this mean? According to the simple model, encoding is a matter of listing the attributes of each term. But which attributes? If you are presented with a series of problems of the sort illustrated in Figure 4.9, this may not seem a serious issue. You just list them all: in the particular example shown in the figure, A is a large, happy man, with a black square hat. But that, of course, is not quite true: A is also a black stick figure on a white background (rather than pink or purple); his face is round and has no nose; his arms and legs end without hands or feet; B is a large female, etc; but she, too, has a round face and no nose, etc., while her skirt is a white triangle. There is, of course, no need to list these further attributes: they are not relevant to the solution of the analogy, because they, and a dozen other attributes, are common to all the terms. As Sternberg (1986) argued, encoding should be *selective*. And as Lohman (2000) noted, you cannot encode, that is, list the relevant attributes of one term of an analogy, until you have taken note of the other terms in order to discover what the relevant attributes might be. One implication of this is that the successful problem solver may well be the one who encodes carefully, and therefore slowly, rather than rapidly. Consistent with this, in a developmental study of analogical reasoning, Sternberg and Rifkin (1979) found that after the age of 9 or 10, an increase in age, although associated with a decrease in the time to execute inference and application components, was also associated with an increase in the time spent on encoding. In terms of Sternberg's later theorizing, this implies that older children differ from younger in the way they allocate resources to the problem, a difference which in this case was partly responsible for their superior performance.

But encoding may be an even more complex operation. One reason why some analogies are harder to solve than others is because they make it difficult to discern what the relevant attributes of the various terms are. A favourite trick is to lead the solver down a garden path by suggesting the wrong attribute to encode, and that is done by providing an obvious relationship between two terms that happens to be the wrong one. Consider the following example from Sternberg (1977) (with apologies to American readers):

Washington is to 1 as Lincoln is to?   (5, 10, 15)

Unless wholly ignorant of American history, no one will attempt to solve this analogy by listing all possible attributes of Washington and Lincoln. The fact that they are both American presidents is obviously the critical attribute they share in common, and it is presumably unnecessary to note that Washington is the capital of the USA, or Lincoln the capital of Nebraska, that Washington is a state in the north-west of the USA, or a town in the north of England where Nissan cars are manufactured, or that Lincoln is an English cathedral city.

The knowledge that Washington was the first president of the USA will add to your confidence. This is about American presidents, and non-Americans will complain that it is not a 'culture-fair' problem because its solution simply depends on knowing whether Lincoln was the fifth, tenth, or fifteenth American president. Maybe it is not *too* unfair, however, since some partial knowledge of American history and politics may be sufficient to suggest the correct answer. Washington would have served as president soon after independence (1776?); Lincoln was president during the civil war (1860?). American presidential terms are four years, and only Franklin Roosevelt served more than two terms. So Lincoln could not have been the fifth president, and could hardly have been the tenth (unless you got your dates a bit wrong, or all his nine predecessors served two full terms). So the answer must surely be 15.

Actually Lincoln was the 16th president (so your reasoning was not far out), and the correct answer is 5, because, although the problem is indeed about US presidents, the relevant connection between Washington and 1 is not that Washington was the first president of the USA, but that his portrait appears on a $1 bill (and Lincoln's on a $5 bill). In other words, you have been misled into encoding the wrong attributes (1 should not be encoded as first) because an irrelevant attribute seemed to make such good sense. Encoding is not the routine, automatic process that is implied by the original, simple model, and, again as noted by Lohman (2000), the study of easy analogies, where the problem of encoding irrelevant attributes hardly arises, may not reveal all the processes engaged in the solution of more difficult problems. Although the original model can claim some success in predicting differences in performance on more difficult problems, the possibility must be acknowledged that prediction is not the same as explanation. It seems likely that a fuller understanding of human reasoning and problem solving will have to appeal to further processes.

A model for Raven's Matrices

All Raven's items are of the same general format (as was illustrated in Chapter 2, but is here shown again in Figure 4.10 with more examples). Figure 4.10a shows the kind of item that appears in the earlier and notably easier part of the Standard Progressive Matrices. It is a simple figural analogy; the transformation from the first to the second figure in the top row is from an outline to a filled in circle; the transformation from the first figure in row one to the first figure in row two is from circle to triangle; applying these two transforms says the answer must be number two. Figure 4.10b shows the kind of item that appears towards the end of the Standard Progressive Matrices or throughout the Advanced Progressive Matrices. With three rows and columns it is easier to see the problems as series completion tasks, but the solution is still a matter of seeing the relationship between the figures in each row and column.

What are these relationships? Carpenter *et al.* (1990) identified five different 'rules' that describe them, listed in Box 4.1 (others have come up with slightly different classifications,

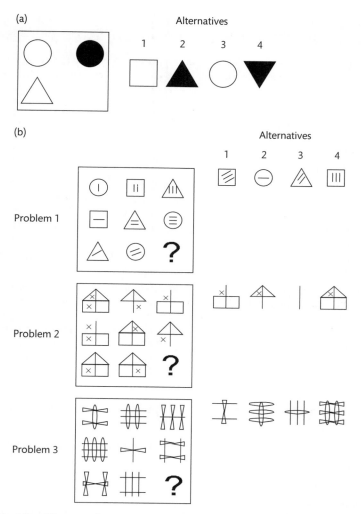

Figure 4.10 Examples of the type of item appearing in Raven's Matrices. (a) An easy problem from the Standard Matrices. (b) Three problems from the Advanced Matrices. The matrix appears here on the left, together with four alternative solutions on the right. These are not, of course, real copies of original Raven's items: among other differences the original advanced items always offer eight alternatives to choose from.

e.g. DeSchon *et al.*, 1995). The application of these rules is illustrated in Problems 1 and 2 of Figure 4.10b. Problem 1 simultaneously illustrates the first three rules:

- C: the inner lines are vertical in row one, horizontal in row two, and oblique in row three.
- PP: the number of these lines increases from one to two to three across each row.
- D3: within each row, the lines are embedded once in a circle, once in a square and once in a triangle.

Therefore the correct answer is number 1.

BOX 4.1 A model for Raven's Matrices

Carpenter *et al.* (1990) proposed a model to account for performance on Raven's Advanced Progressive Matrices (RAPM). Their model assumed that most items could be solved by the application of one or more of the following rules to describe the relations between the items in each row or column:

- C or constant in a row.
- PP or pairwise progression.
- D3 or distribution of three values.
- A/S or addition and/or subtraction.
- D2 or distribution of two values.

The model also assumed that the following processes were required:

- Description and coding of the figures, and finding correspondences between them by pairwise comparison.
- Storing part-solutions in working memory while iterating the above processes and rule discovery on other parts of the problem.
- Employing a goal monitor for planning overall strategy, setting up sequences of sub-goals, satisfying them in turn and moving onto the next appropriate step.

A simple version of the model, called FAIRAVEN, matched the performance of the average college student solving RAPM, with a score of 24 out of 34 items correct; while BETTERAVEN solved 32 of the 34 items, matching the best performance of their students. The difference between the models was that only BETTERAVEN had access to the D2 rule; it also had a superior working memory capacity and used the goal monitor.

Problem 2 simultaneously illustrates the last two rules:

- A/S: an x to the right of the vertical line in column two is subtracted from an x to the left of the vertical line in column one.
- D2: the squares and triangles each appear twice and twice only in each row, with the third value being null.

The correct answer is therefore 3.

In addition to these rules, which correspond to the inference, mapping, and application components of the Sternberg and Pellegrino models, the Carpenter *et al.* model also postulates several additional components shown in the box, not all of which have any corresponding feature in the simpler models.

It is important to note that RAPM is difficult, not just because some of the rules, such as D2, seem quite arbitrary, but because even when you have been told what the possible rules are, it is still not always easy to see how to apply the appropriate rule, or combination of rules, to particular cases. This difficulty is explicitly acknowledged by the model: the description or coding of the relevant attributes of the figures is a matter of searching for correspondences between them, and the induction of the appropriate rule will be possible only if the figures have been coded properly to reveal the relevant correspondences between them. Consider, for example, Problem 3 in Figure 4.10b. Its solution actually depends on the application of the D3 rule, each row should have three values of each of two types of figure. The problem is quite difficult, however, because most people's natural inclination is to suppose that the relevant attributes of the figures are their shapes—cigar, bow-tie, and straight lines. In fact, the relevant attributes are simply whether they are horizontally or vertically orientated. Each row has one instance of one, two, and three vertical figures, and one instance of one, two, and three horizontal figures, regardless of their shape.

The problem, in other words, is one of discovering the appropriate description of the figures, which amounts to seeing which attributes or features are relevant and allowing a solution. And that, it seems probable, will be achieved only if you try out alternative descriptions, to see whether they work, that is, permit the induction of a rule, and if you are willing or able, if they do not work, to go back to the beginning and start again. It seems plausible enough to suppose that one of the hallmarks of the intelligent problem solver is precisely such a willingness to retrace your steps when confronted with an impasse, the ability to question your initial, obvious assumptions rather than persist with them in the face of evidence that something is wrong. Recall the Washington-Lincoln analogy. The model of Carpenter *et al.* at least acknowledges some such idea, but whether it provides a convincing explanation of why and how people differ in this ability may be open to question.

In the same way, their model lists five rules which, between them, are indeed sufficient to solve essentially all items in RAPM. All rules are discovered by comparing items in each row or column. The process involved is much the same as Sternberg's components of inference and mapping. Rules C and PP simply describe the operations that must be applied to an attribute of one figure to transform it into the same attribute of the next figure in a row. Rules D3, A/S, and D2 describe the operations that must be performed on items one and two in each row in order to produce item three.

But where have the rules come from? Do not people differ in their ability to discover them, and are not such differences partly responsible for differences in test performance? Carpenter *et al.* acknowledged that they themselves supplied the rules, so that the task for their model was only to recognize which rules were appropriate for which items, rather than to work out all possible rules from scratch. Their justification was that all their participants correctly and spontaneously identified four of the five rules, so that differences in test performance could not have been due to differences in the availability of those particular rules. Their model did indeed allow the possibility that the fifth rule (distribution of two) might not be available to everyone and that this would account for some differences in test performance (see below). One suspects, however, that had they studied less highly selected subjects than university students, they would have had to allow for the possibility that some of the other rules might equally be more readily discovered by some people than by others. Carroll cites an unpublished study by Tullos, which: 'Found that the primary source of individual differences on the Raven test seemed to be ability to apply rules of inference, along with lack of knowledge of certain types of rule frequently involved in Raven test items' (Carroll, 1993, p. 647).

Carpenter *et al.* acknowledged not only that the D2 rule was harder for their participants to induce than the first four, but also that the other four were not all equally easy: C and PP rules were easier than D3 and A/S. One plausible reason for this is that, as noted above, the C and PP rules can be induced by comparing only neighbouring pairs of items in a row, first items one and two, then items two and three. The D3, A/S, and D2 rules, on the other hand, require the simultaneous comparison of all three items in a row.

The structure of Raven's Matrices

There is reason to believe that different items in RPM and RAPM are not all measuring the same process or processes. Factor analysis of RPM has revealed three distinguishable factors (Lynn *et al.*, 2004). To a very rough first approximation, the types of item that load onto these three factors are like those shown in Figures 4.10a and 4.10b. Early items in the test are all similar to that shown in Figure 4.10a, and Lynn *et al.* labelled this factor 'gestalt continuation'. The distinction between such 'perceptual' items (the term used by Hunt, 1974) and the more 'analytic' items later in the test is also supported by neuropsychological evidence: Villardita (1985) found that patients with right hemisphere damage performed badly on perceptual items, while those with left hemisphere damage performed poorly on analytic items. In a complementary fMRI study (see Chapter 6), Prabhakaran *et al.* (1997) reported that perceptual items resulted in right hemisphere activation, while analytic items resulted in bilateral activation.

The factor analysis by Lynn *et al.* identified two partially distinct analytic factors. The distinction between them is supported by the observation that at age 17, there was a male advantage on items loading onto one factor, but not on those loading onto the other. To the extent that the items that loaded onto one were like those in Problem 1 in Figure 4.10b, and those that loaded onto the other were like those in Problem 2 (the match is certainly not perfect), the distinction might also be described in terms of the rules of Carpenter *et al.*: items requiring PP or D3 rules load onto one factor, while those requiring A/S or D2 rules load onto the other. There is, indeed, some evidence that the male advantage on Raven's may be largely confined to those items requiring A/S or D2 rules for their solution (Mackintosh, 2007; Mackintosh and Bennett, 2005; Colom and Abad, 2007, however, found that males outscored females on all types of item, while Vigneau and Bors, 2008, found that females did as well as males only on D3 items). If there really is a sex difference on one kind of item and not on the other, the implication is that different rules described by Carpenter *et al.* must be engaging rather different cognitive operations. Experimental evidence reinforces this conclusion (DeShon *et al.*, 1995). When participants were required to describe out loud how they were going about solving RAPM items, this interfered with their performance on A/S and D2 items, but not on D3 items. DeShon *et al.* thought that this was because A/S and D2 items are somehow spatial. This would no doubt help to explain the male advantage on these items. But for what it is worth, Mackintosh and Bennett could find no evidence that performance on these items correlated more strongly with performance on a spatial test than did D3 or PP items.

Working memory

As noted earlier, the Carpenter *et al.* (1990) model of RAPM contained two additional components, which have not been discussed yet—working memory for part solutions, and a goal monitor that plans overall strategy and breaks each problem into a series of sub-goals. There is certainly excellent evidence that performance on Raven's Matrices and other measures of Gf correlates with working memory. Larson and Saccuzzo (1989) devised the 'mental counters' task, illustrated in Figure 4.11. The three counters are represented by three horizontal lines, appearing side by side in a display on a computer

Step	Counter display	Counter adjustment	Counter values
0	- - -		0 0 0
1	x - - -	+1 - -	1 0 0
2	x x - - x	+1 −1 +1	2 −1 1
3	x - - - x	−1 - +1	1 −1 2

Figure 4.11 The 'mental counters' test used by Larson and Saccuzzo (1989). A computer screen displays, in succession, the sequence of stimuli shown. Your task is to keep a running track of the value of three 'counters', each corresponding to one of the three horizontal bars on the screen. The three counters start at zero: one is added to a counter whenever an x is shown above its bar; one is subtracted whenever an x appears below the bar.

screen. At the beginning of each trial, all three counters are reset to zero. Each trial consists of a sequence of displays on the screen; in each display an X appears above or below one or more of the counters. An X above a counter is an instruction to add one to the value of that counter; an X below a counter is an instruction to subtract one. Each trial consists of five or seven successive displays, at the end of which participants are required to report the cumulative total of all three counters. Performance on this task correlated 0.50 with scores on RAPM.

Kyllonen and Christal (1990) gave large groups of American Air Force recruits various tasks involving simple operations with letters of the alphabet. In one, called alphabet recoding, the computer briefly displayed three letters, for example:

H, N, C

This was followed by an instruction, for example:

Add 2

To which the answer would be:

J, P, E

As in the mental counters task of Larson and Saccuzzo, the operation, here counting two letters on in the alphabet, is trivially simple. That performance was quite strongly associated (r = 0.45) with people's scores on tests of Gf can only have been because they had to remember the results of one operation, while performing the next, and then the results of both before performing the third.

In another task, called ABC numerical assignment, Kyllonen and Christal gave their participants simple algebraic equations to solve. They were shown three displays, for example:

$$A = B + 2$$
$$B = C - 4$$
$$C = 6$$

The three displays would be followed by a request for the values of A and B. Although the program permitted unlimited time for the study of each display, only one display was shown at a time, and no backtracking was allowed. Thus, participants had to remember each of the first two equations before applying the information that C = 6 to work out the value of B from the second equation, and then use the first equation to work out the value of A from B. In two separate studies, with some 400 recruits in each, performance on this ABC task correlated up to 0.58 with scores on various reasoning tests.

Although solving equations such as these is no doubt more difficult than adding 1 to the value of a counter, or going to the next but one letter of the alphabet, they are really rather simple. Once again it is presumably the requirement to hold the solution to one problem in mind while performing some further operation that is responsible for the correlation with measures of Gf. A study by Stankov and Crawford (1993) provides evidence consistent with this supposition. Their procedure is illustrated in Table 4.2. University students were shown three letters of the alphabet, but in this case, unlike Kyllonen and Christal's experiment, these original letters remained on the screen along with the instructions. In the one-swap condition the instruction was to swap, say, the second and third letters; the two-swap instruction would then add the requirement to swap the (new) first and third letters, and so on, up to three or four swaps. Correlations with performance on Raven's Matrices and a letter series test ranged from zero in the one-swap condition, to 0.20 in two-swap, and 0.46 in the three and four-swap conditions. The one-swap task imposes no load on working memory. It is the requirement to hold the results of this swap in mind while performing further swaps that yields the substantial association with measures of cognitive ability.

The central executive and executive control

The function of the goal monitor in the Carpenter *et al.* (1990) model was to decide the order in which sub-problems should be tackled, keep track of which sub-goals had been satisfied, and to modify the path being taken when a difficulty arose. The selection of an appropriate strategy for tackling a problem, and the deployment and management of lower-order components and resources, are not dissimilar to some of the functions assigned to the 'central executive' by cognitive psychologists, such as Baddeley (2007), or to their 'supervisory attentional system' by Norman and Shallice (1986). The development of a central executive system which can switch attention, compare alternative representations, inhibit inappropriate but prepotent response tendencies, and plan, control, and monitor actions, has been seen by some as the critical mechanism underlying cognitive development in children (e.g.

Table 4.2 Stankov and Crawford's Swaps Task (from Stankov and Crawford, 1993).

Condition	Start	Instructions	Answer
One swap	ABC	Swap 2 and 3	ACB
Two swaps	ABC	Swap 2 and 3; 1 and 3	BCA
Three swaps	ABC	Swap 2 and 3; 1 and 3; 1 and 2	CBA

Russell, 1996). Similarly, others have attributed the decline in Gf in the very old to a decline in executive function (Salthouse, 1992; see Chapter 8). Sternberg has described these and similar functions as 'metacomponents':

> Metacomponents are higher order, executive processes used to plan what one is going to do, to monitor it while one is doing it, and to evaluate it after it is done. These metacomponents include (1) recognizing the existence of a problem, (2) deciding upon the nature of the problem confronting one, (3) selecting a set of lower order processes to solve the problem, (4) selecting a strategy into which to combine these components, (5) selecting a mental representation upon which the components and strategy can act, (6) allocating one's mental resources, (7) monitoring one's problem solving as it is happening, and (8) evaluating one's problem solving after it is done.

> (Sternberg, 1990, pp. 268–9)

An immediate reaction to this list might be that several of these metacomponents are trivial statements of the obvious. It goes without saying that you cannot solve a problem without recognizing the existence of a problem to be solved. Of course you must monitor what you are doing when trying to solve a problem, and then evaluate your solution. No doubt the need for all this seems obvious enough to all readers of this book. But it is not necessarily obvious to everyone. Commenting on some children's attempts to tackle any sort of problem, Binet noted particularly an absence of 'direction and persistence of thought, self-criticism and invention…The child does not reflect…he forgets what he is doing…lacks direction…He does not know that he does not understand' (Binet, 1911, pp. 118–22).

To provide a concrete illustration of some of these ideas, and their relation to Gf, consider a superficially quite different problem from Raven's Matrices, the Tower of Hanoi problem illustrated in Figure 4.12. The task is to move the three discs, A, B, and C (from smallest to largest), from their start position on peg one to their goal position on peg three in as few moves as possible, with the constraints that you are allowed to move only one disc at a time, and at no time can you place a larger disc on a smaller one (C on top of B, or B on top of A). The minimum number of moves required is, in fact, 2^N-1, where N is the number of discs. The problem can be divided into a hierarchy of sub-goals, working back from the final goal (A, B, C on peg three). To achieve that goal, you need to move C onto peg three; to do that, you need to move A and B off peg one, leaving peg three clear; to get A and B onto peg two, therefore, you must first move A to peg three, B to peg two and

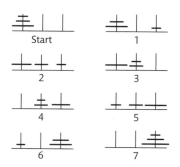

Figure 4.12 The Tower of Hanoi problem. In the start position, three discs are on peg one, with the smallest on top and the largest on the bottom; the goal is to get them onto peg three, again with smallest on top and largest on the bottom (move seven), moving one disc at a time and never placing a larger disc on top of a smaller one. The correct sequence of moves is shown.

then A back to peg two, and so on, as illustrated in Figure 4.12. It is not difficult to see that the problem will become notably harder (and harder to explain!) as the number of discs increases to four, five, or six. But wherein, precisely, lies the difficulty? The individual steps are always similar; the sub-goals are always the same—move the largest disc to peg three, then the next largest, and so on. The difficulty comes at the initiation of the series of moves that will satisfy each sub-goal: which peg do you move the smallest disc to? It is not very difficult to work out that, for the three-disc problem in Figure 4.12, your first move must be A to peg three. But what is the first move for a four, five, or six disc problem? And what is the appropriate next move of a six-disc problem after you have achieved your first sub-goal of placing the largest disc onto peg three? The answer to these questions requires (unless you have succeeded in working out the rule) forward planning: since you always have to use the goal peg, three, for intermediate stacking, you must work out how to start your sequence of moves in a way that will leave the goal peg free to take the largest remaining disc. Quite often the correct move seems to take you further away from your goal, and you must reject a move that *appears* to get you closer. Solution of the Tower of Hanoi problem requires working through a set of moves and keeping track of their consequences (in working memory) before committing yourself.

Having instructed students in the structure of the Tower of Hanoi problem, and how it can be broken down into a series of sub-goals, Carpenter *et al.* (1990) gave them a series of 3–8-disc problems, correcting any errors immediately they occurred. Essentially all errors occurred on moves that initiated each new sub-goal, and the number of errors increased sharply with the number of moves required to complete that sub-goal, that is, the depth of forward processing required. More to the present point, Carpenter *et al.* found a correlation of −0.77 between the number of errors made, and scores on Raven's Matrices. This correlation is not far short of the reliability of the Raven tests, and was obtained in a sample with a relatively restricted range of ability. It implies that, in spite of the marked difference in their surface characteristics, Raven's Matrices and the Tower of Hanoi problem may be tapping closely related underlying operations. A good characterization of those operations would plausibly look like this:

> Before embarking on an action sequence which is novel or complex, we usually spend some time thinking what we are about to do, how best to achieve the goal, in what order to perform the individual actions, and how much time and effort will need to be allocated to the task. Memory is involved in formulating such plans, holding the elements and sequence in mind while the plan is being assembled, evaluated, revised, and implemented . . . [Then] the component actions are assembled in some form of output buffer and the memory system monitors the output of actions from the buffer to ensure that the plan is implemented correctly.
>
> (Cohen, 1989, pp. 17–18)

What is Gf?

Research by cognitive psychologists on how people solve analogical reasoning and related problems, and the role of working memory and planning, have surely gone some way towards illuminating the nature of individual differences in Gf. Moreover, Chapters 5 and 6 will review a growing body of evidence from lesion and brain imaging studies, pointing to the parallels at the neurobiological level between tests of Gf and some tests of executive function. There is a danger, however, that some of the explanations on offer may have done little more than substitute one set of unknowns for another. To say that Gf involves executive control, planning, and the allocation of resources, may have a certain air of plausibility. But what precisely does this mean, and what would count as disproof of such a hypothesis? The language may mark an advance over the notion of general intelligence as mental energy or the efficiency of the brain, but it still falls far short of a tightly specified theory of cognition. Consider again Sternberg's list of metacomponents. The real problem with them is not that they are vacuous or incorrect. It is that they do not specify any precise set of cognitive operations. Planning, monitoring goals and evaluating the consequences of alternative actions are all, presumably, ingredients of the sort of reasoning and problem-solving abilities that are measured by tests of Gf. To locate these operations, either in a physical place (prefrontal and parietal cortex, see Chapter 6) or in a conceptual space (the central executive), has been an important start in that it seems to narrow down the options, but it does not really succeed in dispelling the worry that cognitive psychologists have simply attached fine-sounding labels to processes they do not fully understand. I will take up some of these questions in the next chapter.

Conclusion

Measures of Gc or verbal ability (thus turning Cattell's concept into something closer to Vernon's *v:ed*), typically include tests of vocabulary, general knowledge, reading comprehension, and mental arithmetic. Although some of these seem to be simply tests of acquired knowledge, or of what children are explicitly taught at school, they are more than that. The size of a person's vocabulary, for example, is a good measure of intelligence not because some people have had more opportunity to learn, by rote, the meaning of a larger number of words, but because people differ in their ability to infer the meanings of unfamiliar words from the context in which they appear. People learn the meanings of new words at least in part by a process of inferential reasoning. There is also evidence that differences in verbal IQ are associated with differences in performance on a variety of simple laboratory tasks, which are not plausibly attributed to differences in the familiarity of the material used. Speed of lexical access in letter or word-matching problems shows a modest correlation with verbal IQ, and the magnitude of these correlations is not greatly affected by the common content of IQ test and laboratory task.

Verbal ability seems to be closely associated with the efficiency of working memory, defined as a system that simultaneously operates on some information while holding other information in memory. One implication of this is that 'verbal ability' engages a number of different processes. Another, given the importance of working memory for performance on tests of Gv and Gf, is that some of these processes seem to be shared by tests of other components of intelligence.

Tests of spatial ability or Gv require people to establish accurate representations of objects and scenes that preserve spatial information (what is above, below, left, or right of what else), and to maintain such representations in memory so that they can perform certain operations on them (add new parts, subtract old, rotate it, or 'view' it from a different perspective). The establishment of such representations may, or may not, involve conscious visual imagery: certainly there is essentially no correlation between measures of the vividness of visual imagery and scores on spatial IQ tests. But the execution of such spatial tasks clearly places demands on working memory.

Typical tests of non-verbal reasoning, Gf, or fluid intelligence, are Raven's Matrices, Cattell's tests, or letter-series problems. These are all tests of analogical or inductive reasoning, rather than of deductive reasoning. Attempts to understand the cognitive operations underlying performance on such tests have focused on psychological analyses of the nature of the problems they present, at least as much as on the search for correlates of performance on them. Thus, componential analyses of analogical reasoning or Raven's Matrices have proposed that solving these problems requires such operations as coding of the items, and searching for the rules that describe the transformation of one item into another. However, simple componential models of analogical reasoning, although undoubtedly specifying many of the operations that must be performed in order to solve analogies, fail to acknowledge the interdependence of the various components, something that becomes increasingly important as the problem is made more difficult. Thus, coding of the relevant attributes of each term of an analogy is influenced by the detection of the relationships between the various terms, since those relationships define the relevant attributes. And failure to detect a relationship that will solve the analogy may suggest that your initial coding was incorrect, and require backtracking to start all over again.

This interdependence of different components becomes more evident with more difficult problems, such as those in Raven's Advanced Matrices. And the number of steps that must be worked through and combined in order to solve Raven's problems immediately suggests that one factor limiting performance on such tasks is the efficiency of working memory. Performance on several different working memory tasks does indeed correlate well with performance on tests of Gf.

When the solution to a reasoning problem requires a large number of steps, it seems plausible to suppose that 'metacomponents' of planning and goal monitoring enter into the picture. Performance on Raven's Matrices does indeed correlate strongly with performance on at least one superficially very different task, the Tower of Hanoi, which also requires forward planning. Cognitive psychologists have invoked concepts such as a 'central executive' or 'supervisory attentional system' that perform such functions. Is this just substituting one unknown for another?

 ## Summary

- Tests of Gc, Gv, and Gf all measure a variety of different processes, some of which they share in common: the acquisition of a large vocabulary depends on a process of reasoning, inferring the meaning of a new word from its context.

- Spatial ability or Gv does not depend on visual imagery, and is only misleadingly called visuo-spatial ability. The blind can solve spatial problems.

- Reasoning or the solution of tests of Gf can be decomposed into several processes, the more important of which are attributed to a rather mysterious 'central executive'. Among its functions are decomposing complex problems into component parts, planning, and holding the solution to one part in working memory, while solving other parts.

Further reading

Hunt (1987) provides an excellent review of his earlier work on verbal ability. Two edited books, Miyake and Shah (1999) and Conway *et al.* (2008) provide a variety of perspectives on the concept of working memory. Hegarty and Waller (2005) summarize evidence on the nature of spatial ability, and Lohman (2000) on the nature of fluid ability. The analysis by Carpenter *et al.* (1990) of the nature of the operations needed to solve items in Raven' Matrices remains important.

5 Associative learning, working memory, and executive control

Introduction

One of the second-stratum components of the CHC model is Gr or retrieval from short-term memory. Its importance is underlined by the fact that Johnson and Bouchard (2005) found that incorporating such a factor into the Vernon model significantly improved its fit. Carroll (1993) included a number of tasks that appeared to fall under the general heading of learning and memory. They included: memory span as instanced by the digit span test of the Wechsler scales or Stanford-Binet test; associative memory, where the associations are relatively arbitrary as in most laboratory studies of paired-associate learning—this was contrasted with the case where the material is meaningful and the associations are themselves meaningful in some way; free recall, where a list of items, words, nonsense syllables, or whatever, is studied, and the task is simply to recall as many as possible in any order; visual memory where a number of objects are briefly displayed, and your task might be to recognize later which objects in a larger set had been in the original display.

Performance on all these tasks correlates with other measures of intelligence, but the correlations are usually relatively modest. The digit span test of the Wechsler scales has one of the lowest loadings on the general factor extracted by factor analysis of the entire scale, and that correlation is boosted because the test comes in two parts—forward span and backward span (where the digits have to be recalled in reverse order). Jensen and Figueroa (1975) showed that backward span correlates more strongly with the rest of the test (r = 0.38 and 0.45 in white and black children respectively) than forward span (r = 0.31 and 0.30). The correlation observed between simple paired-associate learning and IQ test scores is only rarely more than 0.20–0.30. These modest correlations imply that *simple* learning and memory tasks will probably not shed much light on the intelligence measured by IQ tests. Unsurprisingly, therefore, attention has come to be focused on slightly different tasks whose correlation with test scores may be substantially higher. The most important of these is the working memory task already mentioned in Chapter 4, but discussed in more detail here; another is a more complex version of paired-associate learning.

Associative learning

Laboratory tests of paired-associate learning or free recall have usually found only a rather weak relationship between the intelligence measured by standard IQ tests and associative learning ability. Jensen (1998), however, has argued that factor analysis of a variety of different learning tasks and IQ tests will extract only a single general factor, the ubiquitous *g*. Although the *g*-loadings of the learning tasks may be lower than those of the IQ tests, they will not be zero. These *g*-loadings, he suggested, will depend on the nature of the task, being low for tests of simple rote learning such as paired-associate learning or free recall, and higher for tasks that rely on perception of the categorical structure of the list of words to be remembered. The results of a study by Underwood *et al.* (1978) are certainly consistent with the first part of Jensen's conclusion. They took 33 different measures from simple learning tasks: the correlations between these measures and students' SAT-V scores ranged from −0.05 to +0.30, with a mean of 0.11. While individual learning tasks thus seem to correlate only very modestly with IQ, a study by Alexander and Smales (1997) suggested that a composite measure of verbal learning, derived from several different tasks, would show a much stronger association: they reported a correlation of 0.56 between Gc and such a verbal learning composite, and one of 0.30 between Gc and a composite measure of figural learning. It is worth noting that Gc was being measured here by tests of reading, spelling, and language use, that is, was rather heavily weighted towards measures of scholastic achievement.

What kinds of learning task will actually load more strongly onto *g*? Williams and Pearlberg (2006) tested university students on Raven's Matrices, simple paired-associate learning and free recall, and on a further measure of associative learning, which they termed 'three-term contingency learning'. The task is illustrated in Table 5.1. As in paired-associate learning, participants are shown a list of stimulus words, but instead of simply being required to associate each stimulus with a single word, here there are three words to be associated with each stimulus, and the correct response is determined by which of three responses the participant is instructed to execute. In the example shown, if the instruction is to perform response *A*, the correct word for *LOG* is *STY*, if *B* it is *COT*, and if *C* it is *RUB*. When the participant has executed all three responses for one stimulus word and been shown the correct answer for each, the next stimulus word is shown, and so on. The correlation between scores on all these tests in Williams and Pearlberg's experiment is shown in Table 5.2. Although there was a significant correlation between

Table 5.1 The three-term contingency learning task studied by Williams and Pearlberg (2006).

Stimulus	Response alternative		
	A	B	C
LOG	STY	COT	RUB
ATE	DIG	FRY	BUN

Table 5.2 The correlation matrix between performance on Raven's Matrices, three-term contingency learning, and (Experiment 1) paired-associate learning (PA) and free recall (FR), and (Experiment 2) measures of working memory (PASAT) and processing speed (ZVT) (data from Williams and Pearlberg, 2006, Tables 2 and 4).

(a)	Experiment 1				(b)	Experiment 2			
	Raven	3-term	PA	FR		Raven	3-term	PASAT	ZVT
Raven	—				Raven	—			
3-term	0.52	—			3-term	0.59	—		
PA	0.13	0.43	—		PASAT	0.36	0.15	—	
FR	0.15	0.31	0.43	—	ZVT	0.42	0.11	0.43	—

three-term contingency learning and both paired-associate learning and free recall, only the former correlated significantly (and rather substantially) with scores on Raven's Matrices. In a second experiment, Williams and Pearlberg also gave measures of processing speed and working memory, the Zahlen Verbindungs Test (ZVT, see Chapter 3) and a paced auditory serial addition task (PASAT), in which a series of random digits is briefly presented one at a time, and the participant's task is to write down the sum of the current and preceding digit in the two-second interval between successive digits (in effect a test of working memory). Once again, as can be seen in Table 5.2b, the best predictor of Raven's scores was the three-term task, although Raven's also correlated significantly with both other tests. More remarkably, it is clear that three-term learning correlated with neither of these other tests: in other words, it predicted Raven's scores *independently* of speed or working memory.

This three-term contingency task is obviously more complex than simple paired-associate learning, but it is rather less obvious what the nature of this increase in complexity could be that drives the stronger association with performance on Raven's Matrices. The puzzle is not resolved by a further study (Kaufman *et al.*, 2009), which confirmed the strong association between three-term learning and measures of Gf (Raven's and Cattell's tests), but a latent variable analysis suggested that both three-term learning and simple paired-associate learning loaded onto a single latent variable of 'associative learning', and the raw correlations between these two measures and the measures of Gf were very similar. Whatever may be the reason for this discrepancy with the results of Williams and Pearlberg, the similarities between the two studies are equally important. Both found that speed, working memory and some, perhaps more complex, measures of associative learning all made significant and largely independent contributions to performance on tests of Gf. What remains quite unclear is which measures of associative learning are critical. Perhaps the most important aspect of these data is that the contribution of associative learning appears to be independent of that of working memory (but see Tamez *et al.*, 2008), which implies that when added to measures of speed of processing they account for a sizeable proportion of the variance in Gf.

Concurrent and competing tasks

The correlation between IQ scores and reaction time in most laboratory tasks, although undoubtedly reliable, is only modest—probably no more than –0.30 (Chapter 3). Lamenting this apparent 0.30 barrier, Hunt (1980) suggested that it might be necessary to introduce competing tasks to get beyond it. As very soon became apparent, he was remarkably prescient. There is indeed evidence that one way of increasing the magnitude of the relationship between IQ and performance on such simple tasks is to require people to perform a second task at the same time. One example of this is a study by Roberts *et al.* (1988), who required students to sort playing cards as rapidly as possible, either by colour (red vs. black, i.e. into two categories), or by suit (four categories), or by number (eight different numbers were used). The total time required to sort a pack constituted, in effect, a measure of two, four, or eight-choice RT, while the task of simply sorting the pack into alternate piles provided a control measure of movement time. As can be seen in Table 5.3, except in this control condition, there was a modest correlation between speed of sorting and scores on Raven's Matrices. The correlation with four-choice RT was rather higher than those typically observed in RT studies, but the remaining data seem very similar, and there was clearly no systematic tendency for the correlation to increase with an increase in the number of alternatives. The important result, however, is that when people were required to perform a second task at the same time (they had to listen to a list of words being read out to them, and verbally report the semantic category of each), the correlations between card-sorting scores and Raven's performance now averaged 0.65. Other examples are provided by Stankov (1988).

It is not necessary to ask people to perform concurrently two separate tasks from quite different domains in order to observe this increase in the strength of the association with cognitive ability. Consider again the difference between forward and backward digit span. Why does backward span correlate with the rest of the WAIS more strongly than forward span? Both tasks require you to remember a list of digits, but while the forward span test simply requires you to read the remembered list off, what is required in the backward span test would seem to be something like this: first, hold the list in memory (in the order in

Table 5.3 Correlations between IQ scores and card sorting when performed as a single task and when performed concurrently with a competing task (data from Roberts *et al.*, 1988, Table 2).

Sorting task	Single task	Competing task
Control condition	0.03	–0.07
Two categories	–0.21	–0.65
Four categories	–0.49	–0.71
Eight categories	–0.30	–0.59

which it was presented, that is, from first to last); read off the last item; go through the list from first to last in order to find the digit preceding the one just given; repeat the process. It seems plausible to suppose that it is this requirement to hold the list in memory while repeatedly performing a further task that makes backward span both more difficult than forward span and causes it to correlate more strongly with the rest of the WAIS.

A study by Vernon and Weese (1993) is consistent with this possibility. They used the PASAT task briefly described above. Students were presented with a list of ten digits shown one at a time, and required to give the sum of each successive pair as they appeared. Thus, to the list:

$$1, 3, 6, 4, \text{etc.}$$

the correct responses would be:

$$4(1 + 3), 9(3 + 6), 10(6 + 4), \text{etc.}$$

The task is rather similar to the more recently developed 'n-back' task (e.g. Friedman *et al.*, 2006; Gray *et al.*, 2003), in which again a series of digits is presented one at a time, and participants are told to report when the currently presented digit is the same as the digit presented n items earlier in the series. In both tasks the difficulty presumably arises from the requirement to hold recently presented items in memory, and to update this list as each new item is presented. In Vernon and Weese's experiment, performance correlated over 0.40 with IQ. Difficulty *per se* was not the critical factor: an increase in presentation rate from one digit every three seconds to one digit a second increased errors from 6.5% to 42%, but only increased the correlation with IQ from 0.45 to 0.47.

Working memory

Tasks that require participants to process new information, or perform some new operation, at the same time as holding some other information in memory, have been given the generic title of working memory tasks (from Baddeley and Hitch, 1974). It is this additional new processing requirement that distinguishes them from simple immediate memory span tests, such as forward digit span. Chapter 4 documented the finding that performance on a wide variety of working memory tasks correlates moderately to quite strongly with a variety of different measures of cognitive ability (a meta-analysis by Ackerman *et al.*, 2005, summarized results from 86 separate samples and nearly 10,000 participants).

Working memory and immediate memory span

There are obvious similarities between simple span and working memory tasks, and there is indeed a significant correlation between the two: in a study where participants were given a variety of simple span and working memory tests, the correlation between the two latent variables was 0.68 (Engle *et al.*, 1999). Moreover, performance on both correlated with IQ test scores. But the correlation between working memory and IQ is usually significantly, and sometimes substantially, greater than that between simple span and IQ: in the meta-analysis by Ackerman *et al.*, the corrected correlation of IQ with working memory was 0.40, with simple span it was 0.26. This may well be an underestimate, since several studies have reported a much wider discrepancy. In Engle *et al.*, the path between the latent variable of simple span and Gf (measured by Raven's and Cattell's tests) was only 0.12, once the variance shared with working memory was taken into account. And in a similar study by Conway *et al.* (2002), structural equation modelling indicated that although the association between working memory and Gf was 0.60, that between simple span and Gf was small and statistically insignificant (0.18). Daneman and Carpenter (1980) reported that correlations between reading span and their students' SAT-V scores or performance on a test of reading comprehension ranged from 0.50 to over 0.70; the correlation between simple word span and these measures of Gc was less than 0.35.

There is evidence that this difference in the strength of the association between intelligence and simple span or working memory is not so pronounced for all measures of intelligence. From the data summarized in the meta-analysis by Ackerman *et al.*, Kovács (2010) calculated that while Raven's scores correlated much more strongly with working memory than with immediate memory (r = 0.50 and 0.21 respectively), for other components of IQ the difference was considerably smaller (r = 0.36 and 0.21 for Gv; r = 0.33 and 0. 26 for Gc; r = 0.27 and 0.23 for Gs). Indeed, contrary to Daneman and Carpenter's results, other studies have reported relatively similar correlations between measures of Gc and either working memory or simple span. In three of four separate experiments, La Pointe and Engel (1990) found that both simple span and working memory correlated significantly with measures of Gc; in only one experiment was there a significant difference in the magnitude of the correlations.

Although there are those who question this conclusion (for example, Colom *et al.*, 2008), differences in working memory are usually a better predictor of differences in ability than are differences in simple span. The question is why? I return to this question later.

Is working memory the unitary basis of *g*?

Baddeley and Hitch's (1974) model of working memory is illustrated in Figure 5.1. A central executive system is responsible for a variety of control and decision making processes, and is supported by two 'slave' systems, a phonological loop responsible for the temporary maintenance of verbal or phonological information, and a visuo-spatial sketchpad responsible for the short-term storage of visual or spatial information. Subsequent development of the model (Baddeley, 2007) added to these two the fourth component shown in the figure—the episodic buffer, which provides a further, modality-free, short-term store that combines

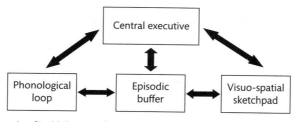

Figure 5.1 A recent version (Baddeley, 2007) of the Baddeley and Hitch model of working memory. See text for further details.

information from the loop and the sketchpad, as well as from long-term memory. But the distinction between verbal and spatial stores has always been maintained, and working memory studies have on the whole supported this distinction.

There is no doubt that performance on a variety of working memory tests correlates with a variety of measures of cognitive ability. But is working memory the basis, or at any rate an important component, of *g*? It should not have escaped the reader's notice that the studies described in Chapter 4 reported correlations between reading span and verbal ability or Gc, and between spatial working memory and measures of Gv or spatial ability. Moreover, the studies of mental counters and alphabet recoding reported correlations only with tests such as Raven's Matrices or other measures of Gf (Kyllonen and Christal, 1990; Larson and Saccuzzo, 1989). Might it be the case that there are as many partially distinct measures of working memory as there are IQ factors, and that each correlates with only one ability factor? Almost certainly not. But there is evidence hinting that there may be some truth in this Thurstonian position.

In addition to their spatial tests, Shah and Miyake (1996) also gave their 50 students a reading span test and recorded their SAT-V scores. Although there was a modest positive correlation, r = 0.23, between verbal and spatial working memory scores, it was not statistically significant. The correlations they observed between the working memory and ability tests are shown in Table 5.4a. As can be seen, while the reading span score predicted verbal ability, it did not predict spatial ability and, conversely, spatial span predicted only spatial ability. The fact that the participants were undergraduates at a relatively selective private university means that these results may not generalize to a wider population, but Mackintosh and Bennett (2003), in a somewhat larger study of sixth-form (senior high school) students, found a very similar pattern of results: the correlation between their verbal and spatial working memory tests was only 0.04, and each test correlated significantly only with its 'own' ability. Similar specificity has been reported by Jurden (1995), Suss *et al.* (2002), and Haavisto and Lehto (2005).

Other studies, however, have observed substantially less specificity. The data summarized by Ackerman *et al.* (2005) in their meta-analysis are shown in Table 5.4b. While the correlations between verbal working memory and verbal ability, and between spatial working memory and spatial ability, are indeed significantly higher than those between working memory in one domain and ability in the other, the latter are statistically

Table 5.4 Correlations between Gc or Gv and verbal or spatial working memory, (a) from Shah and Miyake (1996), and (b) from Ackerman *et al.* (2005).

(a) Shah and Miyake (1996)				(b) Ackerman *et al.* (2005)		
		Working memory				Working memory	
		Verbal	Spatial			Verbal	Spatial
IQ	Gc	0.45	0.07	IQ	Gc	0.43	0.33
	Gv	0.12	0.66		Gv	0.29	0.49

significant and far from zero. Some studies, indeed, have reported very little specificity. In one large experiment, Kane *et al.* (2004) gave a battery of verbal and spatial working memory tests (three of each) as well as 13 ability tests, designed to measure Gc (e.g. reading comprehension), Gf (e.g. Raven's Matrices), and Gv (e.g. paper folding) to a mixed sample of 236 participants that included students from less selective state universities as well as members of the general public. The correlation between reading span and rotation span, the two working memory measures most similar to those used by Shah and Miyake, was 0.59, and both correlated significantly with measures of both Gc and Gv. They reported that a model with a single working memory factor fit the data well. Although a two-factor (verbal and spatial) working memory model also fit the data (but only slightly better), the two factors correlated 0.93, suggesting a high degree of common variance.

It is worth mentioning one further study. Kaufman (2007) gave both verbal and spatial working memory tests to 50 male and 50 female sixth-form students. Although females did somewhat better than males on the verbal working memory test, there was a large and significant male advantage on the spatial working memory test. It would be a mistake to argue that the content of a working memory test is wholly irrelevant.

Baddeley and Hitch's original model of working memory (see Figure 5.1), consisted of a central executive plus two 'slave' systems, a phonological loop and a visuo-spatial sketch-pad. Would this model, now supplemented by the addition of an episodic buffer, be able to account for the partial separation, but equally clear overlap, between verbal and spatial working memory tasks? As noted above, the slave systems are said to be responsible for the temporary maintenance, via rehearsal, of verbal and visuo-spatial information respectively. They are, in other words, engaged by immediate memory span tasks, such as forward digit span or simple spatial span. Although there are parallels between the two systems, and although there is a modest correlation between performance on digit or word span on the one hand and spatial span on the other (r = 0.32 in a study by Smyth and Scholey, 1992), several experiments have shown that operations that interfere with performance on verbal memory span have little or no effect on spatial span, or vice versa. Articulatory suppression significantly interferes with digit span, but not with spatial span (Smyth and Scholey, 1992). Conversely, tasks such as pointing to other targets interfere with spatial span but have no effect on digit span (Smyth and Scholey, 1994). Neuropsychological and brain imaging studies have confirmed the relative independence of simple verbal and spatial span tasks (Logie, 1995; see Chapter 6). Even more important, studies that have explicitly compared the relationship between verbal and spatial immediate memory on the one hand, and verbal and spatial working memory on the other, have consistently found that there is a weaker correlation between the two types of immediate memory span tasks than between the two working memory tasks (e.g. Kane *et al.*, 2004).

There is clear evidence, then, of a distinction between verbal and spatial immediate memory. To the extent that working memory tasks tap at least some of the same processes as immediate memory tasks, which seems both intuitively plausible, and implied by the reliable correlation between the two, one would expect to see at least some separation between performance on verbal and spatial working memory tasks. What about the overlap? In the revised Baddeley and Hitch model, this is partly accounted for by the episodic buffer, which provides a third short-term memory store, capable of integrating information from different modalities. In the original version of the model, this modality-free memory function was assigned to the central executive. The new version simply makes it clear that the control processes undertaken by the central executive should be distinguished from any short-term storage component. Why does the model require this third short-term storage system? Although Baddeley's own reasons are rather different (see Baddeley, 2007), for present purposes the answer must be that one critical difference between working memory and simple span is that the processing component in working memory tasks interferes with participants' ability to rehearse the information they are required to remember. The phonological loop, for example, can only retain information for any length of time if it is rehearsed, so in the absence of rehearsal cannot be responsible for remembering the last word of the first sentence of a reading span test for the length of time it takes people to read five more sentences. Of course, the requirements of any processing component will surely not *completely* prevent rehearsal, so the loop and sketchpad will contribute to performance on verbal and spatial working memory tasks respectively. But to the extent that the processing component does interfere with rehearsal, it is necessary to suppose that people are able to retain information for up to a minute or more without constantly rehearsing it. If the system responsible for this is modality-free, this will explain why there is substantial overlap between performance on tests of verbal and spatial working memory. A similar analysis, albeit couched in rather different terms, has been offered by Unsworth and Engle (2007).

What is the strength of the association between working memory and cognitive ability?

From their meta-analysis, Ackerman *et al.* (2005) concluded that the mean correlation (weighted by sample size) between ten types of working memory test and 12 types of ability test was 0.32, which corrected for attenuation became 0.40. This is considerably smaller than the correlations obtained in many of the studies cited above and in Chapter 4. It is reduced by the inclusion of some studies that correlated verbal working memory with spatial ability, or vice versa, and also because some ability tests, those measuring general knowledge and perceptual speed, correlate much less strongly with working memory than others (such as tests of vocabulary, reasoning, and spatial ability).

Two commentators on Ackerman and colleagues' meta-analysis argued that they underestimated the true underlying association between working memory and *g*, or at least Gf. Kane *et al.* (2005) reported that the average correlation between working memory and measures of Gf in 14 studies with a total of over 3,000 participants was 0.72; while Oberauer *et al.* (2005) suggested a figure of 0.85. Kyllonen and Christal (1990) reported that the correlation between their working memory and Gf factors ranged in different studies from 0.79 to 0.84. Their conclusion, summarized in the title of their paper, was that 'Reasoning ability is (little more than) working memory capacity?!' That is probably too strong. It is safer to go along with Ackerman and his colleagues: 'We feel confident in asserting that the results of the meta-analysis and subsequent analyses support a conclusion that WM [working memory] is not isomorphic to *g*, Gf, reasoning, or any other group factor of intelligence' (Ackerman *et al.*, 2005, p. 44).

But is working memory an important ingredient of *g*, or just of more specific components of psychometric intelligence? It is not in dispute that working memory correlates with tests of Gf such as Raven's and Cattell's, and as noted above Raven's scores correlated much more with tests of working memory than with immediate memory span. But other components of IQ show rather more similar associations with working memory and immediate memory, which suggests that working memory independent of immediate memory is not so important an ingredient of all aspects of IQ. In their meta-analysis, Ackerman *et al.* reported that the corrected correlation between working memory and *g* was 0.48—virtually the same as that between working memory and Raven's (0.50). But their measure of *g* or general intelligence was not the result of factor analysis of any large test battery and the extraction of the general factor; it was simply based on the results of a variety of different tests which were not otherwise categorized, including Cattell's Culture Fair tests, which are better regarded as a measure of Gf rather than *g*. It remains to be seen how strongly working memory, independent of immediate memory, would correlate with a general factor extracted from a large and diverse test battery.

The explanation of the association between working memory and ability

There are, of course, critics who have argued that any attempt to explain *g* or Gf in terms of working memory is tantamount to appealing to one complex unknown to explain another (e.g. Deary, 2000; Detterman, 2002). This seems too pessimistic. However difficult it may be to define complexity, few people would really want to argue that the mental counters task, for example, is as complex as an item in Raven's Advanced Progressive Matrices. Moreover, evidence has begun to accumulate that points to some of the cognitive operations that may underlie performance on working memory tasks, and thus explain their relationship to measures of ability.

It is worth starting with evidence that goes beyond mere correlations between measures of working memory and reasoning ability, and which suggests that there is a genuine causal relationship underlying these correlations. Reasoning problems that place greater demands on working memory are harder than those that place fewer demands, and manipulations to a reasoning task that increase these demands invariably impair performance. Much of this evidence comes from studies of deductive reasoning, in particular syllogistic reasoning, and a discussion of some of this evidence will serve to broaden the scope of this review.

A standard syllogism consists of two premises, one relating A and B terms, the second relating B and C, and requires the solver to decide what relation, if any, might hold between A and C. Thus:

All Artists are Beekeepers.
All Beekeepers are Chemists.

From which it is possible and easy to draw the conclusion:

All Artists are Chemists.

Other syllogisms, however, are rather harder:

Some Artists are Beekeepers
No Beekeepers are Chemists

The valid conclusion is:

Some Artists are not Chemists

Virtually everyone will produce the correct answer to the first problem, but only about two-thirds of students, in one study, got the right answer to the second (Dickstein, 1978). Why this difference? According to one influential account (Johnson-Laird, 2001; Johnson-Laird and Byrne, 1991), people first construct a mental model, or representation, of the state of affairs implied by each premise of a syllogism. Then, in order to determine what conclusion, if any, follows from the premises, they must combine these models in all possible ways to see what states of affairs could be true. Thus, what makes a syllogism difficult is the number of possible ways of combining the representations of the premises, because as soon as there is more than one, you have to hold the implications of the first in working memory, while working out the implications of the second, in order to determine whether there is any conclusion compatible with both.

According to this account, the first syllogism above is easy, because there is only one way of combining the representations of the two premises. The first premise, that all artists are beekeepers, can be represented in a Venn diagram, thus:

The small circle labelled A inside the larger circle labelled B indicates that all artists fall into the category of beekeepers, but there may be some beekeepers who are not artists. Similarly, for the second premise, that all beekeepers are chemists.

Combining these two premises gives the only possible third diagram, from which it follows that all artists are included in the category of chemists.

The first premise of the second syllogism, some artists are beekeepers, is represented by two partially overlapping circles thus:

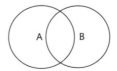

The second premise, no beekeepers are chemists, will be represented by two separated circles thus:

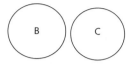

The trouble is that there are two ways of combining these two representations, as follows:

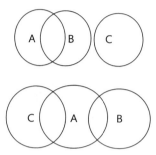

From the first, it would follow that no artists are chemists; from the second, however, it would follow that some are. Since both representations are equally legitimate, but these two implications are incompatible, neither can be a valid inference. The only conclusion that is compatible with both representations is that some artists are not chemists. The problem is difficult because it requires one to hold *both* representations in mind at once, that is, because it imposes a load on working memory.

One simple way of experimentally varying the load on working memory in a syllogistic reasoning task is either to display the two premises of a syllogism on a computer screen until participants produce their answer, or to display them only one at a time, so that participants must remember both premises while trying to work out their answer. This simple change of procedure has a significant impact on errors (Gilhooly *et al.*, 1993). Gilhooly *et al.* also investigated the effects of various dual task requirements on syllogistic reasoning. Participants were allowed to read the premises of a syllogism from a computer display, but from the moment they started viewing them, until they had produced their answer, they had to perform one of three other tasks, in time with a metronome. One simply required them to repeat the digits 1–5 over and over again. The second required them to tap, in sequence, four targets on a board. The third required them to produce a random sequence of the digits 1–5 (e.g. 4, 1, 2, 2, 5, 1, 3, etc.). The three tasks were chosen on the assumption that each would occupy one component of Baddeley and Hitch's working memory system. Simple repetition of a series of digits is articulatory suppression and, as noted above, interferes with immediate memory for verbal material, supposedly by occupying the phonological loop; the tapping task interferes with simple spatial span, supposedly by occupying the visuo-spatial sketchpad. Generating a random string of digits, where you have to remember what digits you have recently given in order to avoid too many repetitions or ascending or descending sequences, is assumed to occupy the central executive. Neither articulatory suppression nor tapping had any effect on the time participants spent studying the premises, or on the accuracy of their solutions. But the random number task significantly increased both the time taken to study the premises and the number of errors people made. Other studies have confirmed that occupying the central executive interferes with inferential reasoning, but have sometimes observed similar interference when participants are required to perform a simple spatial task at the same time (Vandierdonck and De Vrooght, 1997), implying a specifically spatial component to some reasoning tasks (see Chapter 7).

Reasoning tasks do place demands on working memory, and the sizeable correlations observed between people's performance on a working memory task and measures of Gf do seem to represent a true causal contribution of one to the other.

Memory or processing

The hallmark of a working memory task is that, although you are required to remember some information for a short time, you are also required, at the same time, to do something else. Since the same memory span tasks *without* this concurrent processing requirement are less strongly associated with measures of ability, it is presumably the demands of the processing task that drive much of the observed correlation. Perhaps it is simply the *difficulty* of the processing task that is critical. Is it so surprising, after all, that proficient readers should be more successful than those who are less proficient, when required to recall the last word of half a dozen sentences they have been asked to read aloud? If they find the reading task simpler, they will be able to devote more resources to the job of remembering the last word of each sentence.

The argument seems plausible, and is consistent with the suggestion, advanced by Daneman and Carpenter (1980) among others, that the processing and memory demands of working memory tasks compete for a limited pool of resources, and the correlation between working memory and ability simply reflects the fact that more intelligent people have a greater pool of resources. But there is good evidence that this is not the explanation of the relationship between working memory and cognitive ability. For example, Conway and Engle (1996) devised an operation span task in which each item in a list consisted of a simple mental arithmetic problem, followed by a word. Thus:

$$(8 \div 4) + 2 = 4 \text{ (True or False?)} \qquad \text{BIRD}$$

Participants had to read out each problem, decide whether the answer provided was true or false, and read the single word. After three to six such items, they were required to write down, in the correct order, the words in that list. But the mental arithmetic problems had been carefully adjusted to suit each individual's mathematical ability as determined in a lengthy pre-test of similar types of item. In spite of this, word span scores still correlated with scores on SAT-V between 0.50 and 0.60, and continued to do so even when allowance was made for individual differences in viewing time for each problem. Thus, the correlation between working memory and verbal ability is not simply a by-product of differences in the efficiency with which people perform the processing component of the task.

It will be recalled that Shah and Miyake (1996) found that performance on a spatial span task correlated with spatial but not verbal ability, while scores on a reading span test correlated only with verbal, not spatial, ability. They also showed that it was the nature of the memory component of the task that was critical: the correlation between spatial span and spatial ability remained much the same whether the processing component was verbal or spatial; similarly, the association between verbal ability and verbal working memory remained strong even if the processing component of the task was spatial. Kaufman's (2007) study of spatial working memory makes the same point. He found that males outscored females on the spatial task he set them, but there was no sex difference (in fact a small but unreliable female advantage) on a verbal working memory task. But the male advantage on spatial working memory was just as great if the processing component of the task was verbal rather than spatial (in fact exactly the same processing task that was given in the verbal working memory test). The nature or difficulty of the processing component of a working memory task is not as important as one might suppose. What presumably matters is that it prevents rehearsal of the memory component.

A study by Towse *et al.* (1998) provides further evidence. They varied the information content of the various items presented on each trial; all participants received the same set of items on each trial, but under one condition trials started with items that took a long time to process and ended with short items, while this order was reversed in a second condition. Since the same set of items was presented in both conditions, they both placed the same demands on processing resources. The demands on memory, however, were quite different, since they start only *after* the first item has been processed: the longer that takes, the shorter the interval until the end of the trial when you have to recall each item. Performance was significantly better when trials started with items that took a long time to process, implying that it is the load on memory that is critical.

Finally, two procedures greatly increase the strength of the association between simple immediate memory span tasks and measures of Gf. One is to increase the rate at which the items are presented from one per second (Cowan *et al.*, 2005). A plausible explanation is that such a rapid rate of presentation prevents any rehearsal. A second is to present very long lists—well beyond the limit of seven or so items that people can normally recall (Unsworth and Engle, 2006, 2007). Once again, a plausible explanation is that the longer the list, the more impossible it becomes to rehearse any of it.

Speed again

In the absence of rehearsal, information decays rapidly from short-term memory. If asked to listen to a list of words, letters, or digits, and then recall them after a short interval, people will typically recall the last item in the series better than earlier ones—a so-called recency effect. But this recency effect is abolished if, during the delay between being shown the last item and being asked to recall the list, participants are required to do something that prevents rehearsal, for example count backwards in threes from some arbitrary number (Glanzer and Cunitz, 1966).

If information is lost rapidly from short-term memory, then it might seem to follow that the more rapidly it is processed, the greater the chance that it will be adequately processed before being lost. Hence, as Jensen (1998) has argued, maybe working memory capacity is determined by speed of processing, and speed after all really is the basis of *g*. There is good reason to doubt this. Conway *et al.* (2002) took measures of working memory, perceptual speed (Gs), and Gf. The correlation between Gf and Gs was only 0.07; the correlation between Gf and working memory remained significant (and barely affected) after controlling for perceptual speed; while the correlation between speed and Gf was significantly reduced after controlling for working memory.

Memory or attention

One account of the association between working memory and ability, favoured by Conway, Engle, Kane, and their colleagues (e.g. Conway *et al.*, 2011; Kane and Engle 2003), is that if working memory still correlates with measures of Gf after the variance shared by working memory and simple memory span has been partialled out, then it cannot be the *storage* component of working memory tasks that drives the correlation with Gf. It must be the demands on executive attention.

Their argument ignores, however, an important difference between the memory requirements of working memory and immediate memory tasks. While simple span tasks allow you to rehearse the material to be remembered, the processing requirement of a working memory task interferes with this rehearsal. It is possible therefore that what drives the association between working memory and ability is not the demands placed on executive attention, but the requirement to remember some information when you cannot rehearse it. Could it really be the case that differences in intelligence are largely (or even partly) a matter of differences in the ability to remember some information when you are prevented from rehearsing it? On the face of it this seems absurd, but it may not be as nonsensical as it appears at first sight (see below).

In order to address these issues, it will be necessary to consider the role of Baddeley's central executive.

Working memory and executive function

Baddeley (2007) located the important operations of the working memory system in the central executive (see Figure 5.1), and likened its functions to those of the supervisory attentional system (SAS) of Norman and Shallice (1986). Shallice (2002) went further by locating the SAS in physical space, namely, prefrontal cortex, since neuropsychological evidence has long shown that damage to this region of the brain is associated with deficits in planning, responding to new instructions, and inhibiting prepotent or habitual responses. Typical 'frontal' tasks include the Tower of Hanoi and closely related Tower of London tests (see Chapter 4); the Stroop test, where you are asked to state the colour of the ink in which various words are printed, for example the word RED printed in green ink; and the Wisconsin Card Sorting Test (WCST) where you are asked to sort a series of cards containing coloured shapes and patterns first by one rule (e.g. by colour), then by another and another, and so on. I describe some of this evidence in Chapter 6. But it has long been known that lesions to prefrontal cortex may also impair performance on tests of working memory (Baldo and Shimamura, 2000), thus reinforcing the contention that working memory should be included in the list of tests of 'executive function'.

What, however, is the role of the central executive in tests of working memory? Engle *et al.* (1999) were explicit: 'We assume that "working memory capacity" is not really about memory or storage per se, but about *the capacity for controlled, sustained attention in the face of interference or distraction*' (Engle *et al.* 1999, p. 104, italics in original). Is this appeal to the concept of attention helpful? One problem is that 'attention' is used in so many different ways in psychology that its use here hardly helps to narrow down the options. On the other hand, it seems reasonable to suppose that you have to concentrate on (attend to) the task at hand, and not get distracted, if you are to succeed at any working memory test. And it is worth recalling that one explanation of the association between RT or IT and IQ was that low IQ participants were too easily distracted and failed to concentrate on a repetitive and boring task (Chapter 3).

Experimental evidence does indeed suggest that susceptibility to distraction or interference is associated with poor performance on tests of working memory. For example, Kane and Engle (2000) asked people to memorize three separate lists of ten words, with each list consisting of one item from each of ten different categories (such as animals or occupations). The participants were divided into two groups—one with high scores on a test of working memory, the other with low scores. In both groups performance declined over successive lists—a standard proactive interference effect. But although the two groups did not differ in their recall of the first list, the low span group showed a much greater decline than the high spans—implying a greater susceptibility to proactive interference. Proactive interference effects arise because participants confuse items that belong to later lists with those that appeared in earlier lists (did 'leopard' appear in *this* list or in an earlier one?). When the experimenter ensures that items in different lists come from different populations, differences between high and low-span participants disappear (Conway and Engle, 1994). Bunting (2006) showed that the correlation between working memory and Gf increased as proactive interference was built up over a series of trials in which the information to be remembered all came from a single category, but immediately decreased when the category was changed (a procedure that results in release from proactive interference).

The 'cocktail party' phenomenon refers to the finding that when you are required to listen carefully to, or 'shadow', speech coming in at one ear, you may detect your name (but not someone else's) coming in at the other ear, even though you are expressly instructed to listen only to the message coming in at your first ear. Typically some 30–40% of people report hearing their own name. What determines who will and who will not? The answer is working memory. Conway *et al.* (2001) found that 65% of the low-span participants in their experiment, but only 20% of the high-span participants reported hearing their own name. Low-span people are more susceptible to distraction. They are also more susceptible to the Stroop effect. Everyone hesitates when confronted with the word RED printed in green ink, but this effect is more pronounced in those with low span scores (Kane and Engle, 2000).

Differences in working memory span are undoubtedly associated with differences in performance on a variety of tasks where distraction or interference will affect your score. Is this sufficient to support the contention of Engle *et al.* (1999) quoted above, that the core ingredient of working memory and other executive tasks is the ability to maintain attention in the face of distraction? Probably not: executive tasks are more diverse than that. Shallice and Burgess (1998) showed that the correlations between performance on different executive tasks are actually quite low; Delis *et al.* (2001) reported that the median correlation between different tasks was 0.25 in 20–49-year-old adults, rising to 0.33 in people over 50.

For present purposes, however, the critical question is whether the differences in executive function are responsible for the strong association between working memory and intelligence. A study by Friedman *et al.* (2006) suggests that they may not be. They developed a set of nine executive tasks, divided into three groups of three, designed to measure three distinguishable executive processes: inhibition, updating, and shifting. The first involved the inhibition of a prepotent response, as in the Stroop test. Updating tasks required the addition and deletion of information from working memory, as in a spatial two-back task, where different small boxes on a computer screen are illuminated in random order, and you have to say whether the currently illuminated box is the same as one illuminated two trials before. Shifting tasks involved shifting the basis of categorization of the currently presented stimulus depending on the instruction given, as in the WCST: in a colour-shape task, for example, coloured shapes are presented on each trial and you have to respond to either their colour or their shape; the measure of performance taken is difference in reaction time on shift trials and on non-shift trials.

Performance on the three tasks *within* each set correlated sufficiently strongly to suggest each set was measuring a single construct, and thus allowed three latent variables (inhibition, updating, and shifting) to be constructed. Confirmatory factor analysis was used to estimate the correlations between each of the three latent variables and performance on tests of Gf. Although there were significant correlations between all three latent variables, only updating correlated significantly ($r = 0.64$) with Gf. The correlations between inhibition or shifting and Gf were 0.29 and 0.13 respectively, and these associations became even weaker when updating was partialled out. So, although these different executive tasks all shared something in common, they did *not* all share anything in common with Gf: only updating, which is in effect a measure of working memory contributed significantly to performance on tests of Gf. Of course, there are other executive tasks that do correlate with Gf: recall the correlation of −0.77 between Raven's scores and errors on the Tower of Hanoi problem reported by Carpenter *et al.* (1990). But this only serves to reinforce the conclusion that different executive tasks are measuring very different things.

Friedman and her colleagues' results do not stand alone. Ardila *et al.* (2000) found at best only very modest correlations, of 0.30, between children's scores on the WISC and either the WCST or verbal fluency. In a study of 470 youths, aged 8–19, Delis *et al.* (2007) reported equally modest correlations, in the range 0.15–0.35, between performance on four different executive tasks, including fluency and Stroop tests, and scores on an abbreviated version of the WAIS. In another study, with 300 adults, Ardila *et al.* (1998) reported that factor analysis of WAIS, WCST, and a variety of other tests revealed that WCST and WAIS loaded onto quite different factors.

What are the implications of these findings? The first is surely that 'executive function' is not a unitary construct. There may be some overlap between different executive tasks, but they are not all measuring the same thing. The second is that, apart from the Tower of Hanoi, the one executive task that is quite closely related to measures of Gf and several other components of IQ is working memory, and this association is not mediated through other executive tasks. So, there is a distinction between executive function and the intelligence measured by standard IQ tests. Many cognitive scientists and neuropsychologists (see Ardila *et al.*, 1998; Friedman *et al.*, 2006) are, of course, inclined to see their tests of executive function as better measures of intelligence than are IQ tests, and so have concluded that IQ tests have failed to capture important aspects of human cognitive abilities (see Box 5.1).

> **BOX 5.1 Working memory, executive tasks, and intelligence**
>
> The results reported by Ardila, Delis, Friedman and their colleagues may seem rather surprising. There is no doubt that executive tasks measuring inhibition and shifting correlate modestly with updating or working memory. And working memory certainly correlates with a variety of measures of intelligence. However, the fact that A correlates with B, and B with C, does not mean that A will correlate with C. Nor should one be led astray by the clear evidence that performance on all executive tasks, and on measures of Gf, depends on the integrity of prefrontal cortex (Chapter 6). Localization of function is hardly precise enough to allow the inference that two tasks, apparently dependent on the same general region of the brain, must be measuring the same process.
>
> A rather better reason to question some of these results might be that other studies appear to have shown a closer connection between Gf and a variety of measures of executive function. Salthouse *et al.* (2003), for example, reported a correlation of 0.73 between Gf and measures of inhibition, along with ones of 0.87 and 0.93 with updating and dual task performance. The 261 participants in their study ranged in age from 18 to 84, with 70 being over the age of 60. Although these correlations were only slightly reduced by partialling out age, what is not clear is whether they were larger in the older than in the younger participants: there is good reason to believe that old age brings with it a decline in the integrity of prefrontal cortex and a consequent decline in performance on all executive tasks (see Chapter 8). A further consequence will be that executive tasks will correlate more strongly with one another, and all may correlate more strongly with measured intelligence.
>
> If the correlation between many executive tasks and measures of Gf (or indeed any other aspect of IQ) is small or negligible, then they must be measuring distinguishably different cognitive processes or operations. But which is the better measure of 'intelligence'? Perhaps unsurprisingly, as I note, cognitive neuropsychologists have opted for their executive tasks, and concluded that traditional IQ tests have missed out on important aspects of intelligence. It does not seem likely that psychometricians will agree. There can be no doubt that a better rapprochement between the two camps is needed. But it will probably need more time. Do not watch this space—but with luck some other space will provide the answer in years to come.

Conclusion

Among the many definitions or ingredients of intelligence offered by the experts in Snyderman and Rothman's (1988) study was the ability to learn. Most laboratory tests of learning, however, show only modest correlations with IQ, and, as I will show in Chapter 9, measures of so-called 'implicit' learning may not correlate with IQ at all. Set against this background, the discovery by Williams and Pearlberg (2006) of a substantial correlation (about 0.50) between Gf and performance on a novel learning task, which they called 'three-term contingency learning', assumes some significance. Its interpretation remains unclear, in part because although subsequent studies have confirmed the reality of the association, there remain some discrepancies between them. Are measures of ability correlated with the three-term task much more strongly than with simpler paired-associate learning? Is the association between three-term learning and Gf quite independent of speed and working memory? Answers to these questions will be important.

If it would be an exaggeration to say that Gf, or reasoning ability (let alone *g*), is simply a matter of working memory, research on working memory span has, at the least, made a start to the task of unravelling some of the mysteries surrounding the nature of differences in intelligence. Although scores on tests of working memory and immediate memory span are correlated, working memory is more strongly associated with a variety of ability measures. In some studies, at least, the correlation between the two has been as high as 0.70. There is experimental evidence that transcends the merely correlational, suggesting that this association represents a causal relation between the two: manipulations of the load on working memory increase the difficulty of deductive reasoning tasks. There is even evidence that practice on a working memory task may improve your score on a test of Gf (see Box 5.2).

BOX 5.2 How to increase your intelligence in less than 20 days

From time to time there have been excited reports of dramatic improvements in IQ test scores as a function of some relatively brief intervention. Spitz (1986) has provided a distinctly sceptical review of earlier reports. In a more recent study, Jaeggi et al. (2008) gave participants continuous training on an n-back task for 8, 12, 17, or 19 days, and compared their performance on tests of Gf before and after this training, with that of a control group that received no n-back training. Eight days of n-back training had no effect, but beginning with 12 days there was a suggestion of a difference between experimental and control groups that became statistically significant after 17 and 19 days of training.

   The study has attracted much attention, but has also been severely criticized by Moody (2009) and by Conway et al. (2011). For unexplained reasons, the eight-day group, which showed no effect of n-back training, was tested with Raven's Matrices, but the other groups, which did show an effect, were tested with a rather different matrices test. Worse still, although this other test is normally given with a 45-minute time limit, Jaeggi et al. gave their participants only ten minutes. Since the test, like Raven's Advanced Matrices, starts with easy items and progresses to harder ones, all that it can be measuring with a ten-minute time limit is the speed at which participants can solve easy items. Not quite the same as Gf.

   As Conway and his colleagues also note, what is really important to know here is whether the effects of n-back training lasted for any length of time after the training finished. A transient improvement in test scores is hardly the same as an enhancement of intelligence.

Baddeley's model of working memory has separable verbal and spatial short-term rehearsal loops, together with a modality-independent store for retaining information in the absence of the opportunity for rehearsal, and a central executive system. Within this model, the reason why working memory is more strongly associated with ability than is immediate memory, is because the processing component of the former prevents rehearsal of the information you are required to remember, and (less certainly) because working memory tasks place further demands on the central executive's ability to resist distraction or interference.

Has this really shed light on the nature of intelligence, or at least on performance on IQ tests? It makes intuitive sense to suggest that concentration and freedom from distraction are needed to solve items in an IQ test, or indeed any other moderately demanding cognitive task. It is less obvious, as I acknowledged above, why the ability to remember something over a short interval, in the absence of opportunity for rehearsal, should be important. What this ignores is the fact that the solution of many intellectual problems, such as items in Raven's Matrices, often requires you to break the problem down into its component parts, work out the solution to one part, hold that in mind while trying to solve the next part, and then combine the two or more solutions to the two or more sub-parts into a solution to the whole problem (or perhaps, see that the solution to a later part is incompatible with the apparent solution to an earlier part, and start all over again). Consider the problem shown in Figure 5.2. It is in fact a relatively easy item, but it still requires you to apply a particular rule to three distinct attributes of the eight figures shown: each figure needs to be broken down into three parts—an outer shape, which is either black, white, or grey, and an inner set of lines within a central square. Each of rows one and two contains one example of three different outer shapes, one example of the three colours, and one example of three different sets of inner lines. Row three therefore requires completing with an outer circle, which is black, with one line in the inner square. But to see that, you (probably) had to remember that the missing shape in row three was a circle, that the missing colour was black, and that what was needed was a single line. And in a real problem of Raven's Matrices you would have had to remember all this while searching through the eight alternatives on offer to see which pattern matched this triple requirement.

It is not just items in tests of Gf that place these demands on memory. Comprehension of a complicated passage of prose requires the reader to remember earlier sentences while reading later ones. Consider the following:

On the occasion of this first call which, after leaving Saint-Loup, I went to pay on Mme de Villeparisis following the advice given by M. de Norpois to my father, I found her in a

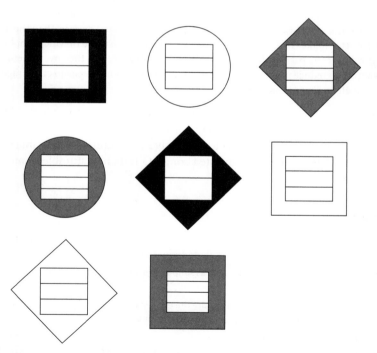

Figure 5.2 Another example of the type of item found in Raven's Advanced Progressive Matrices. See text for further details.

drawing-room hung with yellow silk, against which the settees and the admirable armchairs upholstered in Beauvais tapestry stood out with the almost purple redness of ripe raspberries... Mme de Villeparisis herself, wearing an old-fashioned bonnet of black lace (which she preserved with the same shrewd instinct for local or historical colour as a Breton innkeeper who, however Parisian his clientele may have become, thinks it more astute to keep his maids in coifs and wide sleeves), was seated at a little desk on which, as well as her brushes, her palette and an unfinished flower-piece in water-colour, were arranged—in glasses, in saucers, in cups—moss-roses, zinnias, maidenhair ferns, which on account of the sudden influx of callers she had just left off painting, and which gave the impression of being arrayed on a florist's counter in some eighteenth-century mezzotint.

So, why did the narrator pay a call on Mme de Villeparisis? Why did the settees and armchairs stand out so vividly? Why was Mme de Villeparisis wearing a black bonnet? Why might the innkeeper dress his maids in coifs and wide sleeves? Why had Mme de Villeparisis stopped painting? And this is a passage only two sentences long (admittedly quite long sentences). The load on working memory becomes substantially greater as the passage gets longer. It will also get greater if your task is not just one of parsing and understanding a passage of prose, but of evaluating the validity of a complex argument. To detect a *non sequitur* or other invalid argument, you will have to work out and remember the implications of an earlier set of statements, while reading some supposed further implications of those statements. So, what is the flaw in the following argument?

> The government has announced that it wants to reduce the level of ill-health caused by stress at work. A recent study of 5,000 white-collar workers in America shows what needs to be done. The study found that men who had a high level of control over the way they carried out their jobs had a significantly lower rate of heart disease, a stress-related disease, than those who had less control. This makes it clear that the most stressful jobs are those in which employees have little control over the pace of their work and how it is organized. If the government is serious about wanting to reduce the level of stress-related disease, then it needs to encourage employers to give their workers greater control over their work.

Those who confidently assert that IQ tests fail to measure important aspects of intelligence (recall Medawar's claims, Chapter 1) may need to think again: the analysis of working memory suggests that, no doubt rather fortuitously and certainly without much prior theoretical understanding, those who invented some IQ tests had stumbled onto something quite important.

 ## Summary

- Single laboratory measures of associative learning correlate only weakly with IQ, but the correlation between Gf and one, the 'three-term contingency' task, is about 0.50.
- Measures of immediate memory, such as simple digit span, usually correlate only modestly with IQ.
- But working memory tasks, which require the concurrent processing of other information in addition to short-term memory, correlate significantly more with IQ.
- The addition of the processing requirement means that you must remember information while unable to rehearse it, and that you must simultaneously attend to two tasks. This probably explains why working memory is the more important ingredient of intelligence.

Further reading

Jensen (1998) summarizes early evidence on the relationship between IQ and laboratory measures of associative learning, but this should be supplemented by Williams and Pearlberg (2006). In addition to the Miyake and Shah (1999) and Conway *et al.* (2008) edited books on working memory, Baddeley (2007) and Conway *et al.* (2011) provide further theoretical and empirical analyses, the former touching on the relationship between intelligence, working memory, and executive functions. The difference between various 'executive' tasks, in particular how they differ in their relation to conventional measures of IQ, is well documented by Friedman *et al.* (2006).

Intelligence and the brain

Introduction

In addition to behavioural correlates of IQ, there have been repeated attempts to find the 'biological' basis of intelligence, by looking for an association between test scores and measures of the size of the brain, functioning of the nervous system, or activity in particular regions of the brain. All three lines of research have produced at least some positive findings. Brain size is modestly correlated with IQ. Some measures of event-related potentials (ERPs) recorded to brief auditory or visual stimuli have often shown moderate (and in some early studies high) correlations with IQ, leading Eysenck to suggest, very optimistically as later research made clear, 'that we have come quite close to the physiological measurement of the genotype underlying the phenotypic IQ tests results on which we have had to rely so far' (Eysenck, 1982, p. 6). Since 1990 or so, functional imaging studies have begun to show which regions of the brain become active during performance on IQ tests and other, related, cognitive tasks.

Bigger is better? Brain size and IQ

That there should be a correlation between test scores and *some* measures of the structure or functioning of the nervous system is hardly surprising. Cognitive or intellectual activity is surely mediated by the brain, and differences in such activity are likely to be reflected in differences in the brain. It is more surprising that some commentators should have been so reluctant to acknowledge the possibility. One explanation is no doubt to be found in the crude biologizing of earlier generations of investigators, who did not hesitate to make confident pronouncements about differences in the average intelligence of different human groups as a function of supposed differences in the size or structure of their brains. Gould (1997) provides an entertaining, if not always perfectly accurate, history of these endeavours (see Michael, 1988, for some corrections to Gould's earlier account). Rather remarkably, similar arguments about group differences are still advanced today (Lynn, 2006; Rushton and Jensen, 2005; I briefly discuss their views in Chapters 13 and 14).

Human evolution has been marked by an approximately threefold increase in the size of the brain in the past three million years, from the 450 g brain of Australopithecines to the 1200–1500 g brain of *Homo sapiens*. Yet the human brain is an extremely expensive organ: although comprising no more than 2–3% of body weight, the brain consumes some

20–25% of our metabolic energy. These two observations suggest that the human brain has significant adaptive value, and the popular inference has always been that it is our large brains that have endowed humans with their superior intelligence (an inference that ignores the fact that brain size appears to have decreased rather than increased over the past 100,000 years of human evolution: Aiello and Dean, 1990). Even if the inference is accepted, it would not automatically follow that larger brains were associated with higher IQ scores *within* human populations. Nevertheless, the evidence suggests that they are.

Lacking any direct way of measuring the size or weight of the living brain, earlier investigators relied on less direct measures such as endocranial casts (from the dead) or, even less directly, circumference of the head (obtainable from the living). Van Valen (1974) and Rushton and Ankney (1996) have reviewed a number of studies of the relationship between head size (usually circumference) and IQ. Van Valen reported a weighted mean correlation of 0.27; Rushton and Ankney one of 0.21 from 17 studies of some 45,000 children, and one of 0.15 from 15 studies of over 6,000 adults.

These are very modest correlations. But then the circumference of the head is only an imperfect measure of the size of the brain. The technologies of magnetic resonance imaging (MRI) and computer aided tomography (CAT) allow more direct measures of the size of the brain *in vivo* (see Box 6.2 below). Two reviews (Gignac *et al.*, 2003; McDaniel, 2005) summarized the results from a total of 858 and 1,530 participants respectively: Gignac *et al.* calculated the weighted mean correlation between IQ and brain volume as 0.37, and McDaniel as 0.29, with the correlation being higher in females than in males, and in both males and females higher in adults than in children. A substantial number of these studies reported correlations of 0.40 or higher, and in only one was the correlation negative, and that only –0.05.

Several studies have asked whether these modest correlations are to be found with all measures of intelligence, with some regions of the brain rather than others, or with the grey or white matter (cell bodies or axons) of the brain. Their results have not been entirely consistent. For example, of seven studies reviewed by Gignac *et al.* (2003) that looked at grey vs. white matter correlations, two found stronger correlations with grey matter, three with white matter, and two no difference. There can be no question but that both are significantly correlated with differences in general intelligence (Luders *et al.*, 2009a), and a partial resolution of the discrepancy between different studies appears to be that differences in grey matter are more important in males, while differences in white matter are more important in females (Gur *et al.*, 1999; Haier *et al.*, 2005). The meaning of this sex difference is not entirely understood.

There is evidence that the correlations are stronger in prefrontal, temporal, and parietal cortex than in occipital cortex or cerebellum (Flashman *et al.*, 1998). The important point here is that correlations between intelligence and brain volume are found in *all* these association areas of the cortex (Colom *et al.*, 2009; Haier *et al.*, 2009). General intelligence would seem to be distributed across different brain areas, rather than being localized in a single area. This is consistent with the data on localization of function provided by functional imaging studies (see below).

The highest correlations between intelligence and brain size are with measures of *g* or Gf, although there is a significant correlation with measures of Gc. Surprisingly, however, measures of spatial ability (Gv) seem to be unrelated to brain size (Colom *et al.*, 2009), while Wickett *et al.* (2000) actually reported a small negative correlation between brain size and Gv. On the other hand, Box 6.1 records a rather different result. Speed of processing (Gs) is also unrelated to differences in brain size (van Leeuwen *et al.*, 2009).

Although the overall correlation between brain size and intelligence is not very high, there can be no doubt of its reliability. Its interpretation, however, is another matter. IQ scores are, as I have noted before, modestly but significantly correlated with height (Jensen and Sinha, 1993). No one seriously supposes that greater height somehow endows people with superior intelligence. The correlation must arise for other reasons. As Jensen and Sinha argued, if there really was an intrinsic, causal relation between height and IQ, the correlation would be observed *within* families as well as in the population as a whole. That is to say, if one sibling in a family was taller than another, they would also be likely to differ in intelligence. In the case of height, there is no within-family correlation with IQ: in other words, the correlation in the population as a whole arises because members of taller families have on average slightly higher test scores than members of shorter families—perhaps because they also differ in health, nutrition, social class, or some associated factor.

What of the correlation between brain volume and IQ? Is this observed within families—in other words is the sibling with the larger brain also likely to have a higher test score? The evidence is sparse but mixed. Schoenemann *et al.* (2000) reported an overall correlation of 0.45 between brain volume and a *g* factor score in a sample of 36 pairs of siblings, but the within-family correlation was –0.05. Gignac *et al.* (2003) reported a between-family correlation of 0.37 between *g* factor scores and brain volume, and a within-family correlation of 0.23. There seems little doubt that some or even most of the overall correlation between brain volume and IQ arises between families. These two studies leave open the question whether any of it arises within families.

On the other hand, several twin studies have estimated that the heritability of brain size is high—at least 0.80 (Bartley *et al.*, 1997; Pennington *et al.*, 2000; Posthuma *et al.*, 2002) while another study, which reported a significant relationship between cell density in prefrontal cortex and IQ, also showed that MZ twins were more concordant for cell density than DZ twins (Thompson *et al.*, 2001). This suggests the possibility that a genetically determined difference in brain volume or cell density is the cause of differences in test scores. This may, indeed, be the correct interpretation, but it would still not explain just *why* or *how* a larger brain or more neurons produce greater intelligence. Perhaps, by analogy with computers, a brain with more neurons, like a computer with more transistors, might be able to operate on larger chunks of data at a time, or perform more operations in parallel, and thus get through more jobs in a given time. Set against that, an increase in mere size might slow things down because the signals would have further to travel. Cell density may be more important than sheer volume.

However, it is worth anticipating a point about twin studies and heritability that I make in Chapter 11. The standard twin method for estimating heritability compares MZ and DZ twins. If MZ twins resemble one another significantly more than DZ twins, this is taken as evidence of a significant genetic contribution to similarities and differences in the characteristic under study. But it is worth asking just why it is that MZ twins resemble one another so closely in IQ? At least in part, this may be because their genetic similarity causes them to experience, or create for themselves, very similar micro-environments.

Because they are genetically identical, from an early age two MZ twins will receive, and elicit, from their parents and others very similar treatment; later, they will spend much of their time together, go to the same school together where they sit next to one another. And so on. It may be that this genetically mediated similarity in their environments is the proximal cause of the similarity in their test scores. The observation that MZ twins resemble one another in brain size or cell density just as much as they do in IQ, does not prove that the similarity in their test scores is a direct consequence of the size and cell density of the brains they were born with. For a start, as noted above, the correlation between brain size and IQ is lower in children than in adults. Moreover, in a longitudinal study of some 300 young children followed up to early adulthood, Shaw *et al.* (2006) found a much more complicated picture of the relationship between intelligence and one measure of brain size, cortical thickness. At age 7, there was a *negative* correlation between the two. But the most intelligent children (IQ > 120) then showed a rapid increase in cortical thickness, overtaking the other children, and peaking at age 11–12 before slowly declining to a level similar to the others. As the authors concluded: ' "Brainy" children are not cleverer solely by virtue of having more or less grey matter at any one age. Rather, intelligence is related to dynamic properties of cortical maturation' (Shaw *et al.*, 2006, p. 678).

It is possible that these developmental differences between very intelligent children and those of more average IQ are a consequence of genetically determined differences in the maturation of the brain. But there are other possibilities. Rather than assuming that larger brains automatically generate greater intelligence, it would be equally plausible to suppose that developmental changes in the size of the brain occur in response to the kinds of intellectually stimulating experience that foster cognitive development. In other words, the route from genes to brain size to IQ is mediated through the environment: MZ twins end up with similar sized brains and similar IQ scores, because they experience similarly stimulating or unstimulating environments and these environmental experiences impact on the development of their brains. There is, in fact, excellent evidence that differences in their environment, rather than in their genes, can affect the development of the brain in many different species of animal. For example, rats and mice brought up in large groups, in large cages, with a variety of objects to play with, end up not only better at learning the solution to maze problems, but also with larger brains, than their equally well-nourished littermates reared in isolation in small empty cages (Renner and Rosenzweig, 1987; van Praag *et al.*, 2000; see Box 6.1 for related evidence).

BOX 6.1 Bird brains and London taxi drivers

More specific environmental experiences can have more specific effects on the development of the brain. Many species of bird cache or store food for later consumption. If their caches are not well hidden, they will be pilfered by someone else long before the original storer comes to recover their cache. Successful caching, therefore, requires that birds remember precisely where they have hidden their well-concealed cache. It is not entirely surprising, therefore, that food-storing birds end up with a larger hippocampus than related, but non-storing species. But this increase in the size of the hippocampus only begins to develop *after* the bird has started to cache, and is only maintained if the bird continues to cache (Clayton, 2001). It is the experience of caching that provides the environmental trigger causing the increase in the size of the hippocampus.

A famous study of London taxi drivers (Maguire *et al.*, 2000) showed that they had a larger right hippocampus than other people whose job did not require such spatial skills, and that the magnitude of this increase was correlated with the number of years they had been driving round London.

Differences in brain size seem to be driven by differences in experience.

Brain activity: EEGs and ERPs

If it was plausible to suppose that differences in the size of the brain might be associated with differences in IQ, it is surely inconceivable that there should be no relationship between IQ scores and *some* aspect of the functioning of the nervous system. The search for such relationships has been going on for much of the twentieth century and all of the twenty-first, but for a long time it was hardly crowned with great success. One reason for this, no doubt, is that the problem is a difficult one: if neuroscientists cannot claim to understand the neural basis of learning and memory in the laboratory rat, how could they be expected to understand the neural basis of human intelligence? Deary and Caryl (1993) provided a sympathetic but critical account of the early history of this research, which has been supplemented by Deary (2000).

Changes in neural activity during problem solving

Electrodes attached to the surface of the scalp can record the spontaneous activity of the brain as a series of voltage changes—no doubt the summed activity of many millions of neurons. This is the electroencephalograph or EEG record. The frequency of the EEG record changes when people are in different states, when they are alert and engaged in mental activity, or quiet, drowsy, asleep, dreaming, etc. The question at issue is whether there are differences in the EEG record, in the waking state, associated with differences in IQ. At least some studies have found higher-frequency resting records in people of higher IQ and, more important, smaller changes in activity when they are required to do some mental arithmetic or perform a letter or figure matching task (Doppelmayr *et al.*, 2005; Giannitrapani, 1985; Neubauer *et al.*, 2002). Neubauer and Fink (2009) provide a good review. Rather similar results have been reported by Haier and his colleagues in a number of PET studies (Haier *et al.*, 1992). The technique of positron emission tomography (PET; see Box 6.2) measures the level of activity in different regions of the brain via the uptake of glucose labelled with a radioactive tracer. Glucose metabolic rate increases when people are required to solve Raven's Matrices or other cognitive problems. Once again, however, the magnitude of this increase is *negatively* correlated with measured intelligence.

BOX 6.2 Imaging the brain

PET scanning was the first modern imaging technique applied to the study of intelligence. It involves injecting a low-level radioactive tracer, which carries a positron-emitting isotope into neurons by attaching it to a special glucose. Since glucose is consumed every time a neuron fires, the harder a brain area is working, the more glucose is used, and more of the isotope is deposited in that area. PET scanning simply records the level of radiation in different regions of the brain, thereby providing a measure of glucose metabolic rate and level of neural activity.

Magnetic resonance imaging (MRI) is a non-invasive method for revealing the structure of soft tissue in the body, including of course the brain. It uses magnetic fields and radio waves to produce two or three-dimensional images of brain structures in any plane.

MRI can also be used to produce functional images (fMRI) by rapidly scanning changes in oxygen content in blood. Increased neural activity causes an increased demand for oxygen, and this can be measured as the BOLD (blood-oxygen-level dependent) response. This allows images to be generated that reflect which brain structures are activated (and how) at different times. Since fMRI scanners allow people to be presented with different visual or auditory stimuli, and to perform simple actions such as pressing a button or moving a joystick, fMRI can be used to reveal the brain structures activated while they are performing a variety of cognitive tasks in the scanner (Raven's Matrices, or a test of working memory). Functional MRI is easier to use than PET because no isotopes are required, and the shorter time resolution allows for better experimental control.

Both Haier and Neubauer regard these findings as evidence for a 'neural efficiency hypothesis of intelligence': 'Subjects performing a complex task well may use a limited number of brain circuits and/or fewer neurons, thus requiring minimal glucose use, while poor performers use more circuits and/or neurons, some of which are detrimental to task performance, and this is reflected in higher overall glucose metabolism' (Haier *et al.*, 1992, p. 134). This is, of course, perfectly plausible, although one suspects that a quite different, but equally plausible, explanation could have been found had the correlation between activity and intelligence been positive rather than negative (see below, where several studies have reported exactly such a positive relationship). But a slightly different version of this efficiency hypothesis seems equally possible—that the observed correlation is a consequence, rather than a cause, of greater cognitive ability: the higher someone's IQ, the easier they will find Raven's Matrices, letter series completion tasks, or mental arithmetic problems, and the fewer resources they will need to devote to their solution. It is not so much that more intelligent people have generally more efficient brains; it is more that they simply do not need to work so hard to solve any intellectual problem.

Complexity of ERPs

Other work has relied on recording changes in activity to a particular stimulus or series of stimuli: these are ERPs or event-related potentials. A typical procedure involves a person sitting quietly in a dimly illuminated room listening to very brief tones, played through headphones, or waiting for brief flashes of light. Such stimuli cause changes in brain activity which can also be recorded by electrodes attached to the surface of the scalp. Because the minute changes in electrical potential in response to such signals are embedded in a background of continually fluctuating activity or noise, it is common to repeat the brief signal 50 or 100 times, once every few seconds, and to average the changes recorded over all one hundred trials (hence the earlier term, AEP, standing for averaged evoked potentials).

Although Jensen bluntly characterized early work on ERPs as 'a thicket of seemingly inconsistent and confusing findings' (Jensen, 1980, p. 709), he later took a rather more favourable view, confidently asserting that 'correlations of...AEP variables with IQ typically range between about 0.30 and 0.60' (Jensen, 1998, pp. 153–4). This is surprising, since the thicket of inconsistent findings had certainly not vanished by the time he came to this later conclusion.

The best known of the earliest work was that of Ertl and his colleagues, who claimed to show a high correlation between IQ and latency of the ERP to visual signals—high IQ being associated with shorter latencies to the first response (Ertl and Schafer, 1969). Figure 6.1 illustrates the kind of data they observed. Inspection of these data suggested to Hendrickson and Hendrickson (1980) that the more striking difference between high and low IQ records was not the latency to the first peak or trough, but rather the overall complexity of the waveform—the number and amplitude of deviations from baseline in the first few hundred milliseconds following onset of the signal. They claimed that there was a substantial correlation between this measure of complexity and IQ: high test scores were associated with more complex waveforms. It seems clear that they were wrong (see Box 6.3). The one reliable result that has emerged from attempts to replicate the Hendricksons' experiments is that when participants are required to attend to the brief stimuli presented in a typical ERP experiment, there is a *negative* correlation between complexity and IQ (Bates and Eysenck, 1993a; Bates *et al.*, 1995). Why should high IQ be associated with small changes in ERPs to stimuli which subjects are required to attend to and discriminate (if indeed this relationship is reliable)? An obvious possibility, and the one advanced by Bates and Eysenck and by Bates *et al.*, is that when people are required to pay close attention to particular stimuli, in order to decide whether one is longer, or louder, or of a higher frequency than another,

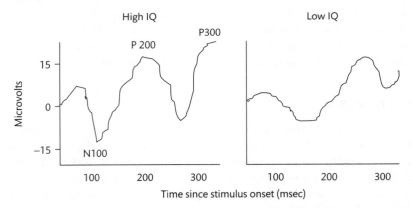

Figure 6.1 A schematic representation of two people's event-related potentials to a briefly presented stimulus turned on at t = 0. These are not real data, but illustrate the kind of difference between people of high and low IQ observed by Ertl and Schafer (1969). The labels N100, P200, and P300 point to particular negative and positive troughs and peaks typically observed in the record at 100, 200, and 300 msec after stimulus onset (see later in chapter).

under conditions where such a discrimination is quite demanding, the lower their IQ the more effort and more resources they must devote to the task. The explanation is, of course, the same as that offered above for the negative correlation between IQ and changes in EEG activity or glucose uptake when people start trying to solve IQ items or perform mental arithmetic.

BOX 6.3 String length and IQ

The Hendricksons devised a measure of ERP complexity which, perhaps inadvisedly, they referred to as 'string length':

> In looking at the records, we noticed that as the waveforms of the low IQ records became smoother, the circumference of the waveform envelope became shorter. If we thought of the waveform as a piece of string, and we went a standard length into the record, cut the string at that point, and pulled it straight the high IQ people would have longer waveform strings than the low IQ people.
>
> (A. E. Hendrickson, 1982, p. 195)

Subsequent studies reported a correlation of 0.72 between Wechsler IQ and ERP string length in a group of 219 schoolchildren (DE Hendrickson, 1982) and one of 0.53 between string length and scores on Raven's Matrices in a group of 33 undergraduates (Blinkhorn and Hendrickson, 1982). The detailed account of the Hendricksons' procedures makes it clear that they worked hard to find measures that yielded such high correlations.

> When a reasonable sample of subjects' data had been processed in the way described above, the 'string' measure...was computed, and correlations were obtained between the string measure and the IQ measures. We were perplexed to find that the correlations were of the order of zero, or even in the 'wrong' direction.
>
> (D. E. Hendrickson, 1982, p. 201)

Hendrickson eventually found a procedure that yielded the correlation of 0.72 cited above. Since the research was clearly at an exploratory stage, it was perfectly legitimate to search around for a measure that resulted in more robust effects. But no faith can be placed in effects obtained after prolonged search of this nature until they have been replicated in independent studies.

As Deary and Caryl (1993) and Deary (2000) have noted, Hendrickson's results were largely consistent with those of an earlier study employing what its authors called a 'map-wheel' measure of ERPs (Rhodes *et al.*, 1969). Since then, however, her data have been replicated in only six rather small studies (and in several of these there remain serious doubts about the procedures and selection of data). Meanwhile, nine other studies have failed to replicate her results (with three of these finding correlations in the opposite direction). In the largest single study, with a sample of 236 students and other adults, Vogel *et al.* (1987) reported correlations ranging from –0.087 to +0.035 between string length and some other measures of visual or auditory ERPs and a battery of IQ tests. Vogel *et al.* acknowledged that there were minor differences between their procedures and Hendrickson's, but regarded it as unlikely that they could have been decisive. Even this faint hope must be dashed by the results of a rather smaller study by Barrett and Eysenck (1992). They exhaustively and systematically attempted to examine the importance of the various procedural details recommended by the Hendricksons, and found correlations ranging from –0.20 to –0.44 between ERP string length and WAIS IQ scores. All eight correlations were negative, that is, in the *opposite* direction to those reported by DE Hendrickson (1982), and four of the eight were significant.

It is a cautionary tale.

Latency and amplitude

It turns out that there *are* measures of ERPs that are genuinely associated with differences in IQ, but the Hendricksons' string length is not one of those measures. Indeed it now appears that Ertl and Shafer (1969) were right all along: it is the latency (and amplitude) of early components of the ERP waveform that are related to IQ, but this relationship holds only when subjects are required to attend to the stimuli being presented in order to make a decision about them—as for example in an inspection time (IT) task. Deary (2000) argued that the critical feature of ERPs that correlates with IQ might be the amplitude of certain components occurring between 100 and 200 msec after the onset of a stimulus—in particular the magnitude of the first major negative deflection at about 100 msec after stimulus onset (N100), or of the first major positive deflection at about 200 msec (P200), or the slope between the two (see Figure 6.1). Zhang *et al.* (1989), Caryl (1994), and Morris and Alcorn (1995) have all reported that measures of the rise time of P200, or of the slope of the gradient from N100 to P200, correlated significantly both with measured intelligence and with inspection time. The N100–P200 interval is generally regarded as the moment when the earliest stages of stimulus detection and identification occur (Deary, 2000), so it seems plausible that different patterns of neural activity over this interval should be associated with differences in IT. There is also good evidence that the latency and amplitude of later components, in particular of the positive peak at approximately 300 msec after stimulus onset, P300, are associated with differences in ability. Most of these studies have employed the 'oddball' task, in which the same brief stimulus is repeatedly presented and participants are required to respond whenever a different stimulus is presented (McGarry-Roberts *et al.*, 1992; Walhovd *et al.*, 2005). Correlations between test scores and P300 latency have been as high as −0.45, but substantially lower, and almost invariably insignificant, in 'passive' conditions when participants are not required to respond to the occasional odd stimulus.

It has taken a long time, but here at last there seems to be a reliable and important finding. A shorter time between stimulus onset and these early components of the ERP waveform implies more rapid detection, analysis, and processing of the stimulus. This will presumably allow both more rapid response to the stimulus in the oddball task and in the related odd-man-out reaction time task (OMO RT, see Chapter 3), and also more accurate discrimination when the stimulus is presented only briefly, as in an IT task. If shorter ERP latencies are associated with higher test scores, the implication is that the correlation between intelligence (or at least the speed component of IQ, Gs) and IT, oddball discrimination and OMO RT, does reflect a genuine difference in speed of initial stimulus processing between people of greater and lesser intelligence.

Localization of function: lesion, PET, and fMRI studies

Much of the evidence reviewed in the previous section looked at the brain as a whole, paying little attention to the possibility that some regions of the brain may be more important than others in determining differences in intelligence. The nineteenth and early part of the twentieth centuries saw a prolonged dispute between those who argued for strict localization of function in the brain and the anti-localizers (for the history of this dispute, see Finger, 1994). It was not in fact until the beginning of the nineteenth century that the importance of the cortex in perception, action, and thought was generally recognized, but by mid-century Flourens, whose lesion studies amply confirmed this, concluded that there was no localization of function *within* the cortex. He was shortly proved wrong by the discovery of Broca's and Wernicke's areas for speech production and comprehension, and by the early twentieth century, experiments on monkeys and studies of brain-injured people had finally identified the primary visual, auditory, somaesthetic, and motor areas of the cortex. But this left the remaining 'association' areas, prefrontal, parietal, temporal, and much of occipital cortex as a last bastion for the anti-localizers. The first breach in their defences came from Jacobsen's demonstration that lesions to prefrontal cortex impaired monkeys' performance on a delayed response task, in which they saw one of two cups being baited with a peanut but had to wait for several seconds before being allowed to choose between them (Jacobsen, 1936). Since then, of course, the localizers have been in the ascendant, to the point where Duncan *et al.* (2000) could claim to have localized *g* to a small area of prefrontal cortex. There is no doubt that prefrontal cortex is implicated in performance on intelligence tests and on a variety of tests of working memory and executive function, but equally little doubt that it is not the whole story.

Lesion studies: dysexecutive syndrome

Neuropsychological studies of patients suffering from damage to different regions of the brain first confirmed Jacobsen's conclusions about the importance of prefrontal cortex for working memory (Baldo and Shimamura, 2000). But, as briefly noted in Chapter 5, such damage has been associated with a wider range of deficits, often referred to as a frontal syndrome, but sometimes characterized functionally as dysexecutive syndrome (Baddeley and Wilson, 1988). Clinical studies led Luria (1966) to conclude that frontal patients' fundamental difficulty was with the formulation of plans and programmes of action: although able to follow explicit step-by-step instructions, they were unable to internalize such instructions to guide a sequence of actions by themselves; they had difficulty ignoring distractions, but equal difficulty in attending to new relevant information which might demand a change of tactics. Experimental research has confirmed and extended many of Luria's clinical insights (Gazzaley and D'Esposito, 2007). In addition to their serious difficulties with problems such as the Tower of Hanoi or the closely related Tower of London tasks (Owen *et al.*, 1990; Shallice, 1988), frontal patients often ignore relevant feedback and are unable to inhibit a prepotent response, as in the Stroop test (Vendrell, 1995). Shallice (2002) located his supervisory attentional system in prefrontal cortex, one of whose functions was to override inappropriate habitual responses when a novel problem presents itself. A nice illustration of the failure of this system is provided by della Malva *et al.* (1993), who tested frontal patients on a modified version of the Wechsler picture arrangement test, where you must arrange a series of pictures in the correct order to tell a story. In one condition, two pictures seemed to go together, but in fact belonged to different parts of the story. Frontal patients were unable to ignore the strong associations between such pictures, and invariably placed them next to one another, thus making no sense of the story.

Watch Left

```
2           6
X           J
W           1
3           D
      +
4           7
M           Q
5           C
P           9
```

Figure 6.2 The task used by Duncan *et al.* (1996) to study goal neglect in frontal patients. The initial instruction, in the example illustrated, is to report any letter that appears on the left; but after four trials, the + sign signals that from this point on they must report letters on the right. See text for further details.

Such patients fail to initiate solutions to novel problems, but once they have eventually solved the problem, persevere with responses that are no longer appropriate in the light of changing circumstances. The Wisconsin Card Sorting Test (WCST) has provided the most popular test of this. Frontal patients, having learned with difficulty the initial categorization, fail to shift to a new rule when informed that their original categorization is no longer correct (Milner, 1963).

A striking example of such perseveration and neglect of instructions was provided by Duncan *et al.* (1996). The task they used is illustrated in Figure 6.2. A computer screen displayed, one at a time, pairs of digits and letters, side by side. The participants' task was to watch out for letters, ignoring all digits, and to repeat out loud each letter as it appeared. However, they were only to watch out for letters on one side of the screen (in Figure 6.2, the initial instruction is to watch left). Finally, they were told that towards the end of each trial, a + or – sign would appear in the centre of the screen: a + sign meant watch right for the rest of the trial (whether or not they had been watching right until then); a – sign meant that they were to watch left. The initial part of each trial was, unsurprisingly, easy enough that virtually no one made errors. But frontal patients were much more likely than controls, or patients with posterior brain damage, to fail to shift sides on those trials when a + or – signalled a change from left to right, or from right to left.

But what, you might ask, is this to do with IQ? I have already shown that not all 'executive' tasks are strongly associated with traditional measures of intelligence (Chapter 5). Although failure to follow instructions would, no doubt, impair anyone's performance on an IQ test, it is hard to believe that such failure is a *major* cause of low test scores. As a matter of fact, however, Duncan *et al.* found that people with below average scores on a test of Gf were much more likely than those of above average IQ to make the same errors as their frontal patients. But there is still a problem with the role of prefrontal cortex in IQ. Hebb and Penfield (1940) reported the case of a patient with intractable epilepsy who received complete bilateral ablation of prefrontal cortex. His pre-operative IQ had been no more than 80. After the operation his IQ was normal. So, far from depressing his score, the removal of prefrontal cortex had enhanced it (this is almost certainly because the deleterious effects of the epileptic focus spread over a much wider area). Reviewing the evidence on the functions of the frontal lobes a quarter of a century later, Teuber (1964) concluded that they had nothing to do with the intelligence measured by IQ tests. The consensus view was that: 'Standard intelligence tests are especially *unsuitable* for revealing frontal impairments. The paradox has been accepted that frontal patients have impaired "planning", "problem-solving", etc., but preserved "intelligence"' (Duncan *et al.*, 1995, p. 262).

As noted briefly in Chapter 5, some cognitive neuropsychologists would go further, arguing that their executive tests provide a better measure of 'intelligence' than traditional IQ tests. It is true that many 'frontal' tasks correlate only very modestly with standard intelligence tests, but the paradox should never have been accepted quite so uncritically, since Hebb himself saw that frontal patients' test scores depended on the nature of the IQ test they were given: they might obtain entirely normal scores on tests such as the Stanford-Binet, but were severely impaired on non-verbal tests (Hebb, 1949). This is exactly what Duncan and his colleagues have confirmed. In one of their studies, three frontal patients obtained scores on the WAIS ranging from 126 to 130, but at the same time their scores on the Cattell Culture Fair test were 108, 97, and 88 (Duncan *et al.*, 1995). Other studies have also found that frontal damage impairs performance on tests of Gf (Waltz *et al.*, 1999). However, the story is not so simple: there are studies of people with extensive damage to prefrontal cortex, who are severely impaired on various 'frontal' tests, but still obtain high scores on Raven's Matrices (e.g. Brazelli *et al.*, 1994). Part of the paradox has not yet been resolved.

Functional imaging

The interpretation of studies of patients who have suffered brain damage is fraught with difficulties: it is virtually impossible to bring together any large group with identical damage; few lesions are precisely limited in scope; if the injury occurred some time earlier, the patient may have learned to compensate in various ways. Since 1990, studies of the role of different brain structures have employed healthy, intact volunteers and relied on the techniques of PET and fMRI (see Box 6.2) to ascertain which regions of the brain are implicated in cognitive functions. Performance on a wide variety of tests of executive function and intelligence has been shown to be associated with an increase in activation of prefrontal cortex (Gazzaley and D'Esposito, 2007; Kane, 2005). The standard procedure of such studies is to compare the activity in various regions of the brain when participants are engaged in some cognitive activity, with that elicited by some 'control' condition. Subtraction of the latter from the former is assumed to reveal those regions specifically engaged by the cognitive demands of the experimental task. As Deary notes: 'There must be sensible scepticism about what that difference represents. For example, subjects might be in a different mood state during the activation task and the different scan pattern might partly reflect that' (Deary, 2000, p. 290). A sensible warning, but one not always heeded.

Prefrontal cortex and executive function

By and large, the results of PET and functional imaging studies have complemented the data obtained from patients with brain lesions. Where performance on a task is disrupted in patients with damage to prefrontal cortex (henceforth PFC), healthy volunteers tested on that task will show an increase in activation of PFC. This applies to the Stroop test (Bench *et al.*, 1993; Collette *et al.*, 2005); Tower of London, where activation levels increase as the problem is made harder (Newman *et al.*, 2003; Wagner *et al.*, 2006); WCST (Buchsbaum *et al.*, 2005); and verbal fluency (Baldo and Shimamura (1998). Performance on several working memory tasks is also associated with increasing PFC activation (see Wager and Smith, 2003, for a meta-analysis). Several studies (Braver *et al.*, 1997; Cohen *et al.*, 1993;

A B C **A** D E F G *F* *E* H I J J **I** G
correct   lure lure   correct

Figure 6.3 The n-back task. A series of letters is presented, one at a time, and your task is to report whenever the current letter is the same as the one that occurred n (here three) trials back. The task is made more difficult by presenting occasional 'lure' trials, when the current letter is the same as that which occurred either two or four trials back.

Gray *et al.*, 2003) used the n-back task illustrated in Figure 6.3: participants listen to a series of digits, letters, or even words, and have to report when a new item is the same as one that had been presented n items earlier: this is of course an example of 'updating' as described by Friedman *et al.* (2006; see Chapter 5). Where n = 1, the task is the trivially easy one of detecting an immediate repetition, but if n = 3, you have to keep a running track of the three most recent items, updating it as each new item appears. PFC activation increases during performance on such tasks, and here, too, the level of activation increases as the memory load increases, from two-back to four-back, or the task is made harder by including 'lure' trials, where the newly presented stimulus matches the one that occurred n + 1 or n − 1, rather than n, trials ago (see Figure 6.3).

In many of these studies, it has been one particular region of PFC that has shown increased activation—dorsolateral PFC on the lateral surface above and behind orbito-frontal PFC. There can be little doubt that the description of executive function tasks as frontal tasks contains an important element of truth. As I shall argue below, this does not mean that all these tasks make the same cognitive demands, let alone that they depend solely on PFC.

Prefrontal cortex and intelligence

Duncan *et al.* (2000) reported that when people were given three different *g*-loaded tasks, one verbal, one numerical, and one figural, the activation common to all three was an area of dorsolateral PFC. Their control condition simply required participants to match a target figure or word. In related studies, Esposito *et al.* (1999) and Prabhakaran *et al.* (1997) compared performance on Raven's Matrices and on control problems which simply required participants to select from several alternatives the one that matched one or all figures in the matrix. In the Esposito study, Raven's items produced bilateral activation of dorsolateral PFC. As briefly described in Chapter 4, Prabhakaran *et al.* compared performance on two types of Raven's items, figural/spatial and analytic. The former problems are solved by what Carpenter *et al.* (1990) called a 'pairwise progression' rule; while 'analytic' items required the 'distribution of two' rule of Carpenter *et al.* (Chapter 4). Both figural and analytic items activated dorsolateral PFC, the latter bilaterally, with additional recruitment of neighbouring areas. Similarly, Lee *et al.* (2006) found that harder Raven's items (Carpenter *et al.* pairwise progression, add/subtract, and distribution of three rules) resulted in a greater increase in activation of dorsolateral PFC than did very easy items (constant in a row). Whether these differences reflect a difference in the nature of the rules required for the solution of these items, or simply a difference in problem difficulty is uncertain.

Finally, Bishop *et al.* (2008) also compared different groups' performance on demanding and easier versions of Gf problems, here derived from Cattell's Culture Fair tests. They observed significant increases in activation of dorsolateral PFC during performance on the more demanding tasks, whether they were verbal or spatial. The verbal tests were associated with left hemisphere, and the spatial tests with bilateral, activation. The difference between the groups was in whether they had zero, one, or two copies of the val allele of the COMT gene. This difference was associated with different levels of activation in dorsolateral PFC (and other critical cortical regions, see below), and also with performance on the demanding version of the Cattell tests. This looks like impressive evidence of association between a single gene and test performance, as well as a neurobiological basis for the association. One puzzling and seriously embarrassing finding should be noted, however: the difference in performance on the demanding Cattell tests was observed *only* when the participants were given the tests while actually in the scanner. When they were given the tests outside the scanner, the difference disappeared.

This has been a rapid and necessarily cursory review of a large and rapidly expanding literature. But it will, I hope, have been enough to establish that there is substantial overlap between the areas of the brain apparently subserving performance on tests of intelligence and tests of executive function. But many questions remain. Is dorsolateral PFC the only area implicated in these tasks? Is it, as once suggested by Duncan *et al.* (2000), the seat of *g*? Is it possible to fractionate the different functions of prefrontal cortex? And above all, why are the correlations between many executive tests and IQ or Gf so often so low?

Prefrontal and parietal cortex

The answer to the first question is clear. Performance on a variety of tests of intelligence and executive function activates not only PFC, but also parietal cortex and the anterior cingulate (which has connections to both PFC and parietal cortex), and some other posterior areas. Many of the studies cited in the preceding section (for example, Bishop *et al.*, 2008; Lee *et al.*, 2006) recorded increases in activation of parietal cortex and anterior cingulate as well as of PFC when participants were engaged in cognitive activity. Reviewing a large number of imaging studies, Jung and Haier reported: 'A striking consensus suggesting that variations in a distributed network predict individual differences found on intelligence and reasoning tasks. We describe this network as the *Parieto-Frontal Integration Theory*' (Jung and Haier, 2007, p. 135).

Neuropsychological studies of patients with damage to parietal cortex have established that such damage results in a variety of impairments (McCarthy and Warrington, 1990). Parietal patients show deficits in spatial attention, including 'unilateral neglect', that is to say, a failure to pay attention to stimuli in, say, their left visual field. They are poor at recognizing faces. And, coming closer to our present concerns, they also show deficits in immediate memory span. Lesions to left posterior parietal cortex result in a severely reduced digit span, while lesions to the corresponding region of right parietal cortex disrupt performance on tests of spatial span. Within the context of the Baddeley-Hitch model of working memory (Chapter 5), left posterior parietal cortex can be seen as the location of the phonological loop, while right parietal cortex is the location of the visuo-spatial sketchpad. Functional imaging studies have confirmed this conclusion (Henson, 2001; Smith *et al.*, 1996). In the latter study, participants were required to study an array of four letters displayed in four particular locations in a larger grid. When later required to report the identity of the four letters, participants showed an increase in activity of left parietal cortex, while the requirement to report the locations of the letters in the grid resulted in an increase in right parietal activity. In a further experiment, participants were presented with an n-back task, where they were required to report whenever the currently displayed letter matched the one that had occurred n back in the sequence. This also resulted in activation of left parietal cortex—but now also of dorsolateral PFC.

This observation implies, what is hardly surprising, that frontal and parietal cortex play different roles in cognitive performance: the frontal-parietal network is not just a single undifferentiated system. But is there any simple way to describe their different functions? The most widely accepted idea is that PFC performs the functions associated with Baddeley's central executive or Shallice's supervisory attentional system, while parietal cortex (and perhaps other posterior regions) perform, among other things, the more domain-specific tasks, short-term storage of verbal or spatial information associated with the phonological loop and visuo-spatial sketchpad (D'Esposito *et al.*, 2006; Henson, 2001; Wager and Smith, 2003). Prabhakaran and Rypma (2007) have gone further, suggesting that parietal cortex alone is engaged in tasks where executive or supervisory requirements are of lesser importance. Their idea is reminiscent of the argument advanced by Haier to explain the negative relationship between regional cerebral blood flow and measured intelligence when people are trying to solve Raven's Matrices or other cognitive tasks: more intelligent people use well-rehearsed and more automatic routines to solve such problems, while the less intelligent have to discard less successful solutions and discover new ways of thinking.

That PFC is not the only region of the brain implicated in performance on cognitive tasks should not come as a surprise. Other studies reviewed earlier in this chapter have established that differences in intelligence are associated with differences in grey matter in several different regions of the brain, including temporal and parts of occipital cortex, as well as parietal and frontal cortex. Intelligence (or at least different aspects of intelligence) is distributed over much of the cortex rather than being strictly localized to a single area.

Fractionation of frontal functions

Lesion and imaging studies have complemented behavioural experiments, for example by confirming the importance both of the overlap and of the distinction between working memory and simple span tasks. Although it is no doubt a crude oversimplification to locate the central executive in prefrontal cortex, and modality-specific, short-term storage systems in parietal cortex, such localization, even if oversimplified, does reinforce the importance of the distinction between these different systems.

The terms frontal or dysexecutive syndrome have become popular for the good reason that frontal patients are impaired on a variety of loosely connected cognitive tasks, but as already noted, the operative word here is 'loosely'. Shallice and Burgess (1996) concluded that 'prefrontal cortex contains a set of subsystems which implement different processes' (p. 140). It is also worth adding that it comprises something like 30% of total cortex in humans (a much greater percentage than in other primates), and that it can be differentiated into a number of different areas, with different connections with other brain structures. Studies with non-human primates, for example, have established a clear dissociation between the effects of dorsolateral and orbitofrontal lesions (Dias *et al.*, 1996). Just because different cognitive tasks seem to be dependent on the integrity of PFC does not mean that they all engage the same systems: 'Frontal lobe involvement does not by itself indicate why, or how, measures of performance on such a wide variety of seemingly different cognitive tasks tend to be correlated with one another' (Salthouse *et al.*, 2003, p. 589–90). Just as it was possible to dissociate different functions of the central executive by behavioural means (Chapter 5), so it is possible to dissociate different functions of PFC. In their meta-analysis of fMRI studies of working memory, for example, Wager and Smith (2003) concluded that although task modality (verbal or spatial) did not seem to activate different regions of PFC, task demands did: tasks such as operation span, which simply required what they termed manipulation of information in working memory, activated more ventral regions, while tasks such as n-back, which required continuous updating activated more dorsal regions (in particular dorsolateral PFC).

Further research is needed to see if more precise localization within PFC will explain the distinction between those frontal tasks that do seem to go together, and those that do not. If differences in performance on tests of working memory, Gf, and Tower of Hanoi, for example, are all correlated quite strongly, is this because these tasks all activate more closely related areas of PFC than do tests that do not seem to correlate so strongly? Esposito *et al.* (1999), for example, reported that although performance on both Raven's Matrices and the WCST activated dorsolateral PFC (as well as the anterior cingulate and inferior parietal cortex), WCST also resulted in activation of ventral anterior PFC, so here is some evidence of a distinction between the two tasks.

Cognitive modules and individual differences

It is important to remember, however, that few of the studies reviewed in this section have necessarily had anything to say about the causes of *individual differences* in g, Gf, or any other component of psychometric intelligence. They have been experiments within the tradition of cognitive neuroscience, whose goal has been to identify and if possible localize particular cognitive modules. They have not studied individual differences. Accept, for sake of argument, that the central executive is located in the prefrontal cortex. As Kane (2005) has noted, that does not necessarily mean that the cause of individual differences in the power or efficiency of the central executive is located in PFC. If this seems difficult to understand, consider the following analogy (Kane uses a slightly different one). If the throttle linkage of a car is damaged or malfunctioning for any reason, this will affect the car's acceleration and top speed. However, the reason why a Ferrari accelerates faster and has a higher top speed than your granny's little runabout is not really because it has a more efficient throttle linkage. It is because the Ferrari has, among other things, a more powerful and efficient engine.

What is needed to address this question are studies that look at individual differences in executive function or intelligence, and associate such differences with differences in activity in PFC, or indeed any other brain region, while people are engaged in trying to solve such problems. Not very many of the studies reviewed so far have done this. Among the exceptions are those by Haier and Neubauer and their colleagues reviewed above, which have consistently found a negative correlation between intelligence and the increase in neural activity as people tackled problems such as Raven's Matrices. This is, indeed, a finding confirmed by others (reviewed by Neubauer and Fink, 2009). For example, Newman *et al.* (2003) reported a negative correlation ($r = -0.67$) between their participants' scores on Daneman and Carpenter's reading span test and the increase in dorsolateral

PFC activation produced by tackling Tower of London tasks. Reichle *et al.* (2000) found that higher scores on the reading span test were associated with less activation of Broca's area when people were using a verbal strategy to solve the sentence verification test (see Chapter 4), while higher scores on the 3-D MRT test were associated with less activation of parietal cortex when they were using a spatial strategy to solve the problem. Consistent with these findings, two studies of age differences in performance on Raven's Matrices and working memory have shown greater recruitment of activity in PFC in older people, whose performance on these tasks was worse than that of younger participants (Esposito *et al.*, 1999; Reuter-Lorenz, 2002). Finally, in several studies, Haier and his colleagues have given participants extensive training on a computer game, which resulted in significant improvement in performance, accompanied by a decrease in brain activity as they played the game (e.g. Haier *et al.*, 1992). As noted above, frontal and parietal regions are activated when people solve analogical reasoning problems, with the increase positively correlated with problem difficulty. Wartenburger *et al.* (2009) confirmed these observations, but also reported that extensive training on such problems both improved performance and resulted in a decrease in such activation.

In contrast to these results, however, Lee *et al.* (2006) found that the increase in PFC and parietal activation when their students were tackling the more difficult Raven's items was significantly *greater* in a high IQ group than in an average IQ group. And a study by Gray *et al.* (2003) provides another example. They tested their participants on Raven's Matrices, and also took fMRI scans while they were performing an n-back task (see Figure 6.3 above; as illustrated there, it was a difficult three-back task). Gray *et al.* included 'lure' trials, where the repeated item had previously occurred not three back, but two or four items back, as well as 'non-lure' trials where the repeated item had occurred either one or six back. As one might expect, errors on lure trials were negatively correlated with Raven's scores. More importantly, however, both Raven's scores and lure trial accuracy were positively correlated ($r = 0.40$ to 0.50) with the magnitude of the increase in activity in PFC, anterior cingulated, and parietal cortex on lure trials. However, consistent with the studies of older people by Esposito *et al.* (1999) and Reuter-Lorenz (2002) described above, Waiter *et al.* (2009) failed to replicate Gray and colleagues' results in a sample of older participants, while a later study once again found a negative correlation between increase in activation during performance on an n-back task and scores on the general factor extracted from an IQ test battery (Tang *et al.*, 2010).

There is a puzzle here, with some studies showing a positive correlation between level of activity and intelligence, and others showing a negative correlation. Taken in isolation, each of these findings may make intuitive sense, but what is needed is a way of reconciling them. Neubauer and Fink (2009) suggest that the key is task difficulty; with easy or moderately difficult tasks, there is a negative correlation between ability and level of activation, since more able people are able to solve the task with fewer resources. With seriously difficult tasks, however, the correlation reverses sign, because only the more able participants are prepared to work to solve the problem: the less able simply give up or guess. This seems plausible enough, but needs a direct experimental test: so far only one study has provided such a test (Doppelmayr *et al.*, 2005), with results at least partially consistent with the idea.

Conclusion

It is surely unsurprising that IQ scores should correlate with some measures of the brain. They do. There is a modest correlation between test scores and the size of the brain (although what this really means is rather less certain), and with the amount of grey matter in many different regions of the brain. There are some correlations between test scores and brain activity, either EEG records or more specific event-related potentials (ERPs). Some of these effects have proved hard to replicate, but there are two that do seem real. Higher IQ is often associated with smaller changes in brain activity when people become engaged in various cognitive tasks. A second is that the higher a person's IQ, the shorter the latency of early components of the ERP to a briefly presented stimulus which they are required to discriminate from other stimuli.

Lesion and imaging studies imply that some areas of the brain are more important for intellectual function than others. Lesions to prefrontal cortex often result in deficits on various 'executive' tasks, including tests of working memory, and sometimes, at least, lead to low scores on tests of Gf. Imaging studies have complemented these results by showing that prefrontal cortex is activated by such tasks. But although all executive tasks seem to depend on the integrity of prefrontal cortex, they do not all correlate strongly with one another, and apart from the Tower of Hanoi and 'updating' tasks that involve working memory, few are strongly associated with difference in measured intelligence.

Imaging studies have also suggested that a frontal-parietal circuit is involved in many cognitive tasks including tests of intelligence, but different regions must surely perform different operations. In only a few cases can it be said that there is good evidence for this supposition: working memory tasks certainly activate parietal as well as prefrontal cortex, and this seems to be a consequence of the modality-specific storage demands: left parietal cortex holds verbal and right parietal cortex spatial information, while the executive demands of the task seem to be more dependent on prefrontal cortex. What is needed, however, in order to understand the neural basis of *differences* in intelligence, are more studies looking at fMRI correlates of differences in intelligence when people tackle different cognitive problems. And one job for such studies will be to explain why higher intelligence is sometimes associated with lower and sometimes with higher levels of activation.

 Summary

- There is a modest correlation between brain size and intelligence. But this does not necessarily mean that more intelligent people are born with bigger brains. Some changes in brain size occur in response to environmental stimulation.

- Some differences in event-related potentials (ERPs), notably a decrease in the latency of early components of the ERP to a stimulus that participants are required to attend to, are associated with higher intelligence.

- Lesion and imaging studies complement each other in showing that prefrontal cortex, and a circuit that includes the anterior cingulate and parietal cortex, are critically important for performance on a variety of 'executive' tasks as well as tests of intelligence.

- In spite of this common dependence on similar regions of the brain, however, different executive tasks correlate only moderately with one another, and few, apart from tests of working memory, correlate with measures of psychometric intelligence.
- An unresolved issue is whether superior intelligence is associated with an increase, or a decrease, in activation of critical brain regions when people are engaged in solving cognitive problems.

Further reading

Finger (1994) recounts the history of research into the relationship between the brain and perception, memory, and cognition, and McDaniel (2005) summarizes the evidence relating brain size to intelligence. The ever accelerating pace of neuroscientific research, taking advantage of ever newer technologies, means that any review of research on the relationship between the brain and cognition or intelligence is soon out of date. Deary (2000, Chapter 9) provides a good account of research on ERPs and intelligence, and the earlier research on functional imaging and intelligence. This last is brought further up to date by Kane (2005) and Jung and Haier (2007, see also several of the commentaries on this paper). Neubauer and Fink (2009) review the evidence bearing on the question whether superior intelligence is associated with increases or decreases in activation of brain regions clearly implicated in performance of various cognitive tasks.

7 Theories of *g*

Introduction

The research reviewed in the last four chapters has (I hope) uncovered a number of important findings about the determinants of performance on a variety of different kinds of IQ test. They have had more to say, however, about particular group factors or components of IQ than about the elusive *g* itself. It is time to turn to the question which many people see as the most important: what is the explanation of *g*?

Although factor analysis of any IQ test battery always reveals a significant general factor, *g*, factor analysis cannot explain *why* all IQ tests are correlated with one another. It did not have to be so: Thurstone tried to devise a set of tests that did not all correlate, but was unable to do so. Why not?

According to Spearman, the explanation was because performance on all mental tests, however diverse, depends, to a greater or lesser extent, on a single, psychological or biological process of general intelligence. Spearman's thesis has been accepted by many later theorists, but it has also been vigorously disputed. According to one version of the critic's argument, Spearman's interpretation of the general factor amounted to: 'The cardinal invalid inference that has plagued factor analysis ever since. He reified it as an "entity" and tried to give it an unambiguous causal interpretation. He called it *g* or general intelligence, and imagined that he had identified a unitary quality underlying cognitive mental activity' (Gould, 1997, p. 281). It is quite easy to find quotations that suggest that at least some psychometricians regard *g* as an 'entity'. For example: 'First discovered by Charles Spearman at the beginning of the twentieth century, *g* has now been shown to exist—alone—at the apex of a hierarchy of mental abilities . . . [It] is both a highly general mental ability and a relatively stable mental trait' (Gottfredson, 2003b, p. 349). But there is a sense in which Gould's argument is at best misleading, at worst plain false. Spearman's inference was invalid only if he believed that the existence of a general factor *necessarily* implied that there must be a single underlying process of general intelligence. That is false. A more sensible reconstruction of Spearman's argument is simply that he was advancing a possible explanation of the general factor. And that explanation is perfectly plausible—for it is not absurd to suppose that the reason why scores on one test correlate with scores on another (or all others) is because both tests (or all tests) tap a single, common psychological or neurobiological process or set of processes. If Spearman's explanation of *g* is plausible, but not necessarily true, then it should be possible to bring evidence to bear on it; equally there will presumably be alternative accounts of *g* which may or may not be equally plausible, but which it should also be possible to test against the evidence.

What is the relation between *g* and Gf?

It will make sense to start with this seemingly rather different question. If *g* is really nothing more than fluid intelligence or Gf, then Chapters 4 and 5 have already provided a psychological account of *g*, and the functional imaging studies reviewed in Chapter 6 have located it in a frontal-parietal circuit. So what is the relationship between *g* and Gf? For some theorists, of course, the question does not arise: the original Horn and Cattell (1966) model had no place for *g*, while the Vernon (1950) model revised by Johnson and Bouchard (2005) has no place for Gf.

Other theorists have expressed varying views. It is not in dispute that within the CHC model, Gf is more closely related to *g* than is any other second-stratum factor, and Gustafsson (1988) among others has argued that this closeness is tantamount to identity. His view has not, however, commanded universal assent. Carroll (2003), although acknowledging that it may sometimes be difficult to distinguish between the two constructs, reported confirmatory factor analyses of two large data sets, in both of which there was clear evidence of both *g* and a second-stratum Gf factor.

In two important studies, which I discuss below, Johnson *et al.* (2004, 2008) calculated the correlations between the *g* factors extracted from a total of nine different test batteries. Their main finding was that the general factor from one test battery was essentially the same as that from another. There was, however, one exception. In their second study, one of the five batteries was simply the Cattell Culture Fair tests—a rather restricted set of tests of Gf. The correlations between the general factor of the Cattell tests and the general factors extracted from the other four test batteries were 0.77, 0.79, 0.88, and 0.96—high, but, except for the last, hardly indicative of identity. Assuming Cattell's tests to be good measures of Gf, then Gf is not *identical* to the *g* extracted from other, more diverse test batteries.

Blair (2006) has also insisted that the two constructs are not the same, and provided a number of arguments to support his position. The Flynn effect provides the most convincing evidence. As noted in Chapter 1, the largest gains in test scores during the course of the twentieth century were observed on Raven's Matrices—a paradigm measure of Gf. Wicherts *et al.* (2004), however, analysed the gains observed on a variety of other test batteries, including Dutch versions of the WAIS and DAT, a Dutch children's test battery and an Estonian National Intelligence Test, and found that they were never gains on the general factors extracted from those batteries. Rushton (1999) also argued that IQ gains over time were not gains in *g*. To establish this, he showed that there was a negative correlation between the magnitude of IQ gains on the various tests in the WAIS and those tests' loadings on the general factor derived from factor analysis of the WAIS. The tests with the highest loadings on the general factor of the WAIS are vocabulary and information, but, as Figure 1.1 showed (p. 28), scores on these two tests have shown the smallest increase over time. In response, Flynn (2000) demonstrated that there was a substantial *positive* correlation between the magnitude of Wechsler test gains and those tests' correlations with performance on Raven's Matrices. The Gf measured by Raven's Matrices is clearly not the same as the general factor extracted from factor analysis of the Wechsler tests.

A final, rather different, argument for distinguishing between the two constructs (which may not persuade everyone) is that the role of the general factor extracted from any comprehensive test battery is to explain why every test in the battery correlates with every other test, and to provide the best possible summary of each participant's score on the test battery. The reason for postulating a factor of Gf is to talk about individual differences in people's ability to solve particular kinds of reasoning problems.

The invariance of *g*

What would count as evidence in favour of Spearman's argument that *g* measures a process of general intelligence that enters into performance on any and every cognitive test? A necessary first condition is surely that the general factor extracted by factor analysis of one test battery should be the same as that extracted from a quite different test battery. Spearman had a rather low opinion of most IQ test batteries, which he thought were little better than a hodgepodge of arbitrarily and idiosyncratically chosen tests. But, he argued, this did not matter, since their very diversity meant that the various specific abilities each test measured cancelled each other out, leaving the general factor, *g*, to shine forth as the true measure of general intelligence. His principle of 'the indifference of the indicator' implied that the precise content of a set of tests was wholly unimportant: all that mattered was their *g*-loadings. Jensen (1998) has followed Spearman, insisting that the general factor extracted from one large and diverse test battery will always turn out, within the limits of measurement error, to be the same as that extracted from another.

Thurstone took strong issue with this particular argument, insisting that *g* could not possibly have any psychological validity, since the general factor extracted from one test battery was not necessarily the same as the general factor extracted from another (Thurstone, 1947):

> A general factor can always be found routinely for any set of positively correlated tests, and it means nothing more or less than the average of all the abilities called for by the battery as a whole. Consequently, it varies from one battery to another and has no fundamental psychological significance...As psychologists we cannot be interested in a general factor which is only the average of any random collection of tests.
>
> (Thurstone, 1940, p. 208)

In principle at least (although perhaps only in principle) Thurstone's argument is surely correct. Factor analysis of any set of intercorrelated tests will always yield a principal factor that accounts for a significant proportion of the variance in those test scores. But this general factor *might* be quite different from that extracted from a different set of tests. Thurstone's illustration of his argument is shown in Figure 7.1. The curved lines are to be seen as forming a triangle on the surface of a sphere, and the small circles are the points where various test vectors, radiating out from the unseen centre of the sphere, intersect with its surface. The twelve tests shown in the left-hand figure yield as their general factor the *g* near the bottom right-hand corner of the triangle; the twelve different tests in the right-hand figure yield a quite different general factor.

Thurstone's argument is not merely hypothetical. Recall the discussion in Chapter 2 of factor analysis of the Wechsler scales. Earlier versions of the WAIS provided a distinctly uneven sampling of the various factors that have since been identified. Most of the tests in

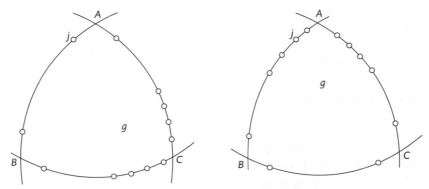

Figure 7.1 An illustration of Thurstone's argument that the identity of *g* varies with the nature of the tests in a battery. The small circles represent the points on the surface of a sphere where 12 test vectors intersect the surface. The three points A, B, and C represent, according to Thurstone, three primary mental abilities or group factors. In the left-hand figure, the majority of the 12 tests happen to load on factor C; in the right-hand figure, the majority happen to load on A.

the verbal scale were measures of Gc, but the performance scale contained a rather motley collection of tests, none of which measured Gf, only one measured Gs, and perhaps two Gv. If you constructed a new test battery which, in addition to the old WAIS tests, included several tests of abstract reasoning, such as matrices or letter or number series completion, as well as some tests of two and three-dimensional mental rotation, the centre of gravity of this new test battery, and therefore its general factor, would surely change.

Given that all IQ tests tend to correlate with one another, however, it must be the case that different test batteries will tend to yield similar, that is, correlated, general factors. The real question is: how similar? Until recently, there was surprisingly little evidence. Carroll (1993), in his survey of factor analytic studies, acknowledged that *g* factors from different data sets 'might be highly correlated…But it is unlikely that they would be perfectly correlated, because the *g* factor for a given data set is dependent on what lower-order factors or variables are loaded on it' (Carroll, 1993, p. 597). Jensen (1998) cited a study by Thorndike (1987), who measured the loadings of a number of tests on the general factors extracted from six independent test batteries. The average correlation between the *g*-loadings of a given test across all six batteries was 0.85 ('highly similar' according to Jensen, p. 87). But in fact the correlations ranged from 0.52 to 0.94: the latter figure suggests something close to identity, but at the low end of the range it is clear that the general factors of the different test batteries cannot have been the same.

Two later studies by Johnson *et al.* (2004, 2008), however, have shown that Spearman and Jensen may be right after all. In the first, they found a sample of 436 people who had completed 42 mental tests taken from three separate test batteries. No test appeared in more than one battery, but each battery included a wide range of tests measuring verbal, spatial, and reasoning abilities, as well as perceptual speed and retrieval. Factor analysis of the correlation matrix of the tests within each battery yielded, as expected, a strong general factor for each test battery. Much more important was the finding that the correlations between these three general factors were 0.99, 0.99, and 1.0. The *g* of one test battery was effectively identical to the *g* of the other two. With one exception (noted above), the results of their second study, with a quite different sample of participants and quite different test batteries, were essentially the same.

Johnson and her colleagues' results are striking and important. They are consistent with Spearman's argument that the general factor arises because all IQ tests are indeed measuring a psychological or neurobiological process or processes which can be called 'general intelligence', and they show that Thurstone rather exaggerated the extent to which the general factor of one test battery will be different from the general factor of another. With sufficiently large and varied test batteries, their general factors will be essentially the same. But the qualification is important: the different test batteries must be large, and they must sample over the range of tests that are included in any IQ test battery. At this point it is perhaps less surprising that their general factors should be very similar indeed. In the limiting case, suppose you took every test of mental ability ever invented, and divided them into two groups, the odd-numbered tests in one group, the even-numbered in the other; if you then extracted the general factor from each group of tests, it would be inconceivable that they would not be the same. And Thurstone's point still needs to be remembered: in practice, most researchers who have extolled the importance and centrality of *g* have extracted their general factors from much more limited test batteries, with little recognition of the possibility that their *g* may differ from someone else's (see Box 7.1).

BOX 7.1 Is *g* invariably invariant?

In spite of Johnson and Bouchard's important results, there is indirect evidence from a variety of other studies supporting Carroll's more sceptical attitude noted above.

Studies of the WAIS have generally yielded a small but reliable sex difference, of the order of 2–3 points in overall IQ, in favour of males (see Chapter 14). Of course, this overall difference conceals a rather wide range of differences on the various tests of the scale, some of which actually favour females. But it so happens that the tests with the greatest male advantage tend to be those with the highest loadings on the general factor extracted from the total test. The consequence is that the sex difference on this general factor is, according to Lynn (1994), even larger than that in overall IQ. Other test batteries, however, have yielded much smaller overall differences in favour of males, and on others females come out ahead. A study of the W-J III test found that there was a very small, but still significant female advantage of 1.2 points on the general factor (Keith *et al.*, 2008). Whatever else this means (I discuss this in Chapter 14), one thing is surely certain: the general factor of the WAIS is not the same as the general factor of the W-J III. On the latest standardizations of the DAT, six of the eight tests yield a female advantage—the main exception of course being the mechanical reasoning test. There is no way that factor analysis of the DAT could yield a general factor on which males outscored females by as much as they do on the WAIS. The same argument must therefore apply here too.

Is there a single process, or set of processes, underlying *g*?

If *g* really were a single psychological or biological process, it should in principle be possible to measure it by some relatively straightforward test that did *not* have all the trappings and complications of a standard IQ test. And it is not wholly unreasonable to accept

Detterman's stringent criterion that the correlation between such a test and IQ scores should be at least 0.80 (Detterman, 2002). If that is accepted, the argument is over—for the time being at least. It is always rash to predict the future, but so far no one has discovered such a measure. Right now, therefore, the conservative conclusion can only be that *g* is probably not reducible to a single process.

This argument clearly applies to the suggestion advanced by Anderson (1992, 2005) and Jensen (1998), that *g* might be reducible to 'speed of information processing'. There is no doubt that performance on tasks such as reaction time, inspection time, OMO reaction time, and the Zahlen Verbindungs test all correlate with IQ test scores, but these correlations are certainly not in the region of 0.80 or higher, and seem to be primarily a correlation with measures of Gs or perceptual speed—an important component of IQ no doubt, but certainly not *g*. The ERP data discussed in Chapter 6 implied that the physical basis of differences in Gs may be partly a matter of differences in the latency of early components of the brain's response to briefly presented stimuli. But the factorial data discussed in Chapter 3 made it clear that Gs is certainly not a simple construct, and can itself be decomposed into several component processes.

Chapters 4 and 5 documented that an efficient working memory system, that is to say, the ability to hold something in mind while operating on other information, is undoubtedly important for the solution of many cognitive problems. Performance on working memory tasks correlates significantly with scores on a variety of measures of intelligence, including tests of Gc and Gv, as well as of Gf. Because there is reasonable evidence of at least some cross-domain generality to these correlations (measures of verbal working memory do often correlate with measures of spatial ability and vice versa), it seems reasonable to suggest that at least some components of a working memory system are engaged by a wide variety of IQ tests, or, put another way, that they form part of the basis of *g*. But there is also evidence of some domain-specificity: tests of verbal working memory correlate more with tests of verbal ability than they do with tests of spatial ability. Moreover, working memory does not correlate with all components of IQ, for example, with simple measures of Gs.

One relatively recent discovery (see Chapter 5) is that performance on Raven's Matrices, a standard measure of Gf, correlates at least as strongly with one particular associative learning task as it does with tests of working memory (Kaufman *et al.*, 2009; Williams and Pearlberg, 2006). Perhaps even more important, there is reason to believe that associative learning, working memory, and speed make relatively independent contributions to Raven's performance. Between them therefore, they may explain a substantial proportion of the variance in test performance. If such findings could be shown to generalize to other components of IQ, Gc, and Gv, it would become more plausible to argue that even if there is no *single* psychological basis for *g*, there may be a *set* of processes that together explain *g*.

Has neuroscience found the physical basis of *g*? Probably not yet. For a start, although the imaging studies reviewed in the final section of Chapter 6 may well have succeeded in identifying regions of the brain implicated in performance on a variety of intelligence tests and other cognitive tasks, relatively few looked at individual differences in the ways in which people performed. Moreover, the large majority of the studies discussed in that chapter gave participants no more than a single IQ test—most commonly Raven's Matrices or other tests of Gf; one exception is the study by Tang *et al.* (2010) which did correlate changes in activation of a frontal-parietal circuit with the general factor from an IQ test battery. No one has pursued the strategy employed by Duncan *et al.* (2000), who gave their participants verbal, figural, and spatial tests, specifically designed to vary in their *g*-loading, and tried to identify regions of increased activation *common* to all three kinds of *g*-loaded test. In the absence of such an approach, most studies can claim only to have discovered something about the nature of Gf. That is undoubtedly important, but it is not the same as discovering something about *g*, if *g* is defined as that which is common to *all* cognitive tests.

There is no doubt that working memory, speed, and probably some aspects of associative learning all contribute to performance on many IQ tests, and may therefore be part of the basis of *g*; without wishing to dispute that conclusion, however, it may be time to move on, and consider other ways of explaining *g*.

General intelligence or general stupidity? Spearman's law of diminishing returns

Spearman (1927) compared the performance of 78 'normal' and 22 'defective' children on a battery of 12 cognitive tests. The average intercorrelation between the 12 tests was 0.47 for former group and 0.78 for the latter. Since the proportion of the variance in any set of test scores accounted for by the first principal component, that is, the magnitude of the general factor, is a reflection of the average intercorrelation between the tests, the implication was that *g* was more important in the retarded than in the normal sample. He termed this discovery a law of diminishing returns: the higher the level of *g*, the less important *g* became. Today it is usually known as the differentiation hypothesis: at higher levels of *g*, abilities become more differentiated.

Detterman and Daniel (1989), using the standardization sample of the WAIS-R, provided good evidence that Spearman was right. They divided the sample into five different bands, with IQs (based on scores on the vocabulary test) of <78, 78–92, 93–107, 108–122 and >122. They then calculated the average intercorrelation between the remaining ten tests for each IQ band. Their results, seen in Figure 7.2, showed a steady and substantial decline in the average intercorrelation as you go from low to high IQ. Lynn (1992) confirmed these

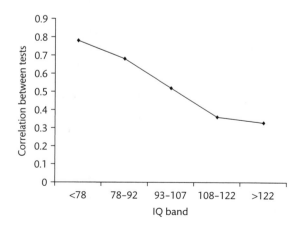

Figure 7.2 The average correlation between the remaining ten tests of the WAIS-R in different groups of the standardization sample defined by their score on the vocabulary test (from Detterman and Daniel, 1989).

findings with the Scottish standardization sample of the WISC-R, and similar results have been found with other test batteries (e.g. Legree *et al.*, 1996; Reynolds and Keith, 2007).

One problem with this type of analysis is that different IQ bands may not have equal variance in test scores, and this may contribute to the differences in their intercorrelations (Jensen, 1998). An alternative way of testing Spearman's hypothesis is to take a high IQ and low IQ sub-group from the standardization sample of an IQ test, but to select the people to be included in each sub-group in such a way as to ensure that the two have equal variances. Employing this type of design with the standardization sample of the WJ-R test, Brand *et al.* (2003) formed a high IQ (mean = 115) and low IQ (mean = 85) group, and found that the first principal component accounted for only 29% of the variance in test scores in the high IQ group, but for 52% of the variance in the low IQ group.

The evidence points fairly convincingly to the conclusion that *g* is more important at lower levels of IQ: the overall positive manifold arises largely because people who perform badly on one IQ test tend to perform badly on others, rather than because people who do well on one do well on others. There is no general intelligence, only general lack of intelligence. One practical implication, of course, is that attempts to understand the nature of *g* are less likely to be successful if they use university students in their experiments. A population of relatively high IQ will not be able to tell one much about general lack of intelligence.

There is also, however, a theoretically more interesting implication of these findings. An increasingly influential suggestion is that a low IQ might be a consequence of the accumulation of an above average number of mildly deleterious mutations (see Chapter 11). The effect of such mutations, it has been argued, might be to impair the 'efficiency' of the system, whatever that might mean. Certainly there is evidence that IQ predicts general health and longevity (Deary and Der, 2005; see Chapter 8). Might it be the case that mildly deleterious mutations could impair the functioning of the central nervous system in such a way as to impair performance on any and every test of cognitive ability? Here would seem to be a hypothesis that is consistent with the possibility that the general factor of intelligence (or rather lack of intelligence) may be due to some very general differences in the efficiency of the brain as an information processing device.

Note, however, that this hypothesis does not require every such mutation to have the same deleterious effect on the functioning of the brain, only that the end result, as far as IQ is concerned, should be the same. Serious learning disability can be the same end product of a large variety of genetic differences (Chapter 11). There are obviously countless different ways in which any complex system can go wrong, and the brain is nothing if not a complex system. One mutated gene may affect the functioning of the brain only indirectly via its effects on another organ: one example of this is phenylketonuria or PKU, a condition caused by two copies of the mutated PAH gene, and which untreated leads to moderately serious learning disability (an average IQ of about 50, see Chapter 11). For present purposes, the important point is that the initial effect of PKU is on the functioning of the liver. Another may have a direct effect on dendritic arborization, yet another on the development of prefrontal cortex. But equally, the effects of others may be mediated via the environment, by increasing susceptibility to pathogens or other environmental insult. In other words, there may be no single process underlying general intelligence, or lack thereof. On the contrary, it seems much more likely that there are many different routes from deleterious mutation to low IQ.

Alternative theories of *g*

Regardless of whether *g* should be conceptualized as general intelligence or general stupidity, it does not necessarily follow that there is any set of processes engaged by all IQ tests. Several other explanations of the positive manifold are possible and need to be considered.

Overlap of multiple processes

The fact that several tests all correlate with one another does *not* necessarily imply that they are all measuring the same process, or even the same set of processes. That strong inference, which seems to have been accepted without question by many psychometricians, can in fact be questioned on a number of different grounds. I start with one. Three tests, A, B, and C may all correlate with one another without there being any process common to all three: A and B may correlate because both measure one common process, X; B and C may correlate because both measure a quite different common process, Y; while A and C correlate because they both measure yet another process, Z (see Ceci, 1996, for a development of this argument). More realistically, if each test in an IQ test battery engages a sub-set of a very large number of elementary processes or operations, there is likely to be some overlap between the processes tapped by one test and those tapped by another.

The idea was first put forward by Thomson in Great Britain (1916, 1939) and by Thorndike (1925) and Hull (1928) in the USA. What they all had in mind was a classic associationist (nowadays it would be called connectionist) theory, which talked of bonds or connections between elementary or neural elements, or the like. Assume, for the sake of argument, a mind consisting of 1,000 such elements. If two tasks each engage 500 of these elements, the chances are that 250 of them will be common to both tasks. But if half the elements operating in task 1 are the same as half the elements operating in task 2, the correlation between performance on the two tasks will be 0.5. In general, if P_1 and P_2 are the proportion of the total set of elements sampled by tasks 1 and 2, the correlation between performance on the two tasks will be $\sqrt{P_1 \times P_2}$. Tests that load strongly on *g*, on this account, are simply tests that sample a high proportion of the available elements, but it does not follow that any one set of elements is common to all tests that show positive correlations.

Bartholomew *et al.* (2009) have resurrected Thomson's theory, and concluded that there is no statistical way of choosing between Spearman's and Thomson's models—both provide equally viable accounts of the positive manifold. A different way of accounting for *g* without appealing to any common processes has been proposed by van der Maas and his colleagues (see Box 7.2).

BOX 7.2 Mutualism

Van der Maas *et al.* (2006) have offered a rather different account of the positive manifold, which again makes no appeal to any process or processes common to all tests. They start from the position that intelligent behaviour depends on a large number of different processes or cognitive operations that are used to solve items in an IQ test battery. Like Thurstone, then, they believe that *g* is a second-order

(continued...)

factor needed to explain the observed correlation between these fundamental mental abilities. Although the resources available for each of these processes are assumed to vary, there is no correlation between the resources available for solving one kind of problem and those available for another. That is to say, while people may differ in the average amount of resources they have, these differences will not result in uniformly good or uniformly poor performance across a variety of different tests. How then does the positive manifold arise? The answer is 'mutualism': 'the assumption that these cognitive processes have mutual beneficial or facilitating relations. Each process supports the development of other processes' (van der Maas *et al.*, 2006, p. 845). Thus, although the different processes start off wholly uncorrelated with one another, during the course of development, any one particularly efficient process will benefit others, and the different processes will end up being correlated with one another. As van der Maas *et al.* point out, one person's high IQ may result from an efficient memory system, another's from good spatial abilities, and another's from a uniformly reasonable, but not outstanding, set of different abilities.

This is undoubtedly ingenious, and will surely explain the positive manifold. But there may be a problem. Other things equal, the theory would seem to predict that *g* will be relatively unimportant in very young children: different skills start off uncorrelated with one another, and it is only in the course of development that they start to be correlated. The theory does not, of course, specify the age at which this transition from uncorrelated to correlated abilities will occur, and this could certainly make it difficult to provide a definitive test. But there is at least some evidence that scores on different IQ tests are *more* highly correlated in young children; and that these correlations become weaker as children grow up, before eventually becoming stronger again in old age (e.g. Li *et al.*, 2004; see Chapter 8).

There is no need to resort to quite such an elementary and structureless theory of the mind as Thomson did. Thurstone relied on what amounts to the same argument to explain why two tests, that supposedly measured different primary mental abilities, correlated with one another. His argument was quite simple: if a test of reasoning correlates with a spatial test, this could be either because part of the reasoning test incorporates spatial content, or because part of the spatial test requires non-spatial reasoning. It may never be possible to devise factorially pure mental tests, that is, tests that tap only a single primary mental ability.

Thomson's and Thurstone's versions of this explanation of *g* may be regarded as two ends of a continuum, Thomson appealing to a very large number of elementary units sampled by different tests, Thurstone to a much smaller number of very much higher-level abilities. Modern cognitive psychology would probably encourage a view somewhere between the two. Cognitive psychologists postulate a variety of different processes or operations involved in the performance of cognitive tasks. At the perceptual level, these would include: sensory analysis, transformation of input, formation of representations, listing of attributes. Beyond this initial perceptual level, they will talk of the focusing or shifting of attention; the input must then be held in some sort of store—iconic memory, working memory, etc. before being elaborated on, and combined with other information to solve a problem, or transferred to longer-term memory from which it may be retrieved at a later date. Executive processes will determine the sequence of operations to be performed, choose between different strategies, or decide to shift from one strategy to another, and so on. Some or all of these processes are likely to be engaged by different questions in IQ tests. The positive manifold might then arise because performance on different IQ tests depends on overlapping sub-sets of these processes. Some of the processes are, no doubt,

Table 7.1 The general factor explained by the overlap between the hypothetical processes engaged by different tests, rather than by any process(es) common to all tests. A + sign indicates that the test engages this particular process. See text for further details.

	Hypothetical processes								
Tests	1	2	3	4	5	6	7	8	9
Gc									
1	+	+	+	+					
2		+	+	+	+				
Gf									
1	+			+	+	+		+	+
2	+		+		+	+	+		+
Gv									
1		+				+	+	+	
2		+					+	+	+

more important than others, in the sense of entering into more tests than others, but there might be no single process, which we could label 'general intelligence', entering into all.

The idea is illustrated in Table 7.1, which shows how it is possible to simulate the important features of the interrelationships between different IQ tests. The table shows six tests, divided into three groups, labelled, Gc, Gf, and Gv. It also postulates nine different hypothetical processes tapped by the six tests. The two tests within each pair share three processes in common with one another, but fewer processes in common with the other pairs of tests. Thus, the two tests of Gf each share two processes in common with each of the tests of Gc and Gv, but the two Gc tests share only one process in common with the two Gv tests. This pattern of shared processes would be sufficient to account for the pattern of intercorrelations actually observed between real tests of Gf, Gc, and Gv. Every test correlates with every other test, but the three pairs of tests form three clusters of high correlations, separated by lower correlations between pairs. The correlation between tests of Gc and Gv is only moderate, and both correlate more strongly with tests of Gf than they do with one another. But notice that no process enters into performance on more than four of the six tests: in other words, there is no single process underlying performance on all.

The hypothesis that the general factor arises as a consequence of this overlap in the multiple processes engaged by different IQ tests sits quite comfortably with many of the findings discussed in previous chapters. The main group factors or components of IQ: Gf, Gc, Gv, Gr, and Gs, are best regarded as clusters of related abilities, dependent on a number of different cognitive operations, some of which overlap with the abilities called for by other components (Chapters 3, 4, and 5).

Differences in crystallized or verbal ability, for example, are measured by vocabulary size or fund of general knowledge (hardly exactly the same thing), and are associated with differences in both working memory and speed of lexical access. But the correlation between vocabulary and speed of lexical access is no more than modest (e.g. one increases, and the other decreases, with age). Since learning the meaning of a new word often requires working it out from the context in which the word appears, the measure of someone's vocabulary will reflect their skill at inferential reasoning, which will explain why measures of Gc and Gf correlate with one another. Measures of specific verbal reasoning correlate both with other measures of Gc and with measures of Gf, depending on the nature of the words presented in the analogy (Lohman, 2000). Verbal fluency is a measure both of vocabulary size and speed of lexical access, and also of the executive processes measured by tests of Gf.

Factor analysis revealed that Gv or spatial ability can be decomposed into a number of different, although of course correlated, abilities. Many years ago, Zimmerman (1954) showed that performance on a particular test, the form board, would correlate with Gs, Gv, or Gf depending on its level of difficulty: simple problems correlated with Gs, the most difficult ones with Gf. There is a comparable difference between simple and difficult mental rotation tasks (Lohman, 1986; Mumaw *et al.*, 1984).

Reasoning ability itself is hardly a unitary skill. Factor analysis of Raven's Matrices (RPM) reveals more than one factor, with males showing a small advantage on items loading onto one of these factors but not others. One possible interpretation of that particular finding is that the solution of some Raven's items depends on spatial ability or Gv. The solution of items in both RPM and RAPM requires the use of a number of different rules (Carpenter *et al.*, 1990), which almost certainly depend on different psychological operations: the solution of some items, but not others, is unaffected by instructions to describe how you are trying to solve the item (DeShon *et al.*, 1995), while the occasionally observed male superiority on RAPM may be confined to, or at least more marked on, only certain items. As is suggested by the strong correlation between performance on RAPM and the Tower of Hanoi problem, the solution of difficult items in RAPM requires forward planning, holding part solutions in working memory, combining them with other part solutions, and backtracking if one part solution is incompatible with another. Finally, performance on Ravens' Matrices appears to be *independently* predicted by performance on tests of working memory, some associative learning tasks, and measures of processing speed (Williams and Pearlberg, 2006). The implication must be that multiple cognitive processes are engaged.

Even Gs, or speed of processing, can be decomposed into a number of subsidiary factors, which are measured by rather different speeded tasks. And some of these tasks almost certainly measure other factors as well. For example, the reason why the Zahlen Verbindungs Test correlates more strongly with measures of Gf than do IT or RT tests, is probably because it also depends on working memory and planning ahead. Equally, some of the speeded tests that appear in IQ test batteries, such as the Wechsler digit symbol test, almost certainly engage other processes beyond mere speed; if you can even partially remember which symbol goes with which digit, you will not have to refer back to the key each time you enter a symbol beneath a particular digit.

Detterman (2002) has provided further evidence that *g* arises from the overlap between the cognitive operations required to solve different kinds of items in IQ tests. Noting that the correlation between IQ scores and any single elementary cognitive task, such as RT or immediate memory, rarely exceeds 0.30, he also showed that the multiple correlation between scores on a battery of a dozen such tasks and IQ may be as high as 0.70 or 0.80. Assume for the sake of argument (it is obviously a serious oversimplification) that each elementary task measures a single cognitive operation, this shows that many different cognitive operations are engaged by the full range of IQ tests.

Strategies

Different people can approach and solve the same problem in quite different ways, and these differences may contribute to the appearance of the positive manifold. For example, some people use a propositional code to solve not only verbal reasoning problems, but also problems that the test constructor has designated as spatial, while others may use a spatial strategy to solve ostensibly verbal problems. To the extent that this is true, the implication would be that there may not actually be any single process, or set of processes, underlying performance on *all* IQ tests in *all* people.

Problems such as the Shepard-Metzler 3-D MRT, for example, are soluble by constructing an analogue mental representation of the target shape, and executing the appropriate set of spatial transformations on it. But an alternative solution is to form a *verbal* or propositional description of the target shape—that it consists of a central stem, four blocks high, with two legs at the top and bottom, one three, the other two blocks long, pointing in opposite directions. Such a verbal description will be quite sufficient to prove that at least some test stimuli could not possibly be the same as the target. Chapter 14 will document that fMRI studies have shown different patterns of activation when males and females attempt items from this test, consistent with the suggestion that males are more likely to use a spatial representation of the shape, and rotate it, while females are, on average, more likely to use a verbal description, as Johnson and Bouchard (2007) proposed.

The cube rotation task devised by Carpenter and Just (1986) described in Chapter 4 also lends itself to different strategies (see Figure 4.8, p. 90). Most people report doing what the experimenter intends, namely rotating the cube, but some people report that they simply compare orientation-free descriptions of the two cubes, for example that in both cubes the top of the A points to the C. This sounds like a rather more verbal strategy. Other studies have suggested that there are different ways of solving paper-folding tests. In addition to the spatial visualization strategy of mentally reversing the folding operations to produce the unfolded piece of paper, and tracking the changing pattern of holes this produces, an analytic strategy would note that if the paper is folded down the middle before the hole is punched, the pattern of holes produced will be symmetrical round that fold. Those of low spatial, but high verbal, ability are more likely to use this strategy (Kyllonen *et al.*, 1984).

A particularly convincing example is provided by analysis of the sentence verification task, described in Chapter 4 (Figure 4.2, p. 80). You are shown a picture, for example of a star above a plus, and have to decide whether a particular sentence, for example 'The star is above the plus', provides a true or false description of the picture. Clark and Chase (1972) proposed that people solve the problem by generating a verbal description of the picture, for example 'A star above a plus', and deciding whether this verbal description matches the sentence provided. If the sentence is true affirmative, the match is easily and immediately

Table 7.2 Partial correlation between Gc or Gv and sentence verification RT (from MacLeod *et al.*, 1978).

	Gc	Gv
'Well-fit' participants (N = 43)	−0.44	−0.07
'Poorly-fit' participants (N = 16)	−0.05	−0.64

made. If the sentence provided is a false affirmative ('The plus is above the star'), the decision will take a bit longer; but negative sentences, whether true or false ('The plus is not above the star' or 'The star is not above the plus') take even longer to match to your verbal description. Group data from experiments such as this have consistently shown that affirmative sentences are indeed confirmed or disconfirmed more rapidly than negative sentences, and that overall RTs correlate moderately with verbal IQ scores. Examination of individual data, however, usually reveals a sizeable minority of people who do not show this pattern of results: they do not respond more rapidly to affirmative than to negative sentences, but show instead a rather smaller difference in favour of true over false sentences; and their overall RTs do not correlate with verbal IQ (MacLeod *et al.*, 1978; Neubauer and Freudenthaler, 1994). That this is not just a matter of random noise in the data is strongly suggested by the observation that their RTs, unlike those of the majority of people, *are* well predicted by their spatial IQ scores. The results of MacLeod *et al.* are shown in Table 7.2.

The implication, consistent with people's own reports of how they solve the problem, is that this minority do so by adopting a spatial strategy: rather than generating a verbal description of the picture, they generate a spatial representation of the sentence (an image of a plus above a star), which they can then match to the picture. As noted in Chapter 6, Reichle *et al.* (2000) showed that use of propositional or spatial strategies to solve the sentence verification task was associated with activation of different regions of the brain.

Different theories of inferential reasoning have stressed the role of either formal, linguistic rules (e.g. Rips, 1994) or of visuo-spatial mental models (Johnson-Laird, 2001; see Chapter 5). Imaging studies have provided support for both, by finding evidence of activation of either left hemisphere, language areas of the brain, or of parietal (spatial) areas, depending on the semantic content of the syllogisms (Goel *et al.*, 2000). Other studies have supported the mental models account by showing a significant correlation between performance on a reasoning task and a measure of Gv (Ruff *et al.*, 2003). It seems possible that both accounts are right, but for different people, with some people (perhaps mostly men?) preferring a spatial strategy, and others (mostly women?) a propositional one (see Chapter 14).

A clear demonstration that different people adopt different strategies to solve transitive inference problems, is provided by Sternberg and Weil (1980). A simple transitive inference problem is:

Adam is taller than Benjamin
Benjamin is taller than Cain
Who is tallest?

The problem can be made harder by reversing the order of the premises, by using negative premises (*Adam is not taller than Benjamin*), and by using so-called unmarked terms in the premises (*Adam is shorter than Benjamin*). One way of solving such transitive inference problems is surely linguistic: you encode the information provided by the premises in terms of underlying meaning or linguistic structure, and then infer the relationship between the two end terms, Adam and Cain, to answer the question. But another solution is spatial: you represent Adam, Benjamin, and Cain in a spatial array, say from left (tall) to right (short), and then read off the answer. These strategies lead to rather different predictions as to which problems will be harder or easier than others. For example, if many more terms are included in the initial training set, which now extends to:

Cain is taller than David
David is taller than Ezekiel
Ezekiel is taller than Farah

You can now be asked to make either a 'near' or a 'far' comparison:

Who is taller, Benjamin or David? (near)
Who is taller, Adam or Ezekiel? (far)

A propositional strategy requires only one intermediate step to solve the near problem, but three intermediate steps to solve the far problem, and implies that people should be slower to answer the far question. But if Adam and Farah and all intermediate names are lined up in a spatial array, the distance between Adam and Ezekiel is greater than that between Benjamin and David, and this should make it easier to read off the answer to the far question.

From a detailed analysis of their participants' performance on a whole series of problems, Sternberg and Weil concluded that the majority employed both verbal and spatial strategies, but some employed only verbal and others only spatial strategies. In those apparently employing verbal strategies, performance on the task correlated 0.76 with verbal ability and only 0.29 with spatial ability. In those apparently employing spatial strategies, however, the correlation with verbal IQ was 0.08 and with spatial IQ was 0.60.

The implications of these studies are of the utmost importance, even if perhaps unwelcome to test constructors. People surely differ in their aptitudes, skills, and abilities; but differences in verbal or spatial abilities are only imperfectly assessed by the tests that psychologists have devised to measure them, since people also, perhaps partly as a consequence of these differences in ability, differ in the strategies they employ to solve various types of problem (in the study by MacLeod *et al.*, for example, a linguistic strategy was associated with a slightly higher average verbal IQ, and a spatial strategy with a significantly higher spatial IQ). But this must mean that there can be no such thing as a pure test of spatial ability, in the sense that everyone who attempts to solve the problem will do so by constructing a set of spatial representations which they then manipulate in certain ways. Some people will always try out other kinds of solution, converting the psychologist's 'spatial' test into one soluble by a verbal description of its terms. Conversely, others will solve a supposedly propositional problem by translating it into a spatial code. If this is true, then, the positive manifold between scores on supposedly quite different kinds of IQ test may arise because, regardless of the name of the tests, many people bring the same strategies to bear on their solution, some translating all problems into a verbal code, others using a spatial representation for all. In a large group of people, this would be quite sufficient to produce an overall positive correlation between their performance on verbal and spatial test batteries, even though verbal and spatial *strategies* or *abilities* tapped no common cognitive processes at all (just as they activate different regions of the brain).

The limits of correlations

As Gould (1997) argued, there is no compelling reason to suppose that a high correlation between scores on two different tests *must* mean that the two tests measure the same process. Two tests may correlate, but still depend on wholly different psychological processes, skills or abilities, provided that possession of the skills required for test 1 happens, for whatever reason, to be correlated with possession of the skills required for test 2. Thus, those who have a high verbal IQ, that is, have a large vocabulary and a wide store of general knowledge, may, as a matter of fact, happen also to be good at solving the sort of series completion and abstract reasoning problems that define Gf. And the reason may be nothing more mysterious than the fact that an environment that encourages the development of one ability may also be the sort of environment that encourages the development of the other. To claim that the same psychological processes underlie performance on two different tasks is to make a claim about the nature of the psychological theories needed to account for such performance. It says nothing about whether people who differ in terms of one set of processes will or will not differ in terms of the other.

Is this nothing more than a hypothetical possibility, which need not really be taken seriously? Probably not. To take a specific example, in the WAIS-III, the correlation between vocabulary and similarities tests is 0.76, not 1.00 of course, but still high. The Flynn effect, however, provides incontrovertible evidence that these two tests must be measuring rather different things: scores on vocabulary have increased by less than five points over the past 50 years; while those on similarities have increased by nearly 25 points, five times as fast (Flynn, 2007; see Chapter 1). If they were really measuring the same thing, either both would have shown an increase of five points or both would have shown an increase of 25 points. In spite of the strong correlation between the two within any one generation, they must be measuring rather distinct abilities. Remember that factor analysis of the WAIS-III places these two tests in the same group factor, verbal comprehension: it is not just that they both load onto *g*. If tests that load onto the same group factor must often be assumed to measure rather distinct cognitive processes, it is surely premature to assume that tests that load onto quite different group factors are at the same time also measuring, at least in part, the same psychological process of *general* intelligence. Absence of correlation, as here in the difference in the magnitude of the Flynn effect, is always more informative than presence of correlation.

Conclusion

Gould (1997) argued that Spearman's and Burt's real error was that they reified *g*. Although this is a charge that can perhaps be levelled against some psychometricians, on the whole both Spearman and Burt were clear about the distinction between a general *factor*, which is the product of a particular statistical technique, factor analysis, and the psychological or neurobiological *explanation* of this general factor.

It is always important to remember that it is the positive manifold, not *g* as such, that needs explanation. Why are people who do badly on one kind of test likely to do equally badly on all other tests, and (to a lesser extent) people who do well on one also likely to do well on others? When put like this, it is not at all obvious that the answer must be because people differ in a single process of general intelligence measured by all the tests. This might be the explanation—and it is certainly consistent with the demonstration that the *g* from one large set of diverse tests is essentially identical to the *g* of another large and diverse test battery. But the search for this single process (or processes) common to all tests, although it has certainly identified some important ingredients of successful performance on a wide variety of tests, such as working memory and processing speed, has not yet provided sufficiently strong evidence to allow the conclusion that the matter is settled.

Other possibilities therefore need at least to be considered. Two equally plausible accounts of *g* are: first that, although there is no process common to all tests, there is significant overlap in the cognitive operations engaged by different tests; and second, that different people use different strategies to solve the same problem. People with high spatial ability may use their spatial skills to solve reasoning problems that others, with high verbal ability, solve propositionally. Conversely, people with low spatial ability may translate what the test constructor has designed as a spatial problem into a propositional code. This would be sufficient to produce a correlation in the population as a whole between performance on tests of Gc and tests of Gv, even though there was no correlation whatsoever between strictly defined verbal and spatial abilities.

Finally, remember that correlations are just that—only correlations. The fact that performance on one test correlates with performance on another does not necessarily imply that the two tests must be measuring the same thing or things, or even that there must be some overlap in the set of processes measured by the two tests.

Summary

- Although Gf is closer to *g* than other second-stratum factors in the CHC model, the two are probably not the same.
- The general factor extracted from one large and diverse test battery is effectively the same as that extracted from another.
- Working memory, speed of processing, and learning ability are all relevant to performance on a variety of IQ tests: whether they are sufficient to explain *g* remains uncertain.
- *g* is more important at low levels of intelligence than at high levels.
- Whether or not there is any process or processes common to performance on all IQ tests (the jury is surely still out), *g* could arise from the overlap of processes engaged by different tests, or from differences in the strategies different people use to solve the same test.

Further reading

The book edited by Sternberg and Grigorenko (2002) brings together a number of chapters taking a different stance on the nature and importance of *g*. But none disputes that factor analysis of any IQ test battery will always reveal a general factor. Jensen (1998) stands at one end of a continuum, and Ceci (1996) at the other, of those who believe that the general factor does or does not imply that there must be some process or processes common to all IQ tests, while van der Maas *et al.* (2006) provide one example of how *g* can be explained without any appeal to any process common to all tests. Blair (2006; see also the commentaries on this paper) argues that *g* is not the same as Gf. Johnson *et al.* (2004) present evidence for the invariance of *g*. Flynn (2007) argues that the enormous difference in the size of the Flynn effect on different tests (which all correlate with one another within any one generation) casts doubt on the assumption that such correlations can possibly show that the tests are measuring the same thing. Reichle *et al.* (2000) document the reality of the different strategies that can be used to solve the sentence verification test.

8 The stability of IQ and the rise and fall of intelligence

Introduction

In order to convince others that their tests really were measuring intelligence, early IQ testers were concerned to establish two points: that their tests were reliable, and that they were valid. The validity of a psychological test is measured by showing, among other things, that the results of the test agree with some independent measure of whatever it is that the test purports to measure. The reliability of a test is an index of the extent to which it measures *anything* or, more precisely, of the extent to which a score on that test reflects anything other than chance. On a perfectly reliable test, if people could be tested again on the same test under exactly the same conditions, they would obtain exactly the same score; on an unreliable test, by contrast, their scores on two separate occasions, being largely a matter of chance, would be unrelated to one another. It will be obvious that reliability is a prerequisite for validity: an unreliable test cannot claim to be a valid measure of anything. The validity of IQ tests has been studied by seeing how well people's IQ scores predict other aspects of their life—how well they do at school, or whether they are any good at their job. I defer discussion of test validity to Chapter 9. The present chapter starts off with a discussion of the reliability of IQ tests and the stability of IQ over the lifetime. But since an IQ score is just a measure of your standing relative to other people of your age, the stability of IQ does not mean that there are no changes in children's ability to answer the questions of an IQ test as they grow older (of course there are such changes), and equally no changes in such abilities as adults grow older (there are, although perhaps there is no 'of course' about this).

Reliability

The reliability of any test can be measured in a variety of ways. 'Split-half' reliability simply involves comparing individuals' scores on, say, odd and even items in the test. Other measures rely on testing people on separate occasions, either on alternate forms of the test (early revisions of the Stanford-Binet test provided alternate forms for measuring IQ on separate occasions), or on the original form again. This last measure, referred to as 'test-retest' reliability, requires, of course, some minimum interval between the two occasions.

The higher the reliability of a test, the higher the correlation between the two scores people obtain. The reliability of individual IQ tests such as the Stanford-Binet or Wechsler tests is, by any reckoning, satisfactory, with reliability coefficients of about 0.95. Multiple-choice group tests generally have slightly lower reliabilities, partly because they are shorter and partly because guesswork can always play a part. A multiple-choice vocabulary test requires you to choose between half a dozen alternatives as the correct definition of each word, but the Stanford-Binet and Wechsler vocabulary tests require you to offer your own definition. Even the sketchiest knowledge, quite insufficient to solve this latter task, may allow you to rule out some of the alternatives in the multiple-choice test and thus affect your chances of guessing correctly. Nevertheless, most multiple-choice IQ tests, such as Raven's Matrices, have reliabilities in the range 0.85 to 0.90 (Jensen, 1980; Court and Raven, 1995, although they report occasional studies of Raven's Matrices with reliabilities as low as 0.75). Anastasi and Urbina (2001) provide a fuller discussion of the reliability of IQ tests.

The stability of IQ

When the test-retest reliability of a particular IQ test is assessed by giving it to the same group of people on more than one occasion, some interval must obviously elapse between first and second tests. Where that interval is, say, a year or more, the question being asked is slightly different, namely, what is the long-term *stability* of an IQ score. Intelligence is surely a *relatively* stable characteristic of any individual. Someone may feel sharper on some occasions than others, or feel slow, stupid, and unable to concentrate when suffering from a bad cold or hangover; some people may function better in the morning than in the afternoon, others the reverse; but you would not expect their intelligence to fluctuate *wildly* from one day or week to the next. So, IQ scores should surely remain relatively stable over time.

Although children may develop at different rates, with some being precocious and others late developers, it would still be surprising if there were no relationship between a child's level of intelligence at age 10, and their adult intelligence some 10–20 years later. Of course a 25-year-old adult would be expected to have a greater fund of general knowledge and larger vocabulary than a 10-year-old child, and thus to get more answers right on most IQ tests, but as noted above, an IQ score is a measure of your relative intellectual standing among people of your own age. If IQ tests purport to measure intelligence, your IQ score today should correlate reasonably well with your IQ score not only tomorrow, but also next year or even perhaps in ten years' time. Contrast this with a test of mood, which might be a perfectly reliable and valid measure, but still give entirely different answers on different occasions, because your mood can change from day to day.

Numerous studies have demonstrated high correlations between scores on the same IQ test taken on two separate occasions up to a year or two apart (Bloom, 1964; Jensen, 1980). For the Stanford-Binet and Wechsler tests, one-year, test-retest correlations average about 0.90. More interesting are the results of several long-term longitudinal studies that have given the same IQ test to the same group of people across intervals of ten or twenty years, or even longer. One such study (McCall, 1977) followed up children from the age of 2–3 until age 40. Figure 8.1 plots the correlation, separately for males and females, between IQ scores taken every year or so from infancy to adolescence, and IQ at age 40. The results suggest

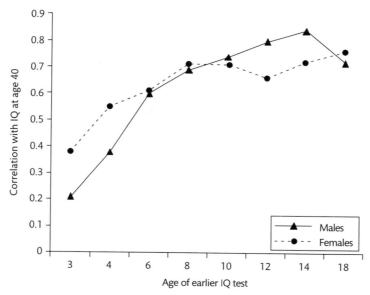

Figure 8.1 The long-term stability of IQ scores in males and females. The ordinate of the figure shows the value of the correlation between earlier IQ and IQ at age 40, and the abscissa shows the age at which the earlier IQ score was measured (data from a study by Honzik, reported by McCall, 1977, Figure 1).

two main conclusions. First, after the age of 8–10, IQ scores remain relatively stable: the correlation between IQ from age 8 to 18 and IQ at age 40 is over 0.70. The correlations are not perfect, which means that significant changes in IQ can and do occur, but these data are evidence of considerable long-term stability, and thus consistent with expectations of a measure of intelligence. Second, however, the correlations of less than 0.50 between IQ scores taken before the age of five and later, adult IQ are distinctly less impressive. Although other data have suggested a slightly higher correlation, nearly 0.60, between IQ at age 2–5 and IQ at age 15 (Wilson, 1986), IQ tests given before the age of 5 are clearly only imperfect predictors of later IQ. I return to this point below.

A Canadian study (Schwartzman *et al.*, 1987) of 260 men who were given an IQ test in their twenties when drafted into the Canadian Army in World War II, retested them on the same test 40 years later when they were in their mid-sixties. The correlation between their verbal IQ scores on the two occasions was 0.82; although the correlation between their non-verbal scores was significantly lower (0.54), this is still rather impressive evidence of the stability of IQ. But the record for a long-term follow-up comes from Scotland. In 1932, the entire population of Scottish 11-year-olds (87,498 children) took the Moray House Test, a general IQ test devised by Thomson. Some 66 years later, 100 of them from Aberdeen, who had been tracked down by Ian Deary and Lawrence Whalley, took the same test again. The correlation between their scores on these two occasions was 0.63 (Deary *et al.*, 2000). In a later study, Deary and his colleagues tracked down some 500 of them living near Edinburgh, and again gave them the same test. A scatterplot of their test scores on the two occasions, separated by just on 70 years, is shown in Figure 8.2; the

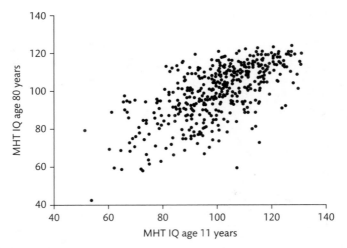

Figure 8.2 Scatterplot of Moray House Test (MHT) IQ scores at ages 11 and 80 for 485 people (reproduced with permission from Deary *et al.*, 2004, Figure 3).

correlation is 0.66 (Deary *et al.*, 2004). As can be seen there are a few outliers, including one with an IQ of over 100 at age 11, but an IQ of only just over 60 at age 80: it seems possible that (as was documented in one case in the earlier study) this person was suffering from the first signs of dementia.

There can be no doubt that people's IQ scores after the age of 10 remain relatively (although far from perfectly) stable for much of the rest of their life. To return to the data shown in Figure 8.1, however: why do IQ scores below the age of 6 fail to predict IQ at age 40? One possibility is that variations in experience in the first year or two of life are not necessarily predictive of the critical variations that will shape IQ later. Perhaps more important, since IQ tests simply measure whether one child is advanced for her age, or another is lagging behind, very young children's scores at any given moment in time will depend on whether they have just mastered a particular accomplishment (pointing to their nose or toes, counting up to four) or whether they are just about to. Minor variations in developmental spurts and lags may have a disproportionate effect on early test scores.

A third possibility is that the accomplishments measured by IQ tests at age 2–3 are simply unrelated to those measured later. This is clearly true of most tests designed for even younger infants. Scores on earlier versions of the Bayley infant scales (Bayley, 1969), show near zero correlation with IQ scores at age 6–10. These scales measured such physical skills as sitting or standing, grasping or looking for objects, and there is no *a priori* reason why the age at which such skills are mastered should predict the later development of the knowledge and skills measured by standard IQ tests.

There is, however, one striking and important exception to this general failure to find early predictors of later IQ. The correlation between measures of habituation to a novel stimulus taken in the first year of life and IQ scores at age 3–11 is at least 0.30 (Kavšek, 2004; McCall and Carriger, 1993). Kavšek's meta-analysis reported even higher correlations, r = 0.49, between habituation scores in the first year of life and IQ measured at ages 7–11. Fagan *et al.* (2007) reported a correlation of 0.34 between infant scores and IQ at age 21.

When presented with a novel visual stimulus, infants direct their gaze towards it, and will fixate it for a certain length of time. Repeated presentation of the same stimulus will result in a decrease in the duration of such fixation, but at this point replacement of the original stimulus with a new one will restore gazing and fixation. There are various measures of such habituation and dishabituation that can be taken: the total length of time the infant fixates the stimulus over a given series of trials; the number of trials needed to produce a given reduction in the duration of fixation; the extent to which fixation is restored by substitution of a novel stimulus; or finally, in a choice test, the proportion of time spent looking at a novel stimulus rather than one seen before. This last test is usually described as a measure of recognition memory. McCall and Carriger (1993) concluded that there was little evidence to suggest that any one of these measures yielded reliably or substantially higher correlations with later IQ than any other, although Kavšek (2004) suggested that habituation might be a better predictor in normal children and dishabituation better in children at risk.

A correlation of 0.30–0.50 may not be dramatically high, but it is certainly higher than those found between any other measure of infants' behaviour and their IQ score up to ten years later. Indeed, one reason why the correlation is not even higher may well be that measures of infant habituation are themselves far from perfectly reliable, and it is a general tenet of test theory that an unreliable test cannot reliably predict performance on any other test. Since the correlation between habituation scores taken on two separate occasions is itself no more than about 0.50, that they should correlate nearly as well with IQ scores taken years later is surely rather impressive, especially since, on the face of it, the two measures seem to have rather little in common.

Any correlation between a measure of an infant's behaviour in the first 6–9 months of life and their later IQ seems hard to reconcile with an extreme environmentalist position, which would say that a child's IQ is a product of years of intellectual stimulation and cannot be measured before those years have been experienced. It is not, of course, necessary to jump to the conclusion that IQ is a fixed, innate property of the brain, in some mysterious way directly measured by rate of habituation, for it is always possible to point to an even earlier environment (perhaps even *in utero*) as a determinant of test performance. Consistent with this, there is evidence that infant habituation scores also predict later IQ for pre-term babies and others identified as at risk from perinatal complications (McCall and Carriger, 1993).

The more interesting question, however, is surely this: measures of habituation, dishabituation, and recognition memory are hardly conventional IQ tests (even if, sensibly enough, later versions of Bayley's developmental scales now include such measures, Bayley, 1993), so the puzzle is to see what they could possibly have in common with conventional IQ tests that would explain the relatively strong correlation between the two over periods of up to ten years.

Habituation tests presumably measure a variety of different psychological processes, any one of which could be responsible for their correlation with IQ. Rapidity of habituation must depend, among other things, on the efficiency and rapidity with which the infant nervous system stores a representation of the repeated stimulus, for in the absence of any such representation of past occurrences all stimuli will always remain equally novel. Dishabituation to a novel stimulus, or preference for the novel stimulus in a test of recognition memory, requires that the stored representation of the familiar stimulus be sufficiently precise that it is discriminated from the novel stimulus. Those who have sought to reduce IQ to the efficiency of sensory registration or basic information processing in the nervous system will want to emphasize these aspects of the habituation task (Chapter 3). But although some such processes must surely be involved in habituation and recognition memory, it does not follow that *variations* in such processes are responsible for variations in speed of habituation or magnitude of dishabituation, let alone for their correlation with IQ. The processes of sensory registration and storing of accurate representations of stimuli might be equally rapid and efficient in essentially all infants, and differences in rate of habituation might have much more to do with the efficiency of mechanisms for inhibiting the initial fixation response (McCall and Carriger, 1993). Such a possibility would be consistent with some neurobiological evidence which points to the maturation of the nervous system, and particularly of prefrontal cortex, as one mechanism subserving the development of the ability to inhibit prepotent responses (Johnson and Morton, 1991; Russell, 1996; see below for further discussion of this as a mechanism of cognitive development). Other possibilities are equally plausible or implausible, and I shall half seriously suggest one later (see Chapter 11). At present there are few grounds for choosing between any of them. But it is not being naively optimistic to suppose that further understanding of the causes of differences in rate of habituation and dishabituation will help to illuminate the nature of the processes being measured by IQ tests.

Stability of intelligence

The data shown in Figure 8.1 imply that IQ at age 10 predicts IQ at age 40 with considerable accuracy, in other words that an adult's IQ at age 40 will be much the same as their IQ as a 10-year-old child. This does not, of course mean that he gets the same number of answers right. If, aged 40, you obtain the same *absolute* score on the same test as the score you had obtained at age 10, something would have gone seriously wrong in your life. The long-term stability of IQ means only that your standing relative to others of your age stays much the same. In the Scottish study, where people were given exactly the same test at age 11 and age 80, their absolute score at age 80 was $1.13d$ higher than it had been at age 11 (Deary *et al.*, 2004).

The development of intelligence

The fact that Binet could use children's age as a criterion against which to assess whether his tests were measuring intelligence only serves to document what everyone knows already—that children's cognitive abilities increase as they grow older. Entire books are devoted to chronicling cognitive development, and it would be presumptuous to pretend that such a topic could be covered in one short section of one chapter. All that I shall try to do is to discuss some of the changes in cognitive abilities that appear to be responsible for changes in test scores as children grow older. Many of these changes are wholly unsurprising: 2-year-old children have a vocabulary of only about 50 to 300 words. By the age of 6, however, the average child has a vocabulary of 14,000 words, which has increased to 40,000 words by the age of 16 (Ellis, 1994). While differences in vocabulary between two different 10-year-olds are probably not entirely attributable to differences in the number of words they have come across (Chapter 4), the difference between a 2-year-old and a 10-year-old must be largely a matter of experience. It is equally obvious that children's store of general knowledge increases as they grow older. That performance on many tests of Gc should improve as children grow up is only to be expected. But neither schools nor (most) parents set out to teach children how to solve Raven's Matrices, so why is the average score obtained by 7–8-year-olds on the Standard Progressive Matrices only about half that of 14–15-year-olds (Raven, 2000)? In fact, although schools may not set out to teach children how to solve the sorts of puzzle set by tests of Gf, there is excellent evidence that the experience of Western schooling has a dramatic effect on young children's ability to solve such puzzles (Chapters 12 and 13).

One marked developmental change is in immediate memory span—as in the digit span test of the WISC. Five-year-olds have a digit span of just over four, and even 12-year-olds have a span of only just over six, still short of the average adult span of about seven (Dempster, 1981). One explanation is that very young children do not systematically use rehearsal strategies: for example, unlike adults, their performance is not seriously disrupted by articulatory suppression, which interferes with rehearsal (Gathercole *et al.*, 1994); another is that they are simply slower to say the words or numbers when they come to recall them, and so increase the length of time they have to hold them in memory (Brown and Hulme, 1995; Hulme *et al.*, 1984). There is indeed evidence that speed of information processing increases as children grow older, and this underlies much cognitive change. Kail and Salthouse (1994) have summarized a great deal of evidence showing very large changes in performance on simple speeded tests between the ages of 5 and 20, and significant decline after the age of 40 (a point I return to below): Figure 8.3 shows the performance of different age groups from the standardization sample on the visual

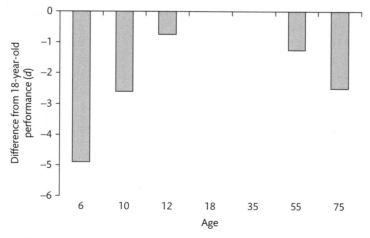

Figure 8.3 Age differences in performance on the visual matching test (a measure of Gs) from the Woodcock-Johnson test battery. The differences are expressed in standard deviation units (*d*) based on 18-year-old performance (data from Kail and Salthouse, 1994, Figure 1).

matching test of the Woodcock-Johnson test battery. At age 5, performance is a full 5.0*d* slower than that of 20-year-olds. Kail (1988, 1991) has shown that this change can be seen in performance on a wide variety of different tasks, and the functions describing these changes are surprisingly uniform across tasks ranging from: mental rotation requiring a decision whether a rotated letter is normal or a mirror image; the digit symbol test from the WISC; memory search where, after studying a short list of digits, participants have to decide whether a single digit presented had or had not been in the study list; and mental addition, where they have to decide whether a simple sum (2 + 6 = 8) is correct or incorrect. Performance on all four tasks speeded up dramatically between the ages of 7 and 12, and more slowly thereafter. More impressively, the exponential function that accurately described these changes had exactly the same decay parameter for all four cases.

It has been argued that changes in processing speed are also responsible for many other changes in test performance as children grow older: Fry and Hale (1996) proposed the idea of a 'developmental cascade', whereby changes in speed result in enhanced working memory capacity, which then results in enhanced fluid intelligence. The idea has been further supported by Kail (2007) and Nettelbeck and Burns (2010). It is certainly true that when differences in speed are partialled out, age differences in performance on Raven's Matrices are very substantially reduced (Kail and Salthouse, 1994). And one theory, of course, says that processing speed is an important underpinning of general intelligence or *g* (see Chapter 3). There is indeed much evidence consistent with these wider arguments. But could changes in speed really be responsible for all cognitive changes as children grow up?

A rather different explanation of the development of logical reasoning as children grow older is the maturation of the brain. Sensory and motor areas develop in the first few years of life, followed by the development of occipital, parietal, and temporal lobes, but the development of prefrontal cortex (widely regarded as the most important part of the brain for Gf, see Chapter 6) continues well into adolescence (Gogtay *et al.*, 2004). Performance on a variety of 'executive' tasks also carries on improving well into adolescence (Romine and Reynolds, 2005). Figure 8.4 shows their summary of this improvement averaged across a number of different tests. This average conceals some substantial differences: the

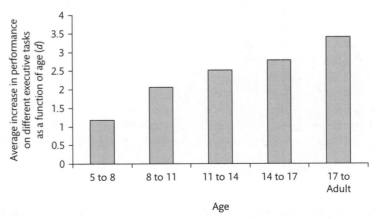

Figure 8.4 Average improvement in performance from one age to the next (5–8, 8–11, and so on) on several different executive tasks (data from Romine and Reynolds, 2005, Table 2).

improvement in performance on the Tower of Hanoi and Tower of London problems was 1.43d between the ages of 5 and 8, a further 1.57d between 8 and 17, and a final improvement of 0.77d between 17 and 22. Performance on tests of working memory (as well as of immediate memory span) also improves substantially from childhood to adolescence. Towse and Hitch (2008) agreed that this was partly due to an increase in speed of processing which reduces the length of time that information must be held in memory, but argued that other factors must also be involved, because controlling for processing speed does not eliminate age differences in working memory (Hitch *et al.*, 2001). They proposed that another factor might be the ability to resist interference from other items at the moment of recall. Siegler and Alibali (2005) have argued that young children's failure to solve various kinds of problem is caused by their inability to use Sternberg's 'metacomponents' (see Chapter 4).

This brings us to a consideration of Piagetian theory. Diamond (1985), for example, has argued that the solution to many of Piaget's tests depends on executive control: young infants initially make the 'A-not-B' error by continuing to search at A, where an object was hidden on the first trial, even after it has been hidden under B on a later trial, because they are unable to coordinate (integrate) the two processes of holding on-line the memory of where the object is placed (B) with the inhibition of the prepotent response to A. The longer the delay between hiding the object at B and allowing the infant to make her response, the greater the probability of an error.

Piagetian theory stresses qualitative changes in children's cognitive abilities, starting with the sensorimotor and pre-operational stages in infancy and very early childhood, where the child learns that there is an external world of other people and objects, whose existence is independent of her own perception of them, and develops the capacity of representational thought. These are followed by the concrete operational stage between the ages of 5 or 6 and 9 or 10, when children learn that objects may retain their identity in spite of differences in their appearance, as when the amount of water in a jug remains the same if poured from a tall thin jug to a short fat one. In the final, formal operational stage, starting at age 11–13, children may begin to understand logical thinking. Although all children supposedly pass through these stages in this fixed order, the theory does, of course, allow some individual differences in the ages at which these stages are reached. And it is also true that performance on Piagetian tests, for example tests of conservation that define concrete operations, show moderate correlations with IQ tests (Case *et al.*, 2001). Rather surprisingly however, given that children's performance on IQ tests has improved over the past 25 years (the Flynn effect), performance on some tests of conservation has declined in Britain over the same period (Shayer *et al.*, 2007).

The qualitative changes from one stage to the next have turned out to be notably less definitive than Piaget himself had supposed. The advent of the concrete operational stage does not mean that children can all at once show conservation across all changes. Conservation of number, when the child sees that spacing the number of beads in a row further apart does not increase their number, usually precedes conservation of liquid, where the child sees that pouring some liquid from one glass into another does not change the amount of liquid, which in turn precedes conservation of volume. These differences presumably reflect the fact that rather different skills and understanding are called for in each task: simple counting will give the right answer to a test of conservation of number;

experience of pouring out a liquid from a jug into a glass will surely soon lead to conservation of liquid. Shayer *et al.* (2007) attributed the decline in British children's performance on some conservation tests to changes in their experience with different kinds of play material. Piaget's theorizing attributed failure on many tasks to the fact that the child had not reached the appropriate stage. In fact, however, such failure can often be explained in rather simpler terms. Just as conservation seems to depend on familiarity with different transformations, so differences in *knowledge*, due to differences in experience or memory, may be responsible for young children's failure on other problems. Piaget argued that children would be unable to solve problems requiring logical reasoning, such as transitive inference or analogical reasoning, until the formal operational stage (Piaget and Inhelder, 1969). But they can at least give the correct answer to such problems at a much earlier age. Although 7 or 8-year-old children *may* fail transitive inference problems, they *can* actually be solved by children as young as 4 or 5. The reason for failures is that children may have difficulty in remembering all the premises. In order to avoid 'end anchor' effects, it is necessary to give at least five premises of the form:

$$A > B; \ B > C; \ C > D; \ D > E$$

So that the test question:

Who is taller B or D?

does not use either the first or last name in the sequence. When steps are taken to ensure that young children can indeed recall all the premises, they have no difficulty with the problem (Bryant and Trabasso, 1971).

Goswami (1992) has shown that the reason why young children may fail to solve analogical reasoning problems is often because they simply do not understand the relationship between some of the terms of the analogy. Provided the relationships are ones they *do* understand, children as young as 3 or 4 can solve analogies. Shown (in pictorial form) the following analogy:

Loaf of bread is to slice of bread as lemon is to?

Some 80% of 4-year-olds selected a picture of a slice of lemon in preference to such alternatives as a slice of cake, a whole lemon, a yellow balloon, or two squeezed lemon halves. But many older children will fail an analogy, such as:

Mare is to stallion as ewe is to (lamb, pony, sheep, ram)

because they do not know that this is about the names of male and female animals.

There are other developmental changes in analogical reasoning. Simple analogies require you to see the relationship between the A and B terms, and apply that transform to C. It is not always necessary to understand the relationship between the A and C terms (there is after all, no important relationship between a loaf of bread and a lemon). But some analogies do require the solver to see the relationship between A and C, and Sternberg and Rifkin (1979) showed that children below the age of 10 do not readily understand the importance, and occasionally the necessity, of mapping the relationship between the A and C terms.

Now most simple analogies can be solved without the need for mapping. For example:

Black is to white as night is to ?

Or:

> Glove is to hand as sock is to ?

can be solved simply by applying the appropriate transform or relationship to the C term (opposite; worn on), without bothering about any possible relationship between the A and C terms. It really is not relevant that nights are usually dark or black, and the relationship of 'opposite' permits the construction of numerous analogies where there is no obvious relationship between the A and C terms at all. For example:

> Black is to white as odd is to ?

However, more difficult analogies are often those where the relationship between A and C terms does become important. Consider the analogy shown in Figure 8.5. Its solution precisely requires one to map the elements of C onto those of A, that is, to see that the three vertical lines in A correspond to the three small lines radiating out from a dot inside the square in C, and the four horizontal lines in A to the four-sided figure of the square in C. Thus, the A:B transform (three to four vertical lines; four to three horizontal lines) implies that D will have four lines radiating out from the dot inside a three-sided triangle. If mapping is an operation ill understood by younger children, it is unsurprising that they should be rather poor at solving certain kinds of analogy.

The decline of intelligence

No one doubts that children grow in intellectual competence as they grow up. It also seems plausible to suppose that there is probably relatively little change in *intelligence* between the ages of, say, 20 and 40. Perhaps the young are often rash and foolish; while as people grow older perhaps they become complacent and stuck in their ways. But even if true, these perceptions are more about differences in cognitive style or attitudes than 'native intelligence'. But what happens as people get still older—at age 60 or 80? Will their intelligence increase, decrease, or stay the same? One point of view, popular with the old, is that old age brings increasing maturity and wisdom, and provides a greater store of knowledge on which to base your sounder judgements. Another, more popular with the young, is that it brings increasing rigidity and inflexibility, that people become increasingly forgetful and slow down as they grow older—and intelligence is partly a matter of being quick on the uptake and bringing relevant information to bear on new problems. It seems, then, that the results of IQ tests over the life span might be quite informative: it is not that test scores *must* stay constant if IQ is to count as a good measure of intelligence. It is just not clear what to expect.

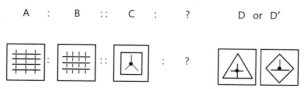

Figure 8.5 Example of a figural analogy that requires you to map the relationship between the A (first) and C (third) terms. See text for further details.

Cross-sectional and longitudinal studies

The first IQ test to provide any serious information on this issue was the Wechsler-Bellevue (the precursor of the WAIS), since Wechsler's original standardization sample included adults stratified by age, as well as some younger children. Later versions of the WAIS provided similar data, and told a similar story: as can be seen in Figure 8.6, both tests showed some decline in test scores, particularly on the performance half of the test. In the WAIS-R data shown in Figure 8.6b, Verbal scores are slightly higher at age 40 than at 22, and decline only very slowly thereafter, so that at age 72 the average score is still at least 90% of the 22-year-old score. Scores on the performance half of the test, however, decline steadily from age 22 on, and by age 72 are less than 75% of the scores obtained at age 20. Not a trivial effect.

Such a pattern of results could be seen as suggesting that the preconceptions of both old and young contain some truth. For what is the explanation of the difference between

(a) Wechsler-Bellevue

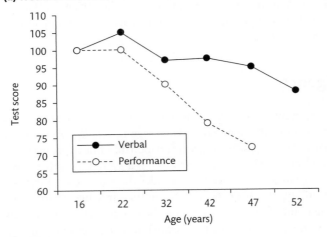

(b) WAIS-R

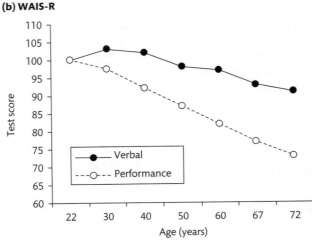

Figure 8.6 Performance on the Wechsler tests as a function of age. The data are from the standardization samples of (a) the original Wechsler-Bellevue test, and (b) the WAIS-R. In both cases, the actual test scores of each age group are expressed as a percentage of the test scores of the youngest age group.

the verbal and performance scales? A plausible answer is that verbal tests, which ask questions about the meaning of words and general knowledge, largely measure accumulated experience or wisdom, while the performance tests require you to solve novel puzzles or problems, often giving bonus marks for rapid answers, and thus measure speed, flexibility, and related aspects of intelligence which do indeed start declining from a relatively early age. Both old and young can thus take comfort from the data, by valuing more highly those aspects of the tests at which they excel. So can Horn and Cattell (1966), since, as was briefly mentioned in Chapter 2, their Gf-Gc theory precisely argued that although Gc was maintained well into old age, Gf declined from a relatively early age.

Although there is no reason to question the accuracy of the data shown in Figure 8.6b, however, they do not necessarily represent what actually happens to people's test scores as they grow older. How can that be? The answer is because the data are *cross-sectional*, and thus confound two quite different things. They were all collected in a given year, about 1980, from people ranging in age at the time from 22 to 72. This difference in age is thus confounded with a difference in the year in which they were born. That is so obvious that it may be hard to see how it could matter. But it does. The critical assumption is that the 72-year-olds obtain lower test scores in 1980 than the 22-year-olds because test performance declines as people grow older. But it is possible that people born in 1910 *always* had lower test scores than those born in 1960, and would have obtained just as low a score if tested, at age 20, in 1930. And the Flynn effect, discussed in Chapter 1, says that this is true. Performance on standard IQ tests has been improving from one generation to the next ever since IQ tests were first invented, and in data from the WAIS and WAIS-R this improvement has been very much greater on the performance tests than on the verbal tests. In general, indeed, it has been greater on tests of Gf than on tests of Gc.

As I shall argue in Chapter 12, the Flynn effect must be a consequence of environmental changes occurring over the course of the twentieth century that made people better at IQ tests. The environment of the 1970s was somehow more conducive to solving IQ-type problems than was that of the 1920s. If this is true, it would seem to follow that the only way to ascertain what happens to IQ test scores as people grow older is to undertake a *longitudinal* study, in which the same group of, say, 20-year-olds is followed up and given a second IQ test at age 60 or more. One such study is that of the Canadian servicemen retested 40 years later at age 65. Schwartzman *et al.* (1987) reported that scores on verbal tests showed no change between the ages of 25 and 65, while scores on non-verbal tests did show a significant decline (from a score of 42.9 to 35.1). Perhaps, then, my dire warnings above were misplaced, and longitudinal and cross-sectional data do tell the same story. Recall, however, that the decline in WAIS-R performance scores shown in Figure 8.6b started from age 22. The Canadian data do not speak to this possibility.

A much larger and more systematic study, the Seattle Longitudinal Study (Schaie, 2005) provides data that allows some answers to these and other questions. The study used a rather complex design that provided both cross-sectional and longitudinal data. Beginning in 1956, Schaie collected data from 500 people ranging in age from 20 to 80, in effect a standard cross-sectional study. However, he also followed up the survivors of this initial cohort every seven years for the next 50 years (by which time, of course, he was studying only the younger members of the original cohort), thus also providing a standard longitudinal study. The final twist was that at each seven-year interval, he also collected data from a new sample of people ranging in age from 20 to 80, and followed them up at seven-year intervals also.

A further important feature of Schaie's study is that he did not rely simply on the Wechsler tests, but used a more systematic series of tests designed to measure the various components of IQ identified by the CHC model. Figures 8.7 and 8.8 summarize some of the main results of Schaie's massive study, with Figure 8.7 showing cross-sectional data

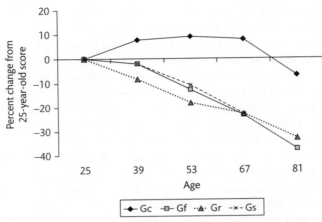

Figure 8.7 Changes in performance on tests of Gc, Gf, Gr, and Gs as a function of age in the Seattle Study. These are cross-sectional data (from Schaie, 2005, Table 4.4).

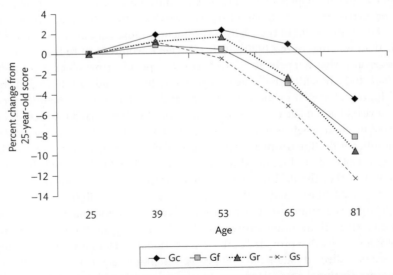

Figure 8.8 Changes in performance on tests of Gc, Gf, Gr, and Gs as a function of age in the Seattle Study. These are longitudinal data. Note the difference in the scale of the ordinate from Figure 8.7 (data from Schaie, 2005, Table 5.8).

and Figure 8.8 showing longitudinal data. Note that the scale of the ordinate is quite different in the two figures. The cross-sectional data show a steady and quite steep decline in performance on tests of Gf, Gv, Gs, and Gr from age 25 to age 80, while scores on tests of Gc actually increase until the age of 50, and show only a modest decline thereafter. The longitudinal data, however, show much smaller changes, and although scores on tests of Gc still hold up better than those on other tests, the relatively steep decline on these other tests does not start until after the age of 60, and only Gs scores showing any decline at all before the age of 60. The data in Figure 8.3 above, showing a decline in performance on a measure of Gs from the standardization sample of the W-J test, were, like those from the WAIS, cross-sectional.

The increase in average test scores over the course of the twentieth century means that cross-sectional data may not give a true reflection of changes in test scores as people grow older. Does that mean that longitudinal data give the true picture? Alas, not necessarily. There are several problems. One is that if you repeatedly give people the same IQ test every seven years or so, they may show a practice effect, getting better and better each time they try the test. There is, indeed, some evidence that this happens, although the effect seems to be small (see Chapter 8 in Schaie, 2005). There are two further problems however. First, people who are willing to sign up for a longitudinal study such as the Seattle study are unlikely to be a wholly representative cross-section of the population: indeed, they were not, being predominantly middle-class, and in fact enrolled in a local health care plan. Since, as I will document below, there are substantial individual differences in the extent to which cognitive abilities are maintained or decline in old age, such a sample will almost certainly underestimate the extent of any decline in the population as a whole. The second problem will exacerbate this effect. Only the more healthy members of the original sample will survive to be tested at age 80, and there is a significant correlation between IQ and health and longevity. If the less healthy and those who die before the age of 60 or 70 drop out of the sample, those remaining will almost certainly show less cognitive decline (Chapter 8 in Schaie, 2005).

So, while cross-sectional studies probably overestimate the extent of cognitive decline in old age (at least while the Flynn effect continues), longitudinal studies probably underestimate any such decline. What is the true picture? The answer is that no one really knows, but presumably somewhere between the estimates provided by the two kinds of study. If that seems a rather feeble compromise, perhaps it does not matter. The *precise* size of the decline in some aspects of the intelligence measured by IQ tests is not the most important issue to discuss. Others are more interesting. Are there any general causes of cognitive decline? Why do some abilities decline faster than others? Why do some people show much greater decline than others?

Older is just slower

Unlike the cross-sectional data, the longitudinal data of Figure 8.8 show that performance on speeded measures of IQ (that together comprise the Gs factor) starts to decline rather sooner than other components. That people slow down as they grow older is, of course, a familiar enough observation. Within psychology, IQ tests are not alone in showing a decline in speed after the age of 30 or so: in cross-sectional studies, reaction time tasks also show a sharp decline in performance after the age of 30 (Cerella, 1985; Nettelbeck and Rabbitt, 1992). Nettelbeck and Rabbitt also observed a decline in performance on an inspection time task. Both these tests arguably provide a more straightforward measure of processing speed than some of the tests of Gs that appear in IQ test batteries, but there is impressive evidence that performance on virtually all speeded tests declines together as people grow older (Salthouse, 1996), just as Kail (1988, 1991) showed that they all improve together as young children grow up.

Whether or not speed of processing declines before any other component of IQ, a popular suggestion has been that changes in speed are the *cause* of the decline in other components. As people slow down, so they find it harder to solve the kind of problem that measures Gf or Gv (Nettelbeck and Rabbitt, 1992; Salthouse, 1996). The idea is consistent with the more general hypothesis, advanced by Anderson (2005) and Jensen (1998), that speed of processing is the biological process underlying general intelligence or *g* (see Chapter 3). Indeed, at one time Salthouse himself embraced this more general hypothesis by arguing that the changes in performance on IQ tests as people grow older are a consequence of changes in *g* rather than in any specific components of IQ, and changes in *g* are largely due to changes in speed of processing.

What would count as evidence for this supposition? A first point, established by Nettelbeck and Rabbitt (1992), Kail and Salthouse (1994), and Salthouse (1996) is that once changes in Gs are partialled out, changes in Gf are very substantially attenuated. This is certainly consistent with the idea that the decline in test scores as people grow older is largely a matter of their slowing down. But do they really force that conclusion? Scores on tests of Gs are correlated with scores on other components of IQ, and it is hardly surprising that if you remove any change in Gs from the equation, the change in other components will reduce. What is minimally needed to establish that an earlier change in speed is the *cause* of subsequent changes in other components of IQ is a longitudinal study that establishes that differences in speed at one age predict differences in other components of IQ at a later age. Deary *et al.* (2009) gave an IQ test and an RT task to 679 people, a representative sample of the population of Glasgow and surrounding area, at age 56, and retested them 13 years later at age 69. Scores at the earlier age were correlated with scores at the later age, both for IQ and for RT. The more interesting question was whether differences in RT at age 56 would predict differences in IQ at 69. They did not. On the contrary, it was IQ at the earlier age that predicted RT at the later age, leading the authors to conclude that higher intelligence may be associated with a lifestyle that preserves processing speed (whatever that might be), rather than changes in speed causing changes in general IQ.

Although processing speed declines quite sharply, and possibly from an earlier age than other components of IQ, speed is probably better seen as one among many components of IQ rather than the cause of all other changes in IQ. As Deary (2000) has noted, controlling for processing speed is not the only way to reduce the age-related decline in other components of IQ. Baltes and Lindenberger (1997) showed that controlling for declining sensory functions (vision and hearing) was just as effective as controlling for processing speed in accounting for changes in cognitive function in old age. The fact is, of course, that a lot of depressing changes occur as people grow older (as well as one or two nicer ones), but they are not necessarily all causally related, let alone a consequence of the same changes in the structure or functioning of the brain. Old age is correlated with a change in hair colour and increased wrinkling of the skin, but this does not make white hair a cause of cognitive decline, or mean that both are a consequence of the same proximal cause. Changing hair colour is simply another correlate of increasing age.

One clear change in the brain as people grow older is an increase in white matter lesions (reminder: white matter is connections between neurons, while grey matter refers to the neurons themselves). Perhaps unsurprisingly, the prevalence of such lesions is associated with declines in speed of processing and also, more modestly, with declines in general intelligence (Rabbitt *et al.*, 2007). But these correlations do not prove that white matter lesions are the cause of the decline in both speed and general intelligence as people grow older. Rabbitt and his colleagues were in fact able to show that when age was taken into account, the prevalence of white matter lesions, although still significantly associated with speed of processing, was completely unrelated to changes in intelligence. The implication is that there is no direct causal link between changes in processing speed and changes in general intelligence. Perhaps this conclusion should not come as too great a surprise: given the large differences in the trajectories of different components of IQ across the life span (see Figures 8.7 and 8.8 above), it does not seem plausible to suppose that all changes in test scores can be attributed to a single underlying cause.

This does not mean that changes in processing speed are unimportant. There is good evidence that changes in speed predict some significant consequences, including death. This was first reported by Birren (1968) and has been confirmed by Deary and Der (2005) and Schaie (2005, Chapter 10). Deary and Der, for example, tested people in their mid-fifties on a reaction time task, and followed them up some 20 years later. Those with the slowest reaction time scores at the earlier age were more likely to have died before the age of 75.

Older is more forgetful

Figures 8.7 and 8.8 showed that performance on tests of Gr or memory starts declining soon after performance on tests of Gs. It is a commonplace observation that the very old may remember what happened to them 40 or 50 years previously, and prove it by boring their listeners to death by telling the same story over and over again. But of course one reason for *that* is that they forget that they have told you the story less than half an hour ago. The decline is in their memory for relatively recent events. What is going on here?

In the laboratory, memory for recent information can be measured in at least three rather different ways (see Table 8.1). All three might start with the experimenter presenting a list of, say, 20 words for people to study. A test of free recall would require them, at some later time, to recall as many words from the list as possible. A recognition test would present them with pairs of words, one word in each pair coming from the original list and the other being new, and ask them to say which one had appeared in the original list. In one common test of implicit memory, stem completion, the first few letters of words in the study list are shown and participants are asked to give a word that would complete the stem. Evidence of implicit memory for the words in the study list would be provided if people are more likely to complete the stem with a study word, for example completing Ele----- with Elephant rather than Election (to ensure that this is not just because everyone is more likely to give

Table 8.1 Schematic design of experiments for studying recall, recognition, and implicit memory.

Study list	Recall	Recognition	Implicit memory
Pigeon	Recall as many words	Which word in each	Fill in the blanks to
Forceful	from the list as you can.	pair was in the list?	complete a word.
Elephant			
Crowded		Pigeon Ostrich	Ele-----
Peaceful		Tiger Elephant	Cro----

Elephant than Election, for other participants, the study list will contain Election instead of Elephant).

Interestingly enough, the difference between old and young people is much greater on tests of free recall than on recognition tests, and many studies of implicit memory have found no significant difference between older and younger participants. That is too optimistic: where there is a difference it is invariably in favour of the young. In a meta-analysis, La Voie and Light (1994) concluded that the effect size in favour of the young was $0.97d$ in studies of free recall, $0.50d$ in recognition tests, and $0.30d$ in implicit memory tests. One explanation of the difference between free recall and recognition is that successful recognition may depend on little more than a sense that one word in each test pair seems more familiar than the other (Box 8.1 describes an ingenious procedure, devised by Jacoby, for distinguishing between recollection and familiarity). The relatively good preservation of implicit memory implies that the decline in performance on tests of free recall must be greatly overestimating the extent to which memory for recent events has simply vanished in the old. The memory is still there, but it cannot be accessed, except indirectly. Why? Deliberate recollection of a past event requires successful encoding of that event at the time it occurred, and successful retrieval of the memory at the time of test. There is reason to believe that older people are in some sense less efficient both at encoding and at retrieval (Zacks *et al.*, 2000).

BOX 8.1 The process dissociation procedure

Jacoby (1991) devised an experimental design which he called the process dissociation procedure, designed to obtain separate measures of, for example, the two routes which people are able to use in order to give an answer in a recognition test. Shown an item which has appeared in an earlier study phase of the experiment, and asked whether it really was in the study list, they could say yes either because they really do remember having seen it in the list, or simply because it seems familiar. How can you separate out these two possibilities?

Jacoby's procedure is as follows. You give people two separate lists to study, and then give them two recognition tests. In one (the inclusion test), they are told to answer yes if the test item had appeared in *either* list; in the other (the exclusion test), they are told to answer yes *only* if it had appeared in one specified list (which could be either the first or the second). You record two measures: the probability of a correct 'yes' (a hit) in the inclusion test, and the probability of an incorrect 'yes' (a false alarm, defined as saying 'yes' to an item that had appeared in the *other* list) in the exclusion test.

In the inclusion test, a hit could occur either because the participant had recollected that the item had indeed occurred in one or other list (R), or because, although he did not recollect having seen it (1 − R), it just seemed familiar (F). This probability of a hit can be expressed as:

$$Pr(hit) = Pr(R) + Pr(1 − R).Pr(F)$$

In the exclusion test, a false alarm occurs when the participant does not recollect which list an item appeared in, but it just seems familiar:

$$Pr(fa) = Pr(1 − R).Pr(F)$$

So, the participant's recollect score (R) is given by the difference between Pr(hit) in the inclusion test, and Pr(fa) in the exclusion test, and once R has been determined it is a simple matter to calculate his F score. Table 8.2 shows the results of a study by Jacoby et al. (2001) with young and old adults. They differ substantially in their recollect score, but not in their familiarity score. In other words, older people may preserve their sense of familiarity about recent events, even though they cannot recollect exactly when they saw it, that is, just why it should seem familiar.

Table 8.2 The results of a study using Jacoby's process dissociation procedure to estimate young and old participants' probability of actually recollecting an item they had studied earlier, in contrast to just saying they recollected it because it seemed familiar (data from Jacoby et al., 2001, Tables 1 and 2).

	Hits (inclusion test)	False alarms (exclusion test)	Process estimates	
			Recollection	Familiarity
Young	0.80	0.35	0.44	0.63
Old	0.73	0.44	0.29	0.62

Gf and executive function

The decline in Gf in old age seen in Figures 8.7 and 8.8 is mirrored by a comparable decline in performance on tests of executive function, Stroop test, Wisconsin Card Sorting Test, Tower of Hanoi, and so on (Raz, 2000). A similar decline is observed on tests of working memory (with notably less decline in immediate memory span, Bopp and Verhaegen, 2005). By now it should come as no surprise to learn that this deterioration in performance is accompanied by a reduction in volume of prefrontal cortex (Raz, 2000; West, 1996). As noted in Chapter 6, imaging studies have also reported that there is greater recruitment of dorsolateral prefrontal cortex in older than in younger people when they are given tests of working memory or Raven's Matrices (Esposito et al., 1999; Reuter-Lorenz, 2002).

Some are luckier than others

The observation that increases in reaction time at one age predict later ill health and death illustrates a more general point, strongly emphasized by Schaie (2005). The picture of cognitive decline shown in Figures 8.7 and 8.8 is an *average*. Some people decline faster than this average (and usually die sooner), others show little or no evidence of decline well into their eighties. What are the causes of these differences? One major cause is general health, and a healthy lifestyle. Cardiovascular disease (heart attacks, strokes) is associated with significant cognitive decline, as is arthritis; while refraining from smoking and drinking, and eating healthy food are associated with maintained cognitive functioning (Chapters 10 and 11 in Schaie, 2005). None of this seems very surprising (even if some people will find it unwelcome). More controversially, there is compelling evidence that the status of people's jobs is associated with maintenance of their cognitive abilities: jobs that are routine and require little in the way of decision making or problem solving result in earlier cognitive decline. Perhaps in compensation for this unfair advantage, retirement from more demanding jobs is associated with a sharper immediate decline in cognitive function than is retirement from more routine jobs (Chapter 11 in Schaie, 2005). One encouraging observation from the Seattle study is that the rate of cognitive decline is itself declining. People born in 1930 or 1940 maintained their cognitive abilities into old age more successfully than those born 20 or 30 years earlier—a further reason, perhaps, for postponing compulsory retirement beyond the age of 60 or 65.

Complementary changes as young children grow older and old adults grow even older

It should hardly be necessary to draw attention to the parallels between the changes in cognitive performance in young children as they grow up and in older people after the age of 50 or 60. Children's reaction times speed up as they grow older, adults' slow down; children's performance on many tests of memory, executive function, and Gf improves between the ages of 5 and 20, adults' eventually deteriorates; prefrontal cortex is the last region of the brain to mature, and the first to go. The parallel may not be complete, for example Nettelbeck and Burns (2010) argued that although increases in processing speed in young children might provide a complete explanation for their improvement in performance on tests of working memory and then Gf, this was not true for the complementary changes after the age of 50 or 60.

It is worth concluding with one further, perhaps more surprising parallel, sometimes referred to as 'differentiation' and 'de-differentiation' effects. Several studies have shown that the correlations between performance on different IQ tests and between performance on different executive tasks is greater in younger than in older children; these correlations remain moderate between the ages of 20 and 50, but then increase again in old age. Although there are many exceptions to this general rule, it seems that cognitive abilities may differentiate as children grow older (Tideman and Gustafsson, 2004), and eventually dedifferentiate again in old age (Baltes and Lindenberger, 1997). A study by Li *et al*. (2004) provides a particularly clear example of both effects: some of their data are shown in Figure 8.9. What is the explanation?

The results are reminiscent of the finding reported in Chapter 7—that *g* is more important, that is, accounts for a higher proportion of the variance in test scores, at lower than at higher levels of IQ. Young children and old adults have lower absolute test scores than

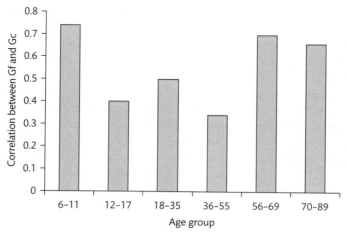

Figure 8.9 Evidence of 'differentiation' and 'de-differentiation': the average correlation between scores on tests of Gc and Gf is high in young children, decreases as they grow older, and then increases again in old age (data from Li *et al.*, 2004, Figure 2).

people aged between 20 and 50, so perhaps it should not be surprising that the correlations between their scores on different tests should also be higher. Of course it will hardly do to suggest that they suffer from a greater number of mildly deleterious mutations (an explanation I offered in Chapter 7), but the later development and earlier decline in prefrontal cortex may have much the same effect. Any decrease in the efficiency of the executive processes mediated by dorsolateral PFC will place greater demands on them and thus increase their contribution to performance on a variety of different tasks. In other words, it will ensure higher correlations between performance on different cognitive tests.

Conclusion

IQ tests are highly reliable. By the age of 8 or so, indeed, childhood IQ predicts adult IQ surprisingly well, and your IQ score remains reasonably stable throughout your adult life. Although traditional IQ tests given at age 2–4 predict later IQ very poorly, one measure taken in the first year of life, rate of habituation to a novel stimulus, correlates with 10-year-old IQ at about 0.50.

However, an IQ score is simply a measure of your relative standing among people of your own age, so a high correlation between IQ at age 10 and at age 70 does not imply that people's absolute level of performance stays the same. Of course it does not: older children do better on IQ tests than younger children, and there is evidence that adults' scores on at least some kinds of test may decline quite sharply after the age of 50 or 60.

That absolute test scores should improve throughout childhood is hardly surprising: a 15-year-old has a larger vocabulary and fund of general knowledge than a 5-year-old. Schools teach children to read and do arithmetic, and although they do not explicitly set out to teach them how to solve the kind of problem that appears in Raven's Matrices, there is good evidence that the experience of school does enhance children's ability to solve this sort of arbitrary, abstract puzzle.

Young children perform worse than older ones on tests of immediate memory span and working memory, differences that may be partly attributable to differences in speed of processing. Although one would perhaps expect that young children should be slower at reaction time tasks than older ones, this speeding up of reaction times continues throughout adolescence, with 20-year-olds being substantially faster than 14-year-olds. This is certainly consistent with the idea that speed of processing is an important ingredient of intelligence. But the development of prefrontal cortex is surely implicated in the development of executive control and improvement in performance on tests of executive function.

It has long been thought that although adults' test performance remains reasonably stable between the ages of 18 and 40, it then declines quite sharply, especially on tests of nonverbal IQ. It turns out that this is partly an artefact of cross-sectional studies. Longitudinal research suggests that IQ test performance holds up rather better. There are, however, significant differences between different components of IQ: performance on tests of Gs starts to decline at an earlier age than other tests, while scores on tests of Gc may actually increase until the age of 60 or more. In many respects, the decline in test performance in old age is the mirror image of the improvement in performance throughout childhood. Older children are faster than younger ones; older people are slower than younger adults; older children are better at any test of short-term memory, and show enhanced executive control; older adults are bad at retrieving recent memories, and show a decline in executive control; and many of these changes are at least correlated with the growth and decline of prefrontal cortex. One of the more important findings about old age and intelligence is that people differ very substantially in the rate of decline in their test scores. These differences are associated with differences in earlier levels of intelligence, with differences in social class, and differences in diet and general lifestyle—all of which are themselves of course correlated.

 ## Summary

- IQ tests are reliable, and after the age of 8 or so, IQ scores remain quite stable for the rest of people's lives.

- The stability of *IQ*, of course, does not mean that absolute test scores remain constant. They increase throughout childhood, and scores on most tests eventually start to decline.

- Changes in speed of processing and in executive control contribute to both the improvement in test scores throughout childhood, and their eventual decline.

- The decline in test scores in old age is exaggerated by cross-sectional studies, but both cross-sectional and longitudinal studies agree that performance on tests of Gc hold up very much better than performance on most other components of IQ.

Further reading

The now classic Scottish studies by Deary *et al.* (2000, 2004) provide the most remarkable evidence for the long-term stability of IQ. Kavšek (2004) summarizes the evidence relating infant habituation to later test scores. Kail and Salthouse (1994) show how speed of processing develops as children grow older, and Fry and Hale (1996) develop this idea into an account of changes first in working memory and later IQ. Salthouse (1996) argues that changes in speed of processing underlie the changes in intelligence as people grow older. Deary (2000, Chapter 8) provides a good review of cognitive ageing, which questions whether this could be a complete account, and Schaie (2005) describes the Seattle longitudinal study. Craik and Salthouse's (2000) edited handbook contains a number of relevant chapters.

9 The predictive validity of IQ—and some limits

Introduction

Earlier chapters have reviewed the attempts of cognitive psychologists to identify some of the component operations or processes that might underlie people's performance on IQ tests. In so far as these attempts have met with at least some success, they have perhaps suggested that the tests have succeeded in measuring something (or things) that could reasonably be called 'intelligence'. For much of the twentieth century, however, IQ testers themselves took a quite different approach. They sought to prove that their tests must be measuring intelligence because they predicted a variety of other important things about people's lives that could reasonably be taken to be indices of intelligence, for example who would be successful and who would not. They relied on establishing the *validity* of their tests, by showing that test performance correlated with other, external criteria of intelligence (see Box 9.1).

BOX 9.1 The varieties of validity

Test theory traditionally distinguishes between three different measures or meanings of validity—concurrent validity, predictive validity, and construct validity. Concurrent and predictive validity are measured by the degree of correlation between test scores and other external criteria: the only difference is that concurrent validity is measured by the correlation with an independent measure taken at the same time, while predictive validity is measured by the correlation between a test score and some independent measure taken at a later date. Thus, if the external criterion is performance on some test of educational attainment, such as school exam results, concurrent validity is measured by the correlation between IQ and exam results both measured at age 12, while predictive validity would be measured by the correlation between IQ at age 12 and exam results at age 16.

Construct validity is a somewhat trickier concept. As put by Jensen:

Construct validity may be defined theoretically as the correlation between test scores X and the construct C the test is intended to measure…In reality, of course, the problem is that we have no direct measure of C. And so the process of construct validation is roundabout, consisting mainly in showing in more and more different ways that the test scores behave as should be expected if, in fact, the test measures the construct in question.

(Jensen, 1980, p. 422)

So the construct validity of an IQ test refers to the extent to which it successfully measures 'intelligence'. And how are we to decide the answer to that? It is easy enough to see that some measures, although correlating with intelligence, have no construct validity as *measures* of intelligence. Recall that the critical insight that allowed Binet to develop the first successful intelligence test was that, in the case of young children, age provided an independent criterion of intelligence. But children grow in height and weight as they grow older, and no one would suggest substituting a tape measure or pair of scales for an IQ test as a satisfactory measure of intelligence. They have no construct validity.

In Chapter 1, I provided a list of requirements that one would expect to see satisfied by any test purporting to measure intelligence (pp. 4–5), and suggested that IQ tests did satisfy these criteria. This was evidence of the tests' construct validity. There is an obvious problem: it is inevitably a matter of judgement whether a particular set of test questions has construct validity as a measure of intelligence: it does not seem likely that Jensen and Gardner would agree in their answer: indeed Gardner would presumably argue that *no* set of paper and pencil questions could have good construct validity as a measure of his intelligences (see Chapter 10).

Two external criteria have traditionally been accepted by most psychometricians: they were both first used by Galton (1869). He argued that eminence and achievement provided one criterion of intelligence: successful generals, judges, politicians, men of affairs, were presumably more intelligent than those less successful in these professions, let alone those who failed to acquire such positions in the first place. And he also used performance at public examinations, specifically at Cambridge University and in the Civil Service, as a second criterion of intelligence. Educational and occupational attainment have been the most popular external validators of IQ tests ever since.

There is good evidence that IQ does indeed predict both educational and occupational success, but the predictions are far from perfect. That should not be any cause for surprise or alarm. Passing exams depends on a certain amount of hard work, as well as intelligence. A reasonable level of intelligence may be necessary if you are to succeed in business, but it is surely not sufficient: many other characteristics are likely to be important—drive, ambition, the desire for money, to name a few. And good luck will probably also help. But it remains possible that some of these other characteristics are cognitive in nature, although not picked up by IQ tests.

Early validity studies

Their failure to correlate with one index of educational attainment, college grades, proved the downfall of Cattell's original mental tests (Wissler, 1901; see Chapter 1). In spite of this, many of the pioneers of intelligence testing took a distinctly cavalier attitude to the need to establish the validity of their tests. Although Binet, for example, noted that his tests succeeded in identifying children classified as 'feeble-minded' (mildly or moderately disabled), he did not regard this as particularly strong evidence for the validity of his tests, since he immediately went on to insist that the tests did this job *better* than current medical practice: 'The typical doctor, when he is confronted with a retarded child, does not examine him by listing, interpreting and classifying each of the symptoms the child presents; he is content to rely on a subjective, global impression, and to make his diagnosis by instinct'

(Binet and Simon, 1905a, p. 168). As for schoolteachers, Binet argued, they were often prepared to classify as subnormal children who were simply ignorant or troublesome. Why, he argued, should one suppose that one has validated an IQ test by establishing its agreement with such an unreliable criterion?

Binet also noted that his test results agreed with one indicator of scholastic ability: children with above average test scores were more likely to be a year or more ahead in school, while those whose mental age was lower than their chronological age were more likely to be a year or more behind at school (Binet, 1911). But although he acknowledged the significance of this finding, it did nothing to qualify his insistence that intelligence and scholastic aptitude were not the same. He was even more dismissive of schoolteachers' assessments of their pupils' intelligence. When he asked teachers how they undertook such assessment, many of their replies seemed to him to be pointless and merely verbose, while others confused knowledge (usually simply the ability to remember what the teacher had told them) with judgement or intelligence. Binet had sufficient confidence in the validity of his own methods for devising tests that he hardly seems to have felt the need for much external evidence of their validity.

In his introduction to the Stanford-Binet test, Terman (1916) dwelt at much greater length on the question of his test's validity. But the impression he gives is that of a salesman eager to extol his wares, rather than of a scientist soberly evaluating the evidence. He begins by arguing that most people have greatly underestimated the extent to which children (and adults) differ in natural intelligence, with the result that on the one hand they do not appreciate the true magnitude of the burden imposed on society by the large number of feeble-minded people, and on the other that they fail to recognize how many exceptionally intelligent children receive an education that does no justice to their abilities. Properly used, intelligence tests will more than pay for themselves.

> Not only in the case of retarded or exceptionally bright children, but with many others also, intelligence tests can aid in correctly placing the child in school...The hour of time required for the test is a small matter in comparison with the loss of a school term [resulting from incorrect placement]...The time is probably not far distant when intelligence tests will [also] become a recognized and widely used instrument for determining vocational fitness...Any business employing as many as five hundred or a thousand workers...could save in this way several times the salary of a well-trained psychologist.
>
> (Terman, 1916, pp. 16–18)

Terman agreed with Binet that teachers cannot be trusted to assess their pupils' intelligence with any degree of accuracy, and provided examples of discrepancies between test scores and teachers' assessments that invariably illustrated the accuracy of the former and the egregious error of the latter. But how did he know that his test scores were right? With little sense of embarrassment, he happily validated the test scores of his standardization sample by reporting 'a fairly close agreement' (p. 73) between IQ scores and teachers' grading of their pupils' schoolwork on a five-point scale from very superior to very inferior. The correlation was in fact only 0.45. Even then he was not content to accept the teachers' gradings as themselves valid, but argued that most discrepancies were caused by teachers' failure to take their pupils' chronological age into account (superior work by a child a year older than the rest of her class would be entirely consistent with an average, or even below average, IQ score). The only other correlation he reported as evidence of the validity of his test was one of 0.48 between IQ and teachers' ratings of intelligence. Here too, whenever there was disagreement, 'the fault was plainly on the part of the teacher' (p. 75).

A similar confidence marked the work of those who sold IQ testing to the US Army in World War I. The tests were given to some 1.75 million recruits, but although their test scores sometimes affected the jobs they were assigned to (frequently being used for selection for officer training, for example), little or no evidence was ever presented to establish that those scores provided a valid indicator of anyone's ability to undertake any military job, or their success at it. This is not really very surprising. The world of adult work does not provide such a convenient testing ground for the validation of IQ tests as does the school classroom. Schoolchildren are routinely assessed by their teachers; they are required to take exams; they can be given other tests of attainment as part of the school system's evaluation of their progress and its own efficiency. There is little difficulty in comparing the results of all these evaluations with those of an IQ test. But what constitutes success in a given job, and how is any assessment of that success to be obtained? Certainly when he came to develop his individual IQ tests for adults, Wechsler had little evidence to which he could point to establish the validity of his tests. He noted that adolescents' scores on his test correlated highly (r = 0.82) with their scores on the Stanford-Binet, and also, moderately well, with teachers' ratings of their intelligence. In the case of adults, he noted that his tests discriminated well between those classified as retarded and those not so stigmatized. For the rest, he simply acknowledged the problem:

> How do we know that our tests are 'good' measures of intelligence? The only honest reply we can make is that our own experience has shown them to be so. If this seems to be a very tenuous answer we need only remind the reader that it has been practical experience which has given (or denied) final validity to every other intelligence test. Regrettable as it may seem, empirical judgements, here as elsewhere, play the role of ultimate arbiter.
>
> (Wechsler, 1944, pp. 127–8)

Regrettable—but certainly honest.

IQ and educational attainment

This brief excursion back into the early history of IQ testing should not be taken to imply that there are no external criteria to which one can point as validators of IQ. Although critics such as Murdoch continue to claim that the tests 'do not test intelligence and have negligible ability to predict academic achievement' (Murdoch, 2007, p. 231), there is no shadow of doubt that test scores correlate moderately well with Galton's two criteria of intelligence, educational and occupational achievement (for a good summary, see Sackett et al., 2008). Since IQ tests were first developed for use in schools, it is not surprising that their validity has been most extensively studied by measuring their correlation with various indices of educational attainment. These indices include: formal tests of reading or mathematics; more general measures of educational attainment, such as public exams (in Britain) or school or college grades (in the USA); whether students stay in school after completing GCSE exams at age 16 (in England) or complete high school (in the USA); whether they obtain undergraduate or graduate degrees; or finally the total number of years of education received. It has been clear for 50 years or more that IQ scores correlate with all these measures.

Correlations between IQ scores and formal tests of reading, mathematics, or other subjects, and between IQ and school exam performance or grades, range between 0.40 and 0.70 (Brody, 1992; Jensen, 1998; Lavin, 1965; Vernon, 1947). The general consensus has been that higher correlations are found with younger children, and that correlations decline as students progress through school, college, or university. Where any decline has been observed, it has been attributed to increasing restriction of range, since those of lower IQ and educational attainment are likely to drop out of school, leaving a more restricted range of scores in older samples. But no one seems to have undertaken the longitudinal study that would test the truth of this assumption: it is not known whether the selected sample of those who stay in education beyond the age of 20 would have shown an equally low correlation between IQ and educational attainment when tested at age 8 or 10.

There is also a significant correlation (of 0.50–0.60) between IQ and total number of years of education (e.g. McCall, 1977; Strenze, 2007), and thus between IQ and educational qualifications. In the USA, for example, there is a 10–15 point difference in average IQ between those who graduate from high school and those who drop out before graduating, and a similar difference between high school graduates and those who go on to obtain a college or university degree (Herrnstein and Murray, 1994).

There can be no reasonable doubt that IQ scores do not just record people's ability to answer the arbitrary questions posed by IQ testers; they say something about how long people stay in the educational system, and the qualifications they obtain, as well as their performance on standard measures of educational attainment. But it is also important to try to understand *why* there should be such pervasive correlations between IQ and educational attainment.

One sceptical answer is that the correlations were built into the tests: IQ tests were constructed precisely with the requirement that their scores should correlate with educational attainment, and therefore included items that simply measured such attainment (Evans and Waites, 1981). Given that both the WISC and Stanford-Binet tests include, for example, an arithmetic test, this argument might seem moderately plausible. But it will hardly do as a sufficient explanation. Binet's and Terman's dismissive attitude towards teachers' judgements should make it clear that they did not go about the business of test construction by carefully selecting items that would agree with them. Nor is there any reason to suspect that Raven's Matrices were constructed with this end in mind.

A second sceptical answer is that the correlation between IQ and some measures of education, such as educational qualifications obtained or total number of years of education received, may reflect the effect of education on IQ as much as the effect of IQ on education (Ackerman and Lohman, 2003; Ceci, 1991). There is after all convincing evidence that schooling is good for your IQ (see Chapter 12), so it is hardly surprising that people who stay in the educational system longer should end up with higher IQ scores than those who leave school at the first opportunity.

How important is this? It is impossible to say. But it can hardly be the whole story, since the correlation between test scores and educational attainment is not just a correlation between two concurrent measures: test scores at one age predict educational attainment at a later age. The IQ scores of kindergarten children predict their performance on tests of reading one, two, or three years later, with no decline in the correlation between the two as the interval between IQ test and reading test increases (Horn and Packard, 1985). In Britain, two large studies, of 14,000 and 70,000 children respectively, reported substantial correlations between 11-year-old IQ scores and performance on GCSE exams at age 16: in one the correlation was about 0.50 (Mackintosh and Mascie-Taylor, 1986); in the other the correlation between *g* and a general factor of exam performance was a remarkable 0.81 (Deary *et al.*, 2007b). American longitudinal studies have shown that as early as age 10, IQ correlates between 0.40 and 0.50 with total years of education or final level of educational qualifications received (McCall, 1977; Strenze, 2007). Finally, there is good American evidence that SAT scores used for college admission predict performance, measured by grade point average (GPA), throughout students' time at college (Sackett *et al.*, 2008).

The consistent finding that IQ at one age predicts later educational achievement suggests that the intelligence measured by the tests does indeed have an impact on educational achievement. It is complemented by a second observation: using a design similar to that employed by Deary *et al.* (2009; see p. 182), termed a cross-lagged panel design, Watkins *et al.* (2007) took measures of IQ and educational achievement in a group of 9-year-old children, and again three years later when they were 12. Consistent with the data reviewed above, they found that earlier IQ predicted later educational achievement, but critically that earlier educational achievement did *not* predict later IQ. To the extent that these results can be generalized (the children were being assessed for possible special education), the direction of causality implied by the correlation between IQ and achievement is from IQ to achievement, not vice versa.

The causal chain may, however, be quite indirect. A young girl with a high IQ score is likely to be doing well at school, and to enjoy school. Teachers will find her rewarding to teach. She is more likely to make friends with other clever children than with those who are struggling. She is thus creating for herself a high IQ environment. She and her friends will want to stay on at school, and then want to go on to university. Conversely, the young boy with a low test score will find school work difficult and unrewarding, will make friends with others who also dislike school, and leave at the first opportunity. To an unknown extent, the effect of differences in intelligence at one age may be to channel children into different paths which reinforce these early differences.

Family background

A final point that needs to be made is that the correlation between IQ and educational attainment is not simply a consequence of family background. Critics have argued that middle-class parents endow their children with a high IQ (whether genetically or by providing a suitable early environment), and also, but independently, teach them to read at an early age, provide them with books and personal computers, place an emphasis on school attainment, supervise their homework, send them to good schools, and can afford to keep them there beyond the minimum school leaving age, and so on. The correlation between children's IQ scores and their educational attainment may not reflect a direct causal link from one to the other, but only the fact that both are determined by the children's family background or social class.

The argument has been expressed most forcibly by Bowles and Gintis (1976). It seems plausible enough, but there are two reasons why it cannot be the whole story. First, with the exception of Bowles and Gintis themselves, essentially every study has shown that the correlation between family background, however measured, and educational attainment, however measured, is smaller than that between children's IQ scores and their educational attainment. Different studies have reported widely differing estimates of the strength of the relationship between family background and educational attainment. One systematic analysis (White, 1982) suggested that the correlation was less than 0.25; a more recent meta-analysis (Strenze, 2007) suggested a somewhat higher figure (r = 0.41). But even this higher figure was smaller than the correlation between children's IQ scores and their subsequent educational attainment in Strenze's analysis. A study of over 600 Brazilian children reported correlations between IQ and educational attainment ranging from 0.44 to 0.69, while the correlations between parental income or education and their children's educational attainment ranged from 0.01 to 0.25 (Colom and Flores-Mendoza, 2007). Second, and even more decisively, the correlation between children's IQ scores and their educational attainment is found within families as well as between families. Even among brothers and sisters living in the same family, differences in IQ predict differences in at least two measures of education—number of years of education received and probability of obtaining an undergraduate degree. From the larger sample of young people whose data were analysed by Herrnstein and Murray (1994), Murray (1998) found some 1,000 pairs of siblings, where one had an average test score (IQ = 90 to 109), while the other had a test score either above or below this range. As can be seen in Figure 9.1, siblings with higher test scores were more likely to obtain a bachelor's degree than their average sibling, while those with lower test scores were very much less likely to. Related to this, of course, there was also a substantial difference in the number of years of education received. These within-family differences imply that family background is not a sufficient explanation of the association between IQ and educational attainment.

Statistical analysis confirms this conclusion. In their larger sample, Herrnstein and Murray (1994) showed that when parental socio-economic status (SES) was held constant,

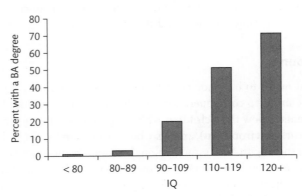

Figure 9.1 The percentage of people obtaining a BA degree as a function of their IQ. Those in the two lower and two higher IQ bands (< 90, or >109) were all siblings of the 'reference group' of people in the 90–109 IQ band (data from Murray, 1998, as presented by Lubinski, 2004, Table 3).

IQ scores were still strongly related to two measures of educational attainment—obtaining a high school diploma and a university degree. But when IQ was held constant, the relationship between parental SES and these educational achievements was quite modest. Strenze's (2007) meta-analysis suggested that Herrnstein and Murray's data underestimated the importance of family background (just as Bowles and Gintis's analysis overestimated it), but still confirmed that controlling for family background did not eliminate the relationship between test scores and educational attainment. Although American critics of the SAT have variously claimed that it should simply be called a wealth test, or that it only measures the size of a student's house, Sackett *et al.* (2008) reported that controlling for SES reduces the predictive validity of the SAT for GPA by only a trivial amount, from 0.47 to 0.44. Strenze was, however, able to dispute a further argument advanced by Herrnstein and Murray that the relative importance of IQ and family background changed over the course of the twentieth century. It might seem reasonable to suppose that entrance to Harvard, Yale, or Princeton in the USA, or to Oxford or Cambridge in England, was more dependent on family background, and less on prior educational attainment (or IQ) in the first half of the twentieth century than it is today. But Strenze's analysis suggests that there is little evidence to support this conjecture.

The relationship between test scores and a variety of measures of educational achievement provide reasonable grounds for accepting that an IQ score measures something other than the ability to answer questions on IQ tests, and that this something is related to success in one sphere of activity where 'intelligence' has traditionally been thought to be relevant.

IQ and occupation

Some people have been willing to accept that IQ scores successfully measure academic intelligence, but immediately gone on to suggest that this is *all* they measure (Neisser, 1976; Sternberg, 1997): IQ tests, they argue, miss out on everyday, practical abilities—those needed for success in the real world outside the school classroom or university ivory tower. It is here that Galton's second criterion of intelligence, worldly distinction or eminence, needs to be considered. How well do IQ scores predict whether people will succeed after they leave full-time education?

More prosaic and jargon-ridden than Galton, IQ testers have sought to validate their tests by showing that they predict occupational status or income, and the ability to perform a job effectively. They have argued that IQ scores correlate with three rather different aspects of occupational achievement: the status of a person's job; the income they earn; and the efficiency with which they perform their job. I shall take up each of these in turn.

Occupational status

There is general agreement that some jobs confer higher status and prestige than others. Table 9.1 lists a range of different occupations; although readers may quibble with the precise rank ordering shown in the table, most would probably agree that the job of lawyer, engineer, or other professional has a higher status than that of typist, tractor driver, barber, or miner. Different classification schemes assign jobs to anywhere between five and twelve

Table 9.1 Average IQ and range of scores in various occupations (from Harrell and Harrell, 1945).

Occupation	Mean IQ	IQ range
Accountant	128	94–157
Lawyer	128	96–157
Engineer	127	100–151
Teacher	123	76–155
Clerk-typist	117	80–147
Machinist	110	38–153
Tractor driver	99	42–147
Crane operator	98	58–147
Barber	95	42–141
Lumberjack	95	46–137
Miner	91	42–139

status bands, the details of which need not concern us. Table 9.1 gives sufficient idea of what is meant by the concept of 'occupational status'. As can be seen, the jobs are also ordered by the average IQ score of their incumbents. Studies of adult job holders, both in Britain and the USA, have consistently reported a significant correlation, of the order of 0.40 to 0.60 between their IQ scores and the status of their jobs (see Harrell and Harrell, 1945, and Vernon, 1947, for early studies and reviews; Gottfredson, 2003a; Herrnstein and Murray, 1994; and Strenze, 2007, provide more recent evidence). Strenze's meta-analysis found that the correlation between IQ before the age of 18 and adult occupational status after the age of 30 was 0.41.

One striking feature of the data shown in Table 9.1 is that people with high IQ can be found in all jobs, but those with an IQ below 75 only in the lower status jobs. There is reason to believe that this first point may no longer be true (see Gottfredson, 2003a, p. 299, for more recent data). But it remains true that few people with an IQ below 100 become lawyers. From this, Jensen concluded that: 'A certain threshold level of intelligence is a necessary but not a sufficient condition for success in most occupations: a diminishing percentage of the population is intellectually capable of satisfactory performance in occupations the higher the occupation' (Jensen, 1980, p. 344). Other commentators (e.g. Herrnstein and Murray, 1994) have also accepted this inference. But it surely requires further justification. It is one thing to show that, as a matter of fact, few lawyers or doctors have an IQ below 100. It is another thing to assert that no one with an IQ below 100 is intellectually capable of performing the job of lawyer or doctor. I return to this point below.

What, then, is the explanation of the correlation between IQ and occupational status? As for the case of educational attainment, so here, a popular explanation has been that both are a by-product of the social class into which one is born. High SES parents not only endow their children with a high IQ, they also pass on, or otherwise ensure their children's entry into, their high-status jobs. There is, it hardly needs saying, a significant correlation between parents' social class and their children's eventual occupation: children born into middle-class families are indeed more likely to end up in middle-class jobs than the children of unskilled or unemployed parents. But most studies suggest that this correlation is no more than 0.30 to 0.35 (Strenze, 2007). If that is so, then just as with the case of educational achievement, so here, parental status cannot possibly be the *sole* cause of the higher correlation (of between 0.40 and 0.60) between a person's own IQ and the status of their occupation. Even when IQ is tested before the age of 20, it is a better predictor of later occupational status than is parental social class.

The relationship between childhood IQ and later, adult status is not simply a consequence of one's parents' status. But that still does not mean that there is a simple, direct causal link from one to the other. In fact there is good evidence that the link is at least partly mediated by education. IQ is well correlated with educational attainment and qualifications; not surprisingly, adult occupational status is also predicted by educational qualifications, if only because many jobs require formal educational credentials. Thus, one reason why people with higher test scores obtain higher-status jobs is probably because they obtain superior educational qualifications. Jencks (1972) indeed suggested that although both IQ and years of education are associated with occupational status, IQ exerts most of its influence by its effect on level of education. The remaining (or direct) effect of IQ on occupation may be quite small. Small, but probably not zero: Strenze's meta-analysis concluded that the relation between academic performance and later occupational status ($r = 0.33$) is rather weaker than that between IQ and status ($r = 0.41$).

Although some critics have tried to argue that IQ *per se* is entirely unimportant as a determinant of occupational status (Bowles and Gintis, 1976; Ceci, 1996; Evans and Waites, 1981), this inference seems no more justified than that which saw the correlation between IQ and status as proof that no one with a low IQ is intellectually up to the demands of a high-status job. In the first place, the effect of IQ is still significant even when other variables such as family background and years of education have been allowed for. But it is also important to see just what analyses such as Jencks's could ever show. No doubt the most important single factor determining whether one becomes, say, a lawyer or a doctor, is the possession of the appropriate educational qualifications (a medical or a law degree, for example). By and large, however, only those with a reasonably high IQ will obtain such qualifications: IQ may not have much further impact because it has already done its work by being necessary for the acquisition of the relevant educational qualifications. Only if you could obtain a medical degree regardless of your IQ would it be reasonable to conclude that IQ scores had no bearing on occupational status. Test scores do have an important bearing on people's job prospects, even if much of their effect is mediated through educational qualifications.

Is that all? Is it simply because they fail to obtain the necessary educational qualifications that people with low test scores do not obtain and hold down high status jobs? Is Jensen right to conclude that the data shown in Table 9.1 above prove that a certain level of IQ is *necessary* for adequate performance on some jobs? On the face of it, the only way to answer the question would be via a highly improbable experiment in which access to a particular set of jobs was deliberately made open to a group of people with test scores below the normal threshold for those jobs. Remarkably enough, the experiment has been done. In 1966, the US Department of Defense inaugurated Project 100,000, which required the military to induct a certain percentage of men whose scores on the AFQT (the Armed Forces Qualifying Test) fell below the cut-off (approximately an IQ of 85) normally required for entry to the military (see Gottfredson, 2003a, for an account of this study). The performance of these New Standards men, as they were called, was compared to that of a control group (all of whom had passed the AFQT) over their first two years of military service. The measures included satisfactory completion of basic and more advanced training, satisfactory performance over the full two years, promotion to higher pay grades, and final ratings as a good or highly effective worker. At all stages of this progression, the large majority (over 80%) of New Standards men passed, but in all cases there were more failures than in the control group. As can be seen in Figure 9.2, therefore, the *cumulative* pass rate showed a steady drop to a level substantially below that of the controls. So, IQ matters. But equally, it is not all-important. At the end of two years, the performance of some 40% of those with test scores below the normal cut-off for acceptance into the US military was rated as good or highly effective. High test scores were *not* a necessary precondition for holding down these particular jobs.

Income

A second measure of occupational status is income. Lawyers and doctors are, after all, usually paid more than secretaries, nurses, or lorry drivers, although, as university professors are the first to point out, the pay associated with a particular job is not always commensurate with its importance or social prestige. Some relatively prestigious jobs (teachers) are no better, and often a great deal worse, paid than other less prestigious ones. Status and income are correlated (if they were not, the concept of socio-economic status would hardly have got off the ground), but the correlation is far from perfect; in American data, no more than 0.40 (Jencks, 1972).

Thus, income does provide a partially independent measure of occupational success, and it turns out that its association with IQ is rather different from that between

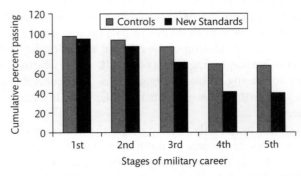

Figure 9.2 Success rates of Control and New Standards men at five stages of military training: 1 = basic training; 2 = skills training; 3 = satisfactory performance over the first two years; 4 = promotion to good pay grade; 5 = good final rating of performance (data from Gottfredson, 2003a, Table 15.5).

status and IQ. In the first place, the overall correlation between IQ and income is notably smaller than that between IQ and occupational status, 0.23 as opposed to 0.45 according to Strenze's (2007) meta-analysis (although one large study reported a correlation of 0.30, Zagorsky, 2007). Once again, of course, these correlations cannot be taken at face value; income is also correlated with other correlates of IQ such as schooling, parental income, parental status, and there is the usual problem of attempting to disentangle the true causal pathway. According to Bowles and Gintis (1976), when these other factors are taken into account there is *no* residual effect of IQ *per se*. Although their conclusion has been frequently cited, their results are again quite atypical. Figure 9.3 shows data from Murray's (1998) sibling study on the average income earned as adults by siblings whose test scores, measured when they were adolescents or young adults, fell into different bands. The difference in income earned by two siblings can hardly be attributed to any difference in family background.

One of the problems in the analysis of IQ and income is that the relationship varies with age, being substantially lower in younger than in older people: in Strenze's meta-analysis, the correlation between IQ and income at age 20–24 was only 0.06, rising to 0.25 at age 35 or over. That is hardly surprising: neither graduate students nor junior doctors are very well paid, and it is not until we are dealing with people over the age of 35 or so that these, and the numerous other cases where a relatively high IQ and prolonged education are initially associated with low income, have disappeared from the analysis. Thus, it is not entirely surprising that Ceci (1996), in an analysis of some two thousand 30-year-olds, should find no relationship between IQ and income once social class and schooling were controlled for. He also reported a more interesting finding—that the effect of their parents' social class on people's income was significantly greater among those of lower IQ than those of higher IQ. This surely inclines one to believe that the less intelligent need the benefit of parental background while the more intelligent can rely on their own ability. Neither of Ceci's observations can justify his conclusion that 'the relationship between IQ and adult income is illusory' (p. 66). On balance the evidence implies that there is a small, but significant, relationship between the two.

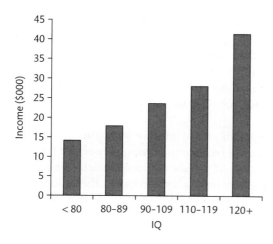

Figure 9.3 Average income as a function of earlier IQ. As in Figure 9.1, those in the two lower and two higher IQ bands (< 90 or >109) were the siblings of those in the 90–109 IQ band (data from Murray, 1998, as presented by Lubinski, 2004, Table 2).

Occupational performance

No one can seriously doubt that income and status are influenced by all manner of educational and social advantages. But the evidence establishes rather clearly that test scores also make a difference. A more direct measure of the importance of such scores, however, would be to see whether they predict how rapidly and effectively people learn the skills needed for a new job, or the efficiency with which they perform their job. And to the extent that some jobs (those of high status) require greater intellectual proficiency, the relationship between IQ and efficiency should be more apparent in some jobs than in others. Not only does this seem a more direct measure of the importance of test scores, it is also, as Gottfredson (2003a) has pointed out, one less likely to be contaminated by extraneous factors such as family background. It is one thing to claim that parental influence is the main reason why the children of wealthy parents obtain a good job, but it stretches the imagination to argue that this parental influence explains why they perform the job better than those with less affluent parents.

Given that test scores predict how well children do at school, and students at college or university, it is not very surprising that they should also predict how well people do on training courses for new jobs (see Ones *et al.*, 2005, for a detailed summary). Different meta-analyses of different data sets have reported values ranging from 0.54 (Salgado *et al.*, 2003), or 0.56 (Schmidt and Hunter, 1998), to as high as 0.68 (Sackett *et al.*, 2008), or 0.71 (Salgado *et al.*, 2003). Salgado and colleagues' meta-analysis is of European studies, and makes it clear that the magnitude of these correlations is directly related to the complexity of the jobs concerned, ranging from 0.36, to 0.53, to 0.74 for jobs of low, medium, and high complexity. American data tell the same story (Schmidt and Hunter, 1998).

It should be pointed out that these are not the raw correlations; they have been 'corrected' for unreliability and restriction of range. How far such corrections are justified is a matter of some dispute, although Sackett *et al.* (2008) have argued persuasively that they are justified in the present case: the true relationship between two variables will be underestimated to the extent that your measure of each is unreliable (subject to error). It is also true that if the pool of trainees has already been selected by excluding any applicant with a test score below some cut-off, then this restriction of range will affect the strength of the correlation observed. The data shown in Figure 9.2 above, from the US Defense Department's Project 100,000, show that trainees with scores below the US military's normal cut-off performed significantly worse throughout their two years of training than those whose scores were above the cut-off. Some correction is surely justified. However, even without correction for range restriction, Hartigan and Wigdor (1989), who applied only a very conservative correction for unreliability of the criterion measure (training performance), still observed correlations ranging from 0.33 to 0.40 between IQ and training for jobs of medium complexity.

Regardless of their absolute magnitude, a possibly more informative picture of the value of IQ scores as a predictor of how well people will respond to training is provided by comparing them with some other possible predictors. If you are an employer screening applicants for a job, what information should you rely on to choose between them? Ree *et al.* (2003) and Schmidt and Hunter (1998) have summarized evidence showing that for a wide variety of jobs a general IQ score (supposedly a measure of *g*) is a better predictor than any of the following: tests of specific abilities, biographical data, references, educational level, college grades, or interviews. Few of these even add any significant further predictive value over and above general IQ. There are, however, exceptions: measures of Gv or spatial ability are good predictors of performance in many jobs (see Chapter 4). How well someone will perform a job may depend on so many factors, some of them idiosyncratic or not easily measured, that prediction will always be imperfect. But IQ predicts performance rather better than these other indices, and IQ is not just a surrogate for years of education or college grades, both of which show lower correlations with performance.

Once they have undergone training, do IQ scores predict how well people will actually perform their job? How is that to be assessed? One measure is provided by supervisors' or managers' ratings; another by supposedly more objective 'work sample' measures, productivity, or rapidity of promotion. The data reviewed by Ones *et al.* (2005) suggest a slightly more variable picture than for training success, but both in Europe (Salgado *et al.*, 2003) and North America (Sackett *et al.*, 2008; Schmidt and Hunter, 1998) the overall corrected correlations can be as high as 0.45–0.60. It does not seem to make very much difference what measure of job performance is used, but as with training, so here, the predictive validity of IQ varies with the complexity of the job, ranging from 0.45 for typists to 0.67 for managers (Salgado *et al.*). Gottfredson (2002) suggests an even wider range: from 0.20 to 0.80 (there are after all substantially less skilled jobs than that of a typist). Her analyses also imply that the importance of intelligence does not diminish with length of time in the job: to the extent that this is true (it is not always, see Hunt, 1995), it implies that test scores do not just predict how rapidly people learn the demands of their jobs. One study, indeed, reported a correlation of 0.38 between test scores taken at the beginning of employment and management level attained after 15 years of employment (Howard and Bray, 1988).

Once again, it must be remembered that most of these correlations are the 'corrected' values: one should not infer that test scores predict actual performance on the job very much better than they predict the type of job you will get or the income you can expect to earn, the values for these latter given above being the raw unadjusted correlations. The raw correlations between test scores and job performance are substantially lower, usually in the range 0.25–0.45.

Conclusion

Although the point is still disputed by some, test scores do predict a variety of indices of educational and occupational attainment. In some cases, this relationship may be partially attributable to factors such as family background, in others the role of IQ may be indirect, largely mediated through its effect on educational qualifications. But neither of these reservations would seem to apply to the important case of how well people actually perform their job. Here, there is evidence that IQ is more important than other measures often taken, such as education, references or performance at interview, and that adding in these other measures often does little to improve prediction.

The contribution of IQ may not be huge, but it is real. It is worth concluding by insisting that the demonstration of a *moderate* correlation between test scores and these other indices of success is the best result the testers could have asked for. If correlations between IQ and other measures had turned out to be zero or negative, there would have been reason to question whether IQ tests could possibly be measuring anything we normally understand by the term 'intelligence'. Paradoxically, however, too high a correlation between IQ and measures of educational or occupational success would have been equally problematic. For these other measures are themselves quite imperfect and unreliable indices of *intelligence*. Not only are teachers' assessments, as Binet and Terman argued, unreliable; more importantly, no one could seriously suppose that intelligence was the sole determinant of educational success: there is ample evidence that other factors are important, perhaps even more important, than intelligence—study skills, determination, self-discipline, and willingness to delay gratification, to name a few (Crede and Kuncel, 2008; Duckworth and Seligman, 2005; Freeney and O'Connell, 2010). A test that purports to measure intelligence, therefore, should not correlate too highly with such an imperfect criterion.

The fact is that there is no such thing as a perfect, independent criterion of intelligence, if only because there is no agreed definition of the nature of intelligence. There is no point, therefore, in insisting that IQ tests must correlate with something that does not exist. And it is equally pointless for a critic such as McClelland (1973) to berate IQ tests for their supposed failure to predict real competence in such walks of life as business management (see Klemp and McClelland, 1986, discussed in Chapter 10). These would be grounds for criticizing IQ tests only if you accept one or other of two assumptions: either that the proper function of the tests is not to measure 'intelligence', whatever that may be, but rather to predict who will, and who will not, be successful in any walk of life; or that 'intelligence' is simply synonymous with every possible competence in every walk of life. Both of these assumptions seem at least open to question. An equally plausible interpretation of the modest correlation between IQ and occupational success is that some people earn more, or are better at certain jobs than others, not because they are more intelligent, but because they are more conscientious, industrious, ambitious, or glib (take your pick). As Chomsky has noted: 'One might speculate, rather plausibly, that wealth and power tend to accrue to those who are ruthless, cunning, avaricious, self seeking, lacking in sympathy and compassion, subservient to authority and willing to abandon principle for material gain, and so on' (Chomsky, 1972, p. 38). Whether or not this is an accurate portrayal of the qualities needed to be a captain of industry or successful hedge fund manager, at more mundane levels the evidence suggests that it is the personality dimensions of conscientiousness and integrity that add to IQ as predictors of success in employment (Schmidt and Hunter, 1998).

Other consequences of differences in IQ

Some of the furore generated by the publication of *The bell curve* arose because Herrnstein and Murray (1994) argued that low IQ was responsible for a whole host of undesirable consequences, damaging both to individuals and to society as a whole—in this following a precedent set by Goddard and Terman at the beginning of the twentieth century (Chapter 1). Those with test scores below 85 or so were not only less likely to obtain good educational qualifications or a high status job, they were more likely to be totally or at least intermittently unemployed, to be in receipt of welfare or benefits and, if female, to have children born out of wedlock. Herrnstein and Murray's data on these and other consequences of low IQ are shown in Table 9.2.

Table 9.2 Relationship between IQ at age 15 to 23 and various other indices (data from Herrnstein and Murray, 1994, Chapters 5, 7, 9, and 11).

IQ band	<76	76–90	91–110	111–125	>125
% Unemployed *	22	19	15	14	10
% Unemployed **	12	10	7	7	2
% Convicted of offence (men)	14	21	15	7	3
% In prison (men)	7	7	3	1	0
% On welfare (women)	31	17	8	2	0
% In poverty	30	16	6	3	2

Unemployed * are men who are described as 'out of the labour force', that is, not looking for work, for a month or more.

Unemployed ** are men registered as unemployed, and looking for work, for a month or more.

To these gloomy figures can be added two further ones. O'Toole and Stankov (1992) reported some data on young Australian males showing that the lower their IQ the more likely they were to die before the age of 40 (this was partly because the probability of dying in a car accident was three times as high in men with an IQ of 80 as in those with an IQ of 115; O'Toole, 1990). Since then, studies of 'cognitive epidemiology' have proliferated, and have convincingly established that differences in IQ are associated with differences in general health and mortality (a special issue of the journal *Intelligence*, November/December 2009, published 14 papers on the topic). For many social scientists, the interpretation of such findings is obvious. Test scores are associated with social class, and so is health: it has long been known that the poor suffer from poorer health, and die at a younger age, than the rich (Elo, 2009). Differences in SES surely have a causal impact on differences in health, but an early study by Lubinski and Humphreys (1992) showed convincingly that differences in IQ were more important than differences in social class. This conclusion has been fully confirmed in subsequent studies from Britain, North America, and Australia (Gottfredson and Deary, 2004; special issue of *Intelligence*): differences in cognitive ability measured in 7-year-old children predicted the probability of dying between the ages of 15 and 57—and this prediction was only very slightly attenuated by controlling for a variety of perinatal factors, father's social class, and number of other children in the family. Although the effect of IQ on mortality is partly explained by accidents and other 'external' causes of death, low IQ also predicts an increase in susceptibility to a variety of diseases, particularly cardiovascular disease, and is quite strongly associated with differences in lifestyle that plausibly contribute to such diseases (see Chapter 8).

A second apparent consequence of low IQ shown in Table 9.2 was first noted and documented by Hirschi and Hindelang (1977): there is a correlation between IQ and crime; on average, criminals have lower test scores than the law-abiding majority. Ellis and Walsh (2003) reviewed over one hundred studies from all parts of the world, and reported that some 90% of studies of delinquency and 80% of studies of adult criminals had found a significant negative correlation between IQ and criminal behaviour. Herrnstein and Murray themselves suggested that the average IQ of convicted criminals was some 8–10 points below the population mean. One rather convincing Danish study (Kandel *et al.*, 1988) followed up a sample of some 1,500 boys considered at risk for later antisocial behaviour; sons whose fathers had served time in prison were more likely than others to end up in prison themselves, but within these families there was a 15-point gap between the IQs of sons who eventually acquired a police record and those that did not. A low IQ predicts getting into trouble with the police independently of family background.

It goes without saying that the vast majority of those with an IQ below 90 or so are not criminals, and that low IQ could not possibly be more than one contributing factor to criminality. It can hardly, after all, explain why some 80% of crimes are committed by young males rather than females. But why should there be any association between the two at all? One popular explanation is that the relationship holds only for those criminals that are actually in prison: intelligent criminals do not get caught; and it is only those of below average intelligence that end up in prison. This seems plausible enough, and may well be part of the explanation. The counter-argument is that the association also holds with self-reports of criminal behaviour—whether resulting in conviction and imprisonment or not. While that is certainly true, there must be some question about the reliability of such self reports: are less intelligent people more likely to boast about crimes they have not even committed? In fact, however, low IQ in young children predicts other aspects of antisocial behaviour that do not come to the attention of the police but do predict later criminal behaviour.

The association between low IQ and criminal behaviour seems genuine (if modest). What is the explanation? The Danish study mentioned above showed that it cannot simply be an effect of family background. Psychometricians have been inclined to argue that low IQ is associated with other unfortunate attributes, such as impulsivity or failure of moral reasoning, once again following a precedent set by Goddard and Terman (Chapter 1). A more prosaic possibility is that it is associated with failure, particularly at school. If you do badly at school, you are more likely to skip school, leave as soon as possible without educational qualifications, and find it difficult to obtain a job. And you must look elsewhere for any boost to your self-esteem. Petty crime may well seem to offer a good solution to all these problems, and petty crime leads to more serious crime.

Exceptional accomplishment

It is time to turn from the apparent consequences of low test scores, to ask a different question. There can be no serious doubt that high test scores are associated with, indeed predict, better than average chances for success—in terms of occupational status and some measures of job performance. But what about seriously superior levels of performance? Does the relationship between test scores and achievement continue to hold at the very highest level? Is the difference between a good doctor or research scientist and a truly excellent one predicted by their IQ scores? Was Galton right to suppose that eminence and genius are reflections of superior intelligence, and if he was, is this superiority captured by an IQ score?

No one has supposed that genius is simply a matter of having an unusually high IQ score, but many writers have thought it probably important (surprisingly enough, even Gardner, 1997, accepts this), and some, such as Eysenck (1995) and Simonton (2003), have argued that a high IQ is a necessary precondition of genius. How, one is inclined to wonder, could anyone know that? The study of genius poses an obvious problem. If you restrict yourself to those universally accepted as a genius, you will end up with a rather small number of mostly historical figures—Julius Caesar, Leonardo, Newton, Wagner, Tolstoy (and so on). And how will you ever decide whether they were intelligent, let alone would have obtained a high IQ score? A larger, contemporary sample could be selected, but it would be on the basis of success, distinction, and eminence—hardly the same as genius.

There has been one heroic attempt to assign an IQ score to a large, historical group of geniuses (Cox, 1926). Cox selected some 300 men and women, living between 1450 and 1850, whose achievements, on the basis of the length of their entry in standard dictionaries of biography, could fairly be described as exceptional (royalty and aristocracy were expressly excluded). She attempted to assess their level of intelligence by examining such biographical information as she could obtain. Although she acknowledged that this was far from perfect and excluded a further eleven possible subjects (among them Rabelais and Shakespeare) for lack of evidence, this did not stop her assigning two IQ scores (one, AI, when they were still young, aged 17 or less; one, AII, as adults), and giving numerical estimates of the reliability of these scores.

There are, no doubt, some cases where sufficiently detailed information of a sufficient range of accomplishments is available that you can be confident that this person was pretty intelligent. Thus John Stuart Mill started learning Greek at the age of 3, was reading Plato when he was 7, having finished writing a history of Rome the year before, and started mathematics, physics, and chemistry the following year. Cox assessed his adolescent IQ at 190, with a reliability of 0.82. But for many of her historical figures (for example Mozart, whose case I discuss in Chapter 10), Cox had no evidence worthy of the name. And that seems inevitable. Jane Austen and George Eliot, for example, were surely, in their very different ways, both unusually intelligent women, but there are simply no reasoned grounds for assigning either of them a specific IQ score. In order to answer the question whether a superior test score predicts a superior level of accomplishment, it will be necessary to return to the contemporary scene, and settle for what can be discovered about the relationship between IQ and more modest degrees of eminence or distinction. Two approaches to this question can be contrasted, one which selects people by IQ and then looks at evidence of their achievements, the other which takes the accomplishments first and then looks at IQ.

The most celebrated example of the former type of study is Terman's, optimistically entitled *Genetic study of genius*. Whatever its defects, and they are many, this massive longitudinal study had the virtue of trying to obtain a broad picture of the accomplishments of a group of individuals with high IQ scores. In a real sense, Terman set out to test Galton's hypothesis that intelligence is an essential ingredient of general eminence.

The study was initiated in 1921. Relying on teachers in various Californian schools to nominate the brightest children in their classes, Terman gave them a series of IQ tests that resulted in a selected group of some 1,500 children, with an average age of 11, and an average IQ of 151 (virtually all with an IQ over 140). The main purpose of the study was to follow the later careers of these children: three final reports (Holahan and Sears, 1995; Oden, 1968; Terman and Oden, 1959) give a detailed account of their adult accomplishments. Table 9.3 summarizes some of them. Although they do not include any Nobel prizes (in spite of the fact that one Nobel laureate was at school in California at the time the study was initiated), by any reckoning they are impressive. But is there any reason to believe that it was the children's IQ scores, rather than some other characteristics correlated with IQ, that predicted their later success? As several critics have noted (Ceci, 1996; McClelland, 1973), the vast majority of the children came from professional families (and those who did not were significantly less successful, see below). The fact that some 80–90% of them (men and women) went to college, compared to less than 20% of the population of California as a whole at that time, is neither here nor there. The proper comparison must be with a group of children from similar backgrounds. Given the large average difference between the IQ scores of members of the same family, the ideal control group would have been their brothers and sisters of lower IQ (as Murray used in his analyses illustrated in Figures 9.1 and 9.3 above).

Terman eventually recognized that a comparison with the general population was not particularly appropriate, and from 1947 on Terman and Oden compared their group of men with all college-educated men for such indices as income. In fact their study did show that family background was important: Terman and Oden (1947, 1959) divided their 700 or so men into the 150 most successful and the 150 least successful. The differences in various standard indicators of success were substantial: twice as many of the former group had graduated from college; five times as many were in professional or managerial jobs, and their income was over twice as high. Although there had been a difference in their initial IQ scores, the difference was small—a mean Stanford-Binet IQ of 155 for the successful group and of 150 for the less successful group. The most notable difference was in their family

Table 9.3 Achievements of Terman's seven hundred men (from Oden, 1968).

Percentage in professional and managerial jobs	86.4%
Median income	$13,464
Members of National Academy of Science or American Philosophical Society	5
Appearing in *American Men of Science*	81
Appearing in *Dictionary of American Scholars*	10
Appearing in American *Who's Who*	46
Number of published books/monographs	200
Number of articles/papers	2,500
Number of patents	50

backgrounds: the fathers of the successful group were over twice as likely to have a college degree and a professional job.

The value of Terman's study, however, does not lie in its demonstration (or failure to demonstrate) that a high IQ will guarantee riches, although in fact his sample did earn somewhat more than other college-educated men. What it surely suggests is that a high IQ is associated with other more notable accomplishments than simply earning a lot of money. Certainly, Table 9.3 lists some impressive achievements, and it is not difficult to show that they cannot easily be attributed to family background alone. For example, in 1959, 70 men (10% of the total) had entries in *American Men of Science*. Even the most generous estimates suggest that no more than 0.1% of American men of comparable age appeared in this volume. In other words, Terman's men were 100 times as likely as the general population to achieve this distinction. Although their family backgrounds were above average, they were certainly not confined to the top 1%.

A more recent series of studies under the umbrella title *Study of mathematically precocious youth*, or SMPY (Lubinski and Benbow, 2006) identified some 1,500 children who had taken the SAT-M by the age of 13, and obtained scores in the top 1% for their age. The study followed them up over the next 30–40 years. As a group, they were much more likely than the general population to go to university, and to go on to obtain a postgraduate degree. Even more impressive is the finding that within this highly selected and well above average group, *differences* in their SAT-M scores predicted significant differences in their accomplishments. In one particular study, for example, those in the top quartile of SAT-M scores were between 3 and 12 times more likely than those in the bottom quartile to have published a scientific paper in a peer-reviewed journal and to have secured one or more patents for an invention (Park *et al.*, 2008).

A high test score as a young child does seem to be associated with a broad range of later accomplishments. What is also needed, however, is the complementary approach: take more or less successful people, perhaps more or less eminent members of a particular profession, and see whether these differences in eminence or success are associated with differences in IQ. Two old studies found little evidence for this. Roe (1953) found no relationship between IQ and a variety of measures of eminence or success in a group of successful scientists. Similarly, MacKinnon (1962) found only a trivially small correlation of 0.11 between IQ and success (estimated by other experts) in a group of 185 successful architects. In one sense, perhaps, these negative results are hardly surprising. These were highly selected people, *all* of whom were relatively successful and all of whom had relatively high IQs. None had an IQ below 105, and the average IQ of the two groups was about 130. But remember the proposition under test: if above-average IQ is associated with above-average success, does it also follow that a *very* high IQ is associated with exceptional success? These two studies at least suggest that the answer might be no.

There is one plausible, but widely ignored, explanation for this, namely that, above a certain level, test scores simply cease to be reliable or valid. A precocious 8-year-old can obtain a high IQ on a standard test by scoring at the level of the average 12 or 14-year-old. But this does not apply for adults. The maximum score obtainable on the WAIS is an IQ of 150, and the difference between an IQ of 150 and one of 140 is a matter of a very small additional number of correct items (some carrying bonuses for speed). The reliability of this difference must be open to question. Lubinski and Benbow (2006) and their colleagues are among the few people to have recognized the importance of this. The reason why they selected children on the basis of their SAT scores at age 13, is that by the time they took the test at age 17–18, when it is normally taken, many were obtaining the maximum score of 800 (a few did so at age 13). As they note, the proposition that exceptionally high test scores predict exceptional accomplishments can only be confirmed or disconfirmed when those scores are not constrained by a ceiling effect.

Where special tests have been constructed for groups of supposedly above average intelligence, the construction of items is usually based on further extrapolation from already difficult items in existing tests. Here one can reasonably question the validity of the new test: by what criterion is one justified in concluding that such extrapolation poses sensible questions that succeed in measuring differences in the same sets of skills as are measured by normal tests? The answer is by no means obvious. For example, verbal IQ can be measured by a vocabulary test: you will obtain a high IQ score if you know the meaning of relatively obscure words, such as lapidary or ordnance. Does it follow that you are even more intelligent if you know that a killergang is something that crushes paper-pulp? Perhaps you just have a fund of esoteric and useless knowledge (or work in a paper mill). Just as there are not enough generally accepted geniuses in the world to undertake a proper study of intelligence and genius, so it has proved difficult to find enough people of very high intelligence to permit the standardization and validation of tests measuring IQ above 140.

Expertise

This is probably protesting too much. Taking Roe's (1953) results at face value, what is it that IQ tests are failing to measure? A clue is provided by her observation that the one feature distinguishing all the eminent scientists she studied was their enthusiasm for their work, which ensured that they spent most of their time actively engaged in it. Perhaps the old saying about the relative importance of perspiration and inspiration in the creation of genius is also true. While this may sound simply like another motivational factor, it also suggests a quite different possibility—that those who are successful in any field of human endeavour are those who have spent a great deal of time learning everything that there is to know about it.

That practice makes perfect, or at least improves things, is a familiar enough proposition. And no one would doubt it, when applied to most sports, the playing of a musical instrument, ballet dancing, juggling, or performing conjuring tricks. These are all activities where prolonged practice may be essential if you are ever to become seriously proficient. But it has not seemed so obvious that a similar truth may apply over a much wider range of activities: what distinguishes the more from the less successful in almost any sphere of human activity may be a difference in the amount of knowledge and expertise acquired about that activity. Successful businesspeople simply know more about their business than less successful ones. Eminent architects spend more time thinking and reading about architecture. Successful professors and researchers work in the evening and at weekends, and throughout the summer vacation, while their less successful colleagues take advantage of the opportunities afforded by the academic life to write detective novels, appear on television, or simply take long holidays. In any profession or occupation, success comes to those who find their work so absorbing that they devote most of their waking hours to it, at the expense of much else in their lives. The expertise thus acquired may be more important than an IQ test score.

According to Ericsson and Charness (1994), for example, by the age of 20, exceptional violinists will have put in some 10,000 hours of concentrated practice, and will continue to practise, four hours a day, seven days a week, in order to maintain their exceptional status. Chase and Simon (1973) also estimated that chess experts had spent some 10,000 hours of practice before attaining expert status. The so-called ten-year rule states that, as a rule of thumb, ten years of deliberate, concentrated practice is necessary for expert status in many different domains (Ericsson, 2006). In what does this expertise consist? And is intelligence important?

In the case of chess, a classic study by De Groot (1965) showed that when expert and novice chess players were given a brief opportunity to view a chess board containing some dozen or so pieces in positions reached after a game had been in progress for some moves, the experts were very much better than the novices at recalling the positions of all the pieces; but when the same pieces were placed at random on the board, their expertise was no longer of any avail: they could recall no more positions than the novices. In a nice twist to De Groot's original study, Chi (1978) and Schneider *et al.* (1993) showed that 10-year-old chess players were substantially better than adult novices at recalling chess positions. Whatever their IQ score, the chess-playing children's mental age must have been well below that of the adults', and as one might expect the children were significantly worse at traditional memory span (digits or letter) tasks than the adults. In a study of adult chess players, Waters *et al.* (2002) found that their scores on a test of visual memory predicted their ability to recall random chess positions, but was wholly unrelated to their chess skill.

The basis for experts' superior recall of real chess positions is that they already have stored in long-term memory many thousands, perhaps as many as 300,000, positions encountered in games of chess, and can therefore compare the positions shown in the test with those stored in memory. Of more practical importance when it comes to playing a real game of chess, they also have stored in memory the moves that led up to, and followed on from, particular positions (Gobet and Charness, 2006). Unlike the novice, therefore, they can select the next move in a game from a far narrower range of possibilities because they do not need to explore the implications of so many possible moves from the current position.

Expertise vs. ability

Practice really does make perfect—or if not absolutely perfect, at least a whole lot better. And this is true over a wide range of human endeavour. Some experts on expertise appear to go even further, arguing that practice is all-important, provided it is sustained, deliberate, and well structured. Can that really be true? It is one thing to acknowledge that prolonged practice and experience are *necessary* for very high levels of achievement. But are they *sufficient*? Could anyone, regardless of their intelligence, aptitude, or talent, become a chess grandmaster or concert pianist if they were willing and able to work hard enough at it?

In the case of musical achievement, at least, there is evidence that the answer is probably no. Carroll (1993) included 'musical sound discrimination and judgement' as one component of his higher-order factor of 'auditory reception', although acknowledging that there were 'few if any trustworthy and *extensive* factor-analytic studies of musical talent' (p. 364). The implication is that people do differ in their talent or aptitude for music. Moreover, several studies have demonstrated moderate correlations between musical accomplishment and more general aspects of measured intelligence. In a study of 10-year-old children by Lynn *et al.* (1989), the correlations ranged from 0.27 to 0.40. Ruthsatz *et al.* (2008) have shown that among high school musicians, undergraduates majoring in music, and students at a musical conservatory, superior musical performance was associated not only with higher levels of musical practice, but also with higher scores on both Raven's Matrices, and on a test of musical ability that is supposedly not much influenced by practice.

What about chess? Is it not an intellectually demanding game? And does this not suggest that grandmasters must be highly intelligent? Perhaps surprisingly, the evidence is at best equivocal. As noted above, a major part of the chess expert's expertise is an astonishingly extensive knowledge base of thousands of possible chess positions—something that must clearly be based on years of practice rather than any particular intellectual skill. And that knowledge base is about *chess*; they do not have exceptional memory for other information.

Several studies have looked for a relation between chess skill and intelligence without success. For example Doll and Mayr (1987), Grabner *et al.* (2006), and Unterrainer *et al.* (2006) all found no correlation between chess skill and scores on a variety of different intelligence tests in groups of 27, 47, and 25 experienced chess players respectively; while Unterrainer *et al.* also found no difference in IQ between their chess players and a control group of non-players matched for age and education. These are of course null results, and based on relatively small numbers of people, but in the absence of any convincing evidence of a positive association between intelligence and chess skill in adults, their cumulative weight cannot be ignored.

There is some suggestion that intelligence may correlate with chess skill in children, who will no doubt have had less experience playing chess than adults (Horgan and Morgan, 1990). Convincing evidence comes from a study by Bilalic *et al.* (2007) of 57 young players, all of whom were attending chess clubs in their schools. An IQ score derived from four sub-tests of the WISC correlated with three different measures of chess skill, r = 0.49 to 0.55. Bilalic *et al.* also took detailed and apparently reliable measures of the amount of time the children had spent practising chess since they first started playing. Here the correlation with the measures of chess skill was even higher, ranging from 0.76 to 0.90. Regression analysis, however, established that IQ and practice made relatively independent contributions to chess skill. In a final part of their study, they looked at a sub-group of 23 exceptionally skilled players, skilled enough to have British Chess Federation ratings based on their performance in competitive matches. Their IQ scores were significantly higher than those of the rest of the children, but rather surprisingly there was a *negative* correlation between IQ and their chess rating. This turned out to be largely because the more intelligent children spent less time practising than the less intelligent. Practice seems more important than IQ as a predictor of chess skill, but intelligence is also important, at least in children who have started playing only quite recently. The results from the elite sub-group suggest that this relationship may hold only in less experienced players, which would help to explain why there seems to be no reliable relationship between chess skill and intelligence in experienced adults.

That measured intelligence contributes to proficiency at early stages of practice in any activity, but becomes less important with prolonged practice is supported by a more trivial example. Rabbitt (1993) reported that in a sample of relative novices, crossword puzzle solving ability was significantly associated with scores on tests of Gf ($r = 0.72$), but in experts this correlation was essentially zero. Perhaps of wider interest is an observation reported by Masunaga and Horn (2001) on ageing and expertise—in this case expertise at the Japanese game of GO (said to be at least as complex as chess). As is well established (Chapter 8), some of the abilities measured by IQ tests start declining in middle age, most notably scores on tests of Gs, Gf, and Gr. When these investigators devised tests of Gf and Gr, but specifically designed to measure these abilities in the context of GO, they found little or no decline in performance in their older participants. At the same time, however, the older experts showed the traditional decline in performance on traditional, domain-free versions of these tests. This interaction between age and domain-specific vs. domain-free tests was not observed in non-experts: older people did worse on both kinds of test.

The claims for the pre-eminent importance of practice rather than any differences in ability have been extended by some writers to encompass creativity. Is prolonged training and deliberate practice all it takes to become a successful composer, artist, or poet? Most people would be sceptical, and their scepticism would be redoubled if you started talking about supreme levels of genius. In Chapter 10 I will argue that there is no good reason to believe that Mozart was exceptionally intelligent. But it is hard to believe that he was not blessed with an exceptional musical talent (whatever that might mean). He may have received an unusually intensive musical education from his ambitious father, but how many people really believe that they could have composed any of his mature works if they had received the same education?

Well, Howe (1999) and Weisberg (2006) have argued that the ten-year rule applies just as strongly to Mozart as to anyone else: it took him at least ten years of concentrated practice before he composed any work that would now be recognized as a masterpiece. That may well be true, but what does it prove? Mozart may have needed the intensive musical education provided by his father, but it does not follow that anyone benefiting (or suffering) from that education would have been able to create the mature Mozart's major compositions. Moreover, given Leopold Mozart's ambition for his son, whose musical education he started at an extraordinarily young age, Mozart would have had to start composing masterpieces before he was well into his teens in order to disprove the ten-year rule. Among classical composers, the case for Schubert, for example, seems rather stronger (see Box 9.2). Poets and other writers provide convincing counter-examples (writing, after all, unlike musical composition, is something that most of us learn to do in the course of our education). Arthur Rimbaud, who can lay claim to have founded the modernist movement in French poetry in the late nineteenth century, composed all his poetry between the ages of 15 and 19, at which ripe old age, he gave up poetry for ever, and travelled in Africa for much of the rest of his short life (Robb, 2000). Similarly, John Keats, having given up his medical education at the age of 14, did not start writing poetry until he was 18. Three years later, having spent all night sitting up with a friend reading Chapman's new translation of Homer, he walked home and next day composed his first much anthologized poem. Three years after that, he composed all his famous odes in a period of a few weeks (Gittings, 1968). Charles Dickens, after jobs in a lawyer's office and as a parliamentary reporter, and having published a number of sketches and a few short stories, sat down to write the first instalment of *Pickwick Papers*, whose publication made him the most famous writer in England (Ackroyd, 1990).

BOX 9.2 Ten years' hard labour? The case of Franz Schubert

Schubert was born in 1797 in a suburb of Vienna; his father was a schoolteacher (Gibbs, 2000). The family was certainly musical, and young Franz learned to play the piano and violin as a boy at home, where he played in the family string quartet. He also received some lessons in counterpoint from the local church organist. But his serious musical education did not start until the age of 11 when he won a choral scholarship to the Imperial College, where he sang in the choir and played the violin in the college orchestra. He also, largely self-taught, started composing small pieces, a long fantasy for piano duet when he was 13, and later (shortly before his fifteenth birthday) more ambitiously an opera, although he never got beyond the first act. His musical abilities were such that the following year he was allowed to start private lessons in music theory and composition with Antonio Salieri, the court Kapellmeister. Over the next 18 months his compositions included several string quartets, overtures, piano duets and trios, as well as songs. He left the college at age 16, and after a year's teacher training took a job as a schoolteacher in his father's school. Over the next three years, aged 17 to 20, while still working as a schoolteacher, he composed four masses, six operas, five symphonies, three string quartets, three piano sonatas, numerous dances and over three hundred songs, several of which (including *Gretchen am Spinnrade* written at the age of 17) are unquestionable masterpieces. At best, he spent no more than 4–5 years in serious and sustained practice as a composer before producing several masterpieces.

In the case of music, more systematic evidence has been provided by Simonton (1991), who obtained estimates for 120 classical composers, of the age at which they started their training in musical composition, and the age at which they composed their first masterpiece (defined as a work still in the repertoire and which has been frequently recorded). The average length of time separating these two events was considerably more than ten years (14 to be precise); more interestingly, however, there was a negative correlation between this time and estimates of the composers' eminence. The greater the composer, the less training they needed before they composed their first masterpiece.

Domain specificity of skill: familiarity breeds success

One secure conclusion can surely be drawn from the study of chess and music: expertise is not only a result of prolonged practice—it is also relatively domain specific. That is hardly surprising: if it takes 10,000 hours to become an expert in one domain, there are simply not enough hours in anyone's life to become expert in many different domains. But it is worth documenting the point that at rather lower levels, people's skills are often confined to areas with which they are familiar and have had practice.

For example, studies of poor, and poorly educated, Brazilian children, living in *favelas* or shanty towns, and supplementing the family income by selling fruit from stalls at street corners or in open markets, have shown that they have impressive mathematical skills (Carraher *et al.*, 1985). The children were first given a series of realistic problems: If one melon costs 35 cruzeiros (Cr$), how much must I pay for six melons? If I buy two coconuts at Cr$ 40 each, how much change will I get from Cr$ 500? From the problems answered correctly by each child, the experimenters constructed for that child a series of formally identical questions in standard arithmetic format: What is 6×35? What is $420 + 80$? The children now solved less than 40% of the problems (see Box 9.3 for another similar example). These and other studies of performance on such Piagetian tasks as class inclusion and conservation make it clear that poor, uneducated children can solve problems when they are presented in a format or context with which they are familiar, but are likely to fail completely when presented with formal or abstract versions of exactly the same problems (see Ceci and Roazzi, 1994, for a review).

BOX 9.3 Computer games: baleful or benign?

Ten-year-old children were given the task of predicting the direction in which a shape on a computer screen would move (Ceci, 1996; Ceci and Roazzi, 1994). The shape would initially appear in the centre of the screen on each trial and after a short time move to another location on the screen, and the children were required to point to where they thought it would move on each trial. The underlying algorithm was simple enough if written down, but not easy to work out from observation. It might, for example, be:

Triangles move left; circles move right; squares move neither left nor right.
Dark shapes move up; light shapes move down.
Large shapes move a long distance; small shapes move a short distance.

After 750 trials, the children were barely above chance, and succeeded only to the extent of having memorized one or two specific instances, for example that a large, dark circle moved to the top right corner of the screen.

The task could be turned into a game by changing some of the surface features without altering any of the underlying algorithms. Triangles, circles, and squares became birds, butterflies, and bees; sound effects were added; and rather than point to the place where they thought the stimulus would move, the children had to move a cursor resembling a butterfly net to capture the animal. Now the children all learned virtually perfectly within 400 trials. As Ceci and Roazzi noted, the children's failure on the first version of the task is consistent with a large experimental literature which says that neither adults nor children are capable of complex, multi-causal reasoning; but any parent who tries their hand at their children's computer games knows better.

Some jobs or daily activities place considerable demands on immediate memory. The barman or waiter who takes orders from a dozen customers at once needs to remember what was ordered and by whom. Bennett (1983) found that waitresses in a cocktail bar could regularly remember up to 20 different drink orders at a time—performance that was well beyond anything achieved by university students who had no practice at the job (a study of dairy workers in Baltimore by Scribner (1986) makes the same point, see Box 9.4).

The plausible inference that the waitresses' achievements were indeed simply the result of prolonged practice is supported by the finding that deliberate, prolonged practice can improve anyone's performance on memory span tasks, even in the arbitrary format in which they appear in the Wechsler and Stanford-Binet tests. Two years of practice allowed one subject, SF, to achieve a digit span (defined as the longest list length that he could recall without error on 50% of trials) of 84, while 4½ years was sufficient for a second subject, DD, to break through the 100 barrier to a digit span of 106 (Chase and Ericsson, 1982; Staszewski, 1990). Neither SF nor DD are described as in any sense out of the ordinary, and their remarkable memory span for digits did not even translate into an unusually good memory span for letters or words.

BOX 9.4 Making light work of shifting the milk

The traditional psychometrician's view is that the higher the status of the job, the greater the intellectual demands it makes: that is why you supposedly need an IQ over 100 to be a lawyer or accountant. An alternative view is that the more menial and boring the job, the more important it becomes to use your intelligence to cut corners and make your life easier. Skilled and experienced workers show considerable ingenuity in this. Thus Scribner (1986) described a study of workers in a dairy in Baltimore. The job of an assembler was to respond to orders from drivers, for example, for:

Ten quarts of wholemilk, six pints of skimmed milk, four pints of buttermilk

Analysis of their performance showed a striking economy of effort that invariably allowed the assemblers to fill each order with the least possible number of moves, given the materials at hand. The first part of this order, for ten quarts of wholemilk, might be satisfied either by adding four to an already partially filled case of six or subtracting two from a case containing twelve. If a case already contained twelve quarts of wholemilk and four pints of skimmed, the complete order would be filled by removing two quarts of wholemilk, adding two pints of skimmed and four of buttermilk. Newcomers, by contrast, responded literally to their instructions, and starting with an empty case would fill it up in the sequence specified by those instructions. Uninstructed practice was quite sufficient to turn a novice into a similarly skilled operator, but when better educated and presumably more intelligent supervisors tried their hands at the job for the first time, they, too, were no better than novices.

It is equally important to use short cuts to reduce the need for mental effort. Scribner described how the drivers solved problems calling for mental arithmetic. Their job included pricing their orders, but rather than operate with the company price list which gave prices per quart or per pint, skilled drivers simplified the problem by recasting it, where appropriate, as price per case. Thus, if asked to work out the cost of 31 pints of chocolate milk at 42 cents a pint, they would not multiply 31×42, but calculate as follows: one case of chocolate milk, which contains 32 pints, costs $31.44 per case, minus one pint at 42 cents comes to $31.02 But given a paper and pencil arithmetic test, drivers whose accuracy on the job was well nigh perfect made numerous errors, even though the problems were formally identical.

In a similar vein, Lave *et al.* (1984) observed that Californian shoppers at a supermarket performed complex feats of mental arithmetic in order to work out which item represented best value for money, at a time when supermarkets carefully refrained from printing unit prices. So which of three bags of rice is the one to buy, when one costs 47¢ for 1 lb, a second 99¢ for 32 oz, and a third $1.39 for 48 oz? The shoppers resorted to a variety of sensible strategies or heuristics to simplify their task. A decision between 20 oz at $1.79 or 24 oz at $1.89 would be made simpler by noting that you got four more ounces for only ten more cents. But just as was the case with the young Brazilian street vendors, there was no correlation between the shoppers' skill in this real-life setting and their performance on formal tests of mental arithmetic.

Domain-specific logic

More general conceptual skills or reasoning abilities may also be confined to particular areas. To take one specific instance, Inhelder and Piaget (1958) reported the case of a 4-year-old girl who knew that, if an apple or pear were cut in half, she would have two pieces of apple or two pieces of pear. But when asked how many pieces there would be if a melon were cut in half, she replied that it depended on how big the melon was. The ability to answer specific questions that fall within your experience is no evidence that your answers depend on the application of a general underlying rule; they may simply reflect specific, associative learning: when an apple is cut by a knife, two pieces of apple will appear. And even the generalization of this rule to melons may not guarantee its generalization to all concrete objects (people, for example) let alone the realization that all manner of things may be divided in half—space, power, etc.

Piaget assumed, however, that the end product of normal cognitive development, the attainment of the formal operational stage, did precisely endow the older child with a general mental logic that could be used for reasoning about anything—an assumption shared by a number of other cognitive psychologists (see Adler and Rips, 2008). But, as Adler and Rips point out, such theories must all face up to one critical finding. If intelligent problem solving is a matter of understanding the abstract logical structure of a problem and then bringing one's mental logic to bear on its solution, you would surely expect that a problem presented in an abstract format would be easier to solve than one presented in a concrete format. However familiar the content of the problem, it would still be necessary to strip that content away to perceive the underlying logical structure. There is ample evidence that this expectation is false. It is not only young children who find familiar versions of a problem easier than an abstract version. Exactly the same holds for well-educated adults, including university students. The content of the premises of a simple syllogism are often critical. For example, from the premises:

All Artists are Beekeepers
Some Beekeepers are Chemists

Does it follow that:

Some Artists are Chemists?

In fact, it does not, although the conclusion is commonly accepted. To see that it is erroneous, it is only necessary to provide a less abstract version of the syllogism (one I tried out at a committee meeting of the Royal Society):

All members of this committee are fellows of the Royal Society
Some fellows of the Royal Society have published no scientific work for the past ten years

Unsurprisingly, no one thought that these premises entailed the following conclusion:

Some members of this committee have published no scientific work for the past ten years

Still one of the more elegant demonstrations of the difficulty that many people have with a simple but abstract logical puzzle is Wason's selection problem, otherwise known as Wason's four-card trick (Wason, 1968; forty years later it still commanded a longer entry in the index of Adler and Rips's (2008) edited book on reasoning than any other topic).

Which cards do you need to turn over to check whether the following rule applies:

If a card has a vowel on one side, it has an odd number on the other.

Figure 9.4 Wason's four-card problem. You are shown the four cards above, and told that each card has a letter on one side and a number on the other. Which cards do you need to turn over to check whether the rule is being broken?

Figure 9.4 shows four cards, two with letters, two with numbers; you are told that each card has a letter on one side and a number on the other, and the problem is to decide which of the four cards must be turned over in order to test whether the following rule is being violated:

If a card has a vowel on one side it must have an odd number on the other.

Virtually everyone sees that they must turn over the A, and nobody wants to turn over the B. A sizeable number of students, up to 10%, want to turn over the 1, presumably to check that it really does have a vowel on the other side (although the rule says nothing about consonants *not* going with vowels, and would not therefore be violated whatever letter appeared on the other side). Even worse, however, only about 20% of students see that they *must* turn over the 2; if it does have a vowel on the other side the rule has, after all, been broken.

These are figures for British undergraduates. Graduate students and research scientists fare only a little better. But there is good evidence that the ability to make the correct choices is related to measures of academic ability: Stanovich and West (2000) reported that those who did choose correctly had substantially higher SAT scores than those who got it wrong.

More intriguingly, however, if the problem is presented in a realistic, concrete format much of the difficulty vanishes. One version asks you to act as a bartender who has to enforce the rule that no one under the age of 18 is allowed to drink alcohol. You are shown four cards: the first says 'Age = 16'; the second 'Age = 20'; the third 'Drinking Coca-Cola'; and the fourth 'Drinking beer'. Nearly everyone sees that you must turn over the first *and* the fourth card.

Why is the second version so much easier than the first? If this were just another example of familiar content making a problem easier, the results would by now hardly be surprising, and would not merit extensive discussion. But there is reason to believe that it is not the *content,* but the nature of the logic, that makes the problem easy or hard. The abstract version of the problem presents an 'if...then' statement familiar to students of the propositional calculus:

If p then q (if a vowel, then an odd number).

This statement is false, if and only if:

p is true, but q is false (there is a vowel, but the number is even).

That is why, if you see an even number, you must check whether there is a vowel on the other side, since if there is, the statement is false.

But the second instantiates a different kind of logic—that concerned with rules, permissions, and obligations (usually termed deontic logic): you are not allowed to drink beer unless you are at least 18. According to Cheng and Holyoak (1985), people are familiar in their everyday life with the logic of permissions and obligations; they have no difficulty in bringing a 'permission schema' to bear on a problem, and therefore no difficulty in seeing when such rules are potentially being violated. When Cheng and Holyoak asked their participants to imagine that they were immigration officials at an international airport, checking arriving passengers to see whether they were entering the country or merely in transit, they had no difficulty in applying the rule:

Passengers entering the country (p) must have a certificate of inoculation for cholera (q), and virtually all turned over the not-q card.

Cheng and Holyoak's critical experiment demonstrated that even a wholly abstract version of a permission rule was solved by the majority of their participants. They were asked to imagine that they were an authority checking whether people were obeying a regulation of the form:

If you are going to take action A, then you must first satisfy precondition P. In other words, in order to be permitted to do A, you must have fulfilled prerequisite P.

The majority turned over the card stating that someone had not satisfied the prerequisite.

Cosmides (1989) added a further twist to Cheng and Holyoak's idea, by suggesting that the critical feature of permission schemata is that they are about social contracts, costs, and benefits: if you wish to gain a particular benefit (drink beer or enter the country), then you must pay the cost (be at least 18 or have been inoculated for cholera). And the reason why people find problems of this sort easy is because our evolutionary history involved learning to live in small cooperative groups, where there was a premium on detecting cheats. In other words, we possess an innate, domain-specific module for thinking about social contracts. The idea is intriguing, but does not easily apply to all permission rules. For example, Manktelow and Over (1990) found that people had no difficulty with the following 'if…then' rule:

If you are going to clean up spilt blood, you must wear rubber gloves.

It is hard to believe that cleaning up spilt blood is a benefit for which one should be prepared to pay the price of putting on rubber gloves, or that you are cheating if you fail to do so. Rather than appealing to an innate cheater-detector module, it seems more sensible to suggest that the logic of permissions and obligations is one that people learn from an early age. The world of the young child is full of things they are allowed to do, and even fuller of things they are not allowed to do. 'You can't have a sweet until you have eaten up your vegetables'; 'You can't go out to play until you have tidied your room'; 'You must finish your homework before you watch TV', and so on. It is hardly surprising that people find it easy to understand new, arbitrary rules when set in this format of permissions and obligations.

Conclusion

Do IQ tests *really* measure intelligence? Studies of the validity, or external correlates, of IQ have shown that an IQ score at age 10 can predict various indices of later educational and occupational success. Such correlations may not always be easy to interpret, but they cannot be explained away by saying that it is differences in social class or family background that are really responsible for the association. They are not. A more interesting problem is that the chain of causation from an IQ score at age 10 to the final level of education achieved by age 25, or the type of job held down at age 40, may be quite complex. Ten-year-old children who obtain high IQ scores probably enjoy school, and their teachers may not only enjoy teaching them, but may also give them more challenging material to learn or stream them in special classes. They will surely be expected to stay in school, and encouraged to apply to a good university. This will not only be good for their IQ, it will also increase their chances of eventually obtaining a prestigious job. It is all too easy to see the rather different fate that may await the 10-year-old with a low IQ, who finds schoolwork difficult, and school a wholly unrewarding experience.

The correlations between IQ and subsequent achievements may not be particularly high, but to the extent that the status of a person's job and the success of their performance depend on their ambition, motivation, and personality, there is no reason to expect more than modest correlations between IQ and success.

At higher levels of achievement, IQ is certainly not the only cognitive factor influencing success. There is no real evidence to prove that genius is a product of an exceptionally high IQ (partly because it is not clear how such evidence could ever be obtained), and although Terman's famous longitudinal study revealed some fairly impressive lifetime achievements of a group of high IQ Californian schoolchildren, there is good evidence that IQ was not the only determinant of their success. Similar conclusions are suggested by studies of successful scientists, architects, and businessmen. In many of these cases, a critical ingredient is simply experience and knowledge: good businessmen are experienced businessmen; good scientists are those who spend all their waking hours thinking about science.

The role of practice in achieving expertise in any domain is by now incontrovertible. Chess players and violinists, so it is estimated, need ten years of sustained, concentrated practice to achieve any serious eminence in their chosen field, and sheer amount of practice is more important than IQ in determining the final level of achievement. At the same time, such practice may produce expertise in only a very narrow domain: years of practice can result in a digit span of 100, but leaves immediate memory span for letters or words no more than average. Similar domain-specific expertise is evident in the ability of young Brazilian street vendors to perform quite complex feats of mental arithmetic in the context of working out the price of six melons or the amount of change a customer is owed, combined with an inability to solve formally identical problems presented in the standard format of a mental arithmetic test. And perhaps even more strikingly, well-educated university students fail to see how to test the truth of a formal 'if...then' statement in Wason's reasoning task, but have no difficulty when the rule is cast in the form of a more familiar statement about permissions or obligations.

 Summary

- The validity of IQ tests has been demonstrated by their ability to predict achievement both in educational settings and in the real world of jobs.
- Success clearly does not depend solely on intelligence, let alone IQ, but also on aspects of personality such as conscientiousness and willingness to delay gratification. So the correlations between IQ and success are rarely more than 0.50, and often less.
- Above a certain level of achievement in many domains (chess for example), expertise seems to be more important than IQ, and expertise depends on prolonged and persistent practice.

Further reading

Although much criticized, Herrnstein and Murray (1994, Parts I–III) are worth reading for evidence that differences in IQ scores predict a lot of other important differences in people's lives. The meta-analyses by Strenze (2007) documents the relationship between early IQ and later educational and occupational attainment. Ceci (1996) should be read for a critical interpretation of some validity studies. Holohan and Sears (1995) provide the latest follow-up to Terman's famous longitudinal study of high IQ Californian schoolchildren. The edited handbook by Ericsson *et al.* (2006) has numerous chapters on expertise in a wide variety of domains.

Is this all? Multiple aspects of intelligence

Introduction

Ever since IQ tests were first developed, a common argument has been that they measure only a narrow aspect of (largely academic) intelligence. Given that IQ predicts not only how well students do at school, but also the kind of job they will later obtain and how well they perform that job (Chapter 9), this is perhaps something of an exaggeration. But that does not mean that IQ tests provide a good measure of *all* aspects of intelligence. Sternberg (1985; Sternberg *et al.*, 1995, 2000) has argued that 'practical intelligence' contributes to people's achievements independently of their academic intelligence. People may use academic intelligence to solve problems that appear in IQ tests or the classroom, but they need practical intelligence to solve the everyday problems that arise in their work. The concept is related to the idea of expertise: successful people in any walk of life are those who know a great deal more about their work than others—and one reason for this is that they have superior practical intelligence. Are there other skills or abilities that deserve the label 'intelligence', but are not measured by IQ tests? One long-standing suggestion has been that they fail to measure social intelligence, something, as I discuss in Chapter 13, which is probably more valued in some cultures than others (and perhaps not valued at all by many professors and research scientists). The best known proponent of the view that IQ tests fail to measure a whole range of different aspects of intelligence is Howard Gardner:

> In the classic psychometric view, intelligence is defined operationally as the ability to answer items on tests of intelligence. The inference from the test scores to some underlying ability is supported by statistical techniques...The apparent correlation of these test scores across ages and across different tests corroborates the notion that...[there is a] general faculty of intelligence, called *g* for short...Multiple intelligences theory, on the other hand, pluralizes the traditional concept. An intelligence is a computational capacity—a capacity to process a certain kind of information—that originates in human biology and human psychology...An intelligence entails the ability to solve problems or fashion products that are of consequence in a particular cultural setting or community. The problem-solving skill allows one to approach a situation in which a goal is to be obtained and to locate the appropriate route to that goal. The creation of a cultural product allows one to capture and transmit knowledge or to express one's

conclusions, beliefs, or feelings. The problems to be solved range from creating an end for a story to anticipating a mating move in chess to repairing a quilt. Products range from scientific theories to musical compositions to successful political campaigns.

(Gardner, 2006, pp. 6–7)

Armed with this definition, Gardner argues that, rather than a single intelligence, *g*, there are at least eight different and independent intelligences.

I start with a discussion of Sternberg's concept of practical intelligence.

Beyond IQ: practical intelligence and tacit knowledge

Experts are people who know a lot about any particular domain. And one major reason why they know a lot about their favourite subject is because they have spent a lot of time learning all about it. This is hardly controversial, although it may be surprising to discover just how important and pervasive the effects of practice are. On the other hand, the evidence for the role of practice in so many fields of human endeavour should make it less surprising that differences in performance, whether it be in school, university, or a job, are only imperfectly predicted by differences in IQ scores. Even if they are less intelligent, conscientious and hard-working students will probably do better at school than lazy, irresponsible ones who never study. All else equal, the doctor who reads medical journals will probably be a better doctor than one who never opens one from one year to the next. The lawyer or accountant who regularly takes work home in the evening will probably be better at their job than the ones who go out to the pub every night. Differences in intelligence can surely be trumped by differences in effort, work ethic, and, no doubt, many other characteristics: there is indeed good evidence that personality characteristics are associated with successful performance of a job (Barrick *et al.*, 2001). None of this should be taken as evidence that IQ is unimportant or that the tests fail to measure 'intelligence in the real world'. The question remains, however, whether IQ scores capture all, or even most, of the relevant *cognitive* determinants of success in many jobs.

There is at least some evidence that they may not. In what they termed 'job competence assessment', Klemp and McClelland (1986) identified a number of outstanding managers in a variety of businesses ranging from industry, financial services, voluntary organizations, military hospitals, and colleges. To be classified as outstanding, the managers had to be nominated as such both by their peers and by senior executives, and to satisfy certain relatively objective criteria. They were then compared with 'average' performers who were nominated by no one and who failed to satisfy the performance criteria. Finally, Klemp and McClelland conducted structured interviews focusing on a few 'key situations', and scored the transcripts of these interviews for the presence of various characteristics or 'competencies'. Many of these were concerned with motivation, personality, and social skills, but many were not. The 'intellectual competencies' identified as distinguishing outstanding from average managers in most, if not all, of the organizations studied are listed in Table 10.1.

Table 10.1 The intellectual competences of successful managers (from Klemp and McClelland, 1986, Table 3).

Label	Indicators
Planning	Sees implications, consequences, alternatives, or if-then relationships. Analyses causal relationships. Makes strategies, plans steps to reach a goal.
Diagnostic information seeking	Pushes for concrete information in an ambiguous situation. Uses questions to identify the specifics of a problem or other situation.
Conceptualization/synthetic thinking	Understands how different parts, needs, or functions of the organization fit together. Identifies patterns, interprets a series of events. Identifies the most important issues in a complex situation. Uses unusual analogies to understand or explain the essence of a situation.

Although presenting no details, Klemp and McClelland claimed that scores on standard ability tests 'tend to be uncorrelated' both with actual proficiency in managerial jobs and with performance on simulated business problems used as part of their assessment programme. This may at first sight seem rather puzzling, since some of the skills listed in Table 10.1 bear more than a passing resemblance to some of the skills tested in standard IQ tests. The ability to see implications, consequences, and alternatives, to identify patterns or interpret a sequence of events, are all surely part of what is involved in solving the sort of deductive or inductive reasoning problems that measure Gf. Why then is there so little connection between the two types of problem? According to Klemp and McClelland, one critical difference is that items in IQ tests set well-defined problems: all the information necessary for solution is given, and there is only one permitted solution. But:

> In real life problems are rarely so clear-cut: before figuring out a solution, one must first figure out the problem. Only then can one know what kind of information to seek out (it is not given) in order to solve it—and then choose a solution, usually from among several possible solutions. The process bears little relationship to the controlled one of an intelligence test...The major differences between outstanding and average managers in intellectual competence are that the former spend more time on the job exercising these capabilities than the latter and employ a greater repertoire of mental responses in doing so. In short, what we discovered is that the difference between capacity to act and disposition to act forms the distinction between average and outstanding senior managerial performance.

(Klemp and McClelland, 1986, pp. 31 and 48)

The charge that IQ tests set problems that are too cut and dried to find any parallel in the real world seems intuitively plausible. There is surely an important difference between being presented with a clearly defined puzzle plus six possible solutions to choose from, and an open-ended problem where you have to work out the solution for yourself, which first requires that you figure out what information might be relevant to its solution. Solving analogies or series completion tasks in an IQ test is not necessarily the same as seeing that there is an analogy between two apparently disparate situations, so that you can use the known solution to one problem to suggest an analogous solution to the other. Consider the following classic problem (from Duncker, 1945):

> A patient has an inoperable stomach tumour. The tumour can be destroyed by radiation, but although weak radiation will not damage normal flesh, it will also not destroy the tumour. Radiation strong enough to destroy the tumour will also destroy normal flesh. How can the surgeon use radiation to treat the tumour?

Given no further clues, only about 10% of university students solve this problem (Gick and Holyoak, 1980, 1983). Gick and Holyoak asked whether the provision of the solution to an analogous problem would increase their chances of success. One such analogous problem was this:

> A general is trying to capture a fortress that can be approached by a number of different roads, all of which have been mined. If he advances his entire army down one road they will set the mines off, but a small group will not. However, a small group will not be sufficient to capture the fortress. For that he needs his entire army. What is he to do?

The solution is simple: divide the army into small groups, all of whom advance down different roads and arrive at the fortress simultaneously. The analogous solution to the tumour problem is, of course, to use a number of independent sources of radiation that converge only on the tumour. If they were just told about the general's problem, with no hint that it might help them to solve the surgeon's, only a minority of students saw the analogy. It was only when they were explicitly asked whether the story of the general might help to solve the tumour problem that a majority of students took the hint. It seems clear that people differ in their ability to see, and make use of, such analogies. Presumably these differences are also found outside the psychological laboratory. But it is at least open to question whether they are measured by standard IQ tests.

Sternberg and his colleagues (Cianciolo *et al.*, 2006; Hedlund *et al.*, 2006; Sternberg *et al.*, 1995, 2000; Wagner and Sternberg, 1986) have drawn a distinction between academic and practical intelligence that expands on that suggested by Klemp and McClelland. In contrast to the cut and dried puzzles that characterize items in an IQ test:

> Work problems often are (a) unformulated or in need of reformulation, (b) of personal interest, (c) lacking in information necessary for solution, (d) related to everyday experience, (e) poorly defined, (f) characterized by multiple 'correct' solutions, each with liabilities as well as assets, and (g) characterized by multiple methods for picking a problem solution.
>
> (Sternberg *et al.*, 1995, p. 913)

The solution of this type of problem requires practical intelligence, which depends on gradually acquired 'tacit knowledge' of the job. It is tacit knowledge that underlies expertise. The main defining characteristics of tacit knowledge are that it is procedural rather than declarative, informal and implicit rather than formal and explicit, and usually acquired without formal, explicit instruction. Tacit knowledge is reflected in your knowing what to do in a given situation (it is procedural knowledge), and getting on and doing it, without necessarily being able to articulate why you are doing it (i.e. without declarative knowledge), and without your having been explicitly instructed or taught what to do.

Are practical intelligence and tacit knowledge valid constructs? Sternberg and his colleagues have used various procedures, ranging from job analysis to interviews with acknowledged experts and others successful in their chosen career, to generate a number of problem situations that might arise in any particular job or profession, along with an expert consensus on the most appropriate solutions to these problems. They then gave the problems to various groups of people, and scored their answers in terms of how well they agreed with the expert answers. In a number of studies, and with jobs including business management, the military, sales, and academic psychology, they found that job experience and status predicted how closely participants' solutions agreed with the experts'. For example, business managers produced 'better' solutions to problems of business management than business graduate students, who in turn produced better solutions than ordinary undergraduates, and the same pattern of differences in solutions to problems of academic psychology was found between university professors of psychology, psychology graduate students, and undergraduates.

Is this so very surprising? What would be surprising, a carping critic might argue (and there has been no shortage of them—see, for example, Gottfredson, 2003b), would be to find that business managers did *not* know more about business management than an undergraduate who had never worked in business. There is, moreover, an element of circularity in these studies: it seems obvious enough that the higher your status in a given profession the more closely your answers to the sorts of questions being posed here will agree with those given by people of even higher status (the experts).

Some further observations, however, serve both to provide at least a partial answer to such criticism, and to suggest that the concept of tacit knowledge may be valid in its own right. Measures of tacit knowledge correlate not only with amount of experience in a given occupation, but also with various measures of competence and success. In one study, for example, business managers who were all participants in the same training programme, were required to work in small groups to solve a variety of practical problems. Evaluations of their performance correlated 0.61 with measures of their tacit knowledge. Although this was by some way the highest correlation in any of Sternberg's studies, the weighted mean of 26 such correlations between measures of tacit knowledge and job performance in a variety of different studies was 0.34, with a range from 0.14 to 0.61 (Sternberg *et al.*, 2000). Moreover, tacit knowledge predicted people's competence at their job or at university *partially* independently of their IQ or other measures of 'academic' intelligence. Tacit knowledge is not the same as IQ. Of 27 correlations between tacit knowledge and measures of IQ summarized by Gottfredson (2003b), only seven were significant, and the average value of these correlations ranged from 0.07 in air force recruits, 0.12 and 0.13 in army officers, 0.14 in business managers, to 0.17 in undergraduates. More importantly, Sternberg *et al.* (2000) have also shown that, although IQ does of course predict job competence (see Chapter 9), the multiple correlation between IQ *plus* tacit knowledge and competence can be significantly and substantially higher: in one study, the addition of a tacit knowledge score to an IQ score predicted an additional 30% of the variance in measures of job competence. In other words, regardless of whether IQ or tacit knowledge is the *better* predictor of job performance, they make relatively independent contributions to that prediction.

In another study, Hedlund *et al.* (2006) gave students entering an MBA programme two different tests of tacit knowledge of business management. Their scores on these tests were unrelated to either their undergraduate grade point average (GPA), or their performance on the standard entrance exam for the MBA, with correlations ranging from –0.06 to 0.08. They did, however, predict to a moderate extent (correlations ranging from 0.16 to 0.30) their final GPA at the end of the MBA course, and did so independently of other predictors.

Whatever it is that these relatively specific tests of tacit knowledge of business management are measuring, it is not the same as IQ. But is it simply experience? That does seem intuitively plausible and is harder to disprove, but in the Hedlund study there was no evidence that differences in the students' actual business experience were associated with differences in their tacit knowledge. And in one study of business managers, correlations between tacit knowledge and salary or level of job, after controlling for age, education, *and* years of experience in the job, ranged from 0.35 to 0.40.

The knowledge assessed in all these studies was quite specific to a particular job or profession. Is there any reason to believe that the concept of tacit knowledge has wider generality, in other words that some people are notably better than others in their ability to deal with life's everyday problems in a way unrelated to any difference in their intelligence as measured by an IQ test? Anecdotal evidence would surely suggest that the answer is yes. University professors, as a group, are probably of above average intelligence. But no one who has worked in a university would want to claim that they are all shining examples of practical ability, common sense, or sound judgement. Alas, I know of no study that has put this perception of the impractical professor to the test, so it had better be dismissed as merely anecdotal.

Cianciolo *et al.* (2006) did, however, devise three questionnaires designed to provide more general tests of tacit knowledge, one labelled 'common sense', a second 'everyday situational judgement', and a third, for students, 'college life'. They all presented participants with brief written or filmed vignettes of everyday situations likely to be encountered in any job, or daily life, such as being asked to work on your day off, how to deal with a difficult person with whom you share a house, or going to a party where you see no one you recognize, along with several alternative lines of action you might take. In one study, the correlation between scores on the common sense questionnaire and supervisors' ratings of employees' performance on the job was 0.39. When students were given all three questionnaires, their scores all intercorrelated, so that factor analysis revealed a strong general factor of tacit knowledge. Scores on each of the three questionnaires showed only modest correlations with Cattell's Culture Fair test, a measure of Gf, or the Mill Hill vocabulary test, a measure of Gc (maximum r = 0.20), suggesting again that differences in tacit knowledge are largely independent of IQ. However, there *was* a substantial and significant correlation between the general factor of tacit knowledge and the general factor of intelligence (r = 0.48), implying considerably more overlap between the two constructs than Sternberg has elsewhere suggested. It seems quite possible that as the concept of tacit knowledge expands to encompass more aspects of life rather than knowledge specific to a particular job or profession, so it will overlap more with conventional measures of intelligence. This needs further examination.

'A day at the races': a special test case?

In 'A day at the races', Ceci and Liker (1986) reported on the achievements of 30 devotees of harness racing (where the rider sits in a small two-wheeled cart pulled by the horse rather than riding the horse as in flat racing or steeplechasing). They initially tested over one hundred men, all of whom had bought a copy of *Early Form*, a paper that contains the relevant past statistics of the runners in the following day's race. Only moderately serious punters will take the trouble to buy a paper whose sole purpose is to give one time to start calculating probable odds of tomorrow's runners. From these one hundred men they selected a group of 30 who displayed greatest knowledge about harness racing, and then asked these 30 men to predict, on the basis of information provided by *Early Form*, the favourite and also the first, second, and third favourites, in ten of tomorrow's races. They chose this as their dependent variable rather than prediction of the actual winners, since it is, in fact, more important for serious gamblers to be able to predict such odds, in order to decide whether it will be worth their while to bet on a particular horse. Fourteen of the 30 men were astonishingly good at this, predicting the favourite with an accuracy of 93%, and the first three favourites in correct order in 53% of races. The remaining 16 were notably less skilled, with accuracies of 55% and 8% respectively. Ceci and Liker then gave a variety of further tests to all 30 men, involving handicapping real races and hypothetical races; the 14 'experts' were substantially better than the 16 less expert men at all these tests. Finally, by detailed analysis of their performance, Ceci and Liker were able to show that the experts were using some seven different variables which they allowed to interact in complex ways to solve their tasks. These variables included: a horse's lifetime's earnings; speed in previous races; jockey; details of prior races, including the opposition; the amount of time spent on the outside trying to pass other carts; speed at different points in the race; and nature of the track. The critical difference between the two groups of 14 and 16 men, however, was in the complexity of the interactions between these variables that the experts employed. Whether a horse has won his last race is, after all, less important than against whom he has won, and on what course; actual speed can only be calculated by taking into account the proportion of time the horse was forced to pass other carts on the outside. And so on. It was the ability to allow for interactions such as these that seemed to be the secret of the 14 experts' success.

By any normal standards, of course, all 30 men were experts; they were all exceptionally knowledgeable about harness racing; they had been to the races at least twice a week for, on average, the past 16 years; even the non-experts were well above chance in their predictions (Ceci and Liker estimated the odds against predicting the first three favourites in each of ten races as something like 40,000:1). But why were they not as good as the 14 experts? Were they perhaps less intelligent? No. The average IQ of the 14 experts was 100.8 (range 81–125), and of the 16 non-experts 99.3 (range 80–130). There was, moreover, no correlation between IQ and success in Ceci and Liker's handicapping tasks, nor between IQ and the extent to which the interactive model provided a good account of each individual's performance. Whatever it was that distinguished the two groups, apart from their success, it was not measured IQ (or educational or occupational level, on which again the two groups were closely matched).

It is hardly surprising that someone who goes to the races every day should end up knowing a lot more about racing than other people. But both groups had done this: indeed the non-experts had spent marginally more years going regularly to the races than had the experts. They were initially selected from a larger group of over one hundred committed racegoers on the basis of their superior knowledge about harness racing. It is, of course, possible that the 14 experts had, in some sense, acquired more relevant information during their years spent going to the races than had the 16 non-experts. But if so, the difference was between one group who knew a great deal more about harness racing than most people would ever want to know, and a second group who knew *even* more.

There remain some unanswered, and probably unanswerable, questions. The strong inference that might be drawn from the study is that, since experts and non-experts had equal opportunity to develop the relevant skills, the experts must have been more intelligent, in ways not measured by an IQ score, to have done so more effectively. That inference may not be justified. Perhaps the difference was one of motivation or actual time spent studying form books at home and trying to beat the system. Perhaps the experts gambled more, and so needed to win more than the non-experts. It is usually possible to appeal to unmeasured and uncontrolled factors in any natural or quasi-natural experiment. Nevertheless, Ceci and Liker's study is important and, although much criticized (in my view not always convincingly, see Box 10.1), its results are certainly suggestive.

BOX 10.1 Some comments on 'A day at the races'

Does the Ceci and Liker study show that IQ tests fail to measure an important aspect of intelligence—one that permitted their experts to perform the handicapping tasks so much more efficiently than their less expert control group? One possible measure of the importance of the study is the number of rebuttals and critical commentaries it has generated (depending on your point of view, of course, this might just imply how seriously flawed the study was). Here, for example, is a comment published some 20 years after the original study appeared:

> Ceci and Liker (1986) found that in a group of race track bettors there was essentially no relation between IQ scores and the ability to predict handicaps at post time. They interpreted this finding as an example of a general lack of relationship between IQ scores and 'real world' performance. Detterman and Spry (1988) pointed out substantial errors in Ceci and Liker's study. As of August 2006, the Ceci and Liker article has been cited 79 times. The Detterman and Spry article has been cited 11 times.
>
> (Hunt and Carlson, 2007, p. 398)

I can do little to redress this imbalance, but I can comment on Detterman and Spry's criticisms.

They do point to one very puzzling feature of the study. Ceci and Liker say that from an initial pool of one hundred men, they selected a group of 30 who displayed greatest knowledge about harness racing, and gave them all an initial ten-item handicapping test. While one would no doubt expect that some would be better than others, indeed that it would be possible to divide the 30 into two roughly equal groups with higher and lower average scores on the test, it seems unlikely that there should have been *no* overlap in the scores of the two groups. But all 14 men in the expert group obtained scores of nine or ten out of ten, while the highest score in the non-expert group was five. From a presumably relatively homogeneous group of 30 men, all deemed to be very knowledgeable, such a bimodal distribution of scores is, to say the least, surprising. But Ceci and Liker are insistent that they selected the 30 men from their initial group of over one hundred solely on the basis of their superior ability to answer their initial questions about harness racing.

Nevertheless, Detterman and Spry argue, the fact that there was no overlap in the two groups' scores means that they cannot be treated as a single homogeneous group, and it is inappropriate to treat them

(continued…)

as such for purposes of statistical analysis. Even if this is accepted, the fact remains that within each group none of the correlations between IQ and scores on the subsequently administered test (prediction of favourite and of first three favourites in correct order) was significant. It is true of course that the group sizes are now quite small. However, if one treats them as two separate groups, then it is clearly appropriate to ask whether the difference in the two groups' handicapping scores was mirrored by a difference in their IQ scores. It was not of course.

Ceci and Liker rightly place much emphasis on their finding that, in spite of their similar IQ scores, the 14 experts used more complicated algorithms to make their predictions than did the 16 non-experts. It is this that led them to argue that the experts' behaviour was more cognitively complex (intelligent?) than that of the non-experts in ways not captured by IQ scores. Detterman and Spry accept that this is 'most interesting', but offer no further comment. In another critique of the Ceci and Liker study, Gottfredson (2003b, p. 370) argued that this is 'not even relevant, because *g* predicts the *correctness*, not the *complexity*, of a solution…complexity and efficiency need not go hand in hand' (italics in original). No doubt that is sometimes true, but the whole point is that it was not true here: the experts used more complex algorithms and were very much more successful. It is hard to believe that there was no causal connection between the two.

Implicit learning, tacit knowledge, and expertise

Artificial grammar and sequence learning

In a typical laboratory experiment on implicit learning, you are shown a sequence of events, for example a series of lights being illuminated on a computer screen or letters of the alphabet (Cleeremans *et al.*, 1998; Shanks, 2005). In the artificial grammar learning task developed by Reber (1967), you are asked to try to memorize some apparently arbitrary letter strings that are actually generated by a Markov process such as that illustrated in Figure 10.1. You are then told that there was a 'grammar' or set of rules that generated the strings you had been studying, and are asked to judge whether some new letter strings are or are not 'grammatical' (see Figure 10.1 for further explanation). Although usually unable to articulate the rules of the grammar, people perform significantly above chance on this final test. In other experiments, a sequence of stimuli appears, in rapid succession, in different positions on a screen, and your task is to respond as rapidly as possible to the appropriate response key below each position. In a control condition, the sequence of stimuli is entirely random, but in an experimental condition it is, at least in principle, predictable. In one version of the task, a particular 16-trial sequence of positions is repeated over and over again (Willingham *et al.*, 1993). In another, the position of the sixth stimulus in each block of six trials is predicted, in a complex way, by the positions of the second and fourth stimuli (Cleeremans and McClelland, 1991). In yet another, the large majority of trials instantiate one particular sequence, but on a minority of trials there is a different sequence (Kaufman *et al.*, 2010). Reaction times are generally speeded up when it is possible to predict the occurrence of the stimulus you are required to respond to. Evidence that people have learned something about the trial sequences in these experiments comes from the observation that they eventually respond faster in experimental (predictable) than in control (random) conditions. Implicit learning tasks can even be made a bit more realistic: people can be asked to 'manage' an imaginary factory and take decisions about purchasing

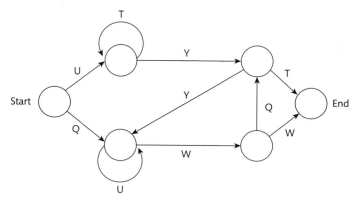

Figure 10.1 A Markov artificial grammar which generates strings of letters. To generate a string, start from the circle marked Start, and follow any arrow to another circle until you reach the circle marked End. Each arrow has an associated letter and the string generated is determined by the path taken. The loops at some circles allow you to repeat the same letter more than once. Examples of 'grammatical' strings would be: UYT, UTTYYWW, QWQT, QUUWW. An 'ungrammatical' string would be QYQW.

policy or employee relations, whose outcomes are dependent on the interaction of a large number of variables (Berry and Broadbent, 1984).

In all these cases, people's performance indicates quite clearly that they have learned something about the task they were set. But their knowledge is usually no more than fragmentary, and they are poor at articulating it. They are certainly unlikely to draw a picture of the Markov process illustrated in Figure 10.1 in Reber's artificial grammar task. According to Reber, their learning is implicit, rather than explicit, with implicit learning being defined as: 'The acquisition of knowledge that takes place largely independently of conscious attempts to learn and largely in the absence of explicit knowledge of what was acquired' (Reber, 1993, p. 5).

Implicit learning as the source of tacit knowledge

Reber's definition of implicit learning should remind the reader of Sternberg's account of tacit knowledge. Wagner and Sternberg defined tacit knowledge as knowledge that is:

Not openly expressed or stated…informal rather than formal, and…usually…not directly taught…We do not wish to imply that such knowledge is completely inaccessible to conscious awareness, unspeakable, or even unteachable, but merely that it usually is not taught directly to most of us…Much tacit knowledge may be disorganized and relatively inaccessible, making it potentially ill suited for direct instruction.

(Wagner and Sternberg, 1986, p. 54)

Two quite independent research traditions have homed in on a very similar set of ideas. Wagner and Sternberg's tacit knowledge, which they assume to underlie practical intelligence or competence, seems plausibly regarded as a product of the implicit learning system studied in some highly contrived laboratory experiments. But can implicit learning be characterized more precisely?

Reber initially described implicit learning as the unconscious acquisition of knowledge about complex, abstract rules. The idea seemed to be that the participants in an artificial grammar learning experiment really had internalized the set of rules corresponding to the Markov process illustrated in Figure 10.1, and since they certainly could not articulate these rules, their knowledge must be unconscious (see Reber, 1993). This interpretation has led to prolonged dispute, it being argued, for example, that sufficiently careful probing of participants' explicit understanding usually reveals fragmentary knowledge of certain brief sequences that would often have been sufficient to explain their performance on test (Perruchet, 1994; Shanks *et al.*, 1994). Fortunately, it is not necessary to try to resolve this dispute: for present purposes it is unimportant whether implicit learning is or is not wholly unconscious. There are other, more interesting ways of characterizing the difference between implicit and explicit learning.

Laboratory studies of implicit learning require people to detect complex contingencies between rapidly occurring sequences of events. This is precisely the function of the general purpose associative system postulated by modern conditioning theory (see Box 10.2). So a plausible characterization of the distinction between implicit and explicit learning, and one later advanced by Reber (1993) himself, is that implicit learning is the product of a basic associative system, probably shared by people and other animals, while explicit learning is the product of a cognitive system which generates and tests hypotheses, detects other kinds of relationships between events, infers rules, and decides between alternative conclusions on the basis of the evidence (see McLaren *et al.*, 1994).

BOX 10.2 Conditioning as the perception of causal relations

Laboratory studies of Pavlovian and instrumental conditioning in animals have a long history and a worse reputation, conjuring up images of dogs helplessly drooling at the sound of the dinner bell, or rats trundling their way through mazes or pressing levers in Skinner boxes on various schedules of reinforcement. But the laws of conditioning reveal an associative learning process nicely tuned to detecting real causal relationships, which thus allows animals to predict, and sometimes control, the occurrence of those events of consequence to themselves that psychologists call reinforcers (Dickinson, 1980; Rescorla, 1988). Just as causes usually immediately precede their effects and do not act at a distance, so conditioning depends on the temporal and spatial contiguity of conditional stimulus, or response, and reinforcer. If the occurrence of an event, X, is preceded by B, then conditioning will occur to B even though B sometimes occurs without being followed by X. But if another event, A, occurs alongside B, but only on those occasions when X does follow, then A is clearly the cause of X and B's occurrence is probably a chance coincidence. Animals will now show good conditioning to A, but little or none to B; A is said to have 'overshadowed' B. Similarly, if animals first learn that A predicts X, and B is later added to A so that the A + B compound is followed by X, they show little or no conditioning to B: the better predictor, A, is said to have 'blocked' conditioning to B. Conditioning occurs selectively to better predictors of reinforcement at the expense of worse predictors, thereby allowing animals to attribute the occurrence of a reinforcer to its most probable cause.

Experiments on contingency learning or causal learning in people show close parallels with the results of conditioning experiments on other animals. Both overshadowing and blocking can be readily observed in such experiments. Although some authors have attributed such selective conditioning effects in both people and other animals to a process of cognitive calculation (de Houwer, 2009), they can be explained by relatively simple, and hardly cognitive, principles of associative learning.

If this distinction is a valid one, IQ tests are presumably more likely to measure the operations of the explicit system than those of the implicit, associative system. There is, indeed, good evidence for this. In a study of 20 American college students, Reber *et al.* (1991) found no correlation between IQ scores and performance on an implicit learning (artificial grammar) task, although a highly significant correlation between IQ and performance on an explicit letter-series-completion task. A much larger study of over 400 14-year-old schoolchildren (Feldman *et al.*, 1995) also found a negligible correlation, r = 0.05, between WISC IQ scores and performance on an implicit sequence learning task, although such explicit knowledge about the sequences that the children did acquire *was* related to their IQ scores. Kaufman *et al.* (2010) found no correlation between sequence learning and the general factor extracted from a battery of IQ tests. Gebauer and Mackintosh (2007) gave German schoolchildren three implicit learning tasks, artificial grammar, sequence learning, and process control, either with standard 'implicit' instructions or, in another condition, with explicit instructions that there were rules governing the sequence of letters or lights, and their task was to try to work out these rules. The results of their study are shown in Table 10.2: under implicit instructions, there was essentially no correlation between the students' performance and their IQ scores (tests of Gc and Gf). But when they were explicitly told that there were rules underlying the sequence of events and their task was to work out what these rules were, their performance showed a modest but reliable correlation with their IQ scores.

As noted earlier, in their studies of tacit knowledge Sternberg and his colleagues have reported reliable correlations between people's performance on different tests of tacit knowledge. When students were given both psychology and business tacit knowledge questionnaires, the correlation between their scores on the two tests was 0.58. In the Cianciolo *et al.* (2006) study, their three different tests of tacit knowledge had loadings on a factor of general tacit knowledge ranging from 0.75 to 0.90. Correlations between different implicit learning tasks appear to be much weaker (Gebauer and Mackintosh, 2007), and it is clear that there is substantial task-specific variance in artificial grammar and the SRT task. However, with a wider range of measures of implicit learning, Gebauer (2003) did find evidence for a general factor of implicit learning that was unrelated to any factor of general intelligence. More importantly, he also reported that this implicit factor predicted some aspects of school performance, namely the students' grades in maths and English (a foreign language since the students were German). The association with maths scores disappeared after partialling out *g*, but that with English remained significant

Table 10.2 Correlations between IQ and measures of learning under implicit and explicit instruction (from Gebauer and Mackintosh, 2007).

Task	Implicit	Explicit
Artificial grammar	0.11	0.37
Sequence learning	0.11	0.23
Process control	0.07	0.32

independently of general intelligence. Kaufman *et al.* (2010) reported exactly the same result in a study of English sixth-form students: their implicit learning scores were correlated with both maths and French GCSE scores, but only the correlation with French remained significant after partialling out *g*.

Theoretical implications

Within cognitive psychology, the idea that there may be two rather distinct systems for learning and problem solving has become increasingly popular (even if still disputed by some, e.g., Keren and Schul, 2009). Different writers have given different labels to the two systems—explicit and implicit, intentional and incidental, deliberate and automatic, intuitive and rational, rule-governed and associative (Evans, 2008; Kahneman, 2003; Kaufman, 2011; McLaren *et al.*, 1994; Stanovich and West, 2000), but the labels differ more than the underlying idea. One system engages in reasoning, tests hypotheses, looks for rules, sees structural parallels between superficially dissimilar problems or situations; it breaks complex problem down into their component parts, works out the solution to one part, holds it in working memory while solving another part, and then combines the sub-solutions into a solution of the problem as a whole. The other stores information about the frequency of particular events, their statistical structure, and the correlations between them. In one version at least, it relies on a basic associative learning system, studied in experiments on conditioning in animals and causal learning by college students, and is readily modelled by standard connectionist networks (see Box 10.2). The distinction is also revealed by functional imaging: knowledge acquired by implicit and explicit learning results in activation of different brain structures (Reber *et al.*, 2003).

Individual differences in explicit learning and problem solving are what IQ tests purport to measure. But they do not measure individual differences in implicit learning. Although there is a modest correlation between IQ scores and many tests of learning studied by experimental psychologists, such as paired associate learning (Chapter 5), that is presumably because the participants in such experiments are engaged in a deliberate attempt to learn the material presented to them. Perhaps the reason why such correlations are usually no more than modest is because the implicit system can also contribute to successful performance.

If implicit learning were no more than a phenomenon studied in the psychologist's laboratory, this would not be a matter of great moment. A plausible hypothesis, however, is that this second, implicit system is a general-purpose system that furnishes people with much of their knowledge of the world in which they live. It may sometimes lead to error, but it also allows people to make rapid, intuitive judgements that are often more reliable than those made after detailed analysis (Kahneman, 2003). It detects contingencies between events, discovers what goes with what, and allows people to predict the future on the basis of past information. It allows some generalization from past instances to new problems, although, by comparison with explicit, rule-based learning, such generalization will be limited. This is because what has been learned is a number of specific instances that occurred in specific contexts, so generalization to quite new contexts will fail (unlike the case of rule-based learning which can transcend context). Hence the domain-specificity of the expertise shown, for example, by Brazilian street vendors (see Chapter 9).

Although Reber (1993) once suggested that implicit learning ability, being 'evolutionarily old' shows little variation in the general population, it is clear that this is not true: other studies have found substantial variation in performance on artificial grammar or sequence reaction time tasks (Gebauer, 2003; Gebauer and Mackintosh, 2007; Kaufman *et al.*, 2010), and significant correlations between implicit learning scores and at least some other outcomes (see Kaufman, 2011). Differences in implicit learning ability, therefore, may have been responsible for the difference between Ceci and Liker's expert and non-expert racegoers: their experts had become exceptionally skilled at predicting the value of an outcome, a horse's starting odds, from the value of a number of independent variables (past races, jockey, etc.) and their interactions. The differences in 'tacit knowledge' that, according to Sternberg and his colleagues, predict differences in performance in a variety of real-world settings, may equally be attributable to differences in implicit learning ability. At present, there is no evidence to support this conjecture, but I believe it is interesting enough to merit further testing.

Gardner's multiple intelligences

Gardner's critique of traditional IQ tests takes an even stronger line than Sternberg's. Here is another quote:

> Suspend for a moment the usual judgment of what constitutes intelligence and let your thoughts run freely over the capabilities of human beings...the brilliant chess player, the world-class violinist, and the champion athlete...Are the chess player, violinist, and athlete 'intelligent' in these pursuits? If they are, then why do our tests of 'intelligence' fail to identify them? If they are not intelligent, what allows them to achieve such astounding feats?

> (Gardner, 2006, pp. 5–6)

One answer to Gardner's second question that should occur to anyone who has read Chapter 9, is that expertise (practice) is probably more important than intelligence. Another that will surely occur to many readers is: the chess player may need to be reasonably intelligent (although the evidence for this is not very strong), but the violinist needs musical talent, and the athlete athletic ability. The central thesis of Gardner's theory of multiple intelligences, however, is that it *is* intelligence that underlies all their achievements, but that there is more than one kind of intelligence. To be precise, there are eight different and quite independent intelligences (see Box 10.3). At times, Gardner seems to be claiming that none of these intelligences are measured by IQ tests, although the first three look suspiciously like Gc, Gf, and Gv. But what are the criteria he has used to identify these particular abilities, skills, or intelligences and no others?

As stated in an earlier quotation from Gardner (pp. 222–3), one criterion is that an intelligence is the ability to solve problems, or to create products, which are valued within one or more cultural settings. The last part of this definition is probably important: as Gardner acknowledges, face recognition would satisfy many of the other criteria he lists, but few people would want to say that the ability to recognize faces was a part of intelligence. Moreover, one theory of the evolution of human intelligence and the human brain has argued that it was driven by sexual selection: superior intelligence allowed someone to appear more dazzling to the opposite sex by being more creative (Miller, 2000).

BOX 10.3 Gardner's eight intelligences and exemplars of each

Intelligence	Exemplar
Linguistic	T. S. Eliot
Logico-mathematical	Albert Einstein
Visuo-spatial	I. K. Brunel
Musical	W. A. Mozart
Bodily-kinaesthetic	Thomas Edison
Naturalistic	Charles Darwin
Interpersonal	Sigmund Freud
Intrapersonal	Marcel Proust

Gardner goes on to list a number of criteria or 'signs' of an intelligence, and although less than systematic in providing evidence of the applicability of all of these criteria for all of his intelligences, he does give some examples of what he means. The most important seem to be:

- Isolation by brain damage: different brain lesions are associated with deficits in linguistic, logical, visuo-spatial, and musical competence.

- The existence of people with special abilities: savants (often people with autism) show remarkable skills in one particular domain, calendar calculating, drawing, musical performance, combined with a below average IQ.

- A developmental history: developmental psycholinguistics charts the development of language (although its evolutionary origins are fairly obscure); Piaget aimed to chart the development of logical thinking.

- An evolutionary history: songbirds are said to tell us something about the evolutionary origins of music, primates about the origins of interpersonal intelligence, and tool-using animals about the origins of bodily-kinaesthetic intelligence.

- An identifiable set of core operations: linguistic intelligence would include sensitivity to subtle differences in meaning (between, for example, 'accidentally' and 'by mistake'), sensitivity to grammatical rules, inflexion, and rhyme.

- A specialized symbol system: obviously true for language, mathematics, and music.

- Consistency with psychometric evidence: a strange one this, given Gardner's poor opinion of IQ testing, but the idea is that the intelligences should be relatively independent of one another, so that if it were possible to devise pure measures of each, they would be uncorrelated.

Some comments

Gardner's theorizing, although popular with educationalists, has come in for a great deal of criticism from psychologists and psychometricians. Much of this criticism seems to me entirely justified, but I shall try my best to acknowledge some of the virtues of his position.

Intelligences, or talents and skills?

In everyday language, 'intelligence' is a singular noun, not plural, and, as I noted above, we usually talk of musical talent, manual skill, and athletic ability (two examples of bodily-kinaesthetic intelligence), rather than musical, manual, or athletic intelligence. To this, Gardner's response is that he does not care whether we call his 'intelligences' skills, competences, talents, or abilities, provided we use the same word for all of them. Otherwise, he argues, those called 'intelligences' will be perceived as more important or valuable than those called mere talents or skills. Is that really true? The majority of the population almost certainly values the skills of professional footballers or popular singers a great deal more than those of professors, lawyers, or accountants. And even university professors should surely be able to allow that 'academic' intelligence is not the only valuable characteristic that people can possess (once again recall the case of Odysseus, Chapter 1). It is not difficult to have some sympathy for Gardner's evident desire that other talents should command respect and admiration. The question is whether calling them 'intelligences' is the way to achieve this desirable goal.

There is nothing necessarily sacrosanct about ordinary language and everyday usage, and science often gives a new, technical meaning to a word—mass, energy, factor, and so on. However, if this new usage simply blurs distinctions enshrined in ordinary language, it is not obvious what it has achieved. Most, but perhaps not all, of the individuals listed in Box 10.3 were probably rather intelligent, as well as being exceptionally talented. But Gardner's usage would not allow one to draw this distinction, and it is one that surely needs to be drawn. Good artists do not necessarily talk intelligently about their art, and often have less of value to say than a perceptive, intelligent critic. Was Mozart really intelligent? In her attempt to ascertain the intelligence of some three hundred historical geniuses, Terman's student Cox (1926) assigned the young Mozart an IQ of 150. The sum of her evidence for this is shown in Box 10.4. It speaks volumes for his precocious musical talent, but as evidence for his *intelligence*, it is frankly derisory. Although Till (1992, p. xi) characterized Mozart as 'one of the most penetrating intellects of his age', he, too, provides no convincing evidence for this claim. Mozart's letters certainly suggest that he was not as foolish and childlike as some earlier commentators implied ('Outside of his genius as a musical artist, Mozart was a *nullity*', wrote one—see Solomon, 1995, p. 14). Nor, although nineteenth century publishers of those letters felt the need for some careful editing to remove the more obscene passages, was he simply the scatological buffoon portrayed in Peter Shaffer's *Amadeus*. The fact is that there is no evidence one way or the other to say how intelligent Mozart really was. Musical genius is not a guarantee of amazing intelligence.

To take another example, we readily distinguish between good athletes and intelligent ones. In cricket, an intelligent bowler is one who has studied the opposing batsman's weaknesses and worked out a strategy to take advantage of them (I am credibly informed that the same would be true of an intelligent pitcher in baseball). But someone would still be counted a good bowler or pitcher if he just relied on simple speed, accuracy, or the ability to spin the ball. David Beckham is probably not nearly as stupid as popular imagination once had it, but even if he was, few people doubted his footballing skill.

BOX 10.4 Was Mozart very intelligent?

The following is the evidence provided by Cox to support her assessment of Mozart's superior intelligence:

WOLFGANG AMADEUS MOZART (1756–1791)
A Celebrated Austrian Composer
AI IQ 150 AII IQ 155

1. Family standing
The Mozart family belonged originally to the artisan class. The grandfather was a bookbinder. The father, determined to rise out of the rank of his ancestors, studied law and also music; he became orchestral director in Salzburg and was the author of many musical compositions as well as a standard work on violin playing. The mother, a daughter of the steward of the convent of St Gilgen, was a good woman, but in no way distinguished.

2. Development to age 17
   (a) Interests: from before his sixth year, Mozart's sole absorbing interest was in music, and even the games he played had some musical element. Whatever he did was done wholeheartedly, but apparently he had few interests unrelated to music, so absorbing was his art. At of the age of 10, however, he mentally constructed an imaginary kingdom of children in which he was king. He had a map of it drawn by a servant, according to specifications which he drew up. At about the same time, he planned to compose an opera to be presented by the children of Salzburg. At the age of 11 he became skilful in card games and a good fencer. Before he was 16, he had felt the pleasures and pains of a first love.
   (b) Education: when Mozart was aged between 3 and 4, he was taught by his father to play the clavier; he learned minuets and other pieces, which he soon played 'with perfect correctness' and in exact time. At the age of 7 he began to receive instruction in singing by an Italian master, and at 14 he was studying and executing the most difficult counterpoint. Meanwhile his general education was not neglected. He studied arithmetic at the usual age, and evidences of a smattering of Latin appear in letters written at 13, while the correspondence of the following years shows that he had picked up some Italian in the course of his travels.
   (c) School standing and progress: no specific record.
   (d) Friends and associates: Mozart's associates were the musicians and the courtiers of Europe. Everyone like the agreeable and talented little fellow and made much of him. His sister was his comrade and confidante.
   (e) Reading: Mozart mentions reading the *Arabian Nights* in Italian when he was 14.
   (f) Production and achievement: at the age of 5 Mozart first felt the impulse to produce, and the little pieces he composed were written down by his father. Three works are recorded before the age of 6: a Minuet and Trio for Clavier (Op. 1), a Minuet (Op. 2), and an Allegro (Op. 3). These are not particularly original, but they exhibit the rounded simple melody always characteristic of their composer.

There follows a further page of the young Mozart's musical accomplishments.

Goleman (1995, p. 37) quotes the following remarks Gardner made in an interview with him:

The time has come to broaden our notion of the spectrum of talents. The single most important contribution education can make to a child's development is to help him towards a field where his talents best suit him…We should spend less time ranking children and more time helping them to identify their natural competencies and gifts, and cultivate those. There are hundreds and hundreds of ways to succeed, and many, many different abilities that will help you get there.

Not everyone will agree (although I am inclined to), but it is surely a reasonable argument. And note that he does not once talk about 'intelligences'.

Independence

Gardner insists that his eight intelligences are all independent of each other. As I noted above, his linguistic, logico-mathematical and spatial intelligences are surely the same as, or at least closely related to, Gc, Gf, and Gv. To the extent that this identification is justified, it is abundantly clear that they are not wholly independent of one another: it is unnecessary to reiterate that all IQ tests correlate with all other IQ tests. Gardner's response is that the correlations between these three kinds of test arise because paper and pencil IQ tests all require linguistic or logical skills. This is not very convincing. Linguistic and logical intelligences are themselves supposed to be quite independent. Individually administered IQ tests such as the Wechsler and Stanford-Binet scales are not paper and pencil tests. Paper and pencil tests of Gv correlate with other, perhaps more realistic, measures of spatial ability such as route finding (Hegarty and Waller, 2005; Hegarty *et al.*, 2006).

Visser *et al.* (2006) devised several measures of each of Gardner's eight intelligences, gave the resulting battery of tests to a sample of two hundred participants (mostly students), and factor analysed the resulting correlation matrix. They found that it was possible to extract a single general factor from their tests, on which they all, except the measures of musical ability and bodily-kinaesthetic intelligence, loaded. Moreover, again with these two exceptions, they all correlated with scores on a general IQ test, mostly with correlations over 0.40. Visser and colleagues' failure to find any correlation between musical ability and IQ is actually rather surprising, since, as noted in Chapter 9, others have reported modest but significant correlations (Ruthsatz *et al.*, 2008). They explained this by noting that the two musical tests they administered were not very reliable. Gardner anyway is simply dismissive, reiterating his argument that paper and pencil tests will correlate with one another solely by virtue of their common format and reliance on language and logic, and saying that he is not interested in testing people for his intelligences anyway. It is difficult to know what to say in response to such a cavalier attitude. He could have given a more sensible answer by following Thurstone, who argued that the reason why a test for one of his primary mental abilities correlated with tests of another was because it is impossible to construct 'factorially pure' tests (Chapter 7). Whether it would really be plausible to argue that any measure of, say, naturalistic intelligence will inevitably also call on one or more of Gardner's other intelligences, remains an open question.

One of Gardner's criteria or 'signs' of an intelligence was the occurrence of 'islands of ability'—people with quite exceptional ability in one domain, but often below average in all others. The talents of savants provided the most striking examples, sometimes of extraordinary musical or artistic abilities combined with a well below average IQ score (Detterman *et al.*, 2000; Hermelin and O'Connor, 1978). Such people are usually diagnosed as suffering from autism, although no more than 10% of people with autism have savant abilities, and exceptional musical or artistic talent is even rarer. The more common savant skills are notably more mundane, for example calendar calculating. A particular 14-year-old boy, studied by Howe and Smith (1988), had an IQ between 50 and 60, but was a calendar calculator who, entirely self-taught, had learned the correct answers to virtually any question of the form:

What day of the week was or will be 28 January 1905, 3 July 1996, 10 August 2052?

Detailed analysis of his performance suggested that, among other things, he had a series of mental images of the possible calendars for any given month. Ignoring the problem of whether a month has 28, 29, 30, or 31 days, there are, after all, only seven different calendars because the only important difference is what day of the week the month starts on. Having also learned which calendar corresponds to which month of each year it becomes a simple matter to 'read off' the answer to the sorts of questions that he was asked; and such a mental representation also made it easy for him to say which of the following was the odd month out: February 1971, September 1972, June 1973, July 1974, August 1975, October 1976. He correctly answered February 1971 because that is the only one to start on a Monday (the rest all start on a Friday).

Here too, however, IQ is not irrelevant. Although most, if not all, savants have below average test scores, skill at calendar calculating is not independent of IQ. O'Connor *et al.* (2000) studied the performance of ten calendar calculators whose IQ scores ranged from 50 to 97. The accuracy with which they answered questions such as those above correlated $r = 0.78$ with their Wechsler full scale IQ.

Modularity and localization of function

Some of Gardner's criteria are quite irrelevant to the task of explaining individual differences in any sort of intelligence. The fact that a particular function is 'localized' in a particular region of the brain, language in Wernicke's and Broca's areas, for example, in no way helps to understand why people differ in verbal intelligence. Indeed, whether or not the brain or mind can be divided up into distinct cognitive 'modules', is a question entirely independent of whether or not individual differences in performance on tests involving one module correlate with individual differences on tests of other modules. Anderson (1992, 2005) and Jensen (1998) have both argued that the general factor, *g*, refers to the efficiency of a central processor that controls the performance of all modules: they did not deny the existence of modules.

Conclusion

Gardner has certainly not succeeded in his quest to get rid of the general factor. The positive manifold remains positive: differences in performance on a surprisingly wide range of apparently diverse cognitive tasks are all correlated. That there are other abilities, talents, and skills (bodily kinaesthetic, for example, according to the evidence of Visser *et al.*, 2006) that are uncorrelated with performance on existing IQ tests is interesting and important; for many people, indeed, these other talents are just as worthy of admiration and respect as are the skills required to do well at an IQ test. That is as it should be, and Gardner's evident wish to see them respected is itself admirable. But calling them all 'intelligences' is not the most sensible way of going about this.

Social intelligence

Gardner describes two of his intelligences as personal: interpersonal and intrapersonal intelligence. In the factor analysis of Visser *et al.* the tests of these two intelligences correlated as strongly with the general factor as did any other test. But throughout the twentieth century many of those who attempted to measure human intelligence argued that conventional IQ tests fail to capture an important aspect of intelligence—social intelligence. More recently, the focus of attention has moved to emotional intelligence. The former seems to correspond to Gardner's interpersonal intelligence, the latter to his intrapersonal intelligence. Perhaps the first question to ask is whether there really is a sharp distinction between the two. Gardner himself discussed them both in the same chapter, and his definitions certainly seemed related:

> *Inter*personal intelligence is the ability to understand other people: what motivates them, how they work, how to work cooperatively with them. Successful salespeople, politicians, teachers, clinicians, and religious leaders are all likely to be individuals with high degrees of interpersonal intelligence. *Intra*personal intelligence...is a correlative ability, turned inward. It is a capacity to form an accurate, veridical model of oneself and to be able to use that model to operate effectively in life.

(Gardner, 1993, p. 9)

If intrapersonal intelligence is a correlative ability, this presumably means that it correlates with interpersonal ability, as indeed it did in the study by Visser *et al.* (2006). Gardner's exemplar of intrapersonal intelligence was Marcel Proust, and of interpersonal intelligence Sigmund Freud. One could readily imagine their roles reversed. Proust's novel is as much a portrait of Parisian society at the turn of the nineteenth and twentieth centuries, as an examination of his inner life. While psychoanalysis is as much a matter of understanding yourself as others, training to become an analyst requires you to undergo psychoanalysis yourself. There are no doubt differences between intra- and inter-personal, or emotional and social intelligence, but equally the two are surely related. A cynical attitude might be that the newer concept of emotional intelligence has taken over from the older concept of social intelligence, because the latter seemed to have failed. To anticipate: attempts to devise tests that measure the two have not as yet established any clear or decisive distinction between them, but in what follows I shall, as far as possible, deal with them separately, and in historical order, looking at social intelligence first.

Early attempts to define social intelligence

The idea that one could distinguish social from other aspects of intelligence has a history dating back at least as far as the early days of IQ testing (see Sternberg, 1985). Common sense and everyday experience both suggest that we spend much of our time engaged in social interactions with others, and that some people seem more successful than others in such interactions. Certainly, one of the aspects of an intelligent person's behaviour emphasized by many of the respondents in the study by Sternberg *et al.* (1981; see Chapter 1) was a factor the authors labelled 'social competence'. Most people would probably agree on a relatively long list of situations calling for social skills or competence: understanding other people, respecting their wishes but also getting them to respect the wishes of others, showing an interest in them, responding to their needs, sympathizing with them when they are distressed, giving them good advice, putting them at their ease, being the life and soul of the party, showing a suitable level of deference to your superiors, encouraging and supporting those who work for you, being considerate and punctual, and so on. Most people would probably also agree that some individuals are better at many of these things than others. So the next step should not be impossibly difficult: what is needed are some tests that measure these skills.

Early attempts to do so were not crowned with success. Thorndike was an early advocate of the idea of social intelligence, defined as 'the ability to understand and manage men and women, boys and girls—to act wisely in human relations' (Thorndike, 1920, p. 228); but he was reluctantly forced to the conclusion that while it was obvious from everyday observation that some people were socially more competent than others, these differences were not easily measured in the laboratory. Later, Wechsler (1944) concluded that social intelligence was simply general intelligence (or perhaps Gc) applied to the social sphere. The earliest published test of social intelligence was the George Washington Social Intelligence Test (GWIST; Hunt, 1928); it included measures of judgement in social situations, memory for names and faces, and recognition of the mental states behind words. Subsequently, Guilford and Hoepfner (1971) devised tests that, among other things, required you to select from a set of photographs of faces the two displaying the same mental state, or to match the emotion shown in a facial expression with that revealed by a tone of voice. Rosenthal *et al.* (1979) devised the PONS test (profile of non-verbal sensitivity), in which people were shown film clips of brief scenes in which a woman displays various emotional states, and their task was to identify that state. Sternberg and Smith (1985) asked their participants to inspect a series of photographs each containing two people; in one series, their task was to decide whether the couple were friends or strangers, in another, in a work setting, to decide which of the two was the supervisor and which the supervisee.

Problems

If people really do differ along a dimension of specifically social intelligence, then two further points should follow: the first is that measures of the various social skills outlined above should tend to correlate with one another. It is precisely this positive manifold that in other domains of IQ allows one to talk of verbal ability, spatial ability, reasoning ability, perceptual speed, or even of g itself. The second is that they should be at least partly independent of g or any other component of IQ: social intelligence should not be reducible to general intelligence applied to the social sphere. In the jargon of test theory, these requirements are for convergent and discriminant validity.

The evidence for either is at best mixed. Hunt (1928) found that aggregate sores on the GWIST correlated $r = 0.54$ with scores on the George Washington Mental Alertness Test, which had been designed as an IQ test, and Woodrow (1939) factor analysed the GWIST along with a larger battery of IQ tests and found no evidence for any distinct factor of social intelligence. Other studies have found little evidence for any positive manifold among different measures of social intelligence. Sternberg and Smith (1985) found no correlation between performance on their tests and on the Rosenthal *et al.* PONS test, or indeed with any other test of social skills. More remarkably, the correlation between the two parts of their test (photographs of couples and of supervisors and workers) was only 0.09. Keating (1978) reported that the average correlation between different measures of social intelligence was only 0.16 (0.28 when corrected for reliability). And this was *lower* than the average correlation between the tests of social intelligence and traditional IQ tests, r = 0.23 (0.33 corrected). A subsequent study by Ford and Tisak (1983) reported rather more encouraging results. Their different social measures did correlate more strongly with one another than they did with measures of academic intelligence, but the difference was not very large: r = 0.36 and 0.26 respectively. However, Marlowe (1986), factor analysing a large battery of social measures, found five factors of social intelligence that were distinct from verbal and abstract intelligence: social interest (concern for others), social skills, empathy, emotionality, and social anxiety. And Schneider *et al.* (1996) found seven distinguishable factors of social competence that were very largely independent of traditional measures of intelligence.

Why should it have proved so difficult to find evidence of a positive manifold in measures of social intelligence? It seems possible that people use a wide variety of rather different skills and traits to cope with the very wide range of demands that social life imposes. Being the life and soul of the party is not necessarily the same as being sensitive to other people's feelings, understanding what they are thinking, or knowing the right thing to do or say in an awkward situation. People who are considerate and punctual may not necessarily be good at flattering their superiors or encouraging and motivating those who work for them.

A second puzzle, however, is why different studies have reported such different results. The answer seems to be that they have used two quite different measures of social intelligence or competence. Some have used relatively objective tests (with right and wrong answers), asking people to choose the appropriate action to perform in particular social situations, to infer the mental state of the protagonists in a story or video clip, to judge the relationship between two people in a photo, to judge the emotion, feelings or thoughts behind a facial expression (or just a picture of someone's eyes, as in the 'Reading the Mind in the Eyes' test; Baron-Cohen, 2003). Other measures rely on self-report questionnaires where you are asked to agree or disagree with statements such as 'I would rather spend the evening reading a good book than go out to a party', or 'I often worry that people don't like me'.

Self-report questionnaires are used in personality inventories. It is not surprising then that measures of social intelligence that employ such questionnaires should correlate with various aspects of personality, in particular with three of the so-called Big Five personality dimensions: extraversion, openness to experience, and agreeableness (McCrae and Costa, 1997). Schneider *et al.* (1996) reported significant correlations between all their self-report scores and these dimensions of personality. Baron-Cohen's (2003) Empathy Quotient test contains 60 statements with which you are invited to agree or disagree (for example, 'I find relationships very difficult'). The correlation between scores on this test and the agreeableness dimension of personality is 0.75 (Nettle, 2007). These relationships have been extensively documented in more recent studies of emotional intelligence where there is a clear separation between objective tests and self-report scales (see below). To the extent that they correlate with well-established dimensions of personality, such self-report questionnaires can hardly be said to have uncovered a new dimension of social intelligence (Petrides *et al.*, 2004).

On the other hand, the studies that have reported significant correlations between measures of social intelligence and more traditional measures of intelligence, such as Hunt (1928) and Keating (1978), used objective measures with right and wrong answers. The difference between Keating's results, where different measures of social intelligence correlated more strongly with other IQ tests than they did with one another, and those reported by Ford and Tisak (1983) where the opposite was true, is probably due to the fact that, in addition to objective measures, the latter included some self-report ratings as well as other people's ratings of social effectiveness.

Schneider *et al.* (1996) concluded that the term 'social intelligence' was a misnomer; one should talk instead of 'social competence', but understand that this is *not* a unitary construct. People who are competent in one area of social life may be quite incompetent in others. Even more important, however, someone may be able to give all the right answers to a paper and pencil test that asks what one should do in a particular situation, or whether a picture shows someone who is sad or frightened, but still *behave* in socially inept ways. This is, in fact, one of Gardner's more cogent criticisms of standard IQ tests: intelligence, he argues, should be measured by actual accomplishment, not by the answers given to theoretical questions in the psychologist's laboratory. In the present context (and perhaps more widely), this seems an eminently fair point. Social competence may be related to social knowledge and understanding, but it is not the same: someone may in principle know the right thing to do in a socially embarrassing situation, but be too shy or anxious to do it. Social competence will depend on personality as well as understanding or intelligence.

Gardner's criteria again

Three of Gardner's criteria for isolating an intelligence were: evolutionary history, developmental history, and islands of ability or disability. All three are applicable to the concept of social intelligence.

Why, asked Humphrey (1976), should apes and monkeys apparently be so much more intelligent than other mammals? It is not as if their daily lives are fraught with practical difficulties: for most of them, their food supply is reasonably plentiful and their predators relatively few. Why do they need to be so intelligent? Humphrey's answer was that the selection pressure that drove the development of their intelligence was social rather than practical. Most primates live in quite large, and often fluid, social groups, and their intelligence evolved to cope with the demands of social life, the need to learn one's place in a social hierarchy, how to interact with one's social superiors and inferiors, how to cooperate with others and how, sometimes, to outwit them (so-called Machiavellian intelligence; Byrne and Whiten, 1988). Humphrey, like other proponents of this 'social function of intellect' hypothesis, originally assumed that social living had resulted in the development of *general* intelligence. This would correspond to Wechsler's idea that social intelligence is simply general intelligence applied to the social sphere. But subsequent versions of the hypothesis have argued that primates have a well-developed, specifically social intelligence. The argument is that in order to predict or manipulate the behaviour of other members of your social group, it is necessary to understand their beliefs and intentions, in other words, to have a 'theory of mind'. A young baboon who is about to be punished by his elders and betters for some transgression pretends that he has just seen a predator in the distance, because he knows that this will distract his attackers' attention. A female chimpanzee stops approaching some food she has just seen when a dominant male approaches, because she knows that if he believes there is some food available he will take it from her. When he starts walking away, she approaches and takes the food, but he, ever suspicious of her intentions, suddenly turns round and catches her at it (both examples from Whiten and Byrne, 1988). Such anecdotal evidence has not convinced all critics (e.g. Heyes, 1998; Penn and Povinelli, 2007), and the issue remains unresolved (Shettleworth, 2010).

Whether or not other animals have a theory of mind, there can be little doubt that, in a loose sense of the term, people do: we routinely use mental predicates to describe and explain the behaviour of others; we attribute hopes and fears, intentions and plans, wishes and motives, beliefs and doubts, knowledge and ignorance to each other, and there is equally little doubt that it takes time for such understanding to develop in young children. It is not until they are about 2 years old that young children can sympathize with another child's distress. A more regrettable consequence of this increase in social understanding is that children gradually learn to become more proficient liars: in order to deceive someone, you must first be able to pretend that something is true which you know to be false, and then understand that your intended dupes do not themselves know the truth (there is no point in lying to someone who will know you are lying). The classic 'false belief' test (see Box 10.5), which requires that the child understand that someone else's beliefs may not be the same as their own, is not passed by most children until the age of 4. So, social understanding or intelligence certainly passes Gardner's test of having a developmental history.

BOX 10.5 The false belief test

Until they are 3 or 4 years old, young children have difficulty understanding that other people may hold beliefs different from their own, and that they may not know something that the child herself knows perfectly well. The classic 'false belief' test assesses whether a child realizes that if one puppet doll, Sally, leaves the room before another puppet, Ann, moves a piece of treasure from one hiding place to another, Sally cannot know that the treasure has been moved, and will therefore look for the treasure in its old hiding place when she returns to the room. Until the age of 4 or so, most children say that Sally will look for the treasure in the place where they themselves know it is now hidden. Children with autism spectrum disorder continue to fail the test until they are significantly older. A highly intelligent graduate student, who suffered from the related Asperger's syndrome, told me that she still had some difficulty understanding these problems, but had simply *learned* that the correct answer was the opposite of the answer she would intuitively give herself.

The case of autism, or autism spectrum disorders, provides evidence for 'islands of disability'. While it is probably too simplistic to describe children with autism as lacking a 'theory of mind module' (Baron-Cohen, 1995), even those described as high functioning autistics, with an IQ in the normal range, fail the false belief test well after the age at which other children pass it. Adults with the related Asperger's syndrome may be highly intelligent: Richard Borcherds, a Cambridge mathematician, won the Fields Medal, the mathematical equivalent of the Nobel prize, but by his own confession cannot understand social situations, and obtained impressively low scores on Baron-Cohen's tests of social competence (Baron-Cohen, 2003). It is hard to believe that social competence or intelligence is *simply* general intelligence applied to the social sphere.

Emotional intelligence

What of emotional or intrapersonal intelligence? The first point to make is that, just as with tests of social intelligence or competence, so here, a distinction needs to be drawn between ability tests with right and wrong answers, such as the Mayer-Salovey-Caruso Emotional Intelligence Test (MSCEIT; Mayer *et al.*, 2002) and the self-report scales devised by Bar-On (1997) and Schutte *et al.* (1998). Brackett and Mayer (2003) and Bastian *et al.* (2005) reported correlations ranging from the very modest to the negligible between the two types of test (r = 0.18 and 0.21 in the former study, r = 0.04 in the latter).

Mayer and colleagues argue that tests of emotional intelligence must satisfy three criteria. First, they must identify a cognitive ability for dealing with particular situations, problems, or sets of issues, rather than a dimension of personality. I have in effect just accepted this criterion. The second is that performance on such tests should improve with age, which was, after all, Binet's original criterion for an intelligence test. Their third is for convergent and discriminant validity: tests of emotional intelligence should correlate with one another, but these correlations should not be attributable to their correlation with *g*.

The MSCEIT shows some promise of satisfying these criteria. It consists of eight sub-tests divided into four groups or 'branches', and two general areas (see Box 10.6). It is an objective measure rather than a self-report questionnaire, that is to say, there are 'right' and 'wrong' answers. But who decides what is right or wrong? The initial idea was by 'consensus scoring': the right answer is that given by most people. But that has been (sensibly) replaced by 'expert scoring', which means the answer given by a majority of psychologists whose speciality is emotion. In fact, the two methods of scoring agree—the correlations between them can be as high as 0.98 (Mayer *et al.*, 2008). The split-half reliability of the total test is reasonable (just over 0.90), although the reliability of three of the four branches (the exception is perception) is only moderate (about 0.80).

Scores on the eight sub-tests are moderately correlated with one another (with r ranging from 0.16 to 0.56), and factor analysis therefore reveals a general factor, *ge*, onto which all sub-tests load, with loadings ranging from 0.40 to 0.68 (Mayer *et al.*, 2002). There has been some dispute about whether any further group factors can be identified, and if so how many. Mayer and his colleagues opted for two (experiencing and reasoning) or four (perception, facilitation, understanding, and management). A meta-analysis of 19 studies, however, suggested that the best-fitting model was one with three group factors (with perception and facilitation collapsed into one), plus a general factor (Fan *et al.*, 2010).

BOX 10.6 The MSCEIT

The four branches of the MSCEIT, each containing two sub-tests, are as follows:

- *Perception*: for example of emotions in faces or a piece of music or picture. Shown a photograph of a face, you must rate how strongly each of five different feelings (happy, sad, afraid, etc.) is being expressed.
- *Facilitation*: what emotions would be appropriate or inappropriate in a given situation? For example, what mood might be helpful if you are organizing a social event (excitement, boredom, anxiety, etc.)?
- *Understanding*: you are asked to describe the feelings of two people in a story, for example a driver who runs over a dog, and the owner of the dog.
- *Management*: of yourself and others, for example how effective various courses of action would be in coping with an annoying situation, or maintaining a friendship with someone who has let you down.

Perception and *facilitation* are combined into the *experiencing area*, and *understanding* and *management* into the *reasoning area*.

Several studies have reported modest correlations in the range 0.25–0.35 between total MSCEIT score and various measures of intelligence, although in one (Schulte *et al.*, 2004) the correlation was as high as 0.45. However, apart from openness (which correlates with traditional measures of intelligence) and agreeableness, most have reported negligible correlations with the other 'Big Five' personality dimensions (Bastian *et al.*, 2005; Brackett *et al.*, 2004, 2006; Mayer *et al.*, 2002; Rode *et al.*, 2008). This is the exact opposite of the pattern of results for self-report measures of emotional intelligence, which correlate quite strongly with several dimensions of personality, but not at all with traditional measures of IQ. Typical data, from the Bastian *et al.* study, are shown in Table 10.3. I shall have little more to say about self-report scales: what they measure may be interesting and important, but they are largely measures of personality, not *intelligence*.

Table 10.3 Intercorrelations between self-report and ability measures of emotional intelligence, Raven's Matrices, and the 'Big Five' dimensions of personality (data from Bastian *et al.*, 2005, Table 2).

	EI	MSCEIT	Raven	Neuro	Extra	Open	Agree	Consc
EI (self-report)	—							
MSCEIT	0.04	—						
Raven's	0.08	0.27	—					
Neuroticism	−0.42	−0.02	−0.18	—				
Extraversion	0.62	0.07	0.05	−0.32	—			
Openness	0.44	0.23	0.35	−0.11	0.33	—		
Agreeableness	0.31	0.19	0.03	−0.34	0.24	0.21	—	
Conscientiousness	0.32	−0.04	−0.02	−0.38	0.11	0.10	0.27	—

Questions

Emotional or social intelligence

The MSCEIT is designed to measure emotional intelligence, which Maier and his colleagues regard as distinguishable from social intelligence. But there is little evidence to support this distinction. When Visser *et al.* (2006) gave their participants two tests of Gardner's interpersonal intelligence and two of his intrapersonal intelligence, the correlations between the interpersonal and intrapersonal tests were actually rather stronger than those between the two tests *within* each domain. The MSCEIT does in fact include questions about social situations, even if it asks about the feelings that people would have in those situations. Moreover, questions about the emotions being shown in pictures of people smiling or frowning form a part of several tests of social intelligence. Attridge (2006) found a correlation of 0.31, in a group of over one hundred sixth-form students, between total MSCEIT scores and one such test of social intelligence, the Reading the Mind in the Eyes test (Baron-Cohen, 2003). What would happen to the factor structure of the MSCEIT if it included more social questions? Would there be partly distinguishable factors of social and emotional intelligence still within a single general factor, or two independent factors?

Discriminant validity

As noted above, the correlation between the MSCEIT and IQ is not negligible. What is the significance of these correlations? Although it is reasonable to expect some correlation between emotional intelligence and traditional measures of intelligence, one worry would be that the intercorrelations between the various components of the MSCEIT arise simply because they reflect differences in general intelligence rather than anything that might be called general emotional intelligence (as so often seemed to be the case for early measures of social intelligence). But that worry may be exaggerated. Attridge was able to show that the intercorrelations between the four MSCEIT branches remained virtually unchanged after partialling out scores on the DAT test of verbal reasoning (see Table 10.4).

MSCEIT scores also correlate with some measures of personality, but with the exception of the study by Schulte *et al.* (2004), where total MSCEIT score correlated significantly with all five dimensions of personality, with r ranging from 0.18 to 0.28, other studies have by and large reported significant correlations only with openness and agreeableness, and

Table 10.4 Intercorrelations between the four branches of the MSCEIT before and after partialling out scores on the DAT verbal reasoning test (from Attridge, 2006).

Raw correlations					Partial correlations controlling for DAT scores				
	P	F	U	M		P	F	U	M
Perception	—				Perception	—			
Facilitation	0.40	—			Facilitation	0.39	—		
Understanding	0.14	0.26	—		Understanding	0.08	0.24	—	
Management	0.22	0.35	0.43	—	Management	0.19	0.33	0.34	—

these correlations seem intuitively plausible. Although Schulte and her colleagues argue that the MSCEIT measures little or nothing new apart from IQ and personality, the totality of the evidence does not seem to support their case.

Predictive validity

What about evidence of predictive validity? Do scores on the MSCEIT predict achievements and success in the real world? There has been no shortage of extravagant claims (see Box 10.7), but rather little evidence to support them. It is worth noting that performance on the MSCEIT improves with age, and that females usually do better than males (e.g. Brackett *et al.*, 2004, 2006), findings which are certainly consistent with expectations of a measure of emotional intelligence. But do young people's scores agree with parents' or teachers' ratings of sociability, friendliness, or social skills? Do adults' scores predict how well they are liked by people who work with them? Mayer *et al.* (2008) summarized a number of studies that found modest but significant correlations with other people's rating of sensitivity and social competence, and the number of their friends, with managers' effectiveness in interactions with others and how well liked they were by their subordinates. In one study of 38 supervisors, for example, their employees' ratings of their performance correlated 0.39 with their total EI score (Kerr *et al.*, 2006). Negative correlations have been reported with deviant behaviour, poor relationships with friends, aggression, and drug use.

BOX 10.7 Selling emotional intelligence

One of the difficulties some academics have with the concept of emotional intelligence is its popularization. Daniel Goleman's book *Emotional Intelligence*, published in 1995, had as its sub-title *Why it can matter more than IQ*, and included such claims as:

> There are widespread exceptions to the rule that IQ predicts success—many (or more) exceptions than cases that fit the rule. At best, IQ contributes about 20 per cent to the factors that determine life success, which leaves 80 per cent to other forces... My concern is with a key set of these 'other characteristics', *emotional intelligence*... No one can yet say exactly how much of the variability from person to person in life's course it accounts for. But what data exist suggest that it can be as powerful, and at times more powerful, than IQ.
>
> (Goleman, 1995, p. 34)

The cover of a paperback edition of the book includes the following extract from a review: 'Forget IQ. Brains may come in useful, as may social class and luck, but as a predictor of who will succeed in any area of life, EQ is the thing to worry about'.

Goleman can hardly be held responsible for claims made by a reviewer, but his own claim is strong enough, and it is one that he has been happy to repeat: 'nearly 90% of the difference between star performers at work and average ones is due to EI' (Goleman, 1998, p. 94). In my own reasonably careful reading of his book I could not find any serious evidence for these claims. Studies of the validity of the MSCEIT have certainly not supported them.

Mayer and Salovey have repeatedly attempted to dissociate themselves from this hyperbole. Their further concern is that Goleman has included a huge array of attributes into his concept of emotional intelligence: 'trustworthiness, adaptability, innovation, communication, team capabilities' (Mayer *et al.*, 2008, p. 505). As they note, it is hardly surprising that some critics should characterize such a concept as 'preposterously all-encompassing' (Locke, 2005, p. 428).

One interesting study suggests that social ability may satisfy more traditional tests of validity. Conti *et al.* (2009) reported that for every extra friend someone had at school, their salary 35 years later was 2% higher. Schoolboys were asked to name their three best friends, and the number of times someone's name was mentioned was used as the measure of the number of friends he had. Although the study is both clever and suggestive, there could be a problem: if schoolboys are tempted to boast about having important friends, they might be more likely to nominate as a friend someone they perceived as important in preference to their actual, but alas undistinguished, best friend. Conti and her colleagues also acknowledge that the number of friends you have at school is not as good a predictor of future earnings as are IQ or years of education (see Chapter 9). Contrary to some popular claims (see Box 10.7), there is no convincing evidence that tests of social or emotional intelligence are a *better* predictor of 'success' than IQ.

On the other hand, although correlations with traditional measures of achievement, such as educational or occupational attainment, have been reported, they have usually disappeared once IQ is partialled out (Attridge, 2006; Mayer *et al.*, 2004; Rode *et al.*, 2008). One study, however, showed that MSCEIT scores did predict supervisors' ratings of job performance, but only in workers of below average IQ (Cote and Miners, 2006): the suggestion is that high emotional intelligence may compensate for low general intelligence. A second exception is a study by Song *et al.* (2010), which found that emotional intelligence predicted college students' grades independently of their IQ. A possible explanation is that the study was conducted in China, and the discrepancy between these results and those reported in American or British studies may reflect a cultural difference. As I discuss in Chapter 13, Chinese culture emphasizes collectivism rather than individualism, and interdependence rather than independence. It seems possible that this difference in cultural values might be reflected in differences in what is important for academic success.

The constructors of the MSCEIT and other similar tests argue that they have succeeded in measuring an important component of human abilities. Is this claim invalidated by this slightly patchy evidence of validity? No. What, after all, would you expect any measure of social or emotional intelligence to predict? Why should you suppose that students who are more socially competent or have superior emotional intelligence would be academically more successful? They might of course be better liked by their teachers, but that is not quite the same. Does occupational success or income necessarily depend on these skills? To look for evidence of validity in these traditional validators of traditional IQ tests seems a bit blinkered. In the world of work, it might be the case, as Gardner supposed (see above), that success in *some* jobs or professions depended on social or emotional intelligence, for example sales, counselling, GP (medical practitioner), some managerial jobs, novelist. But it seems even more obvious that other jobs, such as accountancy, computing, engineering, university professor, or research scientist, make few if any such demands. Recall the case of Richard Borcherds (p. 246).

Conclusion

Several people have argued that IQ tests measure only one, or at best only a few, aspects of intelligence (Neisser, 1976; Sternberg, 1985). This may be true. One candidate for an additional aspect of intelligence that IQ tests fail to capture is Sternberg's concept of tacit knowledge and practical intelligence. The demonstration that experts in any domain are very much more knowledgeable and skilful than those less expert, without necessarily differing in IQ, has always been open to the relatively uninteresting interpretation that the difference between experts and non-experts is simply a matter of the amount of time they have devoted to acquiring the relevant knowledge and skills. But perhaps there is also a difference in the efficiency with which people acquire such knowledge and skills. Wagner and Sternberg proposed that differences in expertise in a particular job are a consequence of differences in 'tacit knowledge' of the manifold demands of that job. But what explains these differences in tacit knowledge? Tacit knowledge is said to be knowledge which is informal, poorly articulated, and relatively inaccessible to conscious introspection. It seems closely related to the concept of implicit learning studied by Reber and others in the laboratory, where people show evidence of having learned something about some rather complex sequential dependences between rapidly occurring events, without being able to articulate the rules underlying those dependences. And implicit learning, in turn, seems closely related to the concept of associative learning as a system for detecting contingencies between events, as exemplified in studies of simple conditioning in animals or contingency learning by college students. People differ in their performance on implicit learning tasks; such differences are uncorrelated with differences in their IQ, but there is suggestive evidence that they may predict such academic achievements as second language learning. A *very* optimistic reading of the evidence would suggest that implicit or associative learning ability may be a second general-purpose cognitive system that is responsible for the acquisition of practical intelligence or competence in a variety of different domains. There is no reason to question that differences in IQ have a significant effect on the acquisition of skill at early stages of practice, and have a significant impact on people's performance of their job. There is even less reason to doubt that experience and practice are essential for high levels of expertise. But it is just possible that variations in implicit learning ability account for an important part of the remaining cognitive variance in the tacit knowledge, practical competence, or expertise that contributes to the efficient performance of a complex job.

There may well be aspects of intelligence not measured by traditional IQ tests. It does not follow that there are eight different and quite independent intelligences, as Gardner would have one believe. Three of his intelligences are clearly much the same as Gc, Gf, and Gv, which are of course correlated with one another. And there is evidence that most of his others also correlate with one another and with traditional measures of IQ. No one should quarrel with Gardner's wish to emphasize the importance and value of other talents, abilities, and skills, but calling them all 'intelligences' is not the best way of going about this.

One of Gardner's criticisms of traditional IQ tests is that they measure only the ability to give the right answer to questions asked in a wholly artificial setting. They do not measure actual accomplishment. A really intelligent person is one who can translate theoretical knowledge into practical achievement, for example by writing a poem or a song, inventing something, or finding the way home from a strange location. The point here is similar to that made by Sternberg when he argues that IQ does not measure *practical* intelligence.

Social or emotional intelligence, Gardner's interpersonal and intrapersonal intelligences, are probably better examples than his others of aspects of intelligence not measured by traditional IQ tests. After a very slow start, there is now evidence that at least one test, Mayer and Salovey's MSCEIT, does provide a measure of what they call emotional (not social) intelligence, that is at least partially independent of the intelligence measured by IQ tests. The evidence is mixed, but that should really come as no surprise. By comparison with the work that has gone into the construction, development, and validation of conventional IQ tests, research on these aspects of intelligence is still in early childhood, if not infancy.

One conclusion that can be drawn from this research is that a distinction needs to be drawn between self-report and ability measures of social or emotional competence. The latter tend to show moderate correlations with conventional measures of intelligence; the former with conventional measures of personality. This, too, should not come as a surprise: it is one thing to have a theoretical knowledge of the appropriate thing to do or say in any particular situation, it is another thing to be able to *act* on that knowledge. In this sense social or emotional competence is surely a blend of ability and personality. Conventional IQ tests show little or no correlation with any of the main dimensions of personality, the only exception being a modest correlation with openness to experience, and apart from Sternberg few researchers have paid much attention to the possibility that there might be an important distinction between theoretical ability and practical competence.

The most pressing question that remains unanswered is surely whether the tests are valid, and the answer to this will require more thought about just what criteria such tests might be expected to predict.

 ## Summary

- There are probably other aspects of intelligence besides those measured by IQ tests.
- Sternberg's tacit knowledge and practical intelligence seem to provide independent prediction of success in many areas. Tacit knowledge may depend on implicit as opposed to explicit learning.
- But the evidence does not support Gardner's contention that there are eight different and independent intelligences.
- Three of Gardner's intelligence correspond to Gc, Gf, and Gv, and several of the rest also seem to correlate with one another, and with IQ.
- Gardner's interpersonal and intrapersonal intelligences, otherwise social and emotional intelligence, *are* probably aspects of intelligence partially independent of IQ.
- But a distinction needs to be drawn between self-report questionnaires, which seem to be largely measures of well-established aspects of personality, and more objective measures which may more reasonably be called measures of intelligence.

Further reading

Sternberg *et al.* (2000) should be consulted for their account of practical intelligence, but their ideas have not commanded universal assent, and a critic such as Gottfredson (2003b) should also be read. I take a more positive view of 'A day at the races' (Ceci and Liker, 1986) than many commentators; you should read their paper, along with comments such as those of Detterman and Spry (1988), to decide whether I have been too favourable. Kaufman (2011) provides a good account of implicit learning and its potential for explaining the acquisition of tacit knowledge. On 'multiple intelligences', there is no substitute for reading Gardner himself (e.g. Gardner, 2006). Mayer *et al.* (2008) provide a thoughtful review of the MSCEIT and the questions about it that remain unanswered, but unfortunately have little to say about the relationship or difference between social and emotional intelligence. Matthews *et al.* (2005) provide a more critical account of emotional intelligence.

Heritability: kinship studies and single genes

Introduction

Darwinian theory implies that members of any population will vary in many characteristics and that much of this variation is inherited. Francis Galton's insight was to suggest that this general truth applied to human intelligence. By the beginning of the twentieth century, it was an idea whose time had come. With the honourable exception of Alfred Binet, the pioneers of IQ testing had no doubt that their tests measured a genetically determined biological reality, innate intellectual capacity, which varied widely in the general population. Their confidence was hardly based on hard scientific evidence, for there was no such evidence. Galton (1869) and Goddard (1914) had attempted to show that genius and feeble-mindedness ran in families. Burt (1912) and Terman (1916) had shown that children's IQ scores were related to their parents' social status. But without further information, these observations are equally consistent with an environmental explanation of variations in intelligence. It was not until the 1920s and 1930s that any relevant data became available.

Since then, the evidence from kinship studies has multiplied, to the point where it is hardly necessary to accumulate any more. Although Kamin could once argue that 'There exist no data which should lead a prudent man to accept the hypothesis that IQ test scores are in any degree heritable' (Kamin, 1974, p. 1), that position is essentially untenable today. There is still plenty of room for disagreement, and I will disagree with at least some of the conclusions taken as read by many behaviour geneticists. But the broad issue is surely settled: both nature and nurture, in Galton's phrase, are important. Today, molecular geneticists are trying to identify single genes that affect IQ.

The meaning of heritability

Heritability is a term from population genetics. It refers to the proportion of the total variation in a given characteristic in a given population attributable to genetic differences between members of that population. Variation not attributable to genetic differences is caused by differences in the environment experienced by members of the population (this is, I argue below, something of an oversimplification, but it will do for the moment). The heritability of a particular characteristic is not immutable, but is a statistic true for a given population at a given time, dependent on the genetic variation within that population and the variation its members experience in relevant aspects of the environment (where 'relevant' means those features of the environment which affect the characteristic in question). Where such environmental differences are large, heritability will be low; at the other extreme, in the limiting case where there are no such differences, heritability will be 1.0.

There is no single answer, therefore, to the question, 'What is *the* heritability of IQ?' It may differ in different societies, or in the same society at different times. To those who profess to see sinister consequences in the possibility that the heritability of IQ might be quite high, and impute sinister motives to anyone who claims that it is, an appropriate response is to suggest that the heritability of IQ has probably increased in Western societies in the past 150 years or so, and that this is a consequence not of the actions of malign governments but, on the contrary, of some modest improvements in the conditions of those societies. Given that genetic and environmental sources of variation in IQ must sum to 1.0, the greater the effect of differences in the environment the lower the heritability. A society in which the heritability of IQ is low will be one that permits significant differences in those environmental circumstances that affect IQ. These circumstances must surely include access to formal education, and probably include many other things which we now take for granted as universal rights: adequate nutrition, reasonable health care, etc. In a society where many children are severely malnourished and live in grossly overcrowded slums, ravaged by infectious diseases, while others live in comfort or even luxury; where many children receive no formal education at all, and few remain in school after the age of 12, there can be little doubt that differences in IQ scores will be partly a result of these environmental inequalities. Any moves towards equality of health care or of educational opportunity, however imperfect, will probably reduce the total variance of IQ in the population, but *increase* the proportion of that variance attributable to genetic differences between members of that population. In other words, the changes in this direction that have occurred in most industrialized countries in the past 150 years have probably been associated with an increase in the heritability of IQ. And any future increases in such equality of opportunity will presumably increase the heritability of IQ further. A low heritability for IQ could be regarded as a mark of an unjust society.

Those who worry about the heritability of IQ often confuse heritability with immutability. A genetic effect, they believe, is fixed for all time, but an effect due to the environment can easily be modified, for the environment can always be changed. This requires a remarkable confidence in the possibility of social engineering: if it turned out that the single most important cause of differences in children's IQ scores was the way that their parents interacted with them in their first five years of life, would it really be so easy to eliminate this difference? More important, however, heritable is not the same as immutable. To say that a particular characteristic has high heritability is to say that it is not greatly affected by *existing* environmental differences experienced in that population. It says nothing about the consequences of new environmental manipulations. Height is a characteristic with very high heritability (probably greater than 0.90 in most populations), but the average height of Europeans and North Americans increased by over 5 cm between 1920 and 1970 (Van Wieringen, 1978), presumably due to improvements in nutrition and a decrease in the incidence of various diseases.

A hypothetical example from the realm of IQ testing may drive the point home. Although hypothetical, some of its premises are certainly true; even if others are not, the example remains instructive. The first observation (which is unquestionably true, see Chapter 13) is that the average IQ of Americans of African origin is significantly lower than that of whites. The second (which is almost certainly true, see Chapter 12) is that high concentrations of lead in the body are associated with low IQ. The third (for which there is some evidence; see Mahaffey *et al.*, 1982) is that the average concentration of lead in the body is higher in American blacks than in whites, even when attempts are made to allow for differences in income and neighbourhood. The hypothesis (for which, as far as I am aware, there is no evidence whatsoever) is that a genetic difference between people of African and European origin causes the former to absorb a higher proportion of lead from the atmosphere. Given the truth of the premises, the hypothesis would constitute a genetic explanation for part of the difference between the average IQ scores of American blacks and whites. But the moral of the story, of course, is that the explanation would imply no inevitability about this difference. It could be eliminated by a relatively modest environmental intervention, a reduction in the level of lead in the atmosphere. Genetically caused differences may be every bit as malleable as those due to environmental variation.

Having, I hope, clarified some misunderstandings about the meaning of heritability, I turn to the question of how it may be estimated. That is a matter of partitioning variance. The broad heritability of a particular phenotypic characteristic in a given population is the proportion of variance in that characteristic attributable to genetic differences between members of that population, the remainder being attributable to environmental factors. But broad heritability may be further divided into additive and non-additive sources of genetic variation (see below). Similarly, it is customary to divide environmental sources of variation into two components, between-family or common environment (CE) and within-family or special environment (SE). The former refers to the effects of environmental factors which members of the same family share in common, but which may differ between families: the standard examples are social class, income, and neighbourhood. The latter refers to the different experiences of different members of the same family: parents do not, after all, treat all their children exactly alike; and those children will pursue their own interests, make their own friends outside the family, will often have different teachers and may even go to different schools.

Finally, behaviour genetic analyses have generally recognized the possibility of two other sources of variation that involve both genes and environment: covariation and interaction. Covariation refers, in general terms, to the possibility that there might be a correlation between genes for, say, high or low IQ and environments conducive towards high or low IQ. Thus, the children of parents of high IQ might inherit genes for high IQ from those parents, and also be brought up in a family environment favourable for the development of high IQ. The importance of different forms of covariation should not be underestimated, and I shall return to this issue later.

The second possibility is that there may be an interaction between genes and environment. It is necessary to understand what is meant here, for some critics of behaviour genetics have implied that such interactions make nonsense of any attempt to estimate heritabilities. According to one version of the critics' argument, all human characteristics

are a product of an interaction between genes and environment
development, and attempting to estimate the independent con'
like asking whether the area of a field is due more to its length (
ment simply reflects a misunderstanding of what estimates of
To repeat: they are attempts to partition variance, that is, to
similarities and differences between members of a populatio'
how much any individual's particular characteristics are due to .
ment. Of course, we are all a product of both, but the question that is be....
resemble, or differ from, one another. It makes perfectly good sense to ask, or a
set of fields, some large, some small, whether the differences in their areas are due mo...
differences in their length or to differences in their breadth.

The only sense in which gene-environment interaction does raise an important issue for
the estimate of heritability is this: it is possible that particular genetic variations might have
different phenotypic effects in different environments. Genotypes that resulted in a high
IQ in one environment, might have no effect on IQ in another, or even a deleterious effect
on IQ in a third. The children of high-IQ parents might develop a higher IQ than those of
low-IQ parents only if both sets of children were brought up in a 'high-IQ' environment. If
brought up in a 'low-IQ' environment, the two groups of children might not differ in IQ at
all, or, less plausibly, the difference might even reverse. The problem is, in principle, a real
one; indeed, in certain extreme cases, such interactions probably do occur. If the two groups
were both brought up in serious deprivation—severely malnourished, provided with no
intellectual stimulation whatsoever, kept out of school, etc., it does indeed seem probable
that they would both end up with low IQ scores. In practice, however, over the normal
range of environments found in Western industrialized societies, there is surprisingly little
evidence to suggest that such dramatic interactions do occur for IQ. Nevertheless, I will
discuss one case later in this chapter.

Measuring heritability: kinship studies

In principle, it is a simple matter to estimate the relative importance of genes and environment in producing similarities and differences in any characteristic. In other animals or
plants, geneticists are free to conduct controlled experiments: they can measure the extent
to which a particular characteristic responds to selective breeding, or they can rear animals in controlled environments. If two strains of mice differ in their behaviour even if
brought up in the same environment, the difference is probably a genetic one. If mice of the
same strain differ in their behaviour when brought up in different environments (but not if
brought up in the same one), the difference is probably environmental. It is, of course, not
possible to perform such experiments on people. Behaviour geneticists can study only what
natural circumstances provide, and for the most part those circumstances inevitably confound environmental and genetic sources of variation. In order to estimate the heritability
of IQ, you need to measure the extent to which increases in either genetic or environmental similarity are associated with increasing resemblance in IQ. In most human societies,
however, people who share genes in common (i.e. are genetically related, because they are

members of the same family), tend to share similar environments. The fact that members of the same family also tend to resemble one another in IQ does not allow one to disentangle the genetic and environmental sources of this resemblance.

Nature and society, however, have given the human behaviour geneticist at least two kinds of natural experiment that go some way towards answering the question (see Box 11.1). Nature has provided twins, and society the practice of adoption. MZ twins are genetically identical, but fraternal or dizygotic (DZ) twins are genetically no more similar than any other pair of siblings, in principle sharing only 50% of their genes (but see Box 11.2). The practice of adoption means both that some biologically unrelated people live together in the same family (adoptive parents and their adopted children; two or more adopted children), and equally that some biologically related people live apart (two siblings or twins adopted into different families, adopted children and their biological parents).

BOX 11.1 Sharing genes

It is worth remembering that all humans share virtually all their genes with all other humans. Indeed, the current orthodoxy is that we share more than 97% of our genes with the common chimpanzee (*Pan troglodytes*) and even more with the bonobo or pygmy chimpanzee (*Pan paniscus*). We even share some 70% of our genes with goldfish. So when behaviour geneticists talk of members of the same family sharing, say, half their genes, and unrelated individuals sharing none, they are talking of only the 0.1% of genes that are not shared by *all* humans. There is no such thing as two wholly unrelated human beings: we are all, distantly, related to one another.

Members of the same nuclear family are more closely related, and therefore share more genes in common. The common assumption is that DZ twins and other brothers and sisters share 50% of their genes (i.e. of those not common to all of us). Token acknowledgement is usually made that the phenomenon of assortative mating (husbands and wives do not choose one another at random) means that this is an underestimate (see p. 273). But few behaviour geneticists are willing to allow that the vagaries of human behaviour may mean that not all biological siblings are actually that. The definition of biological siblings is: children who share the same biological mother and father; but can we be sure that two siblings actually do so? Maternity is usually quite readily ascertained, although the ancient Roman practice of substitution—the secret substitution of another healthy infant for one stillborn or very sickly in order to ensure a family heir, illustrates one pitfall. But paternity is another matter. Both blood group and DNA studies have shown that in a surprisingly (distressingly) high percentage of cases, the putative father of a baby could not actually have been the true father (Bellis *et al.*, 2005; Phillip, 1973).

It is worth bearing in mind that the panoply of biometrical analysis and quantitative modelling deployed by some behaviour geneticists rests on this rather frail foundation: reproduction is an aspect of human behaviour where what is socially acceptable and what actually happens are not always the same thing, and people go to great trouble to conceal the discrepancies between the two.

BOX 11.2 The variety of natural experiments

Virtually all behaviour genetic studies of human characteristics have relied on two natural experiments provided by nature and society, twins and adoption, and I discuss only them in this chapter. Other times and other societies have provided other kinds of natural experiment, and our own time provides at least one other kind of natural experiment, which behaviour geneticists have been slow to exploit.

Beginning in the thirteenth century, many large European cities started to open foundling hospitals, that is to say charitable institutions expressly designed to look after infants and young children abandoned by their parents (Boswell, 1988). Within 50 years of its opening in 1455, the Innocenti Hospital in Florence was receiving 900 abandoned children a year. By the eighteenth century, French records suggest that some 15–30% of *all* newborn children in most large French cities were abandoned to these foundling hospitals. Jean Jacques Rousseau famously abandoned all five of his children to such hospitals. Add to this, the widespread practice in urban middle-class families of farming out their newborn infants to rural wet nurses for the first year of their life (Schama, 1989), and the eighteenth century French social scientist, had he so wished, could have exploited endless possibilities for natural experiments.

Foundling hospitals or orphanages survived into the twentieth century, and one early British study (Lawrence, 1931) did ask an obvious question: given that a group of children living in an orphanage are all exposed to a rather similar environment, does this reduce the variability in their IQ scores as an environmental hypothesis might predict? Lawrence found only a small reduction in variability, and her results have often been cited as evidence of the limited effect of the environment.

Behaviour geneticists have taken little advantage of the new opportunities for natural experiments offered in many modern societies by rising rates of divorce and remarriage. Many families today contain half-brothers and sisters sharing only one biological parent, and stepbrothers and stepsisters sharing none. Many of these children will have lived together, and with a step-parent for much of their life. At the same time, the children of divorced parents may live with one and never see the other. And, although rarer and still more recent, such developments as artificial insemination and the donation of eggs, mean that some children of ordinary nuclear families are no longer genetically related to both their parents.

Table 11.1 summarizes the results of a large number of studies that have reported correlations between MZ and DZ twins, siblings, parents, and their children, both when they live in the same family and when they have been separated by adoption, and also between unrelated individuals living in the same (adoptive) family. Several points are apparent from the table:

- In all cases, kin living together in the same family resemble one another in IQ more closely than those living apart.

- Biologically unrelated people who live in the same family (adoptive parent and adopted child, two adopted children) show some resemblance in IQ. But by the time that they are adult, this correlation is essentially zero.

- But biologically related people living together resemble one another more than biologically unrelated people: compare the correlation between parents and their children with that between adoptive parents and adopted children, or that between siblings with that between two unrelated children living together.

- MZ twins resemble one another in IQ substantially more than DZ twins.

- In all cases, biologically related people living apart show some resemblance in IQ: the most striking, but unsurprisingly also the rarest, example of this is that of MZ twins brought up apart, where the correlation is very substantial.

On the face of it, the first two points imply a significant effect of family environment on IQ (at least in children), while the last three imply a significant genetic effect. If that is accepted, it follows that variations in IQ in the general population are caused by both

Table 11.1 Kinship correlations for IQ. Most of the data are from Bouchard and McGue (1981) as modified by Bouchard (1997) and Plomin *et al.* (2008); the data for separated DZ twins are the weighted average from two reports, Newman *et al.* (1998) and Pedersen *et al.* (1992); the data for two or more unrelated children living in the same home, and when tested as adults, are from McGue *et al.* (1993).

Kinship	Living together	Living apart
MZ twins	0.86	0.75
DZ twins	0.60	0.38
Siblings	0.47	0.24
Parent-child	0.42	0.24
Adoptive parent-adopted child	0.19	—
Two unrelated children	0.25	—
Two unrelated children (when adult)	−0.01	—

genetic and environmental variation in the population. Is there any good reason to doubt that conclusion? Good reason there may not be, but that has not prevented attempts to find reasons. I turn first to the arguments that have been advanced against the evidence pointing to a significant genetic influence.

Analysis of the genetic evidence

MZ and DZ twins

The classic twin method for estimating heritability was first suggested by Galton (see Chapter 1). It remains popular to this day, and not only in studies of IQ. The comparison of MZ and DZ twins provides the largest single source of evidence for the heritability of many, if not most, human characteristics. The studies summarized in Table 11.1 establish that MZ twins resemble one another in IQ substantially more than DZ twins, whether they have been brought up together or apart (although I defer consideration of separated twins until the next section). Is this good evidence for the heritability of IQ?

The conclusion would seem to depend on the assumption that MZ twins do not experience any greater similarity in their environment than DZ twins. Is that a reasonable assumption? The results shown in Table 11.1 suggest that DZ twins resemble one another in IQ somewhat more closely than other brothers and sisters. The obvious interpretation (but see Box 11.1) is that twins share more environmental experiences than siblings of different ages. Might it not be possible that MZ twins experience even more similar environments than DZ twins? It is not only possible; it is almost certainly true (Loehlin and Nichols, 1976). MZ twins are more likely to dress alike, play together, share the same teacher, sleep in the same room, and be treated alike by others than are DZ twins. This is hardly surprising: genetic identity will normally produce marked physical similarity, and perhaps also similarities in character and temperament; it would be surprising if these did not lead to their spending more time together and being treated more alike.

The question remains, however, whether the greater similarity of their environments is sufficient to explain why MZ twins resemble one another in IQ more than DZ twins: it is one thing to show that MZ twins are treated more alike; it is quite another to prove that this is the *cause* of their more similar IQ scores. Loehlin and Nichols themselves argued that it was not, since they could find no evidence that MZ twins who shared more similar experiences resembled one another in IQ more than those who did not. But this does not necessarily justify their conclusion. If all MZ twins share more experiences in common than all DZ twins, then this difference *between* the two groups of twins might still be responsible for the difference between them in similarity of IQ, even though the rather small range of variation in similarity of experience *within* one of the two groups is not associated with variation in resemblance for IQ.

A second possibility is that MZ twins (or at least some of them) shared a more similar prenatal environment than DZ twins. All twins, of course, share a more similar prenatal environment than other siblings, who in turn share a more similar prenatal environment than unrelated children. But for some MZ twins, the similarity goes further. All DZ twins, and some MZ twins, are surrounded by different sacs or chorions in the uterus. But some MZ twins are monochorionic: that is to say, they share the same chorion. If monochorionic MZ twins experience a more similar prenatal environment than dichorionic twins, this might explain why MZ twins, as a group, resemble one another more closely in IQ than DZ twins. The possibility is open to a simple test: dichorionic MZ twins should resemble each other in IQ less than monochorionic twins, and no more than DZ twins. Although one early study found some support for this in a very small sample of white twins, but not in a sample of black twins (Melnick *et al.*, 1978), a later, larger study found that the IQ correlation between dichorionic MZ twins was actually slightly higher than that between monochorionic twins (Sokol *et al.*, 1995).

If it would be implausible to assert that the greater similarity in their environments has nothing to do with the observation that MZ twins resemble one another in IQ more than DZ twins, it would surely be equally implausible to argue that the only reason why MZ twins resemble one another in IQ *at all*, is because they share such similar experiences. The correlation between the IQ scores of MZ twins sometimes approaches the limits of the reliability of the tests, that is to say, the difference in IQ score between two MZ twins is little greater than the difference between the same person's score taken on separate occasions. To assert that this is *entirely* because they have been treated identically is to ignore the fact that there are numerous respects in which MZ twins differ from one another quite markedly. McCartney *et al.* (1990) reviewed studies showing that the average MZ correlation for eight measures of personality, for example, was no more than 0.50 (see also Bouchard *et al.*, 1990); and the concordance of MZ twins for schizophrenia is also no more than 50% (Plomin *et al.*, 2008). If differences in their experience of life have been sufficient to produce differences such as these between two MZ twins, why have they not also resulted in differences in measured IQ? The argument may not convince the determined sceptic, but it is hard to ignore: their genetic identity is probably one reason why MZ twins have such similar IQ scores. Indeed, it is also probably the main reason why they share such similar environments. That is to say, MZ twins spend time together and are treated alike because they look alike, share similar interests, etc., and one reason why they do that is because they are genetically identical. Here, in fact, is a case of gene-environment covariation, but more of this later. It is time to turn to the supposedly decisive evidence for the heritability of IQ, that from studies of MZ twins brought up apart.

Separated MZ twins

It is not hard to see why behaviour geneticists have been so enamoured of separated MZ twins. Provided that they have been 'truly' separated, it would seem that the only explanation of any resemblance between them, in IQ or any other characteristic, must be their identical genotypes.

Unfortunately for the behaviour geneticist, however, separated MZ twins are also rather rare. Table 11.2 gives the summary results of five published studies of such twins, excluding that published by Burt (1966). The grand total in these five studies is only 162 pairs. Whether or not Burt's data were actually fraudulent, as has been suggested, they contain so many errors, inconsistencies, and anomalies that they cannot be relied on (see Box 11.3). One of the more striking of Burt's claims was that all his twins had been separated before 6 months of age and that there was no correlation between the social circumstances of the separate families in which they had been brought up. Of none of the remaining studies is this true. The three earlier studies provided case histories which make it clear that for many of the twins 'separation' is a bit of an exaggeration. In 27 of Shields's pairs, for example, one twin was brought up by the mother and the other by a relative, usually a maternal aunt or grandmother. A majority of the twins in the Newman *et al.* and Juel-Nielsen studies were also both brought up by relatives. In all three of these earlier studies, no more than about half the twins had been separated before the age of 6 months, and about three-quarters were reunited, for shorter or longer periods, at some point in their childhood. None of this should come as any great surprise. The real world does not arrange perfect experiments for the benefit of social scientists. Mothers of identical twins do not obligingly send one twin off to an adoption agency; if, for any reason, they cannot look after both, they ask a friend or

Table 11.2 Correlations between separated MZ twins.

Study	Number of pairs	Mean correlation
Newman *et al.* (1937)	19	0.71
Shields (1962)	37–38	0.75
Juel-Nielson (1980)	12	0.69
Bouchard *et al.* (1990)	42–48	0.75
Pedersen *et al.* (1992)	45	0.78

All studies gave more than one IQ test to each twin, and sometimes not all twins took all tests. The correlations shown are the average for the various tests, except in the Pedersen *et al.* study, where it is for the general factor extracted from a number of different tests.

relative to look after one; an adoption agency receiving two MZ twins may try to keep them together. And in the rare cases where real separation occurs, the twins may not even know of each other's existence, let alone be simultaneously available for study.

BOX 11.3 The strange case of Cyril Burt

Cyril Burt died, aged 88, in 1971, widely honoured as the foremost British educational psychologist and psychometrician of his generation. Among his many empirical contributions, he had published a series of papers reporting the results of what appeared to be an ongoing study of kinship correlations for IQ, the most notable feature of which was data on a sample of separated MZ twins. Starting with a brief mention of 15 pairs of such twins in 1943, he published three updates in the 1950s, with successively 21, 'over 30', and 42 pairs, culminating in a final paper published in 1966 when the sample of such twins had grown to 53 pairs, at that time, and still, the largest study ever published (Burt, 1966). His data were relied on extensively by Jensen (1969) as the best evidence for the heritability of IQ. On the face of it, indeed, they appeared to be: according to Burt, all 53 pairs had been separated before they were 6 months old; there was no correlation between the social circumstances of their adoptive families; and these family backgrounds spanned the full range to be expected in the general population.

Within a few years of his death, Burt's reputation as an empirical scientist had been destroyed. Kamin (1974), found so many anomalies in his data, combined with such inadequate reporting of critical procedural details, that he concluded that 'the numbers left behind by Professor Burt are simply not worthy of our current scientific attention'. His official biographer (Hearnshaw, 1979), indeed, concluded that much of his later research, not only that on the twins, was fraudulent, and the data simply fabricated.

Whether or not the twin data were fabricated, they cannot be relied upon, for one simple reason. The relevant table of correlations for various IQ and other measures for the twins and other kinship categories in the 1966 paper contains 66 (11 measures for each of 6 kinship categories) correlation coefficients, all given to three decimal places. Nearly half of them are *identical* to those published in earlier papers in the series, even though all the sample sizes (not only those for the twins) had changed over time. One or two correlations might, by chance, have remained the same. Thirty could not have, and it must be assumed that Burt had simply copied down a lot of the old numbers. But with the evidence of this sort of carelessness, how can we then believe either these old numbers or the 30 or so new ones?

Many critics took the invariant correlations to be evidence of fraud; if that is true, Burt was not only a fraud, he was a spectacularly stupid one. And Hearnshaw's charges of deliberate fraud have been disputed by Joynson (1989) and Fletcher (1991), whose defence has been accepted by many, rather depressingly usually by those of a hereditarian point of view (e.g. Herrnstein and Murray, 1994). The invariant correlations, it should be clear, are quite insufficient to prove fraud, but there is other evidence that points rather more conclusively to fabrication, not only in the twin data but also in some of Burt's other, later papers (Mackintosh, 1995). In the case of the separated MZ twins, for example, Burt eventually responded to requests for his raw data with a set of IQ scores for all 106 twins, although in his diary he records that he spent a week *calculating* these data (what on earth was there to calculate?). These scores do, indeed, yield the correlation coefficient reported in the 1966 paper, but there are numerous other inconsistencies between these individual scores and other aspects of the data reported not only in that paper but also in earlier papers in the series. A plausible interpretation is that some (or all) of the individual scores he eventually produced were simply invented to produce the desired correlation, but that they could not simultaneously agree with all the other summary statistics published earlier.

Like others at the time (for example, Raymond Cattell, see Chapter 1), Burt was convinced that intelligence was probably declining from one generation to the next. He published a paper (Burt, 1969)

(continued...)

supposedly reporting the results of tests of intelligence and school achievement in six samples of 10-year-old London schoolchildren, sampled approximately every ten years from 1914 to 1965. The same IQ test (Burt's own version of the Binet tests) was used for each sample, and he claimed that there had been no need to restandardize the test. The Flynn effect, of course, means that 10-year-olds in 1965 should have outscored 10-year-olds in 1914 by something in the region of ten points. His data showed a decline of 0.8 points. This beggars belief.

   Leaving aside the question of how far Burt's data were actually fabricated, an issue of rather wider import is why the twin data, for example, were treated with such respect for so long. It did not take a particularly careful inspection to see that they were inadequately reported and riddled with error. It is tempting to see evidence of a hereditarian conspiracy, or at least of a reprehensible readiness to accept, at face value, data that conformed to the reader's prior expectations. A slightly more benign interpretation is that the scientific enterprise is based on trust; by and large, scientists are reluctant to believe that other scientists fabricate their data.

How far, then, is the resemblance in IQ between these supposedly separated MZ twins to be attributed to the similarities in their environments? The data from the 70 odd pairs of twins in the three earlier studies have been subject to prolonged and (depending on your point of view) painstaking or nit-picking analysis—first by Kamin (1974), and later by Taylor (1980), and Farber (1981). These critics have been able to persuade themselves that there was no good reason to accept a genetic explanation of the twins' resemblance, but they have persuaded few other commentators. Bouchard (1997) and Mackintosh (1998, Appendix to Chapter 3) have discussed the critics' arguments in some detail. Of the two later studies, that by Bouchard *et al.* (1990) provides the more detailed analysis of the circumstances surrounding the twins' separation, degree of contact, and similarity of circumstances, and I shall concentrate on it. Table 11.3a provides the relevant information. It can be seen that although these twins were on average separated before the age of 6 months, and had spent only a small part of their lives in contact with one another before participating in the study, when their average age was over 40 (in these respects being better separated than the twins of earlier studies), there was still substantial variation in their degree of separation. But Table 11.3b shows that this variation was not closely related to variation in their resemblance for IQ. Twins separated earlier, for example, were slightly *more* alike in IQ than those separated later; none of the correlations shown in Table 11.3b is significant. Table 11.3c shows that, as in the earlier studies, the twins were not brought up in wholly uncorrelated home environments. In at least some potentially relevant respects, such as fathers' occupation, mothers' education, material possessions in the home, there were significant correlations between their family backgrounds. But, as can also be seen in Table 11.3c, there is actually no evidence that these aspects of the home environment had substantial effects on the twins' IQ scores. The only two variables where there was evidence both of a correlation between the twins' homes and of an effect of this variable on their IQ, were father's occupation and the material possessions in the home. Since these two variables will themselves have certainly been correlated, they cannot have independently contributed to the separated twins' resemblance in IQ, and it is quite evident that most of that resemblance remains unexplained by the factors enumerated in Table 11.3.

Table 11.3 Details of the Minnesota study of separated MZ twins (from Bouchard *et al.*, 1990, Tables 1 and 3).

(a) Measures of separation

Measure	Mean	SD
Age at separation (months)	5.1	8.5
Total amount of contact before testing (months)	9.2	19.2
Age at testing (years)	41.0	12.0

(b) Correlations between separation and differences in WAIS IQ

Measure	Correlation
Age at separation	0.06
Time apart to first reunion	0.08
Total amount of contact	−0.14
Percent of life spent apart	0.17

(c) Correlations between family backgrounds and twins' IQ scores

Background measure	Correlation between twins' families	Correlation with twins' IQ
Father's education	0.13	0.10
Mother's education	0.41	0.00
Father's SES	0.27	0.17
Material possessions	0.40	0.28
Scientific/cultural	0.15	−0.09
Cultural	−0.08	−0.28

Once again, it is possible to appeal to a shared prenatal environment to explain some of the resemblance in separated twins' IQ scores—an argument advanced by Devlin *et al.* (1997), who suggest that this prenatal environmental effect contributes as much as 20% to the resemblance. One result shown in Table 11.1, however, suggests that this is probably an exaggeration. The correlation between separated DZ twins' IQ scores is 0.38, that is, half that of MZ twins. Since DZ twins share only half of their genes, while MZ twins share all their genes, this difference is what would be expected on a simple genetic hypothesis. Since, however, there is no good reason to suppose that MZ twins experience more similar prenatal environments than DZ twins, subtracting 0.20 from both MZ and DZ correlations leaves a residual DZ correlation of only 0.18, substantially less than half the residual MZ correlation of 0.55. It is also worth pointing out that the available evidence suggests that the impact of prenatal environment even on young children's IQ scores is relatively small (see Chapter 12); moreover, there is also good evidence that *differences* in their prenatal environment can cause differences in the IQ scores of MZ twins (Bouchard *et al.*, 1990): sharing the same womb at the same time does not guarantee that MZ twins experience an identical prenatal environment.

Bouchard *et al.* concluded that the IQ correlation between the separated MZ twins in their study is almost entirely attributable to their shared genotypes. That might be too strong a conclusion, but it is surely nearer the truth than an extreme environmentalist position. It would be surprising if the IQ scores of separated MZ twins were wholly unaffected by similarities or differences in their life experiences. It follows, therefore, that in so far as many of the twins in these five studies experienced somewhat similar environments, the observed correlations in their IQ scores may overestimate the heritability of IQ. That seems plausible enough. Is it really plausible, however, to suggest that these studies of separated MZ twins are consistent with the possibility that the heritability of IQ is zero? Writing about the earlier studies, Kamin pointed to the 'glaring tendency' for the environments of so-called separated twins to be highly correlated:

> This tendency, no less than identical genes, might easily be responsible for the observed resemblance in IQs. We cannot guess what the IQ correlation would be if, in a science fiction experiment, we separated pairs of identical twins at birth and scattered them *at random* across the full range of available environments. It could conceivably be zero.
>
> (Kamin, 1981, p. 113)

Of course in no study were MZ twins taken at birth and scattered at random across all available environments; it follows therefore that no one knows exactly what the correlation between the IQ scores of such twins would be. But is it conceivable that it would be zero? To suppose that, is to say that similarity of environment provides a complete explanation of the correlations reported in Table 11.2. But even if every pair of twins had been brought up in related families, which closely resembled one another in social, cultural, and economic circumstances, and even if all pairs of twins had met one another from time to time while they were growing up, it is difficult to see how they could have experienced *more* similar environments than children growing up in the same family. But the kinship studies summarized in Table 11.1 suggest that the IQ correlation between two unrelated children brought up in the same adoptive family is no more than 0.25, and by the time they are 18 or so (the large majority of separated MZ twins were not tested until they were adult) this correlation reduces to zero. Even brothers and sisters living in the same family show a correlation of less than 0.50, and DZ twins one of only 0.60.

To attribute correlations of more than 0.70 to the shared environment of children living in different families, when children living in the same family correlate substantially less, requires a remarkable act of faith. The only sensible conclusion is that, in spite of their inevitable imperfections, these studies of separated MZ twins strongly suggest that the heritability of IQ is substantial. But those imperfections should not be forgotten. The twins were usually not separated at birth, and were certainly not assigned to a random selection of homes spanning the variety of homes to be found in the general population. Bouchard

(1997) acknowledged that the environments experienced by the MZ twins of his study did not span the full range of possible environments; very few of the twins in any of the published studies were brought up in serious poverty or by illiterate parents, and none had an IQ below 70. To that extent, therefore, their data will underestimate the importance of environmental variation found in the general population, and should be extrapolated to the general population only rather cautiously. A final obvious problem is that the studies are *small*. Some 160 pairs of numbers, collected over 50 odd years in a number of different countries, do not provide a very secure basis from which to extrapolate to the population (what population?) as a whole.

Adoption studies

MZ twins comprise about 0.33% of live births, and the proportion of such twins brought up apart must be a minute fraction of the total. What other data for estimating heritability may lack in elegance, they must surely make up for in sheer abundance. In principle, any group of adopted children provides several ways of disentangling genetic and environmental causes of variation in IQ, and adopted children are, at least by comparison with separated MZ twins, plentiful, even if they have become rather less plentiful in most Western countries in the past 50 years.

One obvious question to ask about adopted children, and one that may provide information analogous to that provided by separated twins, is whether their IQ scores resemble those of their biological parents with whom they have lived for only a very small part of their life. It is also informative to ask whether they resemble their adoptive parents in IQ more or less than their biological parents.

From Table 11.1 it can be seen that the average correlation between adopted children's IQ scores and those of their biological parents is 0.24. Since the children were virtually always adopted before the age of 6 months, this is obviously consistent with a genetic effect, but two counter-arguments must be considered. Since the biological parent in question is usually the mother, there is always the possibility of a prenatal effect. Second, the environmentalist can appeal to 'selective placement', arguing that the adoptive home has been carefully selected to match the biological mother's circumstances, and the similarity in IQ between adopted children and their biological mothers is mediated through the adoptive home.

The obvious way to assess the role of prenatal environment is to see whether adopted children resemble their biological father in IQ as much as their biological mother. Unfortunately, of course, the biological fathers have not always been available to have their IQ measured, but one study (Plomin *et al.*, 1997) reported a correlation of 0.32 between 16-year-old adopted children's IQ scores and those of their biological fathers (compared to one of 0.39 with their biological mothers), while another found that adopted children's IQ scores correlated rather more strongly with their biological fathers' level of education than their biological mothers' (the correlations were 0.43 and 0.33 respectively; Scarr and Weinberg, 1983).

The argument that adopted children's IQ scores correlate with those of their biological parents simply because they invariably live in an adoptive home very similar to that which would have been provided by their biological parents, requires that adopted children's IQ scores must correlate *at least* as strongly with those of their adoptive parents as with their

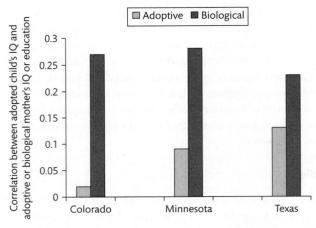

Figure 11.1 Correlations between adopted children's IQ and characteristics of their adoptive and biological mothers. In the Colorado (Plomin *et al.*, 1997) and Texas (Loehlin *et al.*, 1989) studies, the measure is of mothers' IQ; in the Minnesota study (Scarr and Weinberg, 1983) the measure is mothers' education.

biological parents: the argument implies, after all, that it is the former correlation that is responsible for the latter. The summary data shown in Table 11.1 suggest that this is probably not true. More definitive data come from three American adoption studies that have specifically compared the two correlations. Their results are shown in Figure 11.1: in all three studies, adopted children's IQ scores correlate more (sometimes substantially more) with their biological than with their adoptive parents' scores.

Conclusion: IQ is heritable

It has perhaps taken a rather long time to establish a relatively banal conclusion: over the past 80 years or so, the heritability of IQ in Western industrialized countries (where essentially all the data were collected) has been substantially greater than zero. The data are imperfect, the product of necessarily ambiguous, natural experiments rather than of carefully controlled experimentation, but they no longer permit a reasonable person to accept that the heritability of IQ is zero. That is, however, only the first step in the argument. I shall return below to some further questions that can be asked about genetic effects on IQ. But it is time to turn to the environment.

Analysis of environmental evidence

Two features of the data summarized in Table 11.1 strongly suggested that family environment has an impact on children's IQ scores. First, for all kinship categories, MZ and DZ twins, brothers and sisters, parents and their children, people living together in the same family resemble one another in IQ more than those living apart. Second, unrelated people living in the same family, for example adopted children and their adoptive parents, also resemble one another in IQ. The last two rows of the table show the correlation between two or more adopted children living in the same adoptive family, but here the data are divided in two: one row shows the correlations between such children while still young, the other the correlations between such people after the age of 18.

The conclusion that members of the same family resemble one another in IQ at least partly because they live together, will hardly come as a great surprise either to parents or to social scientists, and I do not intend to dispute it. Whether the numbers shown in Table 11.1 provide a precise measure of the importance of family environment is another matter, if only because there is probably no single value for this contribution. There is, after all, evidence that the IQ correlation between members of adoptive families depends on the age of the adopted child: Table 11.1 gives a value of 0.25 when the children are young, but of −0.01 when they are 18 or over. The implication is that the effect of family environment on children's IQ scores decreases as the children grow up. That may seem surprising, but (admittedly with the advantage of hindsight) it should not be. Most young children spend most of their time in the family home, but after the age of 5 or 6 spend as much time at school as at home and, as any parent will know, by the time they are teenagers, they are more influenced by their friends than by their parents. But the results shown in Table 11.1 seem to suggest that there is essentially *no* long-term effect of family environment on IQ. Although that conclusion has been accepted by many behaviour geneticists, it is almost certainly too strong. The numbers shown in Table 11.1 are the average of the results of a number of different studies carried out at different times and places. What is really needed to establish the behaviour geneticists' conclusion is a longitudinal study that follows up a group of adopted children from the age of, say, 7 or 8 until they are teenagers. Three studies have provided the relevant information in the form of correlations between adopted children and their adoptive mothers. They are the Colorado and Texas studies, some of whose results were shown in Figure 11.1, and a different study from Minnesota. The results of all three are shown in Figure 11.2. In the Colorado study the correlation was negligible

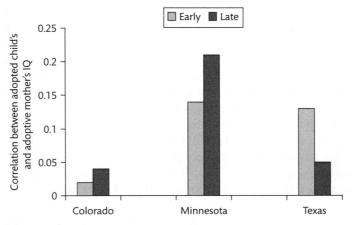

Figure 11.2 Correlations between adopted children's and their adoptive mothers' IQ scores at two ages, 'early', when the children were less than 10 years old, and 'late', approximately ten years later. The Colorado and Texas studies are the same as in Figure 11.1; the Minnesota study (Scarr and Weinberg, 1978) is a different one from that shown in Figure 11.1.

at both ages. In the Minnesota study, the correlation between adopted children's and adoptive mothers' IQ actually increased over time. Only the Texas study shows the expected decline in correlations. The results of these longitudinal studies, therefore, are distinctly equivocal.

On balance, there may be reason to believe that, by late adolescence, adopted children's IQ scores often resemble those of other members of their adoptive family rather weakly. But there is good reason to question the conclusion that in the population as a whole the influence of family environment on children's test scores declines to zero by the age of 18 or so. Since that conclusion rests on data from studies of adoptive families, it would be safe to extrapolate it to the rest of the population only if adoptive families were perfectly representative of the entire population. They are not: Stoolmiller (1999) showed that they are most unlikely to include families from the lowest social class. In addition, adoptive parents are a self-selected group, who have been further selected by adoption agencies who want good, committed parents, and endeavour to reject anyone who might prove to be feckless or irresponsible and neglect their children. They will certainly reject people with a criminal record or a history of drug problems. By comparison with the rest of the population, therefore, *all* adoptive homes are relatively 'good', and this restriction of range will necessarily lower the correlation between adopted children's IQ scores and any measure of the quality of their adoptive homes—including the IQ of their adoptive parents (see Nisbett, 2009).

There is, moreover, evidence from natural families that adolescent children's IQ scores are more affected by their family environment when their parents are from a lower social class and have only a modest level of education (Harden *et al.*, 2007; Turkheimer *et al.*, 2003). Table 11.4 shows the results of the latter study, which compared the resemblance between MZ and DZ twins in well-educated and less well-educated families. As can be seen, in the better-educated families, MZ twins resemble one another much more closely than DZ twins. In the less well-educated families, the difference between MZ and DZ twins is small. Since the difference between MZ and DZ twin correlations provides one of the standard methods of estimating heritability, these results imply that, as shown, the heritability of IQ is substantially higher in better educated families. Twin studies also provide an estimate of the role of family environment (the details of how this is calculated are given in the next section), and as can be seen, while family environment appears to have only a small effect on IQ in the better-educated families, its importance in the less well-educated families is substantial. Not all adoptive parents are necessarily well educated, but even if they are not, they probably share many of the characteristics of other better-educated parents in terms of commitment, conscientiousness, etc. The results shown in Table 11.4 suggest that family background has a more profound effect on children's IQ scores when that background is relatively poor, even if above a certain level there may be rather little long-lasting effect. If most adoptive parents provide a family background above this minimum level, then it is not surprising that differences between different adoptive families are not associated with differences in their children's test scores. The important implication is that correlational evidence from adoptive families underestimates the impact that family environment may have on children's IQ scores: although that effect may decline as the children grow older, there is no reason to suppose that it declines to zero in the population as a whole.

Table 11.4 IQ correlations for MZ and DZ twins in families of high and low SES, together with estimates of heritability (G) and the effects of common family environment (CE) (data from Turkheimer *et al.*, 2003).

	IQ correlations		Estimates	
	MZ	DZ	G	CE
High SES	0.87	0.51	0.72	0.15
Low SES	0.68	0.63	0.10	0.58

Correlational evidence from adoptive families may be suspect, but another kind of adoption study is unambiguous in its implication. Chapter 12 will document the finding that children taken at the age of 4 or 5 from neglectful or abusive parents and placed in good adoptive homes show a substantial increase in their IQ measured ten years later.

Quantitative estimates of heritability

The claim that the heritability of IQ is greater than zero hardly amounts to a very precise estimate. How are such estimates arrived at? How, for example, was Eysenck (1979) able to assert so confidently that the heritability of IQ is approximately 70%, or Lynn (2006) that it is 80%?

Quantitative estimates of heritability require quantitative models. Quantitative modelling, however, requires the modeller to start making a number of assumptions, some plausible enough, others often rather less plausible. In the present instance: any resemblance in IQ between parents and their children can be attributed to the factors (affecting IQ) that they share in common—a shared family environment and some shared genes. The two are inevitably confounded. But a comparison of this correlation with that between adoptive parents and their adopted children, or that between parents and their children sent away for adoption, may allow an estimate of the importance of these genetic and environmental sources of resemblance, provided that certain simplifying assumptions can be made. Table 11.5 illustrates the procedure. As in Table 11.1 above, Table 11.5 shows a list of various kinships—MZ twins brought up together or apart, parents and their children, adoptive parents and their adopted children, etc. The next step is to specify the factors they share in common. The column labelled 'Simple model' makes the simplest possible set of assumptions: first, that MZ twins are genetically identical, while DZ twins, other siblings, and parents and their children all share 50% of their genes (but recall Box 11.1), and unrelated individuals share no genes; and second, that people living in the same family all share exactly the same common family environment, while those who do not, share no common environment.

Armed with these assumptions, it is now possible to estimate the contributions of genetics and environment to similarities in IQ. For example, while the resemblance of

Table 11.5 A simple (unrealistically simple) model for estimating the heritability of IQ from kinship studies.

Kinship	Equation	Estimates	
		G	CE
MZ (t)–DZ (t)	G = 2(MZ t – DZ t)	0.52	
MZ (a)	G = MZ a	0.75	
DZ (a)	G = 2(DZ a)	0.76	
Sib (a)	G = 2(Sib a)	0.48	
Parent-child (a)	G = 2(P – Ca)	0.48	
MZ (t) vs. MZ (a)	CE = (MZt – Mza)		0.11
Sib (t) vs. sib (a)	CE = (Sib t – Sib a)		0.23
Parent-child (t) vs. (a)	CE = (PCt – PCa)		0.18
Unrelated children (t)	CE = Ut		0.25
Unrelated adults (t)	CE = Ut		0.00

MZ, MZ twins; DZ, DZ twins; Sib, Siblings; (t), brought up together; (a), living apart; G, contribution of genetic variance; CE, contribution of common (family) environment.

MZ twins brought up together reflects the contribution of shared genes plus shared family environment, the resemblance of MZ twins brought up apart reflects only that of their shared genes. The *difference* between these two correlations thus reflects the contribution of shared family environment, while the absolute value of the MZ (a) correlation provides a direct estimate of the magnitude of the genetic contribution. The contribution of family environment is equally estimated by the difference between the correlations for any relatives, whether DZ twins, other siblings, or parents and their children, living together and the same relatives living apart. And at the same time, the resemblance between any relatives living apart, which is assumed to be due only to their shared genes, will provide an estimate of the genetic contribution. In the case of parents and their children, or two siblings, however, since they share only 50% of their genes, the full genetic contribution is estimated by doubling the value of the correlation.

Other, indirect estimates of heritability can be achieved by *comparing* the correlations between different kinship categories: the classic twin method of behaviour genetics estimates heritability by subtracting the correlation for DZ twins from that for MZ twins. Since MZ twins share 100% of their genes, and DZ only 50%, the higher correlation for MZ twins reflects the effect of the additional 50% of shared genes, and the difference between the two correlations is doubled to show the genetic contribution. Similarly, the difference between the correlations between parents and children in biological and in adoptive families, or between siblings and two adoptive children living in the same family, is due to the difference between sharing 50% and 0% genes, and can again be doubled to give an estimate of heritability. Estimates of the contribution of common family environment can also be achieved either directly or indirectly: the correlation between adoptive parents and their adopted children, or that between two unrelated children living in the same family, provides a direct measure of common environment; while, as noted above, a comparison between MZ twins, or siblings, brought up together and apart provides an indirect measure.

On the face of it, however, many of the assumptions made in this simple model are demonstrably false. I list only the most obvious, some of which I have already noted in passing:

- The model assumes that all members of a family share the same common environment, to exactly the same degree. But MZ twins living together may well share more experiences in common than DZ twins, who in turn may share more common experiences than siblings of different ages. And can it really make sense to suppose that parents and their children share a similar family environment in exactly the same way as brothers and sisters growing up together? Presumably, much of the effect of family environment must be on young children; there is no reason to expect that the environment parents themselves experienced as young children is the same as that in which they bring up their own children. All these differences in shared environment may well help to explain why, as can be seen in Table 11.5, MZ twins resemble one another more than DZ twins, who resemble one another more than other siblings, who in turn resemble one another more than children resemble their parents.

- There is no allowance for the phenomenon of selective placement. Adoption agencies may attempt to match the child to the home, placing children whose natural parents were well educated with well-educated adoptive parents, and those of poorer natural parents into poorer adoptive homes. To the extent that such selective placement occurs, the correlation between adoptive parents' and adopted children's IQ scores might in principle be partly genetic—a consequence of placing children, who had inherited a high IQ from their natural parents, with adoptive parents who also happened to have a high IQ. While more recent adoption studies, such as the Texas study (Loehlin *et al.*, 1989), have found rather little evidence of selective placement (as measured for example by a negligible correlation between adoptive and biological parents' level of education), in some early studies it was clear that selective placement had occurred (for example Freeman *et al.*, 1928). This issue has, of course, been of concern in the interpretation of the data from MZ twins brought up apart, where the separated twins may have lived in quite similar families.

- Adoptive parents are not a representative cross-section of the population. If all adoptive parents are 'good' parents, studies of adoptive families will not see the effects of poor parenting on children's IQ scores. This restriction of range will reduce the size of any correlation between members of such families, and hence underestimate the role of family environment.

- The genetic assumptions of the model are no more plausible. In the first place, they ignore the well-documented phenomenon of assortative mating, the tendency for husbands and wives to resemble one another in various ways (e.g. education, social class, and height). Bouchard and McGue (1981) reported a weighted mean correlation between husbands and wives in IQ of 0.33. The assumption that DZ twins and other siblings share no more than 50% of their genes is based on the fact that children receive a random 50% of each parent's genes, and on the *assumption* that there is no correlation between their two parents' genes. But if there is assortative mating for IQ, and if IQ is partly heritable, that assumption is false. Sometimes this will result in an overestimation of heritability, at other times in an underestimation. Thus, if siblings share more than half their genes, then a doubling of the correlation between siblings brought up apart will overestimate heritability. On the other hand, if DZ twins share more than half their genes, the difference between DZ and MZ twin correlations reflects a difference of less than 50% genetic similarity, and the model will be underestimating heritability.

- Finally, the model also makes no allowance for the distinction between additive and non-additive genetic variance, and thus ignores the distinction between narrow and broad heritability—the former being that due to additive effects only, the latter being that due to both additive and non-additive effects. Non-additive genetic effects are those due to dominance and epistasis, the former referring to the different phenotypic effects of two alleles of the same gene, the latter to the possibility that phenotypic effects are a consequence of particular *combinations* of genes at different loci. The effect of this would be that even if siblings share, say, 50% of their genes, they might display much lower concordance for a phenotypic character that depended on particular combinations of genes. Since MZ twins, of course, share all their genes, they will necessarily show concordance for such characters. To the extent that such non-additive effects are important, DZ twin and sibling correlations will underestimate broad heritability.

What, then, is the point of attempts to estimate the precise heritability of IQ, if they rely on a model many of whose assumptions appear to be quite untrue? It is possible, of course, that appearances are deceptive, and the assumptions less important than one might have supposed. What would count as evidence of that? Eysenck (1979) argued that the proof of the model was to be found in the fact that different comparisons all converged on very similar estimates of the contributions of genetic and family sources of variance. Table 11.5 shows some half dozen different ways of estimating heritability and a similar number of ways of estimating the contribution of family environment. Eysenck's argument was that they all converged on very similar values. Unfortunately, as can be seen from Table 11.5, this is simply not true (Eysenck's argument had assumed rather different values for some of the correlations on which the estimates are based). If this simple model does not work, would a more complex and perhaps more realistic one fare any better? Chipuer *et al.* (1990) have provided one such model. As can be seen in Table 11.6, it marks several advances over the simple model:

- It acknowledges the distinction between additive and non-additive genetic variance, assuming that although MZ twins are identical in both respects, the value for additive genetic effects for DZ twins and other siblings is 0.5, but that for non-additive effects only 0.25.

- On the environmental side, it assumes that twins share more similar experiences than other siblings, who in turn share more similar experiences with one another than they do with their parents. But it makes no allowance for selective placement, nor for the possibility of restriction of range in adoptive family environments.

- Although not shown in Table 11.6, the model acknowledges the possible importance of assortative mating, and thus allows that the values for shared sources of genetic resemblance in all relatives except MZ twins may be too low.

Chipuer *et al.* (1990) fitted their model to a summary of kinship correlations similar to that shown in Table 11.1. The best estimates for the various parameters of their model are also shown in Table 11.6. Broad heritability (the contribution of additive and non-additive

Table 11.6 A more realistic model for estimating heritability (adapted from Chipuer *et al.*, 1990, Tables 1 and 4).

(a) Contribution of genetic and environmental factors to resemblance in IQ

Kinship	Sources of resemblance
MZ (t)	G (a) + G (n) + E (t)
MZ (a)	G (a) + G (n)
DZ (t)	0.5G (a) + 0.25G (n) + E (t)
Sib (t)	0.5G (a) + 0.25G (n) + E (s)
Sib (a)	0.5G (a) + 0.25G (n)
Parent-child (t)	0.5G (a) + E (p-c)
Parent-child (a)	0.5G (a)
Adoptive parent-adopted child (t)	E (p-c)
Unrelated children (t)	E (s)

(b) Percentage of variance accounted for by different factors

Factor	% Variance
G (a) (Additive genetic variance)	0.32
G (n) (Non-additive genetic variance)	0.19
E (t) (Family environment shared by twins)	0.35
E (s) (Family environment shared by siblings)	0.22
E (p-c) (Family environment shared by parent and child)	0.20
(Unique environment unshared by twins)	0.14
(Unique environment unshared by siblings)	0.27
(Unique environment unshared by parent and child)	0.29

genetic variance) is only 51%; the shared environment of twins is more powerful than that of other siblings or of parents and their children; and in these last two cases, the effects of shared environment are smaller than those of unique, unshared environment.

Although the model provides a reasonable fit to the data, there are still some notable discrepancies. For example, the correlations between MZ and DZ twins brought up apart imply that the broad heritability of IQ is at least 0.75, not 0.51, and the estimate of the effects of common environment provided by subtracting the MZ-apart from the MZ-together correlation is only 0.11, rather than 0.35. What is the explanation of these discrepancies? One possibility, suggested by Devlin *et al.* (1997), is that the resemblance between separated twins is partly due to their shared prenatal environment, and this environmental effect must be subtracted from the observed correlations to get a better estimate of heritability. I have already commented on this argument above.

A perhaps more surprising possibility, which has, however, been endorsed by many behaviour geneticists, to the point where it is accepted as orthodoxy, is that the heritability of IQ increases as children grow older (e.g. Bouchard, 1997; Jensen, 1998). Since separated twins have usually been studied as adults, while most adoption studies have been conducted on young children, this explains why the twin studies give a higher estimate of heritability. There is, as I have already noted, evidence to suggest that the influence of family environment may decrease as children grow older, but the natural interpretation is to say that other, unique environmental factors take over from family environment as sources of influence on IQ, as children start spending more of their time outside the home (Harris, 1998). An alternative possibility, however, is that the decline in the effect of family environment is balanced by an increase in the role of genes. Although it is widely believed, I shall argue that the evidence for this conclusion is decidedly mixed.

The clear implication of the idea that genetic effects become more important with increasing age is that biological relatives brought up apart should come to resemble one another in IQ more and more as they grow older. The obvious place to start looking is separated MZ twins. Not all have in fact been tested as adults. The Newman *et al.* (1937) and Shields (1962) studies both provided individual case histories, which reveal that 12 of their pairs of twins were tested before the age of 20. For what it is worth, the IQ correlation for this set of 12 pairs is 0.77, much the same as that for the entire sample. In other words, there is no evidence that younger separated MZ twins resemble one another any less than older twins.

A second example is provided by adopted children and their biological parents. Does this correlation increase as the children grow older? One study has indeed shown just such an effect: the Colorado study reported a correlation between adopted children's IQ scores and those of their biological mothers of less than 0.20 up to the age of 9, but of 0.38 at age 16 (Plomin *et al.*, 1997). This would seem convincing, except that the Texas study found little or no such effect (Loehlin *et al.*, 1989): the correlation between the children's IQ scores and their biological mothers' at age 8 was 0.23; ten years later the correlation was 0.26, hardly a dramatic increase.

The standard twin method of behaviour genetics compares the resemblance of MZ and DZ twins and assumes that the difference between the two must be due to the greater genetic resemblance of the MZ twins. There is evidence that, as they grow older, so DZ twins begin to resemble one another in IQ rather less, but that this is not true for MZ

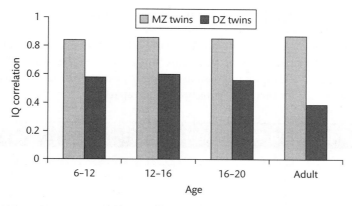

Figure 11.3 IQ correlations for MZ and DZ twins (brought up together), at four different ages, ranging from 6 to 12 years old, to adults over the age of 20 (data from McGue *et al.*, 1993, Figure 2).

twins where the resemblance in their test scores may actually increase (McCartney *et al.* 1990; McGue *et al.*, 1993). In a longitudinal study, Wilson (1983) reported that at age 9 the IQ correlations for MZ and DZ twins were 0.83 and 0.65, but that six years later these correlations were 0.88 and 0.54 respectively. If the difference between MZ and DZ correlations increases as they get older, this implies an increase in the heritability of IQ. Wilson's results do indeed suggest such an increase in heritability from early to later childhood, but not to a figure of over 0.80. A more recent, much larger longitudinal twin study (Davis *et al.*, 2009) reported very similar results, estimating heritability as 0.62 by middle childhood. The study most frequently cited in this context is that by McGue *et al.* (1993), whose results are shown in Figure 11.3. As can be seen, both MZ and DZ correlations remain relatively stable, with a very slight decline (consistent with the Wilson study) in the DZ correlation, between the ages of 6 and 20. But in adulthood the DZ correlation declines from well over 0.50 to just under 0.40. Since the twin method estimates heritability by doubling the difference between MZ and DZ correlations, this decline in the DZ correlation increases the estimate of heritability from about 0.60 to over 0.80, and at the same time decreases the estimate of the contribution of shared environment to zero.

McGue *et al.* (1993) themselves were commendably cautious in their reading of these data, but their caveats have been ignored by those who have seen these results as convincing evidence of an increase in heritability from adolescence to adulthood. As McGue and his colleagues noted, the data are not longitudinal (which must be the proper way to establish that the difference between MZ and DZ correlations increases with age, see Box 11.4); they come from a number of different studies from different countries at different times. By comparison with the data for younger twins, the adult data are sparse, and many of them come from just two Scandinavian studies, Tambs *et al.* (1984) in Norway, and Pedersen *et al.* (1992) in Sweden. Tambs and colleagues explicitly noted that their estimate of heritability seemed unusually high, and suggested that this was because Norwegian society was more homogeneous than either British or North American societies (recall the point made at the beginning of this chapter that in more equal societies the heritability of IQ is likely to be higher). Swedish society, after some 50 years of Social Democratic rule, will have been at least as homogeneous as Norwegian. There are other bizarre features of the Pedersen *et al.* data: while the correlation for MZ twins brought up together was 0.80, that for DZ twins was only 0.22 (yielding an impossible heritability estimate of 1.16), actually less than the correlation of 0.32 for their DZ twins brought up apart.

BOX 11.4 A question of experimental design

Why is a longitudinal study the proper way to investigate changes in MZ and DZ correlations from childhood to old age? The answer is simple. You need to establish that it is the difference in *age* between the children and adults in your study that is responsible for the change in these correlations, not some other difference between the two groups. If the young twins are British and were tested on the Wechsler scales in 2000, while the old twins are Dutch and were given a quite different IQ test in 1950, how can you be sure that one of these other differences was not responsible for the difference in correlations? A recent study (Haworth *et al.*, 2009) illustrates the problem. They reported MZ and DZ correlations at three ages 4–10, 11–13, and 14–34. Their data came from six different samples, three American, with the remaining three from Europe and Australia; only two of these samples could have provided data for all three age groups, while three could have provided data for only one. The IQ tests used ranged from short forms of the Stanford-Binet and Wechsler scales, sometimes in multiple choice format, to Raven's Matrices. So, although they reached the same conclusion as Wilson (1986) and had a much larger total sample size, their data do not provide any stronger evidence for this conclusion than had Wilson's earlier longitudinal study.

Of course, longitudinal studies, especially if they involve a comparison of people differing in age by 25 years or more, are difficult and time-consuming, and it is no doubt a counsel of perfection to insist that only a longitudinal study is acceptable. But it seems reasonable to ask that differences in age should not be confounded with differences in nationality and type of test used. McGue *et al.* (1993) were fully alive to this point also, and reported data from the Minnesota twin studies, where all twins had been given Wechsler tests. The difference between MZ and DZ correlations suggested that 'IQ heritability increases from approximately 50% in preadolescence (11–12-year-olds) to approximately 80% in adulthood (60–88-year-olds)' (McGue *et al.*, 1993, p. 71). Although this might seem to settle the matter, it ignores data they reported from two intermediate groups, aged 17–18, and 30–59. For both of these groups heritability was approximately 0.55. If this is true, it suggests an interesting possibility: the heritability of IQ does not increase to 0.80 in adulthood, but only in old age. And one plausible explanation of that would be to say that it is due to genetic susceptibility to some of the diseases of old age, such as dementia, which affect IQ.

It is worth adding that a further study of some 4,000 MZ and DZ twins, aged 62 to 73, gave a heritability estimate of only 0.30 (Brandt *et al.*, 1993). Unfortunately its measure of IQ was less than satisfactory.

Perhaps it is finally worth noting that it is surely a slightly strange argument to infer an *increase* in the heritability of IQ with age from a *decrease* in the resemblance of biological relatives (DZ twins) as they grow older.

The heritability of IQ certainly increases as children grow older; whether it is substantially higher in adults than in adolescents seems less certain, but the possibility cannot be dismissed out of hand. And the hypothesis should certainly not be dismissed on the grounds of implausibility. It might seem more plausible to suppose that it would be an infant's or young child's intelligence that is affected by their genetic make-up, and that the cumulative effect of environmental experience should become more important when they are grown up. But it is possible that some genes associated with variations in IQ are not 'switched on' until adulthood: for example (as noted in Box 11.4) in old age variation in test scores may be associated with the onset of certain diseases, susceptibility to which is partially genetically determined. There is, in fact, a second, even more interesting explanation why genetic effects should become more important as children grow older, which I pursue below.

What is the best estimate for the broad heritability of IQ? One answer is to say that the question is misplaced, because there is no reason to believe that the heritability of IQ is fixed. It almost certainly varies from one place and time to another, and even within a given society it may well vary somewhat with age. Is it important to come up with a precise figure? Probably not, and a sufficient answer will be to say that the broad heritability of IQ in modern industrialized societies is probably somewhere between 0.40 and 0.70, and that neither the data nor the models justify very much greater precision. The data are too variable, partly because they are necessarily imperfect, but partly because there probably is genuine variation from one age, time, and place to another.

The route from genotype to phenotype

Most early IQ testers described their tests as measures of inborn capacity or innate ability (see Chapter 1). However high the heritability of IQ turned out to be, that would remain a misleading claim. But it is difficult to rid oneself of the belief that if the heritability of IQ is high, this means that some people are born with more, or less, efficient brains than others. This *may* sometimes be true, especially perhaps for certain cases of severe disability associated with errors of brain metabolism. But even here, as I shall argue below, the disability is not always an *inevitable* consequence of the error of metabolism.

Although some of the variation in IQ scores between, say, 70 and 150 in North American and European populations is certainly attributable to genetic differences between members of those populations, it does not follow that it is a consequence of inherited differences in the efficiency of the brain as a processor of information. The route from genotype to IQ may be much more circuitous. Imagine two pairs of separated MZ twins, brought up from birth in four separate adoptive homes. The two twins of one pair not only look alike, they also start behaving alike from an early age. Neither sleeps very much; both seem fractious and easily bored. Their two sets of adoptive parents react to this in similar ways: they have to spend a lot of time with their infant, playing with her and, since she gets bored with familiar toys, constantly providing new ones for her to play with. The two twins in the second pair are both quite different: they are placid and sleep a lot. Again their two sets of adoptive parents react to this in similar ways, each happy to leave their perfectly contented infant alone, rarely bothering to provide him with novel entertainment or new toys since he is quite happy with his old ones. These differences in early experience soon translate into further differences: by comparison with the two boys, the two girls start showing greater curiosity about, and active exploration of, their world; they interact more, not only with their adoptive parents, but also with other children and adults. They start talking sooner and therefore get talked to more, and start learning more about the world; when they go to school, they interact more readily with their teachers, and find learning more rewarding, so their teachers find them more rewarding to teach. As they grow older, the girls continue to find school rewarding and spend more time with other, clever children, while the boys develop other interests. Along with their friends, the girls are more likely to stay on at school and go to university, while the boys leave school as soon as possible. By the age of 20, the two girls will have similar high IQ scores and the two boys similar lower IQ scores. Separated MZ twins, brought up with no knowledge of each other's existence, in quite separate homes, end up resembling one another in IQ—testimony to the power of their genes. But to say that they experienced quite different environments is seriously misleading, and it was the similarity in their environments that was the immediate cause of their similarity in IQ. Now the reason why they experienced such similar environments is, of course, because an initial, genetically influenced similarity in behaviour and temperament elicited similar treatment from their adoptive parents, and one thing led to another. As they grew older, they started to seek out or create for themselves similar environments, which caused further similarities in their behaviour, and so on. The point is that it took time for their identical genes to cause their close resemblance in IQ; and this would give the appearance of an increase in heritability as they grew older.

It is worth noting that this scenario is not wholly fanciful. It is possible to predict 10-year-old children's IQ scores by observing their behaviour, at 6 months, in a habituation experiment (see Chapter 8). The more rapidly infants habituate to, that is, stop looking at, a novel object, and the greater the extent to which they dishabituate, that is, start looking again when the now familiar object is changed for a new one, the higher will be their later IQ: the correlation, across a ten-year span, is about 0.50. Furthermore, when adult separated MZ twins are asked to describe how they were treated by their quite separate sets of adoptive parents, they describe remarkably similar experiences (Plomin *et al.*, 1988). But I acknowledge that although the argument may be plausible, it is far from proven. Much of the data relied upon by Plomin *et al.* consisted of adults' and older children's *recollections* of their early family environment. Separated MZ twins may give similar answers to questionnaires probing their recollections of the past, however, not because they really experienced similar treatment at the hands of their adoptive parents, but because a genetic similarity in temperament predisposes them to answer such questionnaires in a similar manner. Nor should one press too far the argument that MZ resemblances in IQ can be attributed to the similarity of the environments they experienced as a consequence of their genetically based similarities in temperament or personality. MZ twins, whether brought up together or apart, resemble one another in IQ a great deal more than they resemble one another in personality (see above).

The argument has been worth pursuing, however, for several reasons. First, it should serve to illustrate the idea that the route from genotype to phenotype may be circuitous. The two female twins ended up with higher IQs than the two males, not because they were born with more efficient or intelligent brains, but because they were less placid and more easily bored. The more general idea has been termed a 'multiplier effect' (Ceci *et al.*, 2003): an initial small difference between the two sets of twins leads to further differences, which in turn lead to yet further differences, until they end up with dramatically different test scores. The idea was developed by Dickens and Flynn (2001) in the context of the secular increase in IQ scores over the course of the twentieth century (see Chapter 12). But its origins go back further to what the sociologist, Robert Merton (1968) called the 'Matthew Effect' after the verse in St Matthew's gospel: 'For whosoever hath, to him shall be given, and he shall have more abundance: but whosoever hath not, from him shall be taken away even that he hath.' Small advantages and disadvantages eventually turn into big ones. Life is not fair.

To return to kinship studies: they may have unambiguously established that the heritability of IQ is substantial, but, as this example shows, they have done little or nothing to elucidate *how* genetic similarities and differences are translated into similarities and differences in IQ. How will it ever be possible to answer this question? In principle, one way would be by the kind of longitudinal psychological study illustrated in my hypothetical example above. Such an approach will be laborious and difficult, since what will often be needed in order to discover the chain of cause and effect will be a quite unacceptable level of experimental intervention. Why, for example, is later IQ so well predicted by infant habituation scores? Is it, as my scenario suggested, because differences in rapidity of habituation result in the provision of a more stimulating environment? Or do infants who habituate rapidly have a more 'efficient' nervous system, capable of more rapidly establishing an accurate representation of a repeatedly presented stimulus? An obvious way to answer that question would be to ensure that rapidly and slowly habituating infants were not treated differently by others. But what society would contemplate such an experiment?

Second, it provides an illustration of two types of gene-environment covariation: reactive and active. The genetic similarity of the separated twins initially caused other people to react to them in similar ways; eventually, the twins actively sought out similar environments. (Earlier, I also described passive covariation, where, say, children with a high IQ are born to parents with a high IQ, but those parents also provide a 'high IQ' environment, whatever that might be.) In standard modelling procedures, all these effects would be classified as genetic, but they are in fact mediated through the environment. Gene-environment covariation starts to abolish any clear distinction between genetic and environmental effects.

The point is important enough to justify another example. When brought up in the same family, MZ twins resemble one another in IQ significantly more than DZ twins. In an earlier section of this chapter, I discussed whether this is because they are genetically more similar or because they share more similar environments. But, as I hinted there, the distinction between these two possibilities is simply not clear. Of course, MZ twins are genetically more similar to one another than DZ twins, but it is possible that the reason why they are more similar in IQ is because their genetic identity causes them to experience more similar environments, and it is this greater similarity in their environments that results in their closer resemblance in IQ. This possibility cannot be tested by separating the twins, since the genetic identity of MZ twins may continue to ensure that they experience more similar environments even if they are brought up in different families. Nor can it be tested by removing the possibilities of such gene-environment covariation by ensuring that all children are treated exactly alike. In such a science fiction society, there would be no environmental variation at all, and the heritability of IQ, as of any other characteristic, would necessarily by 1.0.

The search for genes 'for' IQ

Longitudinal, developmental studies would, in principle, be one way of elucidating *how* genetic differences between individuals are eventually translated into phenotypic differences in IQ. But the obstacles confronting any such studies should not be underestimated. The alternative would be to search for individual genes associated with differences in IQ, and discover their course of action. How feasible is this?

Abnormal development

On the face of it, some success has been achieved in some cases of serious abnormalities leading to disability. An oft cited example is the case of phenylketonuria (PKU), a condition caused by a number of different recessive alleles of the PAH gene located on chromosome 12 (Plomin *et al.*, 2008). Untreated, PKU is often associated with moderate disability, an average IQ of no more than 50 (the range is quite wide). This disability is, in turn, associated with abnormal development of the nervous system, specifically a failure of myelinization.

This failure is associated with a build up of phenylalanine in the brain, which is caused by the production of an abnormal enzyme in place of phenylalanine hydroxylase, which normally is able to break down phenylalanine into tyrosene. Phenylalanine is an ingredient of much ordinary food, being particularly found in red meat. And the treatment for PKU, as is well known, is to provide a special diet low in phenylalanine. In this environment, there is little build-up of phenylalanine in the brain, no serious failure of myelinization and *relatively* normal cognitive development—although in fact there is evidence that such children may still obtain below average test scores (of only 91 on the WISC in one study, Griffiths *et al.*, 2000). Here again, the important point to note is that the phenotypic effect, low IQ, is not an automatic consequence of the presence of the two recessive alleles; it depends upon an interaction between a particular genotype and a particular environment (here diet). The fact that we are inclined to regard this as the 'normal' environment is beside the point.

Two other examples are worth discussing, since they serve to illustrate some of the limits of this approach. Williams syndrome is caused by the loss of some dozen genes on chromosome 7, and is also often associated with moderate disability (IQs are typically in the range 45 to 85). It has attracted attention because it is also associated with a rather striking pattern of particular abilities and disabilities: apparently preserved social and linguistic skills, good face recognition, but poor numerical and spatial abilities. A popular interpretation has seen this as evidence of the modular nature of the mind, numerical and spatial modules being clearly dependent on the deleted genes, with the preserved abilities equally clearly not. More detailed analysis shows that this is almost entirely false (Karmiloff-Smith, 1998). Williams syndrome children may have a relatively large and apparently sophisticated vocabulary, but they acquire that vocabulary in an unusual way and their syntactic abilities are significantly impaired. Although, both as infants and adolescents, they are good at recognizing faces, they do so in a quite abnormal manner, by concentrating on particular features rather than the overall configuration (as normal controls do). On the other hand, although adolescents with Williams syndrome show very poor numerical skills, infants are sensitive to the numerical differences between items in a display. There is no one-to-one mapping between genes and cognitive modules, but rather a particular pattern of abnormal development, which is associated, for example, with an abnormal pattern of electrical activity in the brain in response to pictures of faces. It seems reasonable to hope that further developments in techniques of non-invasive brain imaging and recording may, in the long run, allow the next generation of neuroscientists to uncover some of the differences in infant nervous systems associated with the development of later differences in IQ and particular cognitive processes. But it seems likely that what they will uncover will be more complexity rather than pleasing simplicity.

Fragile X syndrome is caused by an expanded 'triplet repeat' on the X chromosome. The expansion is adjacent to the FMR1 gene and prevents its transcription. There is evidence that one consequence of this is abnormal dendritic development in the brain. Fragile X is associated with moderate disability, an average IQ of about 50, although here again there is wide variation. The full mutation that causes the syndrome, an expansion to over 200 repeats, is invariably preceded in the parental generation by a 'premutation' of 50–200 repeats (the normal number is between 6 and 50). However, this premutation is associated with entirely normal IQ (Mazzocco and Reiss, 1999). In other words, genetic variation below the level associated with disability is not associated with any variation in IQ in the normal range.

Has the often successful search for genetic mutations associated with disability shed light on the causes of variation in IQ in the 'normal' range? Results such as those of Mazzocco and Reiss have led one commentator to note: 'Not a single gene involved in the development of mental retardation has been shown to be associated with normal variation in IQ' (Grigorenko, 2000). But this is a slight exaggeration. As would be expected for an X-linked condition, Fragile X syndrome is very much more common in males than in females, who would have to have two copies of the mutated gene to show the full syndrome. But heterozygous females do appear to have below average test scores, with a full scale IQ in one study of only 83 (Bennetto et al., 2001). Whether this story will be repeated for other genetic conditions is simply not known.

Genes for high IQ

Whether it is or not, it has seemed to many behaviour geneticists that it will be necessary to mount a specific search for individual genes associated with normal variation in IQ, especially in the range of above average test scores. Plomin and his colleagues have been engaged in just such a search for the past 25 years. The difficulties should not be underestimated. It is one thing to find the genes associated with certain single-gene disorders, such as Huntingdon's disease, or PKU. But normal variations in IQ are surely going to be caused by the combined action of a number of genes, rather than by any one 'major' gene. As I have already argued, although factor analysis yields a general factor, g, IQ is not a unitary construct, and must surely therefore be influenced by many different genes. And, like height, it varies in a continuous way, the standard mark of a polygenic characteristic.

Suppose, for the sake of argument, that the heritability of IQ is 0.50 in today's Western populations. This means that half the observed phenotypic variation in IQ is ascribable to genetic differences between members of those populations. Suppose also that there are 25 genes associated with this variation in IQ, and that each has an equal, additive effect. Then each will be associated with 2% of the observed variation in IQ (at best two points). That is a small effect, not easily distinguished from chance fluctuation.

The history of the search for genes 'for' such interesting characteristics as schizophrenia or manic depression provides ample warning of some likely problems (see Plomin *et al.*, 2008). It is all too easy to find some genetic differences between two groups of people selected for their difference in some phenotypic trait. Chance alone is almost bound to produce some small genetic differences. They are not worthy of serious consideration unless replicated in further independent samples. At one point it seemed possible that, after some false starts, Plomin's group was going to satisfy this minimum requirement. Chorney *et al.* (1998) compared two groups of some 50 children each, between 12 and 15 years old, one of average IQ (a mean of 103), a second of high IQ (a mean of 136). A systematic search of the long arm of chromosome 6 found a significant difference between them in the frequency of different alleles of the IGF2R gene, with allele 5 being more frequent in the high-IQ sample. This difference was replicated in a second sample of 12-year-old children, 50 with an average IQ (a mean of 101) and another 50 with an estimated IQ of at least 160. The probability of the difference arising by chance in both samples was less than 1 in 1,000. So far, so good. Alas, the result did not survive a further attempt at replication (Hill *et al.*, 2002): now allele 5 was found more frequently in the average-IQ group. It should also be noted that the effects observed even in the initial study, although statistically significant, were very small. The critical allele 5 was found in less than half of the high-IQ children, and in nearly one-quarter of the average-IQ group. A more recent study from this group of 7,000 young children examined some 500,000 loci and claimed to identify six associated with differences in IQ, but the highest correlation between any of the six and WISC-III scores was only 0.04 (Butcher *et al.*, 2008).

As noted in Chapter 6, another line of research has suggested that different alleles of the COMT gene are associated with differences in IQ (Bishop *et al.*, 2008).

What is one to make of this? It is easy to get carried away, but the fact is that the discovery of genes associated with variations in IQ is not really very surprising. Even if the heritability of IQ were no more than 0.25, there must be such genes. The importance of the enterprise is said to be that it may make it possible to work out how genetic differences lead to differences in IQ. But that is a promise that may be remarkably hard to deliver. Plomin's work suggests that it is not going to be a simple matter to find these genes. One can be sure that it will be even harder to uncover their mode of action. There may well be some readily detectable differences between the brains of those with an IQ below 50 and those with an IQ of 100 or more. Indeed, as noted above, some such differences have already been discovered. It seems rather less likely that a gene associated with a two-point variation in IQ in the normal range will have such easily discernible effects on brain function. As discussed in Chapter 6, a quarter century or more of research into the relationship between IQ and the brain has made some progress, and will no doubt make much more in years to come, but even the most optimistic neuroscientist would hardly claim that enough is known to be able to find differences in brain structure or function between one person with an IQ of 100 and another with an IQ of 105.

There are other reasons to wonder how rapidly progress will be made. The search for genes associated with variation in IQ will be orders of magnitude harder to the extent that genetic effects on IQ are not additive. Earlier I used the illustrative possibility that IQ was affected by 25 genes, each with an equal, additive effect. But some genetic effects, dominance and epistasis, are not additive. A recessive allele at a particular locus will have one effect on the phenotype if it is accompanied by a dominant allele at that locus, and a quite different effect if accompanied by the same recessive allele. Some harmful recessive genes are maintained in the population because, although harmful or even lethal when two copies are present, they may be beneficial if they are accompanied by a dominant allele which blocks the harmful consequence. The most famous example is sickle cell anaemia, a condition caused by the possession of two copies of a particular recessive gene; heterozygotes, with only one copy, however, gain some protection from malaria. Woolf *et al.* (1975) suggested that the recessive alleles responsible for PKU may have beneficial effects in the heterozygous form, because high levels of phenylalanine reduce the toxicity of ochratoxin A, which is found in mouldy grains and which causes spontaneous abortion. This might explain why PKU is more common in the damp climate of Ireland and western Scotland than in southern Europe.

Another possible example: it has long been known that Ashkenazi Jews have an unusually high average IQ (see Chapter 1); some of them also have the misfortune to suffer from a number of diseases, such as Tay Sachs disease, caused by the possession of two copies of particular recessive genes. One suggestion is that the two are linked: while homozygotes with two copies of the gene develop the disease, heterozygotes with only one copy develop higher than usual intelligence (Cochran *et al.*, 2006).

Epistasis refers to the possibility that phenotypic characteristics are affected by particular combinations of alleles at different loci. For example, it might be the case that allele 5 of the IGF2R gene is associated with high IQ only if it is accompanied by particular alleles at other loci. In their absence, it is accompanied by normal or even low IQ. If that were true, it might help to explain the startling difference between the results of the Chorney *et al.* (1998) and Hill *et al.* (2002) studies. It will surely mean that it will be difficult to detect, and replicate, even quite substantial effects. Is the genetic variance underlying variation in IQ mostly additive? Behaviour geneticists often argue that it is. But the relatively sophisticated attempt to model IQ variation by Chipuer *et al.* (1990), outlined above, while concluding that the overall (broad) heritability of IQ was about 0.50, argued that additive genetic variance accounted for no more than about 30% of the overall variation in IQ, while non-additive effects accounted for some 20%.

A further problem may arise from the possibility of gene-environment interactions: a particular allele may have an effect on IQ only in certain environments. There is now one good example of this. It has often been claimed that breast-feeding can enhance children's later IQ scores by as much as 6–7 points (a claim supported by meta-analysis; Anderson *et al.*, 1999); nevertheless at least one careful and large study found no effect (Der *et al.*, 2006). The resolution appears to be that it all depends on the genes: the beneficial effect occurs in children with one or two copies of the C allele of the FADS2 gene; in children with two copies of the G allele, breast-feeding has no effect on IQ (Caspi *et al.*, 2007). Some of their data are shown in Figure 11.4. Put another way, different alleles of the FADS2 gene are associated with differences in IQ only in a certain environment, one that includes breast-feeding.

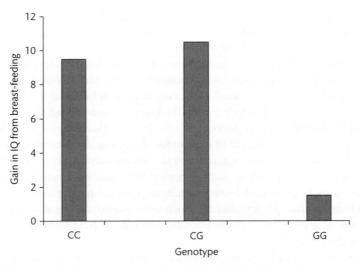

Figure 11.4 The effect of breast-feeding on children's IQ scores depends on their genotype. The figure shows the difference in IQ between breast-fed and non-breast-fed children when they have two, one, or no copies of the C allele of the FADS2 gene (data from the British Birth Cohort analysed by Caspi *et al.*, 2007, Figure 1).

Finally, although no one can sensibly deny that factor analysis will always find a sizeable general factor, this *g* is certainly not the whole story about IQ. The cognitive abilities measured by tests of Gf, Gc, Gv, etc., are partially independent of one another and, as it happens, this is particularly true at higher levels of IQ: scores on different types of IQ test are more strongly correlated in people of below average IQ, than in those of above average IQ (see Chapter 7). Thus, a high-IQ group may contain some people with much higher scores on tests of Gf than Gc, others with higher scores on Gc than on Gv, and so on. If the genes associated with variations in Gc are not the same as those associated with Gv, which in turn differ from those associated with Gf, etc., there will be that much less chance of finding genes consistently associated with a high IQ score. To that extent, Plomin's strategy of looking for genes associated with very high levels of IQ may have been mistaken.

Mildly deleterious mutations

A puzzle usually glossed over by IQ testers is this: if IQ measures intelligence, and high intelligence is of adaptive value, why has low intelligence persisted? Characteristics of significant adaptive value should be selected for, and eventually become fixed in the population. If, as is widely assumed, the evolution of humans' superior intelligence is one of the characteristics that separate us from other primates, why is there still such wide variation in intelligence (at least as measured by IQ tests)?

One answer to this conundrum is to suggest that low IQ is often a consequence of mildly deleterious mutations—mildly deleterious only, since seriously deleterious mutations usually have fatal consequences. There is evidence to suggest that both the number of such mutations which all people carry, and the rate at which new mutations occur in each generation, are much higher than previously supposed (Anderson, 2001; Kondrashov, 1995). If such mutations act to decrease in any way the overall efficiency of the organism, including such systems as the brain, or if they increase susceptibility to pathogens or other environmental insults, one might expect them to contribute to a below average IQ. It would then follow that any variation in the number of such mildly deleterious mutations carried would contribute to variation in the degree of below average IQ. Current estimates suggest that the average number of such mutations carried is about 100 (Kondrashov, 1995): people with fewer than this average might have above average IQ, those with many more might have an IQ in the range 70–80.

Two lines of evidence provide some support for this supposition. First, as noted above, *g* is more important in people of below average IQ than in those of above average IQ. A decrease in the overall efficiency of the system would be more likely to result in poor performance on all IQ tests than on only some, thus increasing the correlation between different tests. Second, several studies have reported a significant correlation, even after controlling for social class, between IQ and such physical factors as overall health and longevity (see Chapter 8), a finding consistent with the idea that low IQ is associated with other indices of lowered efficiency (Lubinski and Humphreys, 1992; Whalley and Deary, 2001). There is also evidence of a small but significant correlation between IQ and bodily symmetry (Banks *et al.*, 2010; Furlow *et al.*, 1997), symmetry being widely regarded as an indicator of biological fitness.

A possibly unwelcome, but surely important, implication of this is that it may be a remarkably difficult task to identify particular genes associated with below average IQ in the population as a whole. A whole range of different genotypes, with quite different mildly deleterious mutations, may be implicated. Some mutations may indeed have the effect of reducing the efficiency of the brain, but even if we understood what that meant, there may be dozens of different ways of doing this. Others may not act directly on the brain at all, but rather increase susceptibility to illness or to a variety of different pathogens, and thus affect IQ only indirectly (for example because children with chronically poor health may miss school, and even when at school may pay less attention to their lessons than their healthier peers). It seems entirely possible that there will be dozens of different genotypes associated with below average IQ, each resulting in much the same outcome, but via wholly different routes.

Conclusion

Estimates of the heritability of IQ have been obtained from comparisons of MZ and DZ twins, from separated twins, and from adoption studies, where biological relatives (adopted children and their biological parents) live apart, and unrelated people (adopted children and their adoptive parents) live together. All such studies point to the conclusion that IQ is substantially heritable, but that the effect of family environment on children's test scores is also substantial. Neither of these conclusions should come as a great surprise.

Two further conclusions are more interesting, and perhaps more surprising, but both should be treated with some caution. The first is that the effect of family environment on children's test scores declines as the children grow up; according to many behaviour geneticists, indeed, it declines to zero. The second is that genetic effects on IQ *increase* as children grow older; according to some behaviour geneticists, the heritability of IQ, which is only about 0.50 in children and adolescents, increases to 0.80 in older adults.

It is true that several adoption studies have found correlations hovering around zero between adopted children and other members of their adoptive family when the children are aged 18 or more. But adoptive parents are a selected and unrepresentative sample of all parents, and it is precisely the families that do not appear in adoption studies where the effect of family environment on test scores is strongest. While there may be some decline over time in the effect of family environment on children's test scores, there is little reason to believe it disappears altogether.

If there really are changes in the effect of genes and family environment over time, they would be best documented by longitudinal studies which followed up a group of children as they grew up. Very little of the evidence thought to show these changes is of this sort: most comes from comparisons between quite different studies, often conducted in different countries, employing different tests. That is why their conclusions should be treated with some caution.

Some further cautions are in order. Although behaviour geneticists have developed a variety of models, some simple, other notably more complex (I have spared the reader some of these), in order to provide quantitative estimates of the heritability of IQ, it is not entirely obvious that such estimates are worth the effort. Quantitative models give a sense of pleasing scientific rigour, but it should always be remembered that the natural experiments which provide the data for such models are inevitably imperfect, and may not bear the weight put upon them. Moreover, of course, heritability is a population statistic and will vary from one population to another, and from one time to another in the same population. Setting all this aside, does it really matter whether the heritability of IQ in, say, western European or North American adults in the twentieth century was 0.40, 0.50, or even 0.70? What difference would it make? You might think that if it were as high as 0.80, there would be little room left for any environmental effect. But recall that a high value for heritability means only that *existing* environmental differences are having rather little effect on the characteristic in question. It says nothing about the possible effects of new environmental changes. Even more important, there really is a sense in which genetic and environmental effects on IQ are inextricably interwoven. The reason why MZ twins end up with very similar IQ scores is doubtless because they are genetically identical. But to an unknown extent, their genetic identity will have its effect on their IQ because it causes them to experience very similar environments; they are treated alike and, more important, they choose to spend time together and follow similar pursuits. To a significant extent, some of this appears to remain true even if they have been separated from an early age.

More interesting than the precise value for the heritability of IQ is to try to understand *how* genetic similarities and differences between people are translated into similarities and differences in their IQ. Do they directly affect the developing brain? Do they affect other systems and therefore have only an indirect effect on the brain? It is noteworthy that the immediate effect of the alleles of the PAH gene responsible for PKU is not on the brain but on the liver. Do they impact on intelligence by affecting people's interests and therefore the immediate environment they experience? It has seemed possible that this question might be answered by identifying single genes associated with differences in IQ. While this may work in the case of serious disability (it already has to a certain extent), it is less obvious that the discovery of such genes associated with differences in IQ in the normal range will be so informative. If the heritability of IQ is greater than zero, there must be such genes, but it has proved remarkably difficult to find them and, what should come as no surprise, those that have probably been identified turn out to have extremely small effects. Some people have thought that their discovery will have sinister eugenic implications in the shape of 'designer babies'. It is always rash to predict the future of any scientific enterprise, but leaving aside the case of single gene disorders and chromosomal abnormalities (where therapeutic abortion is already offered), I do not believe that such fears are going to be realized in the near future.

Summary

- Heritability is a population statistic referring to the proportion of the variance in a given characteristic in a given population attributable to genetic differences between members of that population.

- There is, therefore, no single value for the heritability of IQ: it probably varies from one population to another.

- Twin, kinship, and adoption studies all point to the conclusion that the heritability of IQ in twentieth century Western populations is substantial, probably somewhere between 0.40 and 0.70.

- To an unknown extent, however, genetic effects on IQ are often mediated through the environment.

- Although something is known about the effect of single genes on some types of serious mental disability, the search for genes affecting IQ in the range 70–150 has been rather less successful, and it would seem that any such genes have only a very small effect.

Further reading

The most recent edition of *Behavioral genetics* (Plomin *et al.*, 2008) provides much useful background information, as well as reviews of the literature on genetic effects on general cognitive ability and specific disabilities. Bouchard (1997) reviews the data on separated MZ twins, and Jensen (1998) puts the case for IQ's high heritability. By contrast, Nisbett (2009) cautions against accepting some of the stronger claims made by some behaviour geneticists. Ceci *et al.* (2003) should be read for a discussion of 'multiplier effects', and Anderson (2001) for the possible role of mildly deleterious mutations.

12

The environment: secular changes and social class

Introduction

No one seriously believes that the heritability of IQ is 1.0; indeed, the data reviewed in the last chapter suggested that 0.50 is a more reasonable estimate, at least in children and adolescents. Although many behaviour geneticists argue that between-family environmental effects on IQ become vanishingly small in adulthood (an argument that is readily disputed), they still acknowledge that within-family environmental effects persist. So, no one really doubts that differences in the environment contribute to differences in IQ.

It is obvious enough that extreme environments (being locked up in a cellar with little or no human contact) will have a drastic effect on the developing child's cognitive abilities (and on much else besides); fortunately, however, such extreme environments are rare, and so will have little impact on variations in intelligence in the population as a whole. Here it is easy enough to point to environmental *correlates* of differences in intelligence between different children, but less easy to decide which if any of these correlates actually do have an effect.

I start with a discussion of the changes that have been observed in test scores over the course of the twentieth century, in part because, although they must be largely a consequence of environmental changes, their explanation remains problematic, and thus serves to illustrate some of the problems involved in trying to understand the environmental causes of differences in test scores within any one generation. Here, one of the major correlates of differences in children's intelligence is differences in family background or social class. Disentangling the different factors contributing to this correlation will take up much of the rest of this chapter.

Secular changes in IQ

The secular changes in test scores that occurred in all industrialized countries over the course of the twentieth century, otherwise known as the Flynn effect (Chapter 1), demand explanation. What has caused these remarkable increases of some 20 or more IQ points, and what do they mean? In principle (but only in principle), the explanation might be genetic. A consistent positive relation between IQ and fertility could have produced some increase in test scores from one generation to the next. But to have been responsible for increases of this magnitude, nearly ten points per generation, the positive relation would have had to be astonishingly high, and the weight of the evidence is that the relationship between IQ and fertility throughout the twentieth century was, if anything, slightly negative (Chapter 1). Differential fertility will probably have decreased the magnitude of the Flynn effect. The only other possible genetic explanation is a decrease in inbreeding. There is reasonably good evidence that inbreeding is bad for IQ (among other things): the children of first and second-cousin marriages tend to have lower than average IQ scores (Schull and Neel, 1965). But the effect is small, and although Mingroni (2007) has valiantly advanced the case for its contribution to the increase in test scores, that contribution cannot have been large. Flynn (2007) himself has calculated that even if everyone had married their brother or sister in 1900, this would not be sufficient to provide a complete explanation.

Environmental explanations of the Flynn effect

It is frankly absurd to suppose that the explanation of the Flynn effect is wholly genetic. If not genetic, it must be at least partly environmental. But what are the environmental changes that have produced such dramatic effects? There has been no shortage of suggestions; at least some seem moderately plausible, but counterarguments have been raised against most of them. It is not going to be easy to bring experimental evidence to bear on events that happened in the past (and at least in some countries seem to be coming to an end). On the face of it, all one can do is list some of the changes in society that occurred over the course of the twentieth century in most industrialized countries, and which were therefore correlated with these changes in IQ scores, and suggest more or less plausibly which ones might have contributed to these changes. To be plausible, one might suppose, these factors should be ones known to correlate with differences in IQ scores within any one generation. As I shall argue below, however, that may not be always necessary.

Test sophistication

Cattell (1950) himself attributed the small increase in average IQ he observed in Leicester between 1937 and 1949 to an increase in 'test sophistication'. In the 1930s, IQ tests were new and few children had taken one before. By the late 1940s, they were a fact of school life. The explanation is plausible enough for this limited case; it might equally apply to Tuddenham's comparison of American Army recruits in World Wars I and II, and to other data analysed by Flynn showing an increase in test scores between the 1930s and 1940s (see Chapter 1); but it becomes merely incredible when applied to the data as a whole. There must be a limit to the benefits to be derived from test sophistication, and indeed there is: taking the same test again after a short interval improves one's score by no more than about five points, and further practice leads to negligible further improvement (Jensen, 1980). It is, anyway, difficult to imagine that from 1920 to the present day, each generation of Americans and Europeans has been more accustomed to IQ tests than its predecessor.

Demographic changes

Children's IQ scores are correlated with the social class of their parents. Since 1900 there has been a substantial increase in all industrial societies in the proportion of the population engaged in middle-class occupations at the expense of those in working-class occupations (Huang and Hauser, 1998). In principle, therefore, the gains in test scores may be due to changes in social class. There is one problem for this explanation: the correlation between social class and IQ tends to be higher for tests of crystallized or verbal intelligence, Gc, than for tests of fluid intelligence or Gf (e.g. Ramey *et al.*, 2001; White, 1982). But it has long been known that the increase in average IQ has been very much more marked on tests of Gf than on tests of Gc (Flynn, 1987, 2007). The largest gains have been recorded on Raven's Matrices—an archetypal measure of Gf. Gains in test scores that are more marked for tests less sensitive to differences in social class can hardly be attributed entirely to changes in social class.

Associated with the increase in the size of the middle classes and decrease in the size of the working class in most industrialized countries has been a decrease in family size (Huang and Hauser, 1998). There is, of course, a significant negative correlation between children's IQ scores and the number of other children in their family (Chapter 1); if it is at least in part an environmental effect, this decrease in family size will surely have contributed to the rise in IQ (Sundet *et al.*, 2008; Zajonc and Mullally, 1997).

Nutrition and health

There have also been some general improvements in public health and nutrition since the 1920s. The great depression of the 1930s must have had an adverse effect of standards of nutrition and health care in much of the industrialized world, and World War II can only have added to these effects in most European countries. It seems probable therefore that these improvements were particularly marked in the years immediately following World War II. They have also been sufficient to produce substantial increases in average height in most industrialized countries over the course of the twentieth century (Van Wieringen, 1978). Health and nutrition certainly have some effect on IQ (see below), and it is plausible to suppose that any improvements in them will have contributed to the Flynn effect (Lynn, 1998; Sigman and Whaley, 1998). Once again, however, one may doubt whether this could possibly be the whole story: it is hard to believe that improvements in public health and nutrition continued throughout the 1980s and into the 1990s in such prosperous European countries as Sweden, Norway, and Denmark (Martorell, 1998). Flynn (2007) has argued that such improvements would have benefitted the poor more than the rich, and therefore, presumably, have had a greater impact on the lower half of the IQ distribution. While that has sometimes appeared to be true, it was not true for France and the Netherlands between the 1950s and 1980s.

Moreover, a common perception is that nutritional standards have declined with increasing consumption of junk food in the past 25 years or so; while Rutter (2000) has argued that advances in health care for newborn infants have probably done as much to ensure the survival of damaged infants as to prevent damage to others.

Education

Before World War I, most English children left school by the age of 12. Successive changes increased the minimum school leaving age to 14 (in 1918), 15 (in 1947) and 16 (in 1972). And more and more children opted to stay on in school after the minimum age. Until 1950, no more than 10,000 students a year graduated from English universities; by the end of the twentieth century that number had increased tenfold. Similar increases in the amount of education have occurred in the USA (Huang and Hauser, 1998). Surely they must have had some impact on IQ scores? Once again, however, it can hardly be the whole story since, as noted in Chapter 1, among the earliest evidence of such increases were the Scottish and Leicester data on 11-year-old schoolchildren tested before and after World War II. Here, both the earlier and later generations of 11-year-olds had received the same number of years of formal schooling. Flynn (1984, 2007) has reported American increases on the original WISC and its later revisions in children as young as 4–6, and Lynn and Hampson (1986) reported large increases in Raven's test scores in British 5–11-year-olds between 1949 and 1982.

This is to ignore, however, the increase in pre-school education that has occurred since 1930, which may have had an impact on test scores (see Blair *et al.*, 2005). Moreover, even if all children remained in school until the age of 12 in 1930, thus ensuring that 11-year-olds in 1930 had received the same number of years of formal schooling as 11-year-olds in 1950, the same is not true of 18-year-olds. Much of the European data on rising test scores come from studies of 18-year-old military conscripts. Since they will have received more years of schooling in 1980 than in 1950, part of this rise in test scores may be attributed to an increase in the number of years of schooling.

Perhaps more important than the total number of years of education has been the change in the *type* of education children have received. In at least some countries, the 50 years following World War II are commonly assumed to have witnessed substantial changes in educational theory and practice, with less emphasis on rote learning and more on learning by discovery and conceptual understanding. It is not difficult to imagine how this might have increased children's ability to solve the abstract puzzles and problems that go to make up tests of Gf, without any concomitant improvement in their vocabulary, arithmetic, or general knowledge (Williams, 1998).

Some of these changes have surely been of direct relevance. For example, Blair *et al.* (2005) have noted that teaching of elementary mathematical concepts has increasingly placed reliance on visual rather than verbal material. A (very slightly altered) example of the type of material now used to teach series and sequences is shown in Figure 12.1. This is actually a perfect instantiation of one of the rules needed to solve items in Raven's Matrices, termed pairwise progression by Carpenter *et al.* (1990; see Figure 4.10, p. 97). It is hard to believe that teaching children how to answer these questions would not transfer to their performance on Raven's. Flynn (2007) has argued rather convincingly that increasing

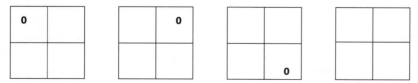

Figure 12.1 An example of the type of figural problem which, according to Blair *et al.* (2006), is nowadays used to teach children about series. In which quadrant of the square should you put the 0 in the fourth square? It is, of course, an instance of the 'pairwise progression' rule described by Carpenter *et al.* (1990) for Raven's Matrices.

familiarity with scientific ways of thinking has been the cause of the dramatic changes in scores on the Wechsler similarities test, where the correct answer requires classification by taxonomic category (a hammer and a spanner are both tools) rather than putting things together that can be used together (a hammer is used to hammer in nails).

Interim conclusion

Each of these suggestions appears to have some merit, but all have come in for criticism. None of them can claim to provide a complete explanation of the Flynn effect. But that does not mean that any of them should be dismissed as irrelevant. The proper inference to draw is surely that there is no single explanation of the rise in test scores: there has been a multitude of contributing factors, some more important at some times and in some countries, others more important at other times and places. Early gains in the 1920s and 1930s may have been partly due to increases in test sophistication; increases from the 1930s to, say, 1960 may have been partly caused by improvements in nutrition, health care, and an increase in the number of years of schooling received by most children; some of the increase since 1950 or 1960 might be attributable to changes in educational practice.

Although this is all very largely speculative, it seems more plausible than the insistence that there has been one single cause of the Flynn effect true for all times and places. However, one problem needs to be acknowledged: correlations do not prove the direction of causation. As Mingroni (2007) has argued, an increase in, for example, the number of years of education received may have been partly a consequence, rather than a cause, of the increase in test scores: more intelligent children find school more enjoyable than less intelligent children, and choose to stay in school longer; they also find exams easier and therefore are more likely to obtain the qualifications that permit them to stay on and go to university. The question whether more education raises test scores or higher test scores lead to more education is one I shall return to later in this chapter. It is hard to decide just how important this confound might be for some of the other factors discussed above, but it cannot, I think, be dismissed out of hand. It is time, however, to turn to a rather different class of environmental explanation—that proposed by Dickens and Flynn (2001).

A multiplier effect

If test scores increased relatively steadily over the entire course of the twentieth century, it follows that the parents of children born in, say, 1920 had lower test scores than the parents of children born in 1950, who in turn had lower scores than the parents of those born in 1980. And so on. In other words, each new generation of children was born into a family with higher test scores and was brought up in a society with higher average test scores. Whatever the environmental variables that affect children's IQ scores may be, it is hard to believe that they do not include the IQ of their parents, siblings, teachers, and friends (at its simplest, this would be a case of passive gene-environment covariation discussed in Chapter 11).

Some behaviour geneticists might argue that many of the suggestions advanced above cannot really explain the rise in test scores, because kinship studies have shown that the effect of family environment on children's IQ scores becomes vanishingly small by the time the children have grown up (Chapter 11). I have already suggested that their data may not justify this strong conclusion. In the present context, moreover, there is a further reason to question their argument. The environmental factors that explain differences in test scores *between* generations may not be the same as those responsible for differences *within* any one generation. The Dickens and Flynn multiplier effect is precisely a between-generation effect. Moreover, as Flynn (2007) has argued, in many respects the differences between the environment in which children were brought up in the 1920s and 1930s and that experienced by children growing up in the twenty-first century, are far greater than any environmental differences experienced by children of the same generation. It is hardly necessary to list the inventions: radio, television, video games, home computers, the Internet, and so on, that have transformed people's lives since 1920, and the increase in leisure time that has allowed people to take advantage of these inventions. If this, too, seems a largely speculative explanation of the Flynn effect, it is not entirely. There is good evidence that exposure to video and computer games can have surprisingly beneficial effects on test scores. Green and Bavalier (2003), for example, showed that naive students given ten hours of practice on certain computer games showed striking improvements on the type of visual search task that appears in certain IQ tests.

Conclusions and implications

It is easy to speculate; it is notably less easy to prove that any of the factors outlined above were actually responsible for the observed changes in IQ test scores. Many of these suggestions amount to little more than a claim to have identified a correlated change in some other variable that might or might not be causally related to the changes in test scores. Few if any have provided unambiguous evidence of causality. As I have said, there is no reason whatsoever to suppose that the same factors have operated in all countries at all times since the 1920s, let alone that a single factor will ever be identified as responsible. It seems much more likely that a wide variety of different factors has been responsible, each contributing a small increment, some more important at one time or place, some more important at others.

There are several messages in all this. The most general is surely plain. IQ is undoubtedly affected by the environment, and there is no difficulty in finding environmental correlates of IQ. But it is quite another matter to establish that any particular environmental factor is actually responsible for variations in IQ, let alone to identify its mode of operation. A second, more specific message is that, just as there is no single gene with a massive effect on test scores, but more probably a large number of genes each with a very small effect, it may be vain to look for a single, magical environmental ingredient that changes IQ by 10 or 20 points. It is at least as probable that there is a whole host of factors, each having some effect on IQ, but none of overriding importance.

It would be a mistake to end on this somewhat negative note. The Flynn effect has implications that transcend any uncertainty about its causes. The drastic difference in the size of the increase in scores on different tests since 1950, ranging from 20 to 25 points on Raven's Matrices and the Wechsler similarities test at one extreme to less than five points on several other verbal tests of the Wechsler scales, for example vocabulary and information (Flynn, 2007), has two important implications. The first, noted in Chapter 7, is to raise a question about the assumptions underlying factor analysis. Factor analysis of the Wechsler tests has similarities loading onto a factor of verbal comprehension, along with vocabulary and information (because they cluster together in the correlation matrix). This is taken to mean that these three tests are to a large extent measuring the same thing. But that inference cannot be entirely true. The second is to reinforce a point made in my initial discussion of the Flynn effect in Chapter 1. Given that some tests have shown large gains while others have not, it follows that today's generation of young people are not necessarily *generally* more intelligent than their grandparents' generation. They are certainly better at some things, but not at everything.

Between and within-family effects: CE vs. SE

It is time to turn to the question of environmental effects on IQ within, rather than between, generations, but before doing so, it is necessary to say a brief word about two different sources of environmental effects. The behaviour geneticists' analysis of kinship studies outlined in Chapter 11 distinguished between environmental effects common to members of the same family and differing between families (CE), and effects unique or special to individual members of the same family (SE). Indeed, the conclusion of their analyses was that CE effects wane in importance as children grow up, while SE effects persist. That did indeed seem plausible enough: as children grow older they spend less time in the family home and more time with their friends, and brothers and sisters may have quite different circles of friends.

On the face of it, the distinction between the two sources is obvious enough: parental social class seems an obvious example of a between-family or CE effect, while a serious illness or accident that affects one child in a family but not her brothers or sisters seems an obvious example of a within-family or SE effect. But the distinction may not always be so clear-cut. Parents' social and other circumstances may, after all, change for the better or worse, with the consequence that older and younger siblings can grow up in rather different environments. Brothers and sisters may not attend the same school. More interestingly, while parents are inclined to believe that they treat all their children alike (and so fairly), their children themselves are more inclined to believe that they are treated quite differently by their parents, and so unfairly. Careful observation of family life suggests that children's perceptions here are more accurate than their parents' (Reiss *et al.*, 2000). To the extent, therefore, that differences in parental treatment may affect their children's test scores, this may be a within-family as well as a between-family source of variation. The same may be said of many other sources of environmental variation. One of the few environmental effects that can be unequivocally assigned to one category rather than the other is birth order: there is evidence that first and second born children are likely to have slightly higher test scores than fourth or fifth born children in the same family, and this is undoubtedly a within-family effect (see below).

In practice, if the goal is to understand what environmental factors do actually influence children's test scores, and how they do so, the distinction between CE and SE effects may not be so very important. In what follows, therefore, I shall pay only passing attention to the question.

Environmental correlates and environmental causes

Whatever else the Flynn effect shows, it suggests that it is one thing to establish a correlation between IQ and some environmental variable, it is another thing to prove that variations in this variable are responsible for variations in IQ. Variables which correlate with children's IQ scores are two a penny. They include: parents' test scores, their level of education, social class, and income; the neighbourhood in which they live; the number of other children in the family, and whether they are older or younger; the child's own height, weight, head circumference, and degree of myopia. The problem is not to establish the existence of such relationships; it is to interpret them correctly. It is a truism of social science that a correlation between A and B may be necessary, but is certainly not sufficient, to prove that A causes B. It is equally possible that B should cause A, or that both A and B should be the consequence of a third variable, X.

Why, for example, should family size correlate with IQ? Does this mean that the experience of growing up with numerous brothers and sisters somehow depresses a child's IQ score, and if so, *how* does this come about? Or is the correlation merely masking some other causal relation? In this particular case, it does not seem very likely that a child's IQ score could affect the number of children his parents might choose to have. But other correlations certainly invite such speculation. Children's IQ scores are correlated, for example, with various aspects of their parents' behaviour. But is this because the parents' behaviour affects the child's IQ, or because children with high IQ encourage their parents to interact with them, constantly asking questions and demanding stories, while those of low IQ are more boring and less demanding of intellectual stimulation? And it seems easy to see how the relationship between IQ and family size might be a consequence of the independent relationship between these two variables and a variety of other factors. Family size is also correlated with social class: there is some tendency for middle-class families to have fewer children than working-class families (Chapter 1). Perhaps, therefore, family size has no effect on IQ at all, and the correlation between the two reflects only the fact that working-class children, who are more likely to come from larger families, have on average a lower IQ than middle-class children. The problem is not, of course, confined to the case of family size: many of the variables mentioned so far, such as parental social class, income and educational level, are correlated with one another. If one of these variables correlates with IQ, therefore, it is hardly surprising that the others should also, but this makes it no easier to decide which, if any, is actually effective.

For it is necessary to acknowledge the possibility that *none* of these factors actually affects children's IQ scores: the correlation might simply be a consequence of a hidden factor X, whose effects have been ignored. One persistent suggestion has been, of course, that the explanation of many of these correlations is a genetic one. If the heritability of IQ is even moderately high, the correlation between parents' and children's IQ scores will be partly a consequence of their shared genes. To the extent that parents of lower IQ have more children than those of higher IQ, children living in larger families may simply inherit their lower IQ from their parents. Moreover, as noted earlier, IQ testers have long argued that their tests were measuring something with profound social consequences, in other words, that a high IQ was necessary for success not only in school but also in life. Social class differences in IQ, they thus argued, must rest in part on genetic differences between those capable of holding down demanding professional or managerial jobs and those capable only of unskilled employment.

There is a multiplicity of factors correlated with a children's test scores, but many of these factors tend to be correlated with one another; some of them (parental genotype) are not directly measurable, while many of those that are, such as family income, can hardly be the immediate, proximal cause of a child's IQ (money does not *directly* buy a high IQ; at most it buys an expensive education or other things that do affect IQ). How can these correlated factors be disentangled, and how will it be possible to ascertain which environmental factors are actually affecting the child's IQ? Although neither will guarantee success, there are two possible answers, one statistical, the other experimental. It is not impossible, at least in principle, to disentangle the effects of correlated variables. There may be a general tendency for family size to be correlated with social class, but there is still wide variation in family size within any one social class, and by studying, for example, professional families with one, two, or more children, it may be possible to determine whether family size is related to IQ independently of social class, or for that matter whether the effect of social class on IQ is independent of family size. The statistical techniques of partial correlation and regression analysis attempt to provide ways of assessing the contribution of one factor, while controlling for the contribution of other, measured factors which are correlated with the first.

The more powerful, experimental answer is to manipulate a particular environmental factor and to observe whether there is any consequential change in IQ. In the case of secular changes in IQ test scores, one can do little more than point to other factors which have changed over the past 75 years, and which are thus correlated with the observed changes in test scores. But although there are obvious limits to the possibilities of social engineering, some natural experiments can be informative, and deliberate, quasi-experimental intervention has sometimes been employed in an attempt to raise IQ scores. Thus, children given up for adoption have often been brought up by adoptive parents who are both richer and better educated than their true, biological parents. If such children also ended up with higher IQ scores than they would otherwise have obtained, this would suggest that family background does exert an environmental influence on IQ. Various forms of educational intervention have also been tried, ranging from relatively brief periods of pre-school education to the massive intervention of the Milwaukee and Abecedarian projects (see below). And finally, there have been explicit experimental manipulations of such specific factors as nutritional intake. With the exception of this last type of manipulation, most forms of intervention have been too global to have succeeded in pinpointing any specific environmental cause of variations in IQ, and this for sufficiently obvious reasons. In many cases, the main purpose of the intervention was not particularly to raise IQ scores at all: this is not, after all, the normal reason why children are given up for adoption. In others, where one goal was indeed to raise the IQ scores of a target group of children, as in many instances of compensatory education, this has been pursued as a practical goal, for the sake of the children in question, rather than for the benefit of the social scientist, who would have sought to identify which precise factor was responsible for changing IQ scores, by varying one at a time while holding all others constant.

The most widely touted correlate of children's IQ scores is their parents' social class or SES. For some social scientists, indeed, IQ tests are little more than thinly disguised measures of social class. Given that the correlation between children's IQ scores and parental SES is little more than 0.30 (see below), this is a singularly foolish assertion. Although it is important to try to understand this correlation, rather than tackle this question right away, I shall first discuss some of the evidence of more specific correlates of IQ, some of which, of course, may well contribute to the global correlation between IQ and SES. I shall consider in turn: physical environmental factors; education; and finally demographic variables. All of these factors are of interest in their own right, and not only for the light they may shed on the relationship between family background or social class and IQ. As I noted above, they may be equally responsible for variations in IQ between members of the same family. Environmental sources of variation in IQ operate just as much within families as between families.

Physical environment

Poverty may cause physical as well as intellectual or cultural deprivation, and some forms of physical deprivation may be indirectly responsible for intellectual loss. Life expectancy is correlated with social class (Elo, 2009), and although part of this correlation may be attributed to differences in the incidence of the diseases of middle and old age, part is due to differences in infant mortality (Maher and Macfarlane, 2004). If children of poor parents are more likely to die than those with better-off parents, they may also be more vulnerable to less lethal forms of physical damage, caused by disease, environmental pollution, or inadequate nutrition, which are still capable of impairing their intellectual development. Perhaps they are also more likely to suffer from prenatal and perinatal complications with similar long-term consequences.

Prenatal environment

There is, indeed, ample evidence of an association between prenatal experience and children's subsequent IQ scores (see Jensen, 1997, 1998). The simplest summary measure of prenatal development is birth weight, and there is a significant correlation between birth weight and later IQ (Breslau *et al.*, 1994; Broman *et al.*, 1975; Mascie-Taylor, 1984). Although the correlation is distinctly modest (for example, only 0.07 in white children and 0.11 in black children in the Broman *et al.* study), this overall correlation conceals a much larger effect at very low birth weights, below 2,500 g, where there is a significant increase in the risk of relatively low IQ persisting through to the age of 17 (Baumeister and Bacharach, 1996; Breslau *et al.*, 1994).

What is the meaning of this relationship? Part of the overall correlation between birth weight and IQ is due to the increased incidence of seriously low test scores in babies who are seriously below weight (Rutter *et al.*, 1970). Their low weight may, of course, be symptomatic of other developmental abnormalities, and genetically caused, rather than the consequence of a poor prenatal environment. Even if it is attributable to prenatal experience, the causal chain linking birth weight and later IQ may be quite indirect, via the later, post-natal environment. It seems often to be implicitly assumed that low birth weight reflects a physical effect on the growth of the embryonic brain; this is certainly sometimes true, but there are other, more mundane possibilities: perhaps very small babies turn into sickly children, whose test scores suffer because they miss so much school.

Are there any more specific prenatal factors that might affect IQ? There is evidence that if a mother smokes during pregnancy, her baby is more likely to have low birth weight (Broman *et al.* 1975), and later a low IQ, even after allowance has been made for other factors (Huizink and Mulder, 2006; Mascie-Taylor, 1984). There is even better evidence for an effect of alcohol. Foetal alcohol syndrome, characterized by low birth weight and poor subsequent growth, as well as microcephaly and retarded brain growth, occurs in approximately one or two live births per thousand, and unsurprisingly rather more often if the mother is an alcoholic (Mayes and Fahy, 2001). At age 7, the children of alcoholic mothers have significantly lower test scores than those of non-alcoholic mothers matched for age, SES, education, race, and marital status (Streissguth *et al.*, 1990).

Numerous studies have examined the effect of prenatal nutrition, but with somewhat conflicting results. In developing countries, nutritional supplements given to pregnant women may have long-lasting effects on their children's cognitive development, but usually only if the children have also received supplements (Grantham-McGregor *et al.*, 2001). Rush *et al.* (1980) randomly assigned a number of African-American pregnant women to one of three groups, one receiving a high-protein supplement to their diet, one receiving a high-calorie supplement, and the third, control group, no supplement. Their one-year-old infants were given a visual habituation test, and those whose mothers had received the protein supplement habituated significantly more rapidly and showed greater dishabituation than either of the other groups. Since habituation and dishabituation scores are reliably correlated with IQ at age 5–11 (Chapter 8), this suggests (even if it does not prove) an effect of maternal diet during pregnancy on young children's IQ, at least in this particular population. But the Dutch famine study suggested equally convincingly that maternal malnutrition during pregnancy may have no long-term effects on IQ. In the winter of 1944–45, the Germans imposed a transport embargo in the Netherlands, causing very severe food shortages in certain parts of the country for about six months. Stein *et al.* (1972) analysed the test scores of men born during the relevant period in towns affected or unaffected by the famine. Although hospital records established that birth weights were lower in the affected towns, absolutely no effect on adult IQ scores could be detected. On balance, except in the case of the severe malnutrition found in some developing countries, there is rather little reason to suppose that prenatal malnutrition alone has any major, long-lasting effects on children's cognitive development.

What to conclude? *Some* differences in prenatal and perinatal environment are certainly associated with differences in later test scores. But while some differences in birth weight (such as those observed between MZ twins, where the lower weight twin usually ends up with a lower IQ, see Lynn, 1990) are a consequence of differences in prenatal environment, others *may* reflect genetic differences. When all is said and done, however, except in the rare cases of *very* low birth weight, the independent contribution of prenatal and perinatal factors to children's IQ scores in industrialized countries seems actually to be rather small. Broman *et al.* (1975) measured some 130 prenatal and post-natal biological variables: none even approached in magnitude the importance of maternal education and social class as a predictor of the child's IQ. Among white children, for example, the latter correlation was 0.42; the addition of all other statistically significant variables raised the correlation only to 0.47 (see also Baumeister and Bacharach, 1996).

Post-natal environment

There is good evidence, but again much of it from developing countries, that chronic ill-health during childhood, and certain specific diseases will affect young children's cognitive development (Alcock and Bundy, 2001). Many of these diseases are virtually unheard of in industrialized countries, and so can hardly be responsible for variations in IQ in those countries. But diphtheria, whooping cough, and measles are not unknown; they may all cause damage to the nervous system, and all are probably still more common in lower income groups than among middle-class children in the West, partly because, although vaccination confers substantial immunity, the proportion of infants vaccinated against these diseases has been a function of social class (Davie *et al.*, 1972; Galea *et al.*, 2005). If serious illness causes prolonged absence from school, which is certainly associated with a decline in IQ scores (see below), mild ill-health may surely lead both to occasional absences and to lapses of attention even when the child is in the classroom.

Evidence on the relationship between health and IQ is, necessarily, almost entirely correlational. However plausible such arguments may seem, therefore, it is difficult to design well-controlled experiments, let alone any form of intervention study, that would establish a causal effect of health on IQ. Indeed, there is convincing evidence that the correlation between the two is partly attributable to an effect of IQ on health, rather than of health on IQ (see Chapters 8 and 9). The Scottish Mental Surveys of virtually all children born in 1921 and 1936 and given an IQ test at age 11, have shown a clear association between IQ at 11 and subsequent health, perhaps most unequivocally indicated by mortality. For example, in the later survey, those still alive in 2000 (aged 63) had 11-year-old test scores some seven points higher than those who had already died (Deary *et al.*, 2000). Gottfredson and Deary (2004) have developed the argument that high IQ promotes healthy behaviour in a variety of different ways. Although it is commonly assumed that social class differences in health are a consequence of poverty and/or access to good health care, the association between childhood IQ and later health is *not* attributable to differences in social class between high and low-scoring children (Deary and Der, 2005; Whalley and Deary, 2001).

Perhaps as a consequence of all this, most of the best studies of the effect of physical environmental factors on IQ have concentrated on two other variables: nutrition and pollution. One apparently convincing instance of a post-natal nutritional effect on young children's IQ scores is that pre-term infants fed on their mothers' breast milk develop higher IQ scores than those given formula diets (Morely, 1996). Whether breast-feeding has an effect on full term babies was for a long time open to dispute. As noted in Chapter 11, the resolution appears to be that it all depends on the genes: some genotypes benefit from breast-feeding, while others do not (Caspi *et al.*, 2007).

There is also more general evidence that children's IQ scores are related to their nutritional status (Grantham-McGregor *et al.*, 2001), but this observation alone is hardly very informative. Malnutrition is, after all, normally a consequence of serious poverty, and the discovery of a correlation between malnutrition and IQ leaves open the possibility that it is some other aspect of social deprivation and poverty that is the effective determinant of IQ rather than nutrition *per se*. Several studies, however, have used matched controls; and some have even compared two or more children from the same family, one severely malnourished, the others not (e.g. Birch *et al.*, 1971; Carmona da Mota *et al.*, 1990). All found a significant difference (up to 11 IQ points) in favour of the better nourished child. It seems possible that there may have been other environmental differences between the two sets of children, but it is also obvious that a family where one child is desperately malnourished is unlikely to provide a wholly satisfactory diet for other children in the family. These studies, therefore, may well underestimate the full extent to which malnutrition can affect IQ. On the other hand, since many were conducted in developing countries, they may be largely irrelevant to the causes of variations in IQ in advanced industrial societies. What is not known is the extent to which there is a relatively abrupt threshold, below which severe malnutrition can lower IQ, but above which variation in diet has little effect.

The effect of nutrition on IQ lends itself readily to an intervention study: do dietary supplements improve IQ scores? A small study by Benton and Roberts (1988) triggered a spate of experiments addressing this question. Benton and Roberts gave an experimental group of 30 Welsh schoolchildren a vitamin and mineral supplement every day for eight months, while control groups received either no treatment or a placebo. At the end of this period, the experimental group had gained some ten points on a test of Gf, while the control groups gained no more than 2–4 points. But subsequent replications have tended to muddy the waters. Some experiments failed to find any significant effect of vitamin or mineral supplements at all (e.g. Crombie *et al*., 1990); others reported positive results, but only in certain groups of children, or only for certain non-verbal tests, or only at some levels of supplementation rather than others (e.g. Benton and Buts, 1990; Schoenthaler *et al*., 1991). Eysenck and Schoenthaler (1997) provided a somewhat optimistic review, in which they noted that even where the effects observed have not been statistically significant, they have usually been in the direction of superior performance on tests of Gf by treatment groups. Certainly, there have been enough positive results to raise the possibility that dietary supplements may affect Gf in some children, but legitimate doubts will not be fully dispelled until specific predictions (who will benefit, on what test, from what sort of supplementation?) have been formulated and successfully tested.

It seems virtually certain that severe, chronic malnutrition, of the sort all too common in some developing countries, has deleterious effects on the IQ of the children in those countries (an effect of perhaps rather less importance than the number of children it kills). But there is less reason to suppose that this is a significant factor affecting IQ in most industrial societies. Here, environmental pollution may well be more important. The possibility that has been most widely canvassed is that atmospheric lead may be detrimental to IQ. Experiments on animals have established that high concentrations of lead can damage the nervous system (Lansdown and Yule, 1986; Lasley *et al*., 1999), and several studies, from countries as far apart as America, Scotland, Yugoslavia, and Australia, have concluded that moderate levels of lead in the body can have a deleterious effect on children's intellectual development (Bellinger and Adams, 2001). As usual there is the problem that children who are exposed to pollution are likely to suffer from various other forms of social disadvantage, and sceptics have questioned this conclusion. A critical review by Kaufman (2001a) raised a number of important questions, but also prompted a whole series of replies in the same issue of the journal. In his reply to his critics, Kaufman (2001b) did not dispute that levels above, say, 25 micrograms per 100 millilitres of blood were likely to have a deleterious effect on children's test scores, and that seems hard to dispute; whether there is a risk from much lower levels may still be open to question (see Bellinger and Adams, 2001; Wasserman and Factor-Litvak, 2001).

In conclusion, IQ is certainly affected both by physical and biological environment, but the magnitude of these effects, within the range of environments found in Western industrial societies, is relatively small. In the Schoenthaler *et al.* (1991) study, for example, the three groups of children who received nutritional supplements, gained on average only 2.1 IQ points over the control group, and the largest gain was only 3.7 points. At the extremes, the effects of lead concentration may be considerably larger than this: McMichael *et al.* (1988) calculated that the highest level of concentration they studied depressed IQ by approximately 15 points. This is a substantial effect, but very few children are unfortunate enough to receive such a high concentration. Nowadays at least, differences in exposure to lead are unlikely to contribute more than a minute fraction to the variability of IQ in the entire population of most Western societies. This may not always have been true: the effect may have been significantly more important 50 or more years ago, since in the USA at least, levels of atmospheric lead have declined substantially in the last 80 years (Kaufman 2001a), to the point where reductions in lead exposure may have contributed to the Flynn effect.

Education and IQ

Scores on IQ tests are related to a wide variety of measures of educational attainment (see Chapter 9). This is hardly surprising, since one of the main purposes of IQ tests was originally to predict children's performance in school, and educational achievements have always served as an external criterion against which IQ tests can be validated. The interpretation of a correlation between IQ and any educational measure, therefore, is likely to be somewhat problematic. To what extent would such a correlation reflect an effect of IQ on educational achievement, rather than an effect of schooling on IQ (the question of interest here)?

Years of schooling

One well-established educational correlate of IQ is the number of years of formal education received, with higher IQ scores being associated with more years of schooling received. But such a correlation is obviously not sufficient to prove that each year of additional schooling will produce an increase in children's test scores. Access to further education is usually dependent on passing exams or the acquisition of the appropriate qualifications, and these will already be correlated with IQ. Sixteen-year-olds with low scores will often choose to leave school as soon as they can; 18-year-olds with only modest test scores may fail to obtain a place at university.

In an attempt to bypass this obvious confound, Harnqvist (1968) obtained test scores from a large sample of Swedish boys, first when they were 13 years old, and five years later when they were 18. This allowed him to take initial IQ into account and then to relate changes in IQ between 13 and 18 to differences in the amount and type of education received. He estimated that such differences could produce a difference in IQ at age 18 of up to ten points. Harnqvist's procedure was ingenious and his results certainly suggest that more, and more demanding, educational experience will enhance test scores. But it is possible to quibble. Even if they obtained exactly the same test score at age 13, after all, there must have been some other differences between a boy who chooses, or is encouraged by his parents to choose, a rigorous academic education, a second who chooses a less demanding one, and a third who opts to leave school at the first opportunity. Perhaps these other differences, in family background, motivation, academic ambition or intellectual interests, were at least partly responsible for the later differences in IQ.

One natural experiment that has seemed to promise a solution to this problem is to rely on the fact that most school systems admit children only at the beginning of the school term or year in which they reach a certain age. There can thus be a difference of up to a year in the age of children within any one class, and a very much smaller difference between the oldest children in one class and the youngest in the class above, although the latter will have enjoyed the benefit of a year's extra schooling. Ceci (1991, 1996) has reviewed a number of studies which have relied on this to measure the effects of schooling on IQ. A particularly clear example is a study of Israeli schoolchildren by Cahan and Cohen (1989). The children were given a total of ten different verbal, mathematical, and figural tests; on all but two of the tests, the estimated effect of an additional year of schooling was greater than the effect of an additional year of age. The results for their vocabulary and matrices tests are shown in Figure 12.2.

These data provide compelling evidence, from which teachers may take comfort, that schooling does influence young children's intellectual development. Figure 12.2 also suggests that the effect of schooling was more pronounced on the vocabulary than on the matrices test, but the difference was not great. Moreover, a study of 10-year-old German schoolchildren found an equal effect of an additional year of schooling on tests of both Gc and Gf (Stelzl *et al.*, 1995). Formal schooling not only teaches children to read, write, and do arithmetic, it also imparts the skills needed to solve some of the reasoning tests that contribute to Gf.

A different line of evidence provides converging support for the conclusion that schooling is good for your IQ. Children who, for one reason or another, are prevented from

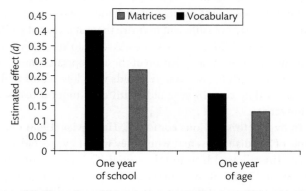

Figure 12.2 The estimated effect of an additional year of school and an additional year of age on young children's scores on a test of vocabulary and a matrices test (data from Cahan and Cohen, 1989, Table 4).

attending school suffer a decline in their IQ scores. In one American case from the 1960s, schools in a county in Virginia were closed for several years in protest against school integration. Local black children received no formal education at all and, compared to a control group, it has been calculated they suffered a decline in IQ of some six points for each year of school missed (Neisser, 1996). De Groot (1951) reported that children prevented from attending school in the Netherlands during World War II, had IQ scores depressed by about five points. Even earlier studies by Gaw (1925) and Gordon (1923) of gypsy and canal boat children in Britain showed a similar effect. The parents' peripatetic lifestyle meant that at best their children moved from one school to another, but more often did not attend school at all. The older the children, the lower their IQ scores dropped. A less extreme case provides further evidence. The long summer vacation enjoyed by American schoolchildren is associated with a decline in test scores (Ceci, 1991).

These and other studies reviewed by Nisbett (2009) leave no doubt that schooling raises children's IQ scores. That is important to know, but the practical significance of some of these findings should not be exaggerated. Up to the age of 16 (or as long as compulsory schooling lasts), the total number of years of schooling children receive will not depend on the accident of their date of birth. So the differences between children in different classes shown in Figure 12.2 will, presumably, wash out by the end of their educational career. Moreover, it cannot be assumed that if the difference between one and two years' worth of schooling is so striking in 6 and 7-year-olds, there will be an equally striking difference between eight and nine years' worth of schooling in teenagers. The effect of a single additional year at school must surely decrease as the total number of years in school increases. But this rather obvious point does not seem to have been entirely assimilated by those who confidently assumed that one or two years of additional schooling before children started their normal school career would have a dramatic and permanent effect on their subsequent educational performance. That was the hope behind the policy of compensatory preschool education, conceived as a noble social experiment, but an experiment which has generated as much academic controversy as practical good.

Compensatory education

'Compensatory education has been tried and it apparently has failed', Arthur Jensen announced in 1969. Project 'Head Start' had been initiated in the early 1960s, as part of President Johnson's war on poverty, in an attempt to break the cycle of poverty and deprivation which seemed to be transmitted from one generation to the next. Children growing up in poverty failed at school, remained poor and thus passed on their own disadvantages to their children, who failed in their turn. Why did the ordinary school system not succeed in breaking this endless cycle? The obvious answer, it seemed to some, was because children from advantaged backgrounds arrived in school with a head start provided by five years of middle-class home life. Thus, for disadvantaged children, the ordinary school system started too late: such children were already doomed to failure when they first arrived at school. The Head Start programme would show the way out by getting to the children before they entered school and providing them with the basic skills they needed to succeed there. The further assumption was that early experience is critical: Bloom's conclusion was widely believed: 'The evidence so far available suggests that marked changes in the environment in the early years can produce greater changes in intelligence than will equally marked changes in the environment at later periods of development' (Bloom, 1964, p. 89).

Jensen's conclusion was fiercely denounced, particularly by those who objected to what they perceived to be his real message—that the reason why compensatory education had failed was because most of its recipients were black. But at the time he was writing, there was little hard evidence that compensatory education programmes had any long-term beneficial effects. The critical question is whether the picture changed later. According to some commentators, at least, it did not (e.g. Herrnstein and Murray, 1994; Locurto, 1991; Spitz, 1986): in spite of widespread hopes and loud claims to the contrary, they have argued, there was little evidence that such programmes had much lasting impact. Even sympathetic reviewers (e.g. Barnett, 1995; Zigler and Muenchow, 1992) have long since stopped claiming that Head Start programmes have any *substantial long-term* effects on IQ scores.

The typical finding has been that pre-school education does indeed have a temporary effect on children's test scores (a gain of up to 7–8 IQ points by the time the programme ends), but that this gain soon fades away, and after a year or two of normal schooling, children in a treatment group are obtaining scores little or no better than those of a control group (Barnett, 1995). One of the better known of these programmes is the Perry Pre-school Project (Schweinhart and Weikart, 1980). Although quite successful in many other respects, its effect on children's IQ scores was no greater: a gain of some ten points when the programme ended and the children entered normal school, which then faded away to nothing by the time they were 9 or 10.

Earlier analyses of Head Start programmes raised the possibility that intervention might have longer-lasting effects on other measures than IQ. If true, this would be more than enough to justify them: in practical terms, it is more important that children should succeed in school than that they have their IQ scores raised by a few points. Garces *et al.* (2002) have provided convincing evidence of such long-term benefits. Analysing a large data set, they were able to show that children who had been in Head Start programmes were significantly more likely than those who had not, both to graduate from high school and to go to college. They also earned more before the age of 30. Some of these comparisons were against their siblings who had not been enrolled in Head Start programmes, thus effectively controlling for any differences in family background as a contributory factor.

The Perry Project also achieved some significant long-terms gains: at age 14, only 14% of children in the control group obtained scores above the tenth percentile on the California Achievement Test, compared to just under 50% of children in the treatment group. Less than half the control group graduated from high school, compared to two-thirds of the treatment group. As adults the treatment group was three times as likely as the control group to be earning over $24,000 a year, and twice as likely never to have been on welfare (Knudsen *et al.*, 2006).

Undaunted by the evidence that pre-school programmes had no lasting effect on children's IQ scores, proponents of early intervention and compensatory education argued that the programmes were still far too short: one or two years of part-time, pre-school

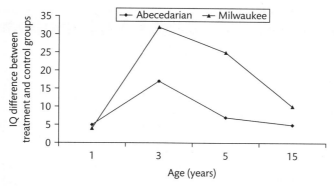

Figure 12.3 Differences in IQ scores of treatment and control children at ages 1, 3, 5, and 15 in the Abecedarian and Milwaukee projects (data from Ramey *et al.*, 2001, Tables 4.2 and 4.3).

education were simply not enough to counteract the cultural and material deprivation in which many children spend the first five years of their life. What was needed was full-time intervention from shortly after birth at least to the point where children enter the ordinary school system. Two studies, the Milwaukee Project (Garber, 1988) and the Carolina Abecedarian Project (Campbell *et al.*, 2002; Ramey, 1993; Ramey *et al.*, 2001), were mounted to see whether such a programme can achieve long-term effects. Both involved full-time day care, five days a week, all year long, from the time the children were a few months old to the time they entered the regular school system and beyond. Both involved intensive training and education by a large staff of professional teachers and psychologists. And finally, both appear to have achieved long-term gains in the children's IQ scores. Figure 12.3 shows the difference between the IQ scores of treatment and control children in both projects, at four points: age 1, 3, 5, and 15 (Ramey *et al.*, 2001). Now for the first time there is evidence of a lasting effect. Although their test scores declined once they left the project and entered normal schools, children in the treatment groups maintained a significant advantage over those in the control groups, about ten points in Milwaukee, and five points in Abecedarian (Campbell *et al.*, 2002, report that this five-point difference was still present at age 21). There seems good reason to believe that pre-school intervention, albeit on a heroic scale, can permanently enhance children's IQ scores.

The question remains whether intervention on this scale is a realistic, practical proposition for every child deemed to be at risk of growing up with a low IQ (see Box 12.1). Estimates of the cost of the Perry Project are approximately $15,000 per child and of the Abecedarian Project over $60,000 per child (Barnett and Masse, 2007): although that seems a lot of money to spend on raising a child's IQ by five points, this ignores the more important long-term benefits, such as increased earnings by the participants when adult, and reduction in welfare and crime costs. It has been calculated that these long-term returns far outweigh the initial costs (Barnett and Masse, 2007; Heckman, 2006; Masse and Barnett, 2002). As Nisbett (2009, p. 152) has argued: 'The economic cost…would be recouped by increasing the productivity of the poor and reducing crime and welfare rates. We would likely do well by doing good.'

BOX 12.1 Miracle in Milwaukee

The Milwaukee Project was initiated in the 1960s. It was extraordinarily ambitious, not in terms of size, for there were only 20 children in each of the two groups (treatment and control), but in the scale of the intervention, which lasted from the time the children were only 3 months old and continued until they were 5 or 6, involved individual or small group tuition five days a week, twelve months a year, and included the mothers as well as the children. The tuition was provided by trained professionals and was expressly designed to stimulate the children's cognitive development. At a total cost of some $14 million (Spitz, 1986), even if we accept the authors' own assessment of the magnitude of the gains, the cost of raising one child's IQ by one point must have been over $30,000.

   Throughout the 1970s, the project was hailed as proof that children at risk of mental retardation could be saved: intelligence was wholly malleable, and it was only lack of political will, aided by false psychological theory, that stood in the way of raising the IQ scores of black inner-city children by 25 points or more. Introductory psychology textbooks cited the study uncritically; the news media lauded it. What is so remarkable is that all this happened in the absence of any proper published report on the study, which did not become available until Garber's book in 1988 (see Page and Grandon, 1981; Sommer and Sommer, 1983, for an account of this history). Another, more spectacular problem was that in 1981, Heber, the original director of the project, was sentenced to jail on charges of embezzlement (thus, perhaps, helping to explain the cost of the project as well as the delay in producing proper reports).

The most serious concern about the effectiveness of the Milwaukee Project is that while the treatment undoubtedly enhanced children's IQ scores, this appears to be *all* it achieved. In virtually all other projects, intervention programmes have been more successful at improving children's school performance than raising their IQ test scores. The Abecedarian Project certainly succeeded in improving children's performance on various school tests as well as on IQ tests (Ramey, 1993; Ramey *et al.*, 2001). But the Milwaukee results are strikingly disappointing. In spite of the ten-point difference in their IQ scores, within a couple of years of their entering the normal school system, there was no difference between the treatment and control groups of children in any formal tests of scholastic attainment.

Indeed in some respects, the children in the treatment group were described as more troublesome than those in the control group. One possibility is that it does not pay for a black child from the inner city to be too clever. Another, equally depressing possibility is that all that the Milwaukee Project succeeded in doing was to teach children how to answer the questions in IQ tests, without having any effect on the 'intelligence' that is supposedly measured by such tests (Jensen, 1989). There is, after all, a finite set of questions that appear in children's IQ tests, and the answers to most of them can be learned.

Demography: family size and birth order

There is a correlation of about −0.30 between children's IQ scores and the number of other children in their family. Given that the correlation between *parental* IQ and the number of children in the family is significantly smaller than this, it seems to follow that at least some of the association between family size and children's IQ scores is environmental in origin. But what is the route via which family size has its effect?

One way to approach this question, it might seem, would be to look at the effect of birth order on children's IQ scores. If, as is suggested by the data shown in Figure 12.4, later born children have lower test scores than first or second born children, is this not evidence that there is a direct effect of family size on children's IQ? It is not quite that simple, since the effects of birth order and family size may be confounded. Third, fourth, and fifth born children simply do not exist in families of one or two. If they have lower scores than first or second born children, they will lower the *average* score of children in larger families. On the other hand, the reason why third, fourth, or fifth born children have on average lower scores than first or second born might be because they come from larger families: the score for second born children is an average of second born children in families of two, three, four, etc., but the score of fifth born children is an average only of children in families of five or more.

If this sounds convoluted, it may perhaps become clearer by considering two ways of looking at birth order effects. The NCDS birth order data shown in Figure 12.4 are based on a survey of some 14,000 children born in Britain in 1958. All first born children regardless of the size of their family are included in the data, but the fifth and later born children, of course, came only from families of five or more. This between-family comparison does produce the confound I have just described. In order to look at the effect of birth order unconfounded by differences in family size, you need to do a *within*-family study. In families of two children, does the first born have a higher score than the second born? In families of four, do the first and second born have higher test scores than the third and fourth born? And so on. Only if such a within-family study reveals a significant effect of birth order, will you be justified in concluding that birth order *per se* is important. At least two large American studies (Retherford and Sewell, 1991; Rodgers *et al.*, 2000) found a significant effect of birth order in a between-family study, which vanished in the within-family analysis. They both concluded that the birth order effect was spurious.

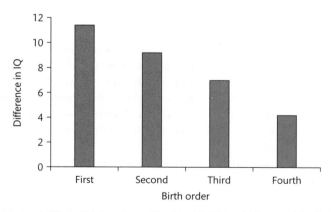

Figure 12.4 The apparent effect of birth order on 11-year-old children's IQ scores. The data shown are the difference between first to fourth born children and fifth and later born children in the NCDS (data from Mascie-Taylor, 1984, Figure 3).

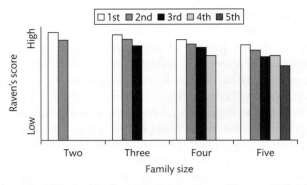

Figure 12.5 The independent effects of family size and birth order on 18-year-old Dutch conscripts' score on Raven's Matrices (selected data from Belmont and Marolla, 1973, Table 3). Belmont and Marolla presented derived rather than actual Raven's scores or their IQ equivalents, so the ordinate of the figure is simply labelled low and high Raven's scores.

That conclusion does not seem justified, or may be valid only for the USA. Several European studies have shown that the effect of birth order can be seen within as well as between families. An English study by Record *et al.* (1969) found a significant birth order effect in a within-family comparison—albeit one smaller than that seen in the between-family comparison. The classic study was by Belmont and Marolla (1973), who analysed Dutch conscripts' scores on Raven's Matrices as a function of the size of their family, and whether they were the first, second, third, or later born child in the family. As can be seen in Figure 12.5, they found that both family size and birth order had a significant effect on the men's scores. One problem with the American within-family comparisons is that the sample size becomes rather small. That problem did not apply to the Dutch study, nor to a Norwegian study of just over a quarter of a million conscripts, all given Raven's Matrices between 1967 and 1998, of whom some 60,000 were brothers and so could provide the needed within-family comparison (Bjerkedal *et al.*, 2007). They reported a significant birth order effect both in the between-family and within-family comparisons, with no difference in the size of the effect between the two.

The effect of family size on children's IQ scores has often been given a eugenic interpretation: irresponsible, low-IQ parents have large numbers of children and transmit their own low IQ to those children. But a within-family birth order effect cannot possibly be explained in this way, and if third, fourth, or fifth born children have a lower IQ than first or second born in the same family, this provides a different (albeit only partial) explanation for the fact that the *average* IQ of children in families of three or more is lower than that of children in families of two.

It remains to explain why birth order has an effect on children's IQ. One explanation has been offered by Zajonc's 'confluence model' (Zajonc, 1983; Zajonc and Mullaly, 1997), which assumes that children's IQ scores will depend on the average 'cognitive level' of the family into which they are born. Unlike IQ, cognitive level is not corrected for age, so adults' cognitive level is higher than that of children, and a first born child will therefore enter a family with a higher average cognitive level than a fifth born child. All else equal (there are other complications to the model with which I will not trouble the reader), the average cognitive level of the entire family will be progressively lower with the addition of each successive child.

A somewhat different theory suggests that young children's intellectual development depends on the amount of time and resources their parents can devote to them (Blake, 1981; Downey, 2001). First born children can receive their parents' undivided attention; by the time the third or fourth child is born, parents are too busy, too tired, or too bored to spend so much time with the child, whose IQ suffers accordingly. Although this makes intuitive sense, as does the confluence model, there are those who resist this kind of environmental explanation. Jensen (1997), for example, has argued that each succeeding pregnancy increases the probability of maternal immune attack on the foetal brain. This and other similar 'biological' prenatal or perinatal environmental effects seem to be ruled out by a further observation from the Norwegian study described above. The large size of the total sample allowed Kristensen and Bjerkedal (2007) to identify a number of later born men whose earlier born sibling had died very young. Their post-natal social environment, therefore, did not match their biological status as later born. It turned out that their IQ score was determined by their social status rather than their biological status.

Parental behaviour and family environment

The effect of birth order on children's test scores points to the unsurprising possibility that the amount of time parents spend with their children can have a modest but significant effect on those children's IQ scores. Perhaps qualitative differences in the way parents interact with their children also affect their IQ. Perhaps, indeed, such differences may help to explain some of the relationship between social class and IQ.

One of the more striking and important findings to emerge from analysis of the British NCDS data is shown in Figure 12.6, which plots the raw, uncorrected differences in IQ

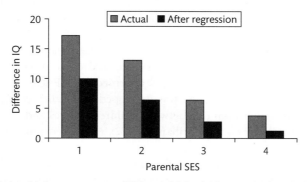

Figure 12.6 The relationship between parental SES and children's IQ scores in the NCDS. As in Figure 12.4, the data shown are the difference in average IQ between children of parents in social class 5 and those in higher social classes. One set of bars represents the actual difference observed, the other the difference after regression analysis has removed the effects of other correlated factors (data from Mascie-Taylor, 1984, Figure 1).

between children in social classes 1 to 5, and the same data once all other factors measured in the study had been taken into account. It is evident that these other factors account for a significant part of the association between social class and IQ, but what is more remarkable is the size of the residual effect. Even after making allowance for differences in birth weight, family size, income, degree of financial hardship, overcrowding, type of accommodation and school, neighbourhood, etc., there is still a ten-point difference in average IQ between children whose fathers are in occupational classes 1 and 5. Since it seems unlikely that a father's occupation could itself be a proximal cause of his children's IQ scores, we must look for other factors, not measured in the study but nevertheless correlated with parental occupation, to mediate the observed relationship. What might these factors be?

The NCDS was a large-scale survey, which obtained a mass of information on children's medical and educational history, but relied on readily obtainable information about their family background. It did not attempt to discover *how* children were brought up, how their parents interacted with them and what their home life was like. If a middle-class upbringing is indeed beneficial for children's test scores, it seems probable that this is because such children are encouraged to read or play educational games, are talked to in a particular manner, and are expected to take school seriously: the fact that they have a lot of money and live in a large house in an expensive neighbourhood may be much less important. Given that IQ tests measure vocabulary and general knowledge, require children to interpret pictures, do jigsaw puzzles and mental arithmetic, it seems plausible that it is the style of parent-child interaction that affects a child's IQ score, rather than the more material factors measured in large-scale social surveys.

It has long been known that many other aspects of family background, even those as readily measured as the number of books owned and newspapers or magazines taken, can predict a child's IQ at least as accurately as parental occupation or income (e.g. Chapin, 1928). The classic American adoption studies of Burks (1928) and Leahy (1935) took a variety of measures of home environment, many of which showed substantial correlations with children's IQ scores in their control (biological) families. In Burks's study, for example, while the correlation between parental income and child's IQ was only 0.24, two 'cultural' indices of the home correlated over 0.40 with the child's IQ. In Leahy's study, children's IQ correlated 0.37 with an economic index of the home, but over 0.50 with its cultural index and environmental status.

These results have been confirmed in more recent studies (Seifer, 2001): not only is there a high correlation, often higher than 0.70, between children's test scores and measures of the cultural aspect of the home (a special index, termed HOME score, Home Observation for Measurement of the Environment, was developed by Bradley *et al.*, 1977); this correlation is invariably higher than that between children's scores and their parents' socio-economic status (Bradley *et al.*; Marjoribanks, 1972). As I noted above, it is not money as such that determines a child's test score.

There remains one problem. However plausible it may be that parental involvement and the provision of appropriate toys, games, and books should be beneficial for a young child's IQ, the establishment of these correlations alone will never prove that one is a direct cause of the other. There are two obvious alternative possibilities. One is that any correlation between the behaviour of parents and their children's test scores reflects the influence of children on their parents rather than that of parents on their children. Do parents raise their children's test scores by reading to them, or do clever children ask to be read to more than less clever ones? Do parents' expectations and pressures affect their children's IQ, or do children's IQs influence the expectations parents entertain for them? Parents may well emphasize the importance of schooling to a child who enjoys school and is doing well, but if their children are clearly struggling at school, they may choose to encourage their other talents, sport, music, or whatever, instead.

The second possibility is that parents influence their children's development at least as much by the genes they pass onto them as by their actual behaviour towards them. Scarr (1997), for example, has argued that attempts to model the influence of parental attitudes and behaviour on their children's intellectual and academic attainments are successful only if they assume some genetic transmission of IQ from parent to child. Indeed, there is an increasing consensus among behaviour geneticists that correlations between parental status, attitudes and behaviour and their children's IQ scores can be almost entirely explained in terms of their shared genes (e.g. Bouchard, 1997; Scarr, 1997), a conclusion they see as reinforced by the evidence from kinship studies said to show that the influence of family environment on children's test scores decreases, virtually to zero, as they grow older. I have already questioned this evidence (see Chapter 11), and will further argue below that studies of both adoptive and biological families suggest that this strong conclusion is indeed too strong.

Many parents will think that the conclusion that parents can influence their children's IQ scores provides another example of academic psychology's 'discovery' of a blindingly obvious truth. No doubt. But wary readers should by now have learned to be suspicious of supposedly self-evident truths about the development of children's intelligence, especially when, as here, they are truths many adults *want* to believe. It would, after all, be depressing (at least for parents) if parents' attitudes and behaviour had no effect on their children's IQ. But it is precisely where an opinion is not only commonly received but also devoutly to be wished that it should be viewed with suspicion. That is a truth which it will be worth bearing in mind in the next section.

Social class

It is time to address what many commentators have seen as the critical question about environmental effects on IQ. Are they a product of differences in social class? In his original standardization of the Stanford-Binet test, Terman (1916) reported that there was a difference of some 16 points between the average IQ scores of children from social class 1 and those from social class 5. More than 50 years later, the British NCDS found a difference of 17 points between children from social class 1 and 5 (see Figure 12.6 above). Similar differences have repeatedly been observed in the restandardizations of the WISC (e.g. Kaufman and Doppelt, 1976). These seem (and are) large differences, but they translate into relatively modest correlations between parental SES and children's IQ. A meta-analysis by White (1982) of numerous, mostly American studies concluded that the best estimate of this correlation was 0.33. Bouchard and Segal (1985) calculated the weighted mean values from five very large studies, totalling some 20,000 children: IQ correlated 0.22 with parental income, and 0.28 with parental occupation. An upper-bound estimate of the correlation between children's IQ scores and their parents' SES is thus perhaps 0.30 to 0.35, with the correlation being rather higher for verbal or crystallized intelligence (Gc) than for Gf or fluid intelligence (Kaufman and Doppelt, 1976; Ramey *et al.*, 2001; White, 1982).

Sociologically minded commentators may be surprised at the modest size of this correlation, but they have rarely questioned the direction of causality it implies: poverty and its associated physical, cultural, and educational disadvantages depress children's test scores. In contrast, as noted above, many behaviour geneticists have followed Burt and Terman in assuming that the correlation is largely, if not wholly, mediated genetically, arguing that differences in family environment contribute little to variation in test scores (e.g. Bouchard, 1997; Scarr, 1997). In what follows I first consider the evidence for an environmental contribution to this correlation, before addressing the evidence that suggests a genetic component.

Social class as environment

It may seem obvious that children suffering from extreme poverty, cultural deprivation, malnutrition, physical illness, or poor education will also obtain low test scores, and that their low IQ will be a consequence of these disadvantages. It is certainly true that many of the factors discussed earlier in this chapter, which appeared to have detrimental effects on children's scores, are found more frequently in low SES families (Nisbett, 2009). This includes prenatal and perinatal problems, since poor mothers are more likely than better-off ones to smoke or drink in pregnancy; their newborn babies are more likely to be of low weight, and less likely to be breast-fed. In the USA at least, they will have less access to good medical care and will therefore continue to be less healthy; they will be likely to attend worse schools, and what is perhaps equally important, more likely to change schools more frequently (remember the difficulty of settling into a new school when you were young?). Above all, there is overwhelming evidence of substantial differences in the way that poor and better-off parents behave towards their children, and the cultural support their homes provide (Hart and Risley, 1995; Lareau, 2003). The general pattern of findings in these studies has been quite consistent, and all point to the conclusion that class differences in parental attitudes and behaviour are the most important influence on differences in their children's test scores. Poorer parents talk less to their children, and when they do, it is often a matter of command and reprimand, rather than interactive conversation. By the age of 3, the children of professional parents will have heard some 30 million words, while working-class children have heard only 20 million, and children of poor black parents will have heard only 10 million. It is hardly surprising, then, that by this age children of professional parents have a vocabulary some 50% greater than those of working-class parents.

One striking observation concerns the effect of the long American summer vacation which, as noted above, is not good for children's test scores. In fact this effect is strongly moderated by social class: in the richest families, test scores may actually improve over the vacation; in middle-income families there may be little change; but in the poorest the decline is substantial (Burkam *et al.*, 2004; Cooper *et al.*, 1996).

In spite of the behaviour geneticists' argument that the effect of family environment on children's test scores becomes vanishingly small by the time that children have grown up, it is hard to believe that all this is without significant long-term consequence. But proof of causality can only come from controlled experiment or intervention—in this case, of course, from adoption studies. Are adopted children's IQ scores affected by the social class of their adoptive parents? In the absence of selective placement, any correlation between the two must be due to an environmental effect of social class on IQ. Bouchard and Segal (1985) reported that, in five adoption studies, the average correlations between children's test scores and their adoptive fathers' education and occupation were 0.16 and 0.10 (compared with values of 0.31 and 0.28 in biological families noted above). The lower value for these correlations in adoptive families may be partly attributable to restriction of range, and a possibly fairer comparison can be seen in the four studies summarized in Table 12.1, where an attempt was made to match adoptive and biological families (in some cases indeed they were the same family, with both biological and adoptive children). As can be seen, there is still some tendency for the correlations to be higher in biological than adoptive families, but, except in Leahy's study, the differences are mostly small. Leaving that aside, the important observation is that the correlations in the adoptive families, although small, are all positive. On the face of it, this is evidence of a modest environmental effect of family background on children's IQ (a conclusion reinforced by a meta-analysis reported by van IJzendoorn et al., 2005).

Of even greater interest, both Burks (1928) and Leahy (1935) reported correlations ranging from 0.12 to 0.25 (median, 0.19) between adopted children's IQ scores and various social and cultural ratings of their adoptive homes, as well as aspects of their adoptive parents' behaviour. These are, no doubt, modest, but they are not zero, and they were larger than the correlations between the children's IQ and their adoptive parents' economic status, occupation, or education. In the absence of alternative explanations, they suggest that children's IQ scores can be affected by their parents' cultural and educational attitudes and aspirations, and by their style of interaction. But there remains a pressing need for longitudinal data which would assess whether adoptive parents' attitudes and behaviour have a lasting impact on their children's test scores as they grow older.

Several adoption studies have demonstrated significant increases in IQ as a result of adoption into a good home. Three French studies are worth describing. Capron and Duyme (1989) found that children adopted into high-status adoptive homes obtained IQ scores, at age 14, some 15 points higher than those of children adopted into low-status homes. The results of the second study, by Duyme et al. (1999), are shown in Table 12.2. Three groups of children were removed from their negligent parents at the age of 4, and placed into

Table 12.1 Correlations between family background and children's IQ scores in biological and adoptive families.

		Burks (1928)	Leahy (1935)	Minnesota (Scarr and Weinberg, 1978)	Texas (Horn et al., 1982)
Biological	SES	—	0.45	0.10	0.20
	Income	0.24	—	0.22	—
Adoptive	SES	—	0.12	0.12	0.16
	Income	0.23	—	0.06	—

Table 12.2 Effects of adoption into different status adoptive homes on neglected children's IQ scores (data from Duyme *et al.*, 1999, Table 1).

SES of adoptive family	Pre-adoption IQ (age 4.5 years)	Post-adoption IQ (age 13.5 years)
Low (N = 24)	78	86
Middle (N = 22)	77	92
High (N = 19)	79	98

low, middle, or high-status adoptive homes. The three groups were well matched for pre-adoptive IQ, but nine years later there was a 12-point difference between the scores of those adopted into the highest and lowest status homes. Note also that all three groups showed some improvement in their IQ as a result of nine years spent in their adoptive homes. This, too, suggests an environmental effect of adoption.

A third French study has also shown that adoption can raise children's test scores. Dumaret and Stewart (1985) traced 32 children abandoned by their working-class mothers at birth and brought up in middle-class adoptive homes. They compared them with 20 siblings (in fact, in virtually all cases half-siblings, with the same mother but a different father) who were brought up either by the mother or a close relative, or occasionally by a nurse, and thus remained in an impoverished environment. The adopted children obtained scores on different verbal and non-verbal IQ tests between 6 and 20 points higher than those obtained by the children staying at home. Since there is no reason to suppose that there was any systematic difference between the two groups of natural fathers, the adopted children's superior IQ scores must surely be attributed to their superior environment. The fact that the difference was about twice as large on verbal as on non-verbal tests is consistent with the general observation that social class differences in IQ are more pronounced on verbal tests (see above), and suggests that this is largely an environmental difference. Although the adopted children obtained scores some eight points lower than those of a control group matched for social class and attending the same schools, other studies summarized by van IJzendoorn *et al.* (2005) have not observed such a difference: adopted children may obtain IQ scores indistinguishable from those obtained by the biological children in their adoptive families.

There remain some question marks. First, the correlation between the SES of the adoptive home and adopted children's IQ scores in the American studies shown in Table 12.1 might be due to selective placement: children may have been placed in high-SES adoptive homes only if their true parents were well educated and from a 'good' background; if so, their high IQ may have been inherited from their true parents rather than moulded by the experience of living in a 'good' home. This is not a problem in any of the three French studies: in the Capron and Duyme study, the two groups of children were carefully matched for the social class of their biological mothers; in the Duyme *et al.* study, the children's pre-adoption IQ scores were known; and in the Dumaret and Stewart study, the two groups of children had the same biological mother. In the American studies, however, there is evidence of some selective placement in the form of correlations between various characteristics of the adopted children's true and adoptive parents. But the effect was never very marked, and in Burks's study, at least, where the correlation between adopted children's IQs and adoptive family income was 0.23, the correlation between the true and adoptive fathers' SES was −0.02. It is unlikely that selective placement is sufficient to account for the full magnitude of the correlations observed in adoptive families.

The second possibility is that these modest correlations may become even more modest, indicating an increasingly negligible effect of family environment on IQ, as the children grow older. But there is surprisingly little evidence to support this conjecture. In all three French studies, the average age of the children was at least 13.5 years old when tested (and many of course were older than this). The 'children' in the Minnesota study, shown in Table 12.2, were adolescents, aged between 16 and 22 at the time of testing. The data for the Texas study also shown in Table 12.2 were divided by Horn *et al.* (1982) into those for children aged 5–7 and those aged 8 or more: both correlations were 0.16. Moreover, in the ten-year follow up of this study (Loehlin *et al.*, 1989), the correlation between children's IQ and adoptive parents' SES showed only a small decline from 0.14 to 0.11 (the difference in initial value being a consequence of the change in the sample available for the longitudinal follow-up). Although it would be highly desirable to have a further follow up of, say, the Duyme *et al.* study, when the children were 20, it is quite clear that the effect of superior adoptive homes on adopted children's IQ scores is still evident when the children are well into adolescence. This all points to the conclusion that the correlation between adopted children's IQ scores and their adoptive parents' social status reflects a true and at least moderately long-lasting environmental effect.

A genetic difference between social classes?

The data from adoption studies may point to an environmental effect of parental social class on children's test scores. But they also suggest the possibility of a genetic effect. The correlation between parental circumstance and children's IQ scores is rather smaller in adoptive than in natural families. It is possible that restriction of range in adoptive families provides one explanation of this: adoptive families of lower occupational status may provide a better environment for developing their children's IQ than do ordinary families of apparently comparable status. But an obvious interpretation of this finding is that in natural families genetic sources of resemblance are added to environmental.

There are indeed reasons for supposing that the correlation between parents' social class and their children's test scores may be at least partly genetic in origin. The correlation between adults' social class and their IQ scores is about 0.50–0.60. But the correlation between the same adults' social class and their *children's* IQ scores is significantly lower— only about 0.30. This difference is illustrated in Figure 12.7a, which shows the average IQ scores of fathers in four different social classes and of their sons. The difference in average IQ between fathers in the highest and lowest classes is over 30 points; the difference between their sons' IQ scores is less than 20. One might suppose from results such as these that the average IQ difference between the social classes was fast disappearing. But this is not true: there is no good evidence that it is smaller today than it was 50 years ago. And in Waller's study shown in Figure 12.7b, the IQ scores of the sons, which correlated only about

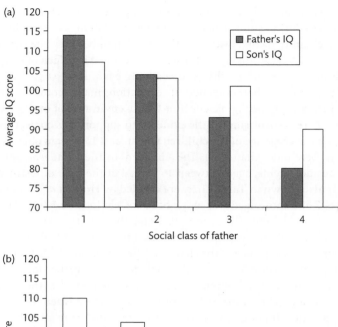

Figure 12.7 Average IQ scores of fathers and their sons. Figure 12.7a shows fathers' and sons' IQ scores sorted according to the fathers' SES. Note that the difference in IQ between SES1 and SES4 is greater for the fathers than it is for their sons. Figure 12.7b shows the IQ of these same sons sorted by their own, later attained SES. Note that the differences in average IQ between the social classes have been restored to nearly the same as they were for their fathers (data from Waller, 1971).

0.30 with the social class of their fathers, correlated over 0.50 with their own, later social class as adults. This, too, is a general enough finding (e.g. McCall, 1977). In other words, the social class difference in IQ is, so to say, recreated in each generation.

It is recreated by social mobility. The social class system of Western industrial societies is not a caste system. People are not necessarily ordained to remain in the social class to which they were born: in the USA, for example, for men born between 1950 and 1980, the correlation between their own attained social class and that of their father was only 0.32 (Beller and Hout, 2006). The degree of social mobility varies quite markedly from one

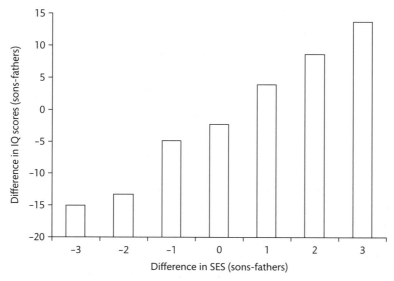

Figure 12.8 The correlation between IQ and social mobility. The figure plots the difference in IQ between fathers and their sons as a function of the difference in their occupational status: sons with higher IQ than their fathers tended to end up in higher status jobs (data from Mascie-Taylor and Gibson, 1978, Table 10).

country to another, being rather higher than this in Scandinavia, Canada, and Australia, and, according to Beller and Hout, lower in Britain and France (although a Scottish study of three generations that span most of the twentieth century reported correlations between fathers' and sons' social class of only 0.23 and 0.18, Johnson *et al.*, 2010). There is direct evidence that one of the factors correlated with social mobility is IQ. Differences in social class between father and son are correlated with differences in their IQ scores; just as a son's eventual social class is not necessarily the same as that of his parents, so he may differ from his parents in IQ (the correlation between fathers' and sons' IQ scores is certainly no more than about 0.50). Studies in both the USA and Britain have shown that the direction of any difference in social class tends to be the same as the direction of any difference in IQ. Sons with higher IQs than their fathers are more likely to be upwardly mobile; those with IQs lower than their fathers are more likely to end up in a lower social class (Mascie-Taylor and Gibson, 1978, whose data are shown in Figure 12.8; Waller, 1971).

There could be no correlation between social mobility and IQ without substantial variation in IQ within each social class. And so there is, especially when you look at children's IQ scores as a function of their parents' social class. In Waller's data shown in Figure 12.7a, the variation in sons' IQ scores within each parental social class was only fractionally less than the variation in the population as a whole. Some sons of fathers in class 1 had lower IQ scores than some sons whose fathers were in class 4. The former were likely to end up in a lower class, the latter in a higher one than their fathers. If social mobility is correlated with IQ in this way, it is difficult to resist the conclusion that such an effect is partly responsible for the maintenance of the correlation between IQ and social class in each generation, and therefore that the direction of causality is partly that IQ differences cause social class differences rather than simply that social class differences cause IQ differences. This may not

Table 12.3 Adopted children's IQ scores as a function of their biological and adoptive parents' SES (data from Capron and Duyme, 1989, Table 2).

		SES of adoptive parents	
		High	Low
SES of biological parents	High	120	108
	Low	104	92

be enough to prove that social class differences in average IQ are partly genetic in origin, but it is clearly consistent with this possibility, and tends to undermine the alternative thesis that they are entirely a consequence of differences in family environment.

In the last analysis, however, the only way to find out whether there might be differences in average IQ genotype between social classes would be via an improbable adoption study, in which children were taken for adoption from two groups of parents who differed in social class, and were then adopted by carefully matched families. A difference in the average IQ scores of the two groups of children would then suggest a genetic difference in IQ potential between the two groups of parents and, by implication, between the two social classes of which they were representative samples. Needless to say no such study has ever been done, but the small French adoption study of Capron and Duyme (1989), already partly described above, approximates to it. Searching through the agency records of children adopted before the age of 6 months, they set out to find four groups of children, two groups born to biological parents of high social class, two to parents of low social class, with one of each group adopted into high status adoptive homes and the other into low status homes. The result is the 'perfect' 2 × 2 factorial design illustrated in Table 12.3, with status of biological and of adoptive parents as the two factors. Understandably enough, the most difficult cell to fill was that of children born to high status parents but adopted into low status homes, and there are only eight children in this group as opposed to ten in each of the others. The results shown in Table12.3 however, suggest that the social class of both biological and of adoptive parents had significant and roughly equal effects on the children's IQ scores. The difference between children adopted into high status and those adopted into low status families provides, as already noted above, an elegant demonstration of an environmental effect of social class on children's IQ scores. But the difference between those born to high and low status biological parents provides, on the face of it, equally strong evidence of a genetic difference for IQ between the two groups of parents. Since there were no differences in birth weight between the two groups of children (i.e. no evidence of prenatal or perinatal environmental differences between the two groups), a genetic hypothesis is certainly the most plausible.

Conclusion

Contemplating the number of inconclusive studies reviewed in this chapter, and the perhaps rather meagre amount of unequivocal information they have provided, it is all too easy to throw up one's hands in despair. It is true that there is much that remains unknown, but despair is probably only a reaction to the disappointment of some unrealistic expectations. Environmentalists have insisted that IQ is malleable, and have railed against the brutal pessimism of those who would assert that a 5-year-old with an IQ of 75 is doomed by virtue of that IQ score to second-class citizenship. But their rhetoric has often implied that it would be a simple matter to intervene and raise such a child's IQ, and that it is only a lack of political will that stands in the way of this being done. Underlying that implication, of course, is a further set of assumptions: that psychologists understand how the environment shapes the developing child's IQ, and that even if they do not have a fully articulated environmental theory of the development of IQ, they can at least point to a small number of general principles governing that development.

Nothing could be further from the truth. Few general principles have emerged from the data reviewed in this chapter. Indeed, the most reasonable conclusion is that there is no single environmental factor that has a magical and permanent effect on children's IQ scores. What the data imply is that there are a very large number of factors, each of which has no more than a small effect on IQ (this is equally true of the environmental factors responsible for the Flynn effect). In most modern societies, many of these factors happen to go together, such that a child benefiting or losing out from one will probably be fortunate or unlucky enough to benefit or lose out from another. But in terms of psychological mode of operation, they are probably quite independent: it is not very likely that lead poisoning, poor nutrition, loss of schooling, and being the youngest of six children in the family, all depress a child's IQ for the same reason.

A list of the environmental factors that affect IQ contains relatively few surprises. From the data reviewed here, such a list would probably include: some prenatal and perinatal factors; health and nutrition; amount and type of parental interaction; the experience of normal schooling. At the same time, however, the data do serve to dispel some myths and point to some conclusions that have not always been recognized. As I noted earlier in this chapter, the most popular candidate for a single environmental determinant of IQ has been social class. There is, of course, a significant correlation between children's IQ scores and their parents' socio-economic status, but it is quite modest (0.30 to 0.35), and it is more probable than not that *part* of this correlation reflects a genetic component. In so far as it does represent an effect of family environment on IQ, it is not so much the sociological or economic concomitants of social class that are important, but rather parents' attitudes, aspirations, and style of interaction with their children. Several studies have shown that children's IQ scores are more strongly associated with 'cultural' than with economic measures of their home environment. Moreover, studies of adoptive families suggest that many of the characteristics of family environments that foster the development of IQ are not necessarily associated with social class at all. Even poor adoptive parents are capable of raising their adopted children's IQ scores. In Leahy's (1935) study, for example, children adopted by semi-skilled workers or 'day labourers' obtained IQ scores some 6–8 points higher than those of control children whose natural parents were in these occupational categories, and only 4–5 points below those of children adopted by professional or managerial parents.

This is one of the more important findings to have emerged from several decades of research. Although many people appear to think otherwise, poverty as such may not be the cause of some children's low test scores and low school achievement. Nisbett's argument that 'if we want the poor to be smarter, we need to find ways to make them richer' (Nisbett, 2009, p. 85) may be an oversimplification (as he goes on to acknowledge). Parental behaviour and attitudes are more important than socio-economic status *per se*, and it is the difference in these attitudes and behaviour between poor and middle-class parents that is largely responsible for differences in their children's intellectual development. If this is true, it makes the prospects of successful social engineering even bleaker: simply throwing money at the problem may not necessarily achieve a great deal (although if poor parents had more money then they might at least have more time to interact with their children).

There is a second message that reinforces and complements this first one. The effect of family environment on IQ cannot be of overriding importance, since members of the same family differ quite widely in IQ. The correlation between siblings for IQ is no more than about 0.40–0.50, and some 75% of the variance in IQ in the population as a whole is to be found among members of the same family. Behaviour genetic analyses suggest that by the age of 15 or so, within-family environmental differences are at least as important as differences between families in their impact on children's IQ scores. What are these environmental factors that cause members of the same family to differ in IQ? Just about the only unequivocally within-family effect identified so far is that first and second born children tend to obtain higher IQ scores than third, fourth, or fifth born children. But even the most optimistic interpretation of the importance of birth order must admit that it can explain no more than a small fraction of the variance in IQ. So what are the other factors?

Parents do not, of course, treat all their children alike, and differences between siblings' IQ scores, therefore, could well be due to differences in parental treatment. One might argue, for example, that parents themselves change over time, not only in their attitudes and aspirations, but also in their own social status and income: people do, after all, sometimes get better jobs, or lose the job they once had. And some parents probably still have different aspirations for their sons and their daughters (many more probably used to). All these factors may contribute to differences between children in one and the same family. Unfortunately, such evidence as there is does not encourage this line of reasoning. Rodgers and Rowe (1985), for example, could detect no tendency for differences in IQ scores between siblings to be affected by the difference in age between them, by the number of other siblings intervening between them, or by whether they were the same sex. This last conclusion has been well documented by numerous larger studies (Bouchard and McGue, 1981).

Once again, it is important to acknowledge that differences in parental treatment, attitudes, and aspirations, even if correlated with differences in their children's IQ scores, may not be the cause of those differences. If parents have higher aspirations for one child than for another, this is just as likely to be in response to pre-existing differences between those children as to be their cause. To the extent that within-family differences in IQ are environmental in origin, they probably reflect a whole variety of chance, one-off events at least as much as any difference in parental attitude. Some of these effects may be prenatal or perinatal, while others may be related to the accident of ill-health (Jensen, 1997). In so far as they are due to the social environment, they may reflect a particular group of friends, or the good or ill fortune to be exposed to an inspiring or a boring teacher at school. And since siblings differ from one another in personality and temperament even more than they do in IQ (sibling correlations for most personality measures are less than 0.20, see Loehlin, 1992), it seems possible that such differences in temperament may lead them to pursue different paths that then impact back on their cognitive development. But at this point, it will be advisable to stop before the merely speculative nature of this analysis becomes too apparent.

One final point should be made. One of the oldest beliefs in psychology is in the pre-eminent importance of early experience. It was reinforced by ethologists' studies of 'critical periods' in such phenomena as imprinting, and by the notion derived from developmental biology that the brain is particularly vulnerable at particular stages of its development. Such a belief, of course, formed part of the philosophy underlying the Head Start programme. But there is remarkably little evidence that environmental factors have a greater impact on children's IQ scores at one age than at another. Early intervention will produce a transient increase in IQ, but the effect washes out unless the intervention is sustained (as it is when the child is adopted). Conversely, years of gross neglect can leave a child with an IQ below 50 (if it can be measured at all), but patient rehabilitation can restore the child to a fully normal level of intellectual functioning (Skuse, 1984). Perhaps early experience is critical only if it pushes the child down an environmental path from which it is difficult to escape.

 ## Summary

- The Flynn effect provides some of the strongest evidence for a sizeable environmental effect on IQ scores. Its explanation is less certain: the best bet is that it reflects the operation of a large number of factors each of limited impact. That is probably just as true of environmental causes of differences in IQ within any one generation.

- Numerous factors are correlated with differences in IQ: parental social class, behaviour and attitudes; prenatal and perinatal complications; nutrition and health; family size and birth order; amount of schooling. This may not make them causes of differences in test scores. In some cases the direction of causation may be from child's IQ to parent's behaviour, rather than vice versa. In others (parental status) there may be a genetic contribution to the correlation.

- Although the behaviour geneticists' modern consensus is that differences in family background have virtually no impact on children's IQ scores after the age of 18 or so, the evidence for this view is less than overwhelming. Nevertheless, it is probable that some environmental sources of variation in IQ operate within families, to make brothers and sisters differ in IQ, rather than between families, to make them the same.

Further reading

Flynn (2007) and the edited book by Neisser (1998) should be consulted for explanations of the Flynn effect. Nisbett (2009) makes a strong case for the power of the environment (especially schools, compensatory education, and family background) to influence children's test scores. The edited book by Sternberg and Grigorenko (2001) has a number of important chapters, especially on physical and biological environmental factors. The books by Hart and Risley (1995) and Lareau (2003) document the great differences in family environment experienced by children from different social classes, especially differences in parental behaviour and attitudes. Van IJzendoorn *et al.* (2005) provide a meta-analysis of adoption studies.

13

Group differences

Introduction

Almost from the start, IQ tests revealed sizeable differences between the average scores obtained by different groups. Chapter 1 briefly mentioned the differences observed by Terman between children from different social classes (a topic taken up in Chapter 12) and, less briefly, the substantial differences shown by the World War I Army tests between Americans originating from different European countries. The 1920s and 1930s saw the publication of a number of studies recording average IQ scores of below 70 in groups of sub-Saharan Africans or Australian aboriginals (e.g. Fick, 1929; Porteus, 1931). The most notorious of all group differences, however, and the one which has attracted attention ever since the Army tests first revealed it, is that between Americans of African and European origin. It is still fiercely debated today, although partially overtaken by the difference now seen between Americans of European and Asian origin. Before turning to these differences, however, it is worth starting by looking at the supposed differences between the indigenous populations of different parts of the world.

National or ethnic differences

In the course of human evolution, the transition from hunter-gatherer lifestyle to settled agriculture and later to urban civilizations first occurred in the Near East, from where it spread to Europe and India. Why there, and rather later, but quite independently, in China and the Far East? Why not in sub-Saharan Africa, North or South America, or Australia? In his book, *Guns, germs, and steel,* Jared Diamond (1998) attempted to answer this question: 'Probably the commonest explanation involves implicitly or explicitly assuming biological differences among peoples...Europeans [are said to be]...genetically more intelligent than Africans, and especially more so than Aboriginal Australians.' But Diamond will have none of this:

> The objection to such racist explanations is not just that they are loathsome, but also that they are wrong. Sound evidence for the existence of human differences in intelligence that parallel human differences in technology is lacking. In fact...modern 'Stone Age' peoples are on the average probably more intelligent, not less intelligent, than industrialized peoples.
>
> (Diamond, 1998, pp. 18–19)

The modern 'Stone Age' people he was talking about are the inhabitants of New Guinea.

A different view is taken by Lynn (2006). The frontispiece of his book, *Race differences in intelligence*, shows a map of the world, with different regions in different colours, ranging from dark green for China, Japan, and Korea, pale green for Europe, orange for most of the Americas, North Africa, and the Indian subcontinent, through to orange-red for sub-Saharan Africa and red for Australia. The colours are said to show the average IQ levels of the indigenous populations of these regions: 105 for China, Japan and Korea, 100 for Europe, 90 for northern Canada, 85 for the rest of North and South America as well for North Africa and India, down to 67 for sub-Saharan Africa and 62 for the Australian aboriginal population. The book closes with the confident assertion that these differences are largely (even if not wholly) genetic in origin:

> The position of environmentalists that over the course of some 100,000 years peoples separated by geographical barriers in different parts of the world evolved into ten different races with pronounced genetic differences in morphology, blood groups, and the incidence of genetic diseases, and yet have identical genotypes for intelligence, is so improbable that those who advance it must either be totally ignorant of the basic principles of evolutionary biology or else have a political agenda to deny the importance of race. Or both.

> (Lynn, 2006, p. 244)

Who is right? I suspect that most readers will side with Diamond (even if questioning his suggestion that the inhabitants of New Guinea are more intelligent than Europeans). But it is only Lynn who provides *any* empirical evidence for his conclusion. His book analyses the results of some 500 studies that have administered IQ tests to indigenous peoples in different parts of the world (including two studies of natives of New Guinea, who obtained scores in the low sixties). It is the results of these analyses that are summarized in his map of the world.

What is one to make of Lynn's data and argument? One point to note at the outset is that his argument rests on a questionable reading of some aspects of human evolution (see Box 13.1). A second is that his summary of the evidence can often be disputed: Wicherts *et al.* (2010) argue that the best estimate of the average IQ of sub-Saharan Africans is nearly 80, rather than 67. But this is little more than minor quibbling. On the face of it, some of his claims seem preposterous: could it really be the case that Australian aboriginals have an average IQ of 62? Assuming a normal distribution and a standard deviation of 15, equivalent to that of a European or North American population, this would mean that the large majority are at least mildly disabled, with one in six having an IQ score below 50, that is, in the moderately disabled range. Australian aboriginals are not even the worst off case: the results of three studies of the San Bushmen of southern Africa give them an IQ of 54. Lynn does, at least for a moment, wonder whether 'people with an average IQ of 54 could survive as hunter-gatherers in the Kalahari desert, and therefore whether this can be a valid estimate of their intelligence' (p. 76). But this worry is soon dismissed. 'An IQ of 54 represents the mental age of the average European 8-year-old child.... [who] would have no difficulty in learning and performing the activities of gathering foods and hunting carried out by the San Bushmen' (p. 76).

BOX 13.1 Races and origins

According to the widely accepted 'Out of Africa' hypothesis, all modern humans originated in Africa, from which they spread out to populate the rest of the world, probably between 50,000 and 70,000 years ago (Lewin and Foley, 2004). Lynn's claim that modern populations have been separated for 100,000 years is at the very upper limit of such estimates: Europeans, for example, seem to have diverged from the population of the Near East and South Asia no more than 50,000 years ago.

The general consensus is that it was an astonishingly small group, no more than a few hundred or so, that first left Africa to become the ancestors of the rest of the world's population. If that is true, it is hardly surprising that the genetic differences between the populations of the rest of the world are smaller than those between different inhabitants of Africa: the genetic diversity of modern Africans is greater than that of the rest of the world put together (Lewin and Foley, 2004; Tishkoff *et al.*, 2009). This makes it all the more implausible to talk of 'the IQ of sub-Saharan Africans'.

Lynn allows that environmental differences, specifically in nutrition and general health, may account for some of these differences in average IQ. 'In broad terms the effect of malnourishment on Africans in sub-Saharan Africa and the Caribbean probably explains about half the low IQs, leaving the remaining half to genetic factors' (p. 185).

This is an astonishingly limited view of the potential scope of environmental influences on test scores. The twentieth century saw an increase in average test scores of at least 20 points in all industrialized countries of the world (Chapters 1 and 12), and one study has documented an increase of 15 points over the course of a mere 14 years in rural Kenya (Daley *et al.*, 2003). Virtually no other commentator has accepted Lynn's argument that these changes are entirely due to improvements in nutrition and health care (Lynn, 1998). No doubt this has been a contributory factor, but a more plausible position is that they are attributable to a whole host of factors, among which are changes in most industrialized societies in the value placed on certain educational styles (Chapter 12). In effect, the culture of many twenty-first century societies is quite different from that of those same societies at the beginning of the twentieth century, and it is in part these cultural changes that have been responsible for changes in test scores. If that is true, then how much greater might be the effect on test scores of the cultural differences between the industrialized economies of Europe and North America on the one hand, and sub-Saharan Africa on the other? There are no grounds for assuming that the modes of thought or reasoning that we take for granted as evidence of intelligence in Western industrial societies, will be the same as those to be found in other societies, let alone among illiterate peasants. The concept of intelligence is, in part, a social or cultural construct, as Sternberg (1985), among others, has insisted. Mary may be more intelligent than her brother John, but the way in which this difference manifests itself would surely be quite different if they were Amazonian Indians or San Bushmen, rather than middle-class Americans. And if they were Amazonian Indians, it remains an open question whether she would obtain a higher score on a Western IQ test than her brother.

Test bias

A popular reaction to the discovery of differences between different groups in average IQ scores is to blame the tests. Writing in a slightly different context, Evans and Waites argued: 'Social class and black-white differences were probably built in when the tests were constructed…The test questions often reflect the white middle-class academic milieu of their constructors rather than any culture free conception of human cognition' (Evans and Waites, 1981, p. 168).

This certainly sounds reasonable: how could a white British middle-class professor of psychology pretend that he knows what constitutes intelligent behaviour in a village in Bangladesh or the shanty towns surrounding Johannesburg? His conception of intelligence, and the tests he constructs to measure it, can only reflect his own parochial prejudices. Is it any wonder that other groups should be penalized when they are measured by these tests?

IQ testers themselves were reasonably quick to see the problems that arose when their tests were given to people from different backgrounds, even if their solution to the problem left much to be desired. The US Army World War I tests came in two forms (Chapter 1), the Alpha tests for those with sufficient schooling to understand written instructions and know, in principle at least, how to do mental arithmetic, and the Beta tests, specifically designed for those whose level of literacy appeared insufficient for the Alpha tests. Many of the Beta tests later found their way into the performance scale of the Wechsler-Bellevue test, and were thought to provide a fairer assessment of the intelligence of minority groups.

It is obvious enough that there must be insuperable problems in adapting most of the verbal tests of the WAIS or WISC, or indeed virtually any other measure of Gc, for a different culture. How, for example, could one possibly establish that the translation of the Wechsler vocabulary test into another language had resulted in a test of comparable difficulty? Even when there is no language difference between two populations, there are likely to be cultural differences. The point is easily illustrated by considering two countries as similar as the USA and Britain. The information test of the original version of the WAIS was modified for the British version of the test—questions about US presidents, for example, being changed into ones about British prime ministers. But the modifications were few and, to put it bluntly, laughably inadequate. Thus, the original American version of the WAIS contained the following item: 'Longfellow was a famous man; what was he?' It remained unchanged for the British version. Unsurprisingly, it turns out to be a harder question for a British than for an American audience. But what should the British translators of the WAIS have done? One obvious answer would be to have substituted a British poet for Longfellow. But who? Chaucer? Donne? Browning? The answer can only be found by trial and error. What is needed is a poet who is as well known to the British as Longfellow is to Americans. And what that in effect means is that the translators must demonstrate that the percentage of the British standardization sample that answers the question correctly is the same as the percentage of the American standardization sample that knew who Longfellow was. But now, when they have done this for every other item in the test, they will have guaranteed that British and Americans obtain identical IQ scores. And what will that have proved?

Do non-verbal tests such as the Army Beta tests solve the problem? Quite certainly not. Gould (1997) took great delight in illustrating some of the items, for example several similar to those appearing later in the picture completion test of the Wechsler tests: two people playing tennis on a court lacking a net, or a man in a bowling alley but with no ball in his hand. Neither seems a wholly appropriate test for a native of New Guinea. Are diagrammatic series completion, classification, and matrices problems any better? Cattell (1940) certainly described his as a 'culture-fair' intelligence test.

Now, as a matter of fact, many of the studies cited by Lynn (2006) documenting the low test scores of sub-Saharan Africans and others employed tests such as Raven's Matrices, Cattell's Culture Fair test, or other measures of Gf. Does this mean that their low scores reflect a real deficit, that is, one that must be largely genetic in origin? The answer is still no. It is quite false to suppose that just because at least some of the performance tests of the WAIS or WISC, Cattell's tests or Raven's Matrices are non-verbal and embody no *superficially* white, middle-class values, they are providing a more direct measure of 'innate intelligence' than do verbal tests. There is, in fact, no evidence to show that the heritability of scores on Raven's Matrices or other supposedly culture-fair measures of Gf is substantially higher than that of scores on measures of Gc such as the Wechsler verbal scale or Stanford-Binet test (Chapter 2), and no reason to suppose that the ability to solve arbitrary abstract problems, such as those found in Raven's Matrices, is any less a learned skill than the ability to do mental arithmetic or answer questions about the meanings of words. The rise in test scores over the course of the twentieth century has been more marked on Raven's Matrices than on any other IQ test (Chapters 1 and 12). Schooling may have just as profound an effect on non-verbal as on verbal IQ scores (Stelzl *et al.*, 1995; Chapter 12). Consistent with this, as is shown in Table 13.1, studies of immigrant children in Britain have found dramatic increases in scores on these tests the longer the children have been resident, and received their education, in Britain.

One problem, therefore, with administering Western IQ tests to people from other countries is simply that they will not be familiar with the material being presented to them. This is surely so obvious that it should hardly need saying, and Chapter 9 provided extensive, and sometimes surprising, documentation of this point. For example, Brazilian children who run street stalls selling fruit become highly skilled at the mental arithmetic required to calculate prices and give the correct change, but completely fail exactly the same problems when they are presented in the abstract form usual in the classroom (Ceci and Roazzi, 1994). In the present context, however, this is only a small part of the problem.

Culture and intelligence

Lynn, and others who think like him, have a wholly unrealistic and impoverished conception of culture. They can see that the comprehension and information tests of the WAIS would be unfair if given to indigenous peoples of other countries, because they are testing

Table 13.1 Indian children's scores on the performance half of the WISC and on Raven's Matrices as a function of the length of their residence in Britain (data from Sharma, 1971).

	WISC performance	Raven's Matrices
Living in India	76	81
Less than 2 years in Britain	84	84
More than 6 years in Britain	99	104

All children were born in a single district of the Punjab in northern India.

knowledge that such people will not have had the opportunity to acquire. But different cultures have different *conceptions* of what it is to be intelligent, and will value and therefore inculcate different attitudes and ways of thought. Consider the following account of African views of intelligence:

> In the subsistence, agrarian societies of Africa, social cohesion is traditionally nurtured through a strong emphasis on cooperation and responsibility. Child-rearing practices in these societies aim to guide the developing minds of children toward those cultural values by requiring them to share with peers, to show respect for elders, and to care for younger children...[In Zambia] the key concept of *nzelu* (which means both wisdom and skill) includes the notions of cleverness (*-chenjela*) and ability to take responsibility (*-tumikila*)...At the heart of this web of meanings lies the principle that cleverness can be deployed either selfishly or in a socially productive way and that only when it is deployed responsibly is it worthy of our admiration.

(Serpell, 2000, p. 550)

Recall that Odysseus, although invariably acknowledged to be clever, has not always been admired (Chapter 1, Box 1.1).

In the 1930s, when the Soviet psychologist Alexander Luria and his colleagues attempted to devise tests of reasoning suitable for illiterate peasants in central Asia, they were careful not to give them traditional 'verbal' tests, and were at pains to use material that would be concrete and familiar to their subjects rather than abstract and unfamiliar (Luria, 1976). It got them nowhere. As a test of syllogistic reasoning, they would present the following kind of problem:

> In the far north, where it snows, the bears are white.
> Nova Zemblya is in the far north, and it is always snowy there.
> What colour are the bears in Nova Zemblya?

The replies they received would be:

> How should I know? I have never been to the north.
> Why are you asking me? You have travelled and I have not.
> So-and-so said the bears were white. But he is always lying.

Does this prove the peasants were incapable of reasoning? Of course not. All these answers, although not those sought by the psychologists, contain evidence of implicit syllogistic reasoning. You cannot believe liars; so-and-so is a liar; therefore even if he says the bears are white, they may not be. Someone who has travelled more widely is more likely to know the answer to questions about far-off lands; you have travelled more than me; so you are more likely than I am to know the answer to your question. Or, people usually only ask questions to which they do not already know the answer; so why are you asking me this silly question? It is not that these peasants could not reason; it is rather that they do not understand the rules of these strange games the psychologists were trying to play.

The similarities test of the Wechsler scales requires the examinee to say in what respect two dissimilar objects, for example a spade and a rake, are alike. Here is a transcript of one of Luria's attempts to administer such a test:

Q: What do a chicken and a dog have in common?
A: They're not alike. A chicken has two legs, a dog has four. A chicken has wings but a dog doesn't. A dog has big ears and a chicken's are small.

Q: You've told me what is different about them. How are they alike?
A: They're not alike at all.
Q: Is there one word you could use for both?
A: No, of course not.
Q: What word fits both a chicken and a dog?
A: I don't know.
Q: Would the word 'animal' fit?
A: Yes.

Has he learned the general principle? The transcript immediately continues with the next example:

Q: What do a fish and a crow have in common?
A: A fish—it lives in water. A crow flies. If the fish just lays on top of the water, the crow would peck at it. A crow can eat a fish but a fish can't eat a crow.

And so on. It will be recalled that the similarities test has shown the largest rise in test score of any of the Wechsler tests during the course of the twentieth century.

A related example is the 'odd-one-out' problem, that appears in the Cattell tests: in Western societies, as children grow older, so they become more likely to sort the world into taxonomic categories: given a knife, fork, spoon, orange, apple, and banana, they sort the first three together as tools, the second three as fruit. So, presented with an odd-one-out classification problem:

Hammer, saw, hatchet, log,

they have no difficulty in saying that the log is the odd one out. Not so Luria's peasants. Typical responses were:

They all belong, you need the saw and hatchet to cut the wood, and the hammer to hammer it.

Told that so-and-so had said the log did not belong, they replied:

He probably has plenty of firewood already. But we do not.

Rather than sort objects into taxonomic categories, they want to put into one group a set of objects that can all be used together to achieve something. Who is to say that one system of classification is more 'intelligent' than another? We happen to regard taxonomic categorization as, in some sense, more intelligent. Others do not. Adult Kpelle peasants shown the utensils and the fruits said that the knife went with the orange because it cuts it, and that this was how a wise man would sort these objects. When asked how a fool would sort them, they promptly put all the utensils in one pile and all the fruit in another (Cole *et al.*, 1971). But when it made sense to them to sort objects taxonomically, they were perfectly capable of doing so: shown a large number of leaves, they sorted them into 'tree' leaves and 'vine' leaves, since for a farmer this is the important distinction.

Standard IQ tests were invented to see how well young children could cope with formal schooling in Western industrial societies, and, more broadly, were designed to measure the knowledge, intellectual skills, and cognitive abilities valued in those societies. They may do a good job of that. But there is no reason to assume that other cultures and societies share the same values. Administering such tests to people of other cultures, who have received little if any formal schooling, may tell you whether they do or do not share the same values.

But it will not necessarily have much to say about their intelligence (Sternberg, 1985). When Evans and Waites (1981, see above) criticized the inventors of IQ tests because their questions reflected their own values rather than any 'culture free conception of human cognition', their error was to suppose that there is any such thing as a culture free conception of human cognition. There is not.

Recall that Kenyan schoolchildren have shown a more dramatic Flynn effect than any observed in any industrialized country—a rise in test scores of 11 IQ points in 14 years. Rash as it is to predict the future, I would hazard a guess that many other underdeveloped countries will show very substantial gains over the next 50 years, and since the Flynn effect seems to be grinding to a halt in at least some European countries, this will mean that the gap between, say, African and European test scores will start to decrease.

East is east

It would be a serious mistake to stop here. The argument so far has been about differences between children or adults who have been exposed to Western schooling and those who have often received little or no schooling. It will not do to suppose that a few years of Western-style education will turn everyone into a replica of a European or North American student. In many of the studies cited by Lynn in support of his hypothesis, the children or young adults being tested were attending, or had attended, school, often the same schools as whites, and in a small number of cases they were students at the same university. The kind of cultural bias described above is surely less plausible here.

Equally surely, however, cultural differences are much wider than this. Nisbett (2003), among others, has argued persuasively for the importance of cultural differences between European and North American societies on the one hand and Chinese, Japanese, and Korean societies on the other. The difference has been described as individualism vs. collectivism, independence vs. interdependence, analytic vs. holistic. It is this last distinction that is of most obvious present concern: analytic thinking classifies the world into taxonomic categories, holistic thinking tries to see the relationship between different things. Shown a picture of a chicken, a cow, and some grass, American children tended to put the chicken and the cow together (they are both animals), while Chinese children tended to put the cow and the grass together (cows eat grass). Americans were more likely to use a rule to classify a series of pictures into one or other of two classes; Koreans were more likely to go on perceptual similarity (Nisbett, 2003, pp. 140–4). It is not difficult to see the impact that these differences might have on performance on supposedly 'culture-fair' tests of Gf (see below).

Heine (2008) has suggested, rather plausibly, that this 'Eastern' style of thought may actually characterize much of the world's population, not just Chinese, Japanese, and Koreans: it is Western thought that is the odd one out. While Cohen (2009) has argued that much 'cultural psychology' has concentrated on cultural differences between countries, ignoring the important cultural differences between different groups within a country—between different religions (think only of Northern Ireland), different regions of the country (north vs. south in both England and the USA), and different socio-economic groups. For present purposes, however, the question is whether these cultural differences are responsible for differences in average test scores. In fact there is little hard evidence to support this conjecture, and in what follows I shall mostly be discussing other possibilities. Although, for example, no one could suppose that in either Britain or the USA, the culture of a black inner-city ghetto is indistinguishable from that of an affluent white neighbourhood, the difference is surely much smaller than that between the black ghetto and an Amazonian tribe or the Bushmen of the Kalahari Desert. What then is responsible for any difference in test scores between different ethnic groups living in the same country? It is time to turn to the numerous studies that have administered IQ tests to ethnic minorities living in Western societies, for example people of African origin living in the USA or Britain.

The black-white test score gap

There can be no serious doubt that African-Americans obtain on average test scores substantially below the white mean (Box 13.2 explains some issues about terminology). This difference showed up in the early World War I Army data, was repeatedly confirmed in subsequent studies between the wars (Shuey, 1966), and has been maintained after World War II. The first American restandardizations of the Wechsler tests (WAIS-R and WISC-R) revealed that there was still a difference of some 15 points (Kaufman and Doppelt, 1976; Reynolds *et al.* 1987). Although there has been no comparably systematic analysis of the position in other countries, no doubt because no other Western industrial society contains such a long established and substantial black minority, there can be little doubt that in the 1970s and 1980s black children in Britain, the majority of West Indian origin, obtained IQ scores significantly below those of the white mean of 100; the results of two national surveys: National Child Development Study (NCDS) and Child Health and Education Study (CHES) of children aged 10 and 11, are shown in Table 13.2. Their scores, particularly in the later study, are higher than those typically reported in the USA at that time and, as can be seen, the results of the earlier study are seriously compromised by the fact that some of the children had only recently arrived in Britain. Those resident in Britain for four or more years before being tested obtained scores no more than 10–11 points below the white mean.

> ### BOX 13.2 Another note on terminology
>
> The 'correct' names for different racial, ethnic, or social groups have changed several times over the past one hundred years. Any attempt to keep up with this ever-changing fashion seems doomed to failure, and I have not particularly tried to do so in this chapter. So I often refer to 'blacks' rather than use the more cumbersome terms 'African-Americans' or 'Afro-Caribbeans', at least partly because I sometimes wish to refer equally to those living in the USA or in Britain. At other times, writing of British studies, I refer to them as West Indians or of West Indian origin, in the same way as I refer to Indians and Pakistanis, without thereby intending to imply that they are not all British citizens, most of whom were born in Britain. Although I sometimes use the generic term 'East Asians' rather than Orientals (let alone Mongoloids), I have usually talked of Chinese, Japanese, or Koreans, sometimes adding Americans, if they are resident in the USA.

Table 13.2 IQ scores of 10 and 11-year old black children in Britain (data from Mackintosh and Mascie-Taylor, 1986, Table 3.1).

	NCDS (1969)		CHES (1980)	
	Verbal	Non-verbal	Verbal	Non-verbal
Blacks (4–)	84	81		
			92	97
Blacks (4+)	90	89		

(4–) = children resident in Britain for less than four years at time of testing.
(4+) = children resident in Britain for four or more years at time of testing.

It is not easy to discuss data such as these rationally, for it would be naive to pretend that they have no social or political impact. In the USA they have in the past been used to argue against the integration of school systems or the provision of compensatory education, in Britain to support bans on further immigration, and in both countries to argue that there is nothing to be done about black poverty or crime because both are inexorable consequences of low black IQ. But however suspect the motives of many of those who have used these data, and however strongly you may deplore their political aims, will anything be gained by pretending that the data do not exist or by refusing to discuss them at all? The trouble with such a response is that it seems to imply that the data really are of the utmost social and political consequence, and that those consequences are too terrible to contemplate. Is that really true? Of course, the results of IQ tests have been used by racists to support their doctrines; but it is absurd to suppose that they *need* such data in order to justify their position. American and European prejudice and discrimination against Jews, Japanese, or Chinese can hardly rest on the claim (which would be the reverse of the truth) that these groups obtain low IQ scores. Conversely, no one has thought to discriminate against identifiable groups, such as MZ twins, whose average IQ scores were at one time lower than those of the rest of the population. The difference in average IQ between blacks and whites is neither a necessary nor a sufficient condition for discriminating against blacks as a group, let alone against individual blacks who may well have IQ scores well above the white mean.

It should be acknowledged, then, without further ado that there is a difference in average IQ between blacks and whites in the USA and Britain. But what is the explanation? On the face of it, there are three possibilities: genetics, environment, or bias in the tests. It has seemed obvious to many commentators that the real question at issue is the genetic one: if the difference were an artefact of the tests, or could be explained in terms of certain environmental differences between black and white populations, would anyone be exercised by it? If bias in the tests were the culprit, that would no doubt give yet further reason to mistrust IQ tests, or alternatively to try to devise better ones. If environmental factors could be shown to cause differences in IQ between blacks and whites, that might make one want to change society. The problem with the genetic explanation is that it seems final and immutable. But this argument is wholly fallacious. It is one thing to establish that IQ scores are affected by the environment; it is another to pinpoint the precise factors responsible, let alone their mode of operation; and it is yet another matter to intervene in such a way as to influence test scores. And even if we did know how, it would not follow that the social engineering required would be socially acceptable. Conversely, genetic effects are not necessarily immutable and are always expressed in a certain environmental context: change that context and the genetically caused effect may disappear (see the discussion of Chapter 11, where I gave one hypothetical example of this in the context of black-white differences).

Nevertheless I shall start with the genetic hypothesis. Is it, in Jensen's words, 'not unreasonable' (Jensen, 1969)? It is important to clear up two very general points at the outset. Human beings form a single interbreeding species and no serious geneticist or anthropologist today would subscribe to a view of fixed and distinct 'races'. But this does not mean, as some have claimed, that the concept of 'race' is wholly meaningless. A better summary is:

> Data from many sources have shown that humans are genetically homogeneous and that genetic variation tends to be shared widely among populations. Genetic variation is geographically structured, as expected from the partial isolation of human populations during much of their history. Because traditional concepts of race are in turn correlated with geography, it is inaccurate to state that race is 'biologically meaningless'. On the other hand, because they have been only partially isolated, human populations are seldom demarcated by precise genetic boundaries. Substantial overlap can therefore occur between populations, invalidating the concept that populations (or races) are discrete types.
>
> (Jorde and Wooding, 2004, p. 32)

Although some writers (e.g. Gould, 1986) have argued that there *could not* be any genetic differences for IQ between people of African and European origin, this seems nonsense. The genetic hypothesis needs nothing more than an average difference in the distribution of the no doubt vast array of genes affecting IQ. One should not attempt to rule it out on *a priori* grounds.

Genetic evidence

So what is the evidence that has persuaded some commentators (Jensen, 1998; Rushton and Jensen, 2005), but has been vigorously disputed by others (Brody, 2003; Nisbett, 2005, 2009) that the black-white test score gap is partly, perhaps largely, genetic in origin? It seems a simple matter to imagine one critical experiment. Take a random sample of black and white children at birth and bring them up in carefully matched adoptive homes or other comparable environments and measure their IQ scores at aged 10 or so. Recall the comparable study by Capron and Duyme (1989; see Chapter 12) which suggested that the difference in average test scores of children born to parents of different social class might be partly genetic in origin. But is the experiment possible? Leaving aside the usual difficulties, common to any study designed to disentangle genetic from environmental sources of variation in IQ, here there is the added problem that it may never be possible, in a racist society, for black and white children to experience comparable environments. No doubt, well meaning white adoptive parents can mitigate the harshness of society, but could they ever eliminate it? Thus, the discovery of a significant difference between the IQ scores of black and white children in this hypothetical study would still not force one to accept the genetic hypothesis.

Black and white children brought up in comparable environments

The argument may seem sound, but says little for the courage of its proponents. For in fact they need not have erected such defences against unwelcome results. No study has achieved the ideal set out above, for no natural experiment ever could, but three have approximated it, and taken as a whole their results provide little support for the genetic hypothesis. The results of the two earlier studies are shown in Table 13.3. In neither case is there any significant difference between the IQ scores of black, or mixed-race, and white children.

The children in Eyferth's (1961) study were the illegitimate offspring of American (and some French) soldiers born to German women during the occupation of Germany after World War II, and brought up by their German mothers or by foster parents. The black children were a representative sample drawn from the approximately 4,000 such children for whom official records were available. The white children were matched to the black for location, school, and mother's circumstances. What could not be ascertained was the status of the fathers, for in most cases their identity was simply not known. This is the most obvious imperfection in Eyferth's study, but is it sufficient to cast doubt on the conclusions suggested by his data? An obvious problem is that the black soldiers in the US Army cannot have been a representative sample of the American black population. The American Army in World War II, as in World War I, used IQ tests to screen all draftees, and since blacks obtain on average lower IQ scores than whites such a procedure necessarily entails the rejection of a higher proportion of blacks than of whites. Flynn (1980) however has calculated that when allowance has been made for this selection, at least 80% of the usual IQ gap between American blacks and whites is left intact. Thus, the trivially small difference between the IQ scores of the two groups of children suggests that there can be no great genetic difference between the two populations from which their fathers came. This conclusion is more or less accepted by Herrnstein and Murray (1994, p. 310), and even Jensen once conceded that the results are 'consistent with a purely environmental hypothesis of the racial difference in test scores' (Jensen, 1998, p. 483).

The second study, by Tizard (1974), was of British children who had lived or were still living in residential nurseries (the majority that had left the nursery were now in adoptive homes). They were all given three separate tests. As can be seen, the white children tended to obtain rather lower scores than children with either one or two black parents. There are at least two problems with this study. First, the children were only 4–5 years old at the time of testing, and test scores at this age do not correlate particularly well with later IQ (see

Table 13.3 IQ scores of black and white children brought up in comparable circumstances.

	Eyferth (1961)	Tizard (1974)
Black	—	107 98 106
Black-white	97	106 99 110
White	97	103 99 101

The three sets of figures under Tizard represent the results of three separate tests given to each child.

Chapter 8). Second, although West Indian families in Britain were on average poorer, less middle class, and scored higher on most indices of social disadvantage than whites at this time (see below), in this sample there was no difference between the proportion of black and white fathers in semi-skilled and unskilled occupations. The black children, therefore, can hardly have been a representative sample of Britain's black population at the time.

The results of a third study (the Minnesota trans-racial adoption study, Scarr and Weinberg, 1976; Weinberg *et al.*, 1992) are shown in Table 13.4. This was an orthodox adoption study, similar in design to those discussed in Chapter 12, and some aspects of its results have already been mentioned. The unique feature of the study is that although the adoptive families were all comfortably off, white, and middle-class, only a small proportion of the adopted children were white; the remainder had at least one black parent. A follow-up study, ten years later (Weinberg *et al.* 1992), traced the majority of the children when they were in their late teens; these results are also shown in Table 13.4.

It is worth concentrating first on the initial data reported by Scarr and Weinberg. At that time, the average IQ of the adoptive parents was approximately 120 and that of their own natural children 117. As can be seen, no group of adopted children achieved average IQ scores of this level, but it is evident that there was no significant difference between the scores of white adopted children and those of mixed parentage. However, the average IQ of the children of two black parents, although well above the mean of the black population, was some 12–14 points below that of the other two groups. Here is the first piece of evidence consistent with a genetic hypothesis, but to complicate matters, there were several clear differences between the circumstances of the children with two black parents and those of the other two groups. The former had been adopted at a later age and had thus been in their adoptive homes a substantially shorter time than the other two groups (at the time of the original test, for three and a half years, on average, as opposed to five or eight). Their biological mothers, unlike the biological parents of any other group, had received less education than was normal for the population from which they came, and their adoptive parents were also less well educated than those of the other two groups of children. In other words the study is far from ideal, and its results are inherently somewhat ambiguous. It is possible that the 12–14 point gap between the adopted children reflects a genetic difference, but it is easy to point to environmental factors that were not matched between the groups.

The most striking feature of the follow-up data shown in Table 13.4 is the apparent decline in the IQ scores of all three groups of adopted children. According to Weinberg

Table 13.4 IQ scores of adopted children in the Minnesota trans-racial adoption study

	Scarr and Weinberg (1976)	Weinberg *et al.* (1992)	
		Initial study	Ten-year follow-up
Black	97	95	89
Black-white	109	110	99
White	112	118	106

et al., this is largely a consequence of changes in test norms. The Flynn effect means that if people are tested with an old IQ test, their scores will be inflated; if they are retested at a later date with a new test, their IQ will appear to have declined. Thus, little should be read into this apparent change. However, one of its consequences is that the children with two black parents now obtained scores hardly different from what one would have expected of a random sample of black children brought up by their own parents in a state such as Minnesota. The implication is that the experience of adoption by a white middle-class family has done little or nothing to raise their IQ scores. There is no doubt that this particular feature of the follow-up data is more consistent with a genetic than with an environmental hypothesis, as Rushton and Jensen (2005), among others, have been quick to point out. But other features of the data should not be ignored: the largest apparent decline in IQ was in fact shown by the white adopted children. It is also important to note that the sub-set of these children available for the follow-up study was a biased sample: their mean IQ score at first testing was 118, as opposed to 112 for the initial, complete sample of white adopted children. Once allowance is made for this six-point difference between the complete sample of white children and the smaller sub-set available at the time of the follow-up, there is no good evidence of any difference in average IQ between white and mixed-race adopted children.

Weinberg *et al.* carried out a stepwise multiple regression analysis to see what factor or factors best predicted the follow-up IQ scores. When biological parents' race was entered into the analysis first, it accounted for 16% of the variance in test scores, and measures of the adoptive homes and the children's adoptive experience accounted for only an additional 7% of the variance. However, when these environmental measures were entered into the analysis first, they accounted for 17% of the variance and biological parents' race accounted for only 6% more. In other words, genetic and environmental sources of variance were largely confounded, and it is impossible to disentangle their relative contributions. Once again, however, it should be acknowledged that the children with two black parents appear to have benefited not at all from adoption into white middle-class families, a finding particularly embarrassing for any environmental hypothesis.

It is hardly surprising that natural experiments should usually fall short of perfection; none of the studies shown in Tables 13.3 and 13.4 is an exception to this rule. So there can be no question of their settling the issue once and for all. Two of the three studies provide no support for a genetic hypothesis at all. The third contains data that are certainly consistent with a partly genetic hypothesis. If it would be rash to argue that they refute the genetic hypothesis, it would surely be absurd to argue that, taken as a whole, they support it. If one recalls the cautionary note sounded at the outset of this discussion, that in a racist society it may never be possible to bring up black and white children in truly comparable environments, the results of these studies are surely consistent with the possibility that if environmental differences between blacks and whites could be miraculously eliminated, the two groups might well obtain approximately equivalent IQ scores.

Degree of white ancestry

Is there any other kind of evidence that would point to a genetic contribution to the difference in average test score between Americans of European and African ancestry? One answer is suggested by the fact that US blacks are not of pure African ancestry, but on average have 20% European ancestry (Chakraborty *et al.*, 1992). So, do blacks with a greater percentage of European genes obtain higher test scores than those with less European ancestry? The data are widely acknowledged to be less than satisfactory: apart from the case of children from mixed marriages, it is not easy to get reliable estimates of the degree of white ancestry. The best method to date has relied on the fact that Europeans and Africans differ in the frequency of different blood groups. According to Rushton and Jensen (2005, p.262), the two studies that used these differences to measure degree of European ancestry (Loehlin *et al.*, 1973; Scarr *et al.*, 1977) 'found that blood groups distinguishing African from European ancestry did not predict IQ scores in Black samples'. Which makes it odd that they should conclude that studies of 'racial admixture' provide support for the genetic hypothesis, since other kinds of study of this question have found no better evidence that degree of white ancestry enhances black test scores. Nisbett's comment is blunt:

> Rushton and Jensen (2005) ride roughshod over the evidence concerning whether the Black-White IQ gap has a hereditary basis. The most directly relevant research concerns degree of European ancestry in the Black population. There is not a shred of evidence in this literature, which draws on studies having a total of five very different designs, that the gap has a genetic basis.
>
> (Nisbet, 2005, p. 309)

Spearman's hypothesis

In an analysis of the US Army data, Spearman had noticed that the black-white difference in test scores 'extended through all ten tests, but it was most marked in just those which are known to be most saturated with *g*' (Spearman, 1927, p. 379). Jensen (1998) developed this idea into a more fully fledged theory, which he termed Spearman's hypothesis: the difference in test scores between blacks and whites is a difference in the general factor (*g*) common to all IQ tests. He showed that in 17 independent data sets (but mostly based on the Wechsler tests), the magnitude of the black-white difference in test scores correlated 0.62 with the tests' *g* loadings. It seems that Spearman's hypothesis is rather better supported than the view of those critics who see the black-white differences as due to a few, patently biased items in the test. However, Flynn (2008) showed that this correlation has shrunk in the most recent Wechsler test, the WISC-IV, where it is only 0.49, while in Eyferth's German data the correlation is only 0.08.

Rushton and Jensen (2005) have argued that the validity of Spearman's hypothesis proves that black-white differences must be genetic in origin (given the WISC-IV data, does this imply that the difference is less genetic in origin today than it was 25 years ago?). It is true that a test's *g*-loading is positively correlated with its heritability (Jensen, 1998; Rushton and Jensen, 2005). There is also some evidence that the magnitude of the black-white difference is correlated with a test's heritability (Rushton, 1995). But does this necessarily prove their conclusion? A modest correlation between two variables implies that they share something in common, but it does not tell you what. Scores on Raven's Matrices are highly heritable, while the Wechsler similarities test is the second most heritable test of the WISC (Rushton, 1995). But these are also the two tests that have shown the largest gains over the past 50 years, in other words two tests that are most influenced by environmental differences between generations (Flynn, 2007). As Flynn (2000) has pointed out, therefore, if black-white differences are more pronounced on these tests than on others, this implies, according to Rushton and Jensen's argument, that black-white differences must be environmental in origin.

In this context, Spearman's hypothesis simply states that black-white differences are in what is central to IQ, not just in one or two special types of item or test, and that they are found in IQ more than in other skills. That, as will become apparent later, is probably true.

Brains and reaction times

Rushton and Jensen (2005) provide other indirect lines of evidence to support their argument. One is that since there is a significant difference in average brain size between Americans of African and European origin, and since brain size is under genetic control and correlated with IQ, it is unsurprising that there should be a significant difference in the two groups' average IQ scores, and obvious that this difference must be at least partly genetic in origin. There are indeed data pointing to a difference in average head circumference and cranial capacity of some $0.20d$ between American blacks and whites (Rushton, 1992), but a difference of this magnitude in a characteristic whose correlation with IQ is no more than 0.20 (see Chapter 6) is never going to explain more than a minute fraction of the difference in test scores, which, they insist, amounts to $1.0d$. Using data from other countries, Lynn (2006) concluded that the difference between the brain size of Africans and Europeans amounted to $1.46d$; assuming a correlation of 0.44 between brain size and IQ (on the optimistic side, see Chapter 6), he calculated that this would explain 28% of the difference between African and European IQs. But that calculation ignored the fact that the measure of brain size in the studies Lynn relied on was again only head circumference, whose correlation with IQ is certainly nowhere near 0.44; it could therefore account for no more than 12–13% of the difference in test scores.

A second argument is that black-white differences are observed not only in IQ but also in other simpler measures, such as reaction times (RT), which correlate with IQ. The implication is that any such difference could hardly be environmental in origin. In fact, however, the only American data (Jensen, 1993) suggested that the black-white difference in single or two-choice RT to lights was negligible (and in two-choice RT actually in favour of blacks), was only slightly larger in OMO RT ($d = 0.19$), and was reasonably substantial only in RT to answer simple arithmetic questions. That is hardly conclusive evidence of a difference in a wholly culture-fair test. It is surprising that Rushton and Jensen never comment on another finding, that there appears to be no difference between black and white children's scores on a variant of the infant habituation/dishabituation test (Fagan, 2000), a test that correlates rather well with later IQ, and seems as likely as simple RT to be culture fair (see Chapter 8).

It is also hard to resist citing a study by Washburn and Rumbaugh (1997), who reported that rhesus monkeys had shorter reaction times than American college students. A difference between two groups in average RT may not really prove that they differ in intelligence.

Environmental causes of black-white differences

So far, at least, there seems to be relatively little reason to suppose that the black-white test score gap has a strong genetic component. Is there any evidence that environmental factors are responsible? Jensen (1998) has been dismissive of many environmentalist arguments. Of course, he acknowledges, the environmental circumstances of blacks and whites differ in many ways. But in some cases, differences in test scores remain even when these differences in circumstance are allowed for, and in others there is simply no evidence that such circumstances affect test performance in the first place. The acid test of an environmental hypothesis, as I argued in Chapter 12, is to manipulate the putative environmental factor and record a change in IQ. If differences in education are responsible for differences in IQ between blacks and whites, Jensen argues, why has compensatory education usually so signally failed to have any *lasting* impact on black children's IQ scores? And why, in spite of all the social engineering and legislation of the 1960s and 1970s in the USA, was the black-white difference in IQ as great in 1980 as it was in 1940? Finally, if poverty and discrimination are the cause of low black IQ, why is it that other ethnic groups, who have also suffered from poverty and discrimination, nevertheless obtain significantly higher test scores?

SES and style of parental interaction

In any Western country with a significant black minority, that minority is poorer and suffers from greater social hardship than the white majority. Since IQ is correlated with SES in the white population, and in the USA at least, where more plentiful data are available, similar (although slightly smaller) correlations are observed between IQ and socio-economic status in blacks (Jensen, 1998), it seems to follow that part of the difference in average IQ between blacks and whites could be accounted for by this massive difference in their social circumstances. Both Jensen (1998) and Rushton and Jensen (2005) have acknowledged that these differences may be relevant, but have insisted that they can do no more than nibble at the edges of the IQ gap, since blacks and whites matched for SES still differ by at least nine or ten IQ points.

This ignores a point made in Chapter 12, that differences in IQ between children from different social classes are caused not so much by differences in their economic circumstances as by differences in cultural aspects of their home and in their parent's behaviour. It seems possible that many white parents' attitudes towards their children, and the way they interact with them, are conducive to the development of high IQ scores, while black parents are likely to have different attitudes and styles of interaction, which may contribute to their children's lower test scores. Phillips *et al.* (1998) found that when differences in HOME scores (see Chapter 12), and other measures of parental interactions with their children, were taken into account, the gap between white and black children's test scores was reduced to some five IQ points.

Moore (1986) compared the IQ scores of black or mixed-race children adopted either by black or by white middle-class families. Her results are shown in Table 13.5. As can be seen, the children adopted by white families obtained IQ scores some 10–15 points higher than those adopted by black families. This is a substantial difference, nearly as large as that found between blacks and whites in the general US population at that time. On the face of it, the implication is that, for whatever reason, children brought up in black families are

Table 13.5 IQ scores of black and black-white children adopted by black and white families (data from Moore, 1986, Table 2).

		Adoptive family	
		Black	White
Children	Black	103	118
	Black-white	106	117

disadvantaged when it comes to taking an IQ test, and Moore's observations on the different ways in which the two groups of adoptive parents interacted with their children when they were attempting to solve a block design problem from the WISC adds further support to this suggestion. The study was not without its problems however. The children were only 7 years old, and a follow-up when they were teenagers would be informative. There may have been differences between the biological parents of the two groups of children. Although the two groups of adoptive mothers were well matched for educational level, the fathers were less well matched, and there may, of course, have been other, unmeasured differences between the adoptive families. But Moore's study certainly suggests that black and white parents differ in the way they interact with their children, and that this contributes to the difference in their children's test scores. Recall from Chapter 12 that while lower SES white children are estimated to have heard some 20 million words by the age of 3, poor black children will probably have heard only 10 million (Hart and Risley, 1995).

An earlier study (Willerman *et al.*, 1974) also pointed to the importance of parental behaviour: they looked at two groups of mixed-race children, one with white mothers and black fathers, the other with black mothers and white fathers. The former group had test scores some nine points higher than the latter. On the assumption (surely reasonable for that time) that mothers spend more time interacting and socializing with their children than fathers, this finding is entirely consistent with Moore's data.

Is the gap disappearing?

To the extent that differences in black and white children's test scores are attributable to differences in their social circumstances, any improvement in black families' social and economic circumstances should ensure an improvement in their children's test scores. It is here that the environmentalists' position has been thought to be weakest: surely there have been massive changes in the socio-economic circumstances of African-Americans in the USA since 1960, but the difference in average test scores, it is said, has remained stubbornly fixed at about one standard deviation. That there have been significant improvements in the relative social circumstances of American blacks over the past 50 years is certainly true. As long ago as the late 1980s, the discrepancy between black and white incomes was significantly reduced when they were matched for educational qualifications (Jencks, 1992); indeed, according to Herrnstein and Murray (1994) the discrepancy was virtually abolished when they matched for IQ. And there is good evidence that discrepancies in educational qualifications have greatly diminished, with a substantial decline in the proportion of blacks dropping out of high school, down from 28% in 1970 to 15% in 1988 (Jencks, 1992), and an equally substantial increase in the proportion attending university (Herrnstein and Murray, 1994).

Have these changes had any effect? They have certainly improved African-American scores on many standardized tests of educational attainment. Several American studies, employing different samples of black schoolchildren and students, have confirmed that the discrepancy in attainment in maths, science, vocabulary, and reading decreased by about 0.30 to 0.40d between the 1960s and the 1990s (Grissmer *et al.*, 1998; Hedges and Nowell, 1998; Herrnstein and Murray, 1994). For reasons which remain rather unclear, these gains seem to have slowed down or even ceased altogether after 1990, but they remain important, for many practical purposes rather more important than the question whether the gap in IQ scores has or has not diminished. But Jensen (1998) and Rushton and Jensen (2005) insist that, in spite of the substantial correlation between tests of scholastic attainment and IQ, a decrease in the size of the black-white gap on the former does not prove that there has been any reduction in the gap on the latter.

In the adult standardization sample of the WAIS-R, tested in 1981, the black-white difference was still 14.6 points. This is, of course, hardly an appropriate measure of the impact of changes in educational and family circumstances, many of which had started only 10–20 years earlier, as a result of the civil rights legislation of the 1960s. But Huang and Hauser (1998) reported a significant decrease in the gap between black and white scores on a short vocabulary test, and more recent standardizations of the Wechsler, Stanford-Binet and the Armed Forces Qualifying tests confirm that the gap has indeed narrowed (Dickens and Flynn, 2006). Their data are shown in Figure 13.1.

A notable feature of these data is that black gains on the WAIS are considerably smaller than those on the WISC. The reason for this is that blacks tend to fall further behind whites as they grow older: on the WAIS, black gains were twice as large for those under the age

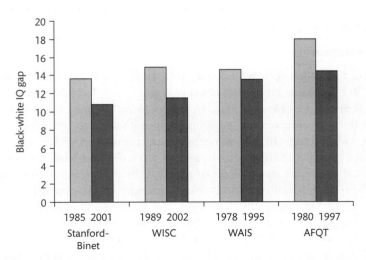

Figure 13.1 The gap between black and white average IQ scores in successive standardizations of the Stanford-Binet, Wechsler, and Armed Forces Qualifying Test (data from Dickens and Flynn, 2006, Table A1).

of 25 as for the entire adult sample, and on the latest standardization of the WISC-IV, the gap between black and white children increased from about five points at age 5–7 to about ten points at age 12–15. So Figure 13.1 underestimates the extent to which young African-Americans have caught up with white children. Flynn (2008) has argued that as they grow older black children tend to fall under the influence of black culture, which may place less value on academic achievement. But there is an alternative explanation of this finding. The 15-year-olds in the WISC-IV were not only ten years older than the 5-year-olds; they were born in 1987, not in 1997. If the gap between blacks and whites has been steadily decreasing over the past 20 years or more, then black children born in 1987 would have scored more than five points below whites even at the age of 5. Just as the Flynn effect means that at any given point in time 60-year-olds will obtain a lower score on Raven's Matrices than 20-year-olds, without that necessarily implying that scores on Raven's decline as people get older; so here, if the black-white gap has been narrowing, this could help to explain why, at any given point in time, older black children will do worse than younger ones.

It has seemed tempting to some environmentalists to extrapolate these trends into the future, and to conclude that in 20, 50, or however many years' time, the gap between black and white test scores in the USA will have disappeared. That may or may not be true. There is one unwelcome factor that may prevent it, however (Flynn, 1992). In Chapter 1, I summarized evidence showing that, for most of the twentieth century, there appears to have been a small negative correlation in the USA between IQ and fertility: by and large, adults of lower IQ tended to have rather more children than those of higher IQ. The effect is not large, and has clearly been counteracted by others that have caused a steady rise in test scores. But there is also evidence that this 'dysgenic' tendency has been larger in some ethnic minorities, including blacks, than in whites (for example, Retherford and Sewell, 1988; see also Flynn, 1992; Herrnstein and Murray, 1994). If that is true, it is likely to have worked against any factor tending to reduce the average black-white difference in the past, and may continue to do so in future.

Specific environmental differences

Although dismissive of most traditional environmental explanations of black-white differences in test scores, such as those that appeal to differences in family background and social class, or to factors unique to the experience of African-Americans—a past history of slavery, white racism, minority status, etc., Jensen (1998) does in fact allow a small but significant contribution from what he calls 'nongenetic biological factors'. By these he means prenatal, perinatal, and immediately post-natal variables, such as maternal age and health, maternal nutrition, smoking and drinking during pregnancy, premature birth, low birth weight, etc. The National Collaborative Perinatal Project (Broman et al., 1975) identified a number of such variables that correlated significantly with 4-year-old IQ scores and also differed between blacks and whites. Excluding those such as maternal education (which, since it is certainly correlated with maternal IQ, is probably partly a genetic factor), Jensen's own conclusion was that these environmental variables probably explained about one-fifth of the difference in test scores between blacks and whites in this study, that is, some three IQ points.

To give some examples: infant mortality rates in the USA are about twice as high among blacks as among whites. Infant mortality is presumably the end point of a continuum of more or less serious prenatal and perinatal pathology, and this implies that black infants probably suffer from many other disadvantages. One obvious one, significantly associated with low IQ, is low birth weight (defined as below 2,500 grams), which is also about twice as prevalent in blacks as in whites. Finally, white mothers are more than twice as likely as black mothers to breast-feed their babies, and breast-feeding benefits many children's test scores (Chapter 12), being particularly beneficial for low birth weight infants (Lucas *et al.*, 1992).

Flynn (2008) has identified a quite different factor that may have a differential impact on black and white children's test scores. Children brought up by a single parent tend to obtain lower test scores than those in two-parent families. In the studies cited by Flynn, the deficit ranged from 5 to 10 IQ points. But the impact of this disadvantage is far greater for the black population than for the white, since in 2002 nearly three times as many black children as white were being brought up in single-parent families in the USA (63% vs. 23%). To forestall those who would attribute this discrepancy to the feckless irresponsibility of black mothers, Flynn pointed to an alternative, rather grimmer explanation. Between the ages of 20 and 45, more than one-third of black males have more or less disappeared from the marriage market: 19% have died, 8% cannot be traced in any records, and 12% are in prison. So, for many black females the choice is stark: either no children or bring them up without a partner.

Conclusion

What is the answer? Is the black-white test score gap (in the USA) entirely due to genetic differences between the two populations, as Lynn (2006) appears to believe? Or is it 80% genetic in origin (Rushton and Jensen, 2005)? Or is it caused by some unknown mixture of genetic and environmental factors (Herrnstein and Murray, 1994)? Or is it entirely environmental (Nisbett, 2005)? There is surely ample reason to reject the 100% genetic hypothesis, and no better reason to accept Rushton and Jensen's estimate of an 80:20 split between genes and environment. Most (perhaps not all) of the genetic evidence reviewed above was consistent with a negligible genetic contribution, and there is rather good evidence that a variety of environmental factors have contributed to the difference in average test scores, which is, at last, now smaller than it was 50 years ago. One could reasonably defend Nisbett's argument that the gap was entirely environmental in origin. But it would probably be even more reasonable to acknowledge that the evidence is simply not sufficient to provide a definitive answer one way or the other—and possibly never will be. Note that this is *not* the same as the answer given by Herrnstein and Murray, who did not doubt that there is some genetic contribution (it is only the magnitude of that contribution about which they were agnostic).

Other ethnic groups

Although the difference in IQ between blacks and whites in the USA has often dominated discussion, it is not the only difference between ethnic groups in average IQ. Quite apart from the national differences, and those between the indigenous populations of different parts of the world, discussed briefly at the beginning of this chapter, there have been numerous studies of the test scores obtained by various ethnic minorities and the majority white population in Europe and North America. Once again, most of the data come from the USA, where differences have been reported between the majority, white European population and American Indian (Native Americans), Latinos (from Cuba, Mexico, and Puerto Rico), and people of Japanese or Chinese ancestry.

A rather longer historical view of the experience of other ethnic groups in the USA may also help to put the black-white difference in test scores in better perspective (Flynn, 1992; Sowell, 1981). At one time or another virtually every group of recent immigrants has been found intellectually wanting. The World War I Army data established that Italians, Poles, and Russians obtained test scores little better than those of blacks. And since at least half the immigrants from Poland and Russia were Jewish, Brigham (1923, p. 190) argued that these data 'disprove the popular belief that the Jew is highly intelligent' (Brigham was of course completely wrong, see Chapter 1). Other studies in the 1920s, cited by Sowell (1978), reported average IQ scores below 90 for Slovaks, Greeks, Spanish, Portuguese, Slavs, Croatian, and Lithuanian immigrants. Irish and Italian immigrants remained most suspect. Although the peak rate of Irish immigration to the USA had been in the middle of the nineteenth century, the Army test data revealed that the test scores of the Irish were below those of every other north European group, and higher only than those of immigrants from southern and eastern Europe. Italian immigrants continued to be a cause for concern and gloom throughout the 1920s and 1930s. Even though the vast majority of Italian immigrants arrived before World War I, Italian children in New York schools still obtained IQ scores well below the national average, and dropped out of school at an earlier age with fewer qualifications than other groups. Few commentators found this surprising: immigration from Italy had been overwhelmingly from the poor, rural south; it was only to be expected that the children of illiterate peasants should remain illiterate. Since they obtained poor scores not only on verbal, but also on non-verbal, IQ tests, and since other non-English-speaking immigrant groups obtained very much better scores on the latter type of test, a common interpretation was that they had inherited their parents' inferior mental capacities (see Sarason and Doris, 1979).

In so far as the descendants of any of these groups could still be identified, by 1960–1970 they were all obtaining IQ scores of at least 100 (Sowell, 1978). What seemed, to an earlier generation of commentators, to be immutable defects of innate character and intellect had blown away as though they had never been. It is a cautionary tale, worth bearing in mind when similar pronouncements are made about the intelligence of American blacks, some of whom were still living in strict segregation in the rural south as recently as the 1960s, and many of whom have continued to receive their education in effectively segregated schools.

East Asians

In the past 25 years, a new group difference has threatened to displace that between blacks and whites as the main focus of American attention and concern. Several commentators have argued that just as blacks lag behind whites, so do whites lag behind one other ethnic or racial group, often referred to as East Asians, more specifically meaning mostly Chinese and Japanese, and to a much lesser extent (since fewer data are available) Korean and

Vietnamese. Vernon (1982) reviewed earlier American studies, some dating back to the 1920s, of children of Japanese and Chinese origin, mostly resident in Hawaii and California. He concluded that although such children had always scored lower than whites on verbal IQ tests, by 1980 this gap was no more than two or three points at most, and since their non-verbal IQ scores had always been some 10–12 points higher than their verbal scores, in the more recent studies they were now obtaining non-verbal scores of 110 or more, well above the white mean. Flynn (1992) argued, rather convincingly, that Vernon's analysis of the earlier American data was misleading, and that up until 1960 or 1970, children in America of Japanese or Chinese origin were not obtaining test scores any higher than the white mean. The largest single study, the Coleman report (1966), showed an average verbal score of 97.6, and a non-verbal score of 99.7. It would indeed have been rather remarkable had they been obtaining test scores above the white mean in the earlier part of the twentieth century. Like other immigrant groups, the Chinese and Japanese initially suffered poverty and discrimination, exacerbated in the case of the Japanese from California by the outbreak of World War II, when they were deprived of much of their property and confined in prison camps (Sowell, 1981). But there is certainly reason to believe that in more recent years they have been obtaining test scores rather higher than the white mean (Herrnstein and Murray, 1994; Jensen and Whang, 1993; Lynn, 1996b). Flynn (2007) concluded that these more recent studies suggest an advantage ranging from eight points in young children to three points in adolescents. He also made the point that one reason for this is that their parents were more likely than the parents of white children to have a college degree and a professional job (see below): arguably, therefore, their test scores should be compared to those of high SES whites.

The data for Chinese and Japanese in China and Japan are also somewhat confusing, since there are questions about how well some tests have been standardized in those countries. A careful and impressive study by Stevenson *et al.* (1985) of children from schools in three cities, one American, one Chinese, and one Japanese, chosen to be reasonably comparable, found that 6-year-old American children tended to obtain higher test scores than either Chinese or Japanese children, while at age 11 there was essentially no reliable difference between the three groups. More recent data, on the other hand, summarized by Lynn (2006), suggest that the average IQ of Chinese and Japanese in China and Japan may be some five points above the white mean of one hundred.

Regardless of whether Chinese and Japanese obtain higher *overall* test scores than whites, a consistent feature of many of these studies is that they obtain higher scores on 'non-verbal' than on verbal tests. This can hardly have seemed surprising in the earlier American studies, given that the children of Chinese or Japanese immigrants would have been living in homes where the first language was not English. But according to Vernon (1982), the discrepancy was just as great when the children spoke only English. The difference was still observed in later American studies, and also in studies of Chinese and Japanese in China and Japan (in for example the Japanese standardization of the WISC-R, see Lynn, 1982). But what does 'non-verbal' mean? In practice it sometimes refers to the performance half of the Wechsler scales, sometimes to tests of Gf, such as Raven's Matrices, and sometimes to tests of visuo-spatial ability or Gv. It is on these last tests (including the WISC block design test) that the difference is most marked (see, for example, Lynn, 1982; Nagoshi and Johnson, 1987). Over all studies, Lynn (2006) calculated the difference between verbal and visuo-spatial scores as 12 points for Chinese and Japanese in China and Japan, and 4.4 points for those resident in the USA.

What is the explanation of this pattern of results? Could it be due to cultural differences between European and East Asian societies? Detecting the differences between the several thousand ideograms of written Chinese or Japanese might put a premium on visuo-spatial discrimination, but this can hardly be responsible for the difference observed today in the USA. Nisbett (2003) argued that cultural differences between West and East actually make tests such as Raven's Matrices and some spatial tests *harder* for Americans of Chinese or Japanese origin. I consider his argument below. There are in fact two reasons for suspecting that their strong spatial abilities may be at least partly genetic. First, there is some evidence that Native Americans, a group genetically related to East Asians, show a similar difference between verbal and visuo-spatial test scores (Lynn, 2006). Second, and much more directly, in a small study of Korean children adopted by middle-class Belgian families, Frydman and Lynn (1989) found that the children obtained substantially higher scores on the performance than on the verbal scale of the WISC (with the highest score of all on block design), a pattern of results strikingly similar to that observed by Lynn (1982) in the Japanese standardization of the WISC.

Test bias

As I noted earlier, one popular reaction to the discovery of group differences in average test scores has been to blame the tests, or the way they are administered. If blacks obtain lower average IQ scores than whites, this must be because the tests contain items that are somehow unfair, or because the experience of being tested somehow impairs blacks' performance. In his book *Bias in mental testing* (1980), Jensen presented some apparently convincing arguments against this position. He dismissed claims that blacks are poorly motivated, suffer from low self-esteem, or perform badly only when tested by a white examiner. Since then, however, a new argument has appeared on the scene: stereotype threat.

Stereotype threat

Steele and Aronson (1995) gave part of the Graduate Record Exam (GRE) to black and white Stanford University undergraduates, matched for SAT scores, under two different conditions. For one group the test was presented as a reliable measure of their intelligence; for another it was said to be simply a set of problems recently devised by the experimenters, who were interested to know what the participants thought of them. The white students obtained similar scores under both conditions, but the blacks obtained significantly worse scores when the test was presented as a measure of their intelligence. Steele and Aronson explained this striking finding by suggesting that the black students were all too aware of the stereotypical view that blacks are less intelligent than whites, were threatened by this thought when asked to take an intelligence test because they feared that they would confirm the stereotype, and were thus unable to concentrate on the test.

As Sackett *et al.* (2004) have pointed out, some commentators have interpreted this finding to mean that the difference in test performance between blacks and whites is abolished when the test is given under unthreatening conditions. This is not what the study showed, nor, of course, what Steele and Aronson claimed. A study of university students (especially at a university such as Stanford) will never tell you that you can eliminate the difference between the test scores of blacks and whites in the population as a whole. In this case, the black and white students had been expressly matched for SAT scores, and their IQ scores would also have therefore been much the same. What the study showed was the black students' GRE scores, unlike the whites', were much worse when they were told they were taking a test of intelligence. That is surely important enough, and implies that the standard procedures for administering IQ tests such as the Wechsler or Stanford-Binet tests to African-Americans, where there is not much pretence that they are anything other than a measure of one's intelligence, can lead to an underestimate of their true ability. The basic result has been confirmed in a number of other studies, including several which have administered standard IQ tests, such as Raven's Matrices (e.g. Brown and Day, 2006). Their results are shown in Figure 13.2. As can be seen, black students obtained lower scores under standard and 'high threat' conditions, when told they were taking either a test of observation and clear thinking (the standard instructions for Raven's Matrices), or an IQ test that provided a reliable measure of their intelligence, while the white students showed if anything the opposite pattern. For reasons noted above, nothing about the difference between blacks and whites in the general American population should be read into the observation that there was no difference between black and white scores under non-threatening conditions. There can be little doubt that stereotype threat contributes to blacks' poor performance on tests of cognitive ability; indeed, it can also affect the performance of other groups on other types of test (see Chapter 14).

Item bias

What of other arguments about bias? Are some items in standard IQ tests unfair for minority groups? The argument seems plausible enough when one stops to look at some

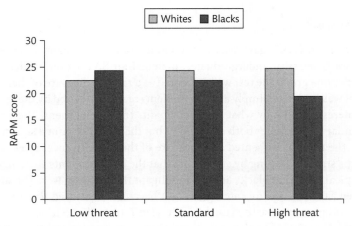

Figure 13.2 The effect of stereotype threat on African-American students' scores on Raven's Matrices (data from Brown and Day, 2006, Table 2).

of the items that actually appear in the Stanford-Binet or Wechsler tests. For example, the aesthetic comparison item from earlier versions of the Stanford-Binet test asked the child to say which of two drawings of faces is the prettier. Block and Dworkin (1976) insisted that this item must discriminate against blacks and other ethnic minorities since the correct answer is invariably the conventional middle-class white face, while the incorrect answer often has features popularly attributed to people from other groups. The comprehension test of the Wechsler scales has equally come in for criticism as a repository of white, middle-class values, with questions that ask for the meaning of various proverbs or what is the right or proper thing to do in certain everyday social circumstances.

However plausible they may seem, few of these arguments withstand serious scrutiny. For example, the standardization of the Stanford-Binet revealed that the aesthetic comparison item was the easiest in the whole test for black children, but only the third easiest for whites (Jensen, 1980, p. 5). Similar analyses of the actual performance of black and white children on various items in the WISC, widely thought to be particularly biased against blacks, have found no evidence that these items are any harder than others for blacks (Gutkin and Reynolds, 1981; McLoughlin and Koh, 1982). There is thus no evidence that these particular items are particularly biased against blacks. Indeed, as is shown in Figure 13.3, the standardization data of the WISC-R made it plain that African-American children obtained, on average, lower scores than whites on *all* tests. The difference was larger on some tests than on others, being particularly small on digit span and symbol, but when one of the largest differences is on the block design test, it is hard to sustain the argument that it is items with transparently white, middle-class values that particularly

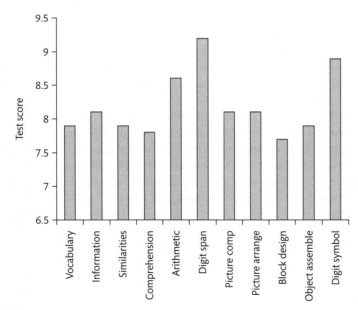

Figure 13.3 Average scores obtained on the 11 tests of the WISC-R by black children in the American standardization sample. A score of ten is the mean test score obtained by the entire standardization sample (data from Gutkin and Reynolds, 1981, Table 1).

discriminate against blacks. There should be no need to pursue this argument further; blacks' relatively poor performance cannot be attributed to a small number of palpably 'unfair' items. Mere inspection of an item in an IQ test is not sufficient to prove that item biased against any particular group. But it is equally insufficient to prove the contrary. The discussion will make no progress until it pauses to ask what it *means* to say that an IQ test is biased against a particular group.

Bias as underestimate of 'true' score

It may help to start by showing what bias does not, and cannot, mean. Taken as a whole, the evidence reviewed earlier did not provide very strong support for the view that differences in IQ between, for example, blacks and whites are substantially genetic in origin. Suppose, for the sake of argument, that new evidence appeared which rendered this conclusion impregnable: a perfectly designed adoption study revealed identical average IQ scores for black and white children brought up in comparable circumstances, and everyone conceded that there is no difference in genetic potential between blacks and whites. Yet there would still be a large difference in measured IQ, for this new evidence would not cause the 5–12-point difference between African-Americans and whites to vanish. Would this not now mean that there must be something wrong with the tests—that they must be biased?

It is important to see just what is wrong with this argument. It contains the unstated premise that IQ tests measure, and are supposed to measure, genetic potential. If this were true then there is no doubt that the conclusion would follow: if IQ tests revealed a difference when none existed, then they would be biased against blacks, for they have underestimated what they purport to measure. But the premise is false: IQ tests do not, and do not purport to, measure anybody's genotypic intelligence. An IQ test provides an estimate of a person's 'intelligence' only if that is understood to mean their actual intellectual accomplishments, knowledge, skills, and abilities, in other words, their phenotypic intelligence. IQ scores are subject both to environmental and to genetic influence, and it is quite possible, therefore, for two people or two groups to differ in phenotypic IQ even though their genetic potential for IQ is exactly the same. Blaming IQ tests for revealing large differences between various groups, as Vernon has remarked, 'is rather like blaming the weighing machine when it shows an undernourished child to be below normal weight' (Vernon, 1969, p. 70). Of course a starved child will weigh less than a well-fed one, and there would be something seriously wrong with the weighing machine that failed to detect this difference; weighing machines are meant to measure what people weigh (phenotypic weight) not their genotype. If IQ scores benefit from a particular environment, and two groups differ in their exposure to that environment, then the group denied exposure will have a lower average IQ than the other. If it is true that black children are often brought up in an environment unfavourable to the development of the knowledge, skills, and abilities measured by standard IQ tests then, of course, they will obtain relatively low IQ scores.

What, then, does it mean to talk about test bias? The proper meaning of bias is quite clear. A test that purports to measure a particular psychological character X is biased against a particular group if it systematically underestimates that group's true level of X. Since IQ tests purport to measure intelligence only in the sense of actual intellectual functioning, they are biased against blacks if they underestimate black people's true level of intellectual functioning: if, say, a black person with an IQ of 85 was in fact performing at the same intellectual level as a white person with an IQ of 100. In order to establish bias, therefore, one needs to ascertain the true level of intellectual functioning of the black population. But how could one do that? It seems to require an alternative, independent measure of intellectual functioning, against which IQ tests could be compared. But what would that be?

There is, of course, no such alternative measure of intelligence. If there were, the question whether IQ tests *really* measure intelligence would have been answered long ago, if indeed anyone had ever bothered to construct an IQ test. All that is available are various more or less imperfect indices of intellectual functioning, for example the traditional criteria against which IQ tests have been validated, such as educational and occupational attainment (see Chapter 9). So all that can be done is to ascertain whether IQ tests underestimate the level of intelligence or intellectual functioning implied by these other indices. Whether that proves that IQ tests are, or are not, biased depends on your views on the validity of these other indices.

Evidence of bias

Since IQ tests were originally designed to distinguish between those children capable of learning effectively in ordinary school classes and those who, for whatever reason, were unable to, performance in school or other assessments of educational attainment have always remained the principal external criterion for validating IQ tests. Thus, if the definition of bias in a test is systematic failure to predict a criterion performance, IQ tests will be deemed biased against blacks or other ethnic groups if they fail to predict how well they do at school.

Despite widespread belief to the contrary, however, there is ample evidence, both in Britain and the USA, that IQ tests predict educational attainment just about as well in ethnic minorities as in the white majority (Herrnstein and Murray, 1994; Jensen, 1980; Mackintosh and Mascie-Taylor, 1986). That IQ tests predict school attainment in whites is established by showing a correlation between the two (Chapter 9). Similar correlations are found in blacks and other ethnic groups. Table 13.6 shows the results of two typical studies. The difference between the overall level of correlation in the two studies (presumably due to differences in the tests employed and perhaps in the ages of the children) is very much greater than any difference between groups within either study.

Table 13.6 shows that, for minority groups as well as whites, a child with a higher IQ is likely to do better on tests of reading and maths than one with a lower IQ. But IQ scores

Table 13.6 Correlations between children's IQ scores and two measures of educational attainment in different ethnic groups in American and British studies.

| | American data (Reschly and Sabers, 1979) | | | | British data (Mackintosh and Mascie-Taylor, 1986) | | | |
	White	Black	Mexican-American	Native American	White	Black	Indian	Pakistani
Reading	0.59	0.64	0.55	0.45	0.74	0.75	0.77	0.75
Maths	0.55	0.52	0.52	0.41	0.74	0.72	0.72	0.74

might still systematically underestimate minority group children's attainments. A black child with an IQ of 100, for example, might do better at reading and maths than one with an IQ of 85, but he might also do better than a white child with an IQ of 100. The possibility can be tested by performing a regression analysis. Figure 13.4 plots the hypothetical scores of a group of white children on an IQ test and on some measure of school attainment. The line drawn through these points is the best-fitting straight regression line to the data, and allows one to predict, for example, that a child with an IQ score of, say, 85 will be likely to obtain a score of 25 on the attainment test, while one with an IQ of 115 would be likely to obtain a score of 45. What will happen if black children's scores are plotted: would their best-fitting regression line fall on top of the white children's, or above or below it? Figure 13.4 shows two possible black regression lines, B1 above, and B2 below, the white regression line W. According to B1, two black children with IQs of 85 and 115 are obtaining attainment scores of 30 and 50, that is, better than those of white children of comparable IQ. With line B2, however, IQs of 85 and 115 are associated with attainment scores of only 20 and 40. If B1 is the appropriate regression line for blacks, their IQ scores do indeed *underestimate* their attainment scores; if B2 is the best-fitting line, IQ *overestimates* attainment; while if their regression line is not significantly different from line W, the IQ scores predict exactly the same attainment scores in blacks as in whites.

The results of a very large number of studies, mostly American but also some British, tell the same story: IQ scores do *not* systematically underestimate the educational attainments

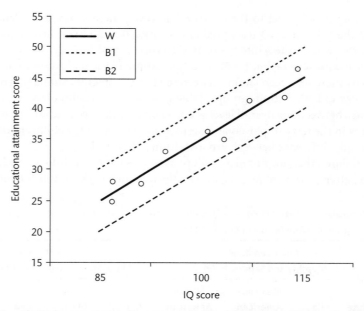

Figure 13.4 Hypothetical scores obtained by a group of white children on an IQ test and on a measure of school attainment. Individual children's scores are shown by the circles. The solid line, W, drawn through these points is the best-fitting regression line. Lines B1 and B2 are two hypothetical regression lines that might be obtained for a group of black children.

of blacks or most other ethnic minorities (Herrnstein and Murray, 1994; Jensen, 1980; Mackintosh and Mascie-Taylor, 1986). The only exception to this generalization is in the case of Americans of Chinese or Japanese ancestry (see below). In the case of blacks and whites, the regression lines relating IQ and attainment tend to be very close. Where there is any discrepancy, it is in the direction of line B2 in Figure 13.4: in other words, IQ scores are, if anything, slightly *overestimating* educational attainment (Jensen, 1980). A similar picture is provided by American data on the relationship between SAT scores, used for college entrance exams, and subsequent performance in college. If college grade point average is used as the measure of attainment, it is predicted by SAT scores just about equally well for blacks and whites (Manning and Jackson, 1984).

There is equally little evidence that IQ tests underestimate blacks' performance on the other traditional criterion used to validate IQ, how well people do their job. IQ scores are used, more commonly in the USA than in Europe, to screen applicants for jobs and to determine job allocation and promotion. Several American studies have sought to justify this practice by examining the relationship between IQ test scores and performance on the job (Hartigan and Wigdor, 1989; Jensen, 1980; Schmidt and Hunter, 1998; see Chapter 9). Over a wide variety of jobs, there is no evidence that test scores show lower correlations with various indices of job performance in blacks than in whites, and no evidence at all of any systematic underestimate of the performance of blacks. As with educational attainment, so with occupational proficiency: where there is any discrepancy, IQ scores *tend* to overestimate job performance (this was true in 60 of the 72 studies reviewed by Hartigan and Wigdor, 1989). It should be stressed that the criterion employed in these studies is usually some index of how well a particular job is being performed, not the status of the job itself. In the quite recent past, blacks often needed higher qualifications than whites in order to obtain a job in the first place. In Great Britain, for example, there was ample evidence in the 1970s of discrimination against blacks in employment, such that a black youth needed significantly better educational qualifications than a white to obtain the same job (Mackintosh and Mascie-Taylor, 1986). Darity and Mason (1998) have reported similar evidence of discrimination in favour of employing white over black job applicants in the USA.

It is of some practical importance to know that IQ scores predict both educational attainment and occupational performance just about as well for blacks as they do for whites, and certainly do not usually *underestimate* black people's proficiency in these areas. IQ tests are still used for purposes of selection in both cases, and if it turned out that they discriminated against black applicants by underestimating their performance, such use would clearly be unjustified. But the point from which this discussion started was not the practical question whether the use of IQ tests for selection is or is not fair; it was whether they are biased against blacks in the sense of underestimating their true level of intellectual functioning. There is an important sense in which this question remains unanswered. True, the data on educational and occupation attainment do not provide any positive evidence of bias against blacks. But it is, after all, entirely possible that educational attainment is just as serious an underestimate of blacks' true level of intellectual performance as are IQ tests themselves. This is hardly a fanciful suggestion: it is not difficult to think of reasons why black schoolchildren might not do as well at school as their abilities dictate. There is ample scope for discrimination and oppression to affect what children actually manage to achieve at school or students at university. Indeed, there is good evidence that teachers' expectations and attitudes have a greater effect on children's performance in school than on their IQ scores (see Box 13.3). If teachers do indeed have a low opinion of the abilities of black children (and they do, see Ferguson, 1998; Mackintosh and Mascie-Taylor, 1986; Weinstein *et al.*, 2004), they are more likely to depress their educational attainment than their IQ scores. It follows, therefore, that actual educational attainment might well be an even more biased measure of black children's intellectual competence than an IQ test.

BOX 13.3 'Pygmalion in the classroom'

The notion that IQ scores could be affected by teachers' expectations was popularized in a once celebrated study *Pygmalion in the classroom* (Rosenthal and Jacobson, 1968), which purported to show that children's IQ scores would increase dramatically if their teachers were led to believe that a special test administered to all children in their class had identified these particular children as 'late bloomers' due to show a marked spurt within the next year. Sure enough, a small number of the late bloomers did show a greater increase in IQ than control children. Although the study achieved widespread fame, it is hard to take it seriously. For one thing the IQ tests were administered by the teachers themselves rather than by a trained tester; thus a teacher who had been told that a particular child should show an increase in IQ over the year was at liberty to ensure that just such an increase occurred. And some of the IQ scores obtained, which ranged from 0 to over 200, must mean either that the test was not being administered properly or that it was an absurd one. More important, although several ingenious and better controlled studies established that a teacher's expectations can significantly affect a child's general performance at school, few have supported Rosenthal and Jacobson's claim that IQ scores can be so affected (Snow, 1995; but see Rosenthal, 1994, for a spirited defence). According to Snow's analysis, the median effect in 16 later studies was to increase IQ by only 0.4 of a point.

The reason for mentioning this somewhat discredited old study is to document the fact that teachers' expectations may well have an impact on their children's academic achievement, if not on their IQ. Given that at least some teachers have rather low expectations of their black pupils' academic ability, it becomes less surprising that black students' IQ scores may overestimate their measured academic achievement.

To round out the picture, it is worth looking at the case of people of Chinese and Japanese ancestry in the USA. For a long time now, they have been one of the most successful groups in American society, obtaining significantly higher educational qualifications and more prestigious jobs than whites. Today, although they comprise no more than 2% of the American population, they constitute 20% of students at Harvard and 45% of students at Berkeley (Nisbett, 2009). As long ago as 1980, the US census showed that 35% of Chinese and Japanese adults had college degrees compared to only 17% of whites, while 43% of Chinese but only 27% of white adults held professional, managerial, or technical jobs (Flynn, 1992). Going even further back, Weyl (1969) analysed the 1960 census and showed that even then Chinese Americans were substantially over-represented in all professions except law. Flynn calculated that these achievements were commensurate with average IQs of 120 and 110 for Chinese and Japanese respectively, relative to a putative white mean of 100. In other words, given the known relationship between IQ and achievement in the white population, a group of whites that matched Chinese in terms of actual achievement would have an average IQ of 120. But no one has suggested that the average IQ of Chinese or Japanese is more than 105, and at least some of this difference between them and whites is due to superior spatial ability. It follows, therefore, that IQ tests are substantially *underestimating* Chinese and Japanese intellectual accomplishments, at least as these are measured by educational and occupational success. Does this mean that IQ tests are biased against them?

As noted earlier, the differences between Western and Eastern cultures summarized by Nisbett (2003) included the following: Westerners look at objects in isolation from their background, Easterners always attend to the context as well; this means that Westerners are more field independent than Easterners; Westerners assign objects to taxonomic categories, Easterners categorize objects by the use to which they can be put; Westerners think logically and conclude that if two propositions contradict one another, one must be wrong, Easterners look for a way of resolving the contradiction, for example by supposing that one proposition may be correct today, but the other will be tomorrow. This is all a gross oversimplification, but it will suffice for present purposes, for it should suggest the possibility that Western IQ tests might favour Western modes of thought and discriminate against Eastern ways of thinking. Classification by taxonomic category is what you are required to do to get the right answers in the Wechsler similarities test; the embedded figures test requires field independence, and the Wechsler block design test shares features with it, requiring you to see how a complex pattern can be constructed from component parts. Nisbett reports a study in which American and Chinese college students and old people were given the sort of speed, short-term memory, and general knowledge tests that appear in many IQ test batteries. The Chinese and American participants were carefully matched for their performance on these tests. They were also tested on items similar to those found in Raven's Matrices and Cattell's Culture Fair tests. On these tests the Americans outscored the Chinese by approximately 0.80d. In other words, these tests of Gf significantly *underestimated* Chinese participants' intelligence as measured by the other tests administered in the study. A reasonable conclusion would be that many Western IQ tests *are* in fact biased against the Chinese. Even though they obtain at least as high scores as white Americans on those tests, their 'true' level of intelligence is even higher, perhaps as high as Flynn's estimate of 120.

There is, of course, another possibility. If two measures, here IQ tests and educational qualifications, give different answers, one certain implication is that they cannot be measuring exactly the same thing. To conclude that IQ tests underestimate Chinese Americans' true level of intelligence implies that educational qualifications are a better measure of their intelligence than are IQ tests. That might be true. But another possibility is that educational qualifications are not solely dependent on intelligence. Hard work, diligence, and ambition may be equally important ingredients of educational (and occupational) success (see Chapter 9). Flynn (1992) and Nisbett (2009) have argued convincingly that it is differences in characteristics such as these between European and Chinese or Japanese Americans, rather than any difference in cognitive ability, that are responsible for their success (see Box 13.4). That seems at least as plausible an interpretation as the suggestion that IQ tests are underestimating their true level of intelligence.

> ### BOX 13.4 East Asian achievement
>
> It is not an easy matter to provide documentary evidence for the proposition that the reason for the superior academic and occupational achievements of East Asians is because they work harder. But work harder they certainly do. According to Nisbett (2009), children in Japan spend on average 60 more days a year in school than children in America. High school students in Japan spend three and a half hours a day studying, compared to one and a half hours a day spent by American high school students (while black students in a study in Detroit spent two hours a *week*). It really does seem likely that these differences help to explain why Japanese schoolchildren can, for example, outscore Americans by 1.30*d* on tests of mathematics (Stevenson *et al.*, 1990).

Adaptive behaviour

Are educational attainment and job performance the only possible criteria against which to validate IQ tests? Surely not. Consider one other use to which the tests have been put—the diagnosis of learning disabilities. According to the World Health Organization, an IQ of 50–70 (approximately) is indicative of mild disability, 35–50 of moderate, 20–35 of severe, and below 20 of profound disability. Earlier classifications added a borderline category in the IQ 70–85 range.

An IQ below 70 is two standard deviations below the mean of 100, and if IQ were normally distributed you would expect some 2.5% of the population to fall into this category. But if African-Americans used to have an average IQ of 85, an IQ of 70 is only one standard deviation below the mean, and you could expect to see some 16% falling into this category. It is difficult to take seriously the suggestion that one in six African-Americans could or should ever have been classified as mildly disabled or worse. And in practice, for a long time now an IQ score alone has not been a sufficient criterion (Detterman *et al.*, 2000): many years ago the American Association on Mental Deficiency defined mental retardation as 'significantly sub-average general intellectual functioning existing concurrently with deficits in adaptive behavior' (see Meyers *et al.*, 1979). A variety of scales have been developed for the assessment of adaptive behaviour; although they differ in their emphasis, they usually include measures of language development and communication, some cognitive skills, such as telling the time or counting money, the ability to interact and cooperate with others in social settings, and the ability to look after oneself: feeding, dressing, etc. (Meyers *et al.*). The reliability of these scales is satisfactory, but, except where they include particular emphasis on language and communication, their correlation with IQ is rarely more than 0.50. Indeed, Mercer and Lewis (1978) reported a correlation of only 0.09 between IQ and performance on their Adaptive Behavior Inventory for Children.

On the face of it, many of the skills assessed by such scales seem more important than an IQ score in determining whether a person is able to live an independent life, outside any sort of institutional setting. In that sense, then, the scales have a certain face validity as an independent measure of intellectual disability or competence. For present purposes, the critical observation is that the relationship between IQ and measures of adaptive behaviour differ in whites and at least some other ethnic groups. Mercer (1973) reported that if IQ alone was used as a criterion of disability, ten times as many blacks as whites would have been classified as disabled; if adaptive behaviour measures were added to IQ, this difference completely vanished. In other words, blacks and whites with similar, low IQ scores differ in measures of adaptive behaviour, with blacks significantly superior to whites.

Here, then, for the first time is evidence that IQ tests *may* be biased against blacks. Certainly, from a practical point of view, this evidence suggests that IQ scores, taken alone, would seriously overestimate the proportion of blacks that should be diagnosed as intellectually disabled and that is an important enough implication in its own right. But it may seem only natural to take the next step, and say that this proves that IQ scores underestimate blacks' true levels of 'intelligence'. Before doing so, it is important to see what is implied by this step: it presupposes that adaptive behaviour scales provide a *better* measure of intelligence than do IQ tests. Whether that is true will surely depend on your definition of intelligence. It may be wiser to accept that the discrepancy simply proves that the two must be measuring rather different things.

Adaptive behaviour scales are intended to measure people's competence in a variety of everyday settings and tasks. People are not born with such competence; they presumably acquire much of it by learning. If black and white children of comparably low IQ differ in competence, this suggests that they may differ in how readily they can learn such simple tasks. Put another way, although blacks and whites may differ in average IQ, they may *not* differ in some aspects of the ability to learn. This may well be true. Black and white students who differed in average scores on a standard IQ vocabulary test, did not differ in their ability to learn the meaning of new words (Fagan and Holland, 2002). More generally, blacks and whites do not differ in speed of paired-associate learning: indeed, if anything, black children are often better at such a task (e.g. Hall and Kaye, 1980). Laboratory measures of associative learning, that is, paired associate learning, do correlate with IQ, but the correlations are often quite modest (see Chapter 5); and measures of incidental or implicit learning are actually wholly uncorrelated with IQ (Chapter 9).

The implication is that differences between some ethnic groups may be confined to only certain aspects of intellectual functioning. The difference between Japanese or Chinese and whites seems to be most marked on one particular group of IQ tests, namely those measuring spatial ability. That between blacks and whites is wider than this, being seen in most types of IQ test, but is still restricted to IQ: there may little or no difference in other aspects of cognitive functioning, which are not measured by IQ tests but which, in some respects at least, are of at least as much practical value. This conclusion is surely of both practical and theoretical importance and, one might have supposed, would be quite welcome to many critics of IQ tests, who have often insisted that the tests fail to measure important aspects of cognitive function. In fact, it has been widely ignored.

Conclusion

Some psychologists have gone to great lengths to show that there are substantial differences in measured intelligence between different populations of the world. While it is certainly true that African peasants and Australian aboriginals, for example, typically obtain substantially lower test scores than white Europeans or North Americans, it requires an astonishing insensitivity to the possibility of cultural differences to conclude that this establishes that they are less intelligent. IQ tests may do a reasonable job of measuring important aspects of intelligence in the populations for whom they were designed (North American and European whites), but other cultures clearly have quite different concepts of intelligence.

The most widely studied group difference in IQ is surely that between blacks and whites in the USA. The difference is usually described as one of 15 points, but it was probably greater than that at one time, and is rather smaller today, at least in young children. In spite of claims to the contrary, there is remarkably little evidence that the difference is genetic in origin: when brought up in *relatively* comparable environments black and white children usually obtain relatively similar test scores; and studies of the degree of white ancestry in American blacks suggest that this has little or no impact on test scores. By contrast, there is quite good evidence that several environmental factors, prevalence of low birth weight, breast-feeding, and especially style of parental interaction, do contribute to the difference in test scores.

There are other ethnic group differences in IQ scores. Chinese, Japanese, and Koreans seem to obtain higher scores than whites on spatial IQ tests, and may obtain higher scores on other non-verbal tests. One small adoption study suggests that this difference may have a genetic basis.

A popular argument is that differences between different groups are not due to real differences in intelligence, but merely reflect bias in the tests. It is worth reiterating and elaborating one or two points that have been made, some implicitly, some explicitly, in the earlier discussion of bias. To say that IQ tests are biased against a given group is to say that they underestimate, in that group, whatever it is that IQ tests purport to measure. IQ tests purport to measure intelligence, but since it is not clear what intelligence is, and there exists no independent measure of intelligence obviously better than IQ tests themselves, it will not be an easy matter to decide one way or another whether the tests are biased. If it is found that IQ tests do *not* underestimate a given group's intelligence as that is indexed by some other, supposed criterion measure, this does not necessarily absolve IQ tests of the charge of bias: the criterion may be equally biased. Thus, the finding that IQ scores do not underestimate black students' educational achievements does not prove they are unbiased. By the same token, however, there can be no good reason to conclude that IQ tests *are* biased even if they do underestimate achievement by some criterion measure. Perhaps the criterion measure is really measuring something else. That is at least a possible interpretation of the difference between black and white scores on IQ and adaptive behaviour tests: perhaps adaptive behaviour depends on a learning process that is partly independent of IQ. Another example is provided by the case of Chinese-Americans. Their IQ scores seriously underestimate their achievements on the two criteria most commonly used to validate IQ tests. Does this mean that IQ tests are biased against them, that is, that they underestimate their true level of intelligence? That is a possible interpretation (and one implied by some cultural differences between European and Chinese ways of thinking about the world), but it requires one to accept that educational and occupational attainments are at least as good a measure of intelligence as IQ tests are. An alternative and perhaps more plausible interpretation is that achievement at school, university, or in a job depends not only on 'intelligence', but also on hard work, conscientiousness, energy, ambition, and so on (see Chapter 9). In other words these criterion measures are measuring many other things besides intelligence. The important point is that it is not a simple matter to decide whether an IQ test is biased. It requires the evaluation of alternative explanations and the balancing of probabilities, rather than confident, glib pronouncements.

Finally, it is important to remember that most of the discussion of ethnic group differences in IQ has concerned different groups living either in Britain or the USA. Even these comparisons are fraught with problems: as numerous commentators have argued, many of these groups have probably created different sub-cultures, and probably differ in their access to the culture of the white majority. Differences in their test scores may, therefore, reflect differences in their values, attitudes, and beliefs. When one turns to comparisons between different nationalities, North American whites against Australian aboriginals or illiterate peasants in sub-Saharan Africa, these problems surely become insuperable, and render such comparisons completely worthless, and probably pernicious.

Summary

- IQ tests apparently reveal large differences between the scores obtained by the indigenous populations of different parts of the world. It would be rash to conclude that these differences reflect real differences in intelligence.

- Within many countries there are reliable differences in the average scores obtained by members of different ethnic groups.

- Blacks in the USA obtain test scores up to 15 points lower on average than whites. There is little (some would say no) good evidence to prove that this difference is genetic in origin.

- A number of environmental causes of these differences have been identified, and there is some evidence that the gap has narrowed in recent years.

- East Asians obtain test scores at least as high as whites, and probably higher on tests of spatial ability.

- It is difficult to know whether IQ tests are biased against particular groups, if only because proof of such bias would need an independent measure of the intelligence supposedly measured by IQ tests.

Further reading

Heine (2008) is a text on cultural psychology, which has useful sections on cognitive differences between different populations of the world. Luria (1976) is worth reading for the transcripts of his interactions with Central Asian peasants, and Nisbett (2003) has an illuminating discussion of Asian conceptions of cognition. Rushton and Jensen (2005) lay out the case for a significant genetic component to the difference in test scores between Americans of European and African origin. Their article appeared in a special issue of the journal *Psychology, Public Policy, and Law*, and was followed by a number of commentaries. The edited book by Jencks and Phillips (1998) has chapters attempting to explain the difference, usually in environmental terms. Flynn (1992) analyses older data on Asian-Americans' test scores; his 2008 book contains interesting analyses of black-white differences in the USA.

Sex differences

Introduction

There have, of course, been exceptions, but on the whole IQ testers have a fairly honourable record when it comes to the question of whether males and females might differ in intelligence. To anticipate: the general consensus has always been that there is probably no reliable difference in overall performance on general IQ test batteries; although still disputed by some, with certain qualifications that consensus seems justified. At the same time, the consensus has suggested that there *are* significant and, in a few cases, substantial differences in performance on certain components of IQ; that seems indisputable (even if that has not stopped some people disputing it). Although it has not always attracted so much attention, there also seems to be a reliable difference in *variability*, with more males than females found both at the upper and at the lower end of the distribution of test scores. The interesting question is: what is the explanation of these results?

The equality of the sexes: fact or artefact?

This record has not always been acknowledged:

> The one exception to the general rule that different groups or populations usually differ in average IQ is that both sexes have approximately the same average IQ on most tests. This is not, however, a true empirical finding but a consequence of the manner in which the tests were first constructed... the two sexes were *defined* to have equal intelligence rather than *discovered* to have equal intelligence.

> (Evans and Waites, 1981, p. 168)

This is a popular argument, endorsed by other commentators (e.g. Rose *et al.*, 1984). But it is a serious misrepresentation of the history of IQ test construction.

Like many men of his generation, Francis Galton had little doubt, even if less evidence to justify his prejudice, that men were more intelligent than women (see Gould, 1997, for entertaining examples of nineteenth century male opinion of female intellect). Neither Burt nor Terman, however, shared this prejudice. Both believed, moreover, that the question of any possible sex differences in intelligence was amenable to straightforward, empirical enquiry. Burt and Moore (1912) devised a variety of tests for measuring perceptual, motor, associative, and reasoning processes in various samples of schoolchildren of both sexes, and correlated the scores they obtained from their tests with assessments of the children's 'general intelligence' provided by their teachers. They found several differences in their test results, some haphazardly favouring boys, others favouring girls, but most very much smaller than the differences measurable in physical characteristics. The one consistent trend was a significant negative correlation between the size of the sex difference on a test and that test's correlation with teachers' assessments of general intelligence, leading Burt and Moore to conclude that 'the higher the process and the more complex the capacity, the smaller, on the whole, become the sex-differences' (Burt and Moore, 1912, p. 379).

That there was essentially no difference between the sexes in general intelligence was confirmed by Terman. Contrary to the implication of Evans and Waites's remarks, there is absolutely no evidence to suggest that either Terman, or Binet before him, had given any thought at all to the question of possible sex differences in deciding what items to include or exclude from their tests. The result was, as Terman wrote in his introduction to the Stanford-Binet test, that he could use the scores of his standardization sample of approximately 1,000 boys and girls, aged 4–16, to provide an empirical answer to the question:

> Many hundreds of articles and books of popular or quasi-scientific nature have been written on one aspect or another of this question of sex differences in intelligence; but all such theoretical discussions taken together are worth less than the results of one good experiment. Let us see what our 1,000 IQs have to offer towards a solution of the problem… When the IQs of the boys and girls were treated separately there was found a small but fairly constant superiority of the girls up to the age of 13 years, at 14, however, the curve for the girls dropped below that for boys… however the superiority of girls over boys is so slight… that for practical purposes it would seem negligible.

(Terman, 1916, pp. 69–70)

Subsequently, the question of sex differences did receive some consideration during construction of new tests. In their introduction to the first revision of the Stanford-Binet, Terman and Merrill wrote: 'a few tests in the trial batteries which yielded largest sex differences were early eliminated as probably unfair' (Terman and Merrill, 1937, p. 34). And Wechsler, commenting on Terman and Merrill's procedure, merely reported 'we have done the same' (1944, p. 106). But the effect of this was not to abolish all sex differences in performance, and in the Wechsler-Bellevue test (the forerunner of the WAIS) as in the original Stanford-Binet, there remained a small difference in overall scores in favour of women, leading Wechsler to say: 'We have more than a "sneaking suspicion" that the female of the species is not only more deadly but also more intelligent than the male' (Wechsler, 1944, p. 107).

The claim that IQ tests were *designed* from the outset to yield equal scores for the two sexes is simply untrue. Terman thought he was making an empirical discovery in 1916 and, whatever the generality or validity of his conclusion, he was surely right. It seems possible that his original finding of essentially no difference between the two sexes had some influence on the subsequent practice of test construction, justifying the rejection of occasional items or sub-tests that seem to run counter to the general rule. The revised version of the Stanford-Binet, on the other hand, found a small but consistent difference in favour of males, which Terman and Merrill attributed to problems with the standardization sample. But unless he and Wechsler were carefully concealing what they were up to, their initial tests *discovered* that there were no more than trivial differences in overall IQ between the sexes.

Are there sex differences in overall IQ (or *g*)?

Having set the historical record straight, the obvious next step is to ask whether Terman's and Wechsler's original conclusions were correct. What do subsequent test batteries say? In what might seem to some as evidence of male conspiracy, later revisions of the Wechsler scales, from the WISC-R and WAIS-R on, have found clear evidence of a slight but statistically significant overall male superiority. The differences in the original standardization samples for the two tests were very small, 1.7 points for the WISC-R and 2.2 for the WAIS-R (Jensen and Reynolds, 1983; Reynolds *et al.*, 1987); but they are still present in more recent standardizations. And Lynn (1994) reviewed a number of other large-scale studies of the Wechsler tests which consistently found significant male superiority, amounting to about three points on various versions of the WAIS. The Spanish standardization of the WAIS-III found a male advantage of 3.6 points. There can be little doubt that the sex difference on the Wechsler tests is reliable, that is, statistically significant and slightly larger for adults on the WAIS than for children on the WISC (see Box 14.1).

BOX 14.1 Are men more intelligent than women because they have larger brains?

Chapter 6 reviewed evidence showing a modest correlation between head circumference or cranial capacity and IQ, and a slightly stronger one between brain size measured by MRI and IQ. There is also reasonably good evidence that men and women differ in average brain size: indeed the difference appears to be substantially larger than that between whites and blacks (Rushton, 1992; Rushton and Ankney, 1996). There are problems in making appropriate allowance for differences in body size between males and females, since there is also a correlation between brain size and body size. However, this is not sufficient to account for the difference in brain size.

Lynn (1994) has argued that this difference in brain size supports his claim that men are more intelligent than women, just as Rushton and Jensen (2005) argued that the black-white difference in brains helped to explain the difference in their intelligence. In the present case, however, the female brain appears to compensate for its smaller volume by being more convoluted, and therefore having at least as great a surface area of cortex (Luders *et al.*, 2009b).

Anyway, is it possible to draw any inference about differences in IQ between two groups from evidence of differences in their brain size plus evidence of a within-group correlation between brain size and IQ? It is a rather simple matter to show that you cannot. Two other correlates of IQ are longevity (Chapter 8), and criminal behaviour—criminals have a lower average IQ than the rest of the population (Chapter 9). Men, however, have a shorter life expectancy than women, and the large majority of criminals are male. By Lynn's argument, therefore, women should be more intelligent than men.

But is this evidence of male superiority confirmed by other test batteries? Figure 14.1 shows that it all depends: some test batteries show a male advantage, others a female advantage. As with the Wechsler data, the differences are mostly small, but because the data are from large standardization samples, they are usually significant. What is one to make of

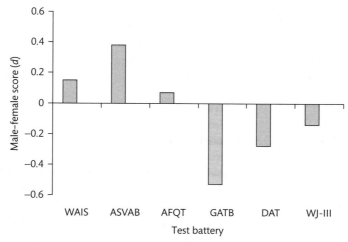

Figure 14.1 The difference between male and female scores on different test batteries, expressed in standard deviation units (*d*): scores above zero indicate male advantage, and below zero female advantage. The WAIS data are from the standardization sample of the WAIS-R (Reynolds *et al.*, 1987); ASVAB = Armed Services Vocational Aptitude Battery (from Jensen, 1998); AFQT = Armed Forces Qualifying Test (a sibling comparison, from Deary *et al.*, 2007a); GATB = General Aptitude Test Battery (from Jensen, 1998); DAT = Differential Aptitude Test (Feingold, 1988); WJ-III = Woodcock-Johnson III (from Keith *et al.*, 2008).

this pattern of results? One implication is that the question whether the two sexes differ in overall IQ is uninteresting, because if by overall IQ is meant the average score obtained on a large diverse test battery, the answer given will depend on the battery. But that is not the same as saying the approximate equality of the sexes is an artefactual consequence of a deliberate decision to balance items favouring one sex with others favouring the other. On the contrary, the wider implication is a more interesting and important one, namely, that the concept of 'overall IQ' may not always be a very useful one.

This is indeed a position endorsed by Jensen, who has argued that 'the simple sum or mean of various subtest scores is a datum without scientific interest or generality' (Jensen, 1998, p. 536). Instead, he argued, the only meaningful answer to the question whether there is a sex difference in intelligence is to see whether males and females differ in the general factor, *g*, derived from factor analysis of a battery of IQ tests. He concluded that they do not, but in fact two of the data points in Figure 14.1, those for the AFQT and for WJ-III test batteries, are precisely *g*-factor scores, and one shows a very small but significant male advantage, and the other a small but significant female advantage. Jensen's argument presupposes that a *g*-factor score is somehow more real, and invariant across different test batteries, than is a simple sum of people's scores on different tests in the battery. It is not obvious why this should be so: Chapter 7 gave some reasons to believe that the general factor from one test battery is not always the same as the general factor of another: *g* necessarily depends on the precise tests included in the battery.

None of this, however, explains *why* different test batteries should give such different results. The answer must be that they are not all measuring exactly the same thing. Test batteries contain a wide variety of different types of item (see Chapter 2), and what both

Terman and Wechsler also found is that, although the overall difference between the sexes was trivial, there were some items or tests on which females did considerably better than males, and others on which males consistently obtained higher scores than females. This has been abundantly confirmed in subsequent studies. Any overall difference between males and females will therefore depend on the precise mix of items included in the test battery.

Sex differences in particular abilities

Both Terman and Wechsler found that males tended to outscore females on tests of mental arithmetic and spatial reasoning, while females outscored males on some verbal tests, immediate memory, and perceptual speed. These differences have been confirmed with other tests of these sorts of abilities. One example is the Differential Aptitude Test battery (DAT). The sex differences for 18-year-olds found in the 1980 American standardization sample for five of these tests are shown in Figure 14.2. As can be seen, females outscored males on the two verbal tests and on the speed test, while males outscored females on the two spatial tests. Moreover, the differences are not trivial, ranging from about 3 to over 13 IQ points. Figure 14.3 shows similar data compiled by Hedges and Nowell (1995) from five large-scale American surveys. Here, with the exception of mechanical reasoning, the differences are rather smaller, but are still mostly significant. It might seem that the male advantage on a measure of mechanical reasoning is something of an outlier, but another test that gives an equally large male advantage is three-dimensional mental rotation (3-D MRT): are the two shapes shown in Figure 4.4 (p. 86) the same or not? In a very large number of studies, males have outscored females by some 10–12 IQ points, a difference of at least $0.75d$ (Masters and Sanders, 1993).

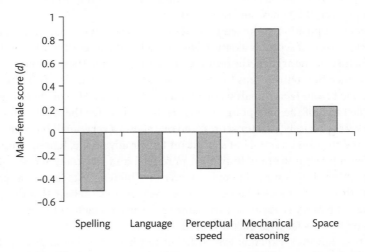

Figure 14.2 The difference between 18-year-old male and female scores on five of the DAT tests (data from Feingold, 1988, Table 1).

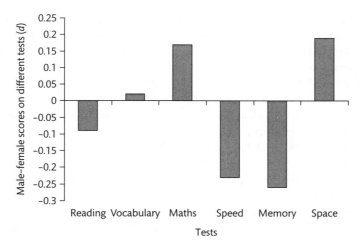

Figure 14.3 The median difference observed in different studies between male and female scores on various different tests (data from Hedges and Nowell, 1995, Table 2).

There can be little doubt that males and females do differ in particular cognitive skills or abilities. The precise nature of these differences, let alone their causes, is still a matter of substantial dispute, and I will discuss some of these details below. For now, it is sufficient to argue that these differences in various components of general intelligence are sufficient to explain the differences between the results of different test batteries. A test battery, for example, that emphasizes spatial and mathematical items will yield a male advantage; one that emphasizes some aspects of language, perceptual speed, and memory will favour females.

Differences in Gf

Factor analysis of IQ test batteries had already revealed that IQ tests measure a number of partially independent abilities (Chapter 2). To that extent there is no great puzzle in finding that males outperform females on some of these abilities, while females outperform males on others. But factor analysis also established that tests of abstract reasoning or Gf are closer to g than are other tests and in the diagrammatic representation of Figure 2.5 (p. 53) lie at the centre of the IQ space. Rather than ask whether males and females differ in overall IQ, or even in g, therefore, it may be more useful to ask whether they differ in Gf. The question seems simple enough. Alas, the answer is rather less simple.

The earliest, and still most widely used, measure of Gf is Raven's Matrices. Lynn and Irwing (2004) and Irwing and Lynn (2005) have reported two meta-analyses suggesting that after the age of 15 there is a male advantage amounting to some 0.30–$0.35d$ or 4–5 IQ points. This is probably an exaggeration, since it ignores the difference between younger and older adults: Lynn and Irwing (2004) reported that the male advantage in people over the age of 40, at $0.32d$, was twice as large as that seen in 18–19-year-olds ($0.16d$). I discuss some possible reasons for this below.

What of other tests of Gf? A Spanish study of some 600 applicants to university suggests that Raven's Matrices may be unusual in yielding evidence of male superiority (Colom and Garcia-Lopez, 2002). The male advantage on Raven's was 0.28d; on Cattell's Culture Fair tests it was only 0.10d (and not significant); while on the inductive reasoning test from Thurstone's PMA test battery, there was a significant female advantage of 0.19d. The DAT, which has been standardized at frequent intervals in several countries, includes three reasoning tests, verbal, abstract, and numerical, on none of which have males consistently obtained higher scores than females. Instead, successive restandardizations of the test in Britain and the USA have shown a rather more interesting pattern—an earlier male advantage giving way to a more recent female advantage (Feingold, 1988; Hyde and Trickey, 1995). The results for 18-year-olds in three American standardizations are shown in Figure 14.4. In 1947, males obtained higher scores than females on all three tests; in 1980 male and female scores were virtually identical; by 1990, females were outscoring males on two of the three. British standardizations of the DAT show a similar pattern (Hyde and Trickey).

What is to be made of these conflicting findings? One conclusion is that data from the middle of the last century are quite unreliable indicators of the position today. This may help to explain why, in Lynn and Irwing's (2004) meta-analysis, male superiority on Raven's was more pronounced in older than in younger adults. A second conclusion is surely that males are not innately superior to females in reasoning ability. If Gf is closer to g than any other group factor, a third is that there are probably no innate sex differences in general intelligence. And this conclusion is not dependent on a judicious selection of items designed to achieve overall balance between those favouring one sex and those favouring the other. There is no evidence of any such policy having dictated the construction of any of these reasoning tests. A final point worth noting is that the male advantage on Raven's Matrices is not necessarily found on all items within the test (see Chapter 4; Lynn *et al.*, 2004; Mackintosh and Bennett, 2005).

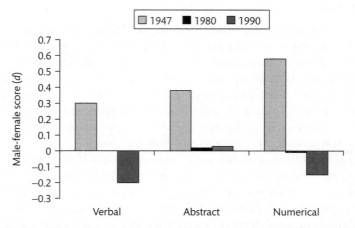

Figure 14.4 Differences between 18-year-old male and female scores on the three reasoning tests from the DAT, in the 1947, 1980, and 1990 standardization samples (data from Feingold, 1988, Table 1, and Hyde and Trickey, 1995, Table 13).

Differences in variability: myth or reality?

It is a commonplace observation that, throughout history, men have more often risen to positions of power and influence than women, and that more men than women have become famous for their achievements in art, music, literature, or science. One striking example: of 557 recipients of Nobel prizes for science up to 2006, all but 12 were male (Deary *et al.*, 2007b). Cultural attitudes, social expectations, females' opportunities (or lack thereof), and male power provide such an obvious explanation for these differences that it might seem perverse to look for any other. But some IQ testers (mostly male) have not hesitated to do so. As several have noted, even a small difference in mean IQ in favour of males would translate into a large difference in the proportion of males and females with an IQ over 140. But the explanation more commonly advanced to account for the existence of more eminent men than women has been the suggestion that there is greater variability among males than among females. The implication is that even if there were no sex difference in average IQ there would be more males than females with an IQ over 140 and, equally, more males than females with an IQ below 70.

In the first serious attempt to measure the variability in IQ of boys and girls, Terman (1916) found no evidence of any difference. But once again his conclusion has been questioned by data from the revised Wechsler scales, where the standard deviation for males is some 5% greater than for females (Jensen and Reynolds, 1983; Reynolds *et al.* 1987).

Although there have been exceptions to this general rule, other general test batteries have usually found more variation in males' than in females' scores, even if the differences have often been slight—less than 3% in Lubinski and Humphreys's (1990) study, and less than 1% in Herrnstein and Murray's (1994). But in a study of over a thousand pairs of opposite-sex siblings who had taken the AFQT, Deary *et al.* (2007b) reported that there were almost twice as many males as females in the top 2% of scores. The Scottish mental surveys of 1932 and 1947, which tested some 80,000 11-year-olds, produced an equally clear result (Deary *et al.*, 2003): boys were over-represented by a factor of 1.4:1 both in the top (IQ > 130) and in the lowest (IQ < 60) band. Similar results were observed in an even larger study of over 300,000 British 11–12-year-old children (Strand *et al.*, 2006). Arden and Plomin (2006) have shown that this difference in variance appears even earlier: they tested children aged 2, 3, 4, 7, 9, and 10 years old. At every age except 2 and 9, the variance in boys' scores was significantly greater than in girls'.

Greater male variance has also been found in tests of more specific abilities. Hedges and Nowell (1995) reported that 34 of 38 different measures showed greater male variability. Feingold (1992) reported that males were more variable than females on four of eight tests of the DAT. The exceptions included the verbal and abstract reasoning tests, a result consistent with many studies of Raven's Matrices, which have also found little or no evidence of greater male variance (Court, 1983; Irwing and Lynn, 2005). The most consistent and reliable difference in variability seems to be in the area of numerical reasoning and mathematics. For example, Lubinski and Humphreys (1990), in their study of some 100,000 American 16-year-olds, reported that boys not only obtained overall maths scores about 0.20*d* higher than girls, the standard deviation of their scores was about 8% greater. The data for this study were collected in 1960, and there is good evidence that the difference in *average* scores has decreased sharply since then, to the point where, at least on some tests, girls may outscore boys (Hyde *et al.*, 1990). Nevertheless, Hyde *et al.* continued to find evidence of greater variability in males, with the consequence that there were more males than females in groups of above average ability. As one instance of this, Benbow (1988) reported that in junior high school students scoring above the mean for college entrants on the SAT-M, there were twice as many males as females, and in the top 5%, this ratio increased to 12 to 1. While this difference has decreased since then, it was still 3:1 in an analysis reported by Spelke (2005).

Analysis of verbal, mathematical, and spatial abilities

The conventional wisdom has been that there is a female advantage in verbal ability, offset by a male advantage in mathematical and spatial ability. Enough empirical research on these abilities has been undertaken to show that this is a serious oversimplification (for reviews see: Ceci *et al.*, 2009; Halpern, 2000; Halpern and Collaer, 2005). By contrast, there has been little or no research into the question why females should do so much better than males on tests of perceptual speed and short-term memory. Readers may make of this what they will.

Verbal ability

Hyde and Linn (1988) conducted a meta-analysis of some 150 studies of verbal abilities. For studies published before 1973, the effect size was $0.23d$ in favour of females, for those published since then, the difference was less than half this, $0.10d$. This seems hardly large enough to be of practical significance, and Hyde and Linn concluded that 'gender differences in verbal ability no longer exist'. One reason why the difference was so small, however, is that in the largest single study included in their survey, of close to one million students taking the SAT-V, males actually obtained slightly higher scores than females. Unlike other tests of verbal ability the SAT-V includes a high proportion of verbal analogy problems.

This suggests that Hyde and Linn's conclusion is misleading, because it blurs distinctions between different measures of verbal ability. It is true, as can be seen in Figure 14.3, that towards the end of the twentieth century there was essentially no difference between males and females on tests of vocabulary; but in the DAT data shown in Figure 14.2, there were large differences in favour of females, amounting to nearly $0.50d$, on two linguistic tests, spelling and language. Halpern (2000) has summarized other data showing that females also outscore males on a variety of measures of language production: they make fewer errors when talking or writing, speak more grammatically, pause less often in their speech, and discriminate more accurately between speech sounds (although few of these skills are measured in conventional IQ tests), and are substantially less likely to stutter or be diagnosed as dyslexic. One measure that does appear in some test batteries is of verbal fluency, for example, give the names of as many flowers as you can, or Christian names beginning with the letter C, in 30 seconds. Here the female advantage is approximately $0.35d$.

As shown in Figure 14.3, there is no real difference between males and females in vocabulary, except at very young ages, since there is good evidence that young girls learn to talk sooner than boys, and have acquired a larger vocabulary by the age of 2 or 3 (Fenson *et al.*,

1994; Huttenlocher *et al.*, 1991). Rather remarkably, the old WISC and WAIS verbal scales yielded evidence of slight male superiority, but that was largely because they included arithmetic and information tests, on both of which males outscored females.

One implication of all this, of course, is to reinforce a conclusion reached earlier (see Chapter 4): 'verbal ability' is hardly a unitary construct.

Mathematics

In most universities, most professors in mathematics departments are male. As a possibly extreme example, in 2007 there were 61 full professors of mathematics at Cambridge University, of whom only one was a female. Why? Larry Summers, then President of Harvard, speculated that it might be partly because, even if there was no difference in *average* aptitude for mathematics between men and women, men's greater variability meant that there was bound to be a preponderance of males at the top (and bottom) of the distribution. In spite of the furore his remarks caused, the data reviewed above suggest that he was right.

A meta-analysis of studies of sex differences in mathematical performance (Hyde *et al.*, 1990) concluded that men were not only more variable than women, but also obtained higher average scores on some, but by no means all, tests of mathematics. The largest single data set came from the SAT-M, taken by American high school students, where the overall male advantage was 0.40d, and the ratio of male to female variance was 1.15:1.

More informative is the breakdown of the other data of Hyde *et al.* by age and type of measure. Some of their findings are shown in Figure 14.5. The first thing to note is that many (although not all) of the differences were trivially small, even zero. But two further points are apparent: up to the age of 14, girls rather consistently outscored boys, but thereafter males started creeping ahead; second, the earlier female advantage was most evident in computation, while the later male advantage was most evident on measures of

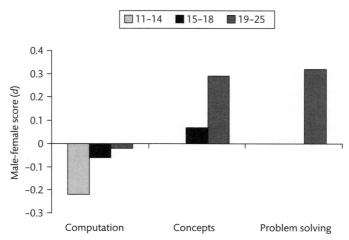

Figure 14.5 Differences between male and female scores on different types of maths tests as a function of age (data from Hyde *et al.*, 1990, Table 4).

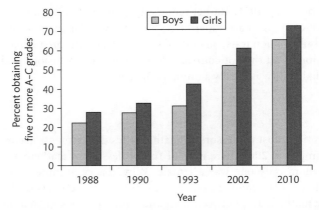

Figure 14.6 The percentage of boys and girls in England obtaining five or more A–C grades (the government target for satisfactory performance) in their GCSE exams between 1988 and 2010.

mathematical problem solving. That girls should tend to obtain better scores than boys up to the age of 12–14 or so should come as no great surprise: this was true, after all, in the original Stanford-Binet test (Terman, 1916) and has been confirmed in studies of Raven's Matrices (Lynn and Irwing, 2004) and the DAT (Colom and Lynn, 2004). It is, of course, also well established that, at age 16, girls obtain higher scores than boys in virtually all subjects (including mathematics) taken for GCSE exams in England (see Figure 14.6). The picture is the same in the USA, where equal numbers of males and females now take advanced high-school maths courses, and females now obtain higher scores (Gallagher and Kaufman, 2005).

What is the difference between those measures of mathematical performance on which there is no sex difference after the age of 14, and those on which males seem to outscore females? Computation involves performance of basic operations, while problem solving requires the application of mathematical techniques to new situations. Geary (1998) has argued that the male advantage here stems from their superior spatial ability, since the solution to many such problems benefits from the ability to translate a verbal description into a visuo-spatial representation. There is good evidence that in many (but not all) samples, scores on the SAT-M correlate significantly with performance on 3-D MRT, and that the sex difference in SAT-M performance can disappear when MRT scores are taken into account (Casey *et al.*, 1995; Nuttal *et al.*, 2005).

In a vigorous attack on the idea that there is any sex difference in mathematical ability at any age, Spelke (2005) has argued that the SAT-M should not be regarded as *the* perfect measure of mathematical ability, and is in fact probably biased against females. She might, of course, be right. But how could one settle the question? As I argued in a slightly different context in Chapter 13, only by finding an alternative, better measure of mathematical ability, which revealed equivalent performance by men and women. According to Spelke, such a measure is provided by high school and college mathematics exams, where there is no evidence that males significantly outscore females. It is a moot question whether this is sufficient to prove Spelke's point: females do better than males at virtually all exams, both at school and at college or university. As was the case with the discrepancy between IQ scores and measures of educational attainment in Americans of Chinese origin, so, here, one might argue that this means that females are more intelligent than, and have just as much aptitude for mathematics as, males. Or that their exam performance is a reflection of some other difference between males and females (see below).

Spatial ability

A meta-analysis reported by Hyde (1981) found an average difference of 0.45d in favour of males on tests of visuo-spatial ability or Gv. But it is clear that the size of the sex difference varies considerably across different kinds of test. For example, in 1980 the DAT space relations test yielded a difference of only 0.15d in favour of males, but the mechanical reasoning test a difference of 0.76d (see Figure 14.1), and by 1995 in the British standardization there was essentially no difference (0.03d) between male and female 18-year-olds in space relations, but still a difference of 0.78d in mechanical reasoning (Hyde and Trickey, 1995). As I discussed in Chapter 4, factor analysis has confirmed that 'spatial ability' is not a unitary construct. Stumpf and Eliot (1995) showed that although one determinant of the size of the sex difference on a particular spatial test was how closely that test correlated with the central factor common to all spatial tests, this was not sufficient to account for the entire pattern of differences. The implication is that the tests were measuring more than one process and that the difference between the sexes was not uniform across the various processes.

This conclusion has been confirmed by the results of two later meta-analyses (Linn and Peterson, 1985; Voyer *et al.*, 1995). Both analyses implied that although men outscored women on all kinds of spatial test, the size of the sex difference varied from less than 0.20d on some kinds of test to over 0.75d on others such as the Shepard-Metzler 3-D MRT task (Masters and Sanders, 1993). Unfortunately, research on sex differences has done remarkably little to elucidate the nature of the differences between various kinds of test, or the differences in the psychological operations they engage.

One question is whether the sex difference observed on tests of Gv translates into differences on other kinds of spatial task. Do males and females differ on *real* measures of spatial skill and knowledge, or are the differences observed only in the artificial paper and pencil tests devised by IQ testers? It depends, of course, on what you mean by a real measure of spatial ability, but the differences are certainly not confined to traditional IQ tests. In a test of geographical knowledge, people can be shown a blank map of the world, with only the borders of each country shown. Given a list of a dozen countries, their task is to fill in their location on the map. Men get more answers right than women (Dabbs *et al.*, 1998). In a route finding task, people can be shown a map of an imaginary small town or village, and asked to learn the shortest route from one point to another. Men on average learn faster than women (Galea and Kimura, 1993). This difference has even been observed in real-world settings: taken outside the laboratory, and asked to find their way round an unfamiliar environment, men learn faster than women (Choi and Silverman, 2003; Saucier *et al.*, 2002). When asked to draw a map of a novel environment they have seen only once, boys' maps are more accurate than girls' (Matthews, 1987).

Since the beginning of the twentieth century animal psychologists have studied spatial learning in mazes and, more recently, in the 'Morris pool' (Morris, 1981): a rat is placed in a circular 2-m diameter pool filled with water and has to find a small hidden platform (which is always in a fixed position relative to the landmarks outside the pool and the room in which it is placed) onto which he can climb to get out of the water. Male rats tend to be better at this task than females (Williams and Meck, 1991). A virtual reality version can be presented on a computer screen, and people asked to find the hidden platform. Men typically learn this task faster than women (Moffatt *et al.*, 1998).

Even more interesting is the reliable finding of a difference in the *way* in which males and females typically solve spatial problems. Male rats are more likely to rely on the geometry of the environment, and females more on local landmarks (Rodriguez *et al.*, 2010). A similar difference is seen in humans. When they are asked to describe the correct route from A to B in a route finding task, men are more likely to talk of distances from one turning to the next and the compass direction in which to turn, while women mention the landmarks that you pass and, to a lesser extent, whether you turn left or right (Choi and Silverman, 2003; Dabbs *et al.*, 1998; Galea and Kimura, 1993). Although memorizing the landmarks you pass as you travel along a route is a perfectly efficient way of learning the route, it should be obvious that it is hardly a specifically *spatial* solution: it simply encodes temporal information about the order in which the landmarks appear. When required to draw a map of a previously seen environment, boys' maps contain more accurate information about the geometrical relationship between different features (Matthews, 1987). When required to find the hidden platform in a Morris pool, men are more likely to use the global geometry of their environment to locate the platform, and women to use one or two local landmarks (Sandstrom *et al.*, 1998).

In Galea and Kimura's (1993) route learning study, the performance of those people, whether male or female, who used directions, distances, and geometrical relationships correlated significantly with their performance on 3-D MRT tasks, while the performance of those who relied on knowledge of landmarks did not. Since, on average, women were less likely than males to show good knowledge of directions and distances, the implication is that males were more likely to be using specifically *spatial* skills (at least those measured by the MRT test) to solve the route learning task. But there is also reason to believe that men and women solve the MRT task itself in different ways: fMRI studies have shown that different regions of the brain are activated in men and women during performance on this test (Hugdahl *et al.*, 2006; Levin *et al.*, 2005). One reading of this evidence is that many females use verbal rather than specifically spatial strategies to solve the MRT task. Johnson and Bouchard (2007) have argued that females use non-spatial strategies to solve a wide variety of supposedly spatial tests, and therefore that the true sex difference in any specifically spatial ability is underestimated by most test results.

There is one striking exception to the general finding of male superiority on spatial tasks. As can be seen in Figure 14.2, women tend to outscore men on tests of short-term memory. An example of this is a test where participants are shown an array of 20 or so different objects; after they have had a minute to study the array, it is hidden and some new items are added to the array. The task is to identify the new ones when the display is shown again. Silverman and Eals (1992), among others, have shown that females are better at this task than males. That is unsurprising. But they were also better than males at a different version of the task, where instead of adding some new items, the experimenter moves some of the items to a different location in the array and your task is to identify the moved items. This is clearly a test of spatial memory, and females were still better than males.

Explanations

What is the explanation of these sex differences in performance on different cognitive tests? A first answer is that there will surely be no single explanation that will cover all cases. Why, for example, should males be more variable than females, so that there are more males than females both at the high and at the low end of the distribution of test scores? It is not easy to imagine how a single factor could be responsible for both these differences. Males are, it is well known, more vulnerable than females, being less likely to survive long enough to be born, and more likely to die sooner even if they do make it to that point. It is not difficult to see how this might lead to a greater preponderance of males at the low end of the distribution, and one genetic explanation of this might be that any harmful recessive gene on the X chromosome will always be expressed in males (who have one X and one Y chromosome) while females (with two X chromosomes) would need two copies for it to be expressed (which is why colour blindness and haemophilia, for example, are more common in males). It is less easy to see how such a sex-linked recessive gene could result in a preponderance of males at the high end of the distribution of test scores, although there has been one famous attempt to provide just such an explanation (see Box 14.2). Environmental explanations for this difference seem more plausible.

BOX 14.2 Spatial ability and the sex-linked recessive gene hypothesis

Any character determined by a recessive gene on the X chromosome will be expressed in any male that carries the gene, but in females only if they carry the gene on both chromosomes. If the frequency of the gene is 50%, it follows that 50% of males but only 25% (0.5 x 0.5) of females will display the trait. If high spatial ability were determined by a single recessive gene on the X chromosome, more men than women would show high spatial ability.

Although surely rather implausible, the beauty of the hypothesis was that it made some quite specific predictions about family resemblances. Sons receive their X chromosome from their mothers and their Y chromosome from their fathers; there should therefore be no correlation between fathers and sons for the trait, and a modest correlation between mothers and sons (only modest because the mother may be heterozygous, and although transmitting the critical recessive gene, may not display the trait herself). Daughters should also resemble their mothers, but less than sons do, since both mother and daughter may carry the gene without displaying the trait. Finally daughters should resemble their fathers more than their mothers, since to display the trait they must have inherited the gene from both parents, and if the father transmitted it he certainly displayed the trait. Indeed the resemblance between fathers and daughters should be the same as that between mothers and sons.

A study by Stafford (1961) reported that familial correlations for spatial IQ were almost uncannily in line with these predictions. What seemed so persuasive was that this pattern of results makes little or no sense from an environmental point of view. The most plausible environmental hypothesis is that familial resemblances will depend on social learning within the family. It presumably, therefore, predicts that sons should resemble their fathers and possibly daughters their mothers. That the

(continued...)

cross-sex correlation should be higher than the same-sex correlation, and that there should be no resemblance between fathers and sons at all, seem inexplicable on an environmental hypothesis. Alas, as T. H. Huxley once remarked, there is no greater tragedy in science than the murder of a beautiful theory by ugly fact. Large-scale replications of Stafford's study, several with hundreds of subjects, have completely failed to confirm the critical pattern of familial resemblance (Boles, 1980).

Test bias

It is worth starting by asking whether any sex difference observed in test scores is simply a consequence of test bias. Do females obtain low 3-D MRT scores, for example, because the test underestimates their true level of spatial ability? I have already provided a partial answer to this question: other, perhaps more realistic, measures of spatial ability, such as map reading and route following, also show females performing less well than males. There seems equally little reason to believe that some of the cases where males do less well than females on tests of language and verbal ability, such as spelling and use of correct grammar, are a consequence of bias in the test.

Evidence of stereotype threat effects on females' performance on tests of mathematics, however, does suggest that such tests may often underestimate their mathematical ability. And one piece of evidence suggests the possibility that IQ tests in general underestimate the true level of female intelligence: a consistent observation, both in Britain and America, is that females outperform males on standard measures of educational achievement (grade point average or GPA in America, and public exams, GCSE and A-levels, in England, see Figure 14.6 above). Since there is no consistent female advantage on IQ tests, do IQ scores underestimate their educational achievements and perhaps therefore their true level of intelligence? Duckworth and Seligman (2006) documented these effects: in two high school studies they showed that the difference between girls' and boys' GPA was over $0.50d$ in favour of girls, while in one case the difference in IQ scores favoured boys. They argued that the reason why girls did so much better than their IQ scores would predict was because they were more self-disciplined. Five different measures of self-discipline, including teachers' and parents' ratings, and measures of impulsivity and delay of gratification, all showed superior performance by girls. When entered into a regression analysis, they accounted for much of the sex difference in academic achievement. As many teachers recognize, it is not that girls are really cleverer than boys, it's that they take schoolwork more responsibly.

Biology

The ubiquity of sex differences in a wide variety of spatial tests, together with the opposite difference that appears on some verbal tests, has encouraged much speculative interpretation. It is obvious enough that boys and girls are treated differently, both by their parents and by the wider society. It is not difficult to see how such differences could eventually produce differences in specific abilities, and there has been no shortage of environmental explanations for such differences. But there has also been a proliferation of more or less 'biological' explanations.

One reason for this is that sex differences in spatial cognition have been observed in very young infants. Moore and Johnson (2008) and Quinn and Liben (2008) reported that male infants showed better discrimination than females between different versions of the Shepard-Metzler 3-D objects used in studies of mental rotation. Another reason is that sex differences in spatial learning and cognition are not confined to people. As noted above, a similar male advantage has been reported in rats (and in a variety of other animals) usually measured by performance in maze learning tasks. An important feature of the animal data is that sex differences in maze learning may be found in some species, but not in other closely related species. This has raised the question: what are the ecological determinants of these differences? The range-size hypothesis says that it is all down to a difference in home range or territory, and this applies to humans because our ancestors were hunter-gatherers (see Box 14.3).

BOX 14.3 The ecology of sex differences in spatial ability

The observation that sex differences in spatial ability are not universal, often being seen in one, but not in another quite closely related, species, opens the way for comparative analysis: are there any particular ecological factors associated with the presence or absence of male spatial superiority? Jones *et al.* (2003) concluded that the best predictor of the sex difference was range size. Where (for whatever reason) males occupy a larger home range than females, they also show evidence of superior spatial ability. In most monogamous species, males and females share the same territory. In polygynous or promiscuous species, on the other hand, where a single male mates with several females, a male's home range or territory will include the home of a number of females. The promiscuous male meadow vole is better than the female at several maze learning tasks (Gaulin and Fitzgerald, 1989), but in monogamous prairie and pine voles, there is no sex difference in spatial learning. Polygynous male deer mice are better than females at spatial learning, but again there is no sex difference in monogamous kangaroo rats (Galea *et al.*, 1994; Langley, 1994).

It is widely believed that our earliest ancestors were hunter-gatherers, and it is clear that in contemporary hunter-gatherer societies men do the hunting while women are engaged in the lower-status (but actually much more productive) task of gathering. Hunting, of course, involves travel over long distances. Thus, over the course of human evolution males would have moved over a wider range of territory than females.

If our ancestors were indeed hunter-gatherers, then it is perhaps less surprising that males should have superior spatial abilities. It is obvious enough that successful hunting will require efficient navigation. Here is one report from an experienced hunter:

> Hunters follow wandering paths in seeking game. They ignore much of the detail of what they pass, and they process and discard much of the information about potential landmarks. In returning home, they prefer using direct routes to retracing their outward paths, and in order to use direct routes they have to know where they are and what direction will take them home.

(Dabbs *et al.*, 1998, p. 90)

Evolutionary psychologists have therefore been happy to trace males' superior performance on various spatial tasks back to our evolutionary origins. The observation noted above, that the parallel between humans and rats extends to a sex difference in the *way* in which males and females solve spatial problems, has encouraged such speculation, especially given that the female strategy of learning a route by memorizing the landmarks is not going to allow a hunter to take the direct route home.

An evolutionary explanation of the origins of a sex difference in spatial cognition in humans may be plausible. But this says nothing about the proximal causes of any such difference. Since one of the major biological differences between the sexes lies in the relative concentrations of the predominantly female hormones, oestrogen and progesterone, and the predominantly male hormones, mostly notably testosterone, it is not surprising that a popular biological explanation of sex differences in cognition should appeal to differences in the relative concentrations of these hormones. Such an explanation is not, in principle, unreasonable, given that these hormonal differences do not just appear at puberty but start prenatally, and that there is ample evidence of hormonal effects on the brain and behaviour (Baron-Cohen *et al.*, 2004). As noted in Chapter 6, there is also, of course, evidence of sex differences in the structure of the brain (see also Box 14.1).

The clearest evidence of hormonal effects on spatial cognition comes from intervention studies in other animals. For example, Roof and Havens (1992) have shown that administration of testosterone to neonatal female rats improves their performance, when adult, on maze tasks, while castration of neonatal male rats has the opposite effect. Even more strikingly, Williams and Meck (1991) reported that these interventions altered the way in which rats solved the problem: treated females were more likely to use geometry, while castrated males were more likely to use landmarks. Unsurprisingly, there have been few such intervention studies in humans, although administration of testosterone to old men has been shown to enhance their performance on spatial tests, in addition to its other more obvious effects (Cherrier *et al.*, 2001); while another study reported that female to male transsexuals administered testosterone as part of their gender reassignment showed an improvement in their spatial ability (Slabbekoorn *et al.*, 1999), and Aleman *et al.* (2004) reported that a single administration of testosterone improved mental rotation scores in young women.

Some natural experiments have tended to support the hormonal hypothesis. Females with congenital adrenal hyperplasia (CAH), a condition resulting in abnormally high prenatal androgen exposure, have sometimes been reported to obtain higher scores on some spatial tests than control females. A meta-analysis concluded that CAH females were better at such tasks than controls, with an overall effect size, $d = 0.43$ (Puts *et al.*, 2008).

The obvious question remains: if hormonal differences are important, how do they achieve their effects on test performance? There is some evidence of an effect on the morphology of the hippocampus (Isgor and Sengelaub, 1998; Roof and Havens, 1992), an area of the brain strongly associated with spatial learning and memory (see Chapter 6). Another possibility is that they affect the development of lateralization of function in the brain. According to Geschwind and Galaburda (1987), high levels of prenatal testosterone slow the development of the left hemisphere, and thus lead to right hemispheric dominance. Since it is generally accepted that in the majority of the population language is predominantly a function of the left cerebral hemisphere and visuo-spatial perception a function of the right (e.g. McCarthy and Warrington, 1990), this might in principle explain why females have an advantage over males in language, while men outscore women on tests of spatial ability.

Environment

Many people find it difficult to accept the idea that sex differences in cognitive abilities might somehow be 'biological', and prefer to point to differences in socialization, sex-role stereotyping, or similar processes. It is important to see that this is often a largely false antithesis. For example, there is no particular reason to suppose that sex differences in lateralization of function, if real, are somehow immutable or hard-wired. According to the 'cognitive crowding' hypothesis (Levy, 1976), they originate in the way parents interact with their children: by talking more to baby girls than baby boys, parents encourage the development of verbal abilities in girls; this results in the spilling over of language functions into the right hemisphere; and the final result is less room for the development of spatial abilities. But why do parents talk to baby girls more than to boys? Perhaps because of a hormonal difference. There is good evidence that males are more aggressive than females, and that hormonal effects are partially responsible for this difference (Halpern, 2000; Maccoby and Jacklin, 1974). If aggression is associated with restlessness, then one reason why baby boys are talked to less than baby girls is simply that they will not sit still long enough.

An alternative hypothesis is that hormones affect children's interests and activities, which then affect their cognitive abilities. A consistent finding from studies of CAH females is that they play more with boys than with girls, prefer boys' toys to girls', and as adolescents and adults are more interested in stereotypically male activities such as sport, and less interested in supposedly typical female activities such as fashion and crafts. To the extent that cognitive abilities are influenced by opportunities to learn, it is hardly surprising that their abilities should follow their interests.

This is, admittedly, merely speculative. Is there any evidence of more direct environmental causes of, for example, sex differences in spatial ability? It is easy to point to differences in parental and societal attitudes and expectations, but here, as elsewhere, environmental correlates are not necessarily environmental causes. What would prove that they were? Intervention studies might be able to do so. Several such studies have shown that spatial skills can be enhanced by specific instruction or education or playing computer games such as Tetris (Baenninger and Newcombe, 1989; Newcombe, 2007). The effects can be large, amounting to an increase of some $0.70d$, that is, about the size of the male advantage on 3-D MRT. But such interventions have rarely, if ever, abolished the sex difference: they are usually equally beneficial to both sexes.

A second approach has been to ask whether sex differences in verbal, mathematical, or spatial abilities are universal, or whether they are confined to a few cultures. If they are not found in other societies, one might want to argue that they must be a product of particular cultural values. A female advantage in the development of reading skills is found in many different countries (Halpern *et al.*, 2005). On the other hand, sex differences in mathematical skills are not uniform across all ethnic groups in the USA (Benbow, 1988), and they are not uniform across all countries (Hyde, 2007). There are, however, few if any exceptions to the general rule that males outscore females on tests of mental rotation. Silverman *et al.* (2007) found that males outscored females on the 3-D MRT test in all seven ethnic groups and in all 40 countries where data were available.

Evidence of an environmental effect on mathematical performance comes from studies of stereotype threat. Women's performance on mathematical problem solving improves if they are told that it is simply an experimental problem rather than a test of mathematical ability (Johns *et al.*, 2005); it suffers if they are told it is a test which typically shows a male advantage, but improves if they are told there is no sex difference, or that if there is one its origins are entirely environmental (Dar-Nimrod and Heine, 2006; Spencer *et al.*, 1999). As was the case with the research on African-American IQ scores, stereotype threat may not provide a complete and sufficient explanation of any sex difference in mathematical test performance, but it certainly shows that some of the difference is readily eliminated.

The best evidence in favour of an environmental account of sex differences in cognitive abilities comes from a relatively consistent pattern of findings that has hitherto been mentioned only in passing. Many sex differences in test performance appear to have declined over the past 50 years. In their meta-analysis of mathematical ability, Hyde *et al.* (1990) reported that the male advantage on the SAT-M had remained constant at $0.40d$ for 20 years or more; more recent data suggest that by 2000 it had decreased to $0.32d$ (Royer and Garofoli, 2005). Going even further back, Hyde and her colleagues found that studies published before 1970 reported larger sex differences than those published after 1970. In the USA, women now obtain nearly half of all BA degrees awarded in mathematics, compared to less than a third 50 years ago. In 1966 only 6% of PhD degrees in mathematics were awarded to women; by the year 2000 this had increased to 21% (Hyde, 2007). Finally, as already noted, in their initial study of young teenagers who obtained scores in the top 1% on the SAT-M, Benbow and Stanley (1983) reported that there were 12 boys for every 1 girl; in some samples, this ratio has now reduced to 3:1 (Spelke, 2005).

The meta-analyses of verbal and spatial abilities undertaken by Hyde and Linn (1988) and Voyer *et al.* (1995) found that here, too, studies published after 1970 or so yielded smaller differences than those published before that date. Although Halpern (2000) has questioned the meaning of this, it certainly suggests that sex differences have decreased in magnitude, and this conclusion is supported by data from successive restandardizations of the DAT between 1947 and 1995 (Feingold, 1988; Hyde and Trickey, 1995). Although there has been rather little change in tests of language and speed, where females obtained higher scores than males, as noted earlier in this chapter, there has been a consistent and substantial decline in male superiority on the two spatial tests, and the complete disappearance (or even reversal) of the earlier male superiority on tests of abstract, verbal, and numerical reasoning.

It is difficult to attribute these changes to any change in the standardization samples. They can hardly reflect changes in, say, relative concentrations of male and female hormones. They must surely be environmental in origin. But as was the case with the secular increase in overall IQ, it is less easy to pinpoint any precise environmental factor, let alone elucidate the manner of its causal action. Most Western countries have undoubtedly seen substantial changes in society's attitudes to women since the 1960s, and it would be perverse to suggest that they have not contributed to these results. But to what extent they have achieved their effects by changing parental behaviour, teachers' behaviour, sex role stereotypes, or self-images may be hard to decide.

Perhaps it does not matter: what is important is that some unnecessary differences have disappeared. But not all; at least on the DAT tests, females' verbal superiority remained substantial; and the difference in favour of males on the mechanical reasoning test remained 10–12 points on an IQ scale. Moreover, other evidence suggests that there has been no

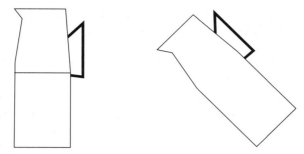

Figure 14.7 The water-level test. Your task is to draw a line representing the surface of the water in the tilted jug. The correct answer is a horizontal line, not one bisecting the jug at right angles to its sides. Significantly more females than males give the incorrect answer.

decrease at all in the size of the sex difference on mental rotation tasks over the past 20 years or more (Masters and Sanders, 1993; Voyer *et al*. 1995). On the 3-D version of this task, the difference was still over $0.75d$, and several more recent studies have continued to report differences of this order of magnitude (e.g. Kaufman, 2007; Mackintosh and Bennett, 2005).

Of course, no one could seriously claim that there are no differences in the attitudes of parents and society towards boys and girls, and it is possible that further changes in society will have yet further effects on the pattern of sex differences. But it would be going well beyond the available evidence to insist that a simple environmental explanation has been found sufficient. It is not easy to see why societal changes should have affected the sex difference on some spatial tests, but had virtually no effect on others. And it does not seem very plausible to suppose that boys spend so much more time than girls pouring water out of jugs that experience alone will explain why about twice as many 10-year-old boys as girls used to pass the water level test shown in Figure 14.7 (see Halpern, 2000). The only sensible conclusion is that there is no complete explanation of the causes of sex differences in various types of IQ test, and those who claim to know what the true cause is, are deceiving themselves.

Conclusion

Some readers will probably have difficulty in accepting that there are any consistent sex differences in any aspects of intelligence, and more will resist all attempts to provide any sort of 'biological' explanation of such differences. Halpern, who does not seek to minimize the role of hormonal effects on the development of the human brain, prefaces her chapter on biological hypotheses with the warning, printed in bold:

> Some of the research and theories described in this chapter may be disturbing to your basic belief systems.
>
> (Halpern, 2000, p. 133)

I do not, I am afraid, share these misgivings. There is a sense in which it can hardly be disputed that the ultimate cause of any sex difference in cognition is genetic: the difference between males and females is, after all, a genetic one, in the vast majority of cases, the possession of two X chromosomes or of one X and a Y chromosome. The question at issue is *how* this genetic difference comes to result in any cognitive difference. It is possible that the visible differences between boys and girls result in their being treated differently from an early age, and as a consequence developing different expectations of life, different attitudes, and interests, all of which contribute to ultimate differences in cognition. The best evidence for this is the observation that at least some cognitive differences have diminished in the past 50 years or more. Others have, however, persisted, and it seems probable that hormonal effects on the development of the brain also contribute to eventual differences in certain cognitive abilities.

Many readers may feel that this chapter (along with Chapter 13) has displayed an unhealthy obsession with the possibility of cognitive or intellectual differences between different groups of people. In the present instance, however, there has been a more important general message. The discussion has strongly suggested that, although it makes rather little sense to wonder whether there is a real difference in *general* intelligence between males and females, there is good evidence that males and females differ in some aspects of the intelligence measured by IQ tests (they also of course differ in some aspects of intelligence *not* measured by the tests, see Chapter 10). Thus, there may be little difference between men and women on many tests of Gf or abstract reasoning, but men outscore women on most tests of spatial ability, while women outscore men on most tests of short-term memory and perceptual speed. The analysis of sex differences suggests some even finer distinctions between different measures: while there may be little or no difference between males and females on tests of vocabulary, males do better on many tests of general knowledge, while females excel on tests of verbal fluency, all of which are usually classified as tests of verbal ability or Gc. Tests of 3-D MRT yield a far greater male advantage than most other tests of spatial ability, while there is a female advantage on tests of object location memory. Even *within* a single test, such as Raven's Matrices, there may be some items that yield a male advantage, and others on which females do as well as males. Even more striking has been the evidence that males and females tend to use different strategies to solve the same problem, with males, for example, more likely to use a genuinely *spatial* strategy to solve both laboratory and real-world spatial problems, and females more likely to use verbal or other strategies.

Factor analysis, of course, has established that any IQ test battery will include a number of partially distinct tests, apparently measuring somewhat distinct cognitive operations, and there is other evidence that different people may use quite different strategies to solve one and the same problem. But the study of sex differences provides, I believe, strong additional evidence of these two points. As such, it seems a fitting conclusion to some of the important themes of this book.

Summary

- The two sexes do not differ consistently in average IQ (different test batteries can show male advantage, female advantage, or no difference), and that conclusion is not simply an artefact of any deliberate policy by IQ testers to eliminate items that favour one sex or the other.

- But males and females do differ reliably in certain components of IQ—the most salient of these differences being that men outscore women on most tests of spatial ability, while women outscore men on tests of perceptual speed and short-term memory.

- Both biological and environmental explanations of the difference in spatial ability have been advanced, but the distinction between the two is not as clear as many writers have implied.

Further reading

Halpern (2000) provides a generally very thorough survey of sex differences, while Halpern and Collaer (2005) review sex differences in spatial ability. Edited books by Gallagher and Kaufman (2005) and Ceci and Williams (2007) contain chapters expressing a variety of views about sex differences in maths and science. Ceci *et al.* (2009) is an excellent examination of these issues. Baron-Cohen (2003) advances a theory of males as 'systemizers' and females as 'empathizers', which ranges more widely but contains some relevant information; Baron-Cohen *et al.* (2004) review evidence on the effects of hormonal differences on the development of the brain.

15 Epilogue

Introduction

The study of human intelligence is surely important: there may be other equally valuable human characteristics, kindness, generosity, loyalty, conscientiousness, or a sense of duty, but it would be silly to pretend that intelligence is not valued. Its study is also interesting, and popular books on intelligence are among psychology's better sellers. Professional psychometricians are apt to bemoan the gap between the message of many of these popular books and that accepted by most, although by no means all, professionals in the field. They want to stress the degree of consensus between professionals, and disapprove of what they see as an irresponsible message being spread by popular writers. But they probably exaggerate and the disagreements are one of the things that make the study of intelligence interesting.

From the beginning, much that was written about IQ testing was intended to have social and political, as well as scientific, impact. Terman was only too anxious to stress the social and political value of the Stanford-Binet test. And Yerkes thought that the Army testing programme provided a unique opportunity to enhance the public status of the fledgling science of psychology, by showing how well IQ could predict at least military competence. The marketing of new IQ tests later became a seriously profitable business, and the success of that marketing depended on claims for the practical utility of the tests. Many of those claims rested on the assertion that an IQ test, taking no longer than an hour to administer, could give a reliable measure of a person's intelligence; that the intelligence so measured was innate and fixed, and was a major determinant of that person's success in all walks of life—of their success in school as a child, of the occupational level and income they could later aspire to, and of the success with which they would perform their job.

Few psychometricians would make *quite* such strong claims today, or at least would modify the language in which they were expressed. But the consensus view they want to stress is not that different. Behaviour geneticists are agreed that the heritability of IQ in adults is probability about 0.80, that the influence of family environment on test scores is essentially zero by the age of 20 or so, and that g is by some way the best predictor of educational and occupational success. I have expressed my own reservations about all these claims throughout several earlier chapters. Perhaps it is time to express some reservations about the claims of the critics. Many of these critics have, in my judgement, done their cause a disservice. Consider this: there can be no serious doubt that the heritability of IQ in modern industrialized societies is significantly greater than zero. Critics who insist on denying this conclusion must be casting some doubts on their own scientific credentials, or at least on their ability to read evidence impartially. More importantly, they must also be sending out a singularly unfortunate message, namely that they believe that dire political consequences will follow from the demonstration that the heritability of IQ *is* greater than zero. The implication is that their conception of the good society is incompatible with there being genetically influenced differences in people's test scores. Do they really believe that? Why? Is it because they have mistakenly identified heritable with immutable, or naively assumed that any environmentally influenced characteristic will readily respond to simple social engineering? Does their reluctance to acknowledge the heritability of IQ extend to other sorts of differences between people—to differences in musical or artistic talent, athletic ability, personality or temperament, personal appearance, or attractiveness to the opposite sex? Is the only just society one consisting of clones? If they single out IQ as the one characteristic which cannot be allowed to be heritable, they are surely investing IQ with even more importance than the most enthusiastic supporters of the tests have ever suggested. They are equating IQ with virtue and merit; they are implying that a high IQ is a necessary prerequisite for any form of success and that a low IQ condemns a person to failure in all walks of life.

This makes it all the odder that so many critics have also insisted, again in the face of good evidence to the contrary, that there is no correlation between IQ and anything else of importance. If IQ scores really are unimportant, why should it matter whether they are heritable? Once again, the implication of the critics' claim is that they fear dire social consequences from any demonstration that IQ scores do predict other things of some social significance. Once again, their cause would surely be better served by acknowledging the probable truth of some moderately well established empirical observations, while questioning some of the more extravagant interpretations that have sometimes been put on those observations.

Use of tests for selection

Arguments about the use of IQ tests in any form of selection, whether for employment or admission to further education, often ignore the fact that the alternative to IQ tests is some other selection procedure. Relatively few employers hire people at random, nor do universities generally admit anyone who applies regardless of their qualifications. It is not that IQ tests are necessarily better than other selection procedures. They may be better in some respects, but worse in others. The point is that many of the issues that need to be discussed are issues about selection, not about IQ.

Where there are more applicants than posts or places to be filled, how will the successful applicants be selected? On a first come, first served basis? Randomly or by lot? At one time the gods could be trusted to see to it that a lottery selected the right winner. Today, we are inclined to believe that we can, and should therefore try to, do better. We believe in selection by merit. But what does that mean? There appear to be, broadly speaking, two distinct approaches: selection on the basis of past accomplishment, or of future potential. In practice, the distinction, like that between tests of achievement and of ability, is notably less clear. It seems only sensible to insist that the accomplishment must somehow be relevant to the position for which applicants are being selected. Only the most eccentric bankers will select their employees by seeing how well they can sing opera arias (although perhaps if they had, they might not have led the world into recession). But what is the reason for insisting on the relevance of past accomplishments other than the belief that, if relevant, they will predict future performance? The reason why doctors are required to pass medical exams is because it is assumed that, in order to practise medicine effectively, they need to have acquired certain knowledge and skills, and that passing the exam is proof they have done so.

Selection by merit, whether past or future, will not differ from selection by lot unless the assessment of merit is moderately accurate. If lotteries are thought to be unjust, therefore, other selection procedures should be valued only to the extent that they are valid. It follows that if an IQ score adds to the predictive validity of a battery of selection tests, an IQ test should be added to that battery. This is, of course, the standard argument of test theory, but it is not an argument specific to IQ tests. It applies equally to any piece of information used for purposes of selection: if that piece of information increases the validity of the selection procedure, it should be used. But the argument is not necessarily quite as persuasive as is sometimes assumed, for there are several problems that need to be borne in mind. For a start, it needs to be recognized that no selection procedure will be perfectly valid, if only because the criterion measure of success is itself often unreliable. It is not just that a supervisor's rating or a brief work sample may provide an imperfect measure of how well an employee is performing. An employee's performance may vary along so many different dimensions that it may be unwise to attempt to capture it in a single rating. One middle-manager may run a section of the company that posts higher profits in a given year; another may be responsible for a major reorganization which, although yielding no immediate profit, promises long-term dividends; a third may be more supportive of her staff, who thus show greater loyalty to the company; and a fourth and fifth may excel in yet other aspects of a manager's job. Although this argument is often an excuse for conservative inertia, it is as well to acknowledge that employers do not always know exactly what they are looking for in applicants for a job, because they do not always know exactly what constitutes success in that job. Concentration on aspects that are easily measured may lead one to ignore others that turn out to be even more important.

There is, however, a more serious consequence of the inevitable imperfection of any selection procedure. It is a simple matter to show that if a particular test is not perfectly valid, its use is almost bound to discriminate in favour of some groups at the expense of others. Imagine a particular test given to members of three groups who are applying for a job. Although imperfect, the test is equally valid for individuals of all three groups, but, as can be seen in Figure 15.1, Group A has a lower mean score on the test than Group B, who score on average below Group C. Figure 15.1 also shows a cut-off score, at Group B's mean: applicants with scores above this cut-off are selected, while applicants with scores below the cut-off are rejected. The test selects a higher proportion of Group C than of A or B, but that, you might think, is right and proper since the test is equally valid for all three groups, and a higher proportion of Group C meets the criterion for selection.

However, the test is not perfectly valid. That is to say, a certain proportion of individuals with scores above the cut-off will actually do worse on the job than a certain proportion of people with scores below the cut-off. The first group were lucky to pass, the

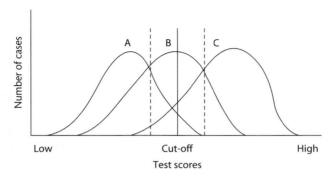

Figure 15.1 Hypothetical distribution of scores obtained by three groups, A, B, and C, on a test used for selecting applicants for a job. The cut-off score for selection is shown by the solid vertical line at Group B's mean: anyone with a score below this cut-off is rejected, and anyone with a score above it is accepted. The two dotted vertical lines on either side of the cut-off encompass a 'zone of uncertainty', where the test has a significant probability of misclassifying applicants. See text for further details.

second unlucky to fail. Such individual cases of injustice are an inevitable consequence of the use of a less than perfectly valid test, and since there is probably no such thing as a perfectly valid test, there is not much that can be done about them. But one should not be so complacent about the systematic injustice done to members of a particular group. To see why such injustice arises, Figure 15.1 shows a 'zone of uncertainty' between the two dotted lines on either side of the cut-off score. Assume arbitrarily that 20% of applicants within this zone of uncertainty were incorrectly placed: that is to say, 10% of those below the cut-off really ought to have been selected, because they would in fact perform the job better than 10% of those above the cut-off. For group B as a whole, these errors cancel out: the number of people below the cut-off that were incorrectly rejected is exactly the same as the number of those above the cut-off that were incorrectly accepted. For Group C, however, the number of incorrect acceptances is far greater than the number of incorrect rejections, while for Group A the number of incorrect rejections is far greater than the number of incorrect acceptances. So use of the test has favoured Group C and discriminated against Group A. There is no need to give real names to these groups to see the social implications of all this.

The discussion of selection sometimes becomes obsessed with the issue of group differences, and whether affirmative action is justified or necessary to counteract them. On the face of it, there is much to be said for the argument that affirmative action or group quotas are unjust, unless there is good independent evidence that the test used for selection is biased against one group and in favour of another. Moreover, the use of group quotas implies that people are being treated as members of a group rather than as individuals, and justice normally requires that people be treated as individuals. Perhaps, in an ideal world, that would be true, although it is not difficult to discern some less lofty motives underlying such arguments, and Figure 15.1 suggests that the argument may be far too simplistic. Moreover, the fact is that people *are* often treated as members of groups, especially when group membership is immediately visible, or otherwise easily ascertained. You may be an excellent driver, not only skilled but also sensible and careful, and thus relatively unlikely to be involved in an accident. But if you are male, under the age of 25, and drive an expensive sports car, you will pay heavily for your insurance. And if you are also black, you are more likely to be stopped by the police on suspicion that the car is stolen, than you would be if you were white, middle-aged, and prosperous looking. Flynn (1996) has argued persuasively that since individual blacks suffer in so many different ways from being treated as a member of a particular group, a small measure of affirmative action in compensation would hardly come amiss.

Whatever your views on these undoubtedly problematic issues, the point to remember is that they are not specific to the use of IQ tests. They concern selection in general, not IQ tests in particular. If IQ tests had never been invented, if their use for any purpose whatsoever were to be banned tomorrow, these issues would not go away. Employers and university admission officers, among others, would still have to decide whether their method of selecting one applicant rather than another was just and fair. They would still need to reconcile fairness to individuals with fairness to groups, and where fairness seemed to conflict with efficiency, they would still have to decide how far to let one win at the expense of the other. The argument often centres round IQ tests, because IQ scores are modestly predictive of success in a variety of settings. But IQ tests are certainly not the only, and not always the best, predictors of success (Chapter 9).

IQ tests and educational selection

It is worth turning from the abstract and general to the concrete and particular. IQ tests have of course been used for purposes of selection; I consider one particular case—the use of the tests for selecting for secondary (high school) education in England. Some critics have seen this as another count against them:

> The IQ test...formed the basis for the selective education system introduced after the Second World War. On the strength of Cyril Burt's enthusiastic argument that a test given to a child at the age of 11 could measure its 'innate intelligence', it was decided to use the results of tests administered to 11-year-olds to 'stream' children into one of three separate—and far from equal—school systems.
>
> (Kamin, 1981, p. 94)

It is certainly true that IQ tests played a part in the 11+ exam in England and Wales, and that after 1944 the results of this exam were used to determine the type of secondary school which a child would attend. But a somewhat longer historical perspective may help to correct the impression given by this quotation (Wooldridge, 1994). Before 1900, the state's provision for public education in England consisted of free elementary schooling up to the age of 12. Secondary schools were fee-paying, with only a handful of scholarships or bursaries. By 1918, the school-leaving age had been raised to 14, and the principle established that there should be a certain proportion of free places in secondary schools, but there continued to be huge differences from one part of the country to another, both in the number of free places and in the procedures used to select children for them. In many cases parental wishes did the job of selection: there was in effect no competition. Where there was, it was done by the headmaster interviewing the parents, with or without their child, or by elementary schoolteachers' assessments, or by some sort of examination, usually of English or mathematics.

It was on this somewhat chaotic scene that IQ tests first appeared. Central government slowly attempted to impose some uniformity both of provision and of selection. The Department of Education received advice from educational psychologists, including Godfrey Thomson as well as Cyril Burt, who argued that IQ tests could provide a more uniform and fairer method of selection. The advice was at least occasionally heeded. By 1945, when the 1944 Education Act had decreed that all children should go on to secondary school and the question was therefore which kind of school they should attend, grammar, technical, or secondary modern, most, but by no means all, local education authorities included some kind of IQ test, as well as tests of English and mathematics, in their 11+ exam.

IQ tests were thus not used to *establish* a system of selective secondary education. That system was already in effect. As late as 1939, only 15% of English children were educated in grant-aided secondary schools. Given that the English system was already highly selective, it is hardly unreasonable to have some sympathy for Thomson's argument that the selection procedure should be efficient and fair. Thomson argued from the very outset, and produced evidence in support of his argument from a study in Northumberland, that IQ tests would succeed in identifying children from deprived backgrounds, or living in remote rural areas, who would otherwise be denied secondary education (Thomson, 1921). Subsequent evidence amply confirmed Thomson's arguments (Vernon, 1957). The classic study was by Floud and Halsey (1957) in Hertfordshire. When the local education authority dropped IQ tests from its 11+ exams, there was an immediate and significant decrease in the proportion of children from working-class families entering grammar schools, and a comparable increase in the proportion of children from professional families. There is equally little doubt that scores on IQ tests predict children's subsequent educational attainments (see Chapter 9), and that, when added to the results of conventional tests of English and arithmetic, they significantly improved the accuracy with which 11+ tests predicted performance at secondary school (Vernon, 1957).

It is not my purpose to attack or defend the varying systems of secondary education prevailing in England at different times since 1900, only to defend IQ tests and their proponents from the charge of *imposing* an unjust system of selection for secondary education, and to suggest that their use was both more valid and fairer than many of the alternatives on offer. Far from being the reactionaries obsessed with social class depicted by Kamin, a more historically informed perspective would characterize people like Thomson and Burt as:

> Meritocrats rather than conservatives and reformers rather than reactionaries. They found their most committed supporters on the left and their most stubborn opponents on the right. They maintained that intelligence testing would open up opportunities and guarantee social justice, and combined a belief in IQ testing with a commitment to a general programme of social reform.
>
> (Wooldridge, 1994, p. 165)

The measure of their eventual success was indeed the 1944 Education Act, which:

> Altered the character and composition of the grammar schools. They ceased to be in part finishing schools for middle-class children of good character and concentrated instead on the education of the ablest—a change which was reflected in numerous complaints that the schools

were being flooded by 'spivs' and 'smart alecks' and that they were losing 'the boy who was not good academically, but who had character, loyalty and other virtues which made him and his kind the backbone of the grammar school [no girls then?]'.

(Wooldridge, 1994, p. 255)

The 11+ exam hardly exists any more in England, although there are still some grammar schools, and from time to time a call for their reintroduction. In so far as there is still selection for free secondary education in England, it is largely done by address: good secondary schools are in middle-class areas where house prices are higher. More formal selection procedures operate at later stages in the educational system, most obviously at entry to university. Not everyone will gain entry to university, especially not to the elite universities. How is admission to be controlled? In America, it has traditionally been through the SAT, which was a multiple-choice test looking a bit like an IQ test. But the SAT has come under increasing fire from those who have lobbied for exams that will test knowledge of the curriculum actually taught in high schools (Atkinson, 2007), and the SAT II does in part now do this. In England, the trend has been in precisely the opposite direction: university entrance has been controlled by A-level exams that are intended to measure knowledge and understanding of the sixth-form (senior high school) curriculum, but there has been increasing dissatisfaction with these exams, and some lobbying for the use of tests of cognitive ability (it would be suicide to call them IQ tests) in addition or in their place. Perhaps the message is that there is no such thing as a perfect selection procedure?

The wider importance of IQ

In their less guarded moments, Herrnstein and Murray (1994) gave the impression that they believed the social consequences of differences in IQ to be of almost boundless significance. They painted, for example, an apocalyptic picture of an American society increasingly segregated by IQ, where a substantial minority of the population was bound, by virtue of its low innate IQ, to live in poverty and squalor, perpetuating a culture of unemployment, crime, drug dependence, and illegitimate births. That there is an 'underclass' in many American cities, the members of which are disproportionately black, is not in dispute. Britain, too, is said to have an underclass, though it is not disproportionately made up of ethnic minorities. The question is how far this lifestyle is to be attributed to low IQ. As many commentators on *The bell curve* (e.g. Ceci, 1996; Fischer *et al.*, 1996; Manolakes, 1997) have noted, Herrnstein and Murray's argument is often oversimplified, and ignores other important factors. Ceci and Fischer *et al.* point out that they ignored the independent role of education. Manelow noted that while white males are more likely to engage in criminal activity the lower their IQ, this relationship is reversed in blacks: more intelligent blacks are more likely to become criminals than those who are less intelligent. Just as there are many other factors that determine how effective people are at their job, so there are many other factors that predict their tendency to engage in a life of crime.

By this point in the book it should hardly need further emphasis that modest correlations (and most of the correlations reported by Herrnstein and Murray were modest, very rarely greater than 0.30) do not necessarily imply direct causal connections. If certain forms of generally undesirable social behaviour really were a simple and direct consequence of a low

IQ, it would follow that it should be possible to eliminate the underclass at a stroke by an intervention that succeeded in raising its members' IQ scores. To make the obvious reply—that this is a merely fanciful suggestion because no one knows how to raise IQ—is to forget that even if it cannot be done overnight, the Flynn effect shows that the environment of all industrial societies has succeeded in doing it over a rather longer time scale. The average IQ of Europeans and of Americans, black as well as white, has increased by some 15 to 20 points since 1945. This dramatic increase in IQ has not been accompanied by any *notable* decrease in crime or teenage pregnancies.

Herrnstein and Murray are not the only ones who occasionally seem to write as though modest correlations between IQ and various indices of social pathology were evidence of a simple causal chain from one to the other. Others have dropped many of the qualifications that *The bell curve* contains. Some are even willing to rely on a within-group correlation to prove that a between-group difference in the incidence of a particular pathology is the consequence of a between-group difference in IQ (an error I discussed in Chapter 14, see Box 14.1). Thus, Gordon (1997) noted that differences in the prevalence of criminal behaviour and HIV infection between blacks and whites in the USA were rather precisely matched by differences in their average IQ scores. Given a $1.0d$ difference between blacks' and whites' IQ scores, it follows that some 16–17% of whites, but 50% of blacks will have an IQ below 85. Gordon then noted, for example, that in various surveys, 17–18% of white youths had appeared before a juvenile court by the age of 18, and some 15% of white males had been arrested for a serious crime at one time or another. In both cases, the incidence among blacks was just over 50%. In other words, the relative proportion of blacks and whites with an IQ below 85 closely matched the relative proportion of blacks and whites falling foul of the criminal justice system. From which Gordon concluded that the IQ difference between blacks and whites must be responsible for this difference.

A charitable response to this suggestion is that it ignores some equally plausible alternatives. An underclass cut off from mainstream society, where adults have few opportunities for legitimate employment and drugs provide the main lubricant of the economy, where children are brought up by single mothers and attend, and soon drop out from, poor schools, may both tempt adolescents into a life of crime and not do much good for their IQ scores. But the simplest reply to Gordon's argument is the same as one made in Box 14.1—that the difference in the incidence of criminal behaviour between blacks and whites is far smaller than the difference between males and females. Although there is evidence that they are catching up, females still commit far fewer crimes than males. Gordon's thesis thus implies that the sex difference in average IQ, in favour of females, should also be very much larger than that between blacks and whites. The only way to avoid this absurd implication is to appeal to some other factor to explain the sex difference in criminality. And why should one not then appeal to some other factor to explain the black-white difference?

Politics and science

There is no doubt that research on intelligence may have social and political implications. If there really is a difference between males' and females' average scores on tests of mental rotation, and if such tests really do predict how well people will succeed in certain professions, such as engineering, architecture, or surgery, it might seem less surprising to find that these are somewhat male-dominated professions. And if males and females really do differ in their average scores on tests of social or emotional intelligence, it might seem unsurprising to find that counselling is a female-dominated profession. If you are someone who insists that males and females should be equally represented in all professions, you might be forced to accept that achieving this may require something more than simply establishing quotas.

The interaction between the science and politics of IQ testing, however, has been good for neither. With a few honourable exceptions, political scientists and sociologists have not made particularly valuable contributions to the scientific study of IQ. And very few IQ testers have made a valuable contribution to political science or social policy. A wider thesis is that science and politics are in principle inseparable when it comes to a discussion of IQ, because any statement about IQ is as much a reflection of your political prejudices as a scientific conclusion. Of course, most scientists have social and political views. And science is not just about the accumulation of factual knowledge, particularly when it must rely on imperfect, natural experiments; science requires the evaluation and interpretation of often ambiguous evidence. Such evaluation requires judgement, and judgement, as cognitive psychologists should know, can be influenced by prior belief or preconception. So much is obvious. Does it really imply that you should accept only those conclusions about IQ advanced by writers whose political views meet with your approval? Of course not. It means that you should strive all the harder to distinguish between matters of fact and matters of opinion (and not be seduced into believing that there is no distinction between the two); that you should scrutinize other people's theories, *and* your own, to decide how strongly they are supported by, and how far they go beyond, the available evidence; that you should scrupulously evaluate both the evidence for, and that against, any conclusion you wish to draw. I do not pretend that I have always lived up to these noble ideals.

A statistical appendix

This is not intended as an introduction to statistics in psychology; there are numerous books available for those who want such an introduction. All I am trying to do is provide a brief and elementary discussion of some of the statistical issues that arise in the literature on intelligence and its measurement.

Experimental psychologists seek to understand the effect of an independent variable on a dependent variable, for example by comparing the performance on a particular task of two or more groups exposed to different levels of the independent variable. The effect of retention interval on memory, for example, can be studied by giving all participants the same opportunity to learn some material, and asking different groups to recall the material after different intervals. Such experiments are sometimes possible in the field of intelligence testing: the effect of nutritional supplements on measured intelligence can be studied by giving two or more matched groups different levels of supplement for different lengths of time, and measuring their intelligence some time later. For obvious ethical reasons, it is not often that intelligence researchers can perform such an experiment, but occasionally a natural experiment is provided for them. The effect of schooling on children's test scores, for example, has been studied by taking advantage of the deplorable decision of a school district to close down their schools for a significant period of time. There are problems with all natural experiments: in this particular example the psychologist did not randomly assign a large number of children to two groups, one continuing to attend school, the other deprived of schooling, so there must be some question whether there were other differences between the children who were able to continue their schooling and those who were not.

Correlations

Much of the research in the field of intelligence, however, does not compare the performance of different groups exposed to different treatments, but looks for associations between two or more variables, and measures the strength of this association by calculating the correlation between them. What is the relationship between children's IQ scores at age 10, and their later educational attainments, or their IQ at age 40 or 80? And how is their IQ related to their parents' social class, or the number of other children in their family?

Such relationships can be depicted graphically by a scatterplot, recording IQ on one axis and educational attainment on the other (see, for example, Figure 8.2, p. 170), but is usually measured by calculating the correlation between the two variables. A correlation coefficient is a measure of the linear association between two variables, and can range from +1.0, for a perfect positive association, through 0, for zero association, to −1.0, for a perfect negative association between the two. The correlation between people's scores on two different IQ test batteries is high, usually in the range 0.70–0.90; that between children's IQ scores and their later educational attainment is moderately strong, about 0.50; that between IQ scores and performance on simple laboratory tasks is modest, usually in the range 0.20–0.50, although sometimes (depending on the nature of the task) as high as 0.65. I usually describe a correlation greater than 0.50 as strong, one between 0.30 and 0.50 as moderate, one less than 0.30 as modest, and one below 0.15 (even if statistically significant) as trivial. But I have not been entirely consistent: the practical (not statistical) significance of a correlation depends, among other things, on your prior expectation. A correlation between scores on two different test batteries of only 0.40 is very low and should lead you to raise questions about at least one of the test batteries; but a correlation between adopted children's IQ scores and the number of books in their adoptive home of only 0.20 is still important, since it implies that quality of family background has an environmental effect on children's test scores.

The correlation coefficient measures the strength of the linear association between two variables. A non-linear association will be missed. If the relationship is U-shaped, scores on variable Y first decreasing as X increases, but then turning round and increasing with further increases in X, the correlation coefficient will not detect this. It will equally fail to tell you that the reason why there is only a modest correlation between X and Y is because, although there is initially a strong positive association between the two, above a certain level of X, Y stays constant (a point probably more relevant in the context of this book).

Multiple regression

Children's IQ scores are correlated not only with their parents' social class, but with dozens of other measures of their family background; with their parents' IQ, level of education, and income (not quite the same as social class); with the number of other children in the family and whether they are the first or last born in the family;

with the neighbourhood in which they live, and the kind of school they attend, and so on. It is obvious enough that many of these other variables will be correlated with one another, which is not going to make it any easier to find out which, if any, really are having any effect on the child's test score. Multiple regression analysis is the technique commonly used to analyse such cases, where a number of different variables are all correlated with a particular outcome or dependent variable. It is designed to ascertain the association between each independent variable and the outcome, one at a time, independently of the contribution of all other independent variables.

Regression analysis can, in certain cases, be very informative. In the present instance, for example, a regression analysis of the contribution of all the above mentioned variables has shown that although the association between parental social class and children's IQ scores is reduced when all these other variables are taken into account, it remains significant and substantial. In other words, the reason why children's IQ scores are associated with differences in their parents' social class is *not* simply due to differences in their parents' income or education, or to the number of other children in the family, etc. (see Chapter 12). That is surely important to know.

The procedure for multiple regression analysis involves entering each independent variable, one at a time, into the regression equation, and seeing whether each new variable adds to the prediction of the outcome, or more formally accounts for a significant increase in the percentage of variance in the outcome explained (the percentage of variance in Y explained by X is the square of the correlation between X and Y). A moment's reflection suggests that a lot is going to depend on the order in which the independent variables are entered into the regression equation. A standard procedure is to enter them in order of the magnitude of their raw correlation with the outcome. But it is far from obvious that this is always appropriate, and where two independent variables are themselves strongly correlated, regression analysis will not necessarily be able to tell you which is really important. As an illustration, consider a study described in Chapter 13, in which Weinberg *et al.* (1992) measured the IQ scores of white, mixed race, and black children, all adopted by white middle-class families. Unfortunately, there were significant differences between the three groups in several aspects of their adoptive homes, and in the age at which they had been adopted. The outcome to be explained was that the three groups of children differed in their average test scores. Why? When the 'biological' variables (biological parents' ethnic group and level of education) were entered first, they accounted for 16% of the variance in the children's test scores, and the adoptive variables only for an additional 7% of the variance. But when the adoptive variables were entered first, they now accounted for 17% of the variance in test scores, and the biological variables only for an additional 6% of the variance. Regression analysis cannot tell you which was more important.

Normal distribution, standard deviation, and effect size

Along with many other measures, the IQ scores of a large, representative sample of the population are approximately normally distributed (see Figure 2.1, p. 34). This means that approximately 68% of the population will obtain a test score within 1 standard deviation of the mean, that is, an IQ between 85 and 115, and only 16% will have an IQ greater than 115. The standard deviation of a test score can be used to calculate the effect size of a difference between two groups' scores on that test: the difference between their mean scores is divided by the average of the two groups' standard deviation, and is referred to as d. Although somewhat unsystematically, I often use d to measure a difference in test scores. A difference of $1.0d$ between two groups' IQ scores amounts to a difference of 15 points. It is particularly useful when you wish to compare the magnitude of the difference on different tests which have quite different standard deviations, for example the difference in IQ with the difference in American SAT scores (where the standard deviation is 100), or the difference in overall Wechsler IQ with the difference in scores on single Wechsler tests (which have a standard deviation of 3.0).

In experimental psychology, a d value of 0.20 or less is deemed small; one about 0.50 moderate, and one greater than 0.80 large, but these labels are not really very informative. Few effect sizes in the realm of intelligence are greater than 0.80 (the obvious counter-example is the supposed difference between European, and African-American IQ scores, which is said to be $1.0d$), but even an effect size of 0.20 can be important, since one of the properties of the normal distribution is that a small difference in the mean scores of two groups translates into a large difference in the ratio of people in each group with a score two or three standard deviations above or below the mean.

Meta-analysis

One important use of effect size as a measure of the difference between two groups is in meta-analysis. This is a technique for bringing together the results of a large number of independent studies that have all examined the same issue, for example whether males and females differ in their performance on tests of verbal ability. Early surveys of this sort of issue, such as Maccoby and Jacklin's (1974) excellent *The psychology of sex differences*, relied largely on listing studies that had looked at such sex differences, annotating each as having found a significant female advantage, significant male advantage, or no significant difference. The trouble is that this may give a wholly misleading impression: if only 4 of 20 studies have found a significant female advantage, and the rest no significant difference between males and females, this might be taken to mean that there probably is no real sex difference in verbal ability. But if 15 of the remaining studies found a non-significant female advantage, and only one a non-significant male advantage, the chances are very high that there really is a modest female advantage in verbal ability. Meta-analysis calculates the effect size obtained in all 20 studies, and then a weighted mean effect size (weighted by sample size), together with an estimate of the probability that the true effect size falls within a particular range, and thus of the statistical significance of the observed effect size. If there is a sufficiently large number of studies, it is possible to look for 'moderator' variables, for example whether the female advantage varies with the type of verbal test, participants' age, or when the study was published.

Meta-analysis is by no means a foolproof method. Its conclusions must depend on the quality of the studies included in the analysis, on how thoroughly the authors have searched the literature, and on the criteria they have adopted for including studies in their analysis. The 'file drawer' problem refers to the possibility that studies that found no difference do not get published, never making it beyond the author's filing cabinet, so there is a danger that published studies overestimate the true size of an effect. Nevertheless, it remains a useful technique for summarizing the results of large numbers of different studies, and I frequently refer to meta-analyses throughout the book.

Bibliography

Ackerman, P. L. (1988). Determinants of individual differences during skill acquisition: Cognitive abilities and information processing. *Journal of Experimental Psychology: General,* 117, 299–318.

Ackerman, P. L. and Lohman, D. F. (2003). Education and *g.* In *The scientific study of general intelligence: Tribute to Arthur R. Jensen* (ed. H. Nyborg). Oxford: Pergamon.

Ackerman, P. L., Beier, M. E., and Boyle, M. O. (2005). Working memory and intelligence: The same or different constructs? *Psychological Bulletin,* 131, 30–60.

Ackroyd, P. (1990). *Dickens.* London: Sinclair-Stevenson.

Adler, J. E. and Rips, L. J. (2008). *Reasoning: Studies of human inference and its foundations.* Cambridge: Cambridge University Press.

Aiello, L. C. and Dean, M. C. (1990). *An introduction to human evolutionary anatomy.* London: Academic Press.

Alcock, K. J. and Bundy, D. A. P. (2001). The impact of infectious disease on cognitive development. In *Environmental effects on cognitive abilities* (eds R. J. Sternberg and E. L. Grigorenko). Mahwah, NJ: Lawrence Erlbaum.

Aleman, A., Bronk, E., Kessels, R. P. C., Koppeschaar, H. P. P., and van Honk, J. (2004). A single administration of testosterone improves visuospatial ability in young women. *Psychoneuroendocrinology,* 29, 612–17.

Alexander, J. R. M. and Smales, S. (1997). Intelligence, learning and long term memory. *Personality and Individual Differences,* 23, 815–25.

Anastasi, A. and Urbina, S. (2001). *Psychological testing* (7th edn). London: Prentice-Hall International.

Anderson, B. (2001). *g* as a consequence of shared genes. *Intelligence,* 29, 367–71.

Anderson, J. W., Johnstone, B. M., and Remley, D. T. (1999). Breast-feeding and cognitive development: A meta-analysis. *American Journal of Clinical Nutrition,* 70, 525–35.

Anderson, M. (1992). *Intelligence and development: A cognitive theory.* Oxford: Blackwell.

Anderson, M. (2005). Marrying intelligence and cognition: A developmental view. In *Cognition and intelligence: Identifying the mechanisms of the mind* (eds R. J. Sternberg and J. E. Pretz). Cambridge: Cambridge University Press.

Arden, R. and Plomin, R. (2006). Sex differences in variance of intelligence across childhood. *Personality and Individual Differences,* 41, 39–48.

Ardila, A., Galeano, L. M., and Rosselli, M. (1998). Toward a model of neuropsychological activity. *Neuropsychology Review,* 8, 171–90.

Ardila, A., Pineda, D., and Rosselli, M. (2000). Correlation between intelligence test scores and executive function measures. *Archives of Clinical Neuropsychology,* 15, 31–6.

Atkinson, R. (2007). College admissions and the SAT: A personal perspective. In R. C. Atkinson, *The pursuit of knowledge: Speeches and papers of Richard C. Atkinson.* Berkeley and Los Angeles: University of California Press.

Attridge, L. C. (2006). The role of emotional intelligence in academic achievement and its relation to other measures of individual differences. Unpublished M.Phil. Thesis, University of Cambridge.

Baddeley, A. D. (1997) *Human memory: Theory and practice.* Hove, UK: Psychology Press.

Baddeley, A. D. (2007). *Working memory, thought, and action.* Oxford: Oxford University Press.

Baddeley, A. D. and Hitch, G. J. (1974). Working memory. In *Recent advances in learning and motivation* (vol. 8.), (ed. G. A. Bower). New York: Academic Press.

Baddeley, A. D. and Wilson, B. (1988). Frontal amnesia and the dysexecutive syndrome. *Brain and Cognition,* 7, 212–30.

Baenninger, M. and Newcombe, N. S. (1989). The role of experience in spatial test-performance: A meta-analysis. *Sex Roles,* 20, 327–44.

Baldo, J. V. and Shimamura, A. P. (1998). Letter and category fluency in patients with frontal lobe lesions. *Neuropsychology,* 12, 259–67.

Baldo, J. V. and Shimamura, A. P. (2000). Spatial and color working memory in patients with lateral prefrontal cortex lesions. *Psychobiology,* 28, 156–67.

Baltes, P. B. and Lindenberger, U. (1997). Emergence of a powerful connection between sensory and cognitive functions across the adult life span: A new window to the study of cognitive aging? *Psychology and Aging,* 12, 12–21.

Banks, G. C., Batchelor, J. H., and McDaniel, M. A. (2010). Smarter people are (a bit) more symmetrical: A meta-analysis of the relationship between intelligence and fluctuating asymmetry. *Intelligence,* 38, 393–401.

Barnett, W. S. (1995). Long-term effects of early childhood programs on cognitive and school outcomes. *The Future of Children,* 5 (3), 25–50.

Barnett, W. S. and Masse, L. N. (2007). Early childhood program design and economic returns: Comparative benefit-cost analysis of the Abecedarian program and policy implications. *Economics of Education Review,* 26, 113–25.

Bar-On, R. (1997). *The Emotional Quotient Inventory (EQ-i): A test of emotional intelligence.* Toronto: Multi-Health Systems.

Baron-Cohen, S. (1995). *Mind blindness.* Cambridge, MA: MIT Press.

Baron-Cohen, S. (2003). *The essential difference: Men, women and the extreme male brain.* London: Penguin.

Baron-Cohen, S., Lutchmaya, S., and Knickmeyer, R. (2004). *Prenatal testosterone in mind: Amniotic fluid studies.* Cambridge, MA: MIT Press.

Barrett, P. T. and Eysenck, H. J. (1992). Brain-evoked potentials and intelligence: the Hendrickson paradigm. *Intelligence,* 16, 361–81.

Barrick, M. R., Mount, M. K., and Judge, T. A. (2001). Personality and performance at the beginning of the new millennium: What do we know and where do we go next? *International Journal of Selection and Assessment,* 9, 9–30.

Bartholomew, D. J. (2004). *Measuring intelligence: Facts and fallacies.* Cambridge: Cambridge University Press.

Bartholomew, D. J., Deary, I. J., and Lawn, M. (2009). A new lease of life for Thomson's bonds model of intelligence. *Psychological Review,* 116, 567–79.

Bartley, A. J., Jones, D. W., and Weinberger, D. R. (1997). Genetic variability of human brain size and cortical gyral patterns. *Brain,* 120, 257–69.

Bastian, V. A., Burns, N. R., and Nettelbeck, T. (2005). Emotional intelligence predicts life skills, but not as well as personality and cognitive abilities. *Personality and Individual Differences,* 39, 1135–45.

Bates, T. C. and Eysenck, H. J. (1993a). String length, attention and intelligence: focused attention reverses the string-length-IQ relationship. *Personality and Individual Differences,* 15, 363–371.

Bates, T. C. and Eysenck, H. J. (1993b). Intelligence, inspection time and decision time. *Intelligence,* 17, 523–32.

Bates, T. C., Stough, C., Mangan, G., and Pellett, O. (1995). Intelligence and complexity of the averaged evoked potential: An attentional theory. *Intelligence,* 20, 27–39.

Baumeister, A. A. and Bacharach, V. R. (1996). A critical analysis of the infant health and development programme. *Intelligence,* 23, 79–104.

Bayley, N. (1969). *The Bayley Scales of Infant Development.* New York: Psychological Corporation.

Bayley, N. (1993). *Bayley Scales of Infant Development* (2nd edn). San Antonio, TX: Psychological Corporation.

Beller, E. and Hout, M. (2006). Intergenerational social mobility: The United States in comparative perspective. *The Future of Children,* 16 (2), 19–36.

Bellinger, D. C. and Adams, H. F. (2001). Environmental pollutant exposures and children's cognitive abilities. In *Environmental effects on cognitive abilities* (eds R. J. Sternberg and E. L. Grigorenko). Mahwah, NJ: Lawrence Erlbaum.

Bellis, M. A., Hughes, K., Hughes, S., and Ashton, J. R. (2005). Measuring paternal discrepancy and its public health consequences. *Journal of Epidemiology and Community Health,* 59, 749–54.

Belmont, L. and Marolla, F. A. (1973). Birth order, family size, and intelligence. *Science,* 182, 1096–101.

Benbow, C. P. (1988). Sex differences in mathematical reasoning ability in intellectually talented preadolescents: Their nature, effects, and possible causes. *Behavioral and Brain Sciences,* 11, 169–232.

Benbow, C. P. and Stanley, J. C. (1983). Sex differences in mathematical reasoning ability: More facts. *Science,* 222, 1029–31.

Bench, C. J., Frith, C. D., Grasby, P. M., and Friston, K. J. (1993). Investigations of the functional anatomy of attention using the Stroop test. *Neuropsychologia,* 31, 907–22.

Bennett, H. L. (1983). Remembering drink orders: the memory skills of cocktail waitresses. *Human Learning: Journal of Practical Research and Applications,* 2, 157–70.

Bennetto, L., Taylor, A. K., Pennington, B. F., Porter, D., and Hagerman, R. J. (2001). Profile of cognitive functioning in women with the fragile X mutation. *Neuropsychology,* 15, 290–9.

Benson, N., Hulac, D. M., and Kranzler, J. H. (2010). Independent examination of the Wechsler Adult Intelligence Scale-Fourth Edition (WAIS-IV): What does the WAIS-IV measure? *Psychological Assessment,* 22, 121–30.

Benton, D. and Buts, J. (1990). Vitamin-mineral supplementation and intelligence. *Lancet,* 335, 1158–60.

Benton, D. and Roberts, G. (1988). Effect of vitamin and mineral supplementation on intelligence of a sample of schoolchildren. *Lancet,* 331, 140–44.

Berry, D. C. and Broadbent, D. E. (1984). On the relationship between task performance and associated verbalisable knowledge. *Quarterly Journal of Experimental Psychology,* 36A, 209–31.

Bilalić, M., McLeod, P., and Gobet, F. (2007). Does chess need intelligence? A study with young chess players. *Intelligence,* 35, 457–70.

Binet, A. (1900). Recherches sur la technique de la mensuration de la tête vivante, plus 4 autres mémoires sur la céphalométrie. *L'Année Psychologique*, 7, 314–429.

Binet, A. (1911). Nouvelles recherches sur la mésure du niveau intellectual chez les enfants d'école. *L'Annee Psychologique*, 17, 145–201.

Binet, A., and Simon, T. (1905). Méthodes nouvelles pour le diagnostic du niveau intellectuel des anormaux. *L'Année Psychologique*, 11, 191–244.

Binet, A., and Simon, T. (1911). *A method of measuring the development of the intelligence of young children*. Lincoln, IL: Courier Company.

Birch, H. G., Pineiro, C., Alcalde, E., Toca, T., and Cravioto, J. (1971). Kwashiorkor in early childhood and intelligence at school age. *Pediatric Research*, 5, 579–84.

Birren, J. E. (1968). Increments and decrements in the intellectual status of the aged. *Psychiatric Research Report*, 23, 207–14.

Bishop, S. J., Fossella, J., Croucher, C. J., and Duncan, J. (2008). COMT val158met genotype affects recruitment of neural mechanisms supporting fluid intelligence. *Cerebral Cortex*, 18, 2132–40.

Bjerkedal, T., Kristensen, P., Skjeret, G. A., and Brevik, J. I. (2007). Intelligence test scores and birth order among young Norwegian men (conscripts) analyzed within and between families. *Intelligence*, 35, 503–14.

Blair, C. (2006). How similar are fluid cognition and general intelligence? A developmental neuroscience perspective on fluid cognition as an aspect of human cognitive ability. *Behavioral and Brain Sciences*, 29, 109–60.

Blair, C., Gamson, D., Thorne, S., and Baker, D. (2005). Rising mean IQ: Cognitive demand of mathematics education for young children, population exposure to formal schooling, and the neurobiology of the prefrontal cortex. *Intelligence*, 33, 93–106.

Blake, J. (1981). Family size and the quality of children. *Demography*, 18, 421–42.

Blinkhorn, S. F. (1995). Burt and the early history of factor analysis. In *Cyril Burt: Fraud or framed?* (ed. N. J. Mackintosh). Oxford: Oxford University Press.

Blinkhorn, S. F. and Hendrickson, D. E. (1982). Average evoked responses and psychometric intelligence. *Nature*, 195, 596–97.

Block, N. J. and Dworkin, G. (1976). *The IQ controversy*. New York: Pantheon Books.

Bloom, B. S. (1964). *Stability and change in human characteristics*. New York: Wiley.

Boles, D. B. (1980). X-linkage of spatial ability: A critical review. *Child Development*, 51, 623–35.

Bopp, K. L. and Verhaeghen, P. (2005). Aging and verbal memory span: A meta-analysis. *The Journals of Gerontology: Series B*, 60, 223–33.

Bors, D. A. and MacLeod, C. M. (1996). Attention, information processing, and IQ. *International Journal of Psychology*, 31, 34–52.

Boswell, J. (1988). *The kindness of strangers*. New York: Pantheon Books.

Bouchard, T. J. Jr. (1997). IQ similarity in twins reared apart: findings and responses to critics. In *Intelligence: Heredity and environment* (eds R. J. Sternberg and E. L. Grigorenko). New York: Cambridge University Press.

Bouchard, T. J. Jr. and McGue, M. (1981). Familial studies of intelligence: A review. *Science*, 212, 1055–9.

Bouchard, T. J. Jr. and Segal, N. L. (1985). Environment and IQ. In *Handbook of intelligence: Theories, measurements and applications* (ed. B. B. Wolman). New York: Wiley.

Bouchard, T. J. Jr, Lykken, D. T., McGue, M., Segal, N. L., and Tellegen, A. (1990). Sources of human psychological differences: The Minnesota study of twins reared apart. *Science*, 250, 223–8.

Bowles, S. and Gintis, H. (1976). *Schooling in capitalist America: Educational reform and the contradictions of economic life*. New York: Harper and Row.

Bowling, A. C. and Mackenzie, B. D. (1996). The relationship between speed of information processing and cognitive ability. *Personality and Individual Differences*, 20, 775–800.

Brackett, M. A. and Mayer, J. D. (2003). Convergent, discriminant, and incremental validity of competing measures of emotional intelligence. *Personality and Social Psychology Bulletin*, 29, 1147–58.

Brackett, M. A., Mayer, J. D., and Warner, R. M. (2004). Emotional intelligence and its relation to everyday behaviour. *Personality and Individual Differences*, 36, 1387–402.

Brackett, M. A., Rivers, S. E., Shiffman, S., Lerner, N., and Salovey, P. (2006). Relating emotional abilities to social functioning: A comparison of self-report and performance measures of emotional intelligence. *Journal of Personality and Social Psychology*, 91, 780–95.

Bradley, R. H., Caldwell, B., and Elardo, R. (1977). Home environment, social status, and mental test performance. *Journal of Educational Psychology*, 69, 697–701.

Brand, C. R. and Deary, I. J. (1982). Intelligence and 'inspection time'. In *A model for intelligence* (ed. H. J. Eysenck). New York: Springer.

Brand, C. R., Constales, D., and Kane, H. (2003). Why ignore the *g* factor? Historical considerations. In *The scientific study of general intelligence: Tribute to Arthur R. Jensen* (ed. H. Nyborg). Oxford: Pergamon.

Brandt, J., Welsh, K. A., Breitner, J. C., and Folstein, M. F. (1993). Hereditary influences on cognitive functioning in older men: A study of 4000 twin pairs. *Archives of Neurology,* 50, 599–603.

Braver, T. S., Cohen, J. D., Nystrom, L. E., Jonides, J., *et al.* (1997). A parametric study of prefrontal cortex involvement in human working memory. *NeuroImage,* 5, 49–62.

Brazzelli, M., Colombo, N., Della Sala, S., and Spinnler, H. (1994). Spared and impaired cognitive abilities after bilateral frontal damage. *Cortex,* 30, 27–51.

Breslau, N., Del Detto, J. E., Brown, G. G., *et al.* (1994). A gradient relationship between low birth weight and IQ at age 6 years. *Archives of Adolescent Medicine,* 148, 377–83.

Brewer, N. and Smith, G. A. (1984). How normal and retarded individuals monitor and regulate speed and accuracy of responding in serial choice tasks. *Journal of Experimental Psychology: General,* 113, 71–93.

Brigham, C. C. (1923). *A study of American intelligence.* Princeton, NJ: Princeton University Press.

Brody, N. (1992). *Intelligence* (2nd edn). San Diego, CA: Academic Press.

Brody, N. (2003). Jensen's genetic interpretation of racial differences in intelligence: Critical evaluation. In *The scientific study of general intelligence: Tribute to Arthur R. Jensen* (ed. H. Nyborg). Oxford: Pergamon.

Broman, S. H., Nichols, P. L., and Kennedy, W. A. (1975). In *Preschool IQ: Prenatal and Early Developmental Correlates.* Hillsdale, NJ: Lawrence Erlbaum.

Brown, G. D. A. and Hulme, C. (1995). Modeling item length effects in memory span: no rehearsal needed? *Journal of Memory and Language,* 34, 594–621.

Brown, R. P. and Day, E. A. (2006). The difference isn't black and white: Stereotype threat and the race gap on Raven's Advanced Progressive Matrices. *Journal of Applied Psychology,* 91, 979–85.

Bryant, P. E. and Trabasso, T. (2001). Transitive inferences and memory in young children. *Nature,* 232, 456–8.

Buchsbaum, B. R., Greer, S., Chang, W.-L., and Berman, K. F. (2005). Meta-analysis of neuroimaging studies of the Wisconsin Card-Sorting Task and component processes. *Human Brain Mapping,* 25, 35–45.

Bunting, M. (2006). Proactive interference and item similarity in working memory. *Journal of Experimental Psychology: Learning, Memory, and Cognition,* 32, 183–96.

Burkam, D. T., Ready, D. D., Lee, V. E., and LoGerfo, L. F. (2004). Social-class differences in summer learning between kindergarten and first grade: Model specification and estimation. *Sociology of Education,* 77, 1–31.

Burke, H. R. (1985). Raven's Progressive Matrices (1938): More on norms, reliability and validity. *Journal of Clinical Psychology,* 72, 247–51.

Burks, B. S. (1928). The relative influence of nature and nurture upon mental development: A comparative study of foster parent-foster child resemblance and true parent-true child resemblance. *Yearbook of the National Society for the Study of Education,* 27. Bloomingdale, IL: Public School Publishing.

Burleigh, M. (1994). *Death and deliverance: 'Euthanasia' in Germany c.1900-1945.* Cambridge: Cambridge University Press.

Burleigh, M. (2000). *The Third Reich: A new history.* Macmillan: London.

Burns, N. R. and Nettelbeck, T. (2003). Inspection time in the structure of cognitive abilities: Where does IT fit? *Intelligence,* 31, 237–55.

Burns, N. R. and Nettelbeck, T. (2005). Inspection time and speed of processing: Sex differences on perceptual speed but not IT. *Personality and Individual Differences,* 39, 439–46.

Burns, N. R., Nettelbeck, T., and Cooper, C. J. (1999). Inspection time correlates with general speed of processing but not with fluid ability. *Intelligence,* 27, 37–44.

Buros, O. K. (1935). *Mental Measurements Yearbook.* Highland Park, NJ: Gryphon Press.

Burt, C. L. (1912). The inheritance of mental characters. *Eugenics Review,* 4, 168–200.

Burt, C. L. (1917). *The distribution and relations of educational abilities.* London: London County Council.

Burt, C. L. (1921). *Mental and scholastic tests.* London: King and Son.

Burt, C. L. (1955). The evidence for the concept of intelligence. *British Journal of Educational Psychology,* 25, 158–177.

Burt, C. L. (1966). The genetic determination of differences in intelligence: a study of monozygotic twins reared together and apart. *British Journal of Psychology,* 57, 137–53.

Burt, C. L. (1969) Intelligence and heredity: some common misconceptions. *Irish Journal of Education,* 3, 75–94.

Burt, C. L., and Moore, R. C. (1912). The mental differences between the sexes. *Journal of Experimental Pedagogy,* 1, 273–84 and 355–88.

Butcher, L. M., Davis, O. S. P., Craig, I. W., and Plomin, R. (2008). Genome-wide quantitative trait locus association scan of general cognitive ability using pooled DNA and 500K single nucleotide polymorphism microarrays. *Genes, Brain & Behavior,* 7, 435–46.

Byrne, R. W. and Whiten, A. (1988). *Machiavellian intelligence: Social expertise and the evolution of intellect in monkeys, apes and humans*. Oxford: Oxford University Press.

Cahan, S. and Cohen, N. (1989). Age versus schooling effects on intelligence development. *Child Development*, 60, 1239–49.

Campbell, F. A., Ramey, C. T., Pungello, E., Sparling, J., and Miller-Johnson, S. (2002). Early childhood education: Young adult outcomes from the Abecedarian Project. *Applied Developmental Science*, 6, 42–57.

Capron, C. and Duyme, M. (1989). Assessment of effects of socioeconomic status on IQ in a full cross-fostering design. *Nature*, 340, 552–3.

Carlson, J. S., Jensen, C. M., and Widaman, K. F. (1983). Reaction time, intelligence and attention. *Intelligence*, 7, 329–44.

Carmona da Mota, H., Antonio, A. M., Leitao, G., and Porto, M. (1990). Late effects of early malnutrition. *The Lancet*, 335, 1158.

Carpenter, P. A. and Just, M. A. (1975). Sentence comprehension: A psycholingusitic processing model of verification. *Psychological Review*, 82, 45–73.

Carpenter, P. A. and Just, M. A. (1986). Spatial ability: An information processing approach to psychometrics. In *Advances in the psychology of human intelligence* (vol. 3), (ed. R. J. Sternberg). Hillsdale, NJ: Lawrence Erlbaum.

Carpenter, P. A., Just, M. A., and Schell, P. (1990). What one intelligence test measures: A theoretical account of the processing in the Raven Progressive Matrices Test. *Psychological Review*, 97, 404–31.

Carraher, T. N., Carraher, D., and Schliemann, A. D. (1985). Mathematics in the streets and in the schools. *British Journal of Developmental Psychology*, 3, 21–9.

Carroll, J. B. (1993). *Human cognitive abilities*. Cambridge: Cambridge University Press.

Carroll, J. B. (2003). The higher-stratum structure of human abilities: Current evidence supports *g* and about ten broad factors. In *The scientific study of general intelligence: Tribute to Arthur R. Jensen* (ed. H. Nyborg). Oxford: Pergamon.

Caryl, P. G. (1994). Early event-related potentials correlate with inspection time and intelligence. *Intelligence*, 18, 15–46.

Case, R., Demetriou, A., Platsidou, M., and Kazi, S. (2001). Integrating concepts and tests of intelligence from the differential and developmental traditions. *Intelligence*, 29, 307–36.

Casey, M. B., Nuttall, R., Pezaris, E., and Benbow, C. P. (1995). The influence of spatial ability on gender differences in mathematics college entrance test scores across diverse samples. *Developmental Psychology*, 31, 697–705.

Casey, M. B., Nuttall, R. L., and Pezaris, E. (2001). Spatial-mechanical reasoning skills versus mathematical self-confidence as mediators of gender differences on mathematics subtests using cross-national gender-based items. *Journal for Research in Mathematics Education*, 32, 28–57.

Caspi, A., Williams, B., Kim-Cohen, J., *et al.* (2007). Moderation of breastfeeding effects on the IQ by genetic variation in fatty acid metabolism. *Proceedings of the National Academy of Sciences*, 104, 18860–5.

Cattell, J. M. (1890). Mental tests and measurements. *Mind*, 15, 373–81.

Cattell, R. B. (1937). *The fight for our national intelligence*. London: King and Sons.

Cattell, R. B. (1940). A culture-free intelligence test, Part I. *Journal of Educational Psychology*, 31, 161–79.

Cattell, R. B. (1950). *Personality*. New York: McGraw-Hill.

Cattell, R. B. (1971). *Abilities: Their structure, growth and action*. Boston: Houghton-Miflin.

Ceci, S. J. (1991). How much does schooling influence general intelligence and its cognitive components? A reassessment of the evidence. *Developmental Psychology*, 27, 703–22.

Ceci, S. J. (1996). *On Intelligence…more or less: A bioecological treatise on intellectual development*. Englewood Cliffs, NJ: Prentice Hall.

Ceci, S. J. and Liker, J. K. (1986). A day at the races; a study of IQ, expertise and cognitive complexity. *Journal of Experimental Psychology: General*, 115, 255–66.

Ceci, S. J. and Roazzi, A. (1994). The effects of context on cognition: postcards from Brazil. In *Mind in context. Interactionist perspectives on human intelligence* (eds R. J. Sternberg and R. K. Wagner). Cambridge: Cambridge University Press.

Ceci, S. J. and Williams, W. M. (eds) (2007). *Why aren't more women in science: Top researchers debate the evidence*. Washington, DC: American Psychological Association.

Ceci, S. J., Barnett, S. M., and Kanaya, T. (2003). Developing childhood proclivities into adult competencies: The overlooked multiplier effect. In *The psychology of abilities, competencies, and expertise* (eds R. J. Sternberg and E. L. Grigorenko). Cambridge: Cambridge University Press.

Ceci, S. J., Williams, W. M., and Barnett, S. M. (2009). Women's underrepresentation in science: Sociocultural and biological considerations. *Psychological Bulletin*, 135, 218–61.

Cerella, J. (1985). Information processing rates in the elderly. *Psychological Bulletin*, 98, 67–83.

Chaiken, S. R. (1993). Two models for an inspection time paradigm: Processing distraction and processing speed versus processing speed and asymptotic strength. *Intelligence, 17*, 257–83.

Chaiken, S. R. (1994). The inspection time not studied: Processing speed ability unrelated to psychometric intelligence. *Intelligence, 19*, 295–316.

Chakraborty, R., Kamboh, M. I., Nwankwo, M., and Ferrell, R. E. (1992). Caucasian genes in American blacks: New data. *American Journal of Human Genetics, 50*, 145–55.

Chapin, F. S. (1928). A quantitative scale for rating the home and social environment of middle class families in an urban community. *Journal of Educational Psychology, 19*, 99–111.

Chase, W. G. and Ericsson, K. A. (1982). Skill and working memory, In *The psychology of learning and motivation* (vol. 16), (ed. G. H. Bower). New York: Academic Press.

Chase, W. G. and Simon, H. A. (1973). Perception in chess. *Cognitive Psychology, 4*, 55–81.

Cheng, P. and Holyoak, K. J. (1985). Pragmatic reasoning schemas. *Cognitive Psychology, 17*, 391–416.

Cherrier, M. M., Asthana, S., Plymate, S., *et al.* (2001). Testosterone supplementation improves spatial and verbal memory in healthy older men. *Neurology, 57*, 80–8.

Chi, M. T. H. (1978). Knowledge structures and memory development. In *Children's thinking: What develops?* (ed. R. S. Siegler). Hillsdale, NJ: Lawrence Erlbaum.

Chipuer, H. M., Rovine, M. J., and Plomin, R. (1990). LISREL modeling: Genetic and environmental influences on IQ revisited. *Intelligence, 14*, 11–29.

Choi, J. and Silverman, I. (2003). Processes underlying sex differences in route-learning strategies in children and adolescents. *Personality and Individual Differences, 34*, 1153–66.

Chomsky, N. (1972). Psychology and ideology. *Cognition, 1*, 11–46.

Chorney, M. J., Chorney, K., Seese, N., *et al.* (1998). A quantitative trait locus associated with cognitive ability in children. *Psychological Science, 9*, 159–66.

Cianciolo, A. T. and Sternberg, R. J. (2004). *Intelligence: A brief history.* Oxford: Blackwell.

Cianciolo, A. T., Grigorenko, E. L., Jarvin, L., *et al.* (2006). Practical intelligence and tacit knowledge: Advancements in the measurement of developing expertise. *Learning and Individual Differences, 16*, 235–53.

Clark, H. H. and Chase, W. G. (1972). On the process of comparing sentences against pictures. *Cognitive Psychology, 3*, 472–517.

Clayton, N. S. (2001). Hippocampal growth and maintenance depend on food-caching experience in juvenile mountain chickadees (Poecile gambeli). *Behavioral Neuroscience, 115*, 614–25.

Cleeremans, A. and McClelland, J. L. (1991). Learning the structure of event sequences. *Journal of Experimental Psychology: General, 120*, 235–53.

Cleeremans, A., Destrebecqz, A., and Boyer, M. (1998). Implicit learning: News from the front. *Trends in Cognitive Sciences, 2*, 406–16.

Cochran, G., Hardy, J., and Harpending, H. (2006). Natural history of Ashkenazi intelligence. *Journal of Biosocial Science, 38*, 659–93.

Cohen, A. B. (2009). Many forms of culture. *American Psychologist, 64*, 194–204.

Cohen, G. (1989). *Memory in the real world.* Hove, UK: Lawrence Erlbaum.

Cohen, J. D., Forman, S. D., Braver, T. S., *et al.* (1993). Activation of the prefrontal cortex in a nonspatial working memory task with functional MRI. *Human Brain Mapping, 1*, 293–304.

Cole, M. (1971). *The cultural context of learning and thinking: An exploration in experimental anthropology.* New York: Basic Books.

Coleman, J. S. (1966). *Equality of educational opportunity.* Washington, DC: US Office of Education.

Collette, F., Van der Linden, M., Laureys, S., *et al.* (2005). Exploring the unity and diversity of the neural substrates of executive functioning. *Human Brain Mapping, 25*, 409–23.

Colom, R. and Abad, F. J. (2007). Advanced progressive matrices and sex differences: Comment to Mackintosh and Bennett (2005). *Intelligence, 35*, 183–5.

Colom, R. and Flores-Mendoza, C. E. (2007). Intelligence predicts scholastic achievement irrespective of SES factors: Evidence from Brazil. *Intelligence, 35*, 243–51.

Colom, R. and García-López, O. (2002). Sex differences in fluid intelligence among high school graduates. *Personality and Individual Differences, 32*, 445–51.

Colom, R. and Lynn, R. (2004). Testing the developmental theory of sex differences in intelligence on 12–18-year-olds. *Personality and Individual Differences, 36*, 75–82.

Colom, R., Abad, F. J., Quiroga, M. A., Shih, P. C., and Flores-Mendoza, C. (2008). Working memory and intelligence are highly related constructs, but why? *Intelligence, 36*, 584–606.

Colom, R., Haier, R. J., Head, K., *et al.* (2009). Gray matter correlates of fluid, crystallized, and spatial intelligence: Testing the P-FIT model. *Intelligence, 37*, 124–35.

Conrad, R. (1979). *The deaf schoolchild.* London: Harper and Row.

Conti, G., Galeotti, A., Mueller, G., and Pudney, S. (2009). *Popularity* (ISER working papers 2009-03).

Colchester, England: Institute for Social and Economic Research.

Conway, A. R. A. and Engle, R. W. (1994). Working memory and retrieval: A resource-dependent inhibition model. *Journal of Experimental Psychology: General,* 123, 354–73.

Conway, A. R. A. and Engle, R. W. (1996). Individual differences in working memory capacity: More evidence for a general capacity theory. *Memory,* 4, 577–90.

Conway, A. R. A., Cowan, N., and Bunting, M. F. (2001). The cocktail party phenomenon revisited: The importance of working memory capacity. *Psychonomic Bulletin & Review,* 8, 331–5.

Conway, A. R. A., Cowan, N., Bunting, M. F., Therriault, D. J., and Minkoff, S. R. B. (2002). A latent variable analysis of working memory capacity, short-term memory capacity, processing speed, and general fluid intelligence. *Intelligence,* 30, 163–84.

Conway, A. R. A., Getz, S. J., Macnamara, B., and Engel de Abreu, P. M. J. (2011). Working memory and intelligence. In *Cambridge handbook of intelligence* (eds R. J. Sternberg and S. B. Kaufman). Cambridge: Cambridge University Press.

Conway, A. R. A., Jarrold, C., Kane, M., Miyake, A., and Towse, J. (eds) (2008). *Variation in working memory.* Oxford: Oxford University Press.

Cooper, H., Nye, B., Charlton, K., and Lindsay, J. (1996). The effects of summer vacation on achievement test scores: A narrative and meta-analytic review. *Review of Educational Research,* 66, 227–68.

Cooper, L. A. (1975). Mental rotation of random two-dimensional shapes. *Cognitive Psychology,* 7, 20–43.

Cosmides, L. (1989). The logic of social exchange: Has natural selection shaped how humans reason? Studies with the Wason selection task. *Cognition,* 31, 187–276.

Cote, S. and Miners, C. T. H. (2006). Emotional intelligence, cognitive intelligence, and job performance. *Administrative Science Quarterly,* 51, 1–28.

Court, J. H. (1983). Sex differences in performance on Raven's Progressive Matrices: A review. *Alberta Journal of Educational Research,* 29, 54–74.

Court, J. H. and Raven, J. (1995). *Manual for Raven's Progressive Matrices and Vocabulary Scales. Section 7: Research and references.* Oxford: Oxford Psychologists Press.

Cowan, N. (1992). Verbal memory span and the timing of spoken recall. *Journal of Memory and Language,* 31, 668–84.

Cowan, N., Elliott, E. M., Saults, J. S., *et al.* (2005). On the capacity of attention: Its estimation and its role in working memory and cognitive aptitudes. *Cognitive Psychology,* 51, 42–100.

Cox, G. M. (1926). *Genetic studies of genius* (vol. 2). Stanford, CA: Stanford University Press.

Coyle, T. R. (2003). A review of the worst performance rule: Evidence, theory, and alternative hypotheses. *Intelligence,* 31, 567–87.

Craik, F. I. M. and Salthouse, T. A. (eds) (2002). *The handbook of aging and cognition* (2nd edn). Mahwah, NJ: Lawrence Erlbaum.

Crawford, J. R., Deary, I. J., Allan, K. M., and Gustafsson, J.-E. (1998). Evaluating competing models of the relationship between inspection time and psychometric intelligence. *Intelligence,* 26, 27–42.

Credé, M. and Kuncel, N. R. (2008). Study habits, skills, and attitudes: The third pillar supporting collegiate academic performance. *Perspectives on Psychological Science,* 3, 425–53.

Crombie, I. K., Todman, J., McNeill, G., Florey, C. D., Menzies, I., and Kennedy, R. A. (1990). Effect of vitamin and mineral supplementation on verbal and non-verbal reasoning of school children. *Lancet,* 335, 744–7.

Cudeck, R. (2000). Exploratory factor analysis. In *Handbook of applied multivariate statistics and mathematical modeling* (eds H. E. A. Tinsley and S. D. Brown). San Diego, CA: Academic Press.

Dabbs, J. M. Jr, Chang, E. L., Strong, R. A., and Milun, R. (1998). Spatial ability, navigation strategy, and geographic knowledge among men and women. *Evolution and Human Behavior,* 19, 89–98.

Daley, T. C., Whaley, S. E., Sigman, M. D., Espinosa, M. P., and Neumann, C. (2003). IQ on the rise: The Flynn effect in rural Kenyan children. *Psychological Science,* 14, 215–19.

Daneman, M. and Carpenter, P. A. (1980). Individual differences in working memory and reading. *Journal of Verbal Learning and Verbal Behavior,* 19, 450–66.

Daneman, M. and Green, I. (1986). Individual differences in comprehending and producing words in context. *Journal of Memory and Language,* 25, 1–18.

Daneman, M. and Tardif, T. (1987). Working memory and reading skill re-examined. In *Attention and performance XII* (ed. M. Coltheart). Hove, UK: Lawrence Erlbaum.

Darity, W. A. Jr. and Mason, P. L. (1998). Evidence on discrimination in employment: codes of color, codes of gender. *Journal of Economic Perspectives,* 12, 63–90.

Dar-Nimrod, I. and Heine, S. J. (2006). Exposure to scientific theories affects women's math performance. *Science,* 314, 435.

Davie, R., Butler, N., and Goldstein, H. (1972). *From birth to seven: A report of the National Child Development Study.* London: Longman.

Davis, O. S. P., Haworth, C. M. A., and Plomin, R. (2009). Dramatic increase in heritability of cognitive development from early to middle childhood: An 8-year longitudinal study of 8,700 pairs of twins. *Psychological Science*, 20, 1301–8.

De Groot, A. D. (1951). War and the intelligence of youth. *Journal of Abnormal and Social Psychology*, 46, 596–7.

De Groot, A. D. (1965). *Thought and choice in chess*. The Hague: Mouton.

de Houwer, J. (2009). The propositional approach to associative learning as an alternative for association formation models. *Learning & Behavior*, 37, 1–20.

de Jong, P. F. and Das Smaal, E. A. (1995). Attention and intelligence: The validity of the Star Counting Test. *Journal of Educational Psychology*, 87, 80–92.

Deary, I. J. (1993). Inspection time and WAIS-R IQ subtypes: A confirmatory factor analysis study. *Intelligence*, 17, 223–236.

Deary, I. J. (1994). Intelligence and auditory discrimination: separating processing speed and fidelity of stimulus representation. *Intelligence*, 18, 189–213.

Deary, I. J. (2000). *Looking down on human intelligence: From psychometrics to the brain*. Oxford: Oxford University Press.

Deary, I. J. (2003). Reaction time and psychometric intelligence: Jensen's contributions. In *The scientific study of general intelligence: Tribute to Arthur R. Jensen* (ed. H. Nyborg). Oxford: Pergamon.

Deary, I. J. and Caryl, P. G. (1993). Intelligence, EEG and evoked potentials. In *Biological approaches to the study of human intelligence* (ed. P. A. Vernon). Norwood, NJ: Ablex.

Deary, I. J. and Der, G. (2005). Reaction time explains IQ's association with death. *Psychological Science*, 16, 64–9.

Deary, I. J., Allerhand, M., and Der, G. (2009). Smarter in middle age, faster in old age: A cross-lagged panel analysis of reaction time and cognitive ability over 13 years in the West of Scotland Twenty-07 Study. *Psychology and Aging*, 24, 40–7.

Deary, I. J. Der, G., and Ford, G. (2001). Reaction times and intelligence differences: A population-based cohort study. *Intelligence*, 29, 389–99.

Deary, I. J., Irwing, P., Der, G., and Bates, T. (2007a). Brother-sister differences in the g factor in intelligence: Analysis of full, opposite-sex siblings from the NLSY1979. *Intelligence*, 35, 451–6.

Deary, I. J., Strand, S., Smith, P., and Fernandes, C. (2007b). Intelligence and educational achievement. *Intelligence*, 35, 13–21.

Deary, I. J., Thorpe, G., Wilson, V., Starr, J. M., and Whalley, L. J. (2003). Population sex differences in IQ at age 11: The Scottish mental survey 1932. *Intelligence*, 31, 533–42.

Deary, I. J., Whalley, L. J., Lemmon, H., Crawford, J. R., and Starr, J. M. (2000). The stability of individual

differences in mental ability from childhood to old age: Follow-up of the 1932 Scottish Mental Survey. *Intelligence*, 28, 49–55.

Deary, I. J., Whiteman, M. C., Starr, J. M., Whalley, L. J., and Fox, H. C. (2004). The impact of childhood intelligence on later life: Following up the Scottish Mental Surveys of 1932 and 1947. *Journal of Personality and Social Psychology*, 86, 130–47.

Delis, D. C., Kaplan, E., and Kramer, J. H. (2001). *The Delis-Kaplan Executive Function System: Technical manual*. San Antonio, TX: The Psychological Corporation.

Delis, D. C., Lansing, A., Houston, W. S., *et al*. (2007). Creativity lost: The importance of testing higher-level executive functions in school-age children and adolescents. *Journal of Psychoeducational Assessment*, 25, 29–40.

della Malva, C. L., Stuss, D. T., D'Alton, J., and Willmer, J. (1993). Capture errors and sequencing after frontal brain lesions. *Neuropsychologia*, 31, 363–72.

Dempster, F. N. (1981). Memory span: Sources of individual and developmental differences. *Psychological Bulletin*, 89, 63–100.

Der, G., Batty, G. D., and Deary, I. J. (2006). Effect of breast feeding on intelligence in children: Prospective study, sibling pairs analysis, and meta-analysis. *British Medical Journal*, 333, 945–8.

DeShon, R. P., Chan, D., and Weissbein, D. A. (1995). Verbal overshadowing effects on Raven's Advanced Progressive Matrices: Evidence for multidimensional performance determinants. *Intelligence*, 21, 135–55.

D'Esposito, M., Cooney, J. W., Gazzaley, A., Gibbs, S. E. B., and Postle, B. R. (2006). Is the prefrontal cortex necessary for delay task performance? Evidence from lesion and fMRI data. *Journal of the International Neuropsychological Society*, 12, 248–60.

Detterman, D. K. (1987). What does reaction time tell us about intelligence? In *Speed of information-processing and intelligence* (ed. P. A. Vernon). Norwood, NJ: Ablex.

Detterman, D. K. (2002). General intelligence: Cognitive and biological explanations. In *The general factor of intelligence: How general is it?* (eds R. J. Sternberg and E. L. Grigorenko). Mahwah, NJ: Lawrence Erlbaum.

Detterman, D. K. and Daniel, M. H. (1989). Correlations of mental tests with each other and with cognitive variables are highest for low IQ groups. *Intelligence*, 13, 349–59.

Detterman, D. K. and Spry, K. M. (1988). Is it smart to play the horses? Comment on 'A day at the races: A study of IQ, expertise, and cognitive complexity' (S. J. Ceci and J. K. Liker, 1986). *Journal of Experimental Psychology: General*, 117, 91–5.

Detterman, D. K., Gabriel, L. T., and Ruthsatz, J. M. (2000). Intelligence and mental retardation. In *Handbook of intelligence* (ed. R. J. Sternberg). Cambridge: Cambridge University Press.

Devlin, B., Daniels, M., and Roeder, K. (1997). The heritability of IQ. *Nature*, 388, 468–71.

Diamond, A. (1985). Development of the ability to use recall to guide action, as indicated by infants' performance on A-not-B. *Child Development*, 56, 868–83.

Diamond, J. M. (1998). *Guns, germs, and steel: The fates of human societies*. London: Vantage.

Dias, R., Robbins, T. W., and Roberts, A. C. (1996). Primate analogue of the Wisconsin Card Sorting Test: Effects of excitotoxic lesions of the prefrontal cortex in the marmoset. *Behavioral Neuroscience*, 110, 872–86.

Dickens, W. T. and Flynn, J. R. (2001). Heritability estimates versus large environmental effects: The IQ paradox resolved. *Psychological Review*, 108, 346–69.

Dickens, W. T. and Flynn, J. R. (2006). Black Americans reduce the racial IQ gap: Evidence from standardization samples. *Psychological Science*, 17, 913–20.

Dickinson, A. (1980). *Contemporary animal learning theory*. Cambridge: Cambridge University Press.

Dickstein, L. S. (1978). The effects of figure on syllogistic reasoning. *Memory and Cognition*, 6, 76–83.

Doll, J. and Mayr, U. (1987). Intelligenz und Schachleistung—eine Untersuchung an Schachexperten. *Psychologische Beitrage*, 29, 270–89.

Doppelmayr, M., Klimesch, W., Sauseng, P., *et al.* (2005). Intelligence related differences in EEG-bandpower. *Neuroscience Letters*, 381, 309–13.

Downey, D. B. (2001). Number of siblings and intellectual development: The resource dilution explanation. *American Psychologist*, 56, 497–504.

Duckworth, A. L. and Seligman, M. E. P. (2005). Self-discipline outdoes IQ in predicting academic performance of adolescents. *Psychological Science*, 16, 939–44.

Duckworth, A. L. and Seligman, M. E. P. (2006). Self-discipline gives girls the edge: Gender in self-discipline, grades, and achievement test scores. *Journal of Educational Psychology*, 98, 198–208.

Dumaret, A. and Stewart, J. T. (1985). IQ, scholastic performance and behaviour of sibs raised in contrasting environments. *Journal of Child Psychology and Psychiatry*, 26, 553–80.

Duncan, J., Burgess, P., and Emslie, H. (1995). Fluid intelligence after frontal lobe lesions. *Neuropsychologia*, 33, 261–8.

Duncan, J., Emslie, H., Williams, P., Johnson, R., and Freer, C. (1996). Intelligence and the frontal lobe: The organization of goal-directed behaviour. *Cognitive Psychology*, 30, 257–303.

Duncan, J., Seitz, R. J., Kolodny, J., *et al.* (2000). A neural basis for general intelligence. *Science*, 289, 457–60.

Duncker, K. (1945). On problem solving. *Psychological Monographs*, 58 (whole number 270), 1–113 (originally published in German in 1935).

Duyme, M., Dumaret, A.-C., and Tomkiewicz, S. (1999). How can we boost IQs of 'dull children'? A late adoption study. *Proceedings of the National Academy of Sciences*, 96, 8790–4.

El Koussy, A. A. H. (1935). The visual perception of space. *British Journal of Psychology*, 20 (Monograph Supplement).

Elashoff, J. D. and Snow, R. E. (1971). *'Pygmalion' reconsidered*. Worthington, OH: Charles A. Jones Publishing.

Ellis, L. and Walsh, A. (2003). Crime, delinquency and intelligence: A review of the worldwide literature. In *The scientific study of general intelligence: Tribute to Arthur R. Jensen* (ed. H. Nyborg). Oxford: Pergamon.

Ellis, N. (1994). Vocabulary acquisition: The implicit ins and outs of explicit cognitive mediation. In *Implicit and explicit learning of languages* (ed. N. Ellis). London: Academic Press.

Elo, I. T. (2009). Social class differentials in health and mortality: Patterns and explanations in comparative perspective. *Annual Review of Sociology*, 35, 553–72.

Engle, R. W., Tuholski, S. W., Laughlin, J. E., and Conway, A. R. A. (1999). Working memory, short-term memory, and general fluid intelligence: A latent-variable approach. *Journal of Experimental Psychology: General*, 128, 309–31.

Ericsson, K. A. (2006). The influence of experience and deliberate practice on the development of superior expert performance. In *Cambridge handbook of expertise and expert performance* (eds K. A. Ericsson, N. Charness, P. Feltovich, and R. R. Hoffman). Cambridge: Cambridge University Press.

Ericsson, K. A. and Charness, N. (1994). Expert performance: Its structure and acquisition. *American Psychologist*, 49, 725–47.

Ericsson, K. A., Charness, N., Feltovich, P., and Hoffman, R. R. (eds) (2006). *Cambridge handbook of expertise and expert performance*. Cambridge: Cambridge University Press.

Ertl, J., and Schafer, E. (1969). Brain response correlates of psychometric intelligence. *Nature*, 223, 421–2.

Esposito, G., Kirkby, B. S., Van Horn, J. D., Ellmore, T. M., and Berman, K. F. (1999). Context-dependent, neural system-specific neurophysiological concomitants of ageing: Mapping PET correlates during cognitive activation. *Brain: A Journal of Neurology*, 122, 963–79.

Evans, B. and Waites, B. (1981). *IQ and mental testing: An unnatural science and its social history*. London: Macmillan.

Evans, J. S. B. T. (2008). Dual-processing accounts of reasoning, judgment, and social cognition. *Annual Review of Psychology*, 59, 255–78.

Eyferth, K. (1961). Leistungen verschiedener Gruppen von Besatzungskindern in Hamburg—Weschler Intelligenztest für kinder (HAWIK). *Archiv für die Gesamte Psychologie,* 113, 222–41.

Eysenck, H. J. (1939). Primary mental abilities. *British Journal of Educational Psychology,* 9, 260–5.

Eysenck, H. J. (1979). *The structure and measurement of intelligence.* Springer Verlag: New York.

Eysenck, H. J. (ed.) (1982). *A model for intelligence.* New York: Springer-Verlag.

Eysenck, H. J. (1995). *Genius: The natural history of creativity.* Cambridge: Cambridge University Press.

Eysenck, H. J. and Schoenthaler, J. J. (1997). Raising IQ level by vitamin and mineral supplementation. In *Intelligence, heredity, and environment* (eds R. J. Sternberg and E. Grigorenko). Cambridge: Cambridge University Press.

Fagan, J. F. and Holland, C. R. (2002). Equal opportunity and racial differences in IQ. *Intelligence,* 30, 361–87.

Fagan, J. F., Holland, C. R., and Wheeler, K. (2007). The prediction, from infancy, of adult IQ and achievement. *Intelligence,* 35, 225–31.

Fagan, J. F. III (2000). A theory of intelligence as processing: Implications for society. *Psychology, Public Policy, and Law,* 6, 168–79.

Fan, H., Jackson, T., Yang, X., Tang, W., and Zhang, J. (2010). The factor structure of the Mayer-Salovey-Caruso emotional intelligence test V 2.0 (MSCEIT): A meta-analytic structural equation modeling approach. *Personality and Individual Differences,* 48, 781–5.

Fancher, R. E. (1985). *The intelligence men: Makers of the IQ controversy.* New York: Norton.

Farah, M. J., Hammon, K. M., Levine, D. N., and Calvanio, R. (1988). Visual and spatial mental imagery: Dissociable systems of representation. *Cognitive Psychology,* 20, 439–62.

Farber, S. L. (1981). *Identical twins reared apart: A reanalysis.* New York: Basic Books.

Feingold, A. (1988). Cognitive gender differences are disappearing. *American Psychologist,* 43, 95–103.

Feingold, A. (1992). Sex differences in variability in intellectual abilities: A new look at an old controversy. *Review of Educational Research,* 62, 61–84.

Feldman, J., Kerr, B., and Streissguth, A. P. (1995). Correlational analyses of procedural and declarative learning performance. *Intelligence,* 20, 87–114.

Fenson, L., Dale, P. S., Reznick,, J. S., Bates, E., Thal, D. J., and Pethnick, S. J. (1994). Variability in early communicative development. *Monographs of the Society for Research in Child Development,* 59, Serial No. 242.

Ferguson, R. F. (1998). Teachers' perceptions and expectations and the black-white test score gap. In *The black-white test score gap* (eds C. Jencks and M. Phillips). Washington, DC: Brookings Institution Press.

Fick, M. L. (1929). Intelligence test results of poor white, native (Zulu), coloured and Indian school children and the educational and social implications. *South African Journal of Science,* 26, 904–20.

Finger, S. (1994). *Origins of neuroscience: A history of explorations into brain functions.* Oxford: Oxford University Press.

Fischer, C. S., Hout, M., Jankowski, M. S., *et al.* (1996). *Inequality by design: Cracking the bell curve myth.* Princeton, NJ: Princeton University Press.

Flashman, L. A., Andreasen, N. C., Flaum, M., and Swayze, V. W. II (1997). Intelligence and regional brain volumes in normal controls. *Intelligence,* 25, 149–60.

Fletcher, R. (1991). *Science, ideology and the media: The Cyril Burt scandal.* New Brunswick, NJ: Transaction.

Floud, J. and Halsey, A. H. (1957). Intelligence tests, social class and selection for secondary schools. *British Journal of Sociology,* 8, 33–9.

Flynn, J. R. (1980). *Race, IQ and Jensen.* London: Routledge and Kegan Paul.

Flynn, J. R. (1984). The mean IQ of Americans: Massive gains 1932 to 1978. *Psychological Bulletin,* 95, 29–51.

Flynn, J. R. (1987). Massive IQ gains in 14 nations: What IQ tests really measure. *Psychological Bulletin,* 101, 171–91.

Flynn, J. R. (1992). *Asian Americans: Achievement beyond IQ.* Hillsdale, NJ: Lawrence Erlbaum.

Flynn, J. R. (1996). Group differences: Is the good society impossible? *Journal of Biosocial Science,* 28, 573–85.

Flynn, J. R. (2000). IQ gains, WISC subtests, and fluid g: g theory and the relevance of Spearman's hypothesis to race. In *The nature of intelligence* (Novartis Foundation Symposium 233), (eds G. R. Bock, J. A. Goode, and K. Webb). New York: Wiley.

Flynn, J. R. (2007). *What is intelligence? Beyond the Flynn effect.* Cambridge: Cambridge University Press.

Flynn, J. R. (2008). *Where have all the liberals gone? Race, class, and ideals in America.* Cambridge: Cambridge University Press.

Ford, M. E. and Tisak, M. S. (1983). A further search for social intelligence. *Journal of Educational Psychology,* 75, 197–206.

Fox, M. C., Roring, R. W., and Mitchum, A. L. (2009). Reversing the speed-IQ correlation: Intra-individual variability and attentional control in the inspection time paradigm. *Intelligence,* 37, 76–80.

Frearson, W. M. and Eysenck, H. J. (1986). Intelligence, reaction time (RT) and a new 'odd-man-out' RT paradigm. *Personality and Individual Differences*, 7, 807–17.

Frearson, W. M., Barrett, P., and Eysenck, H. J. (1988). Intelligence, reaction time, and the effects of smoking. *Personality and Individual Differences*, 9, 497–519.

Freeman, F. N., Holzinger, K. J., and Mitchell, B. C. (1928). The influence of environment on the intelligence, school achievement, and conduct of foster children. *27th Yearbook of the National Society for the Study of Education*, 27, Part I.

Freeney, Y. and O'Connell, M. (2010). Wait for it: Delay-discounting and academic performance among an Irish adolescent sample. *Learning and Individual Differences*, 20, 231–6.

Friedman, L. (1995). The space factor in mathematics: Gender differences. *Review of Educational Research*, 65, 22–50.

Friedman, N. P., Miyake, A., Corley, R. P., *et al.* (2006). Not all executive functions are related to intelligence. *Psychological Science*, 17, 172–9.

Fry, A. F. and Hale, S. (1996). Processing speed, working memory, and fluid intelligence: Evidence for a developmental cascade. *Psychological Science*, 7, 237–41.

Frydman, M. and Lynn, R. (1989). The intelligence of Korean children adopted in Belgium. *Personality and Individual Differences*, 10, 1323–5.

Furlow, F. B., Armijo-Prewitt, T., Gangestad, S. W., and Thornhill, R. (1997). Fluctuating asymmetry and psychometric intelligence. *Proceedings of the Royal Society of London. Series B: Biological Sciences*, 264, 823–9.

Galea, L. A. M. and Kimura, D. (1993). Sex differences in route-learning. *Personality and Individual Differences*, 14, 53–65.

Galea, L. A. M., Kavaliers, M., Ossenkopp, K. P., and Innes, D. (1994). Sexually dimorphic spatial learning varies seasonally in two populations of deer mice. *Brain Research*, 635, 18–26.

Galea, S., Sisco, S., and Vlahov, D. (2005). Reducing disparities in vaccination rates between different racial/ethnic and socioeconomic groups: the potential of community-based multilevel interventions. *Journal of Ambulatory Care Management*, 28, 49–51.

Gallagher, A. M. and Kaufman, J. C. (2005). Gender differences in mathematics: What we know and what we need to know. In *Gender differences in mathematics: An integrative psychological approach* (eds A. M. Gallagher and J. C. Kaufman). Cambridge: Cambridge University Press.

Gallagher, A. M. and Kaufman, J. C. (eds) (2005). *Gender differences in mathematics: An integrative psychological approach*. Cambridge: Cambridge University Press.

Galton, F. (1869). *Hereditary genius: An inquiry into its laws and consequences*. London: MacMillan.

Galton, F. (1883). *Inquiries into human faculty, and its development*. London: MacMillan.

Galton, F. (1908). *Memories of my life*. London: Methuen.

Garber, H. L. (1988). *The Milwaukee Project: Preventing mental retardation in children at risk*. Washington, DC: American Association on Mental Retardation.

Garces, E., Thomas, D., and Currie, J. (2002). Longer term effects of Head Start. *American Economic Review*, 92, 999–1012.

Gardner, H. (1993). *Frames of mind* (2nd edn). New York: Basic Books.

Gardner, H. (1997). *Extraordinary minds*. New York: Basic Books.

Gardner, H. (2006). *Multiple intelligences: New horizons* (revised edn). New York: Basic Books.

Gathercole, S. E., and Baddeley, A. D. (1990). The role of phonological memory in vocabulary acquisition. A study of young children learning new names. *British Journal of Psychology*, 81, 439–54.

Gathercole, S. E., Adams, A.-M., and Hitch, G. J. (1994). Do young children rehearse? An individual-differences analysis. *Memory & Cognition*, 22, 201–7.

Gaulin, S. J. C. and Fitzgerald, R. W. (1989). Sexual selection for spatial-learning ability. *Animal Behaviour*, 37, 322–31.

Gaw, F. (1925). A study of performance tests. *British Journal of Psychology*, 15, 374–92.

Gazzaley, A. and D'Esposito, M. (2007). Unifying prefrontal cortex function: Executive control, neural networks, and top-down modulation. In *The human frontal lobes: Functions and disorders* (2nd edn), (eds B. L. Miller and J. L. Cummings). New York: Guilford Press.

Geary, D. C. (1998). *Male, female: The evolution of human sex differences*. Washington, DC: American Psychological Association.

Gebauer, G. F. (2003). Implicit learning and intelligence. Unpublished Ph.D. Thesis, University of Cambridge.

Gebauer, G. F. and Mackintosh, N. J. (2007). Psychometric intelligence dissociates implicit and explicit learning. *Journal of Experimental Psychology: Learning, Memory, and Cognition*, 33, 34–54.

Geisinger, K. F., Spies, R. A., Carlson, J. F., and Plake, B. S. (eds) (2007). *The seventeenth mental measurements yearbook*. Lincoln, NE: Buros Institute of Mental Measurements.

Geschwind, N. and Galaburda, A. M. (1987). *Cerebral lateralization: Biological mechanisms, associations and pathology*. Cambridge, MA: MIT Press.

Ghiselli, E. E. (1966). *The validity of occupational aptitude tests*. New York: Wiley.

Ghiselli, E. E. (1973). The validity of aptitude tests in personnel selection. *Personnel Psychology*, 26, 461–77.

Giannitrapini, D. (1985). *The electrophysiology of intellectual function*. Basel: Karger.

Gibbs, C. H. (2000). *The life of Schubert*. Cambridge: Cambridge University Press.

Gick, M. L. and Holyoak, K. J. (1980). Analogical problem solving. *Cognitive Psychology*, 12, 306–55.

Gick, M. L. and Holyoak, K. J. (1983). Schema induction and analogical transfer. *Cognitive Psychology*, 15, 1–38.

Gignac, G., Vernon, P. A. and Wickett, J. C. (2003). Factors influencing the relationship between brain size and intelligence. In *The scientific study of general intelligence: Tribute to Arthur R. Jensen* (ed. H. Nyborg). Oxford: Pergamon.

Gilhooly, K. J., Logie, R. H., Wetherick, N. E., and Wynn, V. (1993). Working memory and strategies in syllogistic reasoning tasks. *Memory and Cognition*, 21, 115–24.

Gillham, N. W. (2001). *A life of Sir Francis Galton: From African exploration to the birth of eugenics*. Oxford: Oxford University Press.

Gittings, R. (1968). *John Keats*. London: Heinemann.

Glanzer, M. and Cunitz, A. R. (1966). Two storage mechanisms in free recall. *Journal of Verbal Learning and Verbal Behavior*, 5, 351–60.

Gobet, F. and Charness, N. (2006). Chess and games. In *Cambridge handbook of expertise and expert performance* (eds K. A. Ericsson, N. Charness, P. Feltovich, and R. R. Hoffman). Cambridge: Cambridge University Press.

Goddard, H. H. (1911). Two thousand normal children measured by the Binet measuring scale of intelligence. *Pedagogical Seminary*, 18, 232–59.

Goddard, H. H. (1912). *The Kallikak family: A study in the heredity of feeble-mindedness*. New York: MacMillan.

Goddard, H. H. (1914). *Feeble-mindedness: Its causes and consequences*. New York: MacMillan.

Goddard, H. H. (1916). *Publication of the Vineland Training School*. No. 11. Vineland: N J.

Goddard, H. H. (1917). Mental tests and the immigrant. *Journal of Delinquency*, 2, 243–77.

Goel, V., Buchel, C., Frith, C., and Dolan, R. J. (2000). Dissociation of mechanisms underlying syllogistic reasoning. *NeuroImage*, 12, 504–14.

Gogtay, N., Giedd, J. N., Lusk, L., *et al.* (2004). Dynamic mapping of human cortical development during childhood through early adulthood. *Proceedings of the National Academy of Sciences*, 101, 8174–9.

Goldberg, R. A., Schwartz, S., and Stewart, M. (1977). Individual differences in cognitive processes. *Journal of Educational Psychology*, 69, 9–14.

Goleman, D. (1995). *Emotional intelligence*. New York: Bantam.

Goleman, D. (1998). What makes a leader? *Harvard Business Review*, Nov–Dec, 93–102.

Gordon, H. (1923). *Mental and scholastic tests among retarded children*. London: Board of Education pamphlet no. 44.

Gordon, R. A. (1997). Everyday life as an intelligence test: Effects of intelligence and intelligence context. *Intelligence*, 24, 203–320.

Goswami, U. C. (1992). *Analogical reasoning in children*. Hove, UK: Lawrence Erlbaum.

Gottesman, I. I. (1991). *Schizophrenia genesis*. New York: Freeman.

Gottfredson, L. S. (2002). g: Highly general and highly practical. In *The general factor of intelligence: How general is it?* (eds R. J. Sternberg and E. L. Grigorenko). Mahwah, NJ: Lawrence Erlbaum.

Gottfredson, L. S. (2003a). g, jobs, and life. In *The scientific study of general intelligence: Tribute to Arthur R. Jensen* (ed. H. Nyborg). Oxford: Pergamon.

Gottfredson, L. S. (2003b). Dissecting practical intelligence theory: Its claims and evidence. *Intelligence*, 31, 343–97.

Gottfredson, L. S. and Deary, I. J. (2004). Intelligence predicts health and longevity, but why? *Current Directions in Psychological Science*, 13, 1–4.

Gould, S. J. (1986) *The flamingo's smile*. London: Penguin Books.

Gould, S. J. (1997). *The mismeasure of man* (2nd edn). London: Penguin Books.

Grabner, R. H., Neubauer, A. C., and Stern, E. (2006). Superior performance and neural efficiency: The impact of intelligence and expertise. *Brain Research Bulletin*, 69, 422–39.

Grantham-McGregor, S., Ani, C., and Fernald, L. (2001). The role of nutrition in intellectual development. In *Environmental effects on cognitive abilities* (eds R. J. Sternberg and E. L. Grigorenko). Mahwah, NJ: Lawrence Erlbaum.

Gray, J. R., Chabris, C. F., and Braver, T. S. (2003). Neural mechanisms of general fluid intelligence. *Nature Neuroscience*, 6, 316–22.

Green, C. S. and Bavelier, D. (2003). Action video game modifies visual selective attention. *Nature*, 423, 534–7.

Griffiths, P., Demellweek, C., Fay, N., Robinson, P., and Davidson, D. (2000). Wechsler subscale IQ and subtest profile in early treated phenylketonuria. *Archives of Disease in Childhood*, 82, 209–15.

Grigorenko, E. L. (2000). Heritability and intelligence. In *Handbook of intelligence* (ed. R. J. Sternberg). Cambridge: Cambridge University Press.

Grissmer, D., Flanagan, A., and Williamson, S. (1998). Why did the black-white score gap narrow in the 1970s and 1980s? In *The black-white test score gap* (eds C. Jencks and M. Phillips). Washington, DC: Brookings Institution Press.

Grudnik, J. L. and Kranzler, J. H. (2001). Meta-analysis of the relationship between intelligence and inspection time. *Intelligence, 29*, 523–35.

Guilford, J. P. (1967). *The nature of human intelligence.* New York: McGraw-Hill.

Guilford, J. P. (1982). Cognitive psychology's ambiguities: Some suggested remedies. *Psychological Review, 89*, 48–59.

Guilford, J. P. (1988). Some changes in the structure-of-intellect model. *Educational and Psychological Measurement, 48*, 1–4.

Guilford, J. P., and Hoepfner, R. (1971). *The analysis of intelligence.* New York: McGraw- Hill.

Gur, R. C., Turetsky, B. I., Matsui, M., *et al.* (1999). Sex differences in brain gray and white matter in healthy young adults: Correlations with cognitive performance. *The Journal of Neuroscience, 19*, 4065–72.

Gustafsson, J.-E. (1988). Hierarchical models of individual differences in cognitive abilities. In *Advances in the psychology of human intelligence* (vol. 4), (ed. R. J. Sternberg). Hillsdale, NJ: Lawrence Erlbaum.

Gustafsson, J.-E. and Undheim, J. O. (1996). Individual differences in cognitive functions. In *Handbook of educational psychology* (eds D. C. Berliner and R. C. Calfee). New York: Macmillan.

Gutkin, T. B. and Reynolds, C. R. (1981). Factorial similarity of the WISC-R for White and Black children from the standardization sample. *Journal of Educational Psychology, 73*, 227–31.

Guttman, L. (1957). Empirical verification of the radex structure of mental abilities and personality traits. *Educational and Psychological Measurement, 17*, 391–407.

Haavisto, M.-L. and Lehto, J. E. (2005). Fluid/spatial and crystallized intelligence in relation to domain-specific working memory: A latent-variable approach. *Learning and Individual Differences, 15*, 1–21.

Haier, R. J., Colom, R., Schroeder, D. H., *et al.* (2009). Gray matter and intelligence factors: Is there a neuro-g? *Intelligence, 37*, 136–44.

Haier, R. J., Jung, R. E., Yeo, R. A., Head, K., and Alkire, M. T. (2005). The neuroanatomy of general intelligence: sex matters. *NeuroImage, 25*, 320–7.

Haier, R. J., Siegel, B. V., MacLachlan, A., and Soderling, E. (1992). Regional glucose metabolic changes after learning a complex visuospatial/motor task: A positron emission tomographic study. *Brain Research, 570*, 134–43.

Hall, V. C. and Kaye, D. B. (1980). Early patterns of cognitive development. *Monographs of the Society for Research in Child Development.* Serial no. 184.

Halpern, D. F. (2000). *Sex differences in cognitive abilities* (3rd edn). Mahwah, NJ: Lawrence Erlbaum.

Halpern, D. F. and Collaer, M. L. (2005). Sex differences in visuospatial abilities: More than meets the eye. In *The Cambridge handbook of visuospatial thinking* (eds P. Shah and A. Miyake). Cambridge: Cambridge University Press.

Halpern, D. F., Wai, J., and Saw, A. (2005). A psychobiosocial model: Why females are sometimes greater than and sometimes less than males in math achievement. In *Gender differences in mathematics: An integrative psychological approach* (eds A. M. Gallagher and J. C. Kaufman). Cambridge: Cambridge University Press.

Hanley, J. R., Young. A. W., and Pearson, N. A. (1991). Impairment of the visuo-spatial scratch pad. *Quarterly Journal of Experimental Psychology, 43A*, 101–25.

Harden, K. P., Turkheimer, E., and Loehlin, J. C. (2007). Genotype by environment interaction in adolescents' cognitive aptitude. *Behavior Genetics, 37*, 273–83.

Harnqvist, K. (1968). Relative changes in intelligence from 3–18. I. Background and methodology. *Scandinavian Journal of Psychology, 9*, 50–64.

Harrell, T. W. and Harrell, M. S. (1945). Army General Classification Test scores for civilian occupations. *Educational and Psychological Measurement, 5*, 229–39.

Harris, J. R. (1998). *The nurture assumption: Why children turn out the way they do.* New York: Free Press.

Hart, B. and Risley, T. R. (1995). *Meaningful differences in the everyday experience of young American children.* Baltimore, MD: Paul H Brookes.

Hartigan, J. and Wigdor, A. K. (1989). *Fairness in employment testing: Validity generalization, minority issues, and the General Aptitude Test Battery.* Washington, DC: National Academy Press.

Haworth, C. M. A., Wright, M. J., Luciano, M., *et al.* (2009). The heritability of general cognitive ability increases linearly from childhood to young adulthood. *Molecular Pscyhiatry*, Advance publication, 2 June 2009.

Hearnshaw, L. S. (1979). *Cyril Burt: Psychologist.* London: Hodder and Stoughton.

Hebb, D. O. (1949). *The organization of behavior: A neuropsychological theory.* New York: Wiley.

Hebb, D. O. and Penfield, W. (1940). Human behaviour after extensive removal from the frontal lobes. *Archives of Neurology and Psychiatry, 44*, 421–38.

Heckman, J. J. (2006). Skill formation and the economics of investing in disadvantaged children. *Science, 312*, 1900–2.

Hedges, L. V. and Nowell, A. (1995). Sex differences in mental test scores, variability, and numbers of high-scoring individuals. *Science, 269*, 41–5.

Hedges, L. V. and Nowell, A. (1998). Black-white test score convergence since 1965. In *The black-white test score gap* (eds C. Jencks and M. Phillips). Washington, DC: Brookings Institution Press.

Hedlund, J., Wilt, J. M., Nebel, K. L., Ashford, S. J., and Sternberg, R. J. (2006). Assessing practical intelligence in business school admissions: A supplement to the graduate management admissions test. *Learning and Individual Differences, 16,* 101–27.

Hegarty, M. and Waller, D. A. (2005). Individual differences in spatial abilities. In *The Cambridge handbook of visuospatial thinking* (eds A. Miyake and P. Shah). Cambridge: Cambridge University Press.

Hegarty, M., Montello, D. R., Richardson, A. E., Ishikawa, T., and Lovelace, K. (2006). Spatial abilities at different scales: Individual differences in aptitude-test performance and spatial-layout learning. *Intelligence, 34,* 151–76.

Heil, M. and Jansen-Osmann, P. (2008). Sex differences in mental rotation with polygons of different complexity: Do men utilize holistic processes whereas women prefer piecemeal ones? *The Quarterly Journal of Experimental Psychology, 61,* 683–9.

Heine, S. J. (2008). *Cultural psychology.* New York: Norton.

Hendrickson, A. E (1982). The biological basis of intelligence. Part I: Theory. In *A model for intelligence* (ed. H. J. Eysenck). New York: Springer-Verlag.

Hendrickson, A. E. and Hendrickson, D. E. (1980). The biological basis for individual differences in intelligence. *Personality and Individual Differences, 1,* 3–33.

Hendrickson, D. E. (1982). The biological basis of intelligence. Part II: Measurement. In *A model for intelligence* (ed. H. J. Eysenck). New York: Springer-Verlag.

Henson, R. (2001). Neural working memory. In *Working memory in perspective* (ed. J. Andrade). New York: Psychology Press.

Hermelin, B. and O'Connor, N. (1978). The idiot savant: flawed genius or clever Hans? *Psychological Medicine, 13,* 479–81.

Herrnstein, R. J. and Murray, C. (1994). *The bell curve: Intelligence and class structure in American life.* New York: Free Press.

Heyes, C. M. (1998). Theory of mind in nonhuman primates. *Behavioral and Brain Sciences, 21,* 101–34.

Hick, W. E. (1952). On the rate of gain of information. *Quarterly Journal of Experimental Psychology, 4,* 11–26.

Hill, L., Chorney, M. J., Lubinski, D., Thompson, L. A., and Plomin, R. (2002). A quantitative trait locus not associated with cognitive ability in children: A failure to replicate. *Psychological Science, 13,* 561–2.

Hirschi, T. and Hindelang, M. J. (1977). Intelligence and delinquency: A revisionist review. *American Sociological Review, 42,* 571–87.

Hitch, G. J. (1978). The role of short-term working memory in mental arithmetic. *Cognitive Psychology, 10,* 302–23.

Hitch, G. J., Towse, J. N., and Hutton, U. (2001). What limits children's working memory span? Theoretical accounts and applications for scholastic development. *Journal of Experimental Psychology: General, 130,* 184–98.

Holahan, C. K. and Sears, R. R. (1995). *The gifted group in later maturity.* Stanford, CA: Stanford University Press.

Horgan, D. D. and Morgan, D. (1990). Chess expertise in children. *Applied Cognitive Psychology, 4,* 109–28.

Horn, J. L. (1985). Remodeling old models of intelligence. In *Handbook of intelligence* (ed. B. B. Wolman). New York: Wiley.

Horn, J. L. (1972). Intelligence: Why it grows, why it declines. In *Human intelligence* (ed. J. M. Hunt). Oxford: Transaction Books.

Horn, J. L. and Cattell, R. B. (1966). Refinement and test of the theory of fluid and crystallized general intelligences. *Journal of Educational Psychology, 57,* 253–70.

Horn, J. L. and Knapp, J. R. (1973). On the subjective character of the empirical base of Guilford's structure-of-intellect model. *Psychological Bulletin, 80,* 33–43.

Horn, J. M., Loehlin, J. C., and Willerman, L. (1982). Aspects of the inheritance of intellectual abilities. *Behavior Genetics, 12,* 479–516.

Horn, W. F. and Packard, T. (1985). Early identification of learning problems: a meta-analysis. *Journal of Educational Psychology, 77,* 597–607.

Howard, A. and Bray, D. W. (1988). *Managerial lives in transition: Advancing age and changing times.* New York: Guilford Press.

Howe, M. J. A. (1999). *Genius explained.* Cambridge: Cambridge University Press.

Howe, M. J. A. and Smith, J. (1988). Calendar calculating in 'idiots savants': how do they do it? *British Journal of Psychology, 79,* 371–86.

Huang, M.-H. and Hauser, R. M. (1998). Trends in black-white test score differentials: II. The WORDSUM Vocabulary Test. In *The rising curve: Long-term gains in IQ and related measures* (ed. U. Neisser). Washington, DC: American Psychological Association.

Hugdahl, K., Thomsen, T., and Ersland, L. (2006). Sex differences in visuo-spatial processing: An fMRI study of mental rotation. *Neuropsychologia, 44,* 1575–83.

Huizink, A. C. and Mulder, E. J. H. (2006). Maternal smoking, drinking or cannabis use during pregnancy and neurobehavioral and cognitive functioning in human offspring. *Neuroscience and Biobehavioral Reviews, 30,* 24–41.

Hull, C. L. (1928). *Aptitude testing.* New York: World Book Co.

Hulme, C., Thomson, N., Muir, C., and Lawrence, A. (1984). Speech rate and the development of short-term memory span. *Journal of Experimental Child Psychology, 38,* 241–53.

Humphrey, N. K. (1976). The social function of intellect. In *Growing points in ethology* (eds P. P. G. Bateson and R. A. Hinde). Cambridge: Cambridge University Press.

Humphreys, L. G. and Lubinski, D. (1996). Assessing spatial visualization: An underappreciated ability for many school and work settings. In *Intellectual talent: Psychometric and social issues* (eds C. P. Benbow and D. Lubinski). Baltimore: Johns Hopkins University Press.

Hunt, E. B. (1978). Mechanics of verbal ability. *Psychological Review, 85,* 109–30.

Hunt, E. B. (1980). Intelligence as an information-processing concept. *British Journal of Psychology, 71,* 449–74.

Hunt, E. B. (1985). Verbal ability. In *Human abilities: An information-processing approach* (ed. R. J. Sternberg). New York: Freeman.

Hunt, E. B. (1987). The next word on verbal ability. In *Speed of information-processing and intelligence* (ed. P. A. Vernon). Norwood, NJ: Ablex.

Hunt, E. B. (1995). *Will we be smart enough? A cognitive analysis of the coming workforce.* New York: Russell Sage.

Hunt, E. B. and Carlson, J. S. (2007). The standards for conducting research on topics of immediate social relevance. *Intelligence, 35,* 393–9.

Hunt, E. B., Lunneborg, C. L. and Lewis, J. (1975). What does it mean to be high verbal? *Cognitive Psychology, 7,* 194–227.

Hunt, T. (1928). The measurement of social intelligence. *Journal of Applied Psychology, 12,* 317–34.

Huttenlocher, J., Haight, W., Bryk, A., Seltzer, M., and Lyons, T. (1991). Early vocabulary growth: Relation to language input and gender. *Developmental Psychology, 27,* 236–48.

Hyde, G. and Trickey, G. (1995). *Differential Aptitude Test (DAT) for guidance—manual.* London: Psychological Corporation.

Hyde, J. S. (1981). How large are cognitive gender differences? *American Psychologist, 36,* 892–901.

Hyde, J. S. (2007). Women in science: Gender similarities in abilities and sociocultural forces. In *Why aren't more women in science: Top researchers debate the evidence* (eds S. J. Ceci and W. M. Williams). Washington, DC: American Psychological Association.

Hyde, J. S. and Linn, M. C. (1988). Gender differences in verbal ability: A meta-analysis. *Psychological Bulletin, 104,* 153–69.

Hyde, J. S., Fennema, E., and Lamon, S. J. (1990). Gender differences in mathematics performance: A meta-analysis. *Psychological Bulletin, 107,* 139–55.

Ilai, D. and Willerman, L. (1989). Sex differences in WAIS-R item performance. *Intelligence, 13,* 225–34.

Inhelder, B. and Piaget, J. (1958). *The growth of logical thinking from childhood to adolescence: An essay on the construction of formal operational structures.* New York: Basic Books.

Irwin, R. J. (1984). Inspection time and its relation to intelligence. *Intelligence, 8,* 47–65.

Irwing, P. and Lynn, R. (2005). Sex differences in means and variability on the progressive matrices in university students: A meta-analysis. *British Journal of Psychology, 96,* 505–24.

Isgor, C. and Sengelaub, D. R. (1998). Prenatal gonadal steroids affect adult spatial behavior, CA1 and CA3 pyramidal cell morphology in rats. *Hormones and Behavior, 34,* 183–98.

Jackson, M. (1980). Further evidence for a relationship between memory access and reading ability. *Journal of Verbal Learning and Verbal Behavior, 19,* 683–94.

Jacobsen, C. F. (1936). Studies of cerebral function in primates. I. The functions of the frontal association areas in monkeys. *Comparative Psychology Monographs, 13*(3), 1–60.

Jacoby, L. L. (1991). A process dissociation framework: Separating automatic from intentional uses of memory. *Journal of Memory and Language, 30,* 513–41.

Jacoby, L. L., Debner, J. A., and Hay, J. F. (2001). Proactive interference, accessibility bias, and process dissociations: Valid subject reports of memory. *Journal of Experimental Psychology: Learning, Memory, and Cognition, 27,* 686–700.

Jaeggi, S. M., Buschkuehl, M., Jonides, J., and Perrig, W. J. (2008). Improving fluid intelligence with training on working memory. *Proceedings of the National Academy of Sciences, 105,* 6829–33.

Janssen, R., De Boeck, P., and Steene, G. V. (1996). Verbal fluency and verbal comprehension abilities in synonym tasks. *Intelligence, 22,* 291–310.

Jencks, C. (1972). *Inequality: A reassessment of the effect of family and schooling in America.* New York: Basic Books.

Jencks, C. (1992). *Rethinking social policy: Race, poverty, and the underclass.* Cambridge, MA: Harvard University Press.

Jencks, C. and Phillips, M. (eds) (1998). *The black-white test score gap.* Washington, DC: Brookings Institution Press.

Jensen, A. R. (1969). How much can we boost IQ and scholastic achievement? *Harvard Educational Review,* 39, 1–123.

Jensen, A. R. (1980). *Bias in mental testing.* London: Methuen.

Jensen, A. R. (1987). Individual differences in the Hick paradigm. In *Speed of information-processing and intelligence* (ed. P. A. Vernon). Northwood, NJ: Ablex.

Jensen, A. R. (1989). Raising IQ without increasing *g*? A review of the Milwaukee Project: Preventing mental retardation in children at risk. *Developmental Review,* 9, 234–58.

Jensen, A. R. (1993). Spearman's hypothesis tested with chronometric information-processing tasks. *Intelligence,* 17, 47–77.

Jensen, A. R. (1997). The puzzle of nongenetic variance. In *Intelligence, heredity and environment* (eds R. J. Sternberg and E. Grigorenko). Cambridge: Cambridge University Press.

Jensen, A. R. (1998). *The g factor: The science of mental ability.* Westport, CT: Praeger Publishers.

Jensen, A. R. (2005). Mental chronometry and the unification of differential psychology. In *Cognition and intelligence: Identifying the mechanisms of the mind* (eds R. J. Sternberg and J. E. Pretz). Cambridge: Cambridge University Press.

Jensen, A. R. (2006). *Clocking the mind: Mental chronometry and individual differences.* Oxford: Elsevier.

Jensen, A. R. and Figueroa, R. A. (1975). Forward and backward digit-span interaction with race and IQ: Predictions from Jensen's theory. *Journal of Educational Psychology,* 67, 882–93.

Jensen, A. R. and Reynolds, C. R. (1983). Sex differences on the WISC-R. *Personality and Individual Differences,* 4, 223–6.

Jensen, A. R. and Sinha, S. N. (1993). Physical correlates of human intelligence. In *Biological approaches to the study of human intelligence* (ed. P. A. Vernon). Norwood, NJ: Ablex.

Jensen, A. R. and Whang, P. A. (1993). Reaction times and intelligence: A comparison of Chinese-American and Anglo-American children. *Journal of Biosocial Science,* 25, 397–410.

Johns, M., Schmader, T., and Martens, A. (2005). Knowing is half the battle: teaching stereotype threat as a means of improving women's math performance. *Psychological Science,* 16, 175–9.

Johnson, M. H. and Morton, J. (1991). *Biology and cognitive development.* Oxford: Blackwell.

Johnson, W. and Bouchard, T. J. Jr. (2005). The structure of human intelligence: It is verbal, perceptual, and image rotation (VPR), not fluid and crystallized. *Intelligence,* 33, 393–416.

Johnson, W. and Bouchard, T. J. Jr. (2007). Sex differences in mental abilities: *g* masks the dimensions on which they lie. *Intelligence,* 35, 23–39.

Johnson, W., Bouchard, T. J. Jr, Krueger, R. F., McGue, M., and Gottesman, I. I. (2004). Just one *g*: Consistent results from three test batteries. *Intelligence,* 32, 95–107.

Johnson, W., Brett, C. E., and Deary, I. J. (2010). Intergenerational class mobility in Britain: A comparative look across three generations in the Lothian birth cohort 1936. *Intelligence,* 38, 268–81.

Johnson, W., te Nijenhuis, J., and Bouchard, T. J. Jr. (2008). Still just 1 *g*: Consistent results from five test batteries. *Intelligence,* 36, 81.

Johnson-Laird, P. N. (2001). Mental models and deduction. *Trends in Cognitive Sciences,* 5, 434–42.

Johnson-Laird, P. N. and Byrne, R. (1991). *Deduction.* Hove, UK: Lawrence Erlbaum.

Jones, C. M., Braithwaite, V. A., and Healy, S. D. (2003). The evolution of sex differences in spatial ability. *Behavioral Neuroscience,* 117, 403–11.

Jorde, L. B. and Wooding, S. P. (2004). Genetic variation, classification and 'race'. *Nature Genetics,* 36, S28–33.

Joynson, R. B. (1989). *The Burt affair.* London: Routledge.

Juel-Nielsen, N. (1980). *Individual and environment: Monozygotic twins reared apart.* New York; International Universities Press.

Juhel, J. (1993). Should we take the shape of reaction time distributions into account when studying the relationship between RT and psychometric intelligence? *Personality and Individual Differences,* 15, 357–60.

Jung, R. E. and Haier, R. J. (2007). The Parieto-Frontal Integration Theory (P-FIT) of intelligence: Converging neuroimaging evidence. *Behavioral and Brain Sciences,* 30, 135–54.

Jurden, F. H. (1995). Individual differences in working memory and complex cognition. *Journal of Educational Psychology,* 87, 93–102.

Kahneman, D. (2003). A perspective on judgment and choice: Mapping bounded rationality. *American Psychologist,* 58, 697–720.

Kail, R. V. (1988). Developmental functions for speeds of cognitive processes. *Journal of Experimental Child Psychology,* 45, 339–364.

Kail, R. V. (1991). Processing time declines exponentially during childhood and adolescence. *Developmental Psychology,* 27, 259–66.

Kail, R. V. (2007). Longitudinal evidence that increases in processing speed and working memory enhance children's reasoning. *Psychological Science,* 18, 312–3.

Kail, R. V. and Salthouse, T. A. (1994). Processing speed as a mental capacity. *Acta Psychologica,* 86, 199–225.

Kamin, L. J. (1974). *The science and politics of IQ.* Potomac, MD: Lawrence Erlbaum.

Kamin, L. J. (1981). *Intelligence: The battle for the mind. (H. J. Eysenck versus Leon Kamin).* London: Macmillan.

Kandel, E., Mednick, S. A., Kirkegaard-Sorensen, L., *et al.* (1988). IQ as a protective factor for subjects at high risk for antisocial behavior. *Journal of Consulting and Clinical Psychology,* 56, 224–6.

Kane, M. J. (2005). Full frontal fluidity? Looking in on the neuroimaging of reasoning and intelligence. In *Handbook of understanding and measuring intelligence* (eds O. Wilhelm and R. W. Engle). Thousand Oaks, CA: Sage.

Kane, M. J. and Engle, R. W. (2000). Working-memory capacity, proactive interference, and divided attention: Limits on long-term memory retrieval. *Journal of Experimental Psychology: Learning, Memory, and Cognition,* 26, 336–58.

Kane, M. J. and Engle, R. W. (2003). Working-memory capacity and the control of attention: The contributions of goal neglect, response competition, and task set to Stroop interference. *Journal of Experimental Psychology: General,* 132, 47–70.

Kane, M. J., Hambrick, D. Z., and Conway, A. R. A. (2005). Working memory capacity and fluid intelligence are strongly related constructs: Comment on Ackerman, Beier, and Boyle (2005). *Psychological Bulletin,* 131, 66–71.

Kane, M. J., Hambrick, D. Z., Tuholski, S. W., *et al.* (2004). The generality of working memory capacity: A latent-variable approach to verbal and visuospatial memory span and reasoning. *Journal of Experimental Psychology: General,* 133, 189–217.

Karmiloff-Smith, A. (1998). Development itself is the key to understanding developmental disorders. *Trends in Cognitive Sciences,* 2, 389–98.

Kaufman, A. S. (2001a). Do low levels of lead produce IQ loss in children? A careful examination of the literature. *Archives of Clinical Neuropsychology,* 16, 303–41.

Kaufman, A. S. (2001b). How dangerous are low (not moderate or high) doses of lead for children's intellectual development? *Archives of Clinical Neuropsychology,* 16, 403–31.

Kaufman, A. S. and Doppelt, J. E. (1976). Analysis of WISC-R standardization data in terms of the stratification data. *Child Development,* 47, 165–71.

Kaufman, S. B. (2007). Sex differences in mental rotation and spatial visualization ability: Can they be accounted for by differences in working memory capacity? *Intelligence,* 35, 211–23.

Kaufman, S. B. (2011). Intelligence and the cognitive unconscious. In *Cambridge handbook of intelligence* (eds R. J. Sternberg and S. B. Kaufman). Cambridge: Cambridge University Press.

Kaufman, S. B., DeYoung, C. G., Gray, J. R., Brown, J., and Mackintosh, N. (2009). Associative learning predicts intelligence above and beyond working memory and processing speed. *Intelligence,* 37, 374–82.

Kaufman, S. B., DeYoung, C. G., Gray, J. R., *et al.* (2010). Implicit learning as an ability. *Cognition,* 116, 321–40.

Kavšek, M. (2004). Predicting later IQ from infant visual habituation and dishabituation: A meta-analysis. *Journal of Applied Developmental Psychology,* 25, 369–93.

Keating, D. P. (1978). A search for social intelligence. *Journal of Educational Psychology,* 70, 218–23.

Keith, T. Z., Reynolds, M. R., Patel, P. G., and Ridley, K. P. (2008). Sex differences in latent cognitive abilities ages 6 to 59: Evidence from the Woodcock-Johnson III tests of cognitive abilities. *Intelligence,* 36, 502–25.

Keren, G. and Schul, Y. (2009). Two is not always better than one: A critical evaluation of two-system theories. *Perspectives on Psychological Science,* 4, 533–50.

Kerr, R., Garvin, J., Heaton, N., and Boyle, E. (2006). Emotional intelligence and leadership effectiveness. *Leadership and Organization Development Journal,* 27, 265–79.

Kevles, D. J. (1985). *In the name of eugenics: Genetics and the uses of human heredity.* New York: Knopf.

Klemp, G. O. and McClelland, D. C. (1986). What characterizes intelligent functioning among senior managers? In *Practical intelligence: Nature and origins of competence in the everyday world* (eds R. J. Sternberg and R. K. Wagner). Cambridge: Cambridge University Press.

Kline, P. (1994). *An easy guide to factor analysis.* London: Routledge.

Knudsen, E. I., Heckman, J. J., Cameron, J. L., and Shonkoff, J. P. (2006). Economic, neurobiological, and behavioral perspectives on building America's future workforce. *Proceedings of the National Academy of Sciences,* 103, 10155–62.

Kondrashov, A. S. (1995). Contamination of the genome by very slightly deleterious mutations: Why have we not died 100 times over? *Journal of Theoretical Biology,* 175, 583.

Kovács, K. (2010). A component process account of the general factor of intelligence. Unpublished Ph.D. Thesis, University of Cambridge.

Kranzler, J. H. (1992). A test of Larson and Alderton's (1990) worst performance rule of reaction time variability. *Personality and Individual Differences,* 13, 255–61.

Kranzler, J. H. and Jensen, A. R. (1991). The nature of psychometric g: Unitary process or a number of independent processes? *Intelligence*, 15, 397–422.

Krashen, S. D. (1989). We acquire vocabulary and spelling by reading: Additional evidence for the input hypothesis. *The Modern Language Journal*, 73, 440–64.

Kristensen, P. and Bjerkedal, T. (2007). Explaining the relation between birth order and intelligence. *Science*, 316, 1717.

Kyllonen, P. C. and Christal, R. E. (1990). Reasoning ability is (little more than) working memory capacity?! *Intelligence*, 14, 389–433.

Kyllonen, P. C., Lohman, D. F., and Snow, R. E. (1984). Effects of aptitudes, strategy training, and task facets on spatial task performance. *Journal of Educational Psychology*, 76, 130–45.

La Pointe, L. B. and Engle, R. W. (1990). Simple and complex word spans as measures of working memory capacity. *Journal of Experimental Psychology: Learning, Memory, and Cognition*, 16, 1118–33.

La Voie, D. and Light, L. L. (1994). Adult age differences in repetition priming: A meta-analysis. *Psychology and Aging*, 9, 539–53.

Lansdown, R. and Yule, W. (eds) (1986). *The lead debate: The environment, toxicology, and child health*. London: Croom Helm.

Langley, C. M. (1994). Spatial memory in the desert kangaroo rat (Dipodomys deserti). *Journal of Comparative Psychology*, 108, 3–14.

Langsford, P. B., Mackenzie, B. D., and Maher, D. P. (1994). Auditory inspection time, sustained attention, and the fundamentality of mental speed. *Personality and Individual Differences*, 16, 487–97.

Lansman, M., Donaldson, G., Hunt, E., and Yantis, S. (1982). Ability factors and cognitive processes. *Intelligence*, 6, 347–86.

Lareau, A. (2003). *Unequal childhoods: Class, race, and family life*. Berkeley, CA: University of California Press.

Larson, G. E. and Alderton, D. L. (1990). Reaction time variability and intelligence: Worst performance'-analysis of individual differences. *Intelligence*, 14, 309–25.

Larson, G. E. and Saccuzzo, D. P. (1989). Cognitive correlates of general intelligence: Toward a process theory of g. *Intelligence*, 13, 5–31.

Larson, G. E., Merritt, C. R., and Williams, S. E. (1988). Information processing and intelligence: Some implications of task complexity. *Intelligence*, 12, 131–47.

Lasley, S. M., Green, M. C., and Gilbert, M. E. (1999). Influence of exposure period on in vivo hippocampal glutamate and GABA release in rats chronically exposed to lead. *Neurotoxicology*, 20, 619–30.

Lave, J., Murtaugh, M., and de la Roche, O. (1984). The dialectic of arithmetic in grocery shopping. In *Everyday cognition: Its development in social context* (eds B. Rogoff and J. Lave). Cambridge, MA: Harvard University Press.

Lavin, D. E. (1965). *The prediction of academic performance: A theoretical analysis and review of research*. New York: Russell Sage Foundation.

Lawrence, E. M. (1931). An investigation into the relation between intelligence and inheritance. *British Journal of Psychology* (Monograph Supplement), 16, 1–80.

Lazar, I. and Darlington, R. (1982). Lasting effects of early education: A report from the consortium for longitudinal studies. *Monographs of the Society for Research in Child Development*, 47.

Leahy, A. (1935). Nature-nurture and intelligence. *Genetic Psychology Monographs*, 17, 236–308.

Leather, C. V. and Henry, L. A. (1994). Working memory span and phonological awareness tasks as predictors of early reading ability. *Journal of Experimental Child Psychology*, 58, 88–111.

Lee, K. H., Choi, Y. Y., Gray, J. R., et al. (2006). Neural correlates of superior intelligence: Stronger recruitment of posterior parietal cortex. *NeuroImage*, 29, 578–86.

Legree, P. J., Pifer, M. E., and Grafton, F. C. (1996). Correlations among cognitive abilities are lower for higher ability groups. *Intelligence*, 23, 45–57.

Levin, S. L., Mohamed, F. B., and Platek, S. M. (2005). Common ground for spatial cognition? A behavioral and fMRI study of sex differences in mental rotation and spatial working memory. *Evolutionary Psychology*, 3, 227–54.

Levy, J. (1976). Cerebral lateralization and spatial ability. *Behavior Genetics*, 6, 171–88.

Lewin, R. and Foley, R. A. (2004). *Principles of human evolution* (2nd edn). Malden, MA: Blackwell.

Lewis, E. O. (1933). Types of mental deficiency and their social significance. *Journal of Mental Science*, 79, 293–304.

Li, S.-C., Lindenberger, U., Hommel, B., et al. (2004). Transformations in the couplings among intellectual abilities and constituent cognitive processes across the life span. *Psychological Science*, 15, 155–63.

Linn, M. C. and Peterson, A. C. (1985). Emergence and characterization of sex differences in spatial ability: A meta-analysis. *Child Development*, 56, 1479–98.

Locke, E. A. (2005). Why emotional intelligence is an invalid concept. *Journal of Organizational Behavior*, 26, 425–31.

Locurto, C. (1991). Beyond IQ in preschool programs? *Intelligence*, 15, 295–312.

Loehlin, J. C. (1989). Partitioning environmental and genetic contributions to behavioral development. *American Psychologist*, 44, 1285–92.

Loehlin, J. C. and Nichols, R. C. (1976). *Heredity, environment and personality: A study of 850 sets of twins*. Austin TX: University of Texas Press.

Loehlin, J. C., Horn, J. M., and Willerman, L. (1989). Modeling IQ change: Evidence from the Texas adoption project. *Child Development*, 60, 993–1004.

Loehlin, J. C., Vandenberg, S. G., and Osborne, R. T. (1973). Blood group genes and Negro-white ability differences. *Behavior Genetics*, 3, 263–70.

Logie, R. H. (1995). *Visuo-spatial working memory*. Hove, UK: Lawrence Erlbaum.

Logie, R. H. and Marchetti, C. (1991). Visuo-spatial working memory: Visual, spatial or central executive? In *Mental images in human cognition* (eds R. H. Logie and M. Denis). Amsterdam: North Holland Press.

Logie, R. H., Gilhooly, K. J., and Wynn, V. (1994). Counting on working memory in arithmetic problem solving. *Memory and Cognition*, 22, 395–410.

Lohman, D. F. (1986). The effect of speed-accuracy trade-off on sex differences in mental rotation. *Perception and Psychophysics*, 39, 427–36.

Lohman, D. F. (1988). Spatial abilities as traits, processes, and knowledge. In *Advances in the psychology of human intelligence* (vol. 4), (ed. R. J. Sternberg). Hillsdale, NJ: Lawrence Erlbaum.

Lohman, D. F. (2000). Complex information processing and intelligence. In *Handbook of intelligence* (ed. R. J. Sternberg). Cambridge: Cambridge University Press.

Lubinski, D. (2004). Introduction to the special section on cognitive abilities: 100 years after Spearman's (1904) "General intelligence, objectively determined and measured". *Journal of Personality and Social Psychology*, 86, 96–111.

Lubinski, D. and Benbow, C. P. (2006). Study of mathematically precocious youth after 35 years: Uncovering antecedents for the development of math-science expertise. *Perspectives on Psychological Science*, 1, 316–45.

Lubinski, D. and Humphreys, L. G. (1990). A broadly based analysis of mathematical giftedness. *Intelligence*, 14, 327–55.

Lubinski, D. and Humphreys, L. G. (1992). Some bodily and medical correlates of mathematical giftedness and commensurate levels of socioeconomic status. *Intelligence*, 16, 99–115.

Lucas, A., Morley, R., Cole, T. J., Lister, G., and Leeson-Payne, C. (1992). Breast milk and subsequent intelligence quotient in children born preterm. *The Lancet*, 339, 261–4.

Luders, E., Gaser, C., Narr, K. L., and Toga, A. W. (2009a). Why sex matters: Brain size independent differences in gray matter distributions between men and women. *The Journal of Neuroscience*, 29, 14265–70.

Luders, E., Narr, K. L., Thompson, P. M., *et al.* (2009b). Gender differences in cortical complexity. *Nature Neuroscience*, 7, 799–800.

Luria, A. R. (1966). *Higher cortical functions in man*. London: Tavistock Publications.

Luria, A. R. (1976). *Cognitive development, its cultural and social foundations*. Cambridge, MA: Harvard University Press.

Lynn, R. (1982). IQ in Japan and the United States shows a growing disparity. *Nature*, 297, 222–3.

Lynn, R. (1992). Does Spearman's *g* decline at high-IQ levels? Some evidence from Scotland. *Journal of Genetic Psychology*, 153, 229–30.

Lynn, R. (1994). Sex differences in intelligence and brain size: A paradox resolved. *Personality and Individual Differences*, 17, 257–71.

Lynn, R. (1996a). *Dysgenics: Genetic deterioration in modern populations*. Westport, CT: Praeger.

Lynn, R. (1996b). Racial and ethnic differences in intelligence in the United States on the Differential Ability Scale. *Personality and Individual Differences*, 20, 271–3.

Lynn, R. (1998). In support of the nutrition theory. In *The rising curve: Long-term gains in IQ and related measures* (ed. U. Neisser). Washington, DC: American Psychological Association.

Lynn, R. (2006). *Race differences in intelligence: An evolutionary analysis*. Augusta, GA: Washington Summit.

Lynn, R. (2008). What has caused the Flynn effect? Secular increases in the Development Quotients of infants. *Intelligence*, 37, 16–24.

Lynn, R. (2009). Fluid intelligence but not vocabulary has increased in Britain, 1979–2008. *Intelligence*, 37, 249–55.

Lynn, R. and Hampson, S. (1986). The rise of national intelligence: evidence from Britain, Japan and the USA. *Personality and Individual Differences*, 7, 23–32.

Lynn, R. and Irwing, P. (2004). Sex differences on the progressive matrices: A meta-analysis. *Intelligence*, 32, 481–98.

Lynn, R. and Longley, D. (2006). On the high intelligence and cognitive achievements of Jews in Britain. *Intelligence*, 34, 541–7.

Lynn, R., Allik, J., and Irwing, P. (2004). Sex differences on three factors identified in Raven's Standard Progressive Matrices. *Intelligence*, 32, 411–24.

Lynn, R., Hampson, S. L., and Howden, V. (1988). The intelligence of Scottish children, 1932–1986. *Studies in Education*, 6, 19–25.

Lynn, R., Irwing, P., and Cammock, T. (2002). Sex differences in general knowledge. *Intelligence*, 30, 27–39.

Lynn, R., Wilson, R. G., and Gault, A. (1989). Simple musical tests as measures of Spearman's g. *Personality and Individual Differences*, 10, 25–8.

Maccoby, E. E. and Jacklin, C. N. (1974). *The psychology of sex differences*. Stanford, CA: Stanford University Press.

Mackenzie, B. D. and Bingham, E. (1985). IQ, inspection time, and response strategies in a university population. *Australian Journal of Psychology*, 37, 257–68.

MacKinnon, D. W. (1962). The nature and nurture of creative talent. *American Psychologist*, 17, 484–95.

Mackintosh, N. J. (1998). *IQ and human intelligence*. Oxford: Oxford University Press.

Mackintosh, N. J. (2007). Reply to Colom and Abad (2006). *Intelligence*, 35, 301–2.

Mackintosh, N. J. (ed.) (1995). *Cyril Burt: Fraud or framed?* Oxford: Oxford University Press.

Mackintosh, N. J. and Bennett, E. S. (2002). IT, IQ and perceptual speed. *Personality and Individual Differences*, 32, 685–93.

Mackintosh, N. J. and Bennett, E. S. (2003). The fractionation of working memory maps onto different components of intelligence. *Intelligence*, 31, 519–31.

Mackintosh, N. J. and Bennett, E. S. (2005). What do Raven's Matrices measure? An analysis in terms of sex differences. *Intelligence*, 33, 663–74.

Mackintosh, N. J. and Mascie-Taylor, C. G. N. (1986). The IQ question. In *Personality, cognition and values* (eds C. Bagley and G. K. Verma). Macmillan: London.

MacLeod, C. M., Hunt, E. B., and Mathews, N. N. (1978). Individual differences in the verification of sentence-picture relationships. *Journal of Verbal Learning and Verbal Behavior*, 17, 493–507.

Maguire, E. A., Gadian, D. G., Johnsrude, I. S., *et al.* (2000). Navigation-related structural change in the hippocampi of taxi drivers. *Proceedings of the National Academy of Sciences*, 97, 4398–403.

Mahaffey, K. R., Annest, J. L., Roberts, J., and Murphy, R. S. (1982). National estimates of blood lead levels: United States, 1976–1980. *New England Journal of Medicine*, 307, 573–9.

Maher, J. and Macfarlane, A. (2004). Inequalities in infant mortality: trends by social class, registration, mother's age and birthweight, England and Wales, 1976–2000. *Health Statistics Quarterly*, 24, 14–22.

Manktelow, K. I. and Over, D. E. (1990). Deontic thought and the selection task. In *Lines of thinking: Reflections on the psychology of thinking* (vol. 1), (eds K. Gilhooly, M. Keane, R. Logie, and G. Erdos). Chichester: Wiley.

Manning, W. H. and Jackson, R. (1984). College entrance examinations: Objective selection or gatekeeping for the economically privileged. In *Perspectives on bias in mental testing* (eds C. R. Reynolds and R. T. Brown). New York: Plenum.

Manolakes, L. A. (1997). Cognitive ability, environmental factors, and crime: Predicting frequent criminal activity. In *Intelligence, genes, and success: Scientists respond to the bell curve* (eds B. Devlin, S. E. Fienberg and K. Roeder). New York: Springer.

Marjoribanks, K. (1972). Ethnic and environmental influences on mental abilities. *American Journal of Sociology*, 78, 323–37.

Marlowe, H. A. (1986). Social intelligence: Evidence for multidimensionality and construct independence. *Journal of Educational Psychology*, 78, 52–8.

Martorell, R. (1998). Nutrition and the worldwide rise in IQ scores. In *The rising curve: Long-term gains in IQ and related measures* (ed. U. Neisser). Washington, DC: American Psychological Association.

Mascie-Taylor, C. G. N. (1984). Biosocial correlates of IQ. In *The biology of human intelligence* (eds C. J. Turner and H. B. Miles). London: Proceedings of the 20th Annual Symposium of the Eugenics Society.

Mascie-Taylor, C. G. N. and Gibson, J. B. (1978). Social mobility and IQ components. *Journal of Biosocial Science*, 10, 263–76.

Masse, L. N. and Barnett, W. S. (2002). *A benefit cost analysis of the Abecedarian Early Childhood Intervention*. New Brunswick, NJ: National Institute for Early Education Research.

Masters, M. S. and Sanders, B. (1993). Is the gender difference in mental rotation disappearing? *Behavior Genetics*, 23, 337–41.

Masunaga, H. and Horn, J. (2001). Expertise and age-related changes in components of intelligence. *Psychology and Aging*, 16, 293–311.

Matthews, G., Zeidner, M., and Roberts, R. D. (2005). Emotional intelligence: An elusive ability? In *Handbook of understanding and measuring intelligence* (eds O. Wilhelm and R. W. Engle). Thousand Oaks, CA: Sage.

Matthews, M. H. (1987). Sex differences in spatial competence: The ability of young children to map 'primed' unfamiliar environments. *Educational Psychology*, 7, 77–90.

Mayer, J. D., Salovey, P., and Caruso, D. R. (2002). *Mayer-Salovey-Caruso Emotional Intelligence Test (MSCEIT). Version 2.0*. Toronto, Canada: Multi-Health Systems.

Mayer, J. D., Salovey, P., and Caruso, D. R. (2004). Emotional intelligence: Theory, findings, and implications. *Psychological Inquiry*, 15, 197–215.

Mayer, J. D., Salovey, P., and Caruso, D. R. (2008). Emotional intelligence: New ability or eclectic traits? *American Psychologist*, 63, 503–17.

Mayes, L. C. and Fahy, T. (2001). Prenatal drug exposure and cognitive development. In *Environmental effects on cognitive abilities* (eds R. J. Sternberg and E. L. Grigorenko). Mahwah, NJ: Lawrence Erlbaum.

Mazzocco, M. M. M. and Reiss, A. L. (1999). Normal variation in size of the FMR2 gene is not associated with variation in intellectual performance. *Intelligence*, 27, 175–82.

McCall, R. B. (1977). Childhood IQ's as predictors of adult educational and occupational status. *Science, 197,* 482–3.

McCall, R. B. and Carriger, M. S. (1993). A meta-analysis of infant habituation and recognition memory performance as predictors of later IQ. *Child Development, 64,* 57–79.

McCarthy, R. A. and Warrington, E. K. (1990). *Cognitive neuropsychology.* London: Academic Press.

McCartney, M., Harris, O., and Bernieri, F. (1990). Growing up and growing apart: A developmental meta-analysis of twin studies. *Psychological Bulletin,* 107, 226–37.

McClelland, D. C. (1973). Testing for competence rather than for 'intelligence'. *American Psychologist,* 28, 1–14.

McCrae, R. R. and Costa, P. T. Jr. (1997). Personality trait structure as a human universal. *American Psychologist,* 52, 509–16.

McDaniel, M. A. (2005). Big-brained people are smarter: A meta-analysis of the relationship between in vivo brain volume and intelligence. *Intelligence,* 33, 337–46.

McGarry-Roberts, P. A., Stelmack, R. M., and Campbell, K. B. (1992). Intelligence, reaction time, and event-related potentials. *Intelligence,* 16, 289–313.

McGeorge, P., Crawford, J. R., and Kelly, S. W. (1996). The relationship between WAIS-R abilities and speed of processing in a word identification task. *Intelligence,* 23, 175–90.

McGrew, K. S. (2009). CHC theory and the human cognitive abilities project: Standing on the shoulders of the giants of psychometric intelligence research. *Intelligence,* 37, 1–10.

McGue, M., Bouchard, T. J. Jr. Iacono, W. G., and Lykken, D. T. (1993). Behavioral genetics of cognitive ability: A life-span perspective. In *Nature, nurture and psychology* (eds R. Plomin and G. E. McClearn). Washington, DC: American Psychological Association.

McLaren, I. P. L., Green, R. E. A., and Mackintosh, N. J. (1994). Animal learning and the implicit/explicit distinction. In *Implicit and explicit learning of languages* (ed. N. C. Ellis). London: Academic Press.

McLoughlin, C. S. and Koh, T. H. (1982). Testing intelligence: A decision suitable for the psychologist. *Bulletin of the British Psychological Society,* 35, 308–11.

McMichael, A. J., Baghurst, P. A., Wigg, N. R., Vimpani, V. G., Robertson, E. F., and Roberts, R. J. (1988). Port Pirie cohort study: Environmental exposure to lead and children's abilities at the age of four years. *New England Journal of Medicine,* 319, 468–75.

Medawar, P. B. (1982). *Pluto's republic.* Oxford: Oxford University Press.

Melnick, M., Myrianthopoulos, N. C., and Christian, J. C. (1978). The effects of chorion type on variation in IQ in the NCPP twin population. *American Journal of Human Genetics,* 30, 425–33.

Mercer, J. R. (1973). *Labeling the retarded.* Berkeley, CA: University of California Press.

Mercer, J. R. and Lewis, J. F. (1978). *System of multicultural pluralistic assessment.* New York: Psychological Corporation.

Merkel, J. (1885). Die zeitlichen Verhaltnisse der Willensthatigkeit. *Philosophische Studien,* 2, 73–127.

Merton, R. K. (1968). *Social theory and social structure.* New York: Free Press.

Meyers, C. E., Nihira, K., and Zetlin, A. (1979). The measurement of adaptive behavior. In *The handbook of mental deficiency, psychological theory and research* (2nd edn), (ed. N. Ellis). Hillsdale, NJ: Lawrence Erlbaum.

Michael, J. S. (1988). A new look at Morton's craniological research. *Current Anthropology,* 29, 349–54.

Miller, G. (2000). *The mating mind: How sexual choice shaped the evolution of human nature.* London: Heineman.

Milner, B. (1963). Effects of different brain lesions on card sorting: the role of the frontal lobes. *Archives of Neurology,* 9, 90–100.

Mingroni, M. A. (2007). Resolving the IQ paradox: Heterosis as a cause of the Flynn effect and other trends. *Psychological Review,* 114, 806–29.

Miyake, A. and Shah, P. (eds) (1999). *Models of working memory: Mechanisms of active maintenance and executive control.* Cambridge: Cambridge University Press.

Moffat, S. D., Hampson, E., and Hatzipantelis, M. (1998). Navigation in a 'virtual' maze: Sex differences and correlation with psychometric measures of spatial ability in humans. *Evolution and Human Behavior,* 19, 73–87.

Moody, D. E. (2009). Can intelligence be increased by training on a task of working memory? *Intelligence,* 37, 327–8.

Moore, D. S. and Johnson, S. P. (2008). Mental rotation in human infants: A sex difference. *Psychological Science,* 19, 1063–6.

Moore, E. G. J. (1986). Family socialization and the IQ test performance of traditionally and transracially adopted black children. *Developmental Psychology,* 22, 317–26.

Morley, R. (1996). The influence of early diet on later development. *Journal of Biosocial Science,* 28, 481–7.

Morris, G. L. and Alcorn, M. B. (1995). Raven's progressive matrices and inspection time: P200 slope correlates. *Personality and Individual Differences,* 18, 81–7.

Morris, R. G. M. (1981). Spatial localization does not require the presence of local cues. *Learning and Motivation,* 12, 239–60.

Mumaw, R. J. and Pellegrino, J. W. (1984). Individual differences in complex spatial processing. *Journal of Educational Psychology*, 76, 920–39.

Mumaw, R. J., Pellegrino, J. W., Kail, R. V., and Carter, P. (1984). Different slopes for different folks: Process analysis of spatial aptitude. *Memory and Cognition*, 12, 515–21.

Murdoch, S. (2007). *IQ: The brilliant idea that failed*. London: Duckworth.

Murray, C. (1998). *Income, inequality, and IQ*. Washington, DC: American Enterprise Institute.

Nagoshi, C. T. and Johnson, R. A. (1987). Cognitive ability profiles of Caucasian vs. Japanese subjects in the Hawaii Family Study of Cognition. *Personality and Individual Differences*, 8, 581–3.

Neisser, U. (1976). General, academic, and artificial intelligence. In *The nature of intelligence* (ed. L. Resnick). Hillsdale, NJ: Lawrence Erlbaum.

Neisser, U. (1996). Intelligence: Knowns and unknowns. *American Psychologist*, 51, 77–101.

Neisser, U. (ed.) (1998). *The rising curve: Long-term gains in IQ and related measures*. Washington: American Psychological Association.

Nettelbeck, T. (1987). Inspection time and intelligence. In *Speed of information processing and intelligence* (ed. P. A. Vernon). Norwood, NJ: Ablex.

Nettelbeck, T. (2003). Inspection time and g. In *The scientific study of general intelligence: Tribute to Arthur R. Jensen* (ed. H. Nyborg). Oxford: Pergamon.

Nettelbeck, T. and Burns, N. R. (2010). Processing speed, working memory and reasoning ability from childhood to old age. *Personality and Individual Differences*, 48, 379–84.

Nettelbeck, T. and Kirby, N. H. (1983). Measures of timed performance and intelligence. *Intelligence*, 7, 39–52.

Nettelbeck, T. and Lalley, M. (1976). Inspection time and measured intelligence. *British Journal of Psychology*, 67, 17–22.

Nettelbeck, T. and Rabbitt, P. M. A. (1992). Aging, cognitive performance, and mental speed. *Intelligence*, 16, 189–205.

Nettelbeck, T., Edwards, C., and Vreugdenhil, A. (1986). Inspection time and IQ: Evidence for a mental speed-ability association. *Personality and Individual Differences*, 7, 633–41.

Nettle, D. (2007). Empathizing and systemizing: What are they, and what do they contribute to our understanding of psychological sex differences? *British Journal of Psychology*, 98, 237–55.

Neubauer, A. C. and Fink, A. (2009). Intelligence and neural efficiency: Measures of brain activation versus measures of functional connectivity in the brain. *Intelligence*, 37, 223–9.

Neubauer, A. C. and Freudenthaler, H. H. (1994). Reaction times in a sentence-picture verification test and intelligence: Individual strategies and effects of extended practice. *Intelligence*, 19, 193–218.

Neubauer, A. C., Fink, A. and Schrausser, D. G. (2002). Intelligence and neural efficiency: The influence of task content and sex on the brain-IQ relationship. *Intelligence*, 30, 515–36.

Newcombe, N. S. (2007). Taking science seriously: Straight thinking about spatial sex differences. In *Why aren't more women in science: Top researchers debate the evidence* (eds S. J. Ceci and W. M. Williams). Washington, DC: American Psychological Association.

Newman, D. L., Tellegen, A., and Bouchard, T. J. Jr. (1998). Individual differences in adult ego development: Sources of influence in twins reared apart. *Journal of Personality and Social Psychology*, 74, 985–95.

Newman, H. H., Freeman, F. N., and Holzinger, K. H. (1937). *Twins: A study of heredity and environment*. Chicago: University of Chicago Press.

Newman, S. D., Carpenter, P. A., Varma, S., and Just, M. A. (2003). Frontal and parietal participation in problem solving in the Tower of London: fMRI and computational modeling of planning and high-level perception. *Neuropsychologia*, 41, 1668–82.

Nisbett, R. E. (2003). *The geography of thought: How Asians and Westerners think differently...and why*. New York: Free Press.

Nisbett, R. E. (2005). Heredity, environment, and race differences in IQ: A commentary on Rushton and Jensen (2005). *Psychology, Public Policy, and Law*, 11, 302–10.

Nisbett, R. E. (2009). *Intelligence and how to get it: Why schools and cultures count*. New York: Norton.

Norman, D. A. and Shallice, T. (1986). Attention to action: Willed and automatic control of behaviour. In *Consciousness and self-regulation. Advances in research and theory* (vol. 4.), (eds R. J. Davidson, G. E. Schwarts, and D. Shapiro). New York: Plenum Press.

Nuttall, R., Casey, M. B., and Pezaris, E. (2005). Spatial ability as a mediator of gender differences on mathematics tests: A biological-environmental framework. In *Gender differences in mathematics: An integrative psychological approach* (eds A. M. Gallagher and J. C. Kaufman). New York, NY: Cambridge University Press.

Oberauer, K., Schulze, R., Wilhelm, O., and Suss, H.-M. (2005). Working memory and intelligence—their correlation and their relation: Comment on Ackerman, Beier, and Boyle (2005). *Psychological Bulletin*, 131, 61–5.

O'Connor, N., Cowan, R., and Samella, K. (2000). Calendrical calculation and intelligence. *Intelligence*, 28, 31–48.

O'Connor, T. A. and Burns, N. R. (2003). Inspection time and general speed of processing. *Personality and Individual Differences*, 35, 713–24.

Oden, M. H. (1968). The fulfillment of promise: 40-year follow-up of the Terman gifted group. *Genetic Psychology Monographs*, 77, 3–93.

Ones, D. S., Viswesvaran, C., and Dilchert, S. (2005). Cognitive ability in selection decisions. In *Handbook of understanding and measuring intelligence* (eds O. Wilhelm and R. W. Engle). Thousand Oaks, CA: Sage.

Oswald, W. D. and Roth, E. (1978). *Der Zahlen-Verbindungs-Test (ZVT)*. Gottingen, Germany: Hogrefe.

O'Toole, B. I. (1990). Intelligence and behaviour and motor vehicle accident mortality. *Accident Analysis and Prevention*, 22, 211–21.

O'Toole, B. I. and Stankov, L. (1992). Ultimate validity of psychological tests. *Personality and Individual Differences*, 13, 699–716.

Owen, A. M., Downes, J. J., Sahakian, B. J., Polkey, C. E., and Robbins, T. W. (1990). Planning and spatial working memory following frontal lobe lesions in man. *Neuropsychologia*, 28, 1021–34.

Page, E. B., and Grandon, G. M. (1981). Massive intervention and child intelligence: The Milwaukee Project in critical perspective. *Journal of Special Education*, 15, 239–56.

Palmer, B. R., Gignac, G., Manocha, R., and Stough, C. (2005). A psychometric evaluation of the Mayer-Salovey-Caruso Emotional Intelligence Test Version 2.0. *Intelligence*, 33, 285–305.

Park, G., Lubinski, D., and Benbow, C. P. (2008). Ability differences among people who have commensurate degrees matter for scientific creativity. *Psychological Science*, 19, 957–61.

Pedersen, N. L., Plomin, R., Nesselroade, J. R., and McClearn, G. E. (1992). A quantitative genetic analysis of cognitive abilities during the second half of the life span. *Psychological Science*, 3, 346–53.

Pellegrino, J. W. (1986). Deductive reasoning ability. In *Human abilities: An information-processing approach* (ed. R. J. Sternberg). New York: W. H. Freeman.

Penn, D. C. and Povinelli, D. J. (2007). On the lack of evidence that non-human animals possess anything remotely resembling a 'theory of mind'. *Philosophical Transactions of the Royal Society B: Biological Sciences*, 362, 731–44.

Pennington, B. F., Filipek, P. A., Lefly, D., *et al.* (2000). A twin MRI study of size variations in the human brain. *Journal of Cognitive Neuroscience*, 12, 223–32.

Penrose, L. S. and Raven, J. C. (1936). A new series of perceptual tests: Preliminary communication. *British Journal of Medical Psychology*, 16, 97–104.

Perruchet, P. (1994). Learning from complex rule-governed environemnts: On the proper functions of nonconscious and conscious processes. In *Attention and performance*, XV (eds C. Umilta and M. Moscovitch). Cambridge, MA: MIT Press.

Petrides, K. V., Furnham, A., and Frederickson, N. (2004). Emotional intelligence. *The Psychologist*, 17, 574–7.

Phillip, E. E. (1973). Discussion in *Law and ethics of AID. and embryo transfer*, Ciba Symposium (eds G. E. W. Wolstenholme and D. W. Fitzsimons). Amsterdam: North-Holland/Elsevier.

Phillips, M., Brooks-Gunn, J., Duncan, G. J., Klebanov, P., and Crane, J. (1998). Family background, parenting practices, and the black-white test score gap. In *The black-white test score gap* (eds C. Jencks and M. Phillips). Washington, DC: Brookings Institution Press.

Piaget, J. and Inhelder, B. (1969). *The psychology of the child*. New York: Basic Books.

Plomin, R., DeFries, J. C., McClearn, G. E., and McGuffin, P. (2008). *Behavioral genetics* (5th edn). New York: Worth.

Plomin, R., Fulker, D. W., Corley, R., and DeFries, J. C. (1997). Nature, nurture and cognitive development from 1 to 16 years: A parent-offspring adoption study. *Psychological Science*, 8, 442–7.

Plomin, R., McClearn, G. E., Pedersen, N. L., Nesselroade, J. R., and Bergeman, C. S. (1988). Genetic influence on childhood family environment perceived retrospectively from the last half of the life span. *Developmental Psychology*, 24, 738–45.

Pollack R. H. and Brenner, M. W. (eds) (1969) *The experimental psychology of Alfred Binet; Selected papers*. New York: Springer.

Poltrock, S. E. and Agnoli, F. (1986). Are spatial visualization ability and visual imagery ability equivalent? In *Advances in the psychology of human intelligence* (vol. 3), (ed. R. J. Sternberg). Hillsdale, NJ: Lawrence Erlbaum.

Porteus, S. D. (1931). *The psychology of a primitive people: A study of the Australian aborigine*. Oxford: Longmans.

Posthuma, D., De Geus, E. J. C., Baare, W. F. C., *et al.* (2002). The association between brain volume and intelligence is of genetic origin. *Nature Neuroscience*, 5, 83–4.

Prabhakaran, V. and Rypma, B. (2007). P-FIT and the neuroscience of intelligence: How well does P fit? *Behavioral and Brain Sciences*, 30, 166–7.

Prabhakaran, V., Smith, J. A. L., Desmond, J. E., and Glover, G. H. (1997). Neural substrates of fluid reasoning: An fMRI study of neocortical activation during performance of the Raven's Progressive Matrices Test. *Cognitive Psychology*, 33, 43–63.

Puts, D. A., McDaniel, M. A., Jordan, C. L., and Breedlove, S. M. (2008). Spatial ability and prenatal androgens: Meta-analyses of congenital adrenal hyperplasia and digit ratio (2D:4D) studies. *Archives of Sexual Behavior*, 37, 100–11.

Quinn, P. C. and Liben, L. S. (2008). A sex difference in mental rotation in young infants. *Psychological Science*, 19, 1067–70.

Rabbitt, P. M. A. (1993). Crystal quest: A search for the basis of maintenance of practised skills into old age. In *Attention: Selection, awareness, and control: A tribute to Donald Broadbent* (eds A. D. Baddeley and L. Weiskrantz). Oxford: Oxford University Press.

Rabbitt, P. M. A., Scott, M., Lunn, M., *et al.* (2007). White matter lesions account for all age-related declines in speed but not in intelligence. *Neuropsychology*, 21, 363–70.

Ramey, C. T. (1992). High-risk children and IQ: Altering intergenerational patterns. *Intelligence*, 16, 239–56.

Ramey, C. T. (1993). A rejoinder to Spitz's critique of the Abecedarian experiment. *Intelligence*, 17, 337–45.

Ramey, C. T., Ramey, S. L., and Lanzi, R. G. (2001). Intelligence and experience. In *Environmental effects on cognitive abilities* (eds R. J. Sternberg and E. L. Grigorenko). Mahwah, NJ: Lawrence Erlbaum.

Raven, J. (2000). The Raven's Progressive Matrices: Change and stability over culture and time. *Cognitive Psychology*, 41, 1–48.

Raven, J. C. (1938). *Progressive Matrices: A perceptual test of intelligence*. London: H. K. Lewis.

Raz, N. (2000). Aging of the brain and its impact on cognitive performance: Integration of structural and functional findings. In *The handbook of aging and cognition* (2nd edn), (eds F. I. M. Craik and T. A. Salthouse). Mahwah, NJ: Lawrence Erlbaum.

Reber, A. S. (1967). Implicit learning of artificial grammars. *Journal of Verbal Learning and Verbal Behavior*, 6, 317–27.

Reber, A. S. (1993). *Implicit learning and tacit knowledge: An essay on the cognitive unconscious*. Oxford: Oxford University Press.

Reber, A. S., Walkenfeld, F. F., and Hernstadt, R. (1991). Implicit and explicit learning: Individual differences and IQ. *Journal of Experimental Psychology: Learning, Memory and Cognition*, 17, 888–96.

Reber, P. J., Gitelman, D. R., Parrish, T. B., and Mesulam, M. M. (2003). Dissociating explicit and implicit category knowledge with fMRI. *Journal of Cognitive Neuroscience*, 15, 574–83.

Record, R. G., McKeown, T., and Edwards, J. H. (1969). The relation of measured intelligence to birth order and maternal age. *Annals of Human Genetics*, 33, 61–9.

Ree, M. J., Carretta, T. R., and Green, M. T. (2003). The ubiquitous role of *g* in training. In *The scientific study of general intelligence: Tribute to Arthur R. Jensen* (ed. H. Nyborg). Oxford: Pergamon.

Reichle, E. D., Carpenter, P. A., and Just, M. A. (2000). The neural bases of strategy and skill in sentence-picture verification. *Cognitive Psychology*, 40, 261–95.

Reiss, D., Neiderhiser, J. M., Hetherington, E. M., and Plomin, R. (2000). *The relationship code: Deciphering genetic and social influences on adolescent development.* Cambridge, MA: Harvard University Press.

Renner, J. M. and Rosenzweig, M. R. (1987). *Enriched and impoverished environments: Effects on brain and behavior.* New York: Springer-Verlag.

Reschly, D. J. and Sabers, D. L. (1979). An examination of bias in predicting MAT scores from WISC-R scores for four ethnic-racial groups. *Journal of Educational Measurement*, 16, 1–9.

Rescorla, R. A. (1988). Pavlovian conditioning: It's not what you think it is. *American Psychologist*, 43, 151–60.

Retherford, R. D. and Sewell, W. H. (1988). Intelligence and family size reconsidered. *Social Biology*, 35, 1–40.

Retherford, R. D. and Sewell, W. H. (1991). Birth order and intelligence: further tests of the confluence model. *American Sociological Review*, 56, 141–58.

Reuter-Lorenz, P. A. (2002). New visions of the aging mind and brain. *Trends in Cognitive Sciences*, 6, 394–400.

Reynolds, C. R., Chastain, R. L., Kaufman, A. S., and McLean, J. E. (1987). Demographic characteristics and IQ among adults: Analysis of the WAIS-R standardization sample as a function of the stratification variables. *Journal of School Psychology*, 25, 323–42.

Reynolds, M. R. and Keith, T. Z. (2007). Spearman's law of diminishing returns in hierarchical models of intelligence for children and adolescents. *Intelligence*, 35, 267–81.

Rhodes, L., Dustman, R., and Beck, E. (1969). The visual evoked response: A comparison of bright and dull children. *Electroencephalography and Clinical Neurophysiology*, 27, 364–72.

Rips, L. J. (1994). *The psychology of proof: Deductive reasoning in human thinking.* Cambridge, MA: MIT Press.

Robb, G. (2000). *Rimbaud.* New York: Norton.

Roberts, R. D. and Stankov, L. (1999). Individual differences in speed of mental processing and human cognitive abilities: Toward a taxonomic model. *Learning and Individual Differences*, 11, 1–120.

Roberts, R. D., Beh, H. C., and Stankov, L. (1988). Hick's law, competing-task performance, and intelligence. *Intelligence*, 12, 111–30.

Roberts, R. D., Markham, P. M., Matthews, G., and Zeidner, M. (2005). Assessing intelligence: Past, present, and future. In *Handbook of understanding and measuring intelligence* (eds O. Wilhelm and R. W. Engle). Thousand Oaks, CA: Sage.

Rode, J. C., Mooney, C. H., Arthaud-Day, M. L., *et al.* (2008). An examination of the structural, discriminant, nomological, and incremental predictive validity of the MSCEIT© V2.0. *Intelligence*, 36, 350–66.

Rodgers, J. L. and Rowe, D. C. (1985). Does contiguity breed similarity? A within-family analysis of non-shared sources of IQ differences between siblings. *Developmental Psychology*, 21, 743–6.

Rodgers, J. L., Cleveland, H. H., van den Oord, E., and Rowe, D. C. (2000). Resolving the debate over birth order, family size, and intelligence. *American Psychologist*, 55, 599–612.

Rodríguez, C. A., Torres, A. A., Mackintosh, N. J., and Chamizo, V. D. (2010). Sex differences in the strategies used by rats to solve a navigation task. *Journal of Experimental Psychology: Animal Behavior Processes*, 36, 395–401.

Roe, A. (1953). A psychological study of eminent psychologists and anthropologists, and a comparison with biological and physical scientists. *Psychological Monographs: General and Applied*, 67, Whole No. 353.

Roid, G. H. (2003). *Stanford-Binet Intelligence Scale* (5th edn). Itasca, IL: Riverside.

Romine, C. B. and Reynolds, C. R. (2005). A model of the development of frontal lobe functioning: Findings from a meta-analysis. *Applied Neuropsychology*, 12, 190–201.

Roof, R. L. and Havens, M. D. (1992). Testosterone improves maze performance and induces development of a male hippocampus in females. *Brain Research*, 572, 310–3.

Rose, S., Kamin, L. J., and Lewontin, R. C. (1984). *Not in our genes*. London: Penguin Books.

Rosenthal, R. (1994). Interpersonal expectancy effects: A 30-year perspective. *Current Directions in Psychological Science*, 3, 176–9.

Rosenthal, R. and Jacobson, L. (1968). *Pygmalion in the classroom*. New York: Holt, Rinehart, and Winston.

Rosenthal, R., Hall, J. A., Di Matteo, M. R., Rogers, P. L., and Archer, D. (1979). *Sensitivity to nonverbal communication: The PONS Test*. Baltimore: Johns Hopkins University Press.

Roth, E. (1964). Die Geschwindigkeit der Verarbeitung von Information und ihr Zusammenhang mit Intelligenz. *Zeitschrift für Experimentelle und Angewandte Psychologie*, 11, 616–22.

Royer, J. M. and Garofoli, L. M. (2005). Cognitive contributions to sex differences in math performance. In *Gender differences in mathematics: An integrative psychological approach* (eds A. M. Gallagher and J. C. Kaufman). Cambridge: Cambridge University Press.

Ruff, C. C., Knauff, M., Fangmeier, T., and Spreer, J. (2003). Reasoning and working memory: Common and distinct neuronal processes. *Neuropsychologia*, 41, 1241–53.

Rush, D., Stein, Z., and Susser, M. (1980). *Diet in pregnancy: A randomized controlled trial of nutritional supplements*. New York: Liss.

Rushton, J. P. (1992). Cranial capacity related to sex, rank and race in a stratified random sample of 6,325 US military personnel. *Intelligence*, 16, 401–13.

Rushton, J. P. (1995). *Race, evolution and behavior: A life history perspective*. New Brunswick, NJ: Transaction Publishing.

Rushton, J. P. (1999). Secular gains in IQ not related to the *g* factor and inbreeding depression— unlike black-white differences: A reply to Flynn. *Personality and Individual Differences*, 26, 381–9.

Rushton, J. P. and Ankney, C. D. (1996). Brain size and cognitive ability: correlations with age, sex, social class and race. *Psychonomic Bulletin and Review*, 3, 21–36.

Rushton, J. P. and Jensen, A. R. (2005). Thirty years of research on race differences in cognitive ability. *Psychology, Public Policy, and Law*, 11, 235–94.

Russell, J. (1996). *Agency: Its role in mental development*. Hove, UK: Lawrence Erlbaum.

Ruthsatz, J., Detterman, D., Griscom, W. S., and Cirullo, B. A. (2008). Becoming an expert in the musical domain: It takes more than just practice. *Intelligence*, 36, 330–8.

Rutter, M. (2000). Discussion. In *The nature of intelligence* (Novartis Foundation Symposium 233, 217), (eds G. R. Bock, J. A. Goode, and K. Webb). Chichester: Wiley.

Rutter, M., Tizard, J., and Whitmore, K. (1970). *Education, health and behaviour*. London: Longman.

Saccuzzo, D. P., Larson, G. E., and Rimland, B. (1986). Visual, auditory and reaction time approaches to the measurement of speed of information processing and individual differences in intelligence. *Personality and Individual Differences*, 7, 659–67.

Sackett, P. R., Borneman, M. J., and Connelly, B. S. (2008). High stakes testing in higher education and employment: Appraising the evidence for validity and fairness. *American Psychologist*, 63, 215–27.

Sackett, P. R., Hardison, C. M., and Cullen, M. J. (2004). On interpreting stereotype threat as accounting for African-American white differences on cognitive tests. *American Psychologist*, 59, 7–13.

Salgado, J. F., Anderson, N., Moscoso, S., *et al.* (2003). A meta-analytic study of general mental ability validity for different occupations in the European community. *Journal of Applied Psychology*, 88, 1068–81.

Salthouse, T. A. (1992). *Mechanisms of age-cognition relations in adulthood*. Hillsdale, NJ: Lawrence Erlbaum.

Salthouse, T. A. (1996). The processing-speed theory of adult age differences in cognition. *Psychological Review,* 103, 403–28.

Salthouse, T. A., Atkinson, T. M., and Berish, D. E. (2003). Executive functioning as a potential mediator of age-related cognitive decline in normal adults. *Journal of Experimental Psychology: General,* 132, 566–94.

Samelson, F. (1975). On the science and politics of IQ. *Social Research,* 42, 467–88.

Samelson, F. (1979). Putting psychology on the map: Ideology and intelligence testing. In *Psychology in social context* (ed. A. Buss). New York: Wiley.

Sandstrom, N. J., Kaufman, J., and Huettel, S. A. (1998). Males and females use different distal cues in a virtual environment navigation task. *Cognitive Brain Research,* 6, 351–60.

Sarason, S. B., and Doris, J. (1979). *Educational handicap, public policy, and social history.* New York: Free Press.

Saucier, G. (1992). Openness versus intellect: Much ado about nothing? *European Journal of Personality,* 6, 381–6.

Saucier, D. M., Green, S. M., Leason, J., *et al.* (2002). Are sex differences in navigation caused by sexually dimorphic strategies or by differences in the ability to use the strategies? *Behavioral Neuroscience,* 116, 403–10.

Scarr, S. (1997). Behavior—genetic and socialization theories of intelligence: Truce and reconciliation. In *Intelligence: Heredity and environment* (eds R. J. Sternberg and E. Grigorenko). Cambridge: Cambridge University Press.

Scarr, S. and McCartney, K. (1983). How people make their own environments: A theory of genotype → environment effects. *Child Development,* 54, 424–35.

Scarr, S. and Weinberg, R. A. (1976). IQ test performance of black children adopted by white families. *American Psychologist,* 31, 726–39.

Scarr, S., and Weinberg, R. A. (1978). The influence of 'family background' on intellectual attainment. *American Sociological Review,* 43, 674–92.

Scarr, S. and Weinberg, R. A. (1983). The Minnesota adoption studies: Genetic differences and malleability. *Child Development,* 54, 260–7.

Scarr, S., Pakstis, A. J., Katz, S. H., and Barker, W. B. (1977). Absence of a relationship between degree of white ancestry and intellectual skills within a black population. *Human Genetics,* 39, 69–86.

Schaie, K. W. (2005). *Developmental influences on adult intelligence: The Seattle longitudinal study.* Oxford: Oxford University Press.

Schama, S. (1989). *Citizens.* New York: Knopf.

Schmidt, F. L. and Hunter, J. E. (1998). The validity and utility of selection methods in personnel psychology: Practical and theoretical implications of 85 years of research findings. *Psychological Bulletin,* 124, 262–74.

Schneider, R. J., Ackerman, P. L., and Kanfer, R. (1996). To 'act wisely in human relations': Exploring the dimensions of social competence. *Personality and Individual Differences,* 21, 469–81.

Schneider, W., Gruber, H., Gold, A., and Opwis, K. (1993). Chess expertise and memory for chess positions in children and adults. *Journal of Experimental Child Psychology,* 56, 328–49.

Schoenemann, P. T., Budinger, T. F., Sarich, V. M., and Wang, W. S. Y. (2000). Brain size does not predict general cognitive ability within families. *Proceedings of the National Academy of Sciences,* 97, 4932–7.

Schoenthaler, S. J., Amos, S. P., Eysenck, H. J., Peritz, E., and Yudkin, J. (1991). Controlled trial of vitamin-mineral supplementation: Effects on intelligence and performance. *Personality and Individual Differences,* 12, 351–62.

Schull, W. J. and Neel, J. V. (1965). *The effects of inbreeding on Japanese children.* New York: Harper and Row.

Schulte, M. J., Ree, M. J., and Carretta, T. R. (2004). Emotional intelligence: Not much more than *g* and personality. *Personality and Individual Differences,* 37, 1059–68.

Schulze, R. (2005). Modeling structures of intelligence. In *Handbook of understanding and measuring intelligence* (eds O. Wilhelm and R. W. Engle). Thousand Oaks, CA: Sage.

Schutte, N. S., Malouff, J. M., Hall, L. E., *et al.* (1998). Development and validation of a measure of emotional intelligence. *Personality and Individual Differences,* 25, 167–77.

Schwartzman, A. E., Gold, D., Andres, D., Arbuckle, T. Y., and Chaikelson, J. (1987). Stability of intelligence: A 40-year follow-up. *Canadian Journal of Psychology,* 41, 244–56.

Schweinhart, L. J. and Weikart, D. P. (1980). Young children grow up: The effects of the Perry Preschool Program on youths through age 15. *Monographs of the High/Scope Educational Research Foundation No. 7.*

Scottish Council for Research in Education (1949). *The trend of Scottish intelligence.* London: London University Press.

Scribner, S. (1986). Thinking in action: Some characteristics of practical thought. In *Practical intelligence: Nature and origins of competence in the everyday world* (eds R. J. Sternebrg and R. K. Wagner). Cambridge: Cambridge University Press.

Seifer, R. (2001). Socioeconomic status, multiple risks, and development of intelligence. In *Environmental effects on cognitive abilities* (eds R. J. Sternberg and E. L. Grigorenko). Mahwah, NJ: Lawrence Erlbaum.

Serpell, R. (2000). Intelligence and culture. In *Handbook of intelligence* (ed. R. J. Sternberg). Cambridge: Cambridge University Press.

Shah, P. and Miyake, A. (1996). The separability of working memory resources for spatial thinking and language processing: An individual differences approach. *Journal of Experimental Psychology: General,* 125, 4–27.

Shallice, T. (1988). *From neuropsychology to mental structure.* Cambridge: Cambridge University Press.

Shallice, T. (2002). Fractionation of the supervisory system. In *Principles of frontal lobe function* (eds D. T. Stuss and R. T. Knight). Oxford: Oxford University Press.

Shallice, T. and Burgess, P. (1998). The domain of supervisory processes and the temporal organization of behaviour. In *The prefrontal cortex: Executive and cognitive functions* (eds A. C. Roberts, T. W. Robbins, and L. Weiskrantz). Oxford: Oxford University Press.

Shanks, D. R. (2005). Implicit learning. In *Handbook of cognition* (eds K. Lamberts and R. Goldstone). Thousand Oaks, CA: Sage.

Shanks, D. R., Green, R. E. A., and Kolodny, J. A. (1994). A critical examination of the evidence for unconscious (implicit) learning. In *Attention and performance,* XV (eds C. Umilta and M. Moscovitch). Cambridge, MA: MIT Press.

Sharma, R. (1971). Unpublished Ph.D. Thesis. University of London.

Shaw, P., Greenstein, D., Lerch, J., *et al.* (2006). Intellectual ability and cortical development in children and adolescents. *Nature,* 440, 676–9.

Shayer, M. and Ginsburg, D. (2009). Thirty years on—a large anti-Flynn effect? (II): 13 and 14-year-olds. Piagetian tests of formal operations norms 1976–2006/7. *British Journal of Educational Psychology,* 79, 409–18.

Shayer, M., Ginsburg, D., and Coe, R. (2007). Thirty years on—a large anti-Flynn effect? The Piagetian test Volume & Heaviness norms 1975–2003. *British Journal of Educational Psychology,* 77, 25–41.

Shepard, R. N. (1978). The mental image. *American Psychologist,* 33, 125–7.

Shepard, R. N. and Metzler, J. (1971). Mental rotation of three dimensional objects. *Science,* 171, 701–3.

Shettleworth, S. J. (2010). *Cognition, evolution, and behavior* (2nd edn). Oxford: Oxford University Press.

Shields, J. (1962). *Monozygotic twins brought up apart and brought up together.* Oxford: Oxford University Press.

Shuey, A. M. (1966). *The testing of negro intelligence* (2nd edn). New York: Social Science Press.

Siegler, R. S. and Alibali, M. W. (2005). *Children's thinking* (4th edn). Upper Saddle River, NJ: Prentice Hall.

Sigman, M. and Whaley, S. E. (1998). The role of nutrition in the development of intelligence. In *The rising curve: Long-term gains in IQ and related measures* (ed. U. Neisser). Washington, DC: American Psychological Association.

Silverman, I. and Eals, M. (1992). Sex differences in spatial abilities: Evolutionary theory and data. In *The adapted mind: Evolutionary psychology and the generation of culture* (eds J. H. Barkow, L. Cosmides, and J. Tooby). Oxford: Oxford University Press.

Silverman, I., Choi, J., and Peters, M. (2007). The hunter-gatherer theory of sex differences in spatial abilities: Data from 40 countries. *Archives of Sexual Behavior,* 36, 261–8.

Silverstein, A. B. (1982). Factor structure of the Wechsler Adult Intelligence Scale—Revised. *Journal of Consulting and Clinical Psychology,* 50, 661–4.

Simonton, D. K. (1991). Emergence and realization of genius: The lives and works of 120 classical composers. *Journal of Personality and Social Psychology,* 61, 829–40.

Simonton, D. K. (2003). Genius and *g*: Intelligence and exceptional achievement. In *The scientific study of general intelligence: Tribute to Arthur R. Jensen* (ed. H. Nyborg). Oxford: Pergamon.

Skuse, D. (1984). Extreme deprivation in early childhood—II. Theoretical issues and a comparative review. *Journal of Child Psychology and Psychiatry,* 31, 893–901.

Slabbekoorn, D., van Goozen, S. H. M., Megens, J., Gooren, L. J. G., and Cohen-Kettenis, P. T. (1999). Activating effects of cross-sex hormones on cognitive functioning: A study of short-term and long-term hormone effects in transsexuals. *Psychoneuroendocrinology,* 24, 423–47.

Smith, E. E., Jonides, J., and Koeppe, R. A. (1996). Dissociating verbal and spatial working memory using PET. *Cerebral Cortex,* 6, 11–20.

Smith, E. E., Jonides, J., Koeppe, R. A., Awh, E., Schumacher, E. H., and Minoshima, S. (1995). Spatial versus object working-memory—PET investigations. *Journal of Cognitive Neuroscience,* 7, 337–56.

Smyth, M. M. and Scholey, K. A. (1992). Determining spatial span: The role of movement time and articulation rate. *Quarterly Journal of Experimental Psychology,* 45A, 479–501.

Smyth, M. M. and Scholey, K. A. (1994). Interference in immediate spatial memory. *Memory and Cognition,* 22, 1–13.

Snow, R. E. (1995). Pygmalion and intelligence. *Current Directions in Psychological Science,* 4, 169–71.

Snow, R. E., Kyllonen, P. C., and Marshalek, B. (1984). The topography of ability and learning correlations.

In *Advances in the psychology of human intelligence* (vol. 2), (ed. R. J. Sternberg). Hillsdale, NJ: Lawrence Erlbaum.

Snyderman, M. and Herrnstein, R. J. (1983). Intelligence tests and the Immigration Act of 1924. *American Psychologist*, 38, 986–95.

Snyderman, M. and Rothman, S. (1988). *The IQ controversy: The media and public policy*. New Brunswick, NJ: Transaction Publishers.

Sokol, D. K., Moore, C. A., Rose, R. J., and Williams, C. J. (1995). Intrapair differences in personality and cognitive ability among young monozygotic twins distinguished by chorion type. *Behavior Genetics*, 25, 457–66.

Solomon, M. (1995). *Mozart: A life*. London: Hutchinson.

Sommer, R. and Sommer, B. A. (1983). Mystery in Milwaukee: Early intervention, IQ, and psychology textbooks. *American Psychologist*, 38, 982–5.

Song, L. J., Huang, G.-H., Peng, K. Z., *et al.* (2010). The differential effects of general mental ability and emotional intelligence on academic performance and social interactions. *Intelligence*, 38, 137–43.

Sowell, T. (1978). *Essays and data on American ethnic groups*. Washington, DC: The Urban Institute.

Sowell, T. (1981). *Ethnic America: A history*. New York: Basic Books.

Spearman, C. (1904). General intelligence, objectively determined and measured. *American Journal of Psychology*, 15, 201–93.

Spearman, C. (1927). *The abilities of man*. London: Macmillan.

Spearman, C. and Jones, L. L. (1950). *Human ability*. London: Macmillan.

Spelke, E. S. (2005). Sex differences in intrinsic aptitude for mathematics and science? A critical review. *American Psychologist*, 60, 950–8.

Spencer, S. J., Steele, C. M., and Quinn, D. M. (1999). Stereotype threat and women's math performance. *Journal of Experimental Social Psychology*, 35, 4–28.

Spitz, H. H. (1986). *The raising of intelligence: A selected history of attempts to raise retarded intelligence*. Hillsdale, NJ: Lawrence Erlbaum.

Stafford, R. E. (1961). Sex differences in spatial visualization as evidence of sex-linked inheritance. *Perceptual and Motor Skills*, 13, 428.

Stanford, W. B. and Luce, J. V. (1974). *The quest for Ulysses*. London: Phaidon Press.

Stankov, L. and Crawford, J. D. (1993). Ingredients of complexity in fluid intelligence. *Learning and Individual Differences*, 5, 73–111.

Stanovich, K. E. and West, R. F. (2000). Individual differences in reasoning: Implications for the rationality debate? *Behavioral and Brain Sciences*, 23, 645–65.

Staszewski, J. J. (1990). Exceptional memory: The influence of practice and knowledge on the development of elaborative encoding strategies. In *Interactions among aptitudes, strategies, and knowledge in cognitive performance* (eds W. Schneider and F. E. Wenert). New York: Springer-Verlag.

Steele, C. M. and Aronson, J. (1995). Stereotype threat and the intellectual test performance of African Americans. *Journal of Personality and Social Psychology*, 69, 797–811.

Stein, Z., Susser, M., Saenger, G., and Marolla, F. (1972). Nutrition and mental performance. *Science*, 178, 708–13.

Stelzl, I., Merz, F., Ehlers, T., and Remer, H. (1995). The effect of schooling on the development of fluid and crystallized intelligence: A quasi-experimental study. *Intelligence*, 21, 279–96.

Stern, W. (1912). *Die Psychologische Methoden der Intelligenzprüfung*. Leipzig: Barth.

Sternberg, R. J. (1977). *Intelligence, information processing and analogical reasoning: The componential analysis of human abilities*. Hillsdale, NJ: Lawrence Erlbaum.

Sternberg, R. J. (1985). *Beyond IQ: A triarchic theory of intelligence*. New York: Cambridge University Press.

Sternberg, R. J. (1986). Toward a unified theory of human reasoning. *Intelligence*, 10, 281–314.

Sternberg, R. J. (1990). *Metaphors of mind: Conceptions of the nature of intelligence*. New York: Cambridge University Press.

Sternberg, R. J. (1997). *Successful intelligence*. New York: Plume.

Sternberg, R. J. and Grigorenko, E. L. (eds) (2001). *Environmental effects on cognitive abilities*, Mahwah, NJ: Lawrence Erlbaum.

Sternberg, R. J. and Grigorenko, E. L. (eds) (2002). *The general factor of intelligence: How general is it?* Mahwah, NJ: Lawrence Erlbaum.

Sternberg, R. J. and Powell, J. S. (1983). Comprehending verbal comprehension. *American Psychologist*, 38, 878–93.

Sternberg, R. J. and Rifkin, B. (1979). The development of analogical reasoning processes. *Journal of Experimental Child Psychology*, 27, 195–232.

Sternberg, R. J. and Smith, C. (1985). Social intelligence and decoding skills in nonverbal communication. *Social Cognition*, 3, 168–92.

Sternberg, R. J. and Wagner, R. K. (eds) (1986). *Practical intelligence: Nature and origins of competence in the everyday world*. Cambridge: Cambridge University Press.

Sternberg, R. J. and Weil, E. M. (1980). An aptitude-strategy interaction in linear syllogistic reasoning. *Journal of Educational Psychology*, 72, 226–34.

Sternberg, R. J., Conway, B. E., Ketron, J. L., and Bernstein, M. (1981). People's conceptions of intelligence. *Journal of Personality and Social Psychology*, 41, 37–55.

Sternberg, R. J., Forsythe, G. B., Hedlund, J., *et al.* (2000). *Practical intelligence in everyday life*. Cambridge: Cambridge University Press.

Sternberg, R. J., Wagner, R. K., Williams, W. M., and Horvath, J. A. (1995). Testing common sense. *American Psychologist*, 50, 912–26.

Sternberg, S. (1975). Memory scanning: new findings and current controversies. *Quarterly Journal of Experimental Psychology*, 17, 1–32.

Stevenson, H. W., Lee, S., Chen, C., and Stigler, J. W. (1990). Contexts of achievement: A study of American, Chinese, and Japanese children. *Monographs of the Society for Research in Child Development*, 55.

Stevenson, H. W., Stigler, J. W., Lee, S., Lucker, G. W., Kitanawa, S., and Hsu, C. (1985). Cognitive performance and academic achievement of Japanese, Chinese and American children. *Child Development*, 56, 718–34.

Stoolmiller, M. (1999). Implications of the restricted range of family environments for estimates of heritability and nonshared environment in behavior—genetic adoption studies. *Psychological Bulletin*, 125, 392–409.

Storfer, M. D. (1990). *Intelligence and giftedness: The contributions of heredity and early environment*. San Francisco: Jossey-Bass.

Stough, C. K. K., Nettelbeck, T., and Cooper, C. J. (1990). Evoked brain potentials, string length and intelligence. *Personality and Individual Differences*, 11, 401–6.

Strand, S., Deary, I. J., and Smith, P. (2006). Sex differences in Cognitive Abilities Test scores: A UK national picture. *British Journal of Educational Psychology*, 76, 463–80.

Streissguth, A. P., Barr, H. M., Sampson, P. D., Darby, B. L., and Martin, O. C. (1990). IQ at age 4 in relation to maternal alcohol use and smoking during pregnancy. *Developmental Psychology*, 25, 3–11.

Strenze, T. (2007). Intelligence and socioeconomic success: A meta-analytic review of longitudinal research. *Intelligence*, 35, 401–26.

Stumpf, H., and Eliot, J. (1995). Gender related differences in spatial ability and the K factor of general spatial ability in a population of academically talented students. *Personality and Individual Differences*, 19, 33–45.

Sundet, J. M., Barlaug, D. G., and Torjussen, T. M. (2004). The end of the Flynn effect? A study of secular trends in mean intelligence test scores of Norwegian conscripts during half a century. *Intelligence*, 32, 349–62.

Sundet, J. M., Borren, I., and Tambs, K. (2008). The Flynn effect is partly caused by changing fertility patterns. *Intelligence*, 36, 183–91.

Suss, H.-M. and Beauducel, A. (2005). Faceted models of intelligence. In *Handbook of understanding and measuring intelligence* (eds O. Wilhelm and R. W. Engle). Thousand Oaks, CA: Sage.

Suss, H.-M., Oberauer, K., Wittmann, W. W., Wilhelm, O., and Schulze, R. (2002). Working-memory capacity explains reasoning ability—and a little bit more. *Intelligence*, 30, 261–88.

Tambs, K., Sundet, J. M., and Magnus, P. (1984). Heritability analysis of the WAIS subtests: A study of twins. *Intelligence*, 8, 283–93.

Tamez, E., Myerson, J., and Hale, S. (2008). Learning, working memory, and intelligence revisited. *Behavioural Processes*, 78, 240–5.

Tang, C. Y., Eaves, E. L., Ng, J. C., *et al.* (2010). Brain networks for working memory and factors of intelligence assessed in males and females with fMRI and DTI. *Intelligence*, 38, 293–303.

Taylor, H. F. (1980). *The IQ game: A methodological inquiry into the heredity-environment controversy*. New Brunswick, NJ: Rutgers University Press.

Teasdale, T. W. and Owen, D. R. (2000). Forty-year secular trends in cognitive abilties. *Intelligence*, 28, 115–20.

Teasdale, T. W. and Owen, D. R. (2008). Secular declines in cognitive test scores: A reversal of the Flynn Effect. *Intelligence*, 36, 121–6.

Teichner, W. H. and Krebs, M. J. (1974). Laws of visual choice reaction time. *Psychological Review*, 81, 75–98.

Terman, L. M. (1916). *The measurement of intelligence*. Boston, MA: Houghton Mifflin.

Terman, L. M. (1932). An autobiography. In *A history of psychology in autobiography* (vol. 2.), (ed. C. Murchison). Worcester, MA: Clark University Press.

Terman, L. M. and Merrill, M. A. (1937). *Measuring intelligence*. Boston: Houghton Mifflin.

Terman, L. M., and Oden, M. H. (1947). *The gifted child grows up. Vol 4. Genetic studies of genius*. Stanford, CA: Stanford University Press.

Terman, L. M., and Oden, M. H. (1959). *The gifted group at mid-life. Vol 5. Genetic studies of genius*. Stanford, CA: Stanford University Press.

Teuber, H. L. (1964). The riddle of frontal lobe function in man. In *The frontal granular cortex and behaviour* (eds J. M. Warren and K. Albert). New York: McGraw-Hill.

Thompson, P. M., Cannon, T. D., Narr, K. L., *et al.* (2001). Genetic influences on brain structure. *Nature Neuroscience*, 4, 1253–8.

Thomson, G. H. (1916). A hierarchy without a general factor. *British Journal of Psychology*, 8, 271–81.

Thomson, G. H. (1921). The Northumberland Mental Tests. *British Journal of Psychology*, 12, 201–22.

Thomson, G. H. (1939). *The factorial analysis of human ability*. London: University of London Press.

Thorndike, E. L. (1920). Intelligence and its use. *Harper's Magazine*, 140, 227–35.

Thorndike, E. L. (1925). *The measurement of intelligence*. New York: Teachers College, Columbia University.

Thorndike, R. L. (1987). Stability of factor loadings. *Personality and Individual Differences*, 8, 585–6.

Thurstone, L. L. (1931). Multiple factor analysis. *Psychological Review*, 38, 406–27.

Thurstone, L. L. (1938). *Primary mental abilities*. Chicago: University of Chicago Press.

Thurstone, L. L. (1940). *The vectors of the mind*. Chicago: University of Chicago Press.

Thurstone, L. L. (1947). *Multiple factor analysis*. Chicago: University of Chicago Press.

Thurstone, L. L. and Thurstone, T. G. (1941). *Factorial studies of intelligence*. Chicago: University of Chicago Press.

Tideman, E. and Gustafsson, J.-E. (2004) Age-related differentiation of cognitive abilities in ages 3–7. *Personality and Individual Differences*, 36, 1965–74.

Till, N. (1992). *Mozart and the enlightenment*. London: Faber and Faber.

Tishkoff, S. A., Ree, F. A., Friedlaender, F. R. *et al.* (2009). The genetic structure and history of Africans and African Americans. *Science*, 324, 1035–44.

Tizard, B. (1974). IQ and race. *Nature*, 247, 316.

Towse, J. N. and Hitch, G. J. (2008). Variation in working memory due to normal development. In *Variation in working memory* (eds A. Conway, C. Jarrold, M. Kane, A. Miyake, and J. Towse). Oxford: Oxford University Press.

Towse, J. N., Hitch, G. J., and Hutton, U. (1998). A re-evaluation of working memory capacity in children. *Journal of Memory and Language*, 39, 195–217.

Tresch, M. C., Sinnamon, H. M., and Seamon, J. C. (1993). Double dissociation of spatial and object visual memory: Evidence from selective interference in intact human subjects. *Neuropsychologia*, 31, 211–9.

Tuddenham, R. D. (1948). Soldier intelligence in World Wars I and II. *American Psychologist*, 3, 54–6.

Turkheimer, E., Haley, A., Waldron, M., D'Onofrio, B., and Gottesman, I. I. (2003). Socioeconomic status modifies heritability of IQ in young children. *Psychological Science*, 14, 623–8.

Underwood, B. J., Boruch, R. F., and Malmi, R. A. (1978). Composition of episodic memory. *Journal of Experimental Psychology: General*, 107, 393–419.

Unsworth, N. and Engle, R. W. (2006). Simple and complex memory spans and their relation to fluid abilities: Evidence from list-length effects. *Journal of Memory and Language*, 54, 68–80.

Unsworth, N. and Engle, R. W. (2007). On the division of short-term and working memory: An examination of simple and complex span and their relation to higher order abilities. *Psychological Bulletin*, 133, 1038–66.

Unsworth, N., Redick, T. S., Lakey, C. E., and Young, D. L. (2010) Lapses in sustained attention and their relation to executive control and fluid abilities: An individual differences investigation. *Intelligence*, 38, 111–22.

Unterrainer, J. M., Kaller, C. P., Halsband, U., and Rahm, B. (2006). Planning abilities and chess: A comparison of chess and non-chess players on the Tower of London task. *British Journal of Psychology*, 97, 299–311.

VanCourt, M. and Bean, F. D. (1985). Intelligence and fertility in the United States: 1912–1982. *Intelligence*, 9, 23–32.

Van Daalen-Kapteijns, M. M., and Elshout-Mohr, M. (1981). The acquisition of word meanings as a cognitive learning process. *Journal of Verbal Learning and Verbal Behaviour*, 20, 386–99.

van der Maas, H. L. J., Dolan, C. V., Grasman, R. P. P. P., *et al.* (2006). A dynamical model of general intelligence: The positive manifold of intelligence by mutualism. *Psychological Review*, 113, 842–61.

van IJzendoorn, M. H., Juffer, F., and Poelhuis, C. W. K. (2005). Adoption and cognitive development: A meta-analytic comparison of adopted and nonadopted children's IQ and school performance. *Psychological Bulletin*, 131, 301–16.

van Leeuwen, M., Peper, J. S., van den Berg, S. M., *et al.* (2009). A genetic analysis of brain volumes and IQ in children. *Intelligence*, 37, 181–91.

van Praag, H., Kempermann, G., and Gage, F. H. (2000). Neural consequences of enviromental enrichment. *Nature Reviews Neuroscience*, 1, 191–8.

Van Valen, L. (1974). Brain size and intelligence in man. *American Journal of Physical Anthropology*, 40, 417–24.

Van Wieringen, J. C. (1978). Secular growth changes. In *Human growth* (vol. 2), (eds F. Falkner and J. M. Tanner). New York: Plenum Press.

Vandierendonck, A. and De Vooght, G. (1997). Working memory constraints on linear reasoning with spatial and temporal contents. *The Quarterly Journal of Experimental Psychology A: Human Experimental Psychology*, 50A, 803–20.

Vecchi, T. (1998). Visuo-spatial imagery in congenitally totally blind people. *Memory*, 6, 91–102.

Vendrell, P., Junque, C., Pujol, J., and Jurado, M. A. (1995). The role of prefrontal regions in the Stroop task. *Neuropsychologia*, 33, 341–52.

Verhaeghen, P. (2003). Aging and vocabulary score: A meta-analysis. *Psychology and Aging,* 18, 332–9.

Vernon, P. A. (1993). Der Zahlen-Verbindungs-Test and other trail-making correlates of general intelligence. *Personality and Individual Differences,* 14, 35–40.

Vernon, P. A. and Jensen, A. R. (1984). Individual and group differences in intelligence and speed of information processing. *Personality and Individual Differences,* 5, 911–23.

Vernon, P. A. and Weese, S. E. (1993). Predicting intelligence with multiple speed of information-processing tests. *Personality and Individual Differences,* 14, 413–19.

Vernon, P. A., Nador, S., and Cantor, L. (1985). Group differences in intelligence and speed of information-processing. *Intelligence,* 9, 137–48.

Vernon, P. E. (1947). Research on personnel selection in the Royal Navy and British Army. *American Psychologist,* 2, 35–51.

Vernon, P. E. (1950). *The structure of human abilities.* London: Methuen.

Vernon, P. E. (1957). *Secondary school selection. A British psychological inquiry.* London: Methuen.

Vernon, P. E. (1969). *Intelligence and cultural environment.* London: Methuen.

Vernon, P. E. (1982). *The abilities and achievements of Orientals in North America.* New York: Academic Press.

Vickers, D. (1979). *Decision processes in visual perception.* London: Academic Press.

Vigneau, F. and Bors, D. A. (2008). The quest for item types based on information processing: An analysis of Raven's Advanced Progressive Matrices, with a consideration of gender differences. *Intelligence,* 36, 702–10.

Villardita, C. (1985). Raven's Colored Progressive Matrices and intellectual impairment in patients with focal brain damage. *Cortex,* 21, 627–35.

Vining, D. R. (1995). On the possibility of the re-emergence of a dysgenic trend with respect to intelligence in American fertility differentials: An update. *Personality and Individual Differences,* 19, 259–63.

Visser, B. A., Ashton, M. C., and Vernon, P. A. (2006). Beyond *g*: Putting multiple intelligences theory to the test. *Intelligence,* 34, 487–502.

Vogel, F., Kruger, J., Schalt, E., Schnobel, R., and Hassling. L. (1987). No consistent relationships between oscillations and latencies of visual evoked EEG potentials and measures of mental performance. *Human Neurobiology,* 6, 173–82.

Voyer, D., Voyer, S., and Bryden, M. P. (1995). Magnitude of sex differences in spatial ability: A meta-analysis

and consideration of critical variables. *Psychological Bulletin,* 117, 250–70.

Wager, T. D. and Smith, E. E. (2003). Neuroimaging studies of working memory: A meta-analysis. *Cognitive, Affective & Behavioral Neuroscience,* 3, 255–74.

Wagner, G., Koch, K., Reichenbach, J. R., Sauer, H., and Schlösser, R. G. M. (2006). The special involvement of the rostrolateral prefrontal cortex in planning abilities: An event-related fMRI study with the Tower of London paradigm. *Neuropsychologia,* 44, 2337–47.

Wagner, R. K., and Sternberg, R. J. (1986). Tacit knowledge and intelligence in the everyday world. In *Practical intelligence: Nature and origins of competence in the everyday world* (eds R. J. Sternberg and R. K. Wagner). Cambridge: Cambridge University Press.

Waiter, G. D., Deary, I. J., Staff, R. T., *et al.* (2009). Exploring possible neural mechanisms of intelligence differences using processing speed and working memory tasks: An fMRI study. *Intelligence,* 37, 199–206.

Walhovd, K. B., Fjell, A. M., Reinvang, I., *et al.* (2005). Cortical volume and speed-of-processing are complementary in prediction of performance intelligence. *Neuropsychologia,* 43, 704–13.

Waller, J. H. (1971). Achievement and social mobility: Relationships among IQ score, education and occupation in two generations. *Social Biology,* 18, 252–9.

Waltz, J. A., Knowlton, B. J., Holyoak, K. J., *et al.* (1999). A system for relational reasoning in human prefrontal cortex. *Psychological Science,* 10, 119–25.

Wartenburger, I., Heekeren, H. R., Preusse, F., Kramer, J., and van der Meer, E. (2009). Cerebral correlates of analogical processing and their modulation by training. *NeuroImage,* 48, 291–302.

Washburn, D. A. and Rumbaugh, D. M. (1997). Faster is smarter, so why are we slower? A comparative perspective on intelligence and processing speed. *American Psychologist,* 52, 1147–8.

Wason, P. (1968). Reasoning about a rule. *Quarterly Journal of Experimental Psychology,* 20, 273–81.

Wasserman, G. A. and Factor-Litvak, P. (2001). Methodology, inference and causation: Environmental lead exposure and childhood intelligence. *Archives of Clinical Neuropsychology,* 16, 343–52.

Waters, A. J., Gobet, F., and Leyden, G. (2002). Visuospatial abilities of chess players. *British Journal of Psychology,* 93, 557–65.

Watkins, M. W., Lei, P.-W., and Canivez, G. L. (2007). Psychometric intelligence and achievement: A cross-lagged panel analysis. *Intelligence,* 35, 59–68.

Wechsler, D. (1944). *Measurement of adult intelligence* (3rd edn). Baltimore: Williams and Wilkins.

Wechsler, D. (1958). *The measurement and appraisal of adult intelligence* (4th edn). Baltimore: Williams and Wilkins.

Wechsler, D. (1997). *Wechsler Adult Intelligence Scale—3rd edition (WAIS-III)*. San Antonio, TX: The Psychological Corporation.

Wechsler, D. (2003). *Wechsler Intelligence Scale for Children—4th edition (WISC-IV)*. San Antonio, TX: The Psychological Corporation.

Wechsler, D. (2008). *Wechsler Adult Intelligence Scale—4th edition (WAIS-IV)*. San Antonio, TX: The Psychological Corporation.

Weinberg, R. A., Scarr, S., and Waldman, I. D. (1992). The Minnesota transracial adoption study: A follow-up of IQ test performance at adolescence. *Intelligence, 16*, 117–35.

Weinstein, R. S., Gregory, A., and Strambler, M. J. (2004). Intractable self-fulfilling prophecies fifty years after Brown vs. Board of Education. *American Psychologist, 59*, 511–20.

Weisberg, R. W. (2006). Modes of expertise in creative thinking: Evidence from case studies. In *Cambridge handbook of expertise and expert performance* (eds K. A. Ericsson, N. Charness, P. Feltovich, and R. R. Hoffman). Cambridge: Cambridge University Press.

Weiss, E. M., Ragland, J. D., Brensinger, C. M., *et al.* (2006). Sex difference in clustering and switching verbal fluency tasks. *Journal of the International Neuropsychological Society, 12*, 502–9.

West, R. L. (1996). An application of prefrontal cortex function theory to cognitive aging. *Psychological Bulletin, 120*, 272–92.

Weyl, N. (1969). Some comparative performance indexes of American ethnic minorities. *Mankind Quarterly, 9*, 106–19.

Whalley, L. J. and Deary, I. J. (2001). Longitudinal cohort study of childhood IQ and survival up to age 76. *British Medical Journal, 322*, 819–22.

White, K. R. (1982). The relation between socioeconomic status and academic achievement. *Psychological Bulletin, 91*, 461–81.

Whiten, A. and Byrne, R. W. (1988). Tactical deception in primates. *Behavioral and Brain Sciences, 11*, 233–73.

Wicherts, J. M., Dolan, C. V., and van der Maas, H. L. J. (2010). A systematic literature review of the average IQ of sub-Saharan Africans. *Intelligence, 38*, 1–20.

Wicherts, J. M., Dolan, C. V., Hessen, D. J., *et al.* (2004). Are intelligence tests measurement invariant over time? Investigating the nature of the Flynn effect. *Intelligence, 32*, 509–37.

Wickett, J. C., Vernon, P. A., and Lee, D. H. (2000). Relationships between factors of intelligence and brain volume. *Personality and Individual Differences, 29*, 1095–122.

Widaman, K. F. and Carlson, J. S. (1989). Procedural effects on performance in the Hick paradigm: Bias in reaction time and movement time parameters. *Intelligence, 13*, 63–85.

Wilhelm, O. (2005). Measuring reasoning ability. In *Handbook of understanding and measuring intelligence* (eds O. Wilhelm and R. W. Engle). Thousand Oaks, CA: Sage.

Wilhelm, O. and Schulze, R. (2002). The relation of speeded and unspeeded reasoning with mental speed. *Intelligence, 30*, 537–54.

Willerman, L., Naylor, A. F., and Myrianthopoulos, N. C. (1974). Intellectual development of children from interracial matings: Performance in infancy and at 4 years. *Behavior Genetics, 4*, 83–90.

Williams, B. A. and Pearlberg, S. L. (2006). Learning of three-term contingencies correlates with Raven scores, but not with measures of cognitive processing. *Intelligence, 34*, 177–91.

Williams, C. L. and Meck, W. H. (1991). The organizational effects of gonadal steroids on sexually dimorphic spatial ability. *Psychoneuroendocrinology, 16*, 155–76.

Williams, W. M. (1998). Are we raising smarter children today? School and home-related influences on IQ. In *The rising curve: Long-term gains in IQ and related measures* (ed. U. Neisser). Washington, DC: American Psychological Association.

Willingham, D. B., Greeley, T., and Bardone, A. M. (1993). Dissociation in a serial response time task using a recognition measure: Comment on Perruchet and Amorin (1992). *Journal of Experimental Psychology: Learning Memory and Cognition, 19*, 1424–30.

Wilson, R. S. (1983). The Louisville twin study: Developmental synchronies in behaviour. *Child Development, 54*, 298–316.

Wilson, R. S. (1986). Continuity and change in cognitive ability profile. *Behavior Genetics, 16*, 45–60.

Wissler, C. (1901). The correlation of mental and physical tests. *Psychological Review Monograph Supplement, 3*, no. 6.

Woodrow, H. (1939). The common factors in fifty-two mental tests. *Psychometrika, 4*, 99–107.

Woodrow, H. (1940). Interrelations of measures of learning. *Journal of Psychology, 10*, 49–73.

Wooldridge, A. (1994). *Measuring the mind: Education and psychology in England, c. 1860–c. 1990*. Cambridge: Cambridge University Press.

Woolf, L. I., McBean, M. S., Woolf, F. M., and Cahalanf, S. F. (1975). Phenylketonuria as a balanced polymorphism: the nature of the heterozygote advantage. *Annals of Human Genetics, 38*, 461–9.

Yoakum, L. S. and Yerkes, R. M. (1920). *Army mental tests*. New York: Holt.

Zacks, R. T., Hasher, L., and Li, K. Z. H. (2000). Human memory. In *The handbook of aging and cognition* (2nd edn), (eds F. I. M. Craik and T. A. Salthouse). Mahwah, NJ: Lawrence Erlbaum.

Zagorsky, J. L. (2007). Do you have to be smart to be rich? The impact of IQ on wealth, income and financial distress. *Intelligence, 35,* 489–501.

Zajonc, R. B. (1983). Validating the confluence model. *Psychological Bulletin, 93,* 457–480.

Zajonc, R. B. and Mullally, P. R. (1997). Birth order: Reconciling conflicting effects. *American Psychologist, 52,* 685–99.

Zenderland, L. (1998). *Measuring minds: Henry Herbert Goddard and the origins of American intelligence testing.* Cambridge: Cambridge University Press.

Zhang, Y., Caryl, P. G., and Deary, I. J. (1989). Evoked potential correlates of inspection time. *Personality and Individual Differences*, 10, 379–84.

Zigler, E. and Muenchow, S. (1992). *Head Start: The inside story of America's most successful educational experiment.* New York: Basic Books.

Zimmerman, W. S. (1954). Hypotheses concerning the nature of the spatial factors. *Educational and Psychological Measurement*, 14, 396–400.

Author Index

Subject Index